COLLECTION MANAGEMENT

TREES IN PARADISE

ALSO BY JARED FARMER

Glen Canyon Dammed:
Inventing Lake Powell and the Canyon Country

On Zion's Mount:
Mormons, Indians, and the American Landscape

TREES IN
PARADISE

A California History

JARED
FARMER

W. W. NORTON & COMPANY

NEW YORK   LONDON

For information about permission to reproduce selections from this book,
write to Permissions, W. W. Norton & Company, Inc.,
500 Fifth Avenue, New York, NY 10110

For information about special discounts for bulk purchases, please
contact W. W. Norton Special Sales at specialsales@wwnorton.com or
800-233-4830

Manufacturing by RR Donnelley, Harrisonburg, VA
Book design by Lovedog Studio
Production manager: Anna Oler

Library of Congress Cataloging-in-Publication Data

Farmer, Jared, 1974–
Trees in paradise : a California history / Jared Farmer.
pages cm
Includes bibliographical references and index.
ISBN 978-0-393-07802-2 (hardcover)
1. California—History. 2. Landscape assessment—California—History.
3. Trees—California—History. 4. Giant sequoia—California—History.
5. Coast redwood—California—History. 6. Eucalyptus—California—
History. 7. Citrus—California—History. 8. Palms—California—History.
9. Horticulture—United States—History. 10. Human ecology—United
States—History. I. Title.
F861.F37 2013
634.09794—dc23
          2013021309

634.0979

Farmer, J.

W. W. Norton & Company, Inc.
500 Fifth Avenue, New York, N.Y. 10110
www.wwnorton.com

W. W. Norton & Company Ltd.
Castle House, 75/76 Wells Street, London W1T 3QT

1 2 3 4 5 6 7 8 9 0

In memory of
James Lee Farmer

Contents

List of Maps

In this pleasant soile
His farr more pleasant Garden God ordain'd;
Out of the fertil ground he caus'd to grow
All Trees of noblest kind for sight, smell, taste;
And all amid them stood the Tree of Life,
High eminent, blooming Ambrosial Fruit
Of vegetable Gold

—Milton, *Paradise Lost*, Book IV

By their trees ye shall know them, may be said of
California cities.

—*San Francisco Call* (1904)

A eucalyptus has its implications
where I come from: it means the autumn winds
return each year like brushfires from the desert,
return as dry reminders of the oaks
whose place this was: the valley oak, blue oak,
and the oracle which thrive on little water.
And eucalyptus means the orange groves
once flourished here, that rivers were diverted,
that winter was denied and smoke hung low
over the valley the night of the first frost—
smudgepots warming and darkening the sky . . .

—Kevin Hearle,
"Each Thing We Know Is Changed
Because We Know It"

Introduction

AT CYPRESS POINT ON CARMEL BAY, A PUNCH SHOT AWAY from the fairways and greens of the world-famous Pebble Beach Golf Links, peculiar things grow where surf meets rock. Monterey cypress occurs naturally here and only here. Pruned by salt and bent by wind, the sea-level conifers look positively subalpine. Tourists of an earlier era likened these scenic deformities to pterodactyls, octopuses, gnomes, and wraiths. One travel writer averred that their "queer, unreal, fantastic" shapes were more startling and uncanny than anything imagined by Dante or Doré.[1]

The Pacific Improvement Company, the real estate division of the Southern Pacific Railroad, obtained Cypress Point—part of a former Mexican land grant—in 1880. To stimulate tourism, the firm built a scenic road, 17-Mile Drive. As a stagecoach route, then as a one-way paved automobile tollway, the coastal drive wound through the main 50-acre grove with its approximately eight thousand cypresses. Tour operators spun romantic tales about the botanical attractions, and guidebooks repeated their bogus claims: cypresses as old as Christ, organisms identical with the sacred cedars of Lebanon. Standout specimens acquired names such as Witch Tree and Ostrich Tree. Over the years, many of these arboreal contortions suffered structural damage. Through attrition, the status of landmark fell to Lone Cypress, formerly known as "a lone cypress" or simply "a solitary tree."

It clung to a rocky promontory. Visible from the midway point of 17-Mile Drive, this improbable life-form attracted painters and photographers from the nearby art colony of Carmel-by-the-Sea. Tourists beat a path to the keep, using the tree's exposed roots as steps. The Pacific Improvement Company, fearful that its living property would collapse into the waves, built a retaining wall, attached guy wires, and restricted pedestrian traffic. The next (and current) owner, Pebble Beach Company, increased the vigilance: you can't get closer than 70 yards—near enough for a zoom-lens snapshot. Multiple tour buses stop here every summer day. Lone Cypress is ostensibly the "world's most photographed tree" and one of California's signature sights. It shows up on postcards, calendars, posters, websites. People praise the photogenic plant as an inspirational symbol of fortitude, strength, tenacity, and rugged individualism.

The singular tree has a parallel life as a corporate emblem—"Lone Cypress®, *a trademark of quality*." Pebble Beach Company, a golf resort, calls it the "basis of our brand identity system." The company adopted the tree in 1919 and updated the logo several times over the ensuing decades. The strength of Pebble Beach's trademark was demonstrated in U.S. District Court in 1985, when the company successfully sued a retailer for selling merchandise emblazoned with a stylized cypress and the name Pebble Beach. Although the company did not own the place-name, ruled the judge, it could claim exclusive use of the graphical tree. To protect shoppers from confusion, the judge enjoined competitors from using the company's intangible asset. The trademark applied to the logo, not to the organism. Nevertheless, Pebble Beach sent a few cease-and-desist letters to landscape photographers in 1990 for "illegally" reproducing its branded plant. After "Cypressgate" made the national news—and after experts in trademark law lambasted the company—Pebble Beach retreated to its fallback position: as property owner, it can oblige visitors to refrain from commercial photography; its guests implicitly agree to this "contract" when they pay the admission fee to the scenic drive. The business still alleges that its trademark covers the tree.[2]

The logo may outlive the plant. Lone Cypress is roughly the age of the United States and near the end of its life span. Weakened by past arson attacks and termite invasions, it relies on padded cable supports for stability. Company arborists nurse the tree with supplements of mulch, potash, and phosphorous. Anticipating the inevitable, Pebble Beach has cultivated a future transplant, Lone Cypress Jr., in a secluded spot where onshore breezes will, with luck, train it into a similar wizened appearance.[3]

The concept "naturally occurring" hardly applies to Monterey cypress anymore. Carmel Bay may claim the prototypes, but no longer do you have to travel to Monterey County, or even California, to see the species. Once renowned for being restricted, Monterey cypress is now widespread. Australians and New Zealanders propagated vast quantities of these California trees in the late nineteenth century. In the same era, California farmers and landscapers used cypresses, often in combination with Australasian eucalypts, as hedges and windrows. Away from the windy coast, the species assumes tall, erect, symmetrical, pyramidal forms. Since the Depression, the city of San Francisco has annually illuminated an attractive specimen in Golden Gate Park as its official Christmas tree. Curiously, a species reduced to its "last stand" at Carmel Bay grows with "weed-like rapidity" in other places.[4]

To explain the original island-like isolation of the cypress, Californians formerly turned both to scientific and historical speculation and to flights of fancy. Perhaps ocean currents had carried seeds from cedar groves in Japan. Perhaps the trees had been planted by Franciscans who brought scions from Lebanon; or they might have been cultivated by a race of Syrians, now vanished, that migrated to prehistoric California. The most popular conjecture centered on Chinese monks in North America. This horticultural legend accrued some credibility thanks to the lord abbot of the Buddhist Church of Sacramento, the Venerable Right Reverend Dr. Sri Bishop Leodi Ahmed Mazziniananda Swami. The Golden State was a fitting destination for this protean man. Born in Isfahan, Persia, in 1827, Mazziniananda spent his adolescence in Lhasa, Tibet, studying the priesthood under the Dalai Lama. Later he earned university and postgraduate degrees at Oxford, Heidelberg, Paris, and London, where he became friends with Arthur Conan Doyle. Mazzinianananda came to the United States in 1893 and commenced "spreading the Dharma," gradually working his way west, arriving in California a decade later. He remained in the land of sunshine until his death in 1931. As a lively octogenarian, Mazzinianananda headed the Buddhist Educational Bureau at the 1915 Panama-Pacific International Exposition in San Francisco, where he gave a public lecture that included his etiology of the Monterey cypress.[5]

Here's the story he told: In 420 CE five monks from central China embarked on a quest to locate the Land of the Western Paradise, a transcendent realm described in Buddhist texts. At the end of their journey, they would broadcast the good news of the Supreme Buddha. At China's eastern shore, the monks built a boat and sailed out into the Pacific. Their provisions included Buddhist literature, statues, prayer beads, and seeds and cuttings from the Bodhi Tree, the sacred plant under which Siddhartha achieved nirvana. The long ocean crossing ended on the rocks of Point Lobos at Carmel Bay. The Asian discoverers of America made friends with the natives and taught them the principles of the Enlightened One. Satisfied that they had found the Pure Land, the monks decided to set their seeds and cuttings in the ground and cultivate a Buddhist garden. Two monks eventually returned to China; two more traveled overland to the Aztec capital, Tenochtitlán, where they planted more Bodhi seeds. The final monk stayed behind in Western Paradise, tending the sacred arboretum.

Biological, commercial, mythological: I rehearse these manifestations of Monterey cypress by way of invitation. Read this book, this natural and unnatural history of California trees, and you will never see a living landscape the same way again.

———

CALIFORNIA, U.S.A.—THE GOLDEN STATE, the "cornucopia of the world"—is conventionally regarded as unique and prodigious, even to excess. Statistical distinctions abound. Three of the world's number-one trees—the largest, the tallest, the oldest—grow here. The majority of America's fruits, nuts, wines, salad greens, and winter vegetables originate here. California boasts the highest and lowest elevations, the longest coastline, and the most national parks in the Lower 48. In no other section of America do you find such juxtapositions of cities and wilderness areas, or plantations and wildlife refuges, or farmworker poverty and agricultural wealth (in both of which California ranks first in the Union). The region is a paradox of plenty: more sunshine and smog, beauty and hazard, freedom and unruliness, opportunities and failures, innovations and crises. California, and no other U.S. state, has nurtured its own varietal of the American Dream—the California Dream.

Yet the notion of California as a mythical land predates the Gold Rush, Hollywood, and the promotions of real estate developers. Appropriately, the name California originally referred to an imaginary place. The word first appeared in print in 1510 in a popular romance by Garci Rodríguez de Montalvo, a forerunner of Cervantes. According to the chivalric storyteller, the Island of California lay to the east of Asia, adjacent to Earthly Paradise. The idyllic isle contained gold and beautiful women—and no men. Calafia, queen of California, commanded an army of dark-skinned Amazons who rode griffins through the sky. Conquistadores let this Orientalist romance go to their heads, and the conquest of Tenochtitlán, a city as fantastic as any in legend, engorged their imaginations. When Spanish explorers found an island-like mass off the northwest coast of Mexico, they hoped that truth resembled fiction. Several years later they realized that what they called "California" was actually a long peninsula—what we now call Baja ("lower"). The idea of California as an isle persisted until the mid-eighteenth century and survived on some maps even later. The English perpetuated the cartographic error in their quixotic search for a Northwest Passage linking the Atlantic to the Pacific. In Alta ("upper") California, settlers from the United States appropriated the old Spanish place-name and made it—and the named place—their own. In the process, they remythologized the region.

As an iconic expression, *California Dream* is a post–World War II invention applied retrospectively to the entire period after the discovery of gold. The coinage evokes an optimistic conception of the future as well as of the past. No one has precisely defined it or *American Dream*—an impossible task—but the basic ideological components are exceptionalism and aspiration. Only in America, the idea goes, can an ordinary person achieve the extraordinary thanks to the unique determinants of the Constitution and the free enterprise system. The California species of this genus is different in its environmental insistence. From the Gold Rush to the present, various iterations of the California Dream have begun with the premise that meeting one's aspirations entails packing up and moving to the U.S. region most endowed with rare resources and fine amenities, be they mineral, topographical, climatological, floral. Dream chasers have come for the air, or the surf, or the midwinter promise of flowers—and the sun, always the sun.

Ecologically, California *is* an island. Its fertile lowland areas lie between the fathomless Pacific and formidable mountains and deserts. As a result, much of the state's flora is endemic. Historically, giant sequoias clustered on the flanks of the Sierra Nevada, Monterey pines (like the cypresses) grew in isolation on the central coast, and Torrey pines occupied a single coastal bluff north of San Diego. Several more iconic tree species—coast redwood, coast live oak, California sycamore, California fan palm—barely extend into neighboring states. Two famous arid-zone plants of the U.S. West, bristlecone pine and Joshua tree, here achieve paradigmatic form. California is the world's only polity with three national parks (Sequoia, Redwood, Joshua Tree) dedicated to megaflora.

The genial bioregion between the Sierra and the sea supported North America's most diverse native population north of Tenochtitlán. California's indigenous peoples developed deep relationships with trees and ministered to acorn-bearing oaks. And yet, to our surprise today, much of California, including sun-drenched lowland habitat, was basically treeless before European colonization. Even the coastal ranges were (and remain) more woody than wooded—the California chaparral. Starting in the eighteenth century, Franciscans from Spain introduced many agricultural and ornamental species, Mediterranean fruits and nuts, which they tended at the missions with the help of Indian neophytes. The beautiful mission gardens lasted for about half a century. During the even shorter period of secularization and Mexican independence, Spanish-speaking settlers on the coastal strip of Alta California (people known as Californios) pursued a pastoral rather than a horticultural economy—a rational choice given the small size of the population and the great distance to major markets.

California's savannah and chaparral puzzled American settlers from eastern climes. They missed the shade, the green, and the chatter of songbirds. Accustomed to bosky abundance—and habituated to unthrifty wood use—they desired lumber and firewood, lots of it. Settlers wasted no time "improving" the scene once the United States seized control of the Far West.

Trees in Paradise begins here, in 1848, the year U.S. forces vanquished Mexico and a sawmill worker almost simultaneously chanced upon flakes of gold in the fittingly named American River. After this pivotal moment—the social equivalent of two successive earthquakes of awesome magnitude—settlement took on velocity. Fortune seekers arrived from all parts of the globe. In merely two years, California's nonindigenous population swelled from approximately 10,000 to 200,000. The first chroniclers of San Francisco put it this way in 1855: "California was a hot-bed that brought humanity to a rapid, monstrous maturity, like the mammoth vegetables [giant sequoias] for which it is so celebrated."[6]

Although my book has little to say about the Gold Rush proper, the event served as a touchstone for my primary historical figures— migrants who wanted to soften the coarseness of mining society and ameliorate the prodigal use of California's natural resources. These "improvers" believed they could accomplish good works through *tree culture*, a nineteenth-century term for a body of practical knowledge that included afforestation, horticulture, and landscaping. American settlers in the Far West wanted to "complete" a land blessed with exceptional sun and soil. By adding drought-tolerant trees from other parts of the world, California horticulturists succeeded in making grasslands wooded. Even more importantly, by reallocating the discharge of the Sierra—by draining swamps, by damming and diking rivers, by building canals—they converted dry foothills and arid valleys into high-grade groves of subtropical fruit. Dendrophiles called it "reclaiming" the "wastelands." With imported flora and water, improvers also created shady parks, campuses, and boulevards. They forced grasslands and wetlands to metamorphose into fields, orchards, and garden cities. As a result of rural and urban afforestation, the whole region contains more trees today than at any time since the late Pleistocene. The conquest of California thus begat the greening of California—an outcome easy to see yet easy to miss because it looks so natural.

Back in the Gold Rush era, the connection between expansionism and horticulture was obvious to Americans. In 1857 the nation's leading magazine of tree culture, *The Horticulturalist and Journal of Rural Art and Rural Taste* (founded by Andrew Jackson Downing, the "father of American parks"), shared some California news "more pleasing and humanizing than those of the gold hunter thirsting after sudden riches." The editor had received a copy of the official report of the third annual fair of the California State Agricultural Society. This document announced the dawn of "an era in the history of this Union" because it offered incontrovertible evidence that a variety of valuable Mediterranean and tropical fruits, including olives and oranges, could be cultivated commercially in the Golden State. Writing from Philadelphia, the editor celebrated this horticultural success in jingoistic terms: "A whole new country, falling from the hands of an inert race into the possession of a new and energetic people, has been transformed." The American arborist had replaced the "lazy Spaniard."[7]

We have forgotten the importance of trees in U.S. history. It wasn't just the promise of landownership for white male citizens that set the republic apart from European monarchies. East of the Mississippi River, the land was wooded in a way that Europe had not been for centuries. Americans acclimated to this abundance with profligacy. The nation's founding arboreal stories concern loggers and looters— heroic lumberjacks clearing the way for progress or heedless loggers squandering the patrimony. The character Paul Bunyan personifies both sides of the timbering mythos.

But there is an alternative American tradition, an ethos of tree planting represented by Johnny Appleseed and other real-life amateur scientists as well as professors, bureaucrats, gentleman farmers, nurs- erymen, and urban reformers. These underappreciated middle-class men and women from the nineteenth century created the "fruited plain" celebrated in "America the Beautiful." They agreed with Wil- liam Cullen Bryant—one of the era's leading poets—that "the groves were God's first temples," but they also respected the biblical directive to "be fruitful." Starting in the Northeast in the early national period, arboreal hobbyists formed societies, sponsored meetings and fairs, and published newspapers. They circulated seeds and cuttings among wide networks of correspondents. Through plant breeding and field experimentation, they worked out which species and varieties of vines and trees, introduced or native, grew best in particular American soils and climates. In addition to the goal of "horticultural independence," tree enthusiasts promoted the commercialization of agriculture and business models based on consumer desires. They lent their support to the expansion of governmental power into the realms of forest man- agement, municipal street trees, agricultural experiment stations, and plant quarantining. They pushed for the bureaucratization of botani-

cal and entomological research. Far ahead of other U.S. farmers, horticulturists embraced what we now call biotechnology.

At root, tree culture in the nineteenth-century United States was
an environmental civics movement. If, as American farmers believed,
progress followed the plow, horticulturists believed that high civilization accompanied the grafting knife. They lived in a racist era, so
it should not be surprising that they expounded a kind of horticultural racism. Fruit growers imagined that white people would fulfill
their racial potential in a nation composed of floral smallholdings. As
an extension of their arbo-patriotism, planters tried to cure environmental ailments with disease-killing greenbelts and to improve the
climate with rain-inducing shelterbelts. Their approach to tree cover
was holistic; it united urban, rural, and wild spaces. Tellingly, one of
the movement's leading magazines was called *Garden and Forest*. As
deforestation accelerated in the latter decades of the century, American conservationists worried about the republic's future without trees.
A denuded landscape—the dreaded "timber famine"—endangered
municipal water supplies through stream degradation and threatened
the national economy, even civilization itself. Horticulturists supported public afforestation programs and the professionalization of
American forestry. The same spirit of improvement that had inspired
the removal of forest cover in the East inspired the conservation—
and addition—of trees in the Midwest and Far West.[8]

In the context of western settlement, tree planting in California
after the Gold Rush seems strange yet familiar. Americans systematically introduced trees to other "deficient" parts of the trans-
Mississippi West. Arbor Day began in Nebraska, and its proponents
favored broad-leaved deciduous species native to the temperate East,
Europe, and the British Isles. In Utah, Lombardy poplar became the
floral signature of Mormon colonization. But in lowland California,
the conservative and Eurocentric impulse to propagate trees produced something radically cosmopolitan and mainly evergreen: an
arboreal landscape unlike anything else in North America. Exploiting
California's Mediterranean climate—unique in the United States—

orchardists perfected specialty agriculture and derived unprecedented profit from fruiters. The homogeneity of California's commercial groves was offset by variety in its yards, parks, and streets. Garden enthusiasts shipped in specimens from far-flung regions; to this day, lowlanders cultivate anything and everything, temperate and tropical. This riot of nonnative species—a palm next to a pine, an avocado next to an acacia—gives the coastal California urban forest a distinctive look and smell. Drivers cruise down streets lined with flowering evergreens from colorful genera such as *Ficus*, *Magnolia*, and *Jacaranda*. Although earth tones are the dominant colors of California, most of the street trees here never lose their green.

Of the Golden State's diverse and wondrous flora, an evergreen quartet stands out in significance: redwood, eucalyptus, citrus, and palm. These are my subjects. Studying them requires traveling across the state, from stands of coast redwood in the foggy northwest to oases of fan palm in the desert southeast. Eucalyptus occurs nearly everywhere in California below 1,000 feet, the entire Central Valley as well as the coast. My four arboreal types also inhabit the spectrum of property zones. Sierra redwoods (giant sequoias) are protected in state and national parks, whereas coast redwoods are split between private and public lands. Palms adorn urban streets, travel resorts, and retail spaces, indoor and outdoor; citruses fill tiny backyards in the suburban Southland and massive plantations in the rural San Joaquin Valley; eucalypts occupy regional and municipal parks, university campuses, and state highways. Alone or together, these four kinds of trees add life—and meaning—to a swath of California, from urban to wild, from urban-wild frontier to exurban fringe.

Roughly three-quarters of *Trees in Paradise* concerns plant species outside their native habitat. Ecological newcomers deserve our full attention; almost all the state's human occupants since 1848 originated elsewhere, too. But I start the book with California's supreme indigenous flora, giant sequoias and coast redwoods. At the time of statehood, loggers had never felled a mature sequoia and barely touched the mighty forest of the North Coast. By 1900 private interests had acquired 100 percent of coast redwood habitat, and by 1950 they had clear-cut most of it. Environmentalists fought intense battles in the second half of the twentieth century to save the last totemic remnants of old growth. In the meantime, second growth sprang up. Today there are more California redwoods than there were a century ago. The forest has regenerated, albeit in changed form.

The story of the nonnatives moves inversely. From roughly 1850 to 1950—California's first hundred years as a state—American horticulturists planted innumerable trees in formerly shadeless locales. To use an old-fashioned term, they *emparadised* the land. They imported a profusion of ornamental and commercial species and varietals and created moneymaking orchards and picturesque tree-lined streets. In short, tree planters staged a landscape revolution. By the mid-twentieth century, eucalypts defined the look of lowland California, oranges dominated Southland agriculture, and palms symbolized Los Angeles. Then, in the second half of the century, while native redwoods recovered, this naturalized trio declined, and in some areas disappeared. Whether because of age, disease, infestation, land development—or, just as importantly, because of changing attitudes about which trees belonged where—eucalypts, citruses, and palms entered a period of deterioration. Millions of legacy plantings now approach the limits of their biological life span even as the horticultural ethos needed to sustain or replace them reaches a midlife crisis.

The taking and partial recuperation of native forest trees, the propagation and decline of nonnative garden trees—here is my superstructure. What follows, however, is not a single, linear narrative. Using a thematic approach, I pair each tree type with a cluster of ideas and a facet of the California Dream. Although the four sections of *Trees in Paradise* can be read as individual botanical and cultural histories, together they add up to a reinterpretation of modern California—or an argument for how trees helped make California modern.

In Part One, I investigate ideas of time, history, antiquity, and mortality with the help of the sequoia family. Giant sequoia and coast redwood are famously long-lived and notoriously imperiled. People use these living chronometers to measure epochal durations—the birth and death of civilizations. More than any other vegetation, ancient redwoods contribute to California's reputation as a realm of superlatives. The pith of the California Dream is the idea that the Golden State is different, special, unique, unprecedented. Ancient redwoods—titanic forest beings found nowhere else on earth—inspire unrivaled passions and controversies. They are the ultimate trees.

In Part Two, with eucalypts, I pick up themes of immigration, naturalization, nativeness, and alienness. In pursuit of dreams, people from all over the world have relocated to the West Coast, bringing foreign plants with them. The most cosmopolitan U.S. state has the most varied flora. Eucalypts are native to Australasia; depending on whom you ask in California, the ubiquitous "immigrant trees" (especially Tasmanian blue gum) have become "naturalized citizens" that deserve respect or "invasive aliens" that demand removal. These familiar strangers provide a useful way to think about belonging in California.

I extend my analysis in Part Three, with citruses, to labor, industry, replication, and growth. Modern citrus orchards are industrial plantations supported by an array of technological products and procedures. It takes an abundance of scientific expertise—and physical labor—to cultivate oranges and lemons. My key example is the "parent tree" of Riverside, the genetic progenitor of nearly every commercial navel orange in California. The area around Riverside used to be the world's leading orangery, but not anymore. By narrating the rise and fall of Southern California's groves, I scrutinize the Golden State's conflicted dual status as the nation's leading agricultural economy and its most populous and urbanized state. Growth can produce sprawl, and industry can beget inequality: for some, the "Sunny Southland" cast more shadow than light.

I end the book, in Part Four, with a palmy discussion of beauty, fashion, image, and style. Ornamental palms (which function as trees even though botanically they resemble grass) have been planted more for what they signify than for what they tangibly provide. They are best understood as aesthetic infrastructure. My concluding section takes place mainly on the streets of Los Angeles, the most important city in postwar America, a metropolis built on promotion. From the perspective of urban design, I explore a personal side of the California Dream—the ability to reinvent oneself, to get a makeover. Detractors often refer to Southern Californian culture as "plastic," a word that connotes mutability. Nothing in the Southland's built environment is more plastic than a palm tree.

By transforming the treescape, Californians did more than make dreams reality. They altered ecosystems. In wooded mountains and glens, loggers and preservationists rearranged mixed-age forests into segregated fragments of old growth and second growth. In the Central Valley, meanwhile, horticulturists remodeled species-rich wetlands and grasslands into single-species orchards. In the Bay Area, eucalyptus plantations went wild, producing habitats that favored some birds and butterflies while distressing others and creating fire hazards for certain neighborhoods. The artificial green of Southern California's "Orange Empire" required large doses of chemical treatments to deter injurious fungi and insects. There is a surprising proliferation of bugs in this chronicle of trees. The unprecedented global dissemination of plant stock in the nineteenth century facilitated the invasion of innumerable insect species that stowed away in packages of cuttings and seedlings. To fight "bad" herbivorous insects, state and federal entomologists introduced many "good" six-legged predators. But even after California set the gold standard for plant quarantines—a regime encountered by out-of-state drivers at fruit inspection stations— insects and insect-borne diseases continued to gain entrance to the state, periodically threatening multibillion-dollar industries based on vines and trees and necessitating emergency action. The Golden State's fruited plain is beautiful, bountiful, lucrative—and very costly to maintain.

Conceptually, *Trees in Paradise* is a book about interchanges— between the regional and the global, the native and the introduced, the biological and the cultural, the domesticated and the uncontrollable. The indigenous trees of California changed settlers, and many of those same people changed California with nonnative trees. By considering this biocultural exchange in all its curious detail, we gain a fuller understanding of the successes, failures, and limitations of the California Dream.

MY BOTANICAL DISPATCHES from one extraordinary region also speak to something universal: the human-arboreal bond. Who on earth has no relationship to trees? They provide us basic goods and services. We burn them for fuel, mill them for lumber, pulp them for paper, tend them for food. With simple technology, we can graft, crossbreed, and clone woody plants; our species has practiced these horticultural techniques since ancient times. The Stone Age was also a Wood Age. To erect and furnish the habitat of civilization, humans felled a world of trees. The primacy of wood was renewed by iron and steam. Globalization would have been impossible without tree-derived technology such as ship masts, railroad ties, telegraph and telephone poles, and rubber tires. Industrial deforestation in the nineteenth century inspired countervailing movements in conservation and tree planting. Even as people cleared forests on an unprecedented scale, they institutionalized scientific forestry and created a new arboreal environment: the urban forest. Metropolitan planners found uses for living trees in nearly every sort of built landscape, indoor as well as outdoor. Trees today remain essential. Our companion plants serve us as oxygen makers, carbon sinks, pollution filters, air coolers, sound barriers, windbreaks, water collectors, soil stabilizers, habitat makers, boundary markers, and property enhancers.[9]

Trees supply basic symbolic material, too. Almost every mythology features a sacred tree, often in the form of a Cosmic Tree, Universal Tree, or World-Tree. The Norse called it Yggdrasil. The hadith tradition in Islam tells of Tooba, the tree in Paradise. The landmark 3-D film *Avatar* (2009) is actually an old-fashioned story about a megafloral archetype, the Tree of Life, versions of which appear in the Torah and the Book of Mormon. From the Epic of Gilgamesh to *The Lord of the Rings,* some of humanity's most powerful myths and popular stories feature trees. The veneration of great plants is one of our oldest spiritual impulses. Devotees go to remarkable lengths to preserve offshoots of hallowed specimens such as the Bodhi Tree and to postpone the deaths of botanical icons such as the chestnut in Amsterdam that gave solace to Anne Frank. In the landscape of the imagination, tall trees function as intermediaries between heaven and earth—and, with their roots, the underworld. It takes little mental effort to individuate and anthropomorphize single-trunk plants. Old ones can be imagined as guardians or grandparents. On currencies, stamps, seals, and flags, trees serve as emblems of institutions of every size. They can denote rootedness, fruitfulness, domesticity, ancestry, immortality, resurrection. Countless people make sense of their place in history by creating family trees. Deciduous single-trunk plants are natural signifiers because they manifest our two main conceptions of temporality, linear time (by living, growing, and dying as individuals) and cyclical time (by changing and regenerating with the seasons). The tallest ones, honorary extraterrestrials, help us humans think beyond our earthbound existence.

Botanists don't define trees; regular people do. Any plant-thing we call a tree is in effect a tree. Large nonwoody plants such as bamboo, yucca, and palm can meet the criteria, as can miniaturized woody plants cultivated through the bonsai method. The arborescence of a plant may be legible long after it is dead, processed, even fossilized. Oddments—roots, twigs, leaves, needles, cones, or just a veneer of cambium growth rings—can serve as metonyms; people recognize the essence of a tree in natural history samples, holy relics, and consumer products. People see trees in artificial forms as well. Collapsible, fireproof, artificial Christmas trees stand in for conifers. Chemically preserved palms adorn the atria of American malls, where shoppers make phone calls relayed by metal transmission towers shaped like pines.

In their dual roles as matter and meaning, trees represent the hybrid world that humans cocreate and coinhabit. A single cultivated plant can be a biological member of an urban or agricultural ecosystem, an ornamental feature of the vernacular landscape, and also a living, situated symbol (what academics might call a "site of discourse"). Within cities, organisms often occupy a contested area between private and public property. Because of their multiple natures, trees like the Lone Cypress invite us to think creatively. By taking stock of our plants, we learn a lot about ourselves.

TAKE THE FAMILY OF John Muir, one of California's most beloved figures. The Scottish-born naturalist and conservationist—first president of the Sierra Club—is famed for his affinity for the Sierra Nevada and his spirited defense of its threatened beauties, including the sequoia groves. "Few men whom I have known loved trees as deeply and intelligently," memorialized Charles Sprague Sargent, the preeminent American botanist of his day. By Sargent's account, Muir "loved the Sierra trees the best, and in other lands his thoughts always returned to the great sequoia." We remember Muir as he presented himself in his autobiographical writings: a vagabond poet and amateur geologist at home in the wilderness, the kind of man who, in the midst of a wild Sierra windstorm, decided it was a good idea to clamber to the top of a hundred-foot Douglas fir. "Never before did I enjoy so noble an exhilaration of motion," Muir recalled. "I clung with muscles firm braced, like a bobo-link on a reed." Although the tree made sweeps of 20 to 30 degrees, Muir trusted its "elastic temper" and felt "safe, and free to take the wind into my pulses and enjoy the excited forest."[10]

This was not just a literary performance for the sake of memoir. Back in 1870 a youngish Muir wrote a "woody gospel letter" to his dearest confidant, Jeanne Carr, from his camp in the Sierra Nevada. "Ive taken the sacrament with Douglass Squirrels drank Sequoia wine, Sequoia blood," he exulted. "Drunk & sequoical," Muir "swore his "eternal love" for the "King tree." "Repent for the Kingdom of Sequoia is at hand," preached the great American pantheist.[11]

But there would be another Muir: the man who married late, settled down at an orchard property near Martinez, cultivated Muscat grapes and Bartlett pears, supervised Chinese laborers, and made a lot of money. Muir inherited a fruit ranch in Contra Costa County from his father-in-law, Dr. John Theophil Strentzel (Jan Teofil Strenzel), a political exile from Lublin, Poland. Before coming to America, Strentzel studied medicine and horticulture, two fields that made good use of surgical knives. Even more than Muir, Strentzel personifies the California Dream. He got off the boat at New Orleans in 1840 and proceeded to join a settlement company bound for Dallas. In Texas he married a woman from Tennessee named Louisiana. After the U.S.-Mexican War, Strentzel convinced his wife to move to California with their small daughter. The arduous overland journey through the Sonoran Desert almost killed Louisiana, who suffered from chronic ailments. Although the Strentzels arrived in 1849, they weren't stereotypical forty-niners. They had dreams of agricultural wealth and bodily health in a clement place. Weak lungs troubled the doctor. After an unhappy stint as merchants in the southern gold fields and a disastrous first attempt at farming beside the flood-prone Merced River, Strentzel and his family moved to the sheltered Alhambra Valley near the Carquinez Strait and purchased a choice parcel of a former Mexican land grant. "Here I can realize my long cherished dream of a home, surrounded by orange groves, and all beautiful fruits and flowers, where I can literally rest under my own vine and fig tree," the Polish émigré recalled thinking.[12]

Dr. Strentzel worked diligently to expand his estate from 20 to over 2,000 acres while his wife struggled to regain her health. He organized a local chapter of the National Grange of the Order of Patrons of Husbandry and became Contra Costa County's leading horticulturist, a man recognized as one of the "builders of the commonwealth" by California's enterprising historian Hubert Howe

Bancroft. In his public writings, Dr. Strentzel expressed the grower's ethos: "A tree planted is an heirloom for future generations; it is a sign of expanded culture and civilization." He espoused an agrarian land reformer's vision for California's future: smallholdings of fruited land forming "a great hive of industry, furnishing most desirable homes for the affluent, enjoyable with the beauty of most varied scenery, the mildness and salubrity of its climate, all within easy reach of the metropolis." In 1876, on the occasion of the centennial of the United States, this former Polish revolutionary (of the 1830–31 November Uprising) penned a local survey of horticultural achievement that could not have sounded more chauvinistically American. He looked back on the time leading up to the U.S.-Mexican War, just three decades earlier, when "the halls of Congress resounded with denunciations of California, as being a torrid, barren, desolate country, whose capacity of resources would hardly sustain a population of 10,000 souls; and the plea was plausible." The Spanish mission gardens were in decline, and Californios contented themselves with ranching: "Fruit trees or vines rarely embosomed their homes." On the *ranchos,* the land was parched and sere. Into this dormancy stepped Colonel John C. Frémont, the American "pathfinder of empire." Thanks to Frémont's radiant assessment of the West Coast, a fire was kindled in the breasts of industrious men. Even before the discovery of gold, "before the more potential agent, cupidity, gained its sway, many had resolved to forsake the ungenial climate of the older States, and their cherished homes, exchanging them for the promised land of the olive, the grape and the golden orange." These worshipers of nature, these temple builders for the goddess Pomona, men to whom the "waving grain was more alluring than the golden grains of the placers," founded the state's enduring prosperity. They, not the Mexicans, nor the forty-niners, were the true fathers of California.[13]

Strentzel put forward these flowery statements from an abode of fertility. In addition to extensive commercial plantings of fruiters, the Alhambra ranch included vines and a variety of ornamental species. To beautify his home, Strentzel imported trees from other parts of the state (including California incense-cedar, Monterey pine, giant sequoia), from Texas (Osage orange), and from much farther afield (Tasmanian blue gum and Lebanon cedar, among others). A medley of evergreen and flowering plants surrounded the family's redwood mansion. A ficus set in the ground by the Strentzels' only surviving child grew into a great tree—"Louie's fig." Beneath it, in a bower regarded by the family as "sacred space," Muir wooed his betrothed.[14]

Jeanne Carr, Muir's best friend, served as matchmaker. She was a self-taught botanist and accomplished gardener; her husband, Ezra, Muir's intellectual mentor, was a former professor of natural history and an outspoken advocate of tree culture, a man who once called horticulture "the *original fine art*." The Carrs got to know the Strentzels through the Grange, an agrarian reform movement. Muir often visited Jeanne and Ezra at their retirement home in Pasadena, a Southland settlement that would go on to earn national fame for its love of flowers. Here on the rim of Arroyo Seco, Jeanne fashioned a sylvan sanctuary with trees from every continent, including many species of eucalypts and palms, all lined with hedges of Monterey cypress and Mexican lime. "I suppose nothing less than an *exhaustive* miniature of all the leafy creatures of the globe will satisfy your Pasadena aspirations," Muir told Carr teasingly. In 1877 he wrote a glowing newspaper assessment of this "aristocratic little colony," a horticultural community composed of literary and scientific people whose conversations "smack of mental ozone." The place was growing rapidly, "like a pet tree":

After witnessing the bad effect of homelessness, developed to so destructive an extent in California, it would reassure every lover of his race to see the hearty home-building going on here and the blessed contentment that naturally follows it . . . When a man plants a tree he plants himself. Every root is an anchor, over which he rests with grateful interest, and becomes sufficiently calm to feel the joy of living. He necessarily makes the acquaintance of the sun and the sky. Favorite trees fill his mind, and, while tending them like children, and accepting the benefits they bring, he becomes himself a benefactor.[15]

Muir composed these words during his courtship phase. Once he made vows and put down roots of his own, he did not in fact find contentment. The Strentzel orchard, a virtual dowry, became a duty and a chore. Unlike his father-in-law, Muir grew ambivalent about his horticultural career in the Alhambra Valley, and in multiple interviews in his declining years he repudiated the fruitful estate where he had lived for decades, raised two daughters, and formerly worked as full-time manager. "It is not my home," he said. "Up there [the Sierra] is my home."[16]

The denial rings false. Muir the tree planter and tree tender cannot be divorced from the tree climber and tree savior, any more than he can be separated from his family. Horticulturists of his father-in-law's generation, notwithstanding their elitism and racism, thought of nature holistically: by cultivating trees in all kinds of space—urban, rural, wild—they would preserve, restore, and complete the native promise of the land. As Ezra Carr put it, they believed in tree planting for "rehabilitating the wastes created by a rude and selfish civilization." They worked to develop a "spiritualized civilization" by "preserving the true equilibrium between the animal and vegetable inhabitants." As the term *tree culture* suggests, Arcadians like Carr did not draw a strong normative distinction between the natural and the cultural. This species of environmentalism wilted in the twentieth century as Muir's late-life message—that our "real" home is "out there" in the wild—flowered in U.S. environmental thought. More recently there has been a regrowth of environmental ideas that stress holism, design, and dwelling. Today, in a world where anthropogenic influences seem irrevocably entangled in ecological systems, the arboreal legacy of California's pioneer horticulturists—a hybrid of beauty and folly—is strangely relevant again.[17]

Muir belongs back among the Strentzel family trees. Consider a photographic portrait captured around 1910 outside his manor. Posed in a suit, the great outdoorsman, his beard a shock of white, bows his head beneath the majestic fronds of a Canary Island date palm—the species that, more than any other, signified bourgeois homeownership in California. Cantonese immigrants tended Muir's garden of delight. When he composed some of his most stirring lines about the tonic of wilderness, this was the view from his window. After the naturalist succumbed to pneumonia in 1914, his loved ones buried him at the Strentzel family plot, in the shade of a great manna gum eucalyptus. Reporting on the funeral, a local newspaper claimed that Muir had "often likened this tree to a guardian angel watching over the graves." Engraved Scottish thistle adorned the matching headstones of the naturalist and his wife. John Muir's heterogeneous relationships with plants—embracing indigenous, nonnative, wild, cultivated, public, private, spiritual, and commercial trees—exemplify Californians' complicated kinship with nature in the American period.[18]

MY OWN CONNECTION to far western flora has been distanced by work. People like me follow scholarly appointments to the ends of the earth; I wrote most of this book in the deciduous Northeast. Now when I fly to California for a visit, the treescape appears odd, even Seussian, for the first day or two. Unlike my father, I can't claim the Pacific Coast as native ground, but I lived there long enough to embrace it as an adopted homeland. When my term of residence ended, I said goodbye to the Golden State with mixed feelings of affection, disgust, fascination, and awe. Where else can you see such terrible beauty, such consequential geography? Where else can you hear so many unbelievable true tales of tree fellers, tree planters, and tree huggers? Modern California deserves epic poets as well as narrative historians. It's astounding what Americans carried out at the edge of the continent after 1848. They destroyed and remade entire forests and protected sacred groves; they cultivated the world's most gainful orchards and established garden cities. Most of the Golden State's heritage trees could not bear witness to the Gold Rush, for they weren't even present. Rather, these organisms are living heirlooms of conquest. Come see. Follow me to the westerly Eden.

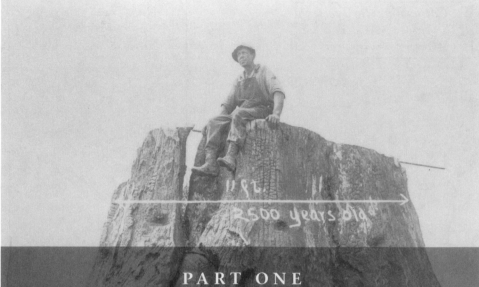

11 ft.
2500 years old

PART ONE

REDWOODS:
THE VALUE OF
LONGEVITY

8 ft.
2000 years old

"More durable
than stone"
894 © PATERSON

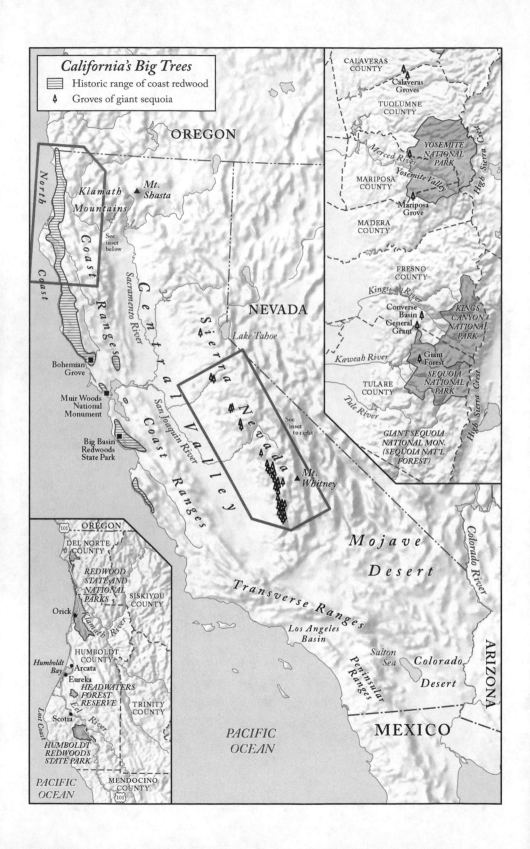

California's Big Trees

▥ Historic range of coast redwood
⚘ Groves of giant sequoia

OREGON

Klamath Mountains

Mt. Shasta

North Coast

Coast Ranges

See inset below

Sacramento River

Central Valley

NEVADA

Sierra Nevada

Lake Tahoe

See inset to right

Bohemian Grove

Muir Woods National Monument

Big Basin Redwoods State Park

San Joaquin River

Coast Ranges

Mt. Whitney

Mojave Desert

Colorado River

Transverse Ranges

Los Angeles Basin

Salton Sea

Colorado Desert

Peninsular Ranges

ARIZONA

PACIFIC OCEAN

MEXICO

CALAVERAS COUNTY

Calaveras Groves

TUOLUMNE COUNTY

Merced River

YOSEMITE NATIONAL PARK

Yosemite Valley

High Sierra Crest

MARIPOSA COUNTY

Mariposa Grove

MADERA COUNTY

FRESNO COUNTY

Kings River

Converse Basin

General Grant

KINGS CANYON NATIONAL PARK

Kaweah River

Giant Forest

SEQUOIA NATIONAL PARK

TULARE COUNTY

Tule River

High Sierra Crest

GIANT SEQUOIA NATIONAL MON. (SEQUOIA NAT'L FOREST)

101

OREGON

DEL NORTE COUNTY

REDWOOD STATE AND NATIONAL PARKS

SISKIYOU COUNTY

Orick

Klamath River

HUMBOLDT COUNTY

Humboldt Bay

Arcata

Eureka

HEADWATERS FOREST RESERVE

TRINITY COUNTY

Scotia

Eel River

Lost Coast

HUMBOLDT REDWOODS STATE PARK

PACIFIC OCEAN

MENDOCINO COUNTY

101

DRIVING ON U.S. 101 IN HUMBOLDT COUNTY, CALIFORNIA, you pass through unincorporated Orick, population 357. Los Angeles is a two-day drive away and might as well be a foreign country. Here on the North Coast, there's no love lost for "southern" California (which from this perspective includes the Bay Area), even though the local economy was long tethered to the Southland. Orick's only product, redwood lumber, once fed housing starts in metropolitan California. With the collapse of the housing boom and the onset of the Great Recession, the Seattle-based California Redwood Company shuttered Orick's sawmill in 2009. What did the future hold for the dozens of local men and women who had lost their jobs? A long-distance rural commute to one of the region's surviving mills? Marijuana cultivation? Or catering to summertime tourists? Orick serves as the gateway for Redwood National Park, a forest reserve created by Congress in 1968 and controversially expanded in 1978. Most visitors don't stop; the town has no stoplight. Orick does have a diner (the Palm Cafe, with incongruous palm trees on its sign); several run-down motels; and even more burl shops, roadside stands where local woodworkers sell chainsaw-carved figures, stumps and driftwood transformed into salmon, eagles, bears, mustangs, gnomes, Indian chiefs, and Lady Liberty. The strangest sculpture is not for

sale. On the south edge of town, next to a gravel pile and filling station, lies a smoothed but somewhat shapeless hunk of redwood, intact
despite years of weathering. Without the two carved bears standing
upright on either side, like guardians, you might assume it's a giant
piece of wooden junk. It is not.[1]

In 1977, at the height of the debate over the expansion of Redwood
National Park, Humboldt County sent a caravan of ten-wheelers
cross-country to Washington, D.C. The fleet carried a variety of
instructional aids to demonstrate that the world-famous coast redwood
was a renewable resource, not a slow-growing, endangered species, as
popularly believed. The payload included specimens of decaying five-
hundred-year-old trunks (evidence that redwoods do not last forever)
and forty-year-old logs 3 feet in diameter (evidence that the redwood
forest regenerates rapidly). Loggers gave away thousands of seedlings
on their eight-day eastbound trip. Most memorably, the first of the
twenty-three logging trucks carried a 116-foot, 17,610-pound log
carved in the shape of an unshelled peanut. Accompanying signs read
IT MAY BE PEANUTS TO YOU, BUT IT'S JOBS TO US and MORE JOBS,
LESS PARKS. The maker of the peanut, a chainsaw artist, had chosen
his material at a local lumberyard. Reputedly the massive log derived
from a tree 170 years old. Officials at the White House indicated that
President Jimmy Carter, a former peanut farmer and self-declared
friend of the workingman, would accept the Paul Bunyan–like gift. A
misunderstanding got in the way. An official at the Interior Department estimated that a log so large must have derived from a thousand-
year-old tree. The carving thus represented an "inappropriate use" of
an ancient redwood. Backpedaling, the president declined the gift
through a low-level emissary. "Would you consider it appropriate if it
were made of plastic?" asked a logger. The official indicated no. "They
said it was a terrible thing to do to a redwood," reported another timberman, dumbfounded, "but we do it all the time in the North Coast;
carving redwoods with a chainsaw is an art with us." The Humboldt
County delegation felt insulted and defeated; their demonstrations
could not compete with the media message broadcast by environ-

mentalists: *Save the redwoods! The world's tallest and oldest trees must be rescued from the brink of doom.* On the National Mall, a North Coast worker called out in resignation: "Come on people, they don't want our peanut. Let's take it home where it will be appreciated!"[2]

After an appearance at the Redwood Empire Logging Olympics, the peanut ended up in Orick. The keepers of the sculpture wanted it as close as possible to the reviled park. Since Orick operated without a mayor, the president of the chamber of commerce spoke for the community: "This location will allow the Peanut to continue proclaiming our stand against the power and growth of governmental control of our land." She organized a meeting at the Palm Cafe in the vain hope of raising enough money to build a redwood house to display the symbol of resistance permanently.[3]

No tree species in modern U.S. history has inspired more passion and controversy than coast redwood. Like its evolutionary cousin, the Sierra redwood or giant sequoia, it grows to astounding age and size. Both tree types have inspired feelings of cupidity and wonder since the early days of California statehood. Though valued as the "oldest living things" on Earth (a distinction now properly given to bristlecone pine), old-growth sequoias and redwoods carried competing commercial value as lumber. By 1900 timber firms had acquired 100 percent of the redwood forest and wastefully consumed the mightiest sequoia grove. But in the Sierra Nevada, two factors—the symbolic importance of giant sequoias and the predominance of public ownership—prevented further destruction. It took much longer for redwoods, California's most valuable extractive resource in the era between gold and oil, to become a national symbol. In the second half of the twentieth century, dramatic warnings and anticipations of the imminent demise of the "last stand" of "virgin" redwoods motivated boisterous environmental campaigns to use public monies to purchase private lands for preserves. Even as logging practices improved, the controversy deepened; even as the North Coast forest began to recover from earlier malpractice and degradation, tree lovers and tree huggers grew more adamant in their opposition to old-growth redwood harvesting. The last and costliest of these timber wars ended in 1999, with loggers and chainsaw artists on the losing side. The idea of the last stand outlasted the symbolism of the peanut. In the end, the aesthetic and ecological values assigned to California's ancient trees transcended their use value.

CHAPTER 1

Twilight of the Giants

DEBUT OF THE BIG TREE

Millions of years ago, redwoods of numerous kinds lived throughout the planet, an arboreal realm on which the sun never set. Now
the wild populations consist of three relict species, each in its own
isolated microhabitat. The deciduous and not-so-lofty dawn redwood
(*Metasequoia glyptostroboides*), first identified in fossilized form and
long assumed to be extinct, persists naturally in one valley in south-
central China—and now grows as an ornamental curiosity throughout
the world. The substantiation of this "living fossil" was *the* botanical
discovery of the twentieth century. The other two species, both evergreens, occur naturally in California and nowhere else. Giant sequoia
(also Sierra redwood, Big Tree, bigtree, or simply sequoia in colloquial
speech) goes by the scientific name *Sequoiadendron giganteum*. Coast
redwood (or simply redwood) goes by *Sequoia sempervirens*. Although
the three members of the Sequoioideae subfamily share a single common ancestor, the evolutionary divergence happened so long ago that
each is effectively sui generis. Each is a genus of one.[1]

Written accounts of coast redwood date to the Spanish period. A
chronicler of the Portolá expedition to San Francisco Bay in 1769
called the tree type *palo colorado* (red tree). A naturalist with the Mala-
spina expedition, a Spanish survey of the Pacific in 1791, collected the

first specimen. Europeans couldn't decide whether the trees should be classified as junipers, cypresses, pines, firs, or larches. An English botanist associated with the Vancouver expedition bestowed the first scientific name, *Taxodium sempervirens*, in 1824. A few years later, the intrepid botanical explorer David Douglas told his botanist friend Joseph Hooker that the enormous evergreen species, the "great beauty of Californian vegetation," gave the coastal mountains "a most peculiar, I was almost going to say awful, appearance—something which plainly tells that we are not in Europe." An Austrian with a philological ken denominated the genus *Sequoia* in 1847. Presumably he knew about the Native American scholar Sequoyah, the inventor of the Cherokee syllabary (an alphabet of syllables), and may have meant to commemorate him with a Latinate name—but no one knows for certain.[2]

For many decades taxonomists grouped the two types of California redwood into a single *Sequoia* genus. Besides geographic proximity, broad affinities exist. Both trees are unusually tall with mighty columnar trunks. Both are wonderfully long-lived—an effective maximum age of 2,000 years for redwoods and 3,500 years for sequoias, though most individuals don't last nearly so long. Both rank among the world's fastest-growing trees. Adapted to fire, they develop protective layers of thick, furrowed, fibrous bark. On the inside, their tannin-rich heartwood resists rot and disease. Sequoias and redwoods shed their foliage as shoots rather than individual leaves and produce tiny cones. Nonscientists routinely conflate the two species, accidentally or deliberately. In 1937 the legislature in Sacramento honored the "California redwood" as the state tree; the attorney general later clarified that the designation applied to both species.

For botanists, fine differences matter. At the genetic level, giant sequoia is diploid, whereas coast redwood is hexaploid—six chromosomes per cell, a unique occurrence in conifers. Redwoods also possess the uncommon ability to reproduce both sexually and asexually. Genetic copies in the form of bright green suckers encircle the trunks of most mature trees; in rare cases, a mutation produces an albino—a white evergreen—that feeds off the parent in lieu of photosynthesis. *S. sempervirens* ("ever-living") can also resprout from the base following a catastrophic disturbance such as a fire—or a chainsaw. Giant sequoia cannot regenerate or resurrect in these ways.

Even untrained eyes can spot some differences in surface appearance. A mature redwood is actually less red than a sequoia. (The *red* in the name refers to the heartwood.) Its bark looks dark ruddy gray-brown, with a patina of green from lichens and moss. On a mature sequoia, the bare shaft is cinnamon red with soot-black fire scars. Compared to a redwood, its bark—its "behemoth-like hide"—is softer and spongier, its foliage rougher and scalier.[3]

Redwoods and sequoias are, in that order, the two tallest plants in creation (though Australia's forests of mountain ash, a eucalyptus species, may have reached greater heights before commercial logging). With ballyhoo, a National Geographic Society expedition "discovered" the world's tallest tree along Redwood Creek in Humboldt County in 1963. The Tall Tree—the "Mount Everest of All Living Things"—subsequently lost some of its height to tip dieback. Officially it ceded its top status in 2000 with the discovery of the Stratosphere Giant in Humboldt Redwoods State Park. Then, in 2006, three more finds by height hunters in Redwood National Park eclipsed them all. The new loftiest, dubbed Hyperion, stands at 379 feet—and growing. By comparison, the Statue of Liberty, including its giant pedestal, rises 305 feet. Amazingly, the widest point on an old redwood may occur near the top. Like candelabra, mature redwoods sport multiple reiterated trunks. Airborne soil and tree litter collect as pockets of humus in these complex networks of limbs. Mosses and ferns and even other species of trees take root literally on top of redwoods; salamanders here may spend their whole lives as supraterrestrials. This high-rise ecosystem, accessible to humans only by roped climbing, also contains epiphytes—nonparasitic vegetation that attaches to the canopy and intercepts nutrients from the air.[4]

Sequoias don't reach quite as high—they seldom exceed 200 feet—but they contain more wood by volume. They are the largest plants in the world. The "mountain-massy" form of a Big Tree is simpler and brawnier than that of a redwood.[5] Over time, an ancient sequoia drops its lower branches; the foliage billows from the bulging upper branches. In silhouette, the tree's shape might be fancied as a titanic stalk of broccoli.

The most salient ecological difference between *Sequoia* and *Sequoiadendron* concerns habitat—one maritime, the other subalpine. True to its common name, coast redwood grows near the Pacific. Its historic range stretches almost 500 miles from the Santa Lucia Mountains of Big Sur in southern Monterey County to a point just beyond the Oregon state line. The redwood corridor is long but narrow—only 1 to 30 miles wide. Though benefiting from ocean proximity, redwoods don't thrive by the shore. They do better above the salt spray. They occur at elevations up to 3,000 feet in the northern coastal ranges, while in the sunnier part of their range, south of Sonoma County, they cluster in canyons and shaded ridges, where they rarely grow to peak size. Redwoods weaken in hot, dry weather; their prime habitat corresponds to California's summer fog belt. North of the Russian River, a continuous forest—a mix of species with localized pure stands of *S. sempervirens*—thrives beneath the clouds. The fog drip captured by redwoods during the otherwise dry season nourishes understory life and provides supplemental moisture for the trees themselves (perhaps 30 percent of their annual intake along the North Coast). To a limited extent, redwood leaves directly absorb water from fog. More importantly, the low marine cloud layer reduces transpiration. Redwoods are inefficient water managers, which explains their stunted, stressed-out appearance when planted in sunbaked environments like the San Joaquin Valley and the Los Angeles Basin. With their shallow roots and wide-open stomata (cell pores), the trees cannot tap external water at great depths or hoard internal water for long periods. Summertime fog allows redwoods to apply their "profligate water use behaviour" toward record-breaking vertical growth.[6]

Far inland, *Sequoiadendron* doesn't form pure stands or occupy a continuous forest in its mountainous redoubt. It occurs in discrete clusters—conventionally called groves—alongside white fir and sugar pine. Only about seventy groves, fewer than 40,000 acres in total, exist in the western foothills of the Sierra Nevada, and nowhere else. The species' semiarid habitat ranges from 3,000 to 9,000 feet in altitude, with 5,000–7,000 being optimal. Sequoias want snowy winters without bitter cold and dry summers without burning heat. The northern two-thirds of the 260-mile-long sequoia corridor encompasses just eight compact, widely scattered groves. The lower third, south of the Kings River, contains a far greater concentration, a mini-belt of Big Trees. Here the concept of "grove" becomes somewhat shaky, as no more than a few miles separate any single stand from another. The most expansive remaining sequoia domain is the Giant Forest in Sequoia National Park, home to the world's biggest tree, the General Sherman.

Groves and forests have different effects on viewers. Usually you can see the monumental form of a sequoia from various angles, whereas the only available perspective for most of the lofty redwoods is looking straight up from the bole. Compared to the North Coast forest, a mature sequoia grove feels open and sunny. "Where are such columns of sunshine, tangible, accessible, terrestrialized?" wrote John Muir in a moment of pantheistic ecstasy.[7] The wide spacing between sequoias provides view corridors like a well-designed park. But even in the denser redwood forest, shafts of light—crepuscular rays—can descend to the understory like missives from God. Pilgrim-tourists draw analogies to church architecture. Standing beneath redwoods is like being inside the nave of a Gothic cathedral, whereas standing next to sequoias is like being outside the main cathedral in a great city.

One more contradistinction is worth mentioning up front because it explains so much of what follows: dissimilar habitats caused divergent economic histories. In the nineteenth century, redwoods were for settlers more accessible and utilizable than sequoias. They grew in thick forests near ocean ports, whereas sequoias grew in isolated groves on roadless mountains. Also, old redwoods made good, strong, durable lumber—arguably the finest in the world—unlike old sequoias, whose massiveness belied brittleness, making them lesser sources of lumber. Largely for these reasons, sequoias preceded redwoods in the transition from a commercial to an aesthetic resource. However, the two stages overlapped for an extended period, producing strange and contradictory outcomes: Americans celebrated and protected the Big Trees even as they felled some of the best specimens and auctioned off the finest grove.

Giant sequoias entered public consciousness in the midst of the Gold Rush and the conquest of California. In the 1850s the discovery of gold, the disclosure of scenery, and the dispossession of native peoples—who of course already knew about the trees—happened in rapid, interrelated fashion. Yosemite Valley was named and publicized by the Mariposa Battalion, a motley crew of deputized gold miners who pursued native bands who had refused to sign treaties drawn up by federal officials. When they couldn't find Indians to apprehend, the campaigners searched for village sites and acorn caches, and burned them. In the middle of the scorched-earth offensive, the battalion entered the valley of waterfalls and immediately recognized that the wonder-spot would become a magnet for tourists—once the Sierra Miwoks had been driven out.

An equally phenomenal scenic revelation in the southern Sierra took place in May of the following year, 1852. A. T. "Gus" Dowd, a long-haired, buckskin-clad big-game hunter, had been employed by a mining company to procure meat for its workers. While tracking down a wounded California grizzly (the now extinct subspecies of bear seen on the state flag), Dowd stumbled into a Big Tree grove in Calaveras County. When no one believed his report, Dowd resorted to a fib. "Boys, I have killed the largest grizzly bear that I ever saw in my life," he supposedly said to campmates. After leading some of them to the Calaveras grove, the hunter exulted: "Now, boys, do you believe my big tree story? That is the large grizzly I wanted you to see." After the fame of the "Great Cedar Tree" grew, other white men claimed (sometimes persuasively, sometimes not) to have seen the trees earlier; they just hadn't told anyone. Back in 1833, the Walker Party emigrants encountered "some trees of the Redwood species, incredibly large," but they had bigger things on their minds, like staying alive during their late-season mountain crossing. Later, the attention of forty-niners was trained on tiny flecks of gold.[8]

In any event, Dowd counts as the first publicist: news of his discovery made it into a local paper, found a national outlet, and so on, until it finally reached Europe in July 1853. The Gold Rush had opened up pathways of communication from the West Coast to the far ends of the earth. Curiosity seekers and collectors soon beat a path to Calaveras. One of the first was William Lobb, an employee of an English nurseryman who sold seeds collected in the New World. Lobb forwarded some of his samples to the eminent British botanist John Lindley, who in December 1853 gave the "vegetable monster" its first name in print. For this ultra-American species Lindley chose the un-American name *Wellingtonia gigantea*, honoring the late Duke of Wellington, the statesman and military hero who had defeated Napoleon at Waterloo. "Emperors and kings and princes have their plants, and we must not forget to place in the highest rank among them our own great warrior," Lindley explained. According to scientific custom, first in print is first in right, but insulted Americans refused to honor the name—a "preposterous piece of cockneyfied nonsense." U.S. chauvinists retaliated against the "British scientific 'stamp acts'" with their own warrior-cult name, *Washingtonia californica*. A French botanist facilitated a truce in 1854 by arguing persuasively that the similarities between the coastal and Sierran redwoods were salient enough to warrant use of the same preexisting genus, *Sequoia*. For the next hundred years, most scientists favored *Sequoia gigantea*, though *Washingtonia* and *Wellingtonia* periodically recurred in U.S. and U.K. publications. (*Washingtonia* ended up as the genus name for the one species of palm native to California; more on that plant later.) The Big Tree's current name, *Sequoiadendron giganteum*, took several decades to gain acceptance after being proposed in 1939.[9]

By any name, no other plant went from obscurity to fame in such a short time. Initially the buzz concerned size. Many outsiders assumed that the stories about gargantuan flora in Calaveras County were a hoax, another frontier tall tale from the land of golden dreams. As early as the 1850s, Californians were bragging only half in jest about their outsized agricultural products—monster cherries that could fill a dinner plate, petite pumpkins that could squash a house, half-acre tree stumps that could accommodate railroad tunnels. California was, in the words of one travel author, "the Brobdi[n]gnag of the vegetable world." In the protophotographic era, the public desired physical proof, and entrepreneurs worked to satisfy. If they couldn't bring the world to the grove, they would bring pieces of the grove to world cities. They promptly killed a pair of giants—bored one down, girdled another—for exhibits on both sides of the Atlantic. "There has been much talk here," wrote a visiting British mining engineer in 1855, "of the Goth-like act of cutting down the tree, the largest and oldest in the world, as the Californians boast." The leveled sequoia was none other than Dowd's "Discovery Tree." Parts of its bark and trunk went to New York and Paris, where botanical enthusiasts paid their entrance fees, satisfied their curiosity, then decried the exhibit as desecration. Many suspected humbuggery. People invented new terms, capitalized for effect, to describe the ne plus ultra: Big Tree, Great Tree, Mammoth Cypress, Great Washington Cedar, Giant Cedar, Giant Tree of California, Monarch of the Forest, Sylvan Mastodon, Giant of the Vegetable Creation, Vegetable Wonder, Eighth Wonder of the World. A member of the Royal Society lectured to his English audience that the *Wellingtonia* was higher than St. Paul's or Salisbury Cathedral. The American West encompassed strange scenes, natural and social, ennobling and disturbing, he said. Instead of inaugurating a golden age, the Gold Rush had inspired "rapine, violence, and blood," like the "breaking loose of hell."[10]

For a few years, the Mammoth Tree Grove—today called the Calaveras North Grove—was the one known domain of the kingly trees. "Nature, by peculiar geognostic arrangements, seems to have isolated [the sequoias], to startle and arrest the attention of mankind," mused one observer.[11] This creekside habitat contained about a hundred mature specimens—now minus two—within a mile-long perimeter. Second in knowledge and fame was Mariposa Grove, "discovered" in 1857 about 20 miles south of the entrance to Yosemite Valley. Whereas private owners acquired Calaveras, Congress protected Mariposa as part of the 1864 Yosemite Grant, the first time in U.S. history that the government reserved public land from private entry to be a national park. After the completion of the transcontinental railroad in 1869, eastern and European tourists on the grand tour of western wonderlands made requisite stops at Calaveras and Mariposa. Until the automobile age, when the Giant Forest at Sequoia National Park became easily accessible, these two groves defined the sequoia experience.

As first impulse, many early tourists tried to temper the enormity. Just as today, cretins carved their names on bark and pinned business cards and calling cards on the inside of fire cavities. Most commonly, visitors humanized the scene by anthropomorphizing the plants. They gave them names. Within a few years, all the giants in the Mammoth Tree Grove bore an engraved marble tablet, varnished metal sign, or painted shingle for identification. To prevent name defacement, people nailed or screwed the markers above eye level. For lesser trees, guides encouraged guests to attach handwritten names on cards, promising to preserve them, only to take them down and make the same promise to subsequent guests.[12]

As the naming convention spread to every sequoia grove, the designations clustered around a few themes, starting with domesticity and gender. Pairs and groups that grew close together received familial titles like Faithful Couple, Mother and Son, Three Sisters, or Siamese Twins and the Guardian. Singular trees were imagined as family-deficient: Old Maid, Bachelor, Hermit. Using analogies to domiciles, people domesticated certain trees with blackened, burned-out hollows: Pioneer's Cabin, Miner's Cabin, Uncle Tom's Cabin. Visitors invoked poetic and literary names such as Three Graces, Satan's Spear, Hercules, and Arborvitæ Queen. Downed giants received

monikers such as Fallen Monarch, Noah's Ark, Goliath. State pride
found ready expression—Granite State, Empire State, and so on—as
did loyalty to cities and universities.

The majority of names commemorated people, including numerous New England luminaries whose light has dimmed with time.
U.S. presidents were of course popular. After 1865 a host of tree
titles honored Civil War figures: General Grant, General Sherman,
J. B. McPherson, Phil Sheridan, Robert E. Lee, Abraham Lincoln,
Edward Everett (the man who gave a two-hour oration at Gettysburg
before Lincoln's two-minute address), and even Lincoln's impeached
successor, Andrew Johnson. (A fallen tree at Mariposa received
the identifier "because it leans toward the South and because the
top was shattered in falling.") Mainly the nicknames served to
Americanize—and masculinize—the trees. In 1871 Elizabeth Cady
Stanton and Susan B. Anthony toured Calaveras after campaigning
for women's suffrage in California and felt discouraged to find the
usual suspects immortalized. Stanton asked for, and readily received,
her guide's permission to tack up "Lucretia Mott" and "Anna Dickin-
son." The matriarchal names were never heard of again.[13]

Refined tourists who composed travel books reacted to arboreal pet
names with distaste; they turned aversion into meditation: *How can
transient man denominate a timeless tree?* The literati marveled at the
age of sequoias more than at their beauty or size. To sensitive eyes, the
bigness seemed inelegantly disproportionate. "There is nothing lovable about a sequoia," divulged one seasoned traveler. A few admitted
to feeling boredom, and many admitted to feeling disappointment,
even "extreme" or "intense" disappointment at first glance. Emotional
letdown became so predictable that guidebooks even warned of it. The
groves let in too much sun to be properly—that is, eerily—sublime.
And the trees didn't seem as monstrous as advertised. Mental comparisons to the Bunker Hill Monument or Nelson's Column didn't
help much. A prominent society woman claimed, tongue in cheek,
that the "average (female) mind" was not "mathematical enough to
admire the work of nature in exact ratio with their size, a very big

tree usually exciting as much satisfaction as one a little bigger." Many tourists reported that their three-dimensional awareness activated over time. In contrast, the antiquity of a sequoia made an immediate, deep impression. The sublime experience came from *thinking*. "None of us were so profoundly impressed at first with the great size of the trees as we had expected to be," shared a Mariposa visitor. "The great space [that the Big Tree] had filled was nothing to the ages it had bridged over."[14]

As easily as visitors felt awe in the presence of biological antiquity, they experienced awfulness—the oppressive weight of time. When comparing themselves to sequoias, people used a vocabulary of temporal alienation: *our own short lives and diminutiveness; the fleeting generations of men; like a meteor in the night, that glows and is gone; man's littleness, his brevity of existence; the utter nothingness of mortal man*. At the same time, visitors found consolation in the sempiternity of sequoias. The same old plants that belittled an individual's life span could ennoble the duration of human history. Reflexively, educated people inserted sequoias into biblical and classical texts. In 1860 two men of letters penned representative ruminations. Describing his trip to the Far West, Horace Greeley, newspaperman and politico from New York City, imagined that the "forest mastodons" were of "very substantial size when David danced before the ark, when Solomon laid the foundations of the Temple, when Theseus ruled in Athens, when Æneas fled from the burning wreck of vanquished Troy, when Sesostris led his victorious Egyptians into the heart of Asia." Similar imagery came from the mind of the celebrated preacher Thomas Starr King, recently transplanted to California from Massachusetts. King wished that the "vegetable Titans" could speak. "Why cannot the dumb column now be confidential . . . Why will not the old patriarch take advantage of that ripple through his leaves and whisper to me his age? Are you as old as Noah?"[15]

In account after account, travel writers filled in this historical scaffolding with purple prose. *This very tree*, they wrote, sprouted from the damp Sierra soil in the time of Abraham or his prophetic successors

Moses and Mohammed. As King Solomon "called his master-masons to refreshment from the building of the Temple," the tree kept growing. It pushed toward the sun during the reign of Sheba. It grew into a lanky youth even as Homer narrated the *Odyssey*, as Herodotus chronicled Xerxes, as Phidias sculpted Zeus, and as Aristotle tutored Alexander the Great. Dew glistened on its branches on the night the Virgin gave birth in a manger. While Rome rose and fell, while Caesar and Constantine lived and died, *this tree* became an adult of full stature. The sequoia completed its second millennium during the tyranny of the papacy. Its girth expanded and its furrows deepened as the world of men convulsed from war (Genghis Khan) and science (Copernicus). The Big Tree "saw the deluge; saw the crucifixion; saw the first Pope, saw Luther; and was here to receive Columbus"; it "witnessed the incarnation, miraculous mission, crucifixion, and ascension of the Messiah." And so on: the pantheon list was multiplied interminably. Historical allusions came fast and thick from the pens of promoters and journalists in 1857 when reassembled bark from a Calaveras tree went on display at London's Crystal Palace. The plant that supplied the "Tree Mountain" was supposedly four thousand years old by the counting of concentric rings—"an astonishing chart of tree time." Two such trees "would span the whole period of recorded time from Adam's days to the present." Not to be outdone, a correspondent with the London *Times* calculated an age of 6,408 years, meaning the specimen had reached maturity "when as yet Adam lived in the Garden of Eden."[16]

People on both sides of the Atlantic synchronized sequoias with gods, prophets, and heroes from the ancient past, but Americans forged a different relationship with antiquity based on distance and desire. For a young nation insecure about its cultural position relative to Europe, natural scenery offered something vaguely compensatory if not commensurate with ruins, myths, and epics. Before the mid-nineteenth century, eastern splendor spots such as the Natural Bridge of Virginia, Niagara Falls, the Hudson River Valley, and the White Mountains of New Hampshire served this nationalistic pur-

pose moderately well. Afterward, the U.S. West provided much better bragging material: taller mountains, deeper valleys. It required a
mental leap, however, to turn inanimate earth forms into emblems
of ancient time. The human dimension was missing. The Grand
Canyon—a radically un-European landscape—became a national
symbol only after scientists convinced the public to intellectualize the
chasm as an open book of *geologic* time. That happened around 1900.
At roughly the same time, the United States appropriated southwestern Pueblo ruins as the cultural property of the nation. But in the
second half of the nineteenth century, the Mammoth Tree Grove
provided the most appealing landscape of antiquity for patriotic
Americans.

Sequoias supervened the enshrinement of historic trees from
America's colonial and revolutionary periods. New Englanders had
painted canvasses and written poems about the "Old Elm" in Boston Common—a plant celebrated for its "antiquity" (that is, the time
before the Puritans)—and turned the Charter Oak of Connecticut
into an icon ("the Mecca of Patriot Pilgrims") on a par with Plymouth
Rock. As elder beings, sequoias merited even greater respect. James
Hutchings, author of the original Yosemite guidebook, asserted: "No
pilgrims to Mohamed's tomb at Mecca, or to the reputed vestment of
our Saviour at Treves, or to the Juggernaut of Hindostan, ever manifested more interest in the superstitious objects of their veneration,
than the intelligent and devout worshippers of the wonderful in nature
and science, of our own country, in their visit to the Mammoth-Tree
Grove." The Sierra Nevada offered a novel kind of heritage tree and
pilgrimage site. Conventionally, historic plants such as the Washington Elm in Cambridge Common had direct (if folkloric) connections to specific place-based events. It didn't take a large stretch of
the imagination to call such trees "witnesses" to the American past.
Giant sequoia couldn't work this way. Its only historical connection
was to indigenous Sierran peoples, and Anglo-Americans didn't
believe that Indians—especially the disparaged "digger Indians" of
California—had much history, much less a past worth remembering.

So the colonizers brought their own history to the groves. The unique western location of the Big Tree stood for the exceptional and manifest destiny of the United States. "They [the sequoias] began with our Modern Civilization," wrote a famous eastern journalist who traveled west with the Speaker of the House to mark the end of the Civil War and the forthcoming completion of the transcontinental railroad. "They were just sprouting when the Star of Bethlehem rose and stood for a sign of its origin; they have been ripening in beauty and power through these Nineteen Centuries; and they stand forth now, a type of the Majesty and Grace of Him in whose life they are coeval."[17]

The insecurity complex of the United States was matched only by its superiority complex. For a people conspicuously lacking in tradition and history, Americans—especially native-born white Protestant citizens who had come of age before the Civil War—felt boldly certain of their country's future. From this position of hubris, the ancient trees of the New World seemed to cut Europe down to size. Thomas Starr King had noted approvingly that even the low estimate for the date of a Big Tree's germination antedated the Norman Conquest and "the foundation stone of the oldest Gothic spire in Europe." As the course of empire moved slowly but inexorably westward, the American trees waited. "What changes have transpired in the condition of people and of States since the germ shot down the roots of those trees," wrote another transplanted Bay Stater, a former forty-niner from Nantucket. "The golden age had not yet dawned on the Roman empire, and the ancestors of the present polished races of *Great Britain*, *France*, and *Germany* were naked and wandering savages, in the bleak and snowy forests of Northern Europe." Many travel writers quoted from a local author's dramatic verse, "The Three Brothers; or, the Mammoth Grove of Calaveras: A California Legend," which had been performed on the stump of the Discovery Tree. The favorite passage imagined the life of this "monarch-father," a sequoia that had germinated in the days after the Flood. "Coeval with Assyrian kings," the branches of the tree spread in dominion; his "sapling heirs with empires grew."

While Art and Science slept,
And ruthless hordes drove back Improvement's stream,
Their sturdy oaklings throve, and in their turn,
Rose, when Columbus gave to Spain a world.[18]

In other words, the tree-father and his patient progeny waited out the "dark ages" until the light of the new Christian dispensation shone on America. Improvement's stream concluded here. It seemed auspicious that the Spanish and the Mexicans had failed to discover both the mother lode and the Big Tree during their tenure in California. Anglo-Americans saw themselves as the culmination of historical progress—the successor to European civilization—and they imagined sequoias as both harbingers and witnesses. "These trees are the only living things that connect us back to ages that are gone," wrote the Congregationalist minister John Todd. "Perhaps before Rome was ever named," he continued, "these minarets of the solitudes . . . were lifting up their young heads, to be ready and waiting for eyes that could appreciate them, when the men of the nineteenth century should gather around them."[19]

All the initial commentators on the Mammoth Tree made a plausible if misleading inference: bigger must mean older. The illustrious Alexander von Humboldt had pronounced categorically that "massive size is indicative of age" in vegetable forms. But the only way to know the true age of a tree was to read a cross-section of its growth rings. Thus botanists reacted with interest, moderated by disgust, to the news that California Mammonites had felled the Discovery Tree. Unfortunately, the basal cut of the "Big Tree Stump" was jagged, making the rings hard to read. On the basis of a small sample of bark, a writer for a popular illustrated newspaper estimated an age of 2,250 years. "When the next of these venerable trees is wantonly destroyed," snorted Asa Gray, America's leading botanical authority, "it is to be hoped that its layers will be accurately counted on the whole section, and the thickness of each century's growth carefully measured on the radius." In 1854 the botanist John Torrey visited Calaveras County and made the first careful reading—only 1,120 layers. "The facts show that the tree lacks almost three centuries of being half as old as it was said to be!" he reported. Far from being disappointed, Torrey marveled at the prodigious capability of a sequoia: "Its enormous size is owing to its continued rapid growth rather than to any extraordinary age." In 1863 the California state geologist J. B. Whitney made the most authoritative count. "The Big Tree is not that wonderfully exceptional thing which popular writers have almost always described it as being," he wrote. He estimated that the tree had lived 1,300 years before dying from vandalism. As Whitney knew, an age of thirteen centuries "is not so great as that assigned, by the highest authorities, to some of the English yews."[20]

Even with this double dose of botanical realism, the age of sequoia trended upward, not downward, in popular imagination. "The age of the Sequoias is the one point most hopelessly befogged to the ordinary tourist," complained a professor at the University of California in 1886. The "wild talk" of three thousand or four thousand years must be "relegated to the realm of absurdity and impossibility." However, the professor did not expect to prevail: "The vaporings and idle imaginings of the newspaper man, I am compelled to believe, are more acceptable both to landlords and tourists, than any presentation of actual facts."[21]

Misinformation derived from reputable sources, too. In 1890 Professor Gustav Eisen of the California Academy of Sciences publicly denounced the logging of monster trees, including a stump he dated at 6,126 years. John Muir, who discovered many new sequoia groves south of the Kings River through his peregrinations in the 1860s and 1870s, spoke of a downed giant with complex and contorted growth rings. He said he had spent a day clearing its charred stump with an ax and counting its rings with a pocket magnifying glass. Interviewed by the *New York Times* in 1891, Muir conjectured that the tree was "probably over 4,000 years old." A few years later, in a book for a popular audience, the "probably" faded away. "I counted over 4,000 rings," wrote Muir, "which showed that this tree was in its prime, swaying in the Sierra winds, when Christ walked the earth. No other tree in the world, as far as I know, has looked down on so many centuries as the Sequoia, or opens such impressive and suggestive views into history." Muir, like Eisen, meant to arouse public support for sequoia preservation. The San Francisco–based Sierra Club, founded in 1892 with Muir as president, took up the cause. Charter member David Starr Jordan, the first president of Stanford University and a noted biologist, expressed his confidence that "many of them [the sequoias] have stood on earth at least 8,000 years." Thanks to Muir and Jordan and other California-based conservationists, Americans of the early twentieth century accepted sequoias as the "oldest living things on earth." The newly created National Park Service repeated this claim, as did the National Geographic Society. Muir's quadrimillennial stump—if it ever existed—has never been seen again.[22]

AMERICAN REMAINS

No amount of deep thinking about the antique age and wondrous longevity of giant sequoia prevented Gold Rush–era Californians from exploiting the species in the service of short-term profit or simple novelty. By peculiar destiny, the age-old trees grew exclusively in the Golden State, a restless place of heedless innovation and creative destruction. American time moved faster here. With the discovery of gold and then the building of the transcontinental railroad, California shifted violently from a premodern economy to industrial capitalism. With astonishing quickness, communal and public domain became private property; rooted trees became liquid assets; wonders of the world became so many shingles, railroad ties, and pay-per-view exhibits.

The avarice inspired by the Sierra redwood—green gold—appeared first at Calaveras. It is worthwhile to go into the details of the death of the Discovery Tree. In July 1853 the brothers Joseph and William Lapham each took out a preemption claim, a legal process by which a citizen-squatter could take possession of 160 acres of public land and obtain title at a rock-bottom price even before the government had surveyed it. William Lapham straightaway sold the Discovery Tree to an entrepreneurial friend, William Hanford, who hatched a plan to put the bark on display. Hanford employed five local miners to strip off 40 vertical feet of the bark in 8-foot sections marked for reassembly. Having girdled the tree, the violators decided to take the whole thing down—why the hell not? Being miners, they attacked the mammoth with tools of their trade. Using 2-inch pump augers, they carved tunnels in the trunk; they bored and cross-bored for twenty days, but the steady sequoia refused to fall. The persistent vandals sawed the wood between the holes; they inserted wedges; they cut down adjacent trees to push into the column like a battering ram. Nothing worked. Finally, the story goes, the sequoia blew over in a breeze while the crew retired at lunch. Vanquished, the great tree crashed into the soft banks of a creek, becoming partially submerged. The force of impact dislodged rocks and roots and threw mud into the air, coating the bark of neighboring plants. The triumphant Lilliputians sawed off a partial cross-section of the exposed butt to obtain a specimen of growth rings.

Thus dismembered, the Discovery Tree was ready to be discovered by the paying public. Hanford arranged for the sequoia shell and the cross-section to be transported by wagon to Stockton and then by steamer to San Francisco. On Bush Street, workers set up the bark to form a hollow trunk—a cozy parlor. It housed wall-to-wall carpet, a piano, and seating for forty—"large enough," one quipped, "to contain all the wives of Brigham Young and all the husbands of Lola Montes."[23] To enter the tree-room cost fifty cents, a considerable sum at the time. In the evenings, couples could attend cotillion parties for three dollars. To ensure customer satisfaction and to preempt complaints of imposture, the proprietor displayed the cross-section nearby as hard evidence.

After a month in residence in the Queen City of the Pacific, the transmogrified tree traveled via clipper around Cape Horn. In early

1854 the boxes of disassembled bark arrived in Manhattan. There Hanford negotiated with P. T. Barnum to show the sequoia at the New York Crystal Palace, a new exposition hall that had, the previous year, hosted America's first world's fair, at Sixth Avenue and 42nd Street (now Bryant Park). Dissatisfied with the terms, Hanford rented his own space on Broadway and prepared advertisements for his "*Gigantea americanum*," three thousand years old. He tarried too long. Before Hanford could open, Barnum began selling tickets to his own "California Cedar Tree." Barnum's specimen was not in fact a giant sequoia but a coast redwood previously procured by a Philadelphia showman and rushed to New York by special arrangement. Flummoxed and incensed, Hanford tried to prove that the illustrious Barnum was a faker, but Barnum outplayed him at the confidence game. The impresario's exhibit, though much smaller, seemed more believable—a hollowed-out one-piece tree cylinder. Hanford's improbably large tree-room, pieced together, looked counterfeit in comparison. The "Vegetable Monster" flopped on Broadway. Before it could be shown again in some other city, the bark from the Discovery Tree burned up in a warehouse inferno.[24]

Meanwhile, back at Calaveras, William Lapham sold the rights to another of "his" trees, the so-called Mother of the Forest, to a pair of local businessmen who wanted to create their own traveling showpiece. Their operation was more professional: workers built scaffolding around the sequoia, with platform supports screwed deep into the inner bark. One section at a time, they excised the shaggy outer bark, up to 2 feet thick, to a height of 116 feet. Marked for reassembly and shipped to the East Coast, the husk found a home at the reimagined Crystal Palace. The glass-domed exhibition space reopened on Independence Day 1855 with an erect trunk, one of the "vegetable wonders of the gold regions," at its center. The protean Horace Greeley, a director of the palace, provided free publicity in his paper, the *Tribune*. The public gaped at the sequoia shaft, which looked like a genuine Big Tree, not a gimmicky tree-room. Invisible internal scaffolding held up the organic construction.

After a yearlong run, the proprietors sent the exhibit across the ocean to England's bigger, better Crystal Palace—a Victorian theme park, the pet project of Prince Albert. The palace had recently been relocated from Hyde Park to Sydenham, South London, where millions of paying guests walked through the iron-and-glass wonderland that celebrated the exploits of empire and engineering. For almost a decade, the *Wellingtonia gigantea*—a red Roman column in arboreal form—drew great crowds. Ornamented with potted cycads, it occupied a prominent location in the Tropical Transept opposite replicas of the colossal Ramses II statues at Abu Simbel. Eight small sphinxes held court beneath the Big Tree. The antiquities of Egypt and California shared the same physical and psychic space in the pleasure dome until 1866, when the prefab ruins turned to rubble and ashes in a fire that consumed the entire menagerie at Sydenham. Probably the 95-foot-tall sequoia shell acted as an intensifying funnel for the flames.[25]

In California, the exfoliated body of the Mother of the Forest remained on display. The matriarch was never cut down. Girdled like no other tree in history, it slowly perished, standing. The last of its greenery fell to the ground in 1861. A British travel writer called the tree "a ghastly object—her sides still transfixed with wooden implements of torture,—the St Sebastian of the forest." Lured by the rickety scaffolding, daredevil visitors carved names and dates into the exposed inner bark as high as they dared to ascend. Over the decades, the workers' platform fell piecemeal to the forest floor, revealing even rows of bore holes in the trunk. Visually startling, the flayed tree attracted the scrutiny of artists. In the 1860s the pioneering photographer Carlton Watkins took a popular series of sequoia images— widely pirated—that included collectible stereoscopic views of the dead Mother. Her visage also appeared in one of the earliest pictorial books on the gold country, *Vischer's Views of California* (1862). The author-artist, the German-born Edward Vischer, had come to San Francisco as a forty-niner after a long business residence in Acapulco. Vischer called the Mammoth Tree Grove "Edenic," in contrast to the "demoniac power of Mammon" on display during the Gold Rush. Despite having witnessed the worst, Vischer believed in a better America. In his book, scenes of social progress and industrial innovation share the same page with wasted minescapes; images of robust sequoias mix with the dead, the fallen, and the fire-damaged. The standout picture shows the Mother of the Forest in two stages, then and now, side by side, partially overlapping—almost like modern rephotography. The Mother on the right carries leaves; the identical tree on the left, in the center of the image, carries a bare crown. The artist inscribed death dates—1855, 1861—on the respective trunks, making them resemble gravestones.[26]

The two exhibition trees taken from Calaveras prompted the earliest outcries against the destruction of sequoias. Objectors often repeated the line "Woodman, spare that tree!" This catchphrase derived from a popular sentimental poem from 1830, an expression of nostalgia for the good old days of country life, a rural childhood untainted by commercialism and industrialization. The Gold Rush, which lured so many men from the used-up farmlands of the Northeast, rekindled that sense of lost innocence. It seems likely that the obituary for the Mother of the Forest motivated the Massachusetts Romantic poet James Russell Lowell to write his 1857 essay "Humanity to Trees," in which he called for a "society for the prevention of cruelty to trees." He praised "our English kinsmen" for their landscape gardening and their "great magnanimity in their treatment of trees." Refined Americans could not believe that fellow citizens had destroyed features unsurpassed in the Old World. In 1853 a Boston newspaper called the demolition of the Discovery Tree "a cruel idea, a perfect desecration," a reflection of the "money-making, go-ahead community" of America. In Europe, it opined, "such a natural production would have been cherished and protected." A writer for a horticultural magazine in 1855 warned that without government action, "trees that in the heathen ages would have been Deified" would be destroyed by lucre-crazed Californians morally polluted by the Gold Rush. In lieu of governmental action, he called on his garden colleagues in England and America to start cultivating sequoias. If the plant would not take to the climate of the North, he wrote, "our chivalrous patriotic, tasteful brethren of the sunny South, must take charge of *The Big Tree.*"[27]

As soon as sequoia seeds became available for purchase in 1854, English gardeners began planting them; soon thereafter, seedlings grew in France, Belgium, Germany, Denmark, and even the colder climes of Scotland, Norway, and Sweden. Many of the first sequoias cultivated in Europe came from a nursery in Rochester, New York, that by 1856 had reared some four thousand plants from a single snuffbox of seeds sent in the mail by an erstwhile gold miner. Botanical collectors galvanized by the species' rarity sometimes facilitated the depredation of wild trees. Andrew Murray, a naturalist in Edinburgh, wanted to propagate sequoias, so he asked his brother, who had gone to the goldfields of California, to procure him some seeds. The Scottish brother outsourced the job to an Irishman, who made a journey to Mariposa Grove in 1859. The cones on the ground lacked seeds, and the trunks were impossible to climb. After abandoning the idea of using a kite to get a rope up a Big Tree, the Irishman tried his aim with a gun. After a few days of meager results, he hired a better shot, an old hunter, but soon realized it would take an army of snipers to bag a good collection of cones. So finally, with the help of some French miners, he cut down four mature sequoias before being stopped by some American vigilantes. It had taken a whole week to take down the smallest one, a tree with a circumference of 24 feet. Murray reported that his brother experienced "mingled feelings of dismay, chagrin, and satisfaction" upon learning about the "sacrilege." Since the expedition obtained between 6 and 8 pounds of seed (300,000–400,000 germs), the naturalist concluded that it had "probably done more good than harm after all."[28]

The motivations of European seed buyers varied. Britons hoped that the great trees could be raised as commercial timber; Germans wanted to use the *Mammutbäume* to avert a timber famine; and the French planned to use them to rehabilitate denuded and eroded lands.

In the end, the species found primary use as ornamentals for estates, parks, arboretums, and avenues. On more than one occasion Queen Victoria ceremonially planted *Wellingtonia* seedlings. When the queen's poet laureate, Lord Tennyson, decided to embed a sequoia at his manor garden on the Isle of Wight, he asked no less a figure than Garibaldi to do the honor. British nurseries switched to propagation by cuttings after getting consistently low yields from seeds. Gardeners multiplied Big Trees out of curiosity and also a sense of responsibility in case the species ceased to exist in the Sierra. Their hobby carried moral implications. Starting in 1856, many correspondents to the London-based *Gardeners' Chronicle* expressed consternation when their saplings grew ill. Over the next few decades in European botanical journals, owners of sequoias swapped tips for potting, transplanting, and sheltering young trees, pruning them, weeding them, watering them, protecting them from nibbling rabbits and blasts of Arctic air. Those who doubted the species could persist in northern Europe felt vindicated when the harsh winter of 1879–80 killed many prize specimens. Even in milder climates, the famed constitutional vigor of *Wellingtonia/ Washingtonia* seemed to wane outside the Golden State. However, for every account of a sickly, blighted, diseased, dead, or dying tree, some other correspondent would offer hopeful evidence about a robust specimen that had gained 9 feet in four years or 37 feet in twelve years. In the favorable Albion climate, thousands of plantings persisted into the next century. "There is scarcely a hilltop or mountain in Great Britain from which a sequoia cannot be seen," quipped a member of the Royal Forestry Commission in the 1970s.[29]

Thanks to their tending, European horticulturists of the 1850s made certain that the Big Tree would not go extinct. But exportation and propagation hardly constituted an efficient conservation strategy. As early as 1854, one English gardener suggested the obvious: the United States should establish a national park or arboretum at Calaveras. Seconding the idea, another Briton called on the Horticultural Society to petition the U.S. ambassador in London.[30]

Instead, the Mammoth Tree Grove became a private tourist park.

In a gesture characteristic of their national culture, Americans simultaneously degraded and sacralized nature's supreme arboreal creation. Hucksters turned the downed trunk of the Discovery Tree into a bowling alley and erected a dance gazebo on its stump. Guests at the nearby hotel could purchase cups and candlesticks derived from the tree or, for a trifle, souvenir pincushions made from its bark. The proprietors of the pleasure ground were not above selling much larger pieces. In 1870 entrepreneurs sawed off a new, clean slice of the Discovery Tree and sent it eastward—the first time a complete sequoia cross-section left the Golden State. During the slab's stopover in Boston, the famed paleontologist and geologist Louis Agassiz, then employed at Harvard, made multiple inspections. Around the same time, P. T. Barnum purchased pieces of an unidentified sequoia and displayed them as part of his "Great Traveling Museum, Menagerie, Caravan, and Hippodrome" in 1871. For that year only, the tree was 837 years old. By the next tour, the specimen had aged over a millennium to reach a ripe old age of 1,937 years. Another Big Tree display—the reconstructed base of a hollowed-out trunk—traveled to Philadelphia in 1876 on the occasion of the centennial exposition, where it ended up in a sideshow. The donor tree had been named Captain Jack after the vanquished Modoc leader Kintpuash, who had recently surrendered to federal authorities in northeastern California in what turned out to be the state's last "Indian war." John Muir reported the tree's age at between 2,100 and 2,300 years. Prior to shipment, the owners set up the exhibit at the Central Pacific yard in San Francisco. The label on the staved sequoia trunk read "four thousand years." At the centenary, crassness met consecration. Albert Bierstadt, the era's most popular painter, unveiled a heroically scaled sequoia—a 10-by-5-foot canvas of a Sierra titan—at Memorial Hall, the fairground's temple of art. The two views of Big Trees in Philadelphia exemplified the amalgamated greatness and pettiness of the United States of America.[31]

LAND GOING TO WASTE

The beginnings of sequoia preservation occurred in the era of exploitation, in the midst of the ruinous Civil War. With no southern votes
in the way, the Republican Congress passed several bills anticipating
the postwar settlement of the U.S. West by "free labor." Most of these
measures encouraged the disposal of land. Federal land policy from
the Northwest Ordinance to the New Deal was nominally straightforward: extinguish Indian title, survey the new public domain,
then convert that territory to private property. To create a citizenry
of white male farmers, the state rationalized and democratized the
process of land entry. From sea to shining sea, federal cartographers
turned America's hills and dales into a perfect mathematical grid,
a collection of small squares (sections) within larger squares (town-
ships). To dispose of sections, the government created an auction
system, and later supplemented that with virtual giveaway programs
such as the Preemption Act (1841) and the Homestead Act (1862).
The post–Civil War government upped the incentives with regard
to the rugged Far West, where climate and topography discouraged
conventional farming. The mountainous West also forced the government to accept the reality that certain lands would never be claimed
and farmed—and also accept the moral imperative that certain lands
should be preemptively closed to privatization.

Americans invented the legal category of the national park, and
they did so in response to two western wonderlands, Yosemite and
Yellowstone. The park at Yosemite came first, in 1864, and it originally came in two parcels. Section 1 of the act signed by Abraham
Lincoln ceded the "'cleft' or 'gorge' . . . known as the Yo-Semite" to
the State of California on the condition that it would be managed for
"public use, resort, and recreation." Section 2 similarly reserved the
"Mariposa Big Tree Grove," though the land grant was very small,
"not to exceed the area of four sections" (4 square miles, or 2,560

acres). A state-appointed Yosemite Commission named Galen Clark, the "discoverer" of Mariposa Grove, as official guardian.[32]

Beyond the famed Calaveras and Mariposa groves, the existence of sequoias remained unknown to science until John Muir entered the scene. After arriving in California in 1868, Muir spent almost a decade as a vagabond-shepherd and field naturalist before getting married, settling down, and becoming a professional orchardist, writer, and conservationist. As of the mid-1870s, when he began publishing his geological and botanical findings, Muir knew more about sequoia distribution than anyone else. Writing for a San Francisco daily, then for the American Association for the Advancement of Science, and finally for *Harper's*, Muir presented good news and bad news. In the isolated groves north of the Kings River, he conceded, the "childless" and "companionless" old sequoias seemed "doomed to a speedy extinction, as being nothing more than an expiring remnant, vanquished in the so-called struggle for life." However, in the "majestic continuous forests of the South," old and young trees flourished side by side. Muir estimated that 90 percent of all sequoias existed here.[33]

Unfortunately, these "noble forests," including the supergrove that Muir named Giant Forest, faced new threats from various economic activities. Lumbermen were moving their mills to the edges of the sequoia belt, having exhausted the magnificent lower-elevation sugar pine forests around Lake Tahoe that fed the underground silver and gold mines at Nevada's Comstock Lode, often called "the tomb of the forests of the Sierra." As wagon roads pushed southward, the Sierra redwoods took on renewed value as quarries and novelties. Muir observed the stump of a colossal specimen (the "Forest King") knocked down in 1870 for a traveling exhibition and the one that went to Philadelphia as a "rustic tub." Yet another attempt to lay low "the biggest sequoia tree in the world" succeeded in 1877. To discourage such destruction, the State of California passed an act in 1874 making it a misdemeanor to "willfully cut down or strip the bark of any tree over 16 feet in diameter in the Big Tree groves of Fresno, Tulare, and Kern counties." This law was purely symbolic, and probably unconstitutional, for the state possessed little or no authority over federal or private lands and no means of enforcement. Muir criticized lawmakers for not addressing the most pernicious threat, fire. Although Muir recognized that wildfire could be beneficial for sequoia seed recruitment, he generally portrayed fire as a baneful force and vehemently condemned the blazes set by muttoneers to move their flocks and improve their pastures. A local newspaper, the *Mariposa Gazette*, criticized the legislation for a different reason. It contended that 16-footers were far less endangered than smaller sequoias, easy targets for the "vandalism of seed hunters, who are slaughtering the beautiful young trees from two to five feet in diameter, more and more wastefully each season, merely for the handful of seeds to be got from them." Muir, too, witnessed "this destructive method of seed-collecting." Out-of-state botanical enthusiasts—most of whom presumably wanted to preserve the species—bought the seed at inflated prices. Galen Clark, the guardian of Mariposa, had a standing order from dealers in San Francisco for all the cones he could procure. Later he sold packets of seeds and seedlings from a nursery near his cabin. In Europe, sellers raised the price as high as $125 per pound. The *Gazette* warned that seed collectors could facilitate the "final extinction of the Groves" if they destroyed the upcoming generation of sequoias.[34]

Tourists, too, behaved badly around the trees. In 1879 an author in the *Pacific Rural Press* criticized the mutilation caused by souvenir hunters who pulled off strips of sequoia bark. Had the body of George Washington been embalmed, he wrote, pilgrims "would not be content without breaking off a piece of an ear or digging out an eye to carry off as mementoes." Photographs of the General Grant from the 1890s show dozens of wooden signs nailed haphazardly to the trunk—a competition to see who could reach highest. For posed photographs, large groups climbed onto the fragile burls of sequoias. Yosemite's Mariposa Grove took the greatest beating. The first land manager, California's Yosemite Commission, did not by today's standards practice much stewardship. Galen Clark once raised his rifle and shot a cone from the Grizzly Giant for the sake of a travel writer who wanted to know if sequoias were still capable of reproducing. Clark and the commission did nothing to stop a stagecoach company from punching a passageway through the basal fire scar of a Big Tree in 1881. The result, the Wawona Tunnel Tree, became one of the most recognizable plants in the world and one of the leading attractions in California. Tourists paid to pass through the bole and bought trinkets such as penknives fashioned from the tree's former core. The tunnel ride proved to be so popular that the stagecoach company bored through a second fire-damaged sequoia, the California Tree, in 1895.[35]

Even more contradictory were the actions of the national government. In 1879 interior secretary Carl Schurz bemoaned the waste and destruction of coast redwood and Sierra redwood and expressed his apprehension that both species would disappear without additional reservations like Yosemite.[36] However, in the 1870s and 1880s Schurz's own department sold or gave away exponentially more sequoia land than had been preserved at Mariposa Grove in 1864. The threats from exhibitioners, sheepmen, and seed collectors paled in comparison to the logging that followed the disposition of forested property in the Sierra Nevada by the General Land Office.

Today this free-for-all seems outrageous; then, it was consistent with the long-standing—and, by European standards, enlightened— policy of creating private property in new western territories. First applied in the Old Northwest (today's upper Midwest), land disposal achieved ferocious speed in post–Gold Rush California. When Mexico ceded its northern territory to its bellicose neighbor in 1848, the United States guaranteed that the property rights of Mexicans in the Southwest would be honored. As it happened, the Senate struck out that article before ratifying the Treaty of Guadalupe Hidalgo. One by one, the large, and in many cases immense, Spanish and Mexican land grants in lowland California—properties known as *ranchos*—fell into the hands of Gold Rush squatters, lawyers, businessmen, legally if not always fairly. In truth, many of the original "Mexican" grantees had been foreign-born immigrants (including some Americans). With nearly 9 million acres of choice land already in grants, post-Mexican California was a paradise for U.S. land monopolists.

For Anglo-Americans, the largesse kept coming. When Congress admitted California to the Union in 1850, it gifted to the state all "swamp and overflowed" lands to sell for revenue. In many instances, surveyors falsely designated forest-rimmed alpine marshes as swamps, thus opening them to public auction. Like other western states, California received millions more acres—the sixteenth and thirty-sixth sections of each township on the grid—to be sold for the benefit of the public school system. All in all, the state obtained more than 8 million acres in federal grants, most of which passed into the private sector. As a common practice, unscrupulous businessmen made a down payment to the state for tracts of redwood forest, cut the trees, then forfeited on the property, thus avoiding full payment and taxation. Similarly, people used the federal Preemption Act to claim, log, and leave. In this climate of corruption, the government potlatch continued. For the benefit of transcontinental railroads, Congress instituted a bonus system: free acreage for every mile of track laid. For the little people, Congress passed the Homestead Act (1862), followed by variants: the Timber Culture Act (1873) and the Desert Land Act (1877), which allowed citizens, for a nominal fee, to claim less desirable farmland that lacked trees or water; and the Timber and Stone Act (1878), which, most consequentially for the sequoias and redwoods, applied to sites where forest cover or rocks made the land unfit for agriculture. Before this law, individuals lacked legal means to buy timberland from the government for the express purpose of logging rather than farming. After 1878, nonarable, nonmineral public land could be purchased at the cut-rate price of $2.50 per acre. The claimant merely had to swear that he meant to use his 160 acres for practical and exclusive use, not speculation or contractual transfer to another party.[37]

Intended by Congress to give honest entrepreneurs a head start, these incentives became fodder for land sharks. Many of the people who made improvements to the land as required by law had no interest in farming or logging; they just wanted to flip the land. By paying "dummies" to file claims, or simply by buying out titleholders, monopolists and speculators soon controlled the best of California's farmland, range land, and forestland. Some consolidation of forestland was necessary and beneficial, since a successful logging venture required more than 160 acres. But consolidation led to widespread fraud. Most notoriously, the California Redwood Company amassed some 64,000 acres (worth about $100 per acre at the time) of prime forestland in Humboldt and Del Norte counties in the early 1880s. The agent operated from an office behind a "notorious saloon" and bribed noncitizens to file entries en masse. "No effort seems to have been made to keep the matter secret," reported the commissioner of the General Land Office in 1886. "Sailors were caught while in port and hurried into a saloon or to a certain notary public's office and induced to sign applications and convey the lands to a member of the firm." This "gigantic scheme" extended all the way to the GLO's main office in Washington, D.C. In an age of graft, this episode might have escaped scrutiny had not the California Redwood Company contracted to sell its assets to a syndicate based in Edinburgh. Foreign ownership upset Washington more than fraud. When it came to the disposal of its domain, the U.S. government had long accepted a certain amount of illegality as inevitable and acceptable. It could not supervise every land transaction. More to the point, until 1891 there was no legal instrument by which a corporate entity could purchase a tract of forested land directly from the government. The state did, however, want logging corporations to thrive. Tellingly, after the Scottish syndicate lost its redwood property in federal court, the land came under the control of U.S. companies, whose stakeholders included some of the same men who had orchestrated the fraud. They proceeded to level the forest without controversy.[38]

In sequoia country, logging companies coveted the southern groves in the watersheds of the Kings, Kaweah, and Tule rivers. Rugged terrain and unnavigable streams had protected these Big Trees for years.

Wagon roads didn't penetrate the region until the 1880s, when GLO surveyors finally completed their mapping of the Sierra Nevada. Once the local survey office in Visalia opened for business, a mini–land rush ensued. Anxious about the tree named in honor of Ulysses S. Grant, hero of the Union, the U.S. general surveyor for California unilaterally (and illegally) withdrew four sections of land around it. The rest of the leafy giants were up for grabs. Three enterprises— two capitalist, one socialist—worked to consolidate landholdings in the groves. The Tule River Lumber Company and the Kings River Lumber Company, both joint stock companies, purchased thousands of acres of prime sequoia land. At the same time, fifty-three social- ists, members of the Co-operative Land Purchase and Colonization Association, used the Timber and Stone Act to assemble their own large tract in the Giant Forest.[39]

Compared to the capitalists, the socialists failed as lumbermen, but they offered a glimpse into an alternative California where settlers might have created a category for age-old trees beyond the dichotomy of the sanctified and the commodified. The cooperative colonists were an eclectic bunch of San Francisco bohemians, including advocates of uniform land taxation, vegetarianism, raw food, phonetic spell- ing, spiritualism, and Swedenborgianism. Their voluntary association became a legal entity known as the Kaweah Co-operative Common- wealth. Members bickered constantly about organization and pro- cedure. Their leader, Burnette Haskell, was a cranky firebrand and former anarchist who had once plotted to blow up the San Francisco County hall of records. He railed against profit and interest; he wanted to create a "perfect medium of exchange" that used the time and effort of human labor, not silver or gold, as the basis of economic value. His utopian colony issued scrip called time-checks—"crystallized labor." A check in the amount of sixty minutes could be traded for an hour of any kind of work by another company member. The resident laborers, whose numbers ebbed and flowed from 15 to 150, spent most of their working hours carving a road into the precipitous granite mountains; it took almost four years before the colony was in position to cut and mill. Despite the road, the commonwealth lacked the financial means to log on an industrial scale and showed no interest in clear-cutting. "It would be nothing short of vandalism to indiscriminately destroy these sentinels of past centuries, as has been done in several parts of California, by ruthless ravagers of the Competitive system," wrote Haskell. He pledged to preserve the old giants "in their primitive glory." In a show of respect, the socialists named the largest tree after Karl Marx.[40]

We'll never know if the colonists would have preserved or destroyed the Giant Forest, for they didn't get a chance to do either. Upon suspicions of land fraud, the GLO withdrew the area from entry in 1885 pending an investigation. Some, like the outdoors-loving editor of the *Visalia Delta*, accused the colonists of being the "unwitting tools of the lumber barons." The editor advocated for a national park around the General Grant Tree and additional groves if possible. The park proposal was seconded by John Muir, picked up by the *New York Tribune* and *Century Magazine*, and eventually adopted by well-placed politicians. In 1890, just as the Kaweahans completed their road, president Benjamin Harrison signed two Sierra bills, one that created a Sequoia National Park and a second a few days later that did much more. To the astonishment of Muir and other conservationists, Congress slipped through a surprise bill that converted Yosemite Grant into a larger, formal national park in line with Yellowstone (1872). The bill also created a miniature national park around the General Grant and enlarged Sequoia to envelop the commonwealth's claims. The GLO never proved any wrongdoing on the part of the claimants, but neither did it ever issue title. By law, the colonists were now trespassers. The government arrested, tried, and convicted four of the commonwealth's trustees for illegal logging. The new guardians of Sequoia, the U.S. Army, had orders to clear out the park; in 1891 mounted officers confronted the Kaweahans at their mill. Already factionalizing, the colony fell apart after this show of federal force.[41]

The army took charge of the three Sierra parks, including Yosemite. The previous managers, the state commission, had attracted controversy and litigation. After years of complaints from tourists, concessionaires, and conservationists, the state legislature conducted a formal investigation in February 1889. At Mariposa Grove, the hot-button issue was fire. The commission admitted that the grove looked unsightly and neglected with heavy undergrowth and a thick litter of deadwood—ample fuel for flames. According to conventional wisdom, only fire could kill a standing sequoia. Americans perceived the ubiquitous smoke stains on old trunks as marks of human negligence or vandalism, not arboreal persistence. They deemed fire unnatural. For past tree injuries, travel writers blamed Indians and their "love of destruction." In truth, the native peoples of the Sierra Nevada had, prior to their eviction, used fire as a tool in their subsistence economy. Burning improved hunting and gathering by promoting food species such as deer and oak. The annual low-level blazes set by Sierra Miwoks rarely destroyed a sequoia; quite the opposite, they promoted seedling recruitment by opening up cones and adding nutrients to the soil. Not understanding this ecological relationship, early visitors to Calaveras and Mariposa believed that blackened sequoias must have been maliciously targeted by Indians or carelessly used as fireplaces or backlogs. One magazine even hypothesized that the limited range of the Big Tree could be explained by the "destructive propensities of the Indians." Whatever the hypothesis, many visitors complained that past fires had degraded the scene, "destroying many trees entirely, ruining the shape of others, and giving a general look of forlornness and smirch to the whole scene." At least one member of the Yosemite Commission rose above prejudice. Under examination, W. H. Mills signaled his openness to a policy of prescribed burning to prevent the buildup of forest fuel at Mariposa and Yosemite. "I have always respected the ability of the Indians to manage that valley," he said. In historic times, "the Indians were Commissioners." To address the fuel-load problem, the commission repeated its long-standing request for an appropriation from the stingy legislature.[42]

As luck would have it, flames swept through Mariposa Grove a few months after the hearing. The fire emboldened political opponents of

the commission to push for federal takeover. Thanks to the surprise
bill, they got their wish sooner than they expected. Army rangers
took the prescribed lesson from the conflagration: fires cause ruin.
The cavalry instituted a complete fire-suppression policy at Mariposa,
clearing the grove with scythe and hoe down to soil level, removing
both deadwood and green undergrowth, scraping lichens from the
tree roots, and constructing a perimeter road. New park rules drawn
up by the interior secretary made it illegal to start or kindle any flame
outside a campfire circle. (Only much later would forest managers
realize that wildfire suppression produces long-term undesirable ecological consequences.)[43]

To supplement Sequoia National Park, President Harrison issued
an order in 1893 that withdrew from entry almost the entire central
and southern Sierra Nevada, more than 4 million acres, thereby creating the Sierra Forest Reserve (the forerunner of Sequoia National
Forest and Giant Sequoia National Monument). Acting on fears of a
national timber famine, Congress had granted authority to the executive branch to establish forest reservations. Harrison, and later Theodore Roosevelt, used this statute boldly to remake the map of the U.S.
West. By government design, the Giant Forest would become a land
of public recreation, limited private enterprise, and no communal
work. The Kaweah Commonwealth's long-labored road, the planned
entrance to a workers' utopia, became instead a conduit for leisure
travelers who paid their respects at the General Sherman—the tree
formerly known as the Karl Marx. The colony's pathway remained
the only access to the Giant Forest until 1934. Despite petitions, the
government never reimbursed the Kaweahans for their toil, a cumulative time-check worth more than $150,000.

Even with the socialist threat removed, ancient sequoias seemed
imperiled by private inholdings, rights-of-way, and mining claims
that riddled the new national parks and forest reserves. A government report issued in 1900 singled out Mariposa as the "only grove
thoroughly safe from destruction" and warned that the "majority of
the Big Trees of California, certainly the best of them, are owned by

people that have every right, and in many cases every intention, to cut them into lumber." This warning applied to the famous Calaveras North (Mammoth Tree) Grove, which had recently been acquired by a lumberman from Minnesota. This land sale inspired a "righteous and lively indignation on the part of Californians after the long period of deathlike apathy," wrote John Muir. Ultimately, in 1931, following women's-club letter-writing campaigns, a congressional resolution, and countless warnings in national periodicals about the grove's imminent wreckage, a group of benefactors, including John D. Rockefeller Jr., met the owner's asking price. The buyers then donated the grove to California to be a state park. It took almost twenty years longer for the state to finalize the purchase of Calaveras South Grove. At Sequoia National Park, the federal government worked for many decades, using various appropriations and private donations, to complete the purchase of inholdings, which in the meantime appreciated in value as summer resort properties. All in all, the great federal fire sale of the post–Civil War period set the stage for long, complicated, inefficient, and costly buy-back programs in the Big Tree groves. (As we will see in the next chapter, a similar story would play out later— to much greater controversy—on the North Coast with the establishment and expansion of Redwood National Park.)[44]

These oppositional threads—public and private, legal and illegal, preservation and destruction, life and death—intertwined most tightly in the pivotal decade of the 1890s. Historians have argued convincingly that the secret instigator of the surprise legislative enlargement of Sequoia National Park was the Southern Pacific Railroad, the most powerful monopoly in California and the largest timber owner in America. Sequoia preservation appealed to the SP for two reasons: the railroad wanted to maintain the mountain watershed to benefit its extensive downstream agricultural landholdings in the Central Valley, and it wanted to carry more tourists on its lines. Throughout the post–Civil War U.S. West, the transcontinental railroads functioned both as the greatest advocates of national parks and the greatest wasters of natural resources. For example, in September 1890 a congressional lobbyist for the SP drew the boundaries of Sequoia National Park; the next month, SP president Collis P. Huntington authorized payment for the procurement of a cross-section from a champion sequoia (the Mark Twain) from just outside the boundaries of that park. The specimen, the megafloral equivalent of a taxidermic bison head, went on display in the American Museum of Natural History. The federal government acted with comparable dualism: after evicting law-abiding socialists from the Giant Forest, it contracted with capitalist loggers, the beneficiaries of giant fraud, to cut down and hollow out a Big Tree for exhibition in the main rotunda of the U.S. government building at the 1892–93 World's Columbian Exposition in Chicago. The eviscerated sequoia was named the General Noble in honor of the late John Noble, who, as secretary of the interior— the office with the greatest responsibility for the stewardship of the nation's public lands—presided over the creation of Sequoia National Park. A spiral staircase inside the 30-foot-tall trunk led to the second floor, a reconstituted cross-section, where fairgoers could touch the tree rings, count the years, and contemplate the millennial course of empire. After its sojourn in the White City, the monumental tree house came to rest on the National Mall, where it stood in front of the Smithsonian until 1932. Mall custodians topped the sequoia hull with a windowed cupola and used it as a toolshed.[45]

The Mark Twain and the General Noble came from the same grove—the densest, grandest expanse of *Sequoiadendron* ever known, an alpine bowl above the Kings River called Converse Basin. By legal and illegal means, the Kings River Lumber Company, incorporated in 1888, acquired this prize property. Only here did the full might of industrial capitalism bore into the Sierra redwood. Immense up-front costs deterred most entrepreneurs. It was expensive enough to build a mill in the mountains, but transporting the extra-large milled lumber downhill required a major engineering feat. The San Francisco–based company rose to the challenge. After amassing a large pool of investment capital, it built a 54-mile-long flume, a giant waterslide perched on a trestle on the edge of steep canyon walls—the technological forerunner of today's amusement park log rides. Transported this way, lumber could arrive at the nearest train depot, 60 miles away, in merely half a day. After a drop of 4,200 feet, the flume ended at the tracks of the SP in the Central Valley town of Sanger, which dubbed itself the "Flumeopolis of the West" on opening day in 1890. Lumber production commenced the next year, when 20 million board feet floated down the wooden flume. (A board foot equals 12 inches by 12 inches by 1 inch.) The heavily leveraged company required even higher output to pay off its debt and turn a profit. It didn't help that the flume constantly needed expensive repairs. In 1895, in the wake of failed reorganization, impatient debt holders took over the firm and renamed it Sanger Lumber. The new ownership decided to gamble on full-scale production. Workers extended the narrow-gauge railroad from the top of the flume into the heart of the basin, where they erected a new sawmill in 1897.[46]

During the Sanger Lumber Company's short life, perhaps eight thousand mature sequoias in the 5,000-acre Converse Basin were downsized to stumps. Only one giant survived. At the northernmost tip of the grove, at the edge of a slope overlooking the jagged mouth of Kings Canyon, loggers spared a single mature tree (now among the world's ten largest), which they named for their foreman, Frank Boole. Even with up-to-date machinery, it took an incredible amount of human labor to level such a plant—up to 300 feet in height and 30 feet in diameter. A grounds crew cleared a "felling bed" while loggers chopped and hewed for days. Despite the bed, the crown of a giant sequoia tended to shatter like glass upon impact. The main trunk was too cumbrous to move, so workers used augers to drill holes into the bark for dynamite charges. If the explosions didn't reduce the prostrate tree to useless bits, the men used steel cables to hitch together sections of the broken timber and hoisted the lumber train with a steam-powered winch over greased skids to the mill. Despite this preparatory deconstruction, the original mill saw couldn't handle the larger sequoias. Sanger had to invest in a "redwood splitter," a bandsaw with a circumference of 90 feet. Lumber output peaked in 1903

at 191 million board feet. The entire operation employed up to seven
hundred men and produced appalling accidents and gross waste. "We
marveled that man had been able by crude methods to do so much
damage; and still more we marveled at the relatively little timber of
the Big Trees that had been worked into lumber or shakes," wrote the
superintendent of Sequoia National Park after a visit, years later, to
the ruins of Converse Basin. "Scores and scores of trunks remained
on the ground, of which not one-fifth of what was commercially valuable had been used." The chief dendrologist of the U.S. Forest Service
estimated the total efficiency of sequoia logging at 25 to 30 percent.[47]

Sanger depleted the most supernal stand of trees without harvesting a profit. A Michigan lumberman bought the business in 1905 and
proceeded to move the main operation out of the Big Tree bowl and
into a lower-elevation mixed-species forest. Afterward his workers
deliberately set the Converse Basin mill ablaze. Secondary logging,
more like scavenging over carrion, continued through the teens. A
Yale professor of English who visited the area felt overcome by melancholy in this "vast and lonely cemetery."[48] In 1935 the U.S. government repurchased the mutilated forest for fifteen dollars per acre.
Today the fields of blackened stumps—surrounded by vigorous second growth—belong to the public as part of Giant Sequoia National
Monument.

CONSUMING THE REDWOODS

In the two decades straddling 1900, loggers felled roughly one-quarter
of all mature sequoias in California—that is, the world. However, the
clear-cutting above the Kings River was not repeated elsewhere in
the sequoia belt, and by the 1950s almost all of the surviving groves
benefited from legal protection as public reserves. The outcome differed radically in the redwood belt. Here, destructive logging practices continued well into the twentieth century.

The histories of California's two greatest tree species diverged for economic and also cultural reasons. Compared to the southern Sierra, the North Coast forest was closer to loggers (because of sea access) but farther away from tourists (because of limited rail access). For travelers, sequoias grew conveniently close to Yosemite Valley, the Golden State's top attraction. Almost instantly, the Big Trees became national icons. The open-air groves allowed people, including major painters and photographers, to single out, name, and romanticize individual specimens. These groves were so small and so few in number that it struck many Americans, even in the free-for-all atmosphere of the Gold Rush, as gross vandalism to cut down an ancient giant. On the North Coast, by contrast, the redwoods occurred in thick forests that seemed to go on forever. A German visitor to Mendocino County came back in 1852 convinced that "California will for centuries have virgin forests, perhaps to the end of Time!" Thirty years later, a botanist with the California Academy of Sciences described the redwood supply as "so prodigious as to be simply incalculable; none but a suicidal and utterly abandoned infanticidal policy, wantonly and untiringly practiced, can ever blot them out." Projections would change. The original historians of Humboldt County, due north of Mendocino, waxed poetic in 1888 of trees of "almost immortal strength, spanning and bridging past centuries," then went on to raise the calamitous possibility of redwood exhaustion through human waste. Commentators tended to adopt a tone of resignation: the Pacific forest would fall to the ax just like the original Atlantic forest. This outcome seemed inevitable because by 1900 the land was all privately owned, and because old redwoods contained the best timber anyone had ever seen. An estimated 60 percent of board material in Humboldt mills was "clear"—solid, vertical-grained, knot-free heartwood—about double the percentage of eastern lumber. "The burly woodsman who attacks the diminutive pine of the East must experience a feeling of remorse, as would a strong man who made war upon a boy," wrote a journalist in 1894. "But here there is something to compel his respect; he must feel that in grappling with these monsters he is doing the work of a Hercules."[49]

In this former era of profligacy, California builders treated redwood—now premium material for specialty uses—as all-purpose building stock. *Sempervirens* was convenient and cheap. All classes of people came into regular contact with it. For the building of California civilization, coast redwood "outranked all other natural resources," including gold, argued Willis Jepson, the state's most distinguished homegrown botanist, a university professor, and a charter member of the Sierra Club.

> The writer of these lines is a Californian. He was rocked by a pioneer mother in a cradle made of Redwood. The house in which he lived was largely made of Redwood. His clothing, the books of his juvenile library, the saddle for his riding pony were brought in railway cars chiefly made of Redwood, running on rails laid on Redwood ties, their course controlled by wires strung on Redwood poles. He went to school in a Redwood schoolhouse, sat at a desk made of Redwood and wore shoes the leather of which was tanned in Redwood vats. Everywhere he touched Redwood. Boxes, bins, bats, barns, bridges, bungalows were made of Redwood. Posts, porches, piles, pails, pencils, pillars, paving-blocks, pipe lines, sometimes even policemen [toys], were made of Redwood.[50]

Jepson's place of residence, Berkeley, was renowned for its Arts and Crafts architecture—houses with unvarnished redwood paneling and unpainted redwood shingling. These homes belonged to the back-to-nature bourgeoisie, the same class of people who filled the Sierra Club's membership roll and advanced the conservationist cause. For their domiciles, tree enthusiasts desired a simple, local, natural style that only redwood consumption could provide. Everything that could be made of wood seemed superior with the close-grained, even-textured heartwood of a centenarian *sempervirens*. Stained or unstained, it looked beautiful.[51]

For technical jobs, meanwhile, redwood earned the highest rating from the USDA's Forest Products Laboratory. It was easy to work with, hard to wreck. No other lumber matched its combination of lightness, evenness, and durability. It almost deserved the extravagant claims of the California Redwood Association, which advertised "nature's lumber masterpiece" as shrink-proof, warp-proof, split-proof, blemish-proof, insect-proof, rot-proof, and waterproof. "The most durable of all building materials," claimed Pacific Lumber, upping the praise. "Concrete and Stucco disintegrate; steel and iron rust; yet Heart Redwood defies decay almost indefinitely." The wood was "more durable than stone." Funeral homes carried caskets made of grade-A redwood—"wood everlasting," "wood that won't rot"— manufactured at a Pacific Lumber factory in Oakland. In one year, 1948, the California casket industry consumed over 21 million board feet of *sempervirens*. Because of modern American death culture—the fear of death and the desire to delay the return to dust—some of the finest lumber ever made was planted six feet under.[52]

The uses of redwood seemed endless. In the first few decades of the twentieth century, before steel-reinforced concrete became the norm, engineers used redwood for egg incubators and battery separators as well as sidewalks, gutters, and roads. The Yolo Causeway, the wetlands-crossing highway between Sacramento and Davis, stood on redwood pilings. To get from San Diego to Yuma, early motorists crossed the forbidding Algodones Dunes on a redwood plank road (a forerunner of I-8). Even the flume that transported lumbered sequoia out of Converse Basin was constructed with redwood. Because it performed well under liquid pressure and because it did not impart any taste, redwood was ideal for water tanks, wine vats, tanning vats, cesspools, and cooling towers. Redwood stave pipes, reinforced with wire hoops, worked for irrigation delivery, sewage disposal, and hydraulic sluicing—and cost less than equivalent metal pipes. Lightweight tongue-and-groove components could be easily transported to remote mountainous locations such as the copper mines of Montana, Utah, and Arizona. In climates as varied as tropical Honolulu, arid Phoenix, and frigid Nome, cities used redwood piping for municipal systems. Until the concrete-and-steel Hetch Hetchy Aqueduct became operational in 1938, San Francisco used redwood troughs to deliver its drinking water. Redwood's resistance to water damage made it the obvious choice for the original bleachers at the Rose Bowl—28 linear miles—as well as Michigan and Notre Dame stadiums.[53]

An incalculable amount of redwood also went up in flames, most notably in San Francisco, which burned *six times* between 1849 and 1851 and again during the earthquake-related firestorm of 1906. At the time of the temblor, the Queen City should have been called the Wooden City, for 90 percent of its building stock consisted of lumber, the highest percentage of any U.S. metropolis. "San Francisco has violated all underwriting traditions and precedents by not burning up," warned the National Board of Fire Underwriters in 1905. Local actuaries believed something different: agents wrote favorable policies for properties made of redwood on the theory that the fire-resistant matter became virtually fireproof as it regularly absorbed moisture from the fog that rolled in through the Golden Gate. The municipal government agreed. Astonishingly, San Francisco's building code of 1903 required builders to use redwood as an insulating "firebreak" within the common walls of adjoining properties. Even after the holocaust, San Francisco's fire department trusted redwood; it argued, plausibly if not intelligently, that the conflagration would have been worse if the city had been built with different material. "We have to thank the California redwood principally for our escape from greater loss," officials told the *Wall Street Journal*. The logging industry used testimonials from city hall and photographs of unburned redwood buildings amid the general devastation to argue that its product had "stopped" the inferno from advancing. Redwood had been "tested by fire." Swayed by the pseudo-evidence, the postdisaster building committee adopted a resolution that obliged builders to obtain a special permit to use any lumber besides redwood. (Requiring setbacks would have been a more prudent response.) Of the 28,507 buildings constructed in the city between the firestorm and the 1914 groundbreaking for the Panama-Pacific International Exposition, 89 percent had wooden frames. To meet the sudden demand, the coastal mills worked over-time. The postquake cut in 1906—660 million board feet—would not be exceeded until the post–World War II economic boom.[54]

Logging the redwoods began in California's colonial period, when Spanish settlers at the Santa Clara Mission and Russian traders at Fort Ross milled a limited number of local trees. Only with the Gold Rush did timbering become commercial. To meet San Francisco's demand, early sawyers concentrated on the forested canyons on the east side of the Santa Cruz Mountains in San Mateo County. From there the lumber went to Redwood City, located on a navigable slough on the bay, a short distance by boat to the instant metropolis. By the mid-1850s, San Francisco had exhausted the easy-to-reach red-wood, including pocket stands in the Berkeley Hills. Loggers moved from the trimmings to the fat: major lumbering shifted northward to Sonoma and Mendocino counties and eventually Humboldt and Del Norte, a foggy stretch of the Pacific Coast where the thickest and tallest trees grew. Here a single plant could supply enough lumber for twenty houses or one larger edifice—for example, the Baptist worship hall in Santa Rosa later made famous by *Ripley's Believe It or Not* as "One Tree Church." But the redwoods north of the Golden Gate initially overwhelmed loggers, who struggled to acquire capital and equipment to match the megaflora. Redwoods were too large, too heavy, and too unwieldy for efficient transport by animals. Where pos-sible, early commercial loggers harnessed gravity. In glens and dales, they skidded logs into gravelly brooks, then waited for winter freshets to run their cut to downstream mills—"flash flood delivery." On the craggy Mendocino coast, timber companies built crazy-stilt chute-ways that led from peninsular bluffs to ocean platforms—"dog-hole ports"—where schooners braved the dangerous surf to capture logs. This was a lot of effort for relatively little profit. Not until the 1870s and 1880s, when railroads replaced rivers and steam winches replaced yoked oxen—and when the once-great sugar pine industry around

Lake Tahoe reached depletion—did capitalists solidify the North Coast "Redwood Empire."[55]

The regional hub was Humboldt Bay, the best ship landing between San Francisco and Portland. Shellfish abounded in the long, thin inlet. Nearby, two major salmon runs, the Klamath and Eel rivers, led into the forested mountains. Before the American period, this resource-rich region hosted a high density of indigenous peoples and a great diversity of languages. Coastal peoples such as the Algonquian-speaking Yurok and the Athabaskan-speaking Tolowa practiced customs of money, inheritance, private property, and permanent architecture. Native artisans made skillful use of fallen redwoods; they split housing planks with elk-horn blades, and carved river and seagoing canoes with mussel-shell adzes. Floral material could also be spiritual matter, for male ceremonial life centered on redwood sweat lodges. Tolowas constructed a lodge at a sacred spot near the mouth of the Smith River where the primeval redwood grew. Yuroks utilized redwood for the reconstruction of their main lodge—a biennial act that symbolized the reconstruction of the world. Whereas siding planks for the lodge could be procured from dead trees, the supporting beams had to derive from one living plant. "I will cut you," invoked the foreman/shaman, "because we are going to have you for holding up the sky." Ritually killed and dismembered into six holy beams, the sacrificial redwood was carried away as an honored funerary corpse and finally resurrected as part of an elaborate ceremony anthropologists call World Renewal.[56]

Largely isolated from the effects of Russian, Spanish, and Mexican colonization, the Indians of northwestern California experienced American invaders as world destroyers. After the discovery of Humboldt Bay's hard-to-find entrance in 1850, the worst kind of fortune seekers flooded the North Coast. George Crook, as a young infantryman with the U.S. Army, witnessed the aftermath. He came to the West Coast straight from West Point, his head full of "marvelous stories" of the "tremendous size of the grizzlies" and "the treachery and cruelty of the Indians." Instead he found the natives generally well disposed, but more frequently forced to take the war path or sink all self respect, by the outrages of the whites perpetrated upon them. The country was over-run by people from all nations in search of the mighty dollar. Greed was almost unrestrained, and from the nature of our government there was little or no law that these people were bound to respect. It was of no unfrequent occurrence for an Indian to be shot down in cold blood, or a squaw to be raped by some brute. Such a thing as a white man being punished for outraging an Indian was unheard of. It was the fable of the wolf and the lamb every time.

Crook penned these recollections as a highly decorated veteran, having earned national fame battling Confederates and vanquishing Lakotas and Apaches. He was the most distinguished Indian fighter in the United States. Thus it meant something when the major general said of Humboldt County, "It is hard to believe now the wrongs these Indians had to suffer in those days. I doubt now there is a single one left to tell their tale."[57]

Many historians contend that anti-Indian violence in northwestern California in the 1850s and 1860s meets the modern legal definition of genocide. This much is indisputable: volunteer companies committed coordinated acts of mass violence, often with community, civic, or state support. For example, voters in Eureka approved a local tax in 1858 to "prosecute the Indian war to extermination." One of many premeditated bloodbaths happened on Indian Island in Humboldt Bay, a place that had been continuously occupied for at least a millennium as evidenced by two vast oyster-shell mounds. For the Wiyot people, this forested islet was the center of the world, the place where time began. Wiyots gathered at the island village Tuluwat in late February 1860 for a weeklong renewal ceremony. After a final night of feasting, singing, and dancing, the young and the old and the women slept in glad exhaustion while most of the men paddled away to resupply. In this moment of predawn peace, killers from Eureka— an irregular army not approved by the state but funded by a subscription that had been publicized in the local newspaper—sneaked onto the island and indiscriminately hunted and hacked with knives and axes. The homicidal strike coincided with two other assaults on Wiyot villages. No one knows how many islanders died that morning; reports suggest 150–200 total. Light sleepers in Eureka awoke to screams and wails carried across the water. "Old women, wrinkled and decrepit, lay weltering in blood, their brains dashed out and dabbled with their long gray hair," reported an indignant Bret Harte from nearby Arcata, before bolting for San Francisco. "Infants scarce a span long, with their faces cloven with hatchets and their bodies ghastly with wounds."[58]

Those Wiyot who survived the pogrom ran up against statutes from Sacramento that condoned the dispossession, relocation, and enslavement of California's Indians. Meanwhile the federal government sold off and otherwise gave away native land without treaty or compensation. In California, unlike every other U.S. state and territory, officials in Washington, D.C., in concession to Gold Rush settlers, acted on the legal fiction that indigenous peoples lacked occupancy rights. In a sense, Wiyot time ended when their sacred island was seized, renamed, deforested, and industrialized. Less than a decade after the massacre, the largest of eleven redwood mills built on Humboldt Bay opened on "Gunther Island."[59]

When Eureka hit its stride in the late 1880s, workers from around the world arrived in search of opportunity. The clamor of shipbuilders, shiploaders, and millworkers rang out in the air. The smoke from coal and wood fires swirled into the coastal fog; the black-and-gray smudge cloaked the stubble on the hills—the remains of dense forests. The bayside town contained rough saloons, rougher shanties, and the appropriated remnants of a former Chinatown. In the opening decades of settlement, immigrant Chinese worked in logging mills and camps and helped build the short-gauge tracks that radiated outward into timbered valleys up the Eel River and its tributaries. For their essential labor, the Chinese were rewarded with spite. Starting in 1885, the last year of a deep recession, Humboldt County systematically drove out its "coolies," starting with a purge in Eureka of over two hundred. In 1890 the local business directory—on the title page, no less—proudly advertised Humboldt as THE ONLY COUNTY IN THE STATE CONTAINING NO CHINAMEN. Labor unionizers and working-class whites scapegoated Chinese workers for low wages and mandatory twelve-hour shifts in the timber industry, and business elites encouraged that notion. The deportation of "foreign" competition did not in reality solve the problem. Before and after, wealth inequality characterized the North Coast. One of the leading anti-Chinese voices, the mill owner John Vance, showed off his fortune by erecting Eureka's finest hotel, named for himself. His main business rival built the singular Carson Mansion, an ultra-Victorian landmark made of redwood and mahogany. At nearby docks, in the regular drizzle, poorly paid workers—predominantly migrants from the timber country of Maine, New Brunswick, and Nova Scotia—loaded boards, beams, posts, stakes, ties, and shingles.[60]

Practically all lumber left Eureka by schooner. Most of the supply didn't travel far—the greater part to wood-hungry San Francisco, the lesser part from there to other parts of California, or Mexico, or Hawai'i. There was the occasional trophy item such as the solid cross-section, a "block of a monster," special-ordered from Vance by William Waldorf Astor in 1897 for installation at his River Thames estate as an "object of interest" (probably not, as widely reported, to settle a drunken wager with members of London's high society, including the prince of Wales, on whether one could seat fifty banqueters around a table made from a single California tree).[61] The East Coast market remained effectively out of reach until 1914, when the North Coast gained a direct rail connection to the transcontinentals and when the Panama Canal opened.

Because of the initial high outlays required, redwood logging did not generate quick profits. To offset start-up costs, timber companies ramped up production; the strategy led to chronic overproduction, which in turn depressed prices. Applying the homestead system to forestland turned out to be a policy mistake: it resulted in too many small timber holders, too many mills, all of them flooding the regional market with the same product as they tried to pay off property taxes and debt. California's population was still relatively small—1.5 million in 1900. It simply didn't need that much high-grade lumber. As excessive supply encountered insufficient demand, business failures piled up. Like most extractive industries, the redwood industry grew fitfully, with booms, busts, and wildly fluctuating prices. Various attempts at cartelization failed. Market stability came in the form of established timber barons from the Midwest, who muscled their way into the Redwood Empire around the turn of the century.[62]

Before chainsaws and tractors, industrial logging in the redwoods required an uneconomical amount of human and animal labor. At least fifty woodsmen worked in each camp. A distinctive North Coast argot described their sequence of tasks. First a two-person team of "choppers" built a protruding platform, like a springboard, above the flared base of a tall redwood. From this elevated workstation, 10 or 20 feet high, choppers used specially made 4-pound double-bitted hickory axes to make a deep undercut, then moved to the other side. Between rounds of cutting, they drove steel wedges into the kerf to force the titan to fall. The job might take a week. In the meantime, other choppers downed small trees (usually yews and firs) in the fall line to cushion the impact. After the fall, woodsmen with different skills began sectioning the redwood. "Ringers" used axes to mark the trunks at even intervals; their gouges provided footholds for the "peelers," who used chisel-headed crowbars to remove the thick, tough, stringy bark, which could gum up the mill saw. Companies typically logged a year's supply of timber in the rainless summer, then burned all the leftover slash, an otherwise impassable mess. Although the fire-resistant timber usually escaped damage, the fire often jumped bounds, destroying adjoining unlogged forest. After the first hard rain cleansed the charred landscape, "buckers" sawed the peeled trunks into logs, 10 to 20 feet long, as previously marked by ringers. If their double-wide saws couldn't span the width of a trunk, buckers called in a "powder monkey" to set a dynamite charge.

Next came yarding, the process of moving lengths of timber to the mill. "Hook tenders" used steel cable and hooks to "dog" the pieces into a "log string" or "train." To "snake in" the logs to the nearest road, workers relied on the "steam donkey," a portable winch powered by a single-cylinder steam engine. This revolutionary machine, invented in 1881 by the Eureka mill owner John Dolbeer, enabled woodsmen to drag trees up ravines and over hills. The "driver" or "puncher" of the machine supervised the "spool tender," who monitored the cable, and the "donkey tender," who fed the upright boiler a constant supply of water and firewood. A "donkey doctor" provided mechanical maintenance. After the logs had been dragged through the forest, they needed to be untied, rehitched, then "swamped out" along a corduroy road, a washboard-like pathway through the mud. Of all the component operations in the timber business, road building required the most money—up to $5,000 per mile. On the West Coast, "swampers" referred to their coarse paths as "skidroads," the source of the colloquial *skid row*. Teams of oxen or horses pulled logs across the lubricated skids. The teamster, better known as the "bullwhacker" or "bullpuncher"—the best-paid man in the whole crew—managed the animals while a "waterslinger" (aka "water packer," "water buck," "bucket man," "sugler," or "skid greaser") applied water or dope, usually animal fat, to reduce friction and make the road "slippy." (Eventually log chutes and larger winches called "bull donkeys" eliminated the need for animal power.) From the end of the road, a short-gauge railroad—a stinky, coal-powered "skunk"—transported the logs to a millpond. Dumped into the water, the wood floated the final distance to the mill for processing.[63]

The drudgery and ingenuity of Humboldt County's early industrial logging was matched only by high costs, excess competition, and flagrant waste. The enterprise resembled mining more than forestry, right down to the abysmal safety record. In quotidian fashion, workingmen lost eyes, fingers, limbs, and lives. The walking wounded had no access to workers' compensation. The industry used up trees, like bodies, in disposable fashion; dismembered redwoods became so much organic slag. The panorama of slash was captured in the first report of the California State Board of Forestry, an advocacy commission created by the legislature in 1885. The board estimated that on average only 29 percent of any felled redwood went to market as finished timber; the rest—the tall stump, the leafy top, the bark, the innumerable sloughed-off pieces—went nowhere. The going price for California lumber did not justify greater efficiency. In the mills, too, the logic of improvidence prevailed. Not until 1885 did North Coast mills begin to invest in band saws. The prior technology, the circular saw, made a savagely wide cut of three-eighths of an inch and transformed up to 40 percent of the milled log into useless sawdust. In the early days, workers simply dumped the wood powder into gullies. Later, conveyors transported all the fine bits, the low-grade material, and the discarded short and odd lengths to a constantly burning bonfire or furnace. The board warned that redwood, a purely Californian resource once considered "exhaustless as the ocean," was "rapidly melting away."[64]

At the national level, Charles Sprague Sargent's official *Report on the Forests of North America* (1884) noted California's "wasteful methods of cutting." For example, "split stuff" crews who made railroad ties simply abandoned any downed redwood that failed to split evenly with the grain. Even at the local level, the chroniclers of Humboldt County seemed scandalized by what Americans had done to the redwoods—"venerable giants" of "almost immortal strength, spanning and bridging past centuries" that had stood "while almost countless generations have come, gone, and passed away." In an oversized, lavishly illustrated commemorative volume from 1888 that celebrated the intelligence and prosperity of settlers and reviled the "California Indian" as the "most degraded of mortals," the authors paused for a melancholic moment:

> No one can contemplate the wholesale destruction of these glorious forests without the saddest feelings. Nothing can be more majestic and impressive than the land clothed with them, nor

The Mother of the Forest, ca. 1865: "A ghastly object—her sides still transfixed with wooden implements of torture." The bark from this flayed giant sequoia went to London for display in the Crystal Palace.

THE STUMP AND TRUNK OF THE MAMMOTH TREE OF CALAVERAS.
Showing a Cotillion Party of Thirty-two Persons Dancing on the Stump at one time.
PUBLISHED BY J. M. HUTCHINGS, S. FRANCISCO.

Merriment at the remains of the Discovery Tree, 1862.

The Big Tree known as the Mark Twain, 1,341 years old at its moment of death in 1891. This champion sequoia was felled at the behest of the American Museum of Natural History.

CALIFORNIA
The Home of the Big Tree

THE famous Big Tree, in the Mariposa Grove, near Yosemite Valley, is 400 feet high. Scientists say its age exceeds **9,000 years.** If placed at the junction of Fifth Avenue and Broadway it would fill Broadway and overtop the new **Flatiron Building** by 114 feet. Cut into one-inch boards it would entirely sheath the building on all sides. ❧ ❧ ❧ ❧

For literature and information concerning the **Mariposa Big Tree Grove, Yosemite Valley,** famous **Hotel Del Monte,** and other **Pacific Coast Resorts,** address the

SOUTHERN PACIFIC

Boston, 170 Washington Street; Baltimore, 109 East Baltimore Street; New York City, 349 and 1 Broadway; Syracuse, 129 South Franklin Street; Philadelphia, 109 South Third Street

L. H. NUTTING, G. E. P. A., New York City

E. O. McCORMICK, P. T. M., San Francisco, Cal.   T. J. ANDERSON, G. P. A., Houston, Tex.

SEAMAN

A 1904 magazine advertisement featuring Yosemite National Park's famous Wawona Tunnel Tree. California flora was legendarily bigger, taller, and older.

Two Humboldt County scenes from the late nineteenth century. *Above*: An oxen team pulls redwood logs; a bucket of lubricating fluid sits on the side of the skid road. *Below*: A steam donkey, the technology that replaced animal power on the North Coast.

Short-gauge railroads carried redwood logs from the ends of skid roads to mills in Eureka.

A chopper rests in the shade of a gigantic undercut log, while axe-wielding ringers work in the distance.

The Pacific Lumber Company's mill in Scotia, with a sawyer milling a huge board of grade-A "clear" redwood, fine-grained and knot-free—"nature's lumber masterpiece."

Cut of Redwood, 15x4 Feet, Sent From Vance's Wood, Humboldt County. to London, England.
From a Photograph.

For his Thames-side estate, William Waldorf Astor special-ordered this solid cross-section. To the left, a eucalypt grows above the redwood stumps.

The Bohemian Grove, one of the largest and most beautiful reserves of old-growth redwood, is closed to the public, and closed to women. This exclusive tract in Sonoma County hosts the Bohemian Club's midsummer retreats, including baroque opening ceremonies befitting an elite secret society.

An Earth First! rally in Eureka during "Redwood Summer," 1990. The sign RESPECT YOUR ELDERS refers to trees. Loggers countered with JOBS FIRST!

One of the last illegal tree-sits on Pacific Lumber property, 2004. Julia Butterfly Hill made tree-sitting famous, but many activists before and after her squatted in redwoods.

more naked, desolate, ragged and uncouth than the land after it is stripped of them. It is in the one case peace, beauty, plenty, virginity and bounty; in the other rags, fire, destruction, rapine, ghastliness and most unsightly death . . . [The redwoods], like the elk they have sheltered, and the poor Indian whose wig-wam they have built, are doomed to fall before the advance of civilization.[65]

The most poetic rendition of these conflicted states of being—immortal/doomed, spiritual/commodified—came from Walt Whit-man, a man who never visited the sunset edge of the continent. Whitman's "Song of the Redwood-Tree" (1873) contains three voices: a poet, a dryadic chorus, and a "mighty dying tree" who speaks a solemn refrain:

> *Farewell, my brethren,*
> *Farewell, O earth and sky—farewell, ye neighboring waters;*
> *My time has ended, my term has come.*

While the great tree and the dryads sing in unison, the lumbermen of Mendocino County make their own "music" with the "crackling blows" of their axes. The unrefined workers cannot hear the forest; only the poet possesses the sensitivity to discern "the mighty tree its death-chant chanting." Though elegiac, Whitman's poem exhibits rough optimism. The redwood and its supporting chorus intone that an epoch has ended, a new age has dawned. After a millennium in the woods, the dryads will retreat to their mountain caves and the Forest King will abdicate his throne—the amplitude of California—to a "superior race" whose arrival has long been predicted. In this bountiful land, pioneers of the republic will have the opportunity to grow "hardy, sweet, gigantic," to tower "proportionate to Nature." The chorus ecstatically praises this New American: "Not wan from Asia's fetiches, Nor red from Europe's old dynastic slaughter-house," but thrifty and inventive, a "swarming and busy race settling and organizing every where." In the Virgin Lands on the Western Shore, the Culminating Man will create an Empire New, the true America.

Whitman wrote "Song of the Redwood-Tree" five months after he lost his mother and nine months after he suffered a debilitating stroke. Death was on his mind. But even before these dual tragedies, Whitman's outlook had darkened. The Civil War changed him, and changed the United States. As a field nurse during the war, Whitman had witnessed the amputations, deformities, and devastations made possible by industrial progress. In the postwar period, he grew increasingly disenchanted with American society, which seemed overly materialistic and commercial. It seems probable that the half-paralyzed poet identified with the figure of the final Forest King—the prophet of a new America he wouldn't live to see. Like so many northerners who experienced the trauma of the Civil War, Whitman located the hope of the nation—and, by extension, Western civilization—in the Far West. "Song of the Redwood-Tree" describes an alternative America, even a utopian America—a New Society no longer possible in the industrial East.

Had the prophetic bard actually visited the Humboldt or Mendocino woods, had he seen the warlike cutting of *Sequoia sempervirens*, he might have lost faith. Even in advance of the Civil War, the Gold Rush made California, the west of the West, the most commercial state in the nation. In the mining and logging camps, society was not just rude; it was rapacious. With the possible exception of the Kaweah colonists, California settlers made a mockery of Whitman's vision: ancient trees intoning their submissive self-sacrifice "to duly fall, to aid, unreck'd at last / To disappear, to serve" a new society proportionate to nature. Pioneers of the redwood forest did not, as the poet imagined, clear the way for populous cities and thrifty farms. After decimating the indigenous population and dislodging Chinese workers, their main achievement was to squander some of the best timberland in the world ahead of market demand and technological efficiency. The amputated forest bore witness to the endemic profligacy of post–Civil War America. The Forest King abdicated to King

Commerce. Looking back on this period from 1920, Willis Jepson remarked, "The only race which is fit to possess this land is one which will use it and at the same time preserve it and be able after 500 years to say that the flush of youth is upon California as it was in the beginning." The botanist lamented the continuing wasteful harvest of redwoods, a practice that would, if continued, make California "old and haggard, wrinkled and dry, skinned down to the bone."[66]

Conservationists, environmentalists, and radical activists of the twentieth century would attempt to stop that day from arriving.

CHAPTER 2

The Perpetual Last Stand

SAVING THE REDWOODS

In the Sierra Nevada, American excursionists from the 1850s onward marveled at sequoias primarily for their age, secondarily for their size and limited distribution. In the category of biological longevity, giant sequoias occupied first place in the American imagination. The Sierra species became a national icon almost immediately after "discovery," and the federal government ultimately preserved most of the Big Tree groves. On the privatized North Coast, by contrast, tourists didn't arrive in great numbers until the twentieth century, and when they did, they stood in awe for a variety of reasons: the height of redwoods, the density of forest cover, and, to a somewhat lesser extent, great age. Saving these trees entailed purchasing them. Conservationists initially directed private monies toward the tallest in the world. In the long run, antibusiness environmentalists succeeded in changing the cultural imagination. They marshaled public assistance for "old-growth" redwoods, which they reclassified as symbolic equivalences of sequoias: ancient relicts, isolated and imperiled.

The expanse of coast redwood at the time of the Gold Rush has been estimated anywhere between 1.3 and 2.1 million acres. The calculation depends on what you count as "redwood forest." *Sequoia sempervirens* occurs in two distinct forest types. More commonly—

though less famously—redwoods mix with species such as Douglas fir and western hemlock on mountain slopes, where they grow less than awesomely tall. The second type is the prime habitat, the narrow alluvial flats along the streams draining the Klamath Mountains and North Coast Ranges. Here the trees take advantage of rich, deep, well-drained soil and a climate with limited diurnal and seasonal variations. The windward edge of low-lying summer fog provides optimal crown wetting. In the shelter of such valleys, redwoods mature into "heavy" stands, also called pure, iconic, diagnostic, superlative, or cathedral stands. These stunning arrays of vertical density constitute the woodiest woodland anywhere. Where trees reach highest, conflicts burn hottest. California's hard-won redwood preserves are largely located in this single rare microhabitat.

As late as 1950 approximately 1 million acres of "original" (pre–Gold Rush) forest still stood, most of it privately owned. By 2000, according to both counting methods, fewer than 100,000 acres of old growth remained, practically all of it publicly owned. Saving that small fraction (perhaps 5 percent) of the historic forest required three distinct, long-lasting efforts, each launched by different interest groups with disparate strategies and goals. First, the Save-the-Redwoods League coordinated land acquisitions for the California state park system (1920s–1930s). Subsequently the Sierra Club, among others, put up a legislative fight for Redwood National Park (1950s–1978); and finally grassroots radical environmentalists litigated and demonstrated for regulatory reform in redwood forestry (1978–2008). As the scraps grew smaller, divisiveness and controversy increased. A conservation campaign gave way to a preservation battle and ultimately a timber war. At each stage, the costs of saving redwoods exponentially grew, requiring more money for less land.[1]

The decades-long conflict played out differently from other famous controversies about western parklands—the proposed damming of the Grand Canyon, for example—because the disputed properties belonged to individuals and corporations. The General Land Office issued the final redwood land patents around 1900, at which point private interests owned 100 percent of *S. sempervirens* as a wild-growing species. Speculators who had been holding on to prime timberland took the opportunity to cash out, and midwestern capitalists with logging experience moved in. Extensive consolidation ensued. By the eve of World War I, twenty-three holders owned 79 percent of the total supply of the species; of that group, fifteen holders owned 66 percent, and six owned 41 percent.[2] Given the subsidiary interests of giants such as Hammond Redwood Company and Pacific Lumber, the concentration was actually even greater. No other species of timber in America belonged to so few. When Woody Guthrie sang the immortal lines "This land is your land, this land is my land . . . from the Redwood Forest to the Gulf Stream waters," he could not have been further from the truth.

Preservation efforts followed the path of devastation. The movement began in the Bay Area, where commercial loggers had cut redwood first. Since the mid-1860s, erudite San Franciscans had warned of the possibility of logging-induced climate change; the region could become a desert, they warned, if fog-condensing redwoods continued to be liquidated. A proposal by the editor of the *San Mateo County Times* for a reserve on the San Francisco Peninsula came and went in the 1880s. By that point, only a few timbered tracts, all privately owned, remained in the canyons of the southern Santa Cruz Mountains. Finally, in 1900–1901, the painter-photographer Andrew Hill of San Jose spearheaded one of the first successful grassroots campaigns in U.S. conservation history. Hill enlisted the support of Stanford president David Starr Jordan, who presided at a planning meeting at the university library. Afterward, two more of Stanford's top science professors, already active in the Sierra Club, joined Hill and Jordan as cofounders of the Sempervirens Club of California.

The club coined a memorable motto—"Save the redwoods"—and rallied various interests into a powerful coalition. Wealthy urbanites wanted a breathing place to camp and play; the Southern Pacific Railroad wanted increased tourism; the University of California wanted a forestry school station; San Francisco wanted to safeguard a potential water supply; and the orchardists of the Santa Clara Valley wanted to maintain the region's climate. Local newspapers like the *San Jose Mercury* championed the conservationists, and regional magazines like *Overland Monthly* blasted the landowners for their destructive habits and their idolatrous worship of the almighty dollar. Bolstered by editorial opinion, philanthropically assisted by Phoebe Hearst (widow of George Hearst and mother of William Randolf Hearst), and organizationally assisted by clubwomen and Catholic church members, the Sempervirens Club shepherded a bill through the state legislature that appropriated a quarter-million dollars for a land purchase. A governor-appointed commission negotiated for 3,800 acres in Santa Cruz County that in 1902 became California Redwood Park, the first state park (since enlarged and renamed Big Basin Redwoods State Park). The following year, sitting president Theodore Roosevelt, speaking at Stanford, emphatically endorsed the effort: "We should not turn into shingles a tree which was old when the first Egyptian conqueror penetrated the valley of the Euphrates."[3]

The next redwood park came into being through individual action and federal fiat. In Marin County, just north of San Francisco, across the Golden Gate, shady Redwood Canyon on Mount Tamalpais sheltered a small relict stand. The businessman William Kent purchased the canyon in 1905 in order to protect the trees and create a quasi-public park accessible by scenic railway. Kent had recently moved to Marin County after making a fortune in Chicago; in short order the industrialist became the county's largest property owner as well as its congressman. After 1906, Kent faced pressure to sell the woods to a private utility in the name of the public interest: postquake San Francisco needed timber and a reservoir site. To avoid the threat of a condemnation suit, Kent donated the property to the U.S. government. Following Kent's suggestion (relayed through chief forester Gifford Pinchot), President Roosevelt turned around and designated the parcel a national monument, using the power Congress granted the executive under the 1906 Antiquities Act. At Kent's request, the monument was named Muir Woods in honor of John Muir—to

Muir's surprise, since he had never met Kent and had spent little time in Marin County.[4]

As a general proposition, it is hard to distinguish the capitalists who spent money saving redwoods from the capitalists who got rich cutting them. Take, for example, the Bohemian Club, an exclusive male fraternity that frolics annually in the woods. In 1898, back when the San Francisco–based club actually contained some bohemians, it preserved a stupendous forested tract along Sonoma County's Russian River; subsequent purchases added to the redwood property. The 3,000-acre Bohemian Grove—nine times larger than the original Muir Woods National Monument—is closed to the public, and all women. It plays host to a famously secretive summer retreat for ultrarich and ultrapowerful men, mainly laissez-faire Republicans. The yearly midsummer retreat, something like a glee camp for Skull and Bones, begins with a ceremony called "the Cremation of Care." After a funeral procession through the trees, a coffin bearing the effigy of Dull Care—the personification of the worldly concerns of the business world—is placed on a pyre on a lakeside altar beneath a 40-foot-high shrine in the shape of an owl. The mocking voice of Care speaks through a dead redwood illuminated by stage lights: "Fools! When will ye learn that me ye cannot slay? Year after year ye burn me in this Grove, lifting your puny shouts of triumph to the stars. When again ye turn your faces toward the marketplace, do you not find me waiting as of old?" Each year, the CEOs-cum-pagans must be content to banish Care for a single weekend holiday; they cheer as their richly costumed high priest, bearing a flame from the Lamp of Fellowship upon the Altar of Bohemia, sets the pyre ablaze to the accompaniment of orchestral music and fireworks. In addition to this baroque opening ceremony, the weekend thespians perform the Midsummer High Jinks, a newly composed pageant-play that may include nature-loving mythological characters such as hamadryads. A theatrical chaser, the Low Jinks, concludes the festivities, not to mention prodigious drinking and boyish urinating on tree trunks. In the early years, campers dressed up in kimonos, slept in tepees under Chinese lanterns, and conducted the main ceremony beneath a giant Buddha. The secret society extended membership privileges to some of California's most prominent politicians, including Herbert Hoover, Richard Nixon, Earl Warren, and Ronald Reagan. (On one of his Oval Office tapes, Nixon can be heard disparaging the forest retreat as "the most faggy goddamned thing you could ever imagine.") In the first half of the twentieth century, the roster included several executives with commercial redwood holdings and many more with investments in timber firms.[5]

The socioeconomic relationship between redwood preservation and destruction shows up glaringly in the early history of the Save-the-Redwoods League, the most forceful conservation group in the Golden State during the interwar wars. Although it took its name from the motto of the Sempervirens Club, the league departed from its predecessor in organization and strategy. Whereas the club was a largely female grassroots local group that focused solely on the San Francisco Peninsula, the league was a male-dominated elite national group that gave its attention to the Calaveras sequoias and especially the North Coast redwoods.

The league's founding triumvirate, Madison Grant, Henry Fairfield Osborn, and John C. Merriam, met at the Bohemian Grove in 1917 as guests of club member Stephen Mather, the millionaire industrialist behind 20 Mule Team Borax, who had just been named the first director of the National Park Service. To attend the retreat, Grant and Osborn traveled all the way from Manhattan. Like their patrician friends Teddy Roosevelt and George Bird Grinnell, Grant and Osborn actively participated in the New York Zoological Society and the Boone and Crocket Club, a hunting and conservation group for gentlemen. Grant, a lawyer by training and a naturalist by inclination, applied his wealth, social capital, and indefatigable energy to the cause of endangered icons of American flora and fauna, including bison, bald eagles, and grizzly bears. Osborn, the paleontologist who named *T. rex*, served for many years as the president of the American Museum of Natural History; he had connections and riches as the son of a railroad tycoon and the nephew of J. P. Morgan. Merriam, another paleontologist and another member of the Boone and Crocket Club, taught at the University of California; eventually he became president of the Carnegie Institution of Washington. It was a distinguished trio.[6]

In the fraternal atmosphere of the Bohemian Grove, the professor from Berkeley intrigued the New Yorkers with talk of taller and grander redwoods. The three men decided to drive to Humboldt County at the close of the Jinks. Just that year, convict workers under the direction of state engineers were putting the finishing touches on a road—later known as U.S. 101—connecting the Bay Area to Eureka. Leaving their car at Bull Creek Flat on the Eel River, the gentlemen wandered into the woods and stood enraptured beneath the cathedral-like trees. A short distance down the road, the wreckage from a fresh logging operation shocked their sensibilities. Smoke filled the air; piles of grape stakes covered the ground. The state highway, which ran through private property, had incentivized loggers as well as sightseers. The newly founded California Redwood Association was aggressively pursuing eastern and international markets recently opened by the Northwestern Pacific Railway and the Panama Canal. Additionally, the resource demands brought on by World War I had prompted the U.S. Railroad Administration, a wartime experiment in socialized industry, to authorize the use of redwood for railroad ties. At military bases in the United States and France, the War and Navy departments installed over 2 million linear feet of redwood piping. All in all, 1917 was a terrible year to be an old redwood.

After their eye-opening trip, Grant, Osborn, and Merriam resolved to organize a conservation group "to preserve the oldest trees in the world." To fill the leadership of the Save-the-Redwood League, they enlisted "better men"—a preponderance of Yale graduates, Progressive Republicans, and mainline Protestants from the Northeast and California. (In 1921 the club appointed a few women—three influential presidents of women's clubs—as councilors.) William Kent and Stephen Mather gave the first large financial gifts; John D. Rockefeller Jr. gave the most. The league recruited additional donors through direct-mail campaigns composed of names drawn from social directories such as *Who's Who*. Generous givers were rewarded with a guided tour of the Eel River forest in a topless touring car. Like the later Nature Conservancy, the league accepted donations from corporations involved in extractive industries, including the redwoods-based Union Timber Company. In deference to the big-business, small-government stance of its membership, the league favored private land purchases. In the words of its longtime chairman, J. D. Grant, a mogul in hydropower, oil, and steel (and proud member of the Bohemian Club), the core principles were "friendly negotiation" and "just compensation" in a "businesslike way" in recognition of the "legitimate interests" of the logging industry.[7]

Showing ideological consistency, league members opposed efforts by other conservationists who wanted to use the state's power of eminent domain to acquire redwoods along the highway and gave only qualified support to the idea of a national park on the North Coast. The leadership preferred the instrument of state parks. League lobbyists deserve substantial credit for the creation of the California State Park Commission in 1927 and the passage of a state bond referendum in 1928 that matched public funds to private donations for parkland purchases. Through insider moves, partisans of the league came to dominate the park commission and its survey of potential land transactions. Although fund-raising became harder during the Depression, the economic crisis opened up a buyer's market. By 1931 California had acquired five small, expensive, and spectacular forest parks—four on the North Coast and one encompassing the northern Calaveras sequoia grove. The league made major contributions to each.[8]

Besides fund-raising, the Save-the-Redwoods League specialized in advertising. To get its message out, the league retained the services of the Drury Company, a San Francisco firm run by two brothers, Aubrey and Newton B. Drury. Newton joined the league as executive secretary before moving on to the directorship of the National Park Service and the California Division of State Parks. Under his guidance, the league sponsored lectures, produced films, printed pamphlets for mass distribution, and placed articles in national periodicals such as *National Geographic* and the *Saturday Evening Post.* The editors at both magazines belonged to the league.[9]

The Drury PR campaign trained the attention of armchair tourists and automobilists on the "Last Stand of the Giants." The league narrowly focused its purchase program on property adjacent to the state highway—the only redwoods most tourists would ever see. In essence, the league wanted to create a wooded parkway. To encourage tourism, the group distributed tens of thousands of copies of a windshield emblem. On the front, it showed a car next to a titanic tree; on the back, it showed a road map. Even the organization's official seal depicted a road running through the woods. The club equated tourism with activism: "See the Redwoods, Save the Redwoods, Travel the Redwoods Highway." A scenic drive made pleasing sightlines in a forest that was otherwise hard to see in full. In its promotions, the league innovated the exploitation of nature photography for political aims. To achieve the desired effect, it juxtaposed two kinds of images, a beautiful "before" shot of a fern-lined touring road and an ugly "after" shot of a logging road lined with stakes, stumps, and slash. The accompanying texts evoked death and destruction— sometimes with allusions to the contemporaneous Great War. The league gave the "estimated life" of the finest roadside groves as five to ten years. The Eel River corridor "resembles devastated France," Osborn declared. In Madison Grant's words, every old stand by the road was "threatened with annihilation." Without action, all would be lost in sixty years; loggers would make a "clean sweep of every standing stick." The scenic Redwood Highway would become an ugly Red Stump Highway.[10]

Grant cared deeply about the fate of America's imperiled animals and plants, starting with the big game and big trees he considered to be noble products of evolution. Just as he worked to save the best of native species, he worked to conserve America's "great race" from extinction. He may be the most seminal eugenicist in U.S. history.

His best-selling *The Passing of the Great Race* (1919) was admired by Nazis and used as evidence for the defense at Nuremberg. Writing from the perspective of 1919, Grant bemoaned "race suicide" on both sides of the Atlantic. In Europe, members of the same racial family, the Germans and the English, had just killed one another by the millions in the trenches; in America, native-born men and women of the "Anglo-Saxon branch of the Nordic race" were producing fewer and fewer children while immigrants of inferior stock were producing more. In his time, Grant sounded like a sage, not a maverick or a crank. Before Hitler gave eugenics a noxious reputation, race breeding was a respectable field of science and social policy, a Progressive cause that appealed to America's best and brightest. David Starr Jordan, a figure of impeccable credentials, lectured and published on the sound principles of sterilizing morons and the scientific hope of breeding the superman.

The council of the Save-the-Redwoods League was a who's who of eugenics, including multiple published authors on the subject and the founder of the Eugenics Society of Northern California. John C. Merriam, in his role as president of the Carnegie, supervised the creation of a topflight eugenics research campus at Cold Spring Harbor, Long Island. Many other league leaders expressed their approval of scientific racism and nativism. In his memoir, *Redwoods and Reminiscences*, J. D. Grant (no relation) wrote about the "survival of the fittest" in frontier San Francisco, noted approvingly that the firestorm of 1906 had "swept clean the plague spot of old Chinatown," and celebrated the triumph of thrifty Anglos over improvident Mexicans and servile Chinese. He praised the "patriotic work" of Madison Grant and the Immigration Restriction League to stem the inflow of "alien hordes"—inferior breeds that "submerged the older stock" and "made the body politic sick unto death."[11]

Not all Progressive-era conservationists supported scientific racism, but a preponderance of the most powerful did, and these influential men evinced keen interest in the preservation of the sequoia taxon, especially *S. sempervirens*. California's supertrees functioned as metaphorical people—as superior individuals. Madison Grant and the other leaders of the Save-the-Redwoods League praised both giant sequoia and coast redwood as descendants of the same noble lineage, but they clearly identified more with the latter. The Big Tree was, Grant wrote, "on the decline," a "battered remnant" whose "shattered ranks remind one of ponderous Roman ruins." Giant sequoia seemed unable to reproduce properly; in the language of eugenics, it seemed unfit. By contrast, coast redwood was a "beautiful, cheerful, and very brave tree" with legendary fitness. By reproducing by sucker and by regenerating from the stump, a vigorous redwood achieved sempiternity without sexuality. It didn't need its seeds to create progeny; it simply cloned itself. An ancient forest thus contained only the fittest of the fit. In contrast to the mixed-species Big Tree groves, the tallest redwood stands were "unmixed" and "pure," like an exclusive club. The Save-the-Redwoods League focused its greatest attention on saving the "best" grove, the home of the "world's tallest tree"—a phallic plant named in honor of Grant, Osborn, and Merriam. "It is an ancient and racial urge that has brought us together today," said a speaker at the dedication of the Founders Tree in 1931.[12]

Memorials became major fund-raising opportunities. With an appropriate donation, wealthy men, women, couples, or organizations could immortalize themselves with trees as old as the Roman Empire. The league preferred to denominate redwoods after "living celebrities" because doing so drew attention to the cause. The purposefully A-list memorial program succeeded in enlisting patrons such as James Irvine and the Rockefeller family. From 1921 to 2001, the league presided at the dedication of more than one thousand trees and groves. The first such grove, the league's inaugural purchase, was strategically named in honor of a dead dignitary, someone who fit the definition of a superior man. Raynal Bolling had graduated from Harvard University and Harvard Law School and worked his way up to general counsel at U.S. Steel. When war came, Bolling put patriotism first: he joined the armed forces, saying goodbye to his wife and children and his Connecticut mansion, Greyledge. Then, in

1918, Colonel Bolling died in France with a revolver in his hand, a German bullet in his heart. THE FIRST AMERICAN OFFICER OF HIGH RANK TO FALL IN THE WORLD WAR, read the unveiled plaque in the Bolling Grove. Speaking at the dedication ceremony, Madison Grant urged his audience to "preserve an America worth fighting for." The tree slaughter in California was robbing Americans of their birthright, much as the war in Europe had left the republic "impoverished of its best stock."[13]

The monumentalization of bluebloods such as Bolling—and especially Grant, a man who never married and fathered no children—may be read as mixed expressions of eugenical pride and concern. What would happen to American civilization if its best trees (best men) died out? In their anxious enthusiasm, Progressive-era conservationists conflated the language of genetic meritocracy with inherited aristocracy. The literature from the period is replete with references to the redwood forest as the last stronghold of the lordliest survivors of a noble race whose kingly dominion once spread across the earth. After conquering time and space, the remnant tree-lords faced an uncertain future. Overall, the early efforts of the Save-the-Redwoods League betray patrician disquiet about excessive democracy and the decline of a white man's republic. Through its publications and activities, the league permitted like-minded people to conflate coast redwood with the Anglo-Saxon American. The great race was also the threatened race, yet that threatened status came not from any inherent lack of virility but simply from the invasion of base elements that could and should be restricted through civic action. To use the ubiquitous language, the great trees were "making their last stand."

In fairness, race-inflected anxiety about California's monarchal flora predated the Save-the-Redwoods League. The viability of giant sequoia drew particular attention. In 1891 the *New York Times* noted that sequoias, "like the other noblest trees of temperate latitudes and all conquering, fighting races, seem to have had their original homes in the North." Driven south by the glaciers, the species occupied its "last retreat" in California, and now, because of human influence, each specimen "cast the shadow of a new-made grave." In 1892 Abbot Kinney, the former state forester, predicted that extinction was the "destiny" of the Big Tree because of its inability to cope with climate change. Kinney found meaning in the "fated forests" of the Sierra Nevada: "The slow but sure disappearance of these magnificent monarchs" because of nonreproduction "is a lesson the people of New England might well take to heart." In the land of the Puritan fathers, the death rate of the "native stock" exceeded the birthrate. "Should this condition continue," wrote Kinney, "the disappearance from the world of this forceful, moral and intellectual race is inevitable."[14]

CLEAN LOGGING

Death, destruction, doom. From the Gold Rush onward, Californians anticipated the undoing of sequoias and redwoods on various scales—individual outstanding specimens, groves or stands, forests, or whole species. In the middle decades of the twentieth century, the dawn of environmentalism, dendrophiles worried most about redwoods on the medium scale. Timber managers focused here, too, but from a silvicultural perspective. Where environmentalists saw the last virgin stand, loggers saw the end of one rotational harvest.

Despite the wasteful lumbering practices of the nineteenth century, perhaps three-quarters of the "original" redwoods remained as of 1900. In the pioneer era, choppers had attacked the heavy stands in the low-lying valleys; they had largely avoided the steep mountain slopes where redwood interspersed with fir. The slopes constituted an untapped resource—provided you could reach them. With new injections of capital, timber firms introduced "skyline logging" from the Pacific Northwest in the early twentieth century. To create a skyline, first a daredevil logger topped off one or more redwoods to form "spar trees" 150 or 200 feet high. Workers attached guy lines to each spar for added stability—like rigging on a mast—and then strung heavy steel cable to logging sites at higher or lower elevations. Along these stationary lines, bicycle-like pulleys transported logs through the air, up and down the mountain. To avoid entanglements, skyline transport demanded "clean logging"—what we now call clear-cutting. Previously loggers had honeycombed the forest each dry season in a process called "high-grading": they cut the best trees and left behind "residuals" that reseeded the land and provided cover for new growth. Unwittingly, pioneer wasters had practiced a form of selective logging—something now associated with sustainability. By contrast, skyline logging offered no geographic or temporal respite; clear-cutting operations on the slopes carried on year-round, even in bad weather. Logging reached the pinnacle of damage around World War I, when companies with skyline equipment responded to strong consumer demand. Unconstrained by regulations or long-term business models, they maximized short-term profits. The upland forests of Sonoma and Mendocino counties fell first.

Less impressively but with sizable cumulative impact, independent crews in the split products industry worked on parcels of individually owned redwood land; there, without the use of mills or machines, splitters converted whole trees, starting with windfalls, into "split stuff" such as railroad ties and grape stakes. These ax-wielding free-lancers, "gyppos," took advantage of the fact that the mature heartwood split easily with the grain into straight, even pieces. Gyppos also sometimes salvaged leftover stumps on industrial logging tracts.

Tax policy encouraged squandering, for the state levied no tax on cut timber, while counties levied an annual property tax on standing timber. This system, the norm throughout the United States, encouraged rapid cutting and discouraged replanting. To avoid the local tax collector, many small-time titleholders cut the valuable redwoods, then vacated their land. The cutover property then reverted to the county for nonpayment of taxes. (The estate tax created a reverse problem for smallholders: to keep the inherited land in the family, an heir often had no choice but to cut redwoods to raise money to pay a tax that had been assessed on those trees when they were standing.) In 1926 voters amended the state constitution to allow the deferment of taxation on second-growth timber for forty years on tracts from which 70 percent of all trees over 16 inches in diameter had been removed. In principle—though not always in practice, for local tax assessors still had considerable discretionary power—the amendment created an incentive for large landowners to bed out a new crop instead of cutting and running. Ironically, environmentalists would later perceive the amendment as an incentive for poor stewardship, for it encouraged the cutting of older, larger trees. In 1976 the legislature finally changed the overall system from a county-based ad valorem tax on standing timber to a state-assessed yield tax on cut timber.[15]

To the extent that sustainability on private redwood lands improved before the 1970s, the industry deserves primary credit. From a starting point of recklessness, it came a long way. In 1891 Eureka's mayor, the wealthy mill owner John Vance, recalled that he had originally "supposed that after the timber had been removed from the land in Humboldt County it would be abandoned and return to its original wildness." Now Vance imagined a different future: cutover redwood land converted to use for fruit trees. His honor owned an orchard of roughly 100 acres. Alas, the fruitfulness of Humboldt failed to meet expectations. Around 1910 several redwood firms, notably the Union Lumber Company of Mendocino County, tried something different: planting eucalypts as a potentially sustainable harvest crop. The experiment withered when the Australasian trees proved susceptible to frost. Whenever it seemed cost-effective, landowners turned cutover land into pastures or bulb farms; to extract massive stumps, they used dynamite, gas- or donkey-powered pullers, and repeated fire. They sold or leased the deforested land to dairymen. One Humboldt County supervisor summarized his preferred approach to silviculture: "I would cut it clean, burn hell out of it, and seed it to grass." In some converted pastures, giant snags—or whole titans, girdled to death, exfoliated—rose above the dairy sod like ghostly sentinels.[16]

Why not replant redwoods in redwood country? According to the ingrained attitude of loggers, *S. sempervirens* was a one-shot crop. The species successfully reproduced only by suckering, they said, and suckered second growth produced commercially worthless wood, knotty and "brashy" (soft, brittle). According to folk wisdom, it took two thousand years for tight-grained heartwood to develop in redwoods. If and when it proved profitable, timber companies were happy to log second growth. In 1922 ten large firms (who together held about two-thirds of all redwoods) formed two allied reforestation associations, one in Mendocino County, one in Humboldt, and asked the University of California to provide technical assistance. The UC School of Forestry had already conducted experiments on extracting, grading, and germinating seeds, and now, at the industry's request, it monitored sample plots of second growth on company land. Encouraged by the initial results, the associations directed employees to hand-plant millions of nursery seedlings on cleaned-up clear-cuts. "We are in on the birth of a forest," exclaimed the San Francisco Chronicle, which played up the "romance" of "artificial reforestation." "Fifty years from now, on that tract that was a battle-scarred ruin after the virgin timber had been logged off . . . will be a stately stand of redwoods, 'to kiss the hem of heaven.'" Unfortunately, about half of the young trees perished. The reasons for high mortality included grazing deer, nibbling rodents, and dehydration. Contrary to popular notion, the North Coast gets hardly any rain during the long foggy season (usually April to November). Discouraged, the reforestation associations dissolved their expensive programs at the end of 1931 as the U.S. economy sank deeper in a hole.[17]

The Depression and war years did, however, lead to unprecedented experiments in uniform—albeit voluntary—business standards in the redwood region. The National Recovery Administration's Lumber Code, written by the industry itself, discouraged clear-cutting and encouraged reseeding. The advisor or code forester for the region was Emanuel Fritz, a straight-talking, cigar-smoking veteran of the U.S. Army Air Service and a professor of forestry at UC Berkeley. Known as "Mr. Redwood," Fritz could speak naturally to academics, loggers, and businessmen. At the Bohemian Grove, club members looked forward to his guided nature walks. Fritz knew more about redwood silviculture than anyone else who ever lived, and he believed in the market value of sustainability. With enough expertise and time, he argued, California could create commercial-grade second growth from seedlings set in selectively logged tracts. The rebuilt forest would be harvested on a rotational basis: inferior trees would be thinned after twenty years for pulp or posts, medium-grade trees cut after forty years for poles, and superior trees allowed to live at least sixty years before being used for sawlogs. The commercial forest would thus always contain redwoods of different ages. True, even the oldest second-growth plant wouldn't provide extra-wide, extra-thick, grade-A boards like a millennial tree, but did that matter? No, argued Fritz. He cited improved methods of construction and veneering. He advised timber firms to think of redwoods in terms of a human generation, not millennia or business quarters. At his suggestion, the California Redwood Association began holding annual regional conferences to share forestry techniques. Although the Supreme Court invalidated the National Recovery Administration in 1935, the association decided to maintain the basic guidelines of the Lumber Code—essentially the Fritz method. Selective logging was becoming more feasible because of cost-saving, gas-powered inventions: drag saws, then chainsaws; tractors, then Caterpillar bulldozers; and logging trucks. The adaptable and powerful diesel engine enabled timber companies to phase out "steam logging"—donkey engines, skylines, and short-gauge railroads.[18]

The industry as a whole signaled its openness to change in 1945 when it and the legislature signed off on the California Forest Practice Act. As drafted by Fritz, the act was modest by design; he merely wanted to codify the principle of selective logging. Without coercion, the law coordinated the industry—a model of what political scientists call corporatism. It divided the private forestland in California into four districts, each with a rules committee. In the Redwood District, the industry wrote its own guidelines about minimum-diameter cutting, slash disposal, and fire prevention under the advisement of

Fritz and a reorganized State Board of Forestry (dominated by industry members). To demonstrate silvicultural techniques, the state purchased 52,000 acres of second growth in Mendocino County as an experimental plot (Jackson Demonstration State Forest) in 1947. About the same time, one large landowner, Simpson Logging Company, inaugurated a private-public partnership with the U.S. Forest Service under the federal Sustained Yield Management Act of 1944.[19]

Greater efficiency did not mean fewer stumps. When the economy rebounded during World War II, a retooled redwood industry revved back into action, escaping the bonds of debt that had stifled innovation. After the war, firms capitalized on the export market to Japan and burgeoning internal demand throughout America. Although engineers no longer needed redwood tanks and pipelines, postwar home buyers coveted the "California look" of redwood siding. Production rocketed to 1 billion board feet per annum by the mid-1950s and remained sky-high for twenty years. At the onset of the go-go years, "fast buck" operators joined the action; from 1940 to 1948, the number of redwood mills increased from 80 to nearly 600. Simultaneously, there was a new round of corporate consolidation, as firms like Simpson and Weyerhaeuser moved to the North Coast from Oregon and Washington. These established companies kept foresters on staff. Like Fritz, they viewed redwood as a rotational crop, something to be harvested, regrown, and reharvested on a fifty- to eighty-year basis. In 1950 the California Redwood Association endorsed the nationwide "tree farm" program, a certification system for tracts managed for repeated harvesting. Big players such as Hammond Lumber Company and Union Lumber Company immediately joined. The industry also demonstrated its commitment to conservation at its mills—once little more than sawdust factories—which now made products such as plywood. Redwood bark, previously burned, could be sold as insulating and packing material (Palco Wool) or as fiber for roofing and textiles. Sawdust was no longer sent away to be upholstery filling or packing material for table grapes but instead recycled and resold as pulp, particleboard, or compressed firewood known as Pres-to-Logs. The industry congratulated itself with new slogans: "Companies Permanize the Industry"; "Logs for Today; Trees for Tomorrow."[20]

Even as redwood logging and milling became exponentially less wasteful, timber companies briskly advanced toward consuming the last of the "virgin" stands. Starting in 1959, Arcata Redwood (a Weyerhaeuser affiliate) revived the practice of clear-cutting, abandoning Emanuel Fritz's method of selective logging. With the exception of Pacific Lumber, every major firm followed suit in the next few years. Companies complained about messy, costly blowdowns of residuals in selectively cut groves. More to the point, in a seller's market they could make more money by clear-cutting. Staff foresters endorsed the change in practice, for they had learned to increase the second-growth recruitment rate with aerial reseeding and herbicide spraying. If a redwood survives the fragile infant stage, it sprouts incredibly fast—a quick-maturing investment. By reseeding—and later by cultivating containerized seedlings cloned from pedigree stock—firms could convert clear-cuts into high-volume, even-age plantations. After putting a stand "to bed," they could leave it alone for decades as the trees converted sunshine into capital. Redwoods thrived with increased light and decreased competition—conditions created by clearing. By maximizing the cut of the forest, companies expedited the growth of a tree farm, a renewable resource. It seemed like a win-win: short-term profit and long-term investment. Corporate plans for maximum-yield harvesting got rubber-stamp approval from the State Board of Forestry in the 1960s. Logging firms ignored Fritz's politically savvy advice to ban roadside logging. In several locations they removed the *screen* or *fringe* (what environmentalists would later call the green façade) along the Redwood Highway that had prevented car tourists from seeing logging operations. Even responsible clear-cuts looked shockingly ugly at first, like a city ruined by atomic attack. Company men installed roadside exhibits designed to reassure sightseers that the stump land had been replanted.

Friends of the redwoods were not mollified, especially now that existing state parks, including the crown jewel, Humboldt Redwoods, appeared under siege. In the 1950s the Save-the-Redwoods League defeated plans to widen and straighten the Redwood Highway inside the park. Instead, road builders gouged a wide path (now the U.S. 101 freeway) through the upslope redwoods just outside the park's boundaries, leaving the Avenue of Giants as a scenic drive. Meanwhile conservationists could do nothing to stop a nearby maze of dirt roads. In the years after World War II, intensive logging came to the fir-covered Bull Creek Basin, located directly upslope from the park's world-famous Rockefeller Forest, including the Founders Tree. "Bulldozer delinquents" dumped logging slash and road detritus into stream channels, using them as landfills. Then, in late 1955, a fire overwhelmed the cutover basin. A torrential rain followed; landslides and flooding resulted. Rocks, gravel, and debris filled Bull Creek and gouged into the Rockefeller Forest. Approximately one-tenth of the wooded alluvial flat washed away; over four hundred trees—some of the tallest in the world—succumbed in one season. Dozens more fell down in the next four winters. Appalled, the Sierra Club became a vocal critic of state forestry regulation.[21]

By a twist of misfortune, another "100-year flood" tore through Humboldt Redwoods the week of Christmas 1964. In this regional disaster, the Eel River destroyed over twenty bridges, drowned more than twenty people, and obliterated ten whole towns. The swirling current undercut the roots of some three hundred bankside redwoods, causing them to topple slowly, almost silently, into the swollen river, which propelled them onward to the ocean, along with thousands of dead cattle and millions of board feet from the drying yards of the Pacific Lumber Company. In the years immediately following the deluge, hundreds more mature trees in the Rockefeller Forest sickened and died. As in 1955, protectionists blamed the logging industry for the losses. The Sierra Club and the California Department of Fish and Game made their case at a special hearing before the State Board of Forestry. Logging companies protested their innocence; experts could not reach consensus. Undeniably, the roads and skid tracks created by tractor logging increased local runoff and erosion, especially on steep slopes. Abandoned logjams from the pioneer era, dislodged by the flood, exacerbated the destruction. Nonetheless, it's probably unfair to assign to logging full responsibility for the damage to Humboldt Redwoods during and after the great flood of 1964. But that's what happened in the court of public opinion. The erosion dispute overlapped with a debate about improving the coast highway through two of the other redwood parks. With increasing urgency, conservationists called for the establishment of a national park to buttress the beleaguered state system.[22]

PARK POLITICS

Before and after its creation, Redwood National Park—now recognized as a World Heritage Site by UNESCO—inspired more discussion and debate than any other nature park in U.S. history. Firm proposals for federal ownership go back to the early 1900s, when clubwomen in Humboldt County advocated for trees and children; they wanted a picnic park where American families could spend quality time beneath the nation's tallest trees. In 1920 a government committee recommended a much larger acquisition of 64,000 acres. The proposal made it through the House but no further. Another option was the national forest system. After doing its best to privatize America's timber supply in the nineteenth century, the U.S. government did an about-face in 1911 with the Weeks Act, which authorized the purchase of huge tracts of private land in the East for conversion into national forests. During the Depression, when many small logging companies shuttered their operations and fell into tax delinquency, the State of California and the supervisors of Humboldt County pushed for the western expansion of this program. The National Forest Reservation Commission initiated a redwood buy-back program, but deficiency of funds prevented large-scale purchases. In the 1940s the retired first chief of the U.S. Forest Service, Gifford Pinchot, proposed to go to Congress for a special appropriation. Pinchot believed that only federal foresters possessed the expertise to facilitate sustainable logging of coast redwood and that the species should be turned over to the benevolent monopoly of his agency. Near the end of his life, Pinchot drafted a bill for the formation of a Franklin Delano Roosevelt Memorial Forest. As introduced by the Los Angeles congresswoman Helen Gahagan Douglas, the bill would have appropriated funds for the purchase of over 2 million acres of private land, including practically all of the North Coast redwoods. Arriving as the postwar economy recovered, this audacious bill ran up against opposition from state and county officials. It never left committee.[23]

The government did not return to the idea of buying redwoods until the 1960s, and by then the goal had shifted to a recreational park rather than a working forest. The proposal built on the precedents of Great Smoky, Shenandoah, and Mammoth Cave national parks, eastern playgrounds that took years to assemble because the 1926 congressional authorization delegated the purchasing responsibility to states and private donors. Later, to fill the new category of national seashore, Congress partially funded the conversion of private lands to public parks at Cape Hatteras (1937) and then principally funded Cape Cod, Fire Island, and Point Reyes (1962–1964). To facilitate future purchases, president John F. Kennedy convinced Congress to set up a government endowment, the Land and Water Conservation Fund, using royalties from offshore oil and gas. Before petroleum money could be spent on redwoods, the boundaries of a preserve had to be agreed upon by Congress and the landowners. Or, more precisely, Congress had to compel the owners to sell in a legal procedure known as "legislative taking." To expedite the process, the National Geographic Society gave the National Park Service a grant to conduct a forest survey—an expense compensated for by the society's exclusive announcement of the 1963 discovery of the new "world's tallest tree." The Tall Tree Grove along Redwood Creek belonged to Arcata Redwood Company.[24]

The debate over the location of the proposed park exposed tensions within the conservation movement, a generational rift between the Save-the-Redwoods League and the Sierra Club. Under the energetic leadership of president Edgar Wayburn and executive director David Brower, the venerable hiking club had reinvented itself as a national environmental group. Self-declared environmentalists distinguished themselves from conservationists in tactics, priorities, and tone. Unlike their genteel predecessors, environmentalists typically assumed an antagonistic stance toward the corporate world and believed in the power of lawsuits and negative campaigning to coerce change. The Sierra Club published a lavish propaganda book, *The Last Redwoods*; distributed a 16mm film, *Zero Hour in the Redwoods*; coproduced an Oscar-winning short documentary, *The Redwoods*; and took out full-page ads in the *New York Times* ("the last chance REALLY to save the redwoods"), all of which relied on visuals of raw clear-cuts. Seen through the club's cameras, the industry's roadside exhibits seemed like a joke: a freshly reseeded "tree farm" resembled a strip mine. In addition to the traditional aesthetic concerns of conservationists, environmentalists emphasized biogeographical coherence. Wayburn and Brower argued for the protection of the entire Redwood Creek watershed in Humboldt County, even though that would involve going up against the "big three" timber companies, Arcata, Simpson, and Georgia-Pacific. For its part, the Save-the-Redwoods League preferred to focus its attention on Mill Creek in Del Norte County, a scenic property owned by one small firm. The league had already saved over 100,000 acres, including most of the "park quality" stands in the alluvial flats, and hoped to minimize conflict by rounding out the existing preserves.

The debate peaked in 1967–68. Governor Ronald Reagan played a limited, lukewarm role ("A tree is a tree—how many more do you need to look at?" he had said during the 1966 gubernatorial campaign), leaving the role of high-level public advocacy to president Lyndon B. Johnson. In his State of the Union address in January 1967, a time of turmoil in race relations and foreign affairs, LBJ took the time to exhort the legislative branch to "save the redwoods." In another speech to Congress a few weeks later, the president repeated his call: "This is a 'last chance' conservation opportunity. If we do not act promptly, we may lose for all time the magnificent redwoods of Northern California." Behind the scenes, Laurance Rockefeller, a Republican with family ties to the Save-the-Redwoods League, worked as Johnson's special advisor, upstaging interior secretary Stewart Udall. Initially the administration endorsed the league's proposal against the objections of the Sierra Club and most mainstream media. Eager to end the stalemate, Georgia-Pacific in early 1968 took out its own boldfaced full-page ad in the *Wall Street Journal* and *New York Times*: "Yes, America's majestic redwoods have already been saved!" The company denounced the vicious attacks, allegations, distortions, and innuendo of the Sierra Club. It rejected the "hue and cry" that redwoods were somehow "vanishing." State parks already safeguarded virtually all the superlative stands, G-P said. Only a tiny fraction of the forest consisted of "cathedral-like groves," and logging would touch none of them.[25]

After a long congressional impasse and many negotiations with the companies—including limited, voluntary moratoriums on logging—the Senate came out with a Johnson-approved compromise that authorized two purchases, one on Mill Creek and one on Redwood Creek. Congressmen such as John Saylor, a wilderness-loving Republican from Pennsylvania's coal country, conferenced feverishly to reconcile the Senate bill with a House bill that authorized a smaller land purchase. In the meantime, G-P and other timber firms logged right up to the proposed boundaries of the park, a practice the Sierra Club called "legislation by chainsaw." The final bill reached LBJ's desk in October 1968.[26]

In its original form, Redwood National Park was an ungainly hybrid, a strip park whose boundaries encompassed three preexisting preserves unrelinquished by California. Thus about half of the 58,000 total acres had prior protection. The other half, including some 11,000 acres of "virgin" redwood, reentered the public domain in return for a combination of purchases and one large land swap. In the end, the deal cost more than triple the $92 million that Congress authorized. For years, no visitor center and few signs called attention to the nation's most expensive park. Ecologically, its boundaries made no sense, for neither watershed had been included in its entirety. At Mill Creek, two wilderness areas sandwiched a logging zone. At Redwood Creek, the Tall Tree Grove received protection, yet the narrow streamside tract—800 yards wide and 8 miles long—was potentially vulnerable to effects from upslope and upstream logging. Only about 10 percent of the watershed had been designated. People likened the odd shape of the Redwood Creek property to a pollywog, a gerrymandered congressional district, and a worm.

The ink had barely dried on the legal documents when logging companies resumed harvesting alternate-patch clear-cuts on lands adjoining "the worm." Just as quickly, environmentalists called for a follow-up congressional bill to enlarge the boundaries of the park to secure the Tall Tree Grove just saved. The "false-front" park was, they said, a Pyrrhic victory, a fraud, a bill of damaged goods. Visitors to the "world's tallest tree" hiked to the sound of chainsaws. Once again activists revived the language of impending death: "time was running out" on the "deadline" to save the "last" of the "vanishing" forest. Haunted by the memory of the Rockefeller Forest after the disastrous winters of 1955 and 1964, environmentalists feared that logging-related aggradation of gravel in Redwood Creek would raise the stream level to the point that the tall trees would drown, or fall over, or otherwise suffer from flood damage. They wanted a ridgetop-to-ridgetop park.

In response, the big three argued that the threat from the advancing gravel "slug" had been overstated; in any case, most of the erosional discharge came from noncompany lands upstream that had been logged in earlier years using techniques no longer allowed under the Forest Practice Act. The timber firms adopted additional voluntary restrictions for logging near "the worm" and entered into cooperative agreements with the National Park Service over management of a buffer zone. From the industry's perspective, they had done their part and more.

During the first round of debates in the 1960s, timber firms had accepted that some kind of park was inevitable and had played defense. The second round went differently: in the 1970s companies took the offensive and portrayed expansion of the park as a harmful extravagance, a threat to private enterprise, a drain on taxpayers, a drag on the local economy, a monument to coercion and misguided emotionalism. They rejected most of the government's requests for voluntary moratoriums on logging and increased their cutting—what opponents called "vendetta logging"—as a bill moved through the Democratic Congress with the help of representative Phillip Burton of San Francisco. Whereas the park's establishment, like environmentalism itself, had been a bipartisan effort, the expansion controversy presaged the political divergence of "pro-job" Republicans and "pro-environment" Democrats.[27]

Environmentalists did not budge: they opposed any logging near the "world's tallest tree." The Sierra Club rushed into print a new edition of *The Last Redwoods* but ceded much of the activism to others, including David Brower's new group, Friends of the Earth. Partly as a stalling tactic, activists turned to litigation. The Sierra Club Legal Defense Fund (a separate entity) successfully sued the secretary of the interior for negligence of duty to protect the public trust. Of greater long-term consequence, the Natural Resources Defense Council won a case in state court against the big three for logging practices along Redwood Creek. The lawsuit contended that the state's recently revamped Forest Practice Act (1973) fell under the purview of the California Environmental Quality Act (1970). Jerry Brown, having just succeeded Ronald Reagan as governor, decided to comply with the ruling rather than appeal. As a result, the newly reorganized State Board of Forestry—whose membership now included members from the public as well as the industry—could compel redwood firms to file environmental impact reports in addition to mandatory timber harvest plans. This was the first fateful crack in the corporatist regulatory system.[28]

Emanuel Fritz, now ninety years old, bemoaned the turn of affairs. He believed that the Sierra Club—to which he belonged— had engaged in a "deliberate attempt to brainwash the public." The way he read environmentalist propaganda, there were only two kinds of redwood landscapes: clear-cuts and cathedral stands. In fact, said Fritz, "Some redwoods most people wouldn't waste a gallon of gas to see." To him, the preservation of a few exceptionally tall trees paled in significance to the reforestation of the whole region. "Scaring the public into believing there soon would be no old-growth forest of redwood for future generations to enjoy when, in fact, the League and the State had already preserved 50,000 acres, was a reprehensible way of deceiving the people," he wrote in a statement to Congress. The mayor of Eureka complained that "about 50" agitators threatened the county's whole economy; these "loud preservationists" wanted to "reverse time" and see the buffalo run again.[29]

Those inclined to believe that "tree huggers" were demented took note when, in 1976, the cult leader and convicted killer Charles Manson issued from jail a "murder list" for the International People's Court of Retribution that included timber executives "responsible for the redwood trees being murdered." On other occasions, Manson execrated clear-cutting as a crime against Earth. The most loyal member of the Manson Family, Lynette "Squeaky" Fromme, made a fervid statement about ecoactivism at her arraignment for the attempted assassination of president Gerald Ford. She threatened the judge if he didn't help to "save the redwood trees." Before being ejected from the courtroom, Fromme avowed that logging redwoods was like "cutting down your arms and legs."[30]

The logging debate reentered mainstream national politics with the election of Ford's successor, Jimmy Carter. The new president sided with environmentalists against the wishes of one of his key electoral backers, the AFL-CIO. The union feared for the future of natural resource jobs. Loggers, most of them gyppos (independent contrac-tors) who worked for union-busting companies, portrayed themselves as conservationists, even resource defenders. "The days of cut out and get out are gone," said one Eureka man. "We're not out to destroy the land and our source of income. We restock every acre harvested." To deliver their message, gyppos snarled traffic in San Francisco with a convoy of one hundred trucks. Carrying logging implements (SIERRA CLUB, KISS MY AXE), they packed meetings of the State Board of For-estry. In solidarity, loggers from other parts of the state converged on federal buildings in Sacramento, Fresno, and Los Angeles. More famously, in May 1977 the "Talk to America" caravan made its way from Eureka—the "westernmost city in the U.S."—to Washington, D.C., sculpted redwood peanut in tow. About five hundred North Coast residents took the trip. Trees are nature's renewable resource, they told the media. They called the "Sierra Clubbers"—a catchall term for environmentalists—liars and thieves; compared park expan-sion to creeping socialism; and, from the steps of the Capitol, chanted, "Save our jobs!" The leader of the caravan, Eureka mayor Sam Sacco ("Sammy Redwood"), became a local hero.[31]

In nearby Arcata, a college town as well as a logging town, the issue divided the community. Humboldt State University, the northern-most campus in the California system, became known as the "envi-ronmental school" in the 1960s and 1970s. Many undergraduates of the era conjoined antiwar and environmental protests and fought against "war in the redwoods"; they joined campus groups such as the Boot and Blister Club. Pro-expansionists in Arcata formed an important advocacy group, the Emerald Creek Committee, which took inspiration from university professor Rudi Becking, who taught forestry as a field of natural resource management and applied ecol-ogy, not (as in Emanuel Fritz's generation) as silviculture. Student activists also found allies at the Northcoast Environmental Center, a coalition founded in Arcata a few years before. Businesses that advertised in EcoNews, the center's publication, found themselves on a blacklist circulated among loggers and millworkers in 1977. When members of the Emerald Creek Committee spoke in favor of expansion at a raucous local hearing, they received taunts and threats.[32]

The bluster was for naught: in March 1978 President Carter signed the controversial bill. In a concession to California, the legislation mandated an unemployment program for displaced loggers. As for actual property, the bill authorized the taking of 48,000 acres, four-fifths of it cutover land, including fresh "moonscapes" of stumps, skid tracks, and bulldozed roads. Congress funded a rehabilitation program for these denuded, erodible lands. Unlike the traditional eminent domain process, title transferred outright; however, the law required the government to compensate for its legislative taking. Federal officials used economic theory to argue that removing billions of board feet from the market (the forested part of the park, or about 15 percent of the merchantable stock of grade-A redwood) actually enhanced the value of the residuals on private land. Timber companies disagreed: the "land grab" not only "locked up" valuable old-growth inventory; it upset their age-class distribution and disrupted their crop rotation schedule, and with it the basis of their business strategy. After years of negotiation, litigation, and interest payments, the final cost of expansion swelled to nearly $2 billion—over five times the original budget. The bill included $100 million in mitigation for the Redwood Employee Protection Program. For about a decade, this entitlement kept Humboldt County afloat, becoming the county's largest payroll. Allegations of loggers collecting illegal benefits attracted the attention of the FBI. Some economists argued that the welfare program created disincentives for laid-off employees to seek new work.[33]

What new work? Locals griped that Humboldt County was becoming the Appalachia of California, and they blamed the park. As a repercussion of 1978, Arcata, Simpson, and Louisiana-Pacific (the successor to Georgia-Pacific) each went through restructuring; all of them scaled back their operations in California. Little of the federal buyout money was reinvested locally; rather, the multinational parent companies planted their money in places with more trees and fewer regulations, including Mexico. In a ripple effect, mill after mill shut down in the 1980s. (L-P eventually sold out and left the Golden State altogether.) If that wasn't bad enough, local salmon runs collapsed, in large part because of long-term cumulative damage to stream habitat from logging. Laid-off fishermen and timbermen did not relish the idea of catering to "park-and-pee" car tourists who wanted to take snapshots of treetops and banana slugs, but any service jobs would be better than joblessness. During the park debates, the Sierra Club had touted economic studies that forecast a dramatic increase in tourism and with it a reinvigoration of the local economy. That benefit never materialized.

Job troubles in Humboldt, a remote county with an undiversified economy, had causes besides the park. The recession of the early 1980s lowered the demand for construction material. Even before, the entire logging sector in the Pacific Northwest began to slump, and it never fully recovered. One factor was the value of the product. Quantity did not always make up for quality: even the best second growth did not command the same price as old growth, most of which was gone. Although young trees contain good, strong fiber, they inevitably carry more sap, more knots, and wider grains. Responding to increased competition from Canada and the U.S. South that further drove down softwood prices, timber firms shipped unprocessed logs overseas as a cost-cutting measure. They also reduced labor expenses—and jobs— through increased mechanization. With grapples, feller-bunchers, and debarkers, a single man could do the work of fifty or one hundred specialized workers in the old days. Harvesting second growth did not require special arboreal knowledge. Since crop trees were all roughly the same grade and the same size—relatively small—they could be toppled and yarded by machine operators rather than lumberjacks. Finally, as the remaining fallers (a local term for loggers) noted in frustration, bureaucratic red tape slowed down work. Environmental- ists had learned to intervene in private enterprise in California using state regulations and also the federal Endangered Species Act (1973).

With each passing year, government agencies issued more restrictions on clear-cutting and road building in the redwoods, new rules about harvesting on slopes and near streams. Although the Sierra Club had assured locals that the "last" battle of the redwood "war" ended with park expansion, the president of Arcata Redwood demurred: "Personally I don't think they will ever stop. I believe they will keep coming back until they have everything so tied up that no will be able to continue operating."[34]

OLD-GROWTH CRUSADE

The businessman was something of a prophet. The war would resume. However, the last legion of environmental activists came mainly from local grassroots organizations, not national groups like the Sierra Club. And the battleground shifted from the alluvial flats to the upland slopes. A paradigm shift accompanied these organizational and geographic shifts. In the wake of environmentalism, greens reevaluated old trees on the Pacific Coast. Before, they fought to protect the tallest and, along with them, the aesthetics of "virgin" stands of "primeval" forest—temporal language that was poetic and metaphorical, not scientific. After, they rallied in defense of "old growth," a semiscientific, semireligious category.

Oldness is a relative concept. In a 1929 speech, Emanuel Fritz criticized the "popular fallacy" that a virgin redwood stand was thousands of years old. From a 30-acre plot, Fritz had taken samples from 567 trees with diameters over 18 inches. Of this sample, the age distribution spread wide; only seventeen specimens had been in place more than one thousand years. The primeval forest was actually an all-age woodland. Professional foresters such as Fritz advocated the selective removal of the senior trees—"overmature," "overage," "overripe," or "decadent"—to promote the healthy development of a younger generation. Fires could do this wastefully, or foresters could do it productively. Old growth was a dynamic and renewable resource that could be scientifically managed, Fritz believed.[35]

Through the looking glass, environmentalists of the 1980s and 1990s viewed the same uneven-age forest as the steady-state culmination of a long natural process. Ecologists once called this idealized temporal stage "climax." According to old-growth defenders, a climax woodland would decline without its decadence—its dying, dead, downed, and decomposing trees. Those high, loose branches that loggers called "widowmakers" were vital to a multilayered habitat. The canopy and the understory supported a whole ecosystem. In its new, enlarged meaning, the "redwood forest" encompassed "biodiversity"—a panoply of life on the ground, in the water, and in the air. It provided homes for salamanders, salmon, and owls. According to the zero-sum thinking of doctrinaire greens—those who equated all logging with clear-cutting—humans could preserve or destroy. To replace an old-growth forest wilderness with an even-age rotational crop was not forestry; it was ecocide.

Although the new definition of *old growth* invoked science, no scientist could quantify how long it took for a stand of redwood to reach that stage. In political practice, the temporal threshold for significance remained the same. The all-important trees predated California's fall from Eden, the Gold Rush. "Old growth" was in fact as much a spiritual as an ecological concept—a reworking of an ancient idea, the sacred grove. An old-growth grove sheltered mystery; here you could *feel* the force of life. No matter that the snaggy trees in the upland slopes were less scenic than the parkland columns in the alluvial flats. For biocentric environmentalists, an ancient redwood forest held significance irrespective of bourgeois aesthetics.[36]

An early version of old-growth spiritualism appeared in *Ecotopia* (1975), by the Berkeley author Ernest Callenbach. Set in 1999, this futuristic novel—a defining product of the 1970s counterculture—depicts Washington, Oregon, and northern California a quarter-century after their successful secession (by threat of atomic terrorism) from the environmentally destructive United States. The Pacific Northwest has become a green utopia—or a cryptofascist totalitarian regime, depending on one's point of view. The main female character, Marissa Brightcloud, is a tree-climbing, tree-hugging, tree-worshiping logging supervisor. As part of a forest practice committee, she enforces sustainable logging in the redwoods: no clear-cutting allowed. Citizens of Ecotopia (capital: San Francisco) must serve as forest laborers before they can build a house with lumber. When not working, Brightcloud enjoys making love in a shrine in the hollow of an ancient redwood.

In real life, the 1980s brought the Reagan revolution—the ascendancy of a Southern Californian who famously despised Berkeley and an administration committed to rolling back environmental regulations. In reaction, a new generation of radicalized activists, including votaries of the Earth First! movement, took biocentrism to its extreme, arguing that the lives and rights of all species had value equal to those of humans. Compared to formerly radical, now mainstream national environmental groups like the Sierra Club, Earth First! was decentralized, even tribalistic; uncompromising, even fanatical; combative, even violent; theatrical, even carnivalesque. Eschewing lawyers and lobbyists, EF! espoused direct action, including neo-Luddite industrial sabotage, which they called monkeywrenching and which detractors called ecoterrorism. In the Southwest, EF! figures such as Dave Foreman and Edward Abbey were too macho to be confused with hippie-dippie peaceniks. But on the North Coast, the movement took major inspiration from the 1970s counterculture as well as the "deep ecology" philosophy popularized by Bill Devall, a professor at Humboldt State University.[37]

EF! found many adherents among the marijuana-growing back-to-the-landers who squatted on and resettled former logging tracts in the remote "Emerald Triangle" (Mendocino, Humboldt, and Trinity counties) in the 1970s. Long after the Bay Area and Southern California transformed into megalopolises, the lightly populated North

Coast remained a "last frontier." The countercultural expats who built shacks in the backwoods thought of themselves as modern home-steaders, but instead of representing the vanguard of American expansionism, the new settlers represented a resistance to American imperialism. Back-to-the-land pioneers didn't get permits for their off-the-grid homesteads, and they didn't pay taxes on their cash crop. They had dropped out of the system to build their own private ecoto-pia. After a brief golden age of isolation, California's sinsemilla farm-ers felt the iron fist of the law: the Campaign Against Marijuana Planting (CAMP), a multiagency initiative begun in 1983 as part of Reagan's War on Drugs. In Humboldt County, CAMP conducted search-and-destroy operations with support from helicopters and U-2 spy planes. In the minds of neolocals, this domestic military incursion connected to the redwoods. Politicized hippies compared the violence of an illegitimate state to the violations against nature by outside cor-porations. They vowed to fight both the Man and the machine.[38]

Redwood radicalism broke out in 1983 in response to Louisiana-Pacific's logging practices in Mendocino County; then in 1986 the movement shifted decisively northward to Humboldt County and the Pacific Lumber Company, the largest private owner of ancient red-woods. PL, or Palco, as its employees affectionately called it, was at first glance an unlikely target—the pioneer era's only surviving red-wood firm, which had been locally controlled by the Murphy family from 1903 to 1972. Even after PL reinvented itself as a holding com-pany, it tried to keep up appearances as a family business. It operated its own mill town, Scotia, population 1,100, where pensioned workers with full benefits lived in company homes at low rent and played in a company recreation center that included a regulation-length basket-ball court made of redwood. Second- and third-generation employees were not uncommon. In an economic sector known for instability, PL offered the closest thing to a nonunion workingman's paradise.[39]

Over the decades, the paternalistic corporation had earned high marks for environmental stewardship. Palco donated acreage to the

Save-the-Redwoods League more than once and reserved other stands of tall timber until the league could raise sufficient money. Longer than any other firm, PL followed Emanuel Fritz's recommendations for selective logging. Until the late 1970s, when the state's tax code changed, the company cut no more than 70 percent of each tract. The forest operation came close to the elusive ideal of sustainability. How? Palco owned a lot of land and maximized stability over profitability. "Fuckin' PL was made to last forever," recalled one worker nostalgically.[40] Except for the tractor roads, its second-growth woodlands looked more like natural forests than tree farms, for they contained large numbers of residual ancient trees, what loggers called "uppers." Palco owned the highest timber volume of any redwood company and a near-monopoly on the "clear"—grade-A heartwood from wide, branchless trunks, the material that well-to-do homeowners prized for indoor paneling, patio furniture, decking, roofing, and siding.

Despite being rich with resources, full of cash, and free from debt, Palco generated modest dividends. The stock market did not reward the company for its conservative approach. In the early 1980s, the logging division of the company initiated a modernization program, including plans to clear-cut. In the midst of these plans, the firm abruptly changed hands. At its undervalued share price, PL was the perfect target for private equity. In 1985 Charles Hurwitz, an investor from Houston with no background in logging, initiated a hostile takeover of PL with $840 million, over 90 percent of it debt money, including $575 million in high-risk securities leveraged by the Beverly Hills broker Michael Milken, inventor of the junk bond. Stunned into submission, Palco's board of directors consented to the sale. Incredibly, the board gave up the company without knowing its true assets, for Palco had not performed a forest inventory ("timber cruise") since the 1950s. As Hurwitz knew from his own secret cruise, Palco owned far more redwood than its books reported. His parent company, MAXXAM (a brassy name always spelled in capital letters), fast-tracked the plans to convert PL's operation from selective harvesting to even-age forestry. The process would take two decades. The first step—the course taken by other firms in the 1960s—was liquidating the major assets: old trees. Each residual now commanded $30,000 to $100,000 as merchantable lumber. MAXXAM needed quick returns to repay high-interest obligations set to balloon in progressively bigger increments starting in 1990. In the short term, Hurwitz hired more loggers and paid them overtime, but he cashed out their pension fund (replaced by annuities from an insurance company that collapsed a few years later under the weight of junk bonds). Stodgy corporate practice gave way to hypercapitalism. "It's like a part of me dying," lamented Woody Murphy, whose family had owned Pacific Lumber. Undeterred by a congressional investigation and by lawsuits from workers, former shareholders, and environmentalists, Hurwitz doubled Palco's output.[41]

For more than a century, the idea of the "last stand" had been a renewable political resource. Conservationists and environmentalists had predicted the not-so-distant day—"in a few years," "in but a decade," "in forty years"—when loggers would assault the "last stand" of virgin redwoods. The final day of reckoning seemed imminent in 1987–89. Congress and the California legislature convened special hearings so representatives could voice outrage at Wall Street. In the national media—even on business pages—reporters uncritically repeated hyperbolic claims that Hurwitz was cutting multimillennial plants, redwoods older than the Declaration and the Magna Carta, trees that had existed at the time of Jesus. And for what? To pay off junk bonds! MAXXAM's takeover of Palco came to represent the excesses of the 1980s—the so-called me decade or greed decade.[42]

Like a TV reality show, the timber war attracted extremes in American culture—the redwood raider versus the ecowarrior. For use as a foil, Hurwitz was gold for militants. Earth First!ers picketed mills, occupied offices, crashed corporate meetings, lay down in front of bulldozers, vandalized and sabotaged logging equipment, barricaded roads, paraded with puppets and effigies and costumes and

masks, chained themselves to trees, and, most famously, perched—
sometimes without clothes—in tall redwoods tagged for harvesting.
From canopies, tree sitters unfurled banners with messages like

TREES = LIFE

EXTINCTION IS FOREVER

CLEAR-CUTTING IS ECO-TERRORISM

TWO THOUSAND YEARS OLD—RESPECT YOUR ELDERS

SAVE THE OLD GROWTH

Of PL's 181,500 acres of timberland, only about 16,000 (or 9 percent)
consisted of primary growth, and government regulations prevented
clear-cutting there. Activists didn't know or forgot that under the
good old management of the Murphy family, these "virgin" stands
would have been selectively logged over time. They now considered
any cutting of *any* ancient trees by the godless new ownership to be
sacrilege. In the age of "think globally, act locally," the redwood forest
became the symbolic equivalent of the imperiled Amazon rainforest.
Trespassers gave poetic names like All Species Grove to PL's relict
stands and drew sacrosanct lines around them. The largest unlogged
area, a remote mountainous tract between Fortuna and Eureka,
became known as Headwaters Forest.

The national media's interest in PL waned even as the Headwaters conflict escalated. In 1990 came "Mississippi Summer in the
California Redwoods"—later shortened to Redwood Summer—a
season-long series of demonstrations and direct actions inspired by
the civil rights movement. In the minds of the "Freedom Riders for
the forest," white people easily identified by countercultural accouter-
ments like African talking drums and crocheted Rasta beanies, the
rights of wild trees seemed analogous to the rights of black southerners. Redwood Summer had been conceived by local radicals Judi Bari
and Darryl Cherney. Bari, a folksinger and labor organizer, spent
much of the season in hospital beds and wheelchairs, trying to recover
from a vicious car bomb attack. Against all evidence and logic, the

FBI and the Oakland police tried to indict Bari—who had previously received multiple death threats—for building the timed pipe bomb that exploded under the driver's seat of her Subaru. Law enforcement wanted to send a strong message to Earth First! The group had gained notoriety in Pacific forest country for spiking old trees scheduled for logging. In 1987 a millworker in Sonoma County had been maimed by shrapnel when his band saw hit an 11-inch nail embedded in a second-growth redwood log—an unsolved crime widely, and probably wrongly, blamed on ecoterrorists. (Antigreens would later try to link EF! with the Unabomber, whose victims included a timber industry lobbyist.) Bari publicly repudiated tree spiking. She wanted to make EF! more appealing to women and workers. She believed that tree defenders and tree harvesters should ally in civil disobedience against corporations. Her post-Marxist "revolutionary ecology" conjoined the exploitation of workers and trees.[43]

The way it played out, Redwood Summer created more antagonism than solidarity. Old-growth protectors were generally tone-deaf to Humboldt County's culture of producerism. A Labor Day march and rally called Redwoodstock did nothing to endear activists to workers, who responded with an angry counterdemonstration. "It's we who are endangered," they said. "Jobs first!" In one logging town, workers erected mock tombstones to represent local families who would "die" without timber jobs. Even though many PL loggers and millworkers hated Charles Hurwitz for endangering the life of their company, they took pride in their own labor: they turned living trees into material for living. They decried pot-smoking hippies and dreadlocked tree huggers as social parasites and welfare cheats. None of them seemed to have a real job; marijuana growers didn't "work for a living," though they, like loggers, harvested a cash crop from the forest. As local police arrested demonstrators during Redwood Summer, federal law officers and active-duty soldiers conducted Operation Green Sweep, a series of drug raids on Humboldt County's Lost Coast.[44]

Grassroots litigants complemented the direct, and sometimes illegal, actions of Earth First! The most important group by far was the Environmental Protection Information Center (EPIC), based in Garberville, the hippie and marijuana capital of Mendocino. EPIC's small, all-volunteer staff included a man who had legally changed his name to The Man Who Walks in the Woods. Hyperlocal yet globally conscious, EPIC did a lot with a little. Remarkably, this band of self-taught lawyers gradually forced a revolution in the system of state governance over private forestland. In 1990 they tried to do it all in one fell swoop. With the backing of a Bay Area millionaire, EPIC placed Proposition 130, "Forests Forever," on the state ballot. The measure would have banned all clear-cutting, ended old-growth harvesting, mandated sustained-yield practices, restructured the State Board of Forestry, and authorized a bond issue for purchasing the Headwaters. Thanks to California's dysfunctional system of direct democracy, the 1990 ballot featured two more initiatives related to the redwood forest. Proposition 128, "Big Green," more or less duplicated the key features of Prop 130 and added a grab bag of expensive environmental programs. To compound the confusion, the timber industry placed a countermeasure on the ballot, the euphemistically titled Global Warming and Clear-Cutting Reduction, Wildlife Protection, and Reforestation Act (maligned as "Big Stump" by greens). None of the initiatives passed, though "Forests Forever" came close. Thus the wild year of 1990 ended with the status quo ante. Hurwitz did offer one token concession: a voluntary five-year moratorium on cutting in the Headwaters.

Over the next many months, old-growth redwood activism moved on the parallel tracks of direct action and litigation. Under the leadership of Alicia Littletree, North Coast Earth First!ers continued to demonstrate (Ecotopia Summer followed Redwood Summer) and took to the road with slideshows. Periodically the national media returned to the Headwaters: "Redwoods: The Last Stand" headlined *Time* magazine in 1994. On the second track, EPIC went back to what it did best, filing lawsuits. With aid from foundations, the group argued in court that PL's timber harvest plans violated the California Environmental Quality Act and the federal Endangered Species Act.

The latter law became relevant in 1989, 1992, and 1997, with the listing of the northern spotted owl, the marbled murrelet (a nesting seabird), and coho salmon as threatened species. Again and again the citizen lawyers beat the corporate suits, all the way up to the state and federal supreme courts. In the end, the last vestiges of the corporatist regulatory regime—a historical legacy of Progressivism and a personal legacy of Emanuel Fritz—crumbled. Under the old system, California had trusted the logging industry to write its own best-practice rules and police itself with the oversight of an appointed committee. Under the new system, citizen watchdogs compelled bureaucrats to enforce state environmental regulations on the industry. Processing comment letters and impact statements took priority over producing timber, even on private land like the Headwaters.

With no resolution in sight, the controversy in Humboldt County kept looping back on itself: a PL timber harvest plan would prompt a legal challenge and a temporary restraining order, followed by direct actions, arrests, and another restraining order, all leading to a long court trial with appeals, ultimately resulting in a new, equally con-tested timber harvest plan. From the industry's point of view, California had become a regulatory nightmare. Assuming the role of business victim and private property martyr, Hurwitz filed a "tak-ings" countersuit, claiming that Washington owed him for losses due to compulsory work stoppages during the April–September nesting season of the marbled murrelet. As enshrined in the Fifth Amend-ment of the Constitution, the government cannot take private prop-erty without just compensation.[45]

After repeated stalemates, a third option—legislation—opened up in 1992 with the election of William Jefferson Clinton, a Democratic majority in Congress, and a local Democratic representative. By this point, redwood preservation had completed its long evolution from a laissez-faire Republican to a bipartisan to a statist Democratic issue. Humboldt County's forest counterculture, outwardly libertarian and localist, demanded federal intervention. Pushed by local greens—and, for the first time, elements of the labor movement—Washington and Sacramento considered various ways of obtaining the Head-waters. The government seemingly gained a wedge in 1995 when both the FDIC and the Office of Thrift Supervision filed lawsuits against Hurwitz, demanding that he repay taxpayers hundreds of millions of dollars for the bailout of a failed savings and loan in Texas owned partially by his holding company. However, Hurwitz's lawyers defeated a proposed debt-for-nature swap and rebuffed proposed land swaps from Sacramento. The CEO from Texas would accept only market-value cash—his definition of "just compensation." The House authorized such an appropriation in 1994 (shortly before the midterm elections and the Republican resurgence), and the Senate followed in 1996 (in time for Clinton's reelection campaign).

As brokered and announced by the California senator Dianne Feinstein, "the Deal" did several things. It pledged federal and state monies for the purchase of the Headwaters Grove, pending nego-tiations. Hurwitz had the right to refuse the final package. In the meantime, PL agreed to create a sustained yield plan for future log-ging and to drop its takings lawsuit. In return, the Clinton admin-istration would prepare a multispecies habitat conservation plan, a legal exemption to the Endangered Species Act. The HCP shielded MAXXAM and the executive branch from lawsuits from environ-mentalists. Thus after 1996 PL enjoyed relative freedom to file timber harvest plans with the State Board of Forestry. The planned cutting included "salvage logging" in mature groves. According to state rules, a private landowner could salvage up to 10 percent of the dead, dying, and diseased trees in an old-growth forest. "Dying" was a loose cate-gory that could be used to describe otherwise "ancient" trees.

Widely praised by the mainstream media, the Headwaters agree-ment divided the various grassroots organizations that had briefly come together in a consensus-based coordinating committee. Most defenders of the ancient forest felt disillusioned by their success and hoped to kill the Deal. EF!ers wanted to save the 60,000-acre "Head-waters wilderness complex," not just the 3,000-acre grove at its core. To them, the HCP was tantamount to a license to kill endangered species. Refusing to compromise, militants used "lockboxes" to fasten their bodies together, forming human obstructions at the Headwaters access road ("Death Road"). Using fishing nets as passageways, they turned six adjoining aerial occupations into one "Ewok Village." Over the last few months of 1996, police arrested more than one thousand protestors, often after spraying pepper in their faces. From the Golden Gate Bridge, Woody Harrelson and other climbers hung a banner (HURWITZ, AREN'T ANCIENT REDWOODS MORE PRECIOUS THAN GOLD?) that, at a minimum, succeeded in creating an enormous traffic jam. Other movie stars expressed their support for a redwood boycott. In Humboldt County, rallies got bigger; a single event at a PL sawmill attracted more than seven thousand demonstrators, overwhelming local law enforcement. And the music got better—not just dudes strumming cheap guitars but actual members of the Grateful Dead.

In this final, unruly phase of the redwood war, recruits arrived from farther away. Along with the usual suspects—undergrads from Arcata, hippies from Garberville, ex-hippies from San Francisco—bourgeois dropouts from Middle America traveled beyond the Redwood Curtain to find truth in the woods. EF! splinter groups formed. Young initiates showed up at "base camps" with bravado but no knowledge of Humboldt County history. They often couldn't see the forest for the trees. In 1998 a "worker outreach" event at an active logging site went horribly wrong when an angry PL logger felled a redwood in the path of an Earth First!er from Texas who went by his "forest name," Gypsy. The impact of the tree cracked Gypsy's head wide open, killing him instantly. The direct-action movement claimed a martyr.[46]

About the same time, the movement acquired a saint in the figure of an ecotopian tree sitter named Julia "Butterfly" Hill. The daughter of a traveling preacher, Hill decided to pursue her own spiritual path after nearly dying in a car accident. She found her calling on a road trip to the West Coast, where she saw redwoods for the first time. Under the awesome canopy, she prayed to the Universal Spirit for guidance. After receiving her message, Hill went back home to Arkansas only long enough to pack her bags. She returned to Humboldt in late 1997 with the intention of joining the Headwaters campaign. Almost immediately, without premeditation or preparation, the twenty-three-year-old took over tree-sitting duties at a residual that Earth First!ers had christened Luna. The tree stood above Stafford, a small town recently devastated by a logging-related landslide. Hill's temporary action became an epic tarriance. Her resolve came from another near-death experience, this time in the canopy. As a wicked storm tossed her about, Hill accepted the fact that she would die. She spoke to Luna; she offered her life to the tree. The redwood spoke back, and told Butterfly to stay. The modern hamadryad didn't touch the ground for two full years and became a polarizing celebrity in the process. Some radicals considered her a grandstander rather than a true tree sitter. From her tiny tarpaulin-covered platform 180 feet in the air, Hill answered fan mail and gave phone interviews. *People* and *Good Housekeeping* ran admiring features. A long line of seekers, including lefty stars such as Bonnie Rait and Joan Baez, climbed the talismanic tree to commune with her. Media cameras took to her pretty, photogenic face: Butterfly didn't look like a "dirty hippie." With her endless talk of love and healing, she sounded more like a New Age motivational speaker than an angry ecowarrior. Despite incessant wind and rain, and various threats, harassments, and indignities, Hill refused to end her trespass until PL promised to sanctify her tree home with a conservation easement. Although Luna stood a considerable distance south of the so-called Headwaters Forest, the she-tree became the arboreal symbol of the campaign.[47]

As the expiration date on the congressional authorization for the buyout drew closer, PL continued to file dozens of timber harvest plans, for Hurwitz still carried a high load of debt. Activists claimed that the CEO was either holding Headwaters hostage for ransom or that he never intended to finalize the Deal, only to use it as a delaying tactic. Certainly Hurwitz played a good game of chicken. PL logged all around the Headwaters, cutting regulatory corners—

losing its state-issued timber license in the process—until the government upped its offer to $480 million. The parties signed the final agreement shortly before the stroke of midnight on March 1, 1999, with seconds remaining on the authorization clock. For half of what Hurwitz paid in securities for the complete assets of Pacific Lumber, the government paid in cash for a collection of small, remote, limited-access properties where government regulations already prohibited clear-cutting. PL agreed to a fifty-year ban on harvesting in "lesser cathedral groves" and in riparian corridors essential for murrelets and salmon. Of the cash payout for the 7,500-acre Headwaters Forest Reserve, one-third came from Sacramento, two-thirds from Washington. With the transfer of title, the old growth became the charge of the U.S. Bureau of Land Management. (So far the reserve doesn't appear on most maps, for the BLM manages it more like a wilderness area than a park.)[48]

Before passions cooled in Humboldt County, a gross act of vandalism occurred. In 2000, around Thanksgiving, someone tried to girdle Luna with a chainsaw, cutting a gash 32 inches deep and 19 feet around. This desecration was not unprecedented. In 1975 some disgruntled person(s) brought down two tall trees in the Lady Bird Johnson Grove at Redwood National Park; and in early 1978, at the height of the park expansion controversy, chainsaw vandals attacked at least sixteen old redwoods in Humboldt County preserves. But none of these trees had a name or a personality. Speaking on NBC's *Today Show*, Julia Butterfly Hill said, "Luna is the greatest teacher and best friend I have ever had. I gave two years of my life to ensure that she could live and die naturally. But two years is nothing compared to the thousands of years she has lived, providing shelter, moisture, and oxygen to forest inhabitants. It kills me that the last 3 percent of the ancient redwoods are being desecrated."[49] Arborists rushed to the scene of the "hate crime" and worked through the night. After injecting organic foam into the wound to help the cambium layer regrow, the botanical doctors inserted steel shims in the gap, bolted braces across the wound, and cut limbs to reduce wind drag. To further reduce the danger of collapse, climbers later attached an oversized collar high on the trunk, with four heavy cables angled downward as anchors. For good measure, caretakers added a mixture of clay and bear saliva to the cut as directed by a "Cherokee medicine healer."

The embers of the conflict took several years to burn out. Environmentalists challenged PL's sustained yield plan, and extremists continued to disrupt individual "timber holocaust plans" with tree sits and lockboxes. EPIC's antilogging lawsuits—the total reached more than twenty—now focused on water quality and Pacific salmon habitat. More visibly, in 2002 a woman representing the Campaign for Old Growth held a fifty-two-day hunger-strike vigil at the state capitol. Although Sacramento had added a new provision to the Forest Practice Act, making it difficult for private property owners to cut any tree predating 1800 CE, dyed-in-the-wool activists wanted a blanket ban—a state heritage tree act to give protective status to all trees older than statehood. Few such residuals remained on PL's property after twenty years of Hurwitz's ownership. In 2007 PL declared bankruptcy, and MAXXAM began to divest. Management claimed that a new set of onerous environmental regulations—state permits required by the Water Resources Control Board, an agency not party to the Deal—had killed a profitable business. From the company's point of view, PL had been tried, convicted, and executed for the crime of practicing capitalism. The state supreme court invalidated PL's sustained yield plan in 2008, even as the company sold its assets. The Fisher family of San Francisco, founders of the clothing retailers Gap and Banana Republic, acquired the logging operation and promised a return to sustainability. When the Fishers convinced the last two tree sitters to come down to earth, a political and economic era closed in Humboldt County. In the aftermath, Scotia looked like a miniature version of a Rust Belt city—a once-proud industrial center operating well below capacity. Many ex-loggers turned to indoor cultivation of marijuana, the number-one cash crop in California. Parts of this shadow economy became barely legal in 1996 when state voters approved a medical marijuana initiative. On the North Coast, America's THC nerve center, cannabis now rivals redwood as the region's leading export.[50]

With the 1999 finalization of the Headwaters deal and the 2000 designation of Giant Sequoia National Monument—an extra layer of protection for Sierra Nevada forestland already owned by the U.S. Forest Service—the history of California redwood entered a new phase with the new millennium. Given that there are no more unprotected groves of primary growth to save, can there be another "last stand"? Has the lifetime of this environmental fetish expired? Again, it depends on how you define *redwood forest*. In the 1970s worker-demonstrators and timber companies carried placards and erected roadside signs with the antipark message THE REDWOODS ARE SAVED. THERE ARE MORE REDWOOD TREES GROWING TODAY THAN EVER BEFORE. If "ever before" referred to historic rather than geologic time, the statement was probably accurate. *S. sempervirens* does not face extinction; the Golden State contains well over a million acres of forest cover with redwood. Compared to some other historic icons of American biological abundance—bison and the passenger pigeon—coast redwood is doing fine. Compared to American chestnut, once the most beloved tree of the U.S. East, redwood has not experienced a species-level catastrophe. In the long run, climate change may change everything, but for the moment there is no reason to continue the deathwatch. However, a certain *idea* about the redwood forest—"wild" and "natural," free of human influence—may yet pass away, if it hasn't already. Likewise, a certain *type* of forest—the "cathedral groves" of tall timber—may yet disappear, if only for a moment in geologic time.

Over the twentieth century, the redwood forest was simplified into two different kinds based on property title: a large checkerboard of even-age second growth on privately owned land (primarily hillsides), and small ribbons of mixed-age old growth on publicly owned land (primarily stream bottoms). The boundaries between the two are immediately obvious in satellite imagery. From a deep-time perspective, the government tree museums are not much more natural than the corporate tree farms. In past millennia, the redwood belt always contained patches of tall growth, but the distribution of mature stands constantly changed as flooding, fire, disease, and succession changed forest composition. The current distribution of ancient trees in small, stationary locations is an artificial outcome, and a risky approach to ecological management, since most of the preserves occupy riparian zones vulnerable to flood damage. These pocket habitats are too small to be managed as an ecosystem. The guardians of the redwood parks lack the regulatory and administrative advantages of the rangers, foresters, and ecologists who watch over the sequoias. In the Sierra Nevada, practically all the Big Tree groves are set within large holdings of public land. On the North Coast, by contrast, most of the forestland is still owned by private interests.

From an idealist's point of view, the two redwood preservation campaigns of the second half of the twentieth century got it backward, compelling the government to take over small parcels of old growth at a high price (financially and socially) instead of facilitating transfer of vast expanses of low-price second growth to the public domain. Rather than privileging the tallest and the oldest, rather than obsessing about the passing of the last stand, environmentalists might have focused on the creation and stewardship of a new redwood forest. On a small scale, the National Park Service has done this by rehabilitating clear-cut lands it acquired through the 1978 enlargement of Redwood National Park. Rangers and volunteers have planted hundreds of thousands of seedlings, which will, if all goes well, be impressively tall trees in time for the park's centennial. California may someday convert the educational-commercial Jackson Demonstration State Forest into a park of future old growth. Sacramento or Washington could conceivably still buy up cutover land on a large scale and, through management techniques such as thinning, burning, and reseeding, create the beginnings of a grand all-age forest. However, centuries-long thinking is not politically expedient. It's hard to imagine a successful movement to commit limited tax dollars to SAVE THE SECOND GROWTH.

And so the financial story of redwood conservation has come full circle: the expansion of preserves once again relies on private capital. But the next preserves may not be parks. In the first decade of the 2000s, two initiatives pointed the way. Without controversy, both the Conservation Fund (a land trust based in Virginia) and the Redwood Forest Foundation (a nonprofit based in California) purchased tens of thousands of acres of young-growth redwood and fir in the coastal mountains of Mendocino County. These free-market, nonprofit experiments—"working community forests"—call for limited, sustainable logging as the land slowly recovers from decades of intensive harvesting. The more immediate goal is simply to prevent these private properties from falling into the hands of developers who would subdivide. At this point, redwood crusaders in California worry about second-home owners and pinot noir growers as much as commercial loggers.

In the original version of "This Land Is Your Land," intended to be a leftist protest song—recorded in 1944 but not released until 1997—Woody Guthrie sang a provocative verse about the righteousness of trespassing. The Okie bard intoned an American contradiction. More than any other country, the United States both worships private property and sanctifies vast areas of its public domain. Inversely, many Americans profess adoration for the national park system—"the best idea we ever had"—while opposing its enlargement and its tax-supported maintenance. The modern history of sequoias and redwoods illustrates this troubled, codependent relationship between real property and the ecological commonwealth. On the North Coast, the tension between property values and the changing value of longevity generated scenes of tragedy and farce. In the name of the public good, the government seized forestland from native peoples without compensation; converted it all to private property through giveaways and auctions, often to fraudulent buyers; and then, much later, prodded by a minority, again in the name of the public good, reacquired a few parcels as state domain, at inflated cost, often against the will of titleholders and local residents. All told, the exploitation and preservation of America's superlative trees speak to the contradictory states of post–Gold Rush California: this is the place that inspired the most naked form of American acquisitiveness, and this is the place that first inspired Americans to set aside national reserves.[51]

Upon the "discovery" of giant sequoia and the onset of industrial logging in the redwood belt, the United States was barely mature, the Golden State not at all. Mammoth stumps offer mute evidence. U.S. settler society allowed, even encouraged, the demolition of some of the grandest, oldest, tallest, largest plants in the world. Environmentalists of the twentieth century looked back on this frontier period with disgust; no wonder they instinctively (if unfairly) mistrusted all timber interests. Radicalism in the redwood forest may be interpreted as a delayed backfire to what historians call the "great barbecue"— the post–Civil War period when capitalist interests acquired western resources by hook or by crook. Extremism of one kind kindled another. This is not the only foundational story of Golden State flora, however. For every lumber looter in the late nineteenth century, the region inspired multiple advocates for afforestation—land speculators, civic boosters, horticulturists alike—who, in the spirit of improvement, brought trees to treeless lands. Before the Gold Rush, California contained many more grasslands, marshes, and desert valleys than groves of giants. After statehood, American settlers did their best to remedy these "wasted" lands and to make up for the wasteful use of redwoods. For every native tree axed to the ground, planters added thousands more nonnatives to woodlots, windrows, orchards, parks, yards, gardens, campuses, sidewalks, and street medians. This arboreal redesign was not innocent; there is no such thing as an innocent landscape. You can't raise a grove without possessing the land, and you can't grow a garden without some clearing and weeding. California's horticultural story is vital and inspiring, if also unsettling. Turn a leaf and see.

PART TWO

EUCALYPTS: THE TAXONOMY OF BELONGING

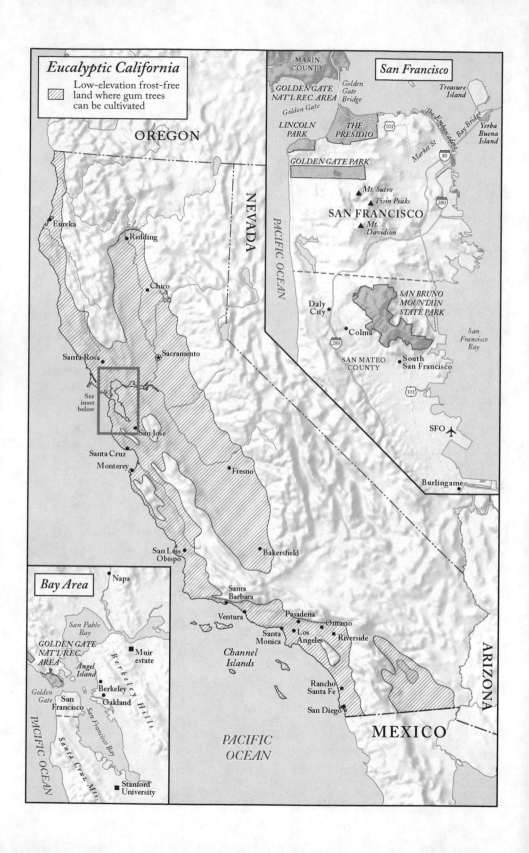

OREGON

NEVADA

PACIFIC OCEAN

Eureka

Redding

Chico

Santa Rosa

Sacramento

See inset below

San Jose

Santa Cruz

Monterey

Fresno

San Luis Obispo

Bakersfield

Napa

Santa Barbara

Ventura

Pasadena

Santa Monica

Los Angeles

Ontario

Riverside

Channel Islands

Rancho Santa Fe

San Diego

ARIZONA

MEXICO

PACIFIC OCEAN

San Francisco

MARIN COUNTY

GOLDEN GATE NAT'L REC. AREA

Golden Gate

Golden Gate Bridge

Treasure Island

LINCOLN PARK

THE PRESIDIO

The Embarcadero

Bay Bridge

Yerba Buena Island

GOLDEN GATE PARK

Market St.

Mt. Sutro

Twin Peaks

SAN FRANCISCO

Mt. Davidson

Daly City

Colma

San Bruno Mountain State Park

San Francisco Bay

SAN MATEO COUNTY

South San Francisco

SFO

Burlingame

Bay Area

San Pablo Bay

GOLDEN GATE NAT'L REC. AREA

Muir estate

Angel Island

Berkeley Hills

Golden Gate

San Francisco

Berkeley

Oakland

San Francisco Bay

PACIFIC OCEAN

Santa Cruz Mts.

Stanford University

April 1970. The Beatles announce their breakup. U.S. forces gather for the invasion of Cambodia. The world has seen better days. Chanting "Give Earth a Chance"—a play on John and Yoko's refrain—U.S. students at some 1,500 schools prepare for a nation-wide "environmental teach-in," better known as the first Earth Day. The time seems right for action. Just months earlier, the Cuyahoga River caught fire—again, and crude oil blackened the beaches of Santa Barbara.

In Ventura County, California, students at Moorpark College act in advance of the demonstration day. On April 8, fifty tree huggers take a stand on local ground: they lay their bodies in front of bulldozers on Los Angeles Avenue, the thoroughfare in unincorporated Moor-park. Politically, this area belongs to Governor Reagan; Moorpark is a long way from Berkeley. Yet even here, "ecology-minded students" (to quote the *Los Angeles Times*) can be found protesting progress—in this case, the widening of the tree-lined road. The police arrest ten. The next day, 150 students picket the site, and the president of the junior college appeals for order. In a show of solidarity, a professor obtains a temporary restraining order against the State Division of Highways. On April 22, Earth Day, seven of the ten defendants are arraigned in juvenile court even as their fellow students gather on campus for a day's worth of speeches with titles like "Here Today but Not Tomorrow." By the end of the week, the trees are gone.[1]

What has been lost? Ancient redwoods? Historic oaks? No. They aren't even native plants. Most of the trees in question are Australasian eucalypts planted in the nineteenth century as ornamentals.

As of 1970, most tree-loving Californians loved eucalypts because they made lowland California look and smell like home. From Redding in the north to San Diego and Yuma in the south, the distinctive blue-green foliage of eucalyptus trees gave character to residential and touring landscapes. In 1956 *Sunset* magazine publicized three sections of highways, two on U.S. 101, one on State Route 99, where an automobilist could drive an entire day without losing sight of eucalypts. Tall specimens even lined the Redwood Highway between Eureka and Arcata in Humboldt County. The *Eucalyptus* genus from Australasia was far more prevalent than redwood, the official state tree, and scarcely less iconic. In the cultural sense, the immigrant had been naturalized.[2]

After 1970 people's ideas began to change. The same ecological awakening that motivated student activists in Moorpark would inspire environmentalists to reevaluate the place of nonnative species. By the 1990s, *Eucalyptus* fell to pariah status in the Bay Area. Here the introduced genus was naturalized in the biological sense: trees had reproduced into forests. Because these woodlands adjoined densely populated areas—and because people had built neighborhoods within them—they presented a fire hazard. The hazard became deadly during the Berkeley Hills firestorm of 1991. In the aftermath, many area residents disowned their eucalypts and, borrowing from conservation biologists, reclassified them as aliens. About the same time, a series of insect infestations caused widespread die-offs of old eucalypts in cities throughout the state. Land managers and ecologists seized the moment to advocate selective habitat restoration. They wanted to bring back pieces of the original lowland landscape, a California marked by grasses more than by trees, by browns more than by greens—and absolutely not by blue-greens.

Restorationists invite controversy. In California, the politicized discourse on immigration can crossbreed with the scientific language of invasion biology. A small but vocal minority of eucalyptophiles defend their favorite tree against "xenophobic" attacks. A larger number of Californians have conflicted feelings. Yes, these Aussie expats can be messy and dangerous, and maybe they don't belong. Then again, can you imagine California without them? Haven't they been here long enough to deserve environmental amnesty or a botanical green card or even arboreal citizenship? Might they be as native as you and I?

CHAPTER 3

Immigration and Naturalization

ACCLIMATIZING WITH BLUE GUM

Eucalyptus trees came to the Golden State from Down Under soon after the Gold Rush. In the next one hundred years, Californians assisted a continuous introduction of "eucs" punctuated by two frenzied periods, one in the 1870s, the other from 1907 to 1913. Planters believed variously that the exotic trees would provide fuel, improve the weather, boost farm productivity, defeat malaria, preserve watersheds, and thwart a looming timber famine. First and foremost, settlers propagated them to domesticate and beautify the land, to give it more greenery. Even when they failed to exploit eucalyptus for specific uses, they succeeded in remaking the landscape. At the end of the planting era, when Californians considered this leafy transformation, they called it good.

Practically from the moment California became U.S. territory, the region was reshaped by waves of newcomers. As luck would have it, the United States concluded its war treaty with Mexico at nearly the exact moment that Americans discovered gold at Sutter's Mill. Tens of thousands of argonauts soon flooded into San Francisco Bay. This disembarkation point became, after 1848, an intercontinental meeting ground—the port of entry for humans, plants, animals, insects, and microbes from around the globe, especially the Pacific Rim.

China and Chile contributed many miners to the Gold Rush; so did Australia. However, the most important newcomer from the island continent was *Eucalyptus*, and it came in seed envelopes. It's unclear who in the 1850s germinated the first eucalypt in American soil, but William Walker's Golden Gate Nursery in San Francisco has been identified as the first business to offer antipodean trees for sale.

San Franciscans wanted trees, period. Their instant city—constructed with wood, fenced with wood, heated with wood—sprang up on a sandy, windswept peninsula. Local supplies of coast live oak and even its scrawny cousin, coastal scrub oak, rapidly diminished. As early as 1860, a local commentator lamented the depletion of flora. The oak lands of Oakland had been "thinned and mutilated," leaving the firewood supply "almost exhausted."[1] In the canyons of the Berkeley Hills, pocket stands of coast redwood fell immediately to the ax.

California's riches—its green gold as well as its precious metals—seemed poorly distributed across vast distances. From San Francisco, it took considerable effort to reach the North Coast redwoods. The great pine forests around Lake Tahoe would become merchantable in the late 1860s with the Central Pacific Railroad, but the pines and sequoias of the southern Sierra Nevada remained isolated. Between the Sierra and the Coast Range, the Central Valley was basically treeless, despite having rich soils, sparkling rivers, and wetlands teeming with wildlife. To settlers, the great valley seemed like a bipolar wasteland, a hot desert that flooded each spring. The chaparral that grew in the milder climates of the central and southern coasts wasn't much better from a timbering point of view. On the inland side of the coastal mountains, majestic oaks grew above a sea of annual grass, but these trees alone could never meet the fuel demands of hundreds of thousands of entrepreneurial settlers.

To make matters worse, the Golden State lacked good coal reserves. In the era before the transcontinentals opened up coal from Rocky Mountain states, California relied on ship-delivered imports from mines in the Pacific Northwest, the British Isles, and Australia. It could at least produce agricultural products that these long-distance suppliers desired in exchange. Thanks to its bountiful environment, the state managed to achieve a high level of prosperity in the late nineteenth century despite its lackluster manufacturing sector and its energy dependence. Firewood and charcoal were critical—and scarce, and thus expensive—resources until the discovery of oil in Southern California in the 1890s. The inflated price of a cord of wood affected the cost of everything from home heating to river freight shipping. The prepetroleum economy took its toll on native trees, especially redwoods and oaks. American settlers in the Bay Area recognized that these natives would have to be replaced.[2]

Americans wanted more than replacements. From the beginning, aesthetic desires as much as economic needs propelled the cultivation of nonnative species. Post–Gold Rush settlers did not feel content with the existing landscape subtly modified by Indians, Spaniards, and Mexicans. It looked deforested. It looked unfinished. A land blessed with so much sunshine, warmth, and fertility demanded more greenery, flowers, and shade. To eyes trained in the American East and northern Europe, California didn't look right. Where nature erred, settlers meant to repair.

In the nineteenth century, Golden State horticulturists tested many trees to fill the oak-land niche, and singled out eucalypts for their amazing growth properties. Evolved to be opportunists, eucalypts scavenge for nutrients in soil that would starve other plants. Like California's native oaks, they can withstand long periods of want. Both are scleromorphs, plants with hard, fibrous leaves. To conserve energy, eucalypts shed senescent branches and used-up bark instead of dropping their nutrient-rich leaves. These resilient evergreens take advantage of feast-or-famine climates by hoarding water and nourishment in special storage roots. From these lignotubers, new buds launch. The trees survive—even thrive after—fires; new shoots sprout from previously dormant epicormic buds buried in the outer bark. Already rapid growers, eucs grew preternaturally fast in frontier California. In the lowland regions of the state, the Australasian genus benefited from ecological similarities and dissimilarities: a familiar semiarid, two-season, fire-prone Mediterranean climate without the insects, birds, mammals, and pathogens that fed on eucalypts Down Under. A branch of the myrtle family, *Eucalyptus* has always been closely identified with Australia, and rightly so. On the island continent, the genus accounts for more than 90 percent of all native trees. The natural range of *Eucalyptus* extends south to Tasmania and north to certain parts of the Malay archipelago, but not east to New Zealand. The genus contains a vast number of species—over seven hundred—though no one agrees on the exact number. "There are as many kinds of eucalyptus as there are varieties of a famous brand of pickles," a California forester once said. [3] Recently botanists broke the single unwieldy genus into three separate but related genera.

Eucalyptus is a Latinate word of Greek derivation; it means "well-covered" and refers to the operculum, a floral lid of fused petals that shields the sexual organs. Each operculum eventually falls off to reveal the showy insides of the flower—all stamens—which can be creamy white, canary yellow, or ruby red. After pollination, the flower bud morphs into a seedpod that functions like a saltshaker for the granular seeds. Taxonomists focus on flowers and seedpods for identification. For laypersons, distinguishing among eucalypts can be vexing. The leaves look different at different stages; they can, for example, shift from ovate (egg-shaped) to falcate (sickle-shaped). To describe the protean nature of their flora, Australians use their own vocabulary. They may group them by size—tall and straight "forest trees," medium-sized and canopied "woodland trees," or small and bushy "mallees." They may also classify them by bark depending on whether a specimen sheds continuously, annually, or never, or whether it sheds in ribbons or in flakes. However, in popular usage through-out the world, people generally recognize just two kinds of eucalypts, ironbarks and gums. Ironbarks secrete a resin called kino that stains and hardens their furrowed bark. Gums "shed" their bark—a process that botanists call decortication—to reveal a smooth pale surface.

In the nineteenth century, Californians grew gums. In fact, to an

overwhelming degree—well over 90 percent—they grew just one species, Tasmanian blue gum (*E. globulus*). *Globulus* means "little button"
and refers to the shape of the fruit. As it happens, the tree's operculums
also look like buttons—the knobby kind you might find on a knit car-
digan in a vintage shop. Piles of detached caps can be found beneath
any mature blue gum, along with copious leaf litter. The thin, falcate
mature leaves have distinctive coloring—somewhat green, almost
blue, slightly gray. The tree's filigreed foliage points downward rather
than outward and casts dappled patterns of shadows. The leaves smell
strongly like menthol. This evergreen—or ever-blue-green—species
can also be identified by its bark, which in summer and autumn sheds
in long ribbons, adding to the litter. The blue gum rivals the female
ginkgo as the messiest tree in the world. It rivals coast redwood as the
fastest sprouter. In early stages of growth it can add 10 vertical feet
per year. The branches of a mature blue gum look massive, muscular,
elephantine. Under optimal conditions, a blue gum will reach up more
than 150 feet with a magnificent crown spread over 100 feet. (One
old specimen in Petrolia occupies the National Register of Big Trees
as a "champion"—the largest hardwood in America. Previously a blue
gum on Clint Eastwood's property in Carmel held that title.) Most
importantly, blue gum tolerates a wide range of habitats, including
warm and dry environments that are positively un-Tasmanian.

California settlers initiated large-scale gum planting in the 1860s
as word spread from San Francisco of a species that seemed to combine
the best traits of redwoods and oaks. They wrote letters to magazines
asking for information: Where could seeds be purchased? How best
to grow them? Horticultural periodicals disseminated knowledge on
varieties, propagation techniques, and wood applications. Since the
Mediterranean climate was unfamiliar to Americans, the first few
decades of farming consisted of trial and error with old as well as new
plants. The *California Farmer* functioned as the first clearinghouse
for news on successes and failures. To promote the blue gum, the
magazine reprinted botanical papers by Australian experts, ran edito-

rials suggesting new uses for the trees, and published ads for nurseries in Oakland, Hayward, and Petaluma. It even offered free packets of seeds to subscribers.[4]

Extension agents and government foresters did not yet exist, but state officials did what they could to support afforestation. In 1868 the California legislature passed the Tree Culture Act, which provided incentives to landowners to add tree cover. The U.S. Congress passed a similar bill, the Timber Culture Act, in 1873. Congressional dendrophiles hoped to change the climate of the Great Plains. According to popular theory, rain followed the tree even more than rain followed the plow. In 1872 hopeful Nebraskans introduced Arbor Day, an observance that soon spread across the country.

George Perkins Marsh awakened many Americans to the importance of tree cover with his seminal book, *Man and Nature* (1864). A diplomat and philologist, Marsh served a long, distinguished term as the first U.S. minister to the Kingdom of Italy. Through research and observation in soil-ravaged parts of the Mediterranean, Marsh deduced a connection between deforestation and erosion. To avoid the fate of Italy, he argued, Americans needed to regenerate damaged or extirpated vegetation or, alternatively, restore equilibrium with new species that mimicked the old or complemented them. In later editions of *Man and Nature*, Marsh discussed the virtues of afforestation. In passing, he noted the growth speed of *Eucalyptus*, "the new vegetable emigrant from Australia."

For nineteenth-century conservationists, state and local efforts to create "artificial forests" on private lands complemented the goal of creating a national forest system on public lands. Horticulture and silviculture had not yet divided into separate fields: a tree-filled garden was not so different from a gardenlike forest. It did not seem out of place for the California State Agricultural Society to offer fifty dollars in 1870 to the person who planted the largest number of trees that year. The cash award went to James T. Stratton, a surveyor who had already earned prominence by mapping and subdividing former Mexican land grants. Stratton covered 45 acres of his private property on Telegraph Avenue outside Oakland with approximately 30,000 blue gum seedlings.

Within a few years, Stratton lost his bragging rights to Santa Barbara County's Ellwood Cooper, the first major eucalyptus planter in Southern California. This Quaker from Pennsylvania bought his Goleta property in 1872 and named it Rancho Ellwood. By 1876 it contained roughly 150,000 blue gums on 100-plus acres. Eager to spread his know-how, Cooper published California's first book on eucalyptology. It began with an exhortation: deforestation and desertification could "threaten the depravation, barbarism, and perhaps even extinction of the [human] species." Cooper called for a two-pronged approach, the preservation of forests and the creation of forests. Californians possessed an unprecedented and exciting opportunity to do the latter. Inadequate rainfall and excessive wind were the only defects in this "near-perfect" land. People could make up the difference: "Moderate the winds, increase the rain, and we have perfection." This could be accomplished by adding a 100-foot-wide belt of blue gums up and down the state, perpendicular to the prevailing winds, and by lining all the roadways with eucalypts. Although this tree cover would take up one-eighth of the state and one-quarter of its arable land, farm productivity would rise. The shelterbelt would increase rainfall, reduce erosion, and protect crops. "With such shelter California would become the paradise of the world," wrote Cooper. The emparadising effects would be environmental, economic, aesthetic, and moral—all four intertwined. The farmer who put in trees "increases the certainty of his crops, decreases one fourth his labor, beautifies his home, improves the climate, doubles the value of his land, receives inspiration from this work of his own hands, elevates his own condition, and adds to the refinement of himself, his family, and all his surroundings."[5]

Cooper did not, like Stratton, cultivate his eucs in even rows like a crop. He grew them in "forest form" to complement his farm operation, which featured dairy cows and walnuts in addition to olives. Cooper became a principal figure in the California olive oil industry and for nearly two decades served as president of the State Board of Horticulture, where he advocated for state-enforced plant quarantines and the biological control of insect pests. "If the great fruit interests of this state ever conceive the idea of erecting a monument to the one who has performed the greatest service for those interests," wrote California's leading entomologist in 1931, "this monument should be to the memory and honor of Ellwood Cooper!"[6]

Ezra Carr of the University of California, Ellwood Cooper's ally and John Muir's mentor, explained the guiding philosophy of pioneer horticulturists: "*Diversified planting*, like diversified farming, will prove the only profitable mode, for California, in the end." Single cropping was akin to soil mining—it depleted the land instead of enriching it. Horticultural reformers prescribed what we would now call sustainable agriculture. According to Carr, "It is only by observing and respecting the methods of Nature that men succeed in gaining mastery over her hidden resources. Now, Nature never plants a field or forest with a single species; she loves an infinite diversity. A plantation of blue gum would be an abomination in her sight, and, we may be sure, she has some chosen parasite in reserve with which to destroy it." Carr recommended the use of rapid-rise gums as nurses for other trees. He urged Californians to consider South American and East Asian plants as well as Australasian ones.[7]

The scientific and economic arguments for polyculture had social and moral implications. Cooper, Carr, and their ilk—white middle-class transplants with a passion for trees—promoted a gendered and racialized vision of California's improvement. They wanted a horticultural commonwealth composed of family-run farms with happy children surrounded by diverse flowering plants. A landscape that was properly domesticated nurtured wives and homes instead of bachelors and bunkhouses. Troubled by the lingering social and environmental effects of the Gold Rush, orchardists such as Cooper wanted intensive, not extensive, farming; balanced cultivation, not monoculture; arboriculture, not viticulture. They were cooperative entrepreneurs rather than aggressive capitalists, reformers rather than arrivistes.

They objected to California's original form of agribusiness, large-scale wheat bonanza farms on former Mexican land grants. They believed that smallholders were better husbandmen; that "fruit growing is a higher order of agriculture, develops a more thoughtful and intelligent man, and conduces to better citizenship." To raise cereal crops in California's special climate was a "perversion of nature's gifts." The Golden State should specialize in trees, not grain. Looking back on U.S. California's first ten years, a member of the State Agricultural Society castigated miners for wasting trees but saved his bile for the wheat farmers, who "could only see that the magnificent evergreen oaks prevented so much more grain to the acre from being grown; and so those vandals laid the ax and fire to the roots of thousands of lovely trees over which the most phlegmatic Englishmen would have waxed eloquent." In the eyes of horticulturists, "wheat kings" compounded their sins by employing Chinese peons and indigenous slaves. After the Civil War and Emancipation, horticulturists gained greater moral authority. Ezra Carr, in his book *The Patrons of Husbandry of the Pacific Coast*, blamed monoculture for slavery and the retardation of progress in the South. California's tree people wanted the opposite outcome. They were receptive to the politics of the reformer Henry George, who railed against land monopolists and "Chinese coolies" alike.[8]

Although this horticultural vision for California was distinctively Anglo-American, the expertise on eucalypts came from foreign sources. The bulk of Elwood Cooper's book *Forest Culture and Eucalyptus Trees* consisted of reprinted material from the great Australian authority on the genus, Ferdinand Jakob Heinrich von Mueller. A European transplant, Mueller eventually earned German baronetcy and British knighthood for his leading role in the eucalyptus diaspora; his baronial coat of arms consisted of a "shield with a golden field, within two erect branches of *Eucalyptus globulus* intertwined at their base."[9] Mueller maintained voluminous correspondences with contacts around the world. His work became known to Cooper through the U.S. consul general in Melbourne.

Mueller, and Cooper by extension, belonged to a global network of self-made scientists who studied "acclimatization." This now-forgotten movement emerged alongside European imperialism. The first, largest, and most important acclimatization society, based in Paris, conducted its main experiments in Algeria. Acclimatizers advertised their science as an alternative to accidental and haphazard introductions of species. They, too, wanted to make "deficient" landscapes more beautiful and useful by adding new species, but they wanted to do it rationally and systematically. In places such as Australia and New Zealand, acclimatization satisfied the nostalgia of settlers for an Albion landscape and the desire of expatriate gentry to hunt foxes and deer. In other contexts, acclimatizers acted out of pure scientific interest; they wanted to test the portability and adaptability of species and organisms.

In general, Americans showed less interest in acclimatization than Europeans, Australians, and New Zealanders. There was no U.S. equivalent to La Société Zoologique d'Acclimatation. With the exception of oysters, game fish, and songbirds, nineteenth-century Americans put little coordinated effort into faunal introductions. They expended far more energy on floral introductions. But only Californians developed a web of individuals, societies, and periodicals that collaborated on the systematic importation of plants and plant-related insects. Horticulture, particularly in regard to citrus and eucalyptus, inspired the greatest collaboration. The transpacific steam connection established between California and Australia in the 1870s aided the two-way travel of knowledge and seeds. At the same time that eucalypts and acacias became popular in coastal California, Monterey pine became popular in southeastern Australia. This Pacific exchange benefited from likenesses between the regions—climate first, but also economy and history. On both sides of the ocean, midcentury gold rushes produced environmental damage that ensuing residents hoped to ameliorate with afforestation.[10]

Thanks to the international acclimatization network, Californians became aware of another perceived virtue of *Eucalyptus*, particularly blue gum: this fast-growing tree was also a "fever-reducing" tree. According to theories of medical geography, malaria and various other maladies resulted from "miasma," or bad air—an infecting vapor that transpired from overgrown bottomlands or marshy areas where vegetable matter decayed. In multiple ways, eucalypts acted as a prophylaxis. By soaking up water, they reduced the size of miasmatic founts. Their pungent leaves and litter disinfected the soil and prevented unhealthful decomposition. As they "inhaled," the purifying trees absorbed the toxic air and exchanged it with "balsamic exhalations"; their essential oils created an atmospheric elixir. Such claims originated in the 1850s with a French botanist working with Mueller's encouragement. Enlisting doctors and sanitation officers, European acclimatizers tested the theory in places such as Córdoba, Valencia, Barcelona, Provence, and Corsica. The most famous success story came from Tre Fontane, a monastery in Rome built around three springs that was the site of Paul's martyrdom. After gum planting, Tre Fontane became less marshy and sickly. Emboldened, colonial authorities spread the antifebrile plant to far-flung lands. The Spanish added blue gum to Cuba; the British did the same to Cape Colony and India, among other territories. The species "furnishes the rare example of a truly Australian tree having become a citizen of the world," wrote a French authority. Most conspicuously, France claimed to have made colonial Mauritius and Algeria more livable with arboricultural medicine. There was, of course, a real connection between wetlands and malaria: mosquitoes breed in water. To the extent that water-greedy eucalypts reduced standing pools, they also reduced the number of disease vectors. (The etiology of malaria remained mysterious until 1880 and disputed until 1900.)[11]

In the Golden State, enthusiasm for the "fever-tree" peaked in the early 1870s. The tree catalog within Elwood Cooper's book described the "once despised" blue gum as "transcendently above any other plants, if not above *all* other plants, in hygienic importance." In 1872 the California Academy of Sciences heard a paper that emphasized the previously unrecognized sanitary properties of the species, and in 1874 the academy heard the testimony of French medical experts.

With the blessing of Australian authorities, California doctors and agriculturalists recommended extensive plantings, especially in the malarial Sacramento and San Joaquin valleys.[12]

Two new agricultural journals, *Pacific Rural Press* and *California Horticulturist*, spread the biomedical news. For example, the president of the board of health in Sacramento, a flood-prone city with a notorious reputation for fever and ague, issued an ordinance for planting eucalypts—the capital city's original public trees. On a smaller scale, the editor of the *Kern County Courier* reported on an experiment at his own farm, where he employed two families of Chinese laborers. In February he gave the family on the north side 2 ounces of eucalyptus seed to sow around their dwelling. The family on the other side got nothing. By the warm season, seeding on the north had resulted in about 1,200 two-foot plants. Their "camphorous" odor could be smelled 100 yards away. The owner pronounced the experiment a success: the family with trees enjoyed "robust health" while the tree-less family got "their usual mildly-distressing fever." The enlightened farmer hoped that Kern County "might soon take rank among the sanitariums of the State." The Southern Pacific Railroad did its part in 1877 by planting a thousand eucs in triple rows to shield the disease-plagued Delano station from the sickly winds of Tulare Lake (a body of water, since drained, that rivaled Lake Tahoe in surface area). Delano reported a reduction in malaria cases that year and attributed it to the trees. Isolated correlation became instant proof.[13]

Encouraged by such anecdotal evidence, Californians began to employ eucalypts to address not only the outdoor environment but also the indoor, the symptoms as well as the causes of disease. For prophylactics, homeowners hung portieres of seedpods or garlands across mantels. They burned the dry leaves in fireplaces or smoked menthol cigars. In closets and trunks, they sprinkled leaf powder to discourage moths. People also invented gum-tree cures. A leaf between the lips supposedly aided throat disease. Eucalyptus tea—or a pillow stuffed with leaves—acted as a sedative. Other folks drank tea to clean out the system or end a cold. The braised pulp of leaves, when applied to the scalp, relieved headaches and, as a bonus, encouraged hair growth in balding men. Hypochondriacs consumed the essential oil in various forms: inhalants, tinctures, gargles, syrups, lotions, injections, capsules, and lozenges. Farm journals provided recipes. According to letters to the editor, the fever-reducing tree could also help with cholera, diphtheria, rheumatism, asthma, pulmonary gangrene, uterine catarrh, and gleets—a detestable malady with an appropriately ugly name.[14]

In short, the initial excitement about *Eucalyptus* in the Golden State was not at first capitalistic. Australian trees made the land more complete, more beautiful, more useful, more healthful. And they relieved the shortage of fence material and fuel. These were good enough reasons for creating a new forest. Afforestation did not require commercial justification.

The sight of eucs thriving did in the long run inspire dreams of speculative profit. Throughout the 1870s readers of farm journals followed the progress of James Stratton's prizewinning grove. "When Gen. Stratton was setting out the trees," reported the *California Horticulturist*, "the neighboring farmers laughed at him, and advised him to desist and attend to his surveying, as he would be dead before the timber would amount to anything; but the laugh is now on the other side." Stratton intended to harvest money, exploiting the market for lumber as well as firewood. Any profit would count as bonus since he had planted the trees on "unproductive" acreage. An esteemed man, Stratton exerted influence both as an example and as a distributor. Going against the conventional wisdom that only Australian-grown seed would germinate, Stratton used and sold his own seed. By the middle of the decade, demand outpaced his supply. Hundreds of small farmers in the central part of the state tried to emulate Stratton by planting blue gums on "wastelands," the dry or hilly or alkaline spots where grain and vegetables could not be germinated. Stratton's first commercial test brought mixed results, however. In 1877 he reported that many of his eucs had reached an impressive 90 feet. Out of them he could make decent telegraph poles but not railroad ties. Firewood, despite being less valuable, brought in the most money, and promised to do so again. Stratton's downed trees sent up second-growth suckers that grew even faster than the first growth.[15]

By the late 1870s, overlapping medical and commercial fads in blue gum had transformed the look of lowland California. In the words of one farmer, *Eucalyptus* had become the "tree of trees—its banners are waving around our State and over all our homes." The Bay Area led the way; the Southland did its best to catch up. A Southland real estate boom (the first of many) created an inexhaustible demand for firewood. The first sizable gum planting south of Santa Barbara occurred in 1875 when the Forest Grove Association put in 190,000 seedlings along the Anaheim branch of the Southern Pacific, 12 miles southeast of downtown Los Angeles. The president of the association was Judge Robert M. Widney, one of the prominent men of the city—the first head of the Chamber of Commerce and later the principal founder of the University of Southern California.[16]

Notwithstanding the endorsement of figures like Stratton and Widney, the voguish tree attracted criticism. In 1877 a San Francisco newspaper printed a satirical editorial about the "craze all over the State":

> Blue gum is supposed to be as sovereign an 'antidote for everything' as blue glass [bottles of medicine] . . . In Australia, where this thing grows wild, the country is so healthy that people have to go to New Zealand to commit suicide . . . This absurd vegetable is now growing all over this State. One cannot get out of its sight. It asserts itself in long twin ranks, between which the traveler must run a sort of moral gauntlet, and crops up everywhere in independent ugliness. It defaces every landscape with blotches of blue, and embitters every breeze with suggestions of an old woman's medicine chest. Let us have no more of it.[17]

Disenchantment grew more obvious as the decade ended. As eucalypts reached maturity, horticulturists reevaluated the benefits and costs of these huge, raggedly, water-loving plants. Even the pro-euc

Pacific Rural Press acknowledged in 1879 that blue gum had fallen from its "high estate." The journal printed a letter from a Riverside grower who had torn out 1,500 gums; he called the blue gum business a "fraud." The *Press* urged prudence. "We have expected too much from the tree," it opined. *E. globulus* was not a bad species; it had just been overplanted, planted in bad places, and harvested too early. The *Press* cited a British authority with experience in India who said that no eucalypt under twelve years of age should be cut for lumber.[18]

Southern Pacific, the California firm with the greatest clout, learned this lesson the hard way. In 1877 the corporation set in about 1 million seedlings on various properties with three goals: first, to advertise to prospective buyers the productive quality of its land; second, to test the value of wood for industrial purposes; and third, to "remove the sterile and forbidding appearance" of its stations. In anticipation of all-around success, the railroad installed two new nurseries, one in the Sacramento Valley town of Chico, another in the San Joaquin Valley town of Tipton. While it waited for the trees to shoot up, the company manufactured about one thousand telegraph poles and two hundred railroad ties from preexisting plantations. The growth of blue gums proved more impressive than the long-term performance of eucalyptus wood. In 1885 the SP reported that poles rotted in the ground and deteriorated at the surface because of beetles. And as ties, the wood checked and cracked "in an extraordinary manner." Blue gum earned "second-class" grading for strength and durability, but second did not merit top-dollar expenditures. The SP immediately shut down its nurseries.[19]

In California's farm country, disillusionment with eucalypts, especially those that had been planted as windbreaks, woodlots, and home ornamentals, peaked in the 1880s. In letters to the *Pacific Rural Press*, farmers complained that blue gums fell down too easily in the wind. More distressingly, their dispersive root system acted as a "venomous feeder upon moisture and soil nutriment," stunting nearby plants. The "insatiable thirst" of these "vegetable monsters" could suck a well dry. For this reason, prominent Santa Barbarans began to tear out the "Australian weeds" from locations near homes. (At the same time, the

Santa Barbara Press called for *more* of these "natural scavengers" next
to Chinese washhouses, where open pools of wastewater offended the
senses.) The trustees of Alameda declared *Eucalyptus* a public nuisance because of obstruction of street lamps. After just a decade, a
blue gum overshadowed a house instead of shading it. Inside, as firewood, it produced a "perpetual detonation and fizzing." A San Mateo
County man uprooted hundreds of blue gums on his property after
time showed them to be "anything but ornamental." He declared
them worthless: "I do not think I would accept a gift of a tract of land
covered with them unless I could simultaneously bargain with some
one for their removal, root and branch." Tellingly, James Stratton sold
20 acres of his famous plantation in 1880 to a party who promptly cut
down the gums and replaced them with stone-fruit trees.[20]

In hindsight, the mid-1880s can be seen as the end of the first
phase of eucalyptus cultivation in California—a phase marked by
the predominance of blue gums, the high significance of therapeutic
afforestation, the relative unimportance of lumber compared to firewood, and the authority of farm journals. A second frenzied phase
was yet to come.

NEW VARIETIES, NEW AUTHORITIES

Early planters rarely knew what kind of eucalyptus they grew. Seed
distributors did not provide reliable information, and without taxonomic training and a microscope, it was virtually impossible to identify species by seed. California sellers and buyers used a simplified
schema: beyond "blue gums," they called everything "red gums."
(Whereas *blue* referred to the color of leaves, *red* referred to the color
of the wood.) The State Board of Forestry, a botanical authority created in 1885, helped Californians make sense of what they were doing
to the landscape.

In its original incarnation, the board functioned more as an educational and promotional organization than as a regulatory agency. It

had no timber reserves to manage; it could do nothing to slow or halt the devastation of the redwood belt. But it could at least encourage the establishment of a new forest bank for the day when the redwoods would be cashed out. The board deplored the improvidence, the gross abuse, the waste and destruction that augured the extinction of forests and the degradation of water supplies. It promoted fire suppression, warned against desertification, and aided the scientific search for a eucalyptus lumber tree to replace redwood. In response to overharvesting by the tanning industry—peelers strip-mining the lowland forests of northern California, excoriating tannin-rich tanoaks and leaving them to die—the board warned of "bark famine." State foresters called for the introduction of rapid-growing, tannin-rich *Acacia* species. Australasian trees would, they hoped, save Californians from their general profligacy with native flora. To learn how different species of eucalypts and acacias grew in different microclimates, the board set up experimental stations on donated land at Chico and Santa Monica. The latter offered seedlings at a discount with the request that buyers send back arboreal progress reports. Thousands took up the offer in the late 1880s and early 1890s.[21]

With the help of the State Board of Forestry, horticulturists refined their catalogs and augmented their short list of favorite trees. Four new eucalyptus species made the grade: river red gum, manna gum, forest red gum, and sugar gum. The first three, although not arid-land species, took well to the heat of the Central Valley. Sugar gum, a billowy grower, favored the southern coastal strip between Santa Barbara and San Diego. By contrast, blue gum performed best in cool, moist areas, especially places with fog drip such as the Bay Area and the central coast. Even as they tried out new species, Californians found unexpected uses for existing blue gums. In the 1880s an Oakland company figured out that the foliage, once stripped, could be reduced to a dark liquid (sold as Downie Boiler Incrustation Preventative and Remover) useful for cleaning steam engines. Other entrepreneurs worked to enlarge the domestic market for medicinal and cosmetic products containing the leaves' essential oils. "The eucalyptus has so many economic uses," wrote one booster, "that it is likely to be the 'tree of California' quite as much as the noble redwood."[22]

Despite past disappointments, blue gums continued to be planted. While farmers turned against the species, urbanites—especially those in the Bay Area—embraced it as an ornamental. San Francisco, which dreamed of becoming New York City's western equivalent, undertook an audacious effort in the 1870s and 1880s to transform an expansive tract of shifting sand into a public pleasure ground larger than Central Park. Borrowing from European reclamation practices, the superintendents of Golden Gate Park, notably John McLaren, imposed an artificially accelerated process of ecological succession. First the gardeners sowed grasses to stabilize the surface of the dunes. Then they stippled the fragile lawn with north-to-south fences and bedded out fast-growing species (eucalypts as well as acacias, tamarisk, Monterey pine) on the sheltered eastern side. To help these trees stretch their roots into the sand and their branches into the fog, the park staff spread loam and manure. Finally, when the gums reached sufficient size, gardeners put second-stage plants in their shadows.[23]

Adolph Sutro, a man who personified the wealth and ambition of San Francisco, added a private landscaping effort to the public one. In 1880 this Prussian-born Jewish mining magnate used his fortune from the Comstock Lode, an operation responsible for the consumption of millions of Sierra pines, to buy Rancho San Miguel, the area around 900-foot-high Twin Peaks and Mount Sutro (home today of the giant, alien-looking Sutro Tower radio antenna). Eventually Sutro came to own about 10 percent of the city's real estate. In addition to two years of service as a mayor, Sutro gave tangible gifts to San Francisco. At Lands End, he built a public recreation complex, Sutro Baths and Cliff House. And on the hilly portions of his property, the millionaire oversaw the addition of blue gum, Monterey pine, and Monterey cypress. Unlike the baths, Sutro Forest was not open to the public, and Sutro may have had an ulterior motive for afforestation, given that the city offered a tax break for forested properties. In any case, the private greenbelt served to beautify the public viewspace.

In 1886 Sutro helped to organize San Francisco's first Arbor Day for his own lands and also the city's military tracts—the Presidio, Fort Mason, and Yerba Buena Island, where children set trees in the form of a giant cross. Speaking to the assembled volunteers, Sutro envisioned a future day when the people of the Pacific Coast would "wander through the majestic groves rising from the trees we are now planting, reverencing the memory of those whose foresight clothed the earth with emerald robes and made nature beautiful to look upon."[24]

Arboreal beautification sometimes conflicted with other municipal improvement programs. In the 1890s many California cities installed their first modern, comprehensive public sewer systems. To protect their expensive new waterworks from the invasive roots of gums—"the greatest destroyer of sewers known to municipalities"—many cities passed ordinances forcing homeowners to fell their big trees. Once thought to improve sanitation, eucalypts now threatened it. In 1900 the city of Berkeley banned eucs anywhere within 70 feet of sewer lines.[25]

Where Australian trees didn't interfere with progress, they remained popular with the Golden State's cultural elite, especially in the south. "The eucalyptus is *the* tree of Southern California for elegance and style," wrote one visitor of the mid-1880s.[26] Here the arboreal landscape—indeed, the entire built landscape—looked different from San Francisco and Berkeley. From the moment that the residential real estate market heated up in the 1880s, Los Angeles County rejected the eastern (and European) model of nucleated growth. Town builders designed the region to be different, neither urban nor rural. Its fruit colonies offered country living for city people. The exemplar was Pasadena, an artistic yet conservative city that has always taken beautification—and moral improvement—very seriously. The city remains renowned for its Rose Parade, a celebration of flowers that recalls the founding generation's commitment to genteel horticulture. Here people created gardens *with* eucalypts rather than forests *of* eucalypts.

Pasadena's leading garden, Carmelita, belonged to Jeanne Carr,

wife of the professor Ezra Carr and confidant of the naturalist John
Muir. In just three years after moving to Pasadena in 1877, Jeanne
Carr assembled a collection of 120 tree species at her arboretum (now
the site of the Norton Simon Museum). She referred to her private
park as a "forest station." For Carr, forestry and gardening were indi-
visible. She interpreted the popular interest in "floriculture, arboriculture, and landscape gardening" as an encouraging sign "indicating
the final triumph of man over wild nature, and over his own selfish
and destructive instincts, which have hitherto allowed one generation to impoverish many succeeding ones, by the reckless destruction
of forests." The "floral adornment" of cities would engender positive
social effects. For every dollar spent on parks, she said, a dollar could
be deducted from law enforcement. If gardeners performed their duty,
Southland society would never endure a month without the civilizing
influence of flowers. Of eucalypts, Carr preferred red-flowering gum,
an undersized tree with oversized blooms.[27]

One of Carr's part-time neighbors, Abbot Kinney, made a point
of advancing new ornamental species. In the process, he succeeded
Ellwood Cooper as the leading eucalyptus expert in Southern California. Whereas Cooper was a middle-class horticulturist, Kinney
was a tennis-playing upper-class real estate developer and public servant (a characteristically Californian combination). A native of New
Jersey, Kinney inherited a fortune from his family's cigarette business
(including the popular brand Sweet Caporal) and moved out west for
his asthma. Today he is mainly remembered for dreaming up Venice, a canaled real estate development near Santa Monica. Kinney
also owned a country place, Kinneloa, on the outskirts of Pasadena,
where he cultivated citrus and mingled with other cultured plant lovers. A self-made multilingual intellectual, Kinney pontificated on
social theory, moral education, and conservation. Over the course of
his life, he served as a federal surveyor, a U.S. Indian commissioner,
and the first chairman of California's State Board of Forestry. Kinney
hoped to convince fellow Golden State transplants of the threat of
desertification and the promise of afforestation. He wanted to safe-

guard modern California from the fate of the ancient Mediterranean, a region that had degenerated from civilized, tree-covered landscapes to "desolate wastes, the haunts of the hyena and the reptile."[28]

In his book *Eucalyptus* (1895), Kinney celebrated the genius of Anglo-Californians in transforming unlovely gums—"scrawny," "ashey," "monotonous and depressing" in their native Australian bush—into hardy adornments. He urged cities to systematically plant ornamental eucalypts along streets and highways. The Southland's two most eminent fruit colonies, Ontario and Riverside, had recently laid out magnificent boulevards—Euclid Avenue and Magnolia Avenue, respectively—that prominently featured eucalypts. The chronicler of the American Horticultural Society's convention in Riverside in 1888 praised "the California method as it related to trees": rows of eucs and pepper trees bordering the main roads. Kinney championed this Southland parallel to the eastern elm-lined avenue. In his capacity as street warden of Santa Monica, he tended a stately twin row of gums that lined the westernmost section of Wilshire Boulevard (formerly Nevada Avenue), an arboreal landmark until road widening in 1924. At his home in Santa Monica, Kinney tended a large collection of eucalyptus from which he distributed seed. Like Carr, Kinney urged property owners to look beyond the wonderfully average blue gum. He felt partial to the sugar gum. Nonetheless, he praised the earlier eucalyptus "apostles" for spreading *E. globulus*. "The introduction of this tree has done more to change radically the appearance of wide ranges of country in California than any other one thing," he wrote. With blue gum, a "brown parched expanse of shadeless summer dust" could, in a year or two, be reclaimed into a vale of clustered trees. It "worked almost like magic."[29]

Notwithstanding his boosterish tone, Abbot Kinney had written the best book yet published in the United States on the Australasian genus; he even included a decent guide to taxonomy. Kinney foreshadowed a trend in professionalization. When the State Board of Forestry dissolved in 1893, the University of California superseded it as a eucalyptus authority and assumed control of the state nurseries in Santa Monica and Chico. Extension agents from the College of Agriculture subsequently gave away millions of seedlings in the name of research and experimentation.

Professionals at the federal level soon added their voices. In 1902 a member of the USDA's Bureau of Forestry, Alfred McClatchie, former research assistant to Kinney, published the new standard American textbook on eucalyptus cultivation. His illustrated volume carried the imprimatur of the Government Printing Office. Working out of Arizona, McClatchie hoped to spread eucalypts beyond the West Coast. He recommended afforestation throughout the desert Southwest, where, he said, endless expanses of barren hills produced nothing but flash-flood debris. Chapter by chapter, he enumerated the uses of eucalypts: as forest cover, as shade, as timber, as windbreaks, as fuel, as a source of oil and honey, even as an improver of health and climate. On the last subject, McClatchie chose his words carefully, given that scientists had by 1900 discredited miasma theory. Citing anecdotal evidence of the antimalarial effects of gum trees, the eucalyptologist concluded vaguely that it "is entirely reasonable to believe that to a certain extent they beneficially affect the atmosphere in the region of their growth."[30]

The only thing missing from McClatchie's nearly comprehensive volume was a detailed how-to section on cutting, seasoning, and processing. After half a century's experience with eucalypts, Californians still did not know how to make lumber out of them. From 1903 to 1905, Dwight Whiting, a large landowner in Orange County, put in close to a million trees—the largest plantation to date—but admitted his ignorance about their "technical values for manufacturing into useful articles, or when they should be felled, or how to cure the timber when sawn." Despite his formless plan, Whiting expressed confidence to an Australian contact that "at the rate that our native forests are being devastated by axes and fires it won't be long before each and every tree I have will be worth ten shillings a piece or more." In neighboring Los Angeles County, growers put in at least eight blue gum plantations in the early years of the century, including four groves alongside Central Avenue between Watts Station and the village of Compton—now the concrete heart of L.A.'s least-loved district.[31]

Businessmen like Whiting were banking on a national or even worldwide "timber famine." In the eighteenth century, Europeans had experienced a similar "wave of deforestation phobias" (to use a German historian's phrase); now America took its turn. In books such as *Trees and Tree-planting* (1888), by the former Union general James S. Brisbin, campaigners cautioned against the evil consequences of forest destruction, highlighted the ruination of redwoods, and trumpeted the climatic and social blessings of shelterbelts. Warnings of catastrophic wood shortages, made with increasing urgency after the Civil War, prompted Congress in 1891 to grant the power of land reserve to the executive branch. Benjamin Harrison, Grover Cleveland, and especially Theodore Roosevelt used this power to create vast forest reserves in the Far West—too late for coast redwoods but just in time to protect many sequoia groves. To manage these perpetually public domains, Congress replaced the federal Bureau of Forestry with the full-fledged National Forest Service in 1905, the same year that the California legislature reconstituted the State Board of Forestry. The bugbear of scarcity reached maximum strength in the following few years. The first chief of the Forest Service, the German-trained Gifford Pinchot, never wasted an opportunity to talk about the looming crisis.[32]

In 1907 Pinchot's agency sounded a more specific alarm about an impending "hardwood famine." *Hardwood* refers to angiosperms (flowering plants), specifically broadleaf deciduous trees, whereas *softwood*—which can actually be quite hard—refers to conifers. In the United States, carpenters traditionally favored hardwoods such as maple, oak, ash, and birch. Every middle-class homeowner aspired to own well-crafted wooden items such as grandfather clocks and rocking chairs. With the invention of the flooring matcher in 1885, hardwood floors became de rigueur in middle-class homes. At the time, hardwood output largely derived from the Ohio River Valley and the Upper Midwest. Astoundingly, the region's prodigious reserve had been squandered by 1907. The Forest Service identified Appalachia as the last hope for eastern hardwood production. Unless scientific foresters intervened, the nation possessed only "about a fifteen years' supply."[33]

BOOM AND BUST

This one statement in a seemingly obscure government circular about the hardwood prospects of the Appalachian Mountains yielded a singular and phenomenal change to the California landscape. In the words of the environmental historian Stephen Pyne, "The resulting bubble was perhaps rivaled only by the tulip mania that swept seventeenth-century Holland."[34] Something about the precision of the latest prediction—*fifteen years*—excited the imagination of investors. They found it easy to believe that the Golden State possessed a natural monopoly: if *Eucalyptus* was the only hardwood capable of reaching full size in a decade and a half, and if California was the only U.S. state with the right climate—not to mention the expertise and the infrastructure—for mass plantings of the genus, then money here would truly grow on trees.

The "bubble" or "boom" of 1907–1913 differed qualitatively from the "craze" or "excitement" of the 1870s. Back then, Ellwood Cooper and other horticulturists worked to complement their small, diversified farms with beautifying and climate-changing windbreaks. Blue gum might provide a nice side profit as firewood, but its reason for existence was principally noncommercial. Cooper's wife, Sarah, publically stated her hope that "every ranch might have its botanical garden" to foster intelligence and refinement in children.[35] By contrast, the new exponents of gum trees did not care about beauty, health, or even fuel. Their sole concern was salable lumber. Speculators, not farmers, led the way. Unlike the Coopers, the new planters saw eucalypts as an extensive, monocultural cash crop—instant industrial forests.

Euc boosters couched commercialism in terms of national service. They connected the fall of empires with the felling of forests: "In the wake of timber exhaustion, invariably will be found decaying civilization, race disintegration, national corruption and dissolution." Supposedly, nomads and barbarians lived in treeless environments. Babylon, Lebanon, and China had all declined, morally as well as economically, because of deforestation. A hardwood shortage could potentially stagger the United States, or give it a knockout blow. Californians embraced both the opportunity and the obligation to save America: "We lack forests; we must make them." Eucalyptus producers would make up for the "lumber looters" and "timber barons" who had treated redwoods like a bonanza mine. Solving the hardwood problem was paramount to building the Panama Canal, intoned authorities such as Stanford University's president, David Starr Jordan. Even Elwood Cooper endorsed a booklet that hyped a eucalyptic response to the crisis.[36]

Today it's hard to relate to these people on their terms. We inhabit a built environment dominated by concrete, asphalt, steel, and plastic, and it takes a feat of historical imagination to appreciate the former importance of hardwood. Yet it wasn't so long ago that most goods were durable goods, and most of them, from toys to coffins, derived from lumber. Moreover, the primary building materials, for foundations, walls, ceilings, roofs, and floors, came from trees. In the industrial age of wood, it did not seem far-fetched to imagine future travelers walking on eucalyptus street-paving blocks, riding in eucalyptus buggies, and driving automobiles on wheels with eucalyptus spokes. Or trains speeding along tracks laid across gum-tree ties; boatmen parking their eucalyptic vessels at wharves supported by eucalyptic pilings; recreationists bowling on gum-wood alleys and drawing beer from gum-wood kegs; and occupants furnishing homes with unbreakable tables and everlasting chairs. *Eucalyptus* boosters echoed the promotional language of the redwood industry. Gums— the hardwood of the future, the king of hardwoods—outperformed all other trees. Here in the dominion of "California mahogany," the reign of hickory, birch, and oak would end. Eastern furniture companies and their skilled workmen would relocate, making the Golden State the hardwood center of America.

For the first time in the history of eucalypts in California, urban dailies and suburban magazines played a major role in disseminating information and hype. They acted ambivalently. In 1908–9, the peak time for speculative investment, the *Los Angeles Times* swung back and forth. The editors ran many articles by self-interested authors who encouraged the little guy to get in now while riches could still be made. On other occasions, the *Times* issued stern editorial warnings about the "fakes" who "cleverly twist" government reports to give "gross exaggerations" about eucalypts. Don't gamble on trees, the paper said. Trust the farmer, not the promoter.

The commercial literature from the period makes for amusing reading today. Start-up companies lured investors with promises such as FORESTS GROWN WHILE YOU WAIT and ABSOLUTE SECURITY AND ABSOLUTE CERTAINTY. To lend authority to their words, they printed certified letters from businessmen and unauthorized photographs of U.S. chief forester Gifford Pinchot. They misquoted Forest Service experts. No hyperbole went too far. The eucalyptus industry was as solid as the Rock of Gibraltar; a gum plantation offered surer returns than a mother lode. The Miracle Tree (also Wonder-Tree, Tree of Hope, Tree of Fulfillment) offered more potential wealth to California than the Gold Rush—or even gold, oil, and citrus combined. Whereas the fruit market was volatile, the timber proposition was steady. From foresightedness came fortune. Just as millions had been made deforesting America, millions would be made reforesting America. The nation's extremity provided the opportunity of a lifetime. Eucalyptus, the HARDWOOD TREE OF THE TWENTIETH CENTURY, the MOST VALUABLE TREE IN THE WORLD, grew almost overnight. The rapid-rise plant could be cut and cut again. This tree was like a machine. When coppiced, a eucalypt sent up *two* new trees that grew in *one-fifth* the time of the original, which already grew *five times* faster than a normal tree. Even better, the second growth produced higher-quality wood. Everything from the tree, right down to the leaves, could be utilized. Just as Chicago meatpackers used all but the squeal of a hog, California foresters would use all but the breeze that sighed through the branches of eucs. These perpetual income producers opened the way to a permanent home on Easy Street. In short, this vegetable treasure house was as sound as national growth, as certain as progress and civilization, as logical as the law of supply and demand.[37]

To evaluate such assertions, aspiring stockholders and landowners had no shortage of advice from ostensibly disinterested outside experts vetted by investigative committees. For example, the Forestry Society of California praised the value and versatility of *Eucalyptus*. One of the society's advisory board members, state forester George B. Lull, gave his opinion in a statewide magazine in 1909. He examined whether the boom had a "stable foundation" or would "fall of its own weight." He noted that thirty-eight timber companies had formed in the past two years, not counting the many associated real estate companies. He warned of a few "wild-cat" organizations lacking scruples, but mainly he commended timber companies, noting that they had recently formed an industrywide body to standardize their promotional claims. For the most part he felt cheery: "It would appear to require no wizard's mind" to foresee that eucalypts would assume a high place in California's economy.[38]

Soon after, a U.S. Forest Service official, George Peavy, added his voice to the discussion. In a four-part magazine article, the forester counted no fewer than one hundred companies involved in the eucalyptus industry. He, too, drew attention to the "extra-optimistic" outfits that seemed "more interested in obtaining the widow's mite" than in propagating plants. Nonetheless, he stated unequivocally that eucalypts could check the timber famine, now predicted to strike in exactly sixteen years. Nature had given California a "prospective corner" on the hardwood market. He reminded readers, though, that gums grew best in specific environmental conditions and that the market for eucalyptus wood as posts, poles, and ties was restricted because of poor field results. He was more positive about piling and manufacturing material. For "conservative businessmen," *Eucalyptus* was "comparatively sure" to bring "moderate returns." "After all," Peavy wrote, "the eucalypts are only trees . . . Treated rationally, they are sure to become a valuable resource. Exploited like a bonanza mine, they are sure to yield disappointment."[39]

This mild expression of circumspection from the feds did not sit well with Sacramento. In response, State Forester Lull sent a letter to the editor. In Lull's opinion, Peavy had "erred on the other side" in his attempt to correct the hyperbole of unscrupulous promoters. There actually was, Lull argued, an unprecedented opportunity to make a forest of money. To help it happen, the State Board of Forestry had already published two editions of a handbook. In 1908 the UC Agricultural Experiment Station added its own bullish report on eucalyptus culture. When a freethinking agronomist with the university dared to tell an audience in Stanislaus County that their land was "too valuable for the planting of eucalyptus trees," local growers demanded an apology or resignation. A more pliant expert, former assistant state forester C. H. Sellers, wrote his own pro-euc book. Endorsed by the forestry board for its "authentic data," Sellers's publication contained breathless testimonials and page after page of illustrations of products that could and would be made from eucalyptus wood, including cribbage boards, rocking chairs, and tables. In other words, this government document resembled a promotional pamphlet.[40]

With so much expertise and authority behind the boom, people began to believe irrationally, almost religiously, in *Eucalyptus*. The value of already mature plantations skyrocketed. People couldn't put in the fast-growing trees fast enough. Men with means invested in gums.

"I have read endless volumes & pamphlets & forestry bulletins on the subject, and am confident that my conclusions are correct," wrote Jack London in 1910. "Everything I can raise and scrape I am sinking into the planting of eucalyptus trees." Despite his dire indebtedness, London, a wheeler and dealer as well as a popular author and erstwhile socialist, ordered some 100,000 forest red gum seedlings for his Sonoma County hacienda. He dashed off short stories for magazines to pay for the immigrant Italian laborers who did the planting. A native of Oakland, London proudly realized his California "dream-ranch" by cultivating a forest of gums and building a house of redwood. Writing an endorsement letter to an investment company, London paraphrased the prophet Jeremiah: "There is no getting away from the fact that the man who 'builds houses and plants trees'—the man who PRODUCES is the man who is most fully a man." The Eucalyptus Timber Corporation advertised hardwood, along with London's "latest and greatest novel," *Burning Daylight*, by repeating the novelist's expectation that his grove would someday make him "richer than the oil kings, steel kings and beef barons." *Burning Daylight* followed the exploits of an unscrupulous businessman relocated to the Bay Area from the Alaska gold camps, a gambler and scoundrel who falls in love with a heroine who begins to domesticate him with a horticultural suggestion:

> Now do you know what I would do if I had lots of money and simply had to go on playing at business? Take all the southerly and westerly slopes of these bare hills [above Oakland]. I'd buy them in and plant eucalyptus on them. I'd do it for the joy of doing it anyway; but suppose I had that gambling twist in me which you talk about, why, I'd do it just the same and make money out of the trees . . . I'd be making thousands and thousands of cords of firewood—making something where nothing was before. And everybody who ever crossed on the ferries would look up at these forested hills and be made glad.[41]

In fact, someone tried this. The entrepreneur Frank C. Havens bought up large sections of the eroded Berkeley Hills in Alameda County and started a blue gum forest from 1910 to 1913. His Mahogany Eucalyptus and Land Company included three nurseries, a sawmill, and scores of employees. Havens had competitors throughout the state. In Mendocino County, the Union Lumber Company experimented with blue gum on its redwood stump lands. In San Luis Obispo County, speculators seeded two huge tracts, one at Montaña de Oro, just south of Morro Bay, and another at Nipomo Mesa, just east of Arroyo Grande. Further inland, in Tulare County, along the tracks of the Southern Pacific, a variety of investors, notably the Los Angeles–based Eucalyptus Timber Company, cultivated trees by the million starting in 1908. The powerful chief engineer of Los Angeles, William Mulholland, secured the services of an Australian botanist to study the feasibility of planting eucs along the entirety of the Los Angeles Aqueduct. Jotham Bixby, the "father of Long Beach," added gums to some 3,000 acres of his seaside ranch. In Riverside County near Ontario, the Pacific Electric Railway Company—the empire of Henry E. Huntington—greened up 2,000 acres. The largest single plantation in California resulted from the Atchison, Topeka & Santa Fe. In 1906 the railroad bought Rancho San Dieguito in San Diego County, renamed it Rancho Santa Fe, and by 1910 put in some 3 million trees on almost 9,000 acres with the expectation of producing railroad ties. The AT&SF was either unaware or unconcerned that its rival, SP, had long ago attempted the same thing and failed.[42]

In this feverish atmosphere, people ignored or explained away a stern word of caution from the Forest Service. The new chief, Henry Graves, issued a public advisory in 1910 about the exaggerated predictions of eucalyptus companies. He complained that his agency had been repeatedly misquoted and announced a new government study that would resolve the gum-tree question. The authors of this report stopped short of criticizing their agency or colleagues such as McClatchie but conceded that "extravagant estimates" about eucalypts had led many people to form "an altogether false idea" about investment potential. Experiments conducted in cooperation with the University of California indicated that young eucalyptus wood tended to shrink, warp, and check. The researchers presented evidence from the U.S. consulate that lumbermen in Australia never cut eucs under thirty years old; sixty and up was better; one-hundred-plus was best. For the industry to succeed in California, a seasoning process needed to be devised, they said. Their study detailed how Australians allowed lumber to dry in stacks in the open for over a year, or they girdled the standing trees and let them die and shrink slowly before cutting. The foresters held out hope for a technological fix, a kiln method that would allow quick drying without warping. Follow-up tests were under way; uncertainty remained. But even these bearers of bad news expressed optimism that under proper conditions eucalyptus timber could become profitable.[43]

Before the bubble finally burst, something strange happened in Southern California: the new commercial interest in eucalyptus revived an older conservationist impulse. American settlers in the Los Angeles Basin had long hoped to green and beautify the chaparral-covered Transverse Ranges. The center of hope was Pasadena, home to thousands of prairie-state transplants, including Theodore Lukens. This banker, real estate developer, one-time mayor, and self-taught forester has since been honored with a place-name: Mount Lukens, a prominent flat-topped massif (now capped with an antenna farm) that juts above the basin. Lukens worked tirelessly on behalf of afforestation, sometimes in the employment of the Forest Service, sometimes as a businessman. Cooperative horticulture, public service, and private speculation overlapped in the social world of Golden State conservationists. Groups such as the California Water and Forest Association, organized in 1899, lobbied to improve logging practices, fight forest fires, and plant new forests.[44] Lukens practiced his passion by founding the Henninger Flat nursery in the foothills near Pasadena, adjacent to the Angeles Forest Reserve (now Angeles National Forest). The nursery experimented with various species to determine what grew best in the Transverse Ranges. It also supplied many trees for the emerging landscapes of Griffith Park and the Huntington Botanical Gardens.

In historical accounts, Lukens has been nicknamed the "Johnny Pineseed" of California and the "John Muir of Southern California." The latter analogy seems credible when one remembers that Muir, in the last stage of his life, presided over a remunerative orchard and vineyard. In 1911 Muir sent a holiday card to his friend Lukens with a watercolor depicting gum trees and a poem evoking the "cloistered aisles," "silvery spires," and "living incense" of eucalypts.[45]

In the environmental thinking of figures such as Lukens and Muir, forest cover was key to the whole hydrological system: trees and tree litter encouraged rainfall, captured fog drip, increased rainfall retention, decreased transpiration, and regulated steam flow. Without forest cover, the San Gabriel Mountains would eventually succumb to the creeping influence of the Mojave Desert. Cities like Pasadena would lose their aquifers and, by extension, their groves of planted fruit trees. As Abbot Kinney put it succinctly, "No forests, no farms." To ease the long-term threat of desertification and the short-term threat of catastrophic flooding, Lukens worked to regrow woodland recently consumed by fire. Just as importantly, he worked to plant trees on naturally treeless lands. Conservationists of his generation did not draw a hard distinction between reforestation and afforestation. More trees meant more health and beauty, in the largest sense of those words. To use the historian Ian Tyrrell's terminology, foresters like Lukens and Kinney were not environmental restorationists but *renovationists*. To renovate means to repair and also to improve.[46]

About the time that Lukens retired from government service, Henninger Flat turned its attention from pines to eucalypts. Between 1906 and 1910, the nursery raised tens of thousands of seedlings. At first the Forest Service distributed gums to various public reserves and private parties. Then, in 1908, the agency began planting in the San Gabriels. To aid the effort, it authorized a second nursery near San Bernardino. Before the program ended in 1910, government agents added something like 100,000 red gums to the mountain front. The Forest Service concentrated on riparian zones below the frost line of 2,500 feet. But even here the trees didn't take. They couldn't compete with native chaparral that had adapted to the soil and climate of Southern California's foothills. A follow-up report did not mince words: introducing eucalypts to the Angeles National

Forest was "folly." Given the narrowness and isolation of the viable habitats, *Eucalyptus* could not, even in the best scenario, significantly alter water supply. If anything, the untidy trees would increase the fire danger. A chastened Forest Service shut down both nurseries by 1912.[47]

While the government tried and failed to establish eucalypts, Theodore Lukens moved on to the last major project in his life—wooded real estate. Lukens and two Iowa-based business associates filed the incorporation papers for the Los Berros Forest Company in 1909. As secretary and forester, Lukens decided what land to buy—8,000 coastal acres on Nipomo Mesa in southern San Luis Obispo County, prime habitat for blue gums. In 1908–9 Lukens oversaw mass plantings. His company planned to sell parcels of its forested land to anyone who would buy—timber companies, speculators, or farmers.

Lukens, a transitional figure, was not the only eucalyptus booster who mixed progressive ideals with pecuniary instincts. In 1911 the U.S. Forest Service inspector Stuart Flintham, who went on to become the forester of Los Angeles County, presided over the addition of thousands of sugar gums to the Whittier Hills property of the Murphy Oil Company, where oil wells and access roads exacerbated erosion. The fast-growing, drought-tolerant trees worked to stabilize the soil and promised future revenue for the company. "The success of this plantation shows what can be done in Southern California along the lines of reforestation," said Flintham.[48] An even better example of progressive eucalyptus planting—an amazing true story—comes from San Diego. There a city officer tried to reform the prison and welfare system with a menthol forest cultivated by hobos.

It happened like this. The Mexican government had given the pueblo of San Diego a 48,000-acre land grant. After Americans took over in 1848, they proceeded to sell off the city's inheritance indiscriminately. By 1908, when officials finally came to their senses, only 7,000 acres remained in reserve. These "pueblo lands" were located just south of Torrey Pines Mesa, near present-day La Jolla. In 1910 the city passed an ordinance providing for the "improvement" of the property and created the new position of pueblo forester.[49] The job went to the evangelically industrious Max Watson. The son of a Unitarian minister, Watson spent his childhood in Los Angeles and attended high school in San Diego. As a teenager he worked as a ranch hand in the hills east of town and there became familiar with *Eucalyptus*. Straight out of school he started his own nursery specializing in the genus. His timing was perfect—just in time for the hardwood boom. Many large property owners in Southern California commissioned him to plant trees. Just two years later, Watson applied for and won the city post. Although barely into his twenties, the new pueblo forester did not lack for big ideas. He wowed the city with a plan to erase the municipal debt with hardwood.

In the fall of 1910 Watson cleared 50 acres of coastal scrub and let the land lie fallow during the winter rains. In March he set in about 50,000 trees, mostly sugar gum. By the end of the year, the neat rows of eucs had shot up 8 feet. Roughly 150,000 more went in the ground the following winter and spring, and this time Watson relied on help. Because of its pacific climate, San Diego served as a wintering place of last resort for seasonal workers and the homeless. In the early twentieth century, most San Diegans viewed the "tramps" as an invading army of professional beggars. Yet during the winter of 1912, the pueblo forester, working with the city, provided the indigent with up to ten days of paid employment clearing brush and planting trees. Roughly four hundred men took advantage of the program. Some additional workers appeared involuntarily: city judges began to send drunks and petty scofflaws to the pueblo lands for rehabilitation, with the forester's blessing. Young Watson earned a new title: probation officer.

The media loved the story. A large entourage from the Editorial Association of Southern California took a tour of the "open-air prison." Reporters quoted the "Boy Reformer" saying that chain gangs and rock piles would be obviated by "penal farms," a more humane and more profitable alternative. Caught up in Watson's enthusiasm, reporters suggested that San Diego might someday be able to eliminate city taxes altogether. Watson planned to complement his money-making forest with a "drug plant farm" that could produce high-value pharmaceuticals, including eucalyptus oil. In his mind, environmental, social, and civic problems could be solved together. "I believe the farming and reforestation of waste lands by municipalities is the easiest and best solution of the unemployed problem," he said. Noting that many of his men suffered from alcoholism, he recommended longer stints so that the therapeutic effects of outdoor work had time to sink in. "If I had my way, I should like to see every jail, workhouse and penitentiary wiped off the face of the earth," pronounced Watson.[50]

San Diego's civic forest has been largely forgotten. Historians do not generally portray the city as a cradle of progressive politics—for good reason. In early 1912 Watson's farm served as a velvet glove on the city's iron fist. Even as the Boy Reformer spoke of revolutionizing the welfare system for the underclass, police and vigilantes from San Diego made war on a unionized segment of the working class, the Industrial Workers of the World. In 1911 the California IWW shifted its off-season recruitment campaign from Fresno to San Diego. Many local Wobblies had recently spent time across the border in Baja California in support of Ricardo Flores Magón's offshoot of the Mexican Revolution. Horrified, San Diego followed Fresno's example by outlawing public assembly and free speech in the section of downtown used by Wobblies. Those who defied the city's abrogation of the First Amendment were arrested as conspirators—a felony charge. By the end of February 1912, some 175 agitators had been jailed. To protest this breach of civil rights, thousands of union members and sympathizers poured into San Diego in hopes of gumming up the judicial system. The city and county called on the governor for state troops. Rebuffed, supervisors authorized vigilance committees to patrol the county's boundaries.

In this context, the city's eucalyptus forest takes on a darker shade. City hall did not share Max Watson's pure motives. By sending unemployed men to the work camp, city officials probably figured they could more easily distinguish between run-of-the-mill hobos and radical unionists. They might also deny the IWW potential recruits. In 1912, when police patrols intercepted bindlestiffs on the outskirts of town, they presented a choice: work at the Pueblo Forest or be escorted out of San Diego. Those who chose the first option received fifty cents a day for their labor. After the maximum ten days, the once again unemployed received five dollars—just enough to get an out-of-town ticket, as they were strongly encouraged to do. Meanwhile, vigilantes targeted nonworking Wobblies. In cooperation with police, citizen groups roughed up and in some cases killed activists. They corralled hundreds and forced them onto trains and trucks. Deportees were told not to return on pain of death. When the celebrity anarchist Emma Goldman came to town to show her support for the union, vigilantes kidnapped her partner and sodomized him. Brute force carried the day. By summer San Diego had crushed the IWW. As a consequence of violence, the Boy Reformer couldn't find enough field hands that summer and fall. The sugar gums continued to reach skyward, but the farm operation went moribund.[51]

Max Watson eventually relocated to the Bay Area, where he built a distinguished career as Santa Clara County's first adult probation officer. Around 1960, as a retiree, Watson revived his interest in horticulture and created a private arboretum of eucalypts at his home in San Jose. He opened a business, the Down-Under Nursery, from which he supplied trees to parks, college campuses, and highway departments.[52]

In a different political climate, could Watson have succeeded in San Diego? Probably not. For all his avidity for eucalyptus culture, Watson possessed no practical plan for converting sugar gum into marketable lumber. His oversight was symptomatic. In the half century following the introduction of eucs to California, countless treatises had been written on how to start the seeds in boxes, how to water the seedlings, how and when to transplant them, how to space them, and so on. Planters could consult detailed charts showing the comparative qualities of species in terms of growth rate, volume, strength, and durability. But no one published a comparable disquisition on wood technology for California-grown eucalypts. It was simply an article of faith that a tall, healthy-looking gum would behave in the mill like any other hardwood.

Like many faith-based initiatives, this one turned out to be mis-guided. The end of the cult of the blue gum can be dated to 1913. Early that year Frank Haven's operation in the Berkeley Hills shut down, barely two years after opening. Trees from his 14-mile-long, 3,000-acre forest had been subject to long-term seasoning experi-ments by the Forest Service. The industrial trade magazine *Hardwood Record* published the final results that autumn. The report, written by H. D. Tiemann of the USDA's Forest Products Laboratory, can only be described as devastating. Tiemann said flatly that Golden State eucalyptus grew on fictions, delusions, and fallacies. Most of the wood "cannot be regarded as lumber in any true sense," he wrote. For commercial utilization, every kind of euc grown in California was more or less bad, Tiemann said, but the worst of all was the spe-cies used most, Tasmanian blue gum. Even though botanical author-ities had consistently identified jarrah as the best Australian lumber tree, no one in California established a jarrah plantation because the species grew slowly. Blue gum accounted for an estimated 90 percent of all eucalypts in the state.[53]

How did this happen? After disappointing experiences with *E. globulus* in the 1870s and 1880s—an episode Willis Jepson, the state's leading botanist, recalled as the "Blue Gum Epidemic"—why did people return to it? There are at least five overlapping explanations. Familiarity comes first. Californians grew blue gum because Amer-icans in California had always grown blue gum; it seemed almost indigenous. Seeds and seedlings were easy and cheap to procure. Sec-ond, the tree grew well in a variety of climate and soil conditions. It was, as Abbot Kinney said, a "jack-of-all-trades" or "all around util-ity" tree. The third reason is historical ignorance. Urbanites—often out-of-state capitalists—drove the twentieth-century boom. These people would not have been familiar with the extensive discussion of blue gums in nineteenth-century farm journals and horticultural reports. The fourth answer is hubris. Those who did know history could argue that they had rectified mistakes from the past instead of repeating them. Nineteenth-century planters followed a "system of neglect." The new commercial eucalypts, "scientifically" grown on "ideal" land, would be physically superior to these old ornamentals haphazardly seeded on leftover lands. The final component is artful deception or advertising. Speculators needed to assure investors that they could produce a hardwood forest in fifteen years. They needed a poster species, and long experience had shown that blue gum, despite its drawbacks, grew faster than any other hardwood. It seems probable that many eucalyptus real estate companies suspected that blue gum would fail as lumber but didn't care because they intended to flip the property.[54]

Paradoxically, the problem with blue gums, and eucalypts in general, stemmed from their vigor in California. Because of the absence of native pests, the trees grew more robustly here than in their native environment. To Australian eyes they looked freakishly robust, with not a single leaf chewed by beetles or koalas. Imagined as a human being, the archetypical California euc was a lanky, athletic teenager in a perpetual growth spurt. Like young bone, young wood has certain characteristics. To withstand the shearing action of wind—and to resist gravity's encouragement to fall down—top-heavy gums developed a high amount of tension wood. Cutting a juvenile tree released the wound-up growth tension, causing the inner bark to check into quarters. Worse, when sawed into planks for drying, the tree's already checked wood began to warp like a washboard as it released its high water content. In some cases, the green logs contained so much water they wouldn't even float. In Australia, lumbermen had devised methods for shrinking eucalyptus wood without warping it. But even a state-of-the-art imported kiln-drying process would not have saved the California industry. Australian lumberers worked from a large supply of old growth. In the Golden State, young growth was the only supply.

Chronic optimists could point to a few bright spots. California

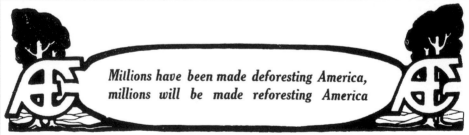

Millions have been made deforesting America, millions will be made reforesting America

In the early twentieth century, a coalition of eucalyptophiles—foresters, conservationists, journalists, boosters, and speculators—spread the message that California-grown Australian trees were the only things standing between the United States and "hardwood famine." The scientific cultivation of gum trees would also make up for the profligate waste of redwood trees.

Despite its failure as a commercial plant, the "adopted tree" became a beloved landscape feature—"as indigenously Californian as the redwoods, the poppy fields, the long white coastal beaches, the gleaming granite of the High Sierra." In this Ansel Adams photograph, Edward Weston, wearing his darkroom apron, rests on the durable base of a sequoia-sized blue gum near his studio in Carmel.

This Depression-era image by Dorothea Lange—part of her iconic "Migrant Mother" series—shows poverty and squalor backed by a naturalized blue gum plantation, a legacy of the "eucalyptus boom."

A contemporaneous image of the Atchison, Topeka & Santa Fe's failed eucalyptus plantation being repurposed into Rancho Santa Fe, an upscale wooded residential development.

A San Francisco newspaper illustration referencing a 1930 zoning controversy in Burlingame.

Orange County, ca. 1920. In the early automobile age, practically every highway in lowland California was lined with ornamental eucalypts. As roads were widened and improved, crews tore out hundreds of miles of row trees. Only a few cities, notably Burlingame, saved their arboreal sentries.

Touring Topics

JANUARY 1926

Touring Topics Has a Larger Circulation *Than Any Other Motoring Magazine in the* United States

Like cars, eucalypts and palms became symbols of California modernism. This charming cover of *Touring Topics*, the magazine of the Automobile Club of Southern California, shows a eucalypt and two popular kinds of palm surrounded by the distinctive sickle-shaped foliage of gum trees.

After the Oakland-Berkeley Hills fire of 1991 (*above*), many Bay Area residents redefined naturalized blue gums as "gasoline trees" and "invasive aliens." Although eucalypts can explode in hot fires (*lower left*), their hazard in California has often been exaggerated. In the Southland, thousands of gum trees succumbed in the 1980s after the eucalyptus longhorned borer beetle (*lower right*) hitched a ride across the Pacific.

Only in California's fog belt—locations such as the Marin Headlands (*above*)—have blue gums expanded beyond their original plantings, becoming moderately invasive populations. The presence of eucalyptus in coastal California has hurt some native species but helped monarch butterflies (*below*).

Today it's hard to recall the time when eucalypts were unambiguous symbols of California beauty and belongingness. A 1921 platinum print by Karl Struss, a member of the Photo-Secession (and subsequent winner of the first Academy Award for cinematography), evokes that lost era.

blue gums proved acceptable as underwater pilings, for they resisted the boring of teredos (wormlike mollusks, or shipworms). A few landowners—those with slightly older plantations or diversified operations—made a profit selling poles to wharves at Oakland, Santa Barbara, Long Beach, and San Diego, among other places. And in the Southland, the market for firewood remained favorable. "As a fuel producer in a region of scant forest and no coal, they [eucalyptus] have been a gift as of the very gods," wrote the Pasadena naturalist Charles Saunders. Most cleverly, the AT&SF transformed its tree farm at Rancho Santa Fe into a wooded real estate development for an exclusive clientele. The railroad proved yet again that it is easy to make money if you can afford to lose some. Small investors who placed their hopes and savings on hardwood manufacturing learned a harder lesson. Timber speculators strung them along to the bitter end. In 1919 one A. H. Crofut appealed to the U.S. Forest Service for evaluation of the financial claims of the San Diego Eucalyptus Company, based in Chicago, Crofut's city of residence. Having become suspicious, Crofut withheld his final two payments on 7.5 acres of California property he had never seen. "They claim the trees on my land are now 6 years old," he wrote, "and that when they reach the age of 10 years, there is an easy market for them. They claim there is a big demand for eucalyptus as a substitute for mahogany and hard woods."[55]

Some honest dreamers refused to concede. In 1914, near the end of his life, Theodore Lukens published a promotional brochure on cultivating blue gum for profit. According to him, the recent collapse of the market had merely separated the tares from the wheat. Heedless "boomers"—people who believed *E. globulus* could thrive anywhere—had been weeded out. In proper locations, like the acreage he offered for sale, tree farming still offered a "safe and remunerative investment" that would surpass any life insurance policy for future income. Lukens, like many others, cited the example of Gillespie's Hardwood Planing Mill of San Jose, the oldest of the handful of wood manufacturers that specialized in *Eucalyptus*. The owner, T. J. Gillespie, made furniture, vehicle parts, implements, and insulator pins. However, he did not use trees from recent commercial plantations. His best lumber came from local gums seeded in the 1870s. He claimed, moreover, that the "San Jose gum" was a hybrid species that performed better than regular blue gum. Whatever the case, no one succeeded in replicating Gillespie's success. Most of the millions of eucalypts planted in the state between 1907 and 1913 were not cut, much less processed.[56]

It goes without saying that the U.S. economy—and American civilization—did not collapse because of insufficient hardwood. Americans avoided a timber famine in part because they shifted technologies. Measured both in total board feet and in per capita consumption, timber use in the United States peaked in 1909. The sheer abundance of wood in the nineteenth century had encouraged wasteful practices like balloon framing and discouraged the creation and acceptance of new building technologies. In the early twentieth century, the United States reached an economic tipping point: steel and concrete grew cheaper and more available even as timber became more expensive and less available. Builders demonstrated the efficacy of a new building method—concrete reinforced with twisted steel bars—in 1903 with the completion of the sixteen-story Ingalls Building in Cincinnati. Reinforced concrete went on to become the standard construction method for large buildings. Simultaneously, railroad companies, the single largest user of timber, replaced untreated hewn ties with creosoted sawed ties, a technological shift that saved timber in both the short and the long term. Railroad engineers developed more efficient designs for trestles and instituted a timber grading system so that each variety and specimen of wood could be matched with its best use.[57]

Notwithstanding concrete, steel, and chemically treated wood, the U.S. economy did require new timber supplies. Large landholding companies seized the opportunity. Most famously, the Weyerhaeuser Company moved its base of operation from the Upper Midwest to the Pacific Northwest in 1900 after purchasing over 1 million acres of Northern Pacific Railroad land grants. Weyerhaeuser proceeded to clear-cut the mountainous Douglas fir forest with the aid of gas-powered machinery. Taking a different approach, other firms set up shop in the Gulf Coast and planted fast-growing yellow pine to create extensive artificial forests.

Judged in hindsight, U.S. conservationists exaggerated the wood shortage problem. They failed to anticipate that scarcity would create market incentives for more efficient uses of wood—a kind of conservation. Figures such as Gifford Pinchot focused narrowly on forest management and silviculture. America's first generation of professional foresters—people who knew that hyperbole helped their cause—wanted to conserve "virgin" or "primeval" (what we generally now call "old-growth") forest cover. They did not prioritize forest product research. Nor did they show much appreciation for second-growth tree cover—reforested woodlands in places such as New England and the mid-Atlantic. Once decimated, the eastern forests recovered remarkably fast, albeit in different form. This recovery long eluded policymakers. While the federal government counted the volume of cut wood, it did not conduct a census of living trees. Only belatedly did Washington acknowledge that the U.S. East, not just the West, deserved representation in the national forest system.

SENSE OF PLACE

Though superfluous to the nation, California's gums made a difference to the state, starting with the look of the land. Precisely because they fell short economically, boom-era plantations aided afforestation. In 1924 a botanical investigator estimated that the state contained 40,000 to 50,000 acres of solid eucalyptus, broken down as 80 percent blue gum, 15 percent "red gums," 4 percent sugar gum, and 1 percent others.[58] In the semiarid, urbanizing Southland, most commercial groves did not have the ability or the opportunity to self-reproduce, so they failed to naturalize in the biological sense. But in the cooler, moister central coast region, gums generally thrived on neglect. The downward-facing foliage of eucalypts pulled down its own rain in the form of fog drip. In certain prime habitats, like the Berkeley Hills, planted blue gums and river red gums expanded into feral forests. In somewhat drier habitats, like Montaña de Oro and Nipomo Mesa, plantations merely maintained their size.

The euc bust did not, surprisingly, bring large-scale eucalyptus cultivation to an end. Farmers in the Southland still grew woodlots for firewood, a commodity in high local demand. And the citrus industry found a productive use for standing gums. Fruit ranchers put in windrows to shield their perishable crops from hot Santa Ana winds, cool coastal breezes, and frosty winter blasts. Long lines of eucalypts became a familiar part of the skyline in the Salinas Valley and horticultural hot spots to the south: Orange County, the Oxnard Plain, and the San Fernando, San Gabriel, San Bernardino, Santa Clara River, Ojai, and Coachella valleys. By the early twentieth century, pomology in the Golden State had become another monocultural agribusiness, not the promised alternative. A single large citrus operation, Fontana Farms Company, contained 550 linear miles of eucalyptus windbreaks. The company president reported in 1925 that the average wind speed had dropped 50 percent since blue gum planting began in 1912. To fill in its windrows, the company topped the trees in the second or third year to encourage more branch formation. The trees also received fertilizer. Thanks to industrial methods, the big-time citrus rancher avoided the gum problem that had bedeviled the small-time stone-fruit farmer of the 1870s—thirsty, overcompetitive roots. Irrigation now provided plenty of water. And the roots of "robber trees" could easily be "pruned" with the blade of a gas-powered tractor.[59]

With horticulture co-opted by agribusiness, the old garden ideal— mixed plantings of floral, fruitful plants in a domestic setting—now relied on suburbanites for survival. In Greater Los Angeles, homeowners cultivated an array of evergreen flowering trees in the famed "semi-tropical" climate. A well-tended postage-stamp yard might feature an orange, a lemon, an avocado, a pomegranate, and one or more decorative eucalyptus, acacia, palm, or pepper trees for good measure. In the first third of the twentieth century, Southland gardeners popularized a new set of Australian species, smaller eucs that looked more graceful and sophisticated than Tasmanian blue gum. Home landscapers now recoiled from greedy giants that buckled sidewalks and broke sewer lines. (Oakland's superintendent of streets maligned blue gum as the "octopus among trees" for its "depredations.")[60] For shading bungalows, medium-sized trees such as swamp mahogany, silver dollar gum, flooded gum, red ironbark, and white ironbark worked fine. The two ironbarks had the added benefit of producing showy flowers. Many dwarf species were introduced purely for their spectacular red stamens. Red-flowering gum and coral gum looked like trees in miniature; mottlecah and rose mallee looked more like shrubs. Another small eucalypt, silverleaf mountain gum, produced skewerlike cordate foliage that became a standard addition to floral arrangements.

To learn about these and other species, flower-loving Angelenos did not peruse farm journals or forestry reports. In the post-boom era, expertise shifted to gardening books, regional lifestyle magazines such as *Sunset*, the Sunday gardening section of the newspaper, and the local garden supply store. Once the subject of agricultural and silvicultural investigation, the *Eucalyptus* genus now fell under the purview of gardeners and landscapers.

Flower and garden experts for the *Los Angeles Times*, writers who tended to be women, used familial discourse to describe the domestication of gums. A 1927 article on "California's adopted tree" said that eucalypts "seem more essentially California than many a native plant; so completely has it adopted California, and so entirely has California adopted it, that without its sheltering beneficence our droves and vineyards would be like Home without a Mother." Other contributors echoed the sentiment: *They are so thoroughly domiciled here by long residence that they have become the next thing to native. It is natural to think of blue gum as native. We Californians are apt almost to revere this adopted child for the marvelous transformation wrought on the landscape. This adopted son fits in harmoniously.*[61]

Even Theodore Payne, Southern California's leading authority on native plants and native landscaping, was a lover of gums. Payne immigrated to the Pacific Rim from Great Britain in 1893; a decade later, he opened a nursery in Los Angeles. Over the next fifty-eight years, his seed store and mail-order catalog specialized in native flowers and nonnative flowering eucalypts. During the euc boom, Payne made a tidy profit as the nation's leading distributor of gum seedlings and seeds. He and his workers collected from old woodlots throughout California; one year they bagged 1,800 pounds of the minute seeds. Rare specimens came from contacts in Australia. In reverse fashion, Payne's sent seed to international destinations such as Libya. After the bust, Payne continued to advocate ornamental plantings of the genus. He laid out an Australasian arboretum at the Ojai summer estate of a Standard Oil executive. In 1957, on the occasion of the centennial of the arrival of *Eucalyptus*, Payne wrote an appreciation about "the most remarkable tree in the world." Yet all the while, as a landscaper, he championed native flora in words and deeds: he laid out the first public garden in Los Angeles (within Exposition Park) devoted to regional flora and helped to design the Rancho Santa Ana Botanic Garden, a large private property devoted to indigenous California species. Today the Theodore Payne Foundation for Wildflowers & Native Plants downplays the now embarrassing pro-euc activities of its namesake.[62]

The former wide acceptance of eucs found expression in landscape art as well as landscape design. Artisans associated with California's thriving branch of the Arts and Crafts movement created a variety of decorative objects—ceramic tile panels, earthenware vases, tin and oyster-shell tea screens—that featured billowy gums or their falcate leaves. In the fine arts world, Giuseppe Cadenasso, an immigrant from Genoa, claimed to have been the first Californian to discover the painterly potential of the tree. "When I first began to paint it, people laughed at me," he said in 1907. "Now they all see it, because I have opened their eyes." Cadenasso called his studio on Russian Hill in San Francisco "the Sign of the Eucalyptus." An active member of the Bohemian Club, Cadenasso went on to join the art faculty at

Mills College, a campus noted for its eucalyptic landscaping. When he died in 1918, a local newspaper eulogized the painter's studio as "the Mecca of art lovers."[63]

Cadenasso had allies and imitators. From about 1910 to 1930, a regional style of American *plein air* impressionism flourished in California, particularly in the Southland art colonies at Laguna Beach and Arroyo Seco. Art historians conventionally refer to this lovely, bland style as the Eucalyptus School. A representative oil painting, which can fetch a fine price today, features a grand gum in the middle foreground backed by rugged mountains, all done in medium pastel tones suggesting warm hazy sunlight. Painters such as Paul Lauritz sold their work in upscale hotel galleries. As coined by Merle Armitage, the classical music impresario of Los Angeles, the term *Eucalyptus School* was pejorative, a metonym for "harmless" and "imitative" art. Writing in rebuttal, a city arts observer defended the painters precisely because they appealed to local, popular tastes; for that they deserved credit for laying "the most hopeful ground-work for a really genuine indigenous Southern California art." After visiting Laguna Beach, the travel writer J. Smeaton Chase commented on the artists' landscape of inspiration: "The eucalyptus, especially the *globulus* variety that has become so common throughout the State, has so truly native an appearance that it seems as if its introduction from Australia must have been more in the nature of a homecoming than of an adoption. The wide, treeless plains and valleys which once lay unrelieved and gasping under the summer sun, and inspired similar sensations in the traveller, are now everywhere graced by ranks and spinneys of these fine trees, beautiful alike, whether trailing their tufty sprays in the wind, or standing, as still as if painted, in the torrid air."[64]

The trees seemed as old as California civilization. Small wonder that *The Curse of Capistrano* (1919), the pulp novel that introduced the character Zorro, includes an anachronistic scene in which the Robin Hood of Alta California hides his steed in the shadow of a towering gum. The author, Johnston McCulley, probably didn't know better. By the time he moved to California from Illinois, the pioneer gums were preternaturally huge. In 1940, Orange County's Knott's Berry Place, which first earned fame for its fried chicken restaurant, added a "Ghost Town Village" within its eucalyptus windbreak. This simulacrum of a Wild West mining camp—the beginnings of the amusement park— including a gum festooned with a macabre noose: the conventional "hangman's tree." Even Ansel Adams, the man most responsible for disseminating images of "wild California" in the twentieth century, had a soft spot for these pseudo-archaic trees. On several occasions he took large-format portraits of eucalypts that mimicked the style of nineteenth-century views of giant sequoias. A 1969 Polaroid shows a mighty euc at the edge of the redwood fence that encloses Fort Ross, the reconstructed Russian settlement in Sonoma County, the oldest European outpost in California. In an image from 1945, Adams posed his friend and fellow photographer Edward Weston on the base of a gargantuan blue gum not far from Weston's darkroom in Carmel Highlands. Both photographs conveyed the impression that eucalypts were deeply rooted beings worthy of veneration.[65]

The parks and arboretums of Southern California—its outdoor art museums—reproduced this neoindigenous look. More than any other tree type, eucalyptus decorated the region's first two prominent public greens, Balboa Park in San Diego and Elysian Park in Los Angeles. (Spectators at Dodger Stadium enjoy a scenic view of the park's river red gums.) Thanks to the aesthetic advocacy of well-placed landscapers such as Kate Sessions in San Diego; Jeanne Carr, Abbot Kinney, and Theodore Payne in Greater Los Angeles; Francesco Franceschi in Santa Barbara; and John McLaren and Max Watson in the Bay Area, eucalypts entered the standard vocabulary of California landscape design. The region's two largest arboretums later added to the consensus about the belongingness of antipodean trees. In the 1950s the Los Angeles County Arboretum in Arcadia added a world-class Australian section to its collection. In nearby San Marino, the Huntington Botanical Gardens formally opened an Australian Garden in 1964.[66]

Parklike academic campuses likewise acclimated residents to eucalyptic landscapes. To this day, the original University of California—the flagship campus in Berkeley—features a skyscraping stand of blue gum near the west entrance. This enchanting grove along Strawberry Creek contains some of the state's tallest hardwoods, a relict of the 1870s craze, when the managers of the new university did their landscaping on the cheap, producing what one critic called a "foolish monotony of surplus Eucalyptus-trees." Over time, the landscape grew on locals. In 1900, when the university grounds superintendent starting thinning the groves, many faculty and residents of Berkeley howled in protest. Taken as a whole, the UC system could be considered an Australian arboretum. The hospitals of UC San Francisco are backed—even overwhelmed—by Mount Sutro's skyscraping blue gums. The campus at Santa Barbara was at the time of its founding boxed in by a rectangular eucalyptus windbreak, a holdover from a decommissioned military base. Another postwar campus, UC San Diego, grew out of a donated portion of San Diego's Pueblo Forest. Today the tight rows, including well over 200,000 sugar gums, form a 112-acre greenbelt. The 40 to 70-foot-tall eucalypts still follow the dense grid positioned by Max Watson and his hobo assistants in 1912. The original plants have all regrown from stumps, having been coppiced sometime before the university opened to students in 1960. Recently UCSD made a formal planning commitment to preserve its "signature open space" by replacing dead sugar gums and by adding irrigation. "The eucalyptus grove helps to define the place," said the director of physical planning. "I think it is what people identify with UCSD." To complement its artificial forest, the university has used art funds to commission three eucalyptic sculptures.[67]

Partly by accident, Stanford University boasts the greatest eucalyptus stands of any California campus. In 1880 Leland Stanford, railroad baron and ex-governor (and future senator), decided to transform part of his 8,000-acre Palo Alto Stock Farm into an arboretum. His landscapers began by planting a blue gum shelterbelt. The plan was to remove these low-value nurses when the rare exotics became established. After Leland Stanford Jr. died in 1884, Governor Stanford and his wife, Jane, added to the master plan: they would build a museum, mausoleum, and memorial university next to the tree garden. The grieving parents hired the nation's best landscape architect, Frederick Law Olmsted of Boston. Olmsted and the Stanfords considered raising a university forest, but as things turned out, the sandstone-and-tile buildings initially received far more attention than the plants. The grandiose main quadrangle began hosting students in 1891. Just two years later, Leland died, leaving his estate in disarray because of a government lawsuit against his corrupt railroad. Suddenly cash-strapped, the Leland Stanford Junior University relegated tree planting to the bottom of its priority list. Most of the plants perished, while the blue gums thrived. In 1910, at the height of the euc boom, Palo Alto founder Timothy Hopkins urged the university's board of trustees to use its unproductive parcels of land to enter into the hardwood business. Belatedly, in 1916, the university experimented with a tightly packed plantation-style grove on some property adjacent to its ungroomed arboretum. The trees were never harvested. As Stanford's endowment became solvent and eventually overflowing, landscapers decided to maintain the parklike groves of *E. globulus*. The leftover gums came to function as an arboreal gate between the campus and downtown Palo Alto; they made "the Farm" feel even more like an academic retreat. In the mid-twentieth century, university arborists added many other types of gums to the sprawling campus; an arboreal census in 1984 counted ninety-four *Eucalyptus* species. Generations of Stanford students have delighted in walking, jogging, tailgating, and powwowing amid towering columns of fragrant trees.[68]

Real estate developers sometimes exploited the feeling of remove engendered by mature eucalyptus groves. They told wealthy white clients that they deserved the peace and privacy of a forested lot. For example, when a developer acquired a portion of San Francisco's Sutro Forest in 1910, he proceeded to build a high-end residential project called Forest Hill. In addition to winding driveways, terraced stairways, and urns—all set within gums—the developer touted the "restrictions that safeguard the person of taste and refinement who seeks exclusiveness. There are no Mongols, Africans or 'shack builders' allowed." Similarly, the homeowners' association at Rancho Santa Fe near San Diego enforced a racially restrictive covenant and strict architectural code that complemented the botanical uniformity of its eucalyptic haciendas.[69]

Developers could successfully, and profitably, market the novel combination of red-tiled houses and blue-green trees because Anglo-Californians had appropriated both design elements. In the context of California Mission Revival, the neonative eucalyptus complimented the retro-modern "Spanish" architecture. The style exemplified at Rancho Santa Fe was at the time a fusion of modernity and quaintness. This distinctively Californian eclecticism—a pastiche of Spanish, Islamic, and Romanesque motifs with added eucs and palms—was the cutting edge of regionalism before the ascendance of modernism in the 1930s through the 1950s. California Mission Revival began with the Stanford campus and the California state building at the 1893 World's Fair in Chicago. One of the largest surviving examples is the Mission Inn in Riverside. The movement evolved into the more codified, and nationally influential, Spanish Colonial Revival, a style strongly influenced by Spanish baroque, as represented by the fairgrounds erected for San Francisco's Panama-Pacific International Exposition (1915) and San Diego's Panama-California Exposition (1917). At both fairs—celebrations of the future heralded by the construction of the Panama Canal—landscapers made conspicuous use of gums. A fair-going journalist from Sydney marveled at the "Australian-made park" by the Golden Gate: "Almost every tree, every shrub, every plant there is Australian!"[70]

On the road, too, eucalypts simultaneously signified the romanticism of the premodern past and the excitement of modernity. As early car owners, the technophiles of their day, traveled away from Los Angeles, they passed through a touring landscape dominated by eucs. The citrus districts surrounding the metropolis contained long lines of blue gum or manna gum windbreaks. To reach wilderness getaways such as Sequoia National Park, Death Valley, and Palm Springs, weekend motorists drove through eucalyptic landscapes along dirt roads also lined with eucs. They felt a sense of modern adventure as they sped beneath a canopy of gums on the Arrowhead Trail Highway at 30 miles per hour. The Automobile Club of Southern California (founded in 1900) encouraged its members—30,000 of them by 1920—to explore what lay beyond the tree-lined horizon by signposting country roads and by issuing a collectible series of strip maps. In the twenties the club's mass-circulation magazine, *Touring Topics*, put graphical eucalypts on its cover, published romantic scenes of gum trees by pictorialist photographers, and ran advertisements for Studebaker dealers showing luxury high-performance Big Six touring cars backed by falcate foliage.[71]

In many towns, the colossal sentries of blue gum or river red gum that lined the main road symbolized rootedness. They anchored place-based identities. Alas, these living landmarks often stood in the way of modern paved automobile highways—the Auto Club's incessant demand—which required extra width for shoulders, medians, and passing lanes. Businessmen complained, too, that the big trees obscured new billboards. Improvements led to smoother, straighter thoroughfares with more signs and less dust—and less shade, less charm. In 1930, through voter-approved zoning regulations, Burlingame (south of San Francisco) saved its signature eucalyptus row on El Camino Real. This was not the usual outcome, as seen the same year in Glendale (north of Los Angeles), where city crews chopped down the famous Lomita Avenue gum row, purportedly the oldest eucalypts in North America. The city prevailed in its road improvement plan at the close of a bitter twelve-year legal battle, including petitions, lawsuits, a court injunction, and a recall drive, all led by determined activists, including clubwomen and two stars of the silent screen. On Melrose Avenue in Los Angeles, street crews simply tore out the "magnificent blue gums which met in a vast arch overhead."[72] During the long process of turning the San Jose–Los Angeles section of El Camino into the four-lane, divided U.S. 101, thousands of fully grown eucalypts fell to the ax and blade. In Santa Maria, for example, the state used the power of eminent domain in 1949 to condemn the property at the town's southern entrance, paving the way for the removal of the city's gateway gums, despite the protests of locals. Hoping to avoid a similar outcome, supervisors in Ventura County declared the blue gums along the 101 at Camarillo a "cultural landmark" in 1968.

Even as it ripped out old eucalypts, the state Division of Highways added thousands more young ones during the great freeway boom after World War II. The colorful trees somewhat softened the harsh landscape of concrete and asphalt. "I don't know what we would do without the Eucalyptus as far as planting our State highways is concerned," wrote the supervising landscape architect in 1961. "We use the Eucalyptus far and above all the other varieties combined. Its ability to withstand varied climatic and soil conditions and the economy of maintenance makes it decidedly outstanding."[73] The division favored red ironbark and various compact species such as bushy yate and dwarf blue gum, a commercial cultivar developed in the 1920s. It grew as fast as the parent species but shorter and denser, an ideal combination for a visual and sonic barrier.

In pedestrian settings, Southland landscapers popularized yet another species, lemon-scented gum. This gorgeous tree sheds its outer bark just once to reveal a creamy white underlayer. Its foliage, which smells bizarrely similar to artificial "fresh lemon scent," is delicate, not shaggy, and sits high in the branches. The tree accepts various styles of pruning and can assume sculptural forms. Its smooth shaft works nicely as an architectural accent; like many modernist buildings, a lemon-scented gum looks clean and spare and draws attention to its structural base. Henry E. Huntington personally chose two specimens to shade his neoclassical marble mausoleum. Perhaps the only drawback of the species is frost intolerance, which makes it a poor fit for northern California.

Even as lemon-scented gum became a common sight in the metropolitan Southland, blue gum lost major ground. In Los Angeles and Orange counties, postwar subdivisions replaced citrus orchards and their windbreaks. Rows of giant gums could not, like individual oranges, be incorporated into tiny house lots. They had to be bull-dozed. Plantations dating to the euc boom fared no better. Long Beach's landmark gum grove at Bixby Ranch was razed in 1961 in deference to an adjacent naval air station. One of the few privately owned gum groves that escaped the cut was financially useful as a film prop: the eucalyptic backlot of Universal Studios served as a stage for many westerns, including the hit TV series *The Virginian* (1962–1971), ostensibly set in Medicine Bow, Montana.

Since environmentalism was a suburban outgrowth, it follows that tree activists of the 1960s made room for gums. The California jer-emiad *Eden in Jeopardy* by Richard Lillard praised the "mystery and adventure" of eucalyptus groves, places where generations of young-sters played in secret bivouacs. Gigantic gums "add heroic virtue and make rare but welcome suggestions of permanence," Lillard wrote. Harold Gilliam, the nature columnist for the *San Francisco Chroni-cle*, pumped up the lyricism. In the Central Valley, eucalypts hovered over farms and communities "like the Gothic towers over the cathe-dral towns of Europe." On the peaks of San Francisco, "they grow in woods as dense and dark as the legendary Schwartzwald." At Mills, Berkeley, and Stanford, they are "the veritable Groves of Academe." Gilliam arrived at this rousing conclusion: "The Eucalyptus seems an indispensable element of this State's landscapes, as indigenously Californian as the redwoods, the poppy fields, the long white coastal beaches, the gleaming granite of the High Sierra."[74]

In the San Fernando Valley, suburban environmentalists rallied to the defense of blue gums endangered by development. "The beauty of the trees is one of the reasons we bought our homes here," said one angry housewife in Granada Hills in 1963. Emboldened, local chapters of women's clubs conducted a valley-wide eucalyptus cam-paign. Most dramatically, homeowners in Canoga Park, on the val-ley's west side, staged a summer-long campaign in 1971 to save 142 mature blue gums that added beauty and shade to Orcutt Ranch, a city-owned historic park that encompassed an oil executive's former vacation home and citrus orchard. The controversy erupted after the Los Angeles County Flood Control District began to build a new concrete storm channel in the path of the trees. This ordinary project had been approved by the city council without comment. The reaction on the ground was extraordinary. Mothers and children sat in front of bulldozers; residents held twenty-four-hour vigils beneath the boughs. A hastily formed neighborhood committee secured a restraining order from a judge, who required them to post a $10,000 bond within the week, which included the Fourth of July. Flag-waving children staged a bicycle rally as their parents went fund-raising door to door. When the eucalyptophiles came up $4,500 short, the judge, moved by their effort, lowered the bond. The *Los Angeles Times* closely covered the suburban drama. Soon the state's deputy attorney general threw his hat in the ring. He invoked the new California Environmental Quality Act, passed in 1970 in the wake of Earth Day, which required environmental impact statements for government projects. Ultimately the city council called for a redesign, an expensive proposition because the contractor required a settlement fee for breach of contract. The Flood Control District reluctantly complied. Bemused, the district's assistant engineer noted that thousands of eucalypts had been removed in past years for street-widening projects without a word of complaint. Earth Day caught him and his boss unawares. The chastised chief engineer announced that the district would henceforth hold public hearings about all of its projects "in response to the environmental wave."[75]

As this wave crested, crashed, and subsided, it left something behind—a new way of thinking about eucalyptus, a novel language to describe what belongs in California.

CHAPTER 4

Natives, Aliens,
and (Bio)diversity

PUTTING OUT FIRES

After the Gold Rush, California horticulturists added exotic plants
to treeless and deforested environments to improve and renovate the
land and to create likenesses of familiar landscapes. At some point
the most prominent of these exotics became familiarized: *Eucalyptus* seemed at home. "It is so much a part of the everyday scene that
it would be difficult to picture the state without the graceful tree,"
pronounced the *Oakland Tribune* in 1952. From the late 1950s to
the early 1970s, Bay Area members of the Sierra Club annually visited the gravesite of John Muir and, as a memorial gesture, linked
hands around the adjacent manna gum—one of Muir's favorite
trees—and sang "Auld Lang Syne." Today this dendrophilic ritual
would be unthinkable to local environmentalists. From Earth Day
to the turn of the millennium, the discourse about California eucalypts turned upside-down. Tasmanian blue gum went from being a
marker of belonging to a vexed symbol of nonnativeness. The leafy
boom-and-bust of 1907–1913, formerly remembered as an endearing
blooper or "beloved failure," now seemed like an odious mistake, a
disastrous get-rich-quick scheme. Residents of the Bay Area were the
first to change their minds. Trees once admired as enterprising survivors now induced apprehension as hazardous, hard-to-kill invaders.

Strange scenes unfolded: euc-hating environmentalists defied tree huggers; habitat restorationists worked against landscape preservationists. In Southern California, different ecological and rhetorical conditions prevailed: eucalypts proved to be all too mortal—victims of development, age, drought, and insect infestations—and people talked more about whether to replace them than to eradicate them.[1]

The winter of 1972–73 marked the beginning of the gum tree's change in status from welcome to unwelcome, from adopted to disowned. The epicenter of change was the Berkeley Hills. Back in the 1930s the East Bay Regional Park District used a districtwide property tax to acquire most of the remains of Frank Havens's plantations of blue gum and river red gum, which became parts of Sibley Volcanic Regional Preserve, Redwood Regional Park, and other units. The district's crown jewel, Tilden Regional Park, likewise contained large tracts of introduced blue gum and Monterey pine. This string of parks formed the backyard of postwar neighborhoods carved into the afforested uplands of El Cerrito, Berkeley, and the Montclair district of Oakland. This scenic real estate came with fire hazard. The "Diablo winds"—the Bay Area version of Southern California's Santa Anas—bring hot, dry air in the late summer and early fall, when the thick understory nourished by winter rains has turned to tinder. Berkeley's "great fire" of 1923 destroyed some six hundred homes. Such a conflagration had been predicted in the pages of the *Oakland Tribune* the year before after a freak heavy snowstorm brought down limbs throughout the "splendid eucalyptus groves."[2] On a smaller scale, flames returned to the hills in 1929, 1931, 1933, 1937, 1940, 1946, 1955, 1960, 1961, 1968, and 1970. During that time span, developers kept building within the trees, and land managers kept practicing fire suppression. From an ecological perspective, the fuel-rich Berkeley Hills needed to be cleaned out with a blaze. Instead, humans and eucalypts increased the fuel budget with wooden houses and tree litter.

In December 1972 a rare multiday cold wave hit northern California; lows in the East Bay dropped to the teens. Eucalypts do not tol-

erate temperatures much below the freezing point, and by February
the blue-greenery had turned brown. Residents of the hills began to
fret. Initial reports suggested that 2 or 3 million trees over 2,500 to
3,000 dispersed acres had died. The worst crown kill occurred above
1,000 feet, where frostbitten eucs dropped their limbs left and right.
"If the picnic areas in the eucalyptus groves are used, you're going to
have dead kids," warned an arborist at the neighboring University of
California.[3] The problem extended beyond parkland. Oakland estimated that 450 of its 650 affected acres were privately owned.

Like the even wealthier homeowners of fire-prone Malibu in
Southern California, the East Bay highlanders relied on others to
solve their problem. In February 1973 Oakland directed "court assign-
ees," people working off misdemeanor convictions, to cut eucalypts on
city-owned open space. Labor also came from youth probationers and
scout troops. As a supplementary measure, Oakland ordered over five
thousand homeowners to remove dead trees from their property by
June 1. To help meet the deadline, more than a dozen fly-by-night
businesses sprouted up. Their fee often exceeded $1,000 per tree, and
homeowners complained of price gouging. Defending the choppers,
one professional noted how eucalypts were different from pines: "They
grow the way smoke goes."[4] The trunks of blue gums twisted and
bent in every direction, making them difficult to cut down. Homeowners who could afford to pay for removal could also direct their
accountants to claim a casualty loss deduction. Others flouted the
city's order, either because they couldn't absorb the cost or because
they held out hope for a government bailout.

Local governments appealed to Sacramento for help with their
outstanding bill, estimated in the millions of dollars. When the legislature failed to act expeditiously, locals turned their attention to
the state disaster fund. The governor's office responded coolly: the
fund provided disaster relief, not disaster prevention. Nonetheless, in
April, Ronald Reagan declared a state of emergency, freed up a little
bit of money ($300,000), and sent in crews from the National Guard,
the Division of Highways, and the new Ecology Corps. Unable to

repair the hillside forest, state workers concentrated on creating a 200-foot wide, 13-mile-long firebreak. Oakland offered free firewood to anyone with a chainsaw and a flatbed truck. The combined efforts seemed paltry: local news coverage became hyperbolic and hysterical—a countdown to catastrophe. Without action, a "hill area holocaust" seemed certain.[5]

Just as the East Bay turned to Sacramento, Sacramento turned to Washington. The Nixon administration initially rejected California's plea because the anticipated disaster did not meet the governmental standard of "imminence." Pressure from Reagan and senator Alan Cranston forced a reversal. In May the executive branch opened up limited federal disaster funds ($1 million) and told California to seek the remainder from Congress. Cranston shepherded an $11 million appropriation bill through the Senate, but the House decided to hold hearings before voting on the "predisaster assistance" bill, which included a reimbursement for homeowners. Congressmen from eastern states listened skeptically. In September a large House majority killed the spending bill (dubbed the "you-clipped-us" bill by one fiscal conservative). Even representatives from Southern California joined the chorus of "no" voices.[6]

In the end, most of the frost-damaged trees were never cut owing to lack of funds—and a lessening of alarm. By summer it became clear, thanks to infrared aerial photography, that the news of the great die-off had been greatly exaggerated. It takes more than a deep freeze to kill a blue gum. In the Berkeley Hills, more than 90 percent of roots and trunks survived; only the extremities had perished. New shoots sprang up from lignotubers and epicormic buds, and reached the height of an adult person in six months. New stumps likewise resprouted, just as former tree farmers had hoped they would. "Like science fiction aberrations," reported the *San Francisco Chronicle* in 1977, "they grow and grow, mostly impervious to chainsaw and ax." For a few years, the hills appeared distinctly shaggy as new branches sprouted and dead ones fell. The limb fall added to the already large buildup of litter. A team of university scientists quantified the danger-

ously high fuel load in the hills and recommended mechanical thinning and prescribed burning. Instead, homeowners in the East Bay
returned to a state of complacency as their neighborhoods returned
to a state of verdure. When the regional park forester, a self-declared
"sucker-basher," tried to arrange volunteer tree removal activities, he
couldn't find enough volunteers.[7]

The blue gums of the East Bay would someday return to the
attention of crisis managers. In the meantime, without any pressure
from locals, Washington and Sacramento became newly involved in
eucalypts—in contradictory ways. Following the Arab oil embargo
of 1973–74, the Department of Energy investigated domestic energy
alternatives such as oil shale in Colorado and, more surprisingly,
trees in California. As part of the Division of Solar Technology, the
DOE conducted a feasibility study for eucalyptus energy farms that
could convert sunlight into biomass. At the state level, University of
California scientists worked on techniques to derive synfuels from
eucs; the California Department of Forestry created a Forestry Wood
Energy Program; and the legislature incentivized tree farms. State
scientists established about a dozen experimental groves in locations
such as Mendocino, Napa, and Riverside counties. Interested entrepreneurs started their own small plots—federal tax write-offs. "Strike
back at the oil cartel with a eucalyptus stick!" read one investment
brochure. For a few years, before the program withered and died,
"eucfuel" promised to be the "energy for the '80s."[8]

Big government begets bureaucratic contradiction. While the
DOE and the USDA encouraged new plantings of eucs on private land, another part of the executive branch, the Department of
the Interior, began to remove old plantings from public parks. In 1982
the natural resources management plan for Golden Gate National
Recreation Area (GOGA) sanctioned the expunging of nonnative
blue gum from the Marin County portion of the park—about 600
forested acres total. The National Park Service called attention to the
encroachment of gums on native plant communities and emphasized
hazard by rekindling memories of recent fires in Los Altos (1985) and

Berkeley (1980). The Park Service hoped to set a forthright example of tree removal at its self-contained federal property, a situation seemingly more straightforward than the awkward patchwork of property ownership and agency oversight in the Berkeley Hills.

GOGA was, however, an atypical national park unit. It had been assembled from various private and military landholdings purchased or transferred to the Park Service, starting in 1972. Encompassing wilderness, ranchland, brownfields, and historic sites, GOGA defied simple categories of urban, rural, and wild. In its attempt to restore much of the park to a "natural" state, the NPS ran up against area residents who had grown accustomed to thinking of GOGA's open spaces as their scenic backyard, their favorite haunt—a place to jog after work, to walk the dog. The idea of park rangers chopping down century-old trees hit a nerve. In a poor public relations move, the Park Service chose Arbor Day in 1986 to announce its removal plan. During the initial public comment period for the proposed action, the superintendent of GOGA received letters from more than 350 citizens and petitions signed by hundreds more.

The respondents, mostly Marin County residents, expressed outrage: *I'm sure the people who came up with this idea are not native, either. America is a melting pot of many races, as well as species of flora and fauna. Stop the Marin Chainsaw Massacre!* They characterized the proposal as ludicrous: *This approach would ultimately lead to our giving the land back to the Indians! Should we reinstate the Miwok Indians (if you could find two of them) and go back to where we came from ourselves?* They dismissed the Park Service's claims that blue gums posed a threat to person and property, and they rejected the reclassification of the plants as nonnative. *Should we remove the palms from Southern California while we're at it? Should we remove the nonnative vineyards from Napa Valley, too?* Above all, euc lovers focused on aesthetics and emotions. They considered the big old gums to be awesome, inspiring, majestic, graceful, stately, beautiful, peaceful, scenic, and unique. *We love them like friends and family. Their loss would be a heartbreaking blow. We were brought up under these eucalyptus groves and we took picnics under them as children and we want to die under them.* The grandfather trees sounded good when the onshore breeze rustled their boughs. The textured bark and the filigreed foliage added variety to the landscape, unlike the flat and monotonous native vegetation. Eucalypts made Marin feel like Marin. Their aroma takes me back to my formative camping trips in the Bay Area, said one Marinite. Those trees sustained me during postpartum depression, said another. *The eucalyptus trees are landmarks like the cable cars of San Francisco. They're part of California heritage.* The depth of opposition took federal land managers by surprise. Barraged with negative comments, including opposition from the county board of supervisors, the Park Service relented. It scaled back its restoration project to a single demonstration site.[9]

The GOGA proposal coincided with a controversial removal program initiated by a different government agency, the California Department of Parks and Recreation (DPR). In 1984 voters approved a state bond that earmarked $5 million for the Natural Heritage Stewardship Program, which allowed the DPR to finally start implementing two resource management directives from 1979: "Exotic plant species capable of naturalizing . . . should be replaced by natives," and "aggressively invading exotic vegetation will be systematically removed." Having designated *Eucalyptus* as an aggressive, noxious, and exotic invader, the agency chose Annadel State Park in Sonoma County as a test site. When the removal process—downing the trees and applying herbicide to the hydralike stumps—proved effective on nearly 100 acres, the DPR moved on to two densely vegetated park units, Montaña de Oro and Angel Island.

In both places, the state encountered support as well as opposition. In San Luis Obispo County, some locals indicated they would rather see tall trees than native coastal scrub at Montaña de Oro, a former blue gum plantation. Fiscal conservatives argued that it would be a better use of tax dollars to improve visitor facilities than to tear down groves. Some called the canopy sacred; others countered that eucalypts were monstrous, evil-smelling weeds. In response, one letter writer said, "Would you also send home the nation's immigrants?

Please, let's stop using labels like 'introduced exotic' and 'noxious weed'—or for that matter 'nigger,' 'honky,' 'wop' or 'wetback'—as an excuse to loose destruction and violence on the planet. It is in our own best interest to save these trees. They have much to teach us in the way of peace."[10]

The plan for Angel Island stirred up much more divisiveness, despite being a showcase project for ecological restoration and land stewardship. The largest island in San Francisco Bay—a miniature mountain topping out at 788 feet—Angel Island is visible to millions of residents and commuters in multiple counties. Accessible by ferry, the island has become a popular destination for hiking, camping, and historic tourism since joining the state park system in 1958. Previously it hosted a variety of military and security installations. In the Civil War era, the U.S. Army established a camp on the island, which later became a fort. For shade and wind protection, soldiers planted some 23 acres with blue gum, which grew to 86 acres (13 percent of the island) by the 1980s. Branches obscured the panoramic view of the Golden Gate. Dave Boyd, the presiding state ecologist, told a reporter that the site looked like a "trashed-out mess" when it should be an "island of naturalness." DPR's management plan called for the restoration of the "natural" landscape that had existed before European contact.[11]

Hundreds submitted comments to the agency. Their message: *Don't nuke the eucs!* A Marin County opposition group, Preserve Our Eucalyptus Trees (POET), accused the DPR of prejudice, phobia, "speciesism," and "plant racism." The group's cofounder noted that "eucalyptus has been in California for 100 or more years, and many of us regard them as a natural part of the state's landscape." Other pro-euc partisans argued that vehicle tracks from the "tree mining" would cause erosion and that the use of herbicide would delay the succession of other vegetation, exacerbating the erosion. Blue gums enhanced the recreational resource, benefited deer (another species introduced by the army), and helped ameliorate the greenhouse effect and even repair the ozone layer. Tree huggers felt particularly offended that the "Deforest Service" had contracted to sell the felled gums to a pulp mill; it smacked of commercial logging. The state countered that it was being fiscally responsible. Nonetheless, the San Francisco Board of Supervisors passed a resolution calling for the immediate cessation of "clear-cutting," and legislators questioned the DPR director. A local columnist with the Hearst Corporation spared no defaming label: state ecologists were "purists," "zealots," "cultists," and "Luddites" who would "mutilate" and "slaughter" beautiful trees and replace them with "scruffy" native plants in a quixotic effort to "time-freeze" nature at some arbitrary point in the past. At the eleventh hour, POET and other plaintiffs succeeded in obtaining an injunction that forced the state to conduct a new environmental review. Most mainstream environmentalists supported the removal plan; the Sierra Club even condoned the use of the reviled herbicide Roundup. One advocate wrote that it seemed "mind boggling that such a sensible project should be delayed—almost as though a Committee to Save the Rabbit might have prevailed in Australia in the 19th Century."[12]

The final plan, approved with minimal fuss in 1990, mandated the preservation of 6 acres of "historically significant" gums near the old army barracks. This local compromise illustrated three important statewide developments. First, land management opinion about eucalyptus had changed overwhelmingly to the negative. Second, a large share of the public still valued the trees, and a vocal minority would fight for them. Third, certain stands of nonnative gums were now sufficiently old to be eligible for "historic" or "heritage" status. As it happened, this middle ground on eucalyptus quickly eroded—or, more precisely, burned up. In the Bay Area, at least, it became harder to praise and easier to malign eucalyptus after 1991, the year that the Oakland-Berkeley firestorm anticipated in 1973 finally happened.

Various factors catalyzed the calamity. A freeze the previous December caused widespread dieback and limb fall. The rains fell lightly: the fourth dry winter in a row. Summer brought nothing but sunshine. Then October rolled around with record high temperatures and abnormally low humidity. Residents of the hills, a mix of hippies, professors, and white-collar professionals, stayed cool only because their homes were swallowed up in vegetation, a mixture of garden plantings and naturalized Monterey pines and eucs. Most of the shacks, bungalows, and mansions featured wooden sides, wood shake roofs, and redwood decks. Only two access roads, narrow, winding, and steep, led in and out of the neighborhood. Wildlife roamed throughout this exurban paradise of wood.

What is now officially known as the Tunnel Fire began on Saturday, October 19, as a minor grass burn near Grizzly Peak above Berkeley. By nightfall, the 35-acre fire had been contained and local firefighters had gone home. All night long, embers smoldered under the surface. A Sunday morning fire crew returned to the site to mop up the hot spots, but they got there too late, at not quite 9:00 A.M. By 11:00 the Diablo winds started howling from the east, and by 11:45 the grass burn had metastasized into a forest firestorm. In a matter of minutes, the flames leaped 2,000 feet across Highway 24 (over the Caldecott Tunnel) to reach the Oakland section of the hills. Extremely hot fires create thermal convection columns, atmospheric pillars of supercharged gas. Sometimes a column turns into a fiery tornado, but here in the hills, the Diablo winds produced a different effect. With sustained speeds at 20 mph and gusts much higher, they turned the convection column on its side and pushed it forward and downward. The result was like a blow-dryer combined with a flame-thrower, or even a heat ray gun. The windborne heat stream primed the vegetation for ignition and in some cases caused it to combust spontaneously. As the blaze jumped from canopy to canopy, oil-rich eucalypts exploded, projecting brands into the air.

Most of the fatalities happened between 11:30 and 12:00, when hundreds of homeowners attempted to leave at once; they clogged the narrow access roads with cars and collided in the smoke. At half past noon the backpedaling Oakland Fire Department desperately called San Francisco for help. By evening a combined force of 1,500 firemen from 440 engine companies battled the blaze. Breakdowns in radio communication as well as leadership hurt the coordination. Many citizen volunteers, young men with no more protection than T-shirts, carried equipment and grappled with water hoses. The emergency work suffered from low water pressure, depleted water supply, and nonstandard threaded connections on local fire hydrants that required special coupling adapters.

Firemen made their stand at the historic Claremont Hotel at the base of the Berkeley Hills. This magnificent white structure—another legacy of the real estate developer Frank Havens, the man responsible for the gum plantations—is one of the tallest wooden-frame buildings in America. Firefighters wanted to preserve the five-story Mediterranean-style palace, but even more they wanted to prevent the wooden building from transmitting the inferno to Berkeley proper. They saved the hotel, but they didn't curtail the fire. Nature did. Around sunset, the balance between inland high pressure and ocean low pressure shifted, and the wind abruptly reversed direction. A cool, moist, onshore breeze blew in through the Golden Gate. By Monday morning the last of the flames died out.

Now the grim calculations of coroners and actuaries began. The one-day weekend fire consumed 25 lives, more than 2,500 single-family dwellings, and almost 450 apartment units, leaving some 5,000 people homeless. Roughly 2,000 cars had melted on the street. All the residential landmarks were gone; the neighborhood looked like central Europe in 1945. By presidential declaration, this high-end real estate became a federal disaster area. Damage claims totaled over $1.5 billion, making the Oakland-Berkeley firestorm the third most costly conflagration in U.S. history (behind Chicago in 1871 and San Francisco in 1906) as well as the deadliest wildfire in California history, even though it scorched only 1,520 acres. Coming almost exactly two years after the Loma Prieta earthquake, the disaster troubled an already shaken Bay Area populace.[13]

Everyone, it seemed, deserved part of the blame: firefighters, city officials, developers, homeowners. Litigation ensued. Nonhuman factors also contributed to the fire, but not all of them seemed blameworthy. Freezes, droughts, and dry downslope winds occur naturally in the East Bay. Not true of blue gum, which covered some 20 percent of the burned area and contributed an estimated 70 percent of the fuel load. While the leaves on the trees were relatively fire-resistant, the copious debris of leaves and bark, dry and oily, intensified the fire. Blue gum produces much more litter than California bay and coast live oak, the two native species that fill the same ecological niche. While gums hardly caused the catastrophe, they certainly made it worse. And of the manifold contributing factors, they could be blamed most conveniently because they seemed less natural, and thus more culpable, than climatic factors. The nonnative annual grasses that covered the treeless parts of the hills—plants that burned more easily than the former native perennial grasses—also magnified the fire, but it's easier to demonize trees than grasses. And unlike people, trees can't talk back, or sue. After the smoke cleared, the discourse about the Bay Area's eucalypts quickly assimilated the language of violence and hazard: blue gums were ticking time bombs with leaves like oil-soaked rags. Oakland firefighters disparaged them as gasoline trees, giant matchsticks, green charcoal. After the Tunnel Fire, local newspapers portrayed eucalypts as murderous and villainous, the story of the California Dream gone awry. In *Why Things Bite Back*, a book about the unintended negative consequences of technological solutions, the science journalist Edward Tenner singled out the story of gum trees in California as a perfect example of the "revenge effect."[14]

TREE HAZARDS

The burning of the Berkeley Hills was one sign of many that the Golden State's eucalypts may have outlived their welcome. In the Southland, gums planted during the craze of the 1870s and the boom of the early twentieth century reached a difficult stage in their life cycle. Older trees are more susceptible to various ailments, including rot, structural collapse, and infestation; old ones stressed from prolonged drought are especially vulnerable to insect attack. *Eucalyptus* in California managed to survive several dry periods in the twentieth century—1929–1934, 1947–1950, 1959–1961, and 1976–77—without major damage only because its herbivorous enemies remained quarantined on the island continent. This position of containment eroded rapidly in the 1980s and 1990s, when, for reasons that remain mysterious, about a dozen Australasian euc-eating insects appeared in western North America in rapid succession. The worst infestation coincided with a new cycle of drought in 1987–1992.

The eucalyptus longhorned borer (ELB) is a 1-inch flying beetle with exceptionally long antennae—longer than the body itself. Members of this species get aroused by the pheromones released into the air by water-stressed eucalypts. A female will, after mating, deposit up to three hundred eggs in batches under exfoliating bark or within cracks in the trunk. Once hatched, the larvae bore into the inner bark and gorge on the phloem and xylem, the layers that transmit fluids throughout the tree. After pupation, beetles emerge as adults from the afflicted plant and fly in the night up to several miles in search of a new host. They leave the previous host riddled with larval galleries, or even girdled from the inside.

A nuisance in Australia, ELB became a pestilence in Southern California, where the statewide drought hit hardest. Presented with ample food and mild weather, the beetles could produce three generations in a single year. ELB struck first in 1984 at Lake Forest, a former eucalyptus plantation in Orange County that had been converted into a master-planned tree community, complete with a municipal seal adorned with eucalypts. Within twenty-one months, the tiny herbivores colonized every Southland county; firewood sales hastened dispersal. Canopied communities in Orange County and San Diego County implored the powerful California Department of Food and Agriculture for assistance. Unmoved by the aesthetic threat posed by the borers (and preoccupied with a medfly invasion that affected the citrus industry and a glassy-winged sharpshooter invasion that affected the wine industry), the CDFA did not commit any funds.

Help came instead from the entomology laboratory at UC Riverside. University scientists traveled to Victoria, Australia, to learn about three species of parasitoid wasps, one that preys on ELB in its egg stage and two that prey on its larvae. Parasitoids are different from parasites. A parasitic organism merely drains the life force from another organism; the draining may lead to the death of the host, but that outcome is not in the interest of the attached parasite. By contrast, a parasitoidal organism must kill its host in order to effect its reproductive strategy (like the titular creature of the *Alien* film series). For example, *Syngaster lepidus* is a tiny wasp with an amazingly long and tough ovipositor. Using this egg-depositing stinger, a female wasp pierces eucalyptus bark in search of a beetle larva, which it paralyzes and fills with its eggs; when they hatch, the larvae devour the host from the inside. With USDA approval and with the help of Australian entomologists, UCR scientists imported members of *S. lepidus* in 1987–88.

Captive breeding of any kind is slow and difficult, and even more so with insufficient funding. To complete its biological control program, UCR relied on some unlikely donors. Caltrans kicked in $50,000—a small amount compared to the potential cost of removing thousands of dead gums from state highways. Another $20,000 came from the board of directors of the Rancho Santa Fe Association (whose official stationery features an image of a eucalypt), with the understanding that the municipality would be the first release site. Roughly 20 percent of the 100,000 gums in Rancho Santa Fe had been infested. Homeowners described eucalyptus as the heart and soul of the community, part and parcel of the identity of the ranch. Residents felt unnerved by the constant clicking of millions of mandibles chewing on cambium, a collective sound likened to gentle rain, a muffled choir of crickets, or the crackle of Rice Krispies in milk. By the mid-1990s, release of three kinds of parasitoid wasps put down the local infestation, but not before ELB alighted in northern California, doing particular damage to the canopies at Stanford University and Mills College. Stanford president Donald Kennedy, a noted biologist, included a beetle specimen in a time capsule buried in the Inner Quad for the university's centennial in 1991.

No one knows how ELB made its way to western North America. Its arrival was probably just one more consequence of globalization— in this case, increased cargo shipping and increased nonstop air travel across the Pacific. California newspapers speculated that the "immigrant" insect "hitchhiked" or "smuggled itself" in eucalyptus-wood crates bound for the ports of Los Angeles and Long Beach. In 1986 a forester with the San Francisco Recreation & Parks Department imagined a more sinister scenario as he braced for the borer's northward land migration. He feared that "avid eucalyptus haters" would hasten the invasion by deliberately transporting the insects. Other commentators raised the specter of "ecological zealots" and "tree terrorists."[15]

Such wild speculation seemed almost credible given the unprecedented introduction of other insects evolved to feed on eucalypts. In 1983, about the same time that ELB arrived, two types of sap-feeding psyllids made their appearance. Then, in the 1990s, at least ten other pests—a kind of ecological reunion—landed in quick succession: another boring beetle, five more psyllid species, a leaf-eating tortoise beetle, a leaf-eating snout beetle (weevil), and two kinds of wasps that chemically induce the growth of galls on eucalyptus leaves for use as larval shelters. Building on the success of the ELB control program, entomologists introduced various host-specific egg parasitoids to address the defoliating beetles and the first wave of psyllids. The second wave presented a greater challenge.[16]

Psyllids, sometimes called "jumping plant lice," are true bugs related to aphids and whiteflies. Insects of this type suck nutrients from the veins of leaves, thereby reducing the host plant's intake of photosynthetic energy. From the human perspective, the tiny pale bugs are less noticeable than their liquid excrement. Clear, thick, and sugary, this "honeydew" is collected by bees and eaten by ants, wasps, and people. The manna described in the Bible was probably some kind of sucrose-rich bug shit. Various Native Americans as well as Mormon pioneers collected "Indian honey" as a treat, or a last-resort calorie source. Australian Aborigines historically used psyllid honeydew as sugar.

On the island continent, certain psyllids have evolved to put their sweet waste to productive use: they build conical shelters on the underside of leaves to protect themselves in the nymph stage. Safe inside their protective domes, the psyllids eat with relative impunity. Entomologists, borrowing from the Aboriginal language, refer to these encrustations as *lerps*. The presence of numerous lerps can compromise a leaf's photosynthetic ability. They can also add enough weight to cause a leaf to fall, prompting growth of a tender new shoot, an even more appetizing meal for the insects. If a beleaguered leaf manages to survive, emptied-out lerps will eventually fall off by themselves like stray strings of cotton candy. The ground beneath a lerp-covered euc becomes a sticky white mess. In urban settings, lerps can become a major nuisance, dropping goo on sidewalks and vehicles. Pedestrians unavoidably track leaf-fall into buildings.

Unlike ELB, psyllids are mainly monophagous: they prefer one species for food. California is now home to blue gum psyllid, lemon gum psyllid, spotted gum lerp psyllid, and so on—a primitive neo-Australian food web. But the most damaging species, red gum lerp psyllid, has proven to be quite omnivorous, feeding on almost thirty species of *Eucalyptus*. It does, however, greatly favor river red gum, and to a lesser extent flooded gum. Specimens of these species are concentrated in the Central Valley and Southern California. Not counting Stanford University, the Bay Area, dominated by blue gum, largely avoided the lerp outbreak of the late 1990s.

Euc haters, concentrated around San Francisco Bay, viewed the Southland infestations as nature's poetic justice, a just reward for nonnative fire-prone trees that had outstayed their welcome. This "anti-immigrant" discourse did not resonate as much in Southern

California, where eucalypts tended to be street trees and urban park trees rather than urban-proximate naturalized forests. "We're not natives either," grumbled San Diego County's chief entomologist in defense of the county's signature tree genus.[17] Perhaps 40 percent of San Diego's eucalypts were river red gums; the figure reached 80 percent in Rancho Santa Fe. A little to the north, in Orange County, Lake Forest alone contained some 33,000 river red gums, a third of which became infested. In Los Angeles, more than 5,000 city-owned gums had to be removed. For travelers, the psyllid damage appeared most evident on U.S. 101 between Santa Barbara and Santa Maria, where Caltrans eventually cut down hundreds of sick trees that overhung the road, and along the I-10 corridor between Fontana and Redlands, where scores of evergreens, after multiple successive defoliations, became leafless skeletons that exposed motorists to the ugliness of warehouse rows.

By overlapping in time, the borer and psyllid infestations bedeviled the human response. The best defense against borers—constant watering to increase sap production so as to drown out the larvae—made the trees more inviting to sap-loving psyllids. Los Angeles tried pesticide sprays, and Lake Forest resorted to poison injections. But the greatest hope lay with biological control. After an unsuccessful experiment with 1.5 million ladybugs, Los Angeles committed research funds to UC Berkeley's Center for Biological Control. The lead scientist, the entomology professor Donald Dahlsten, felt gratified to provide an alternative to pesticides but sounded ambivalent about the life-forms he worked to save. "People plant things where they don't belong," he said. "Planting eucalyptuses in California was a mistake. We continue to suffer from that mistake." In 1999 Dahlsten brought back from Australia some "mummified" red gum lerp psyllids, insects that had already been colonized by various unknown parasitoids. When the organisms hatched, Dahlsten had eight species of parasitoid wasps on his hands. Two were actually *hyper*parasitoids—wasps that fed on wasps that fed on psyllids. Captive breeding identified one species (*Psyllaephagus bliteus*) that preys exclusively on red gum lerps. After a long, frustrating effort to get the males and females to mate, Dahlsten's team released some 50,000 wasps at dozens of sites between 2000 and 2004. Once again, wealthy Rancho Santa Fe arranged to be first in line. Temporarily, California repelled the red gum psyllid "invasion" and redirected its offensive in the "bug war" to lemon gum psyllid.[18]

There are limits to biological control. Today only four of the sixteen euc-feeding insects in California have been abated. Practically every leaf on every blue gum and river red gum in the state now bears injuries from insects. California's eucalypts will never regain the amazing health they possessed between the 1850s and the 1980s. The UC Riverside entomologist Timothy Paine, Dahlsten's intellectual successor, has come to the debatable conclusion that one or more ecosaboteurs must have inaugurated the new ecological regime through deliberate introductions. He works to ameliorate the damage of nonnative insects even though he understands the critique against nonnative plants. In 2012 Paine told a reporter, "Is it worth allowing millions of trees to die because there is the potential that some of them can be a pest?"[19]

In city halls and administrative offices, the managers of California's cities aren't interested in such bioethical debates. Instead they are concerned with budgets. The recent outbreaks of insects prompted many cities to conduct comprehensive tree surveys to evaluate the health of their eucalypts. In the process, city arborists discovered many insect-free eucs that suffered from other problems, including root rot and structural instability. Prudence prompted their removal.

Prudence is another word for liability. In recent decades, a series of well-publicized accidents in Southern California has helped to create an impression that gums present a public safety risk. Whereas some northern Californians worry about eucalyptic forests catching fire, worrywart Southlanders imagine individual eucs crashing down on them. In 1977 a young girl died at the Los Angeles County Arboretum when a tree in the Australian Garden collapsed. The parents filed a wrongful death suit and settled out of court for $1.6 million.

A similar event occurred at the San Diego Zoo in 1983. When a falling branch killed a four-year-old girl at a Highland Park grade school in 1990, the Los Angeles Unified School District rushed to prune all its estimated 750 eucalypts. In 2001 UCLA ignored student objections and knocked down some of Westwood's oldest and largest trees—gums at the main entrance planted by the Daughters of the American Revolution in honor of U.S. presidents. One of the giants had collapsed on a car the previous year. UC officials knew that Pomona College in Claremont had faced lawsuits after two students in a vehicle died when a campus eucalypt fell across a road in 1998. In 2003 a woman walking her dog in San Diego's Old Town died when a 90-foot gum toppled in a windstorm. In 2011 a minor earthquake hit coastal Orange County; hours later, a 10-ton, 50-foot-high blue gum, already weakened by boring insects and root rot, crushed a Hyundai in Costa Mesa, killing the driver. Within days, city contractors chainsawed the other 104 "killer trees" in the street's median row and arborists initiated a full-scale inspection of the city's gums.[20]

Local media often responded to accidents with sensationalism. One San Diego columnist described eucalypts as "land mines" and "deadly aliens." Resorting to a hoary botanical metaphor, he suggested that native oaks never fall over because their sturdy roots reach deep into soil whereas immigrant trees have shallow roots. A freelance arborist in San Diego who moonlighted as an expert witness for personal injury and wrongful death lawsuits echoed this sentiment. Of approximately 150 court cases on his résumé, the great majority involved eucalypts. "The trees are from Australia," he explained. "They're used to struggling and reaching out with their roots under very adverse conditions, to explore the soil." But here in urban California, he said, the sprinklers run constantly, and the "lazy" roots grow shallow and weak. The top-heavy plants become "death traps" and "widowmakers."[21]

Are gums inherently more hazardous than other large trees? Probably not. Every tree in the world will eventually undergo structural failure, provided something doesn't kill it first. Any tree can be eaten by beetles, weakened by fungus, stressed by drought, buffeted by wind. Members of many species drop branches out of the blue. "In periods of hot dry stillness large limbs suddenly give way, with an explosive report, in the crowns of Eucalyptus trees," wrote the botanist Willis Jepson in 1945. He was sleeping under gums at his family ranch near Vacaville and escaped death in the night when a solid 12-foot branch broke off "like a rifle shot" and fell some 100 feet to a spot near his bedroll. "Summer branch drop" is a recognized, if poorly understood, arboreal phenomenon, but it is hardly unique to eucalyptus. California's oaks fail in large numbers, too, and failures of Monterey pine have spiked in recent years because of the effects of pine pitch canker (a fungal disease).[22]

Nonetheless, people interpret tree failure differently for different species. Hazard—meaning the potential failure of an engineered system—is a cultural and legal concept, not a botanical one. When a naturally occurring native oak collapses onto a bicyclist, it can be legally categorized as an act of God. When a nonnative eucalyptus does the same thing, it can be construed as a liable offense, because the tree wouldn't be there unless humans played god. And since Californians planted a large percentage of the state's eucs at roughly the same time, the arboreal age distribution, and thus the hazard, is now top-heavy. In other words, this cohort of California gums, now in its sunset years, may currently be disproportionately more hazardous than other trees. For fear of personal injury lawyers, many cities have removed older eucalypts from parks and schoolyards. Simi Valley performed a comprehensive survey of its gums in 1999 and identified about half of the three hundred as hazards. The city then set about cutting them—not because they were imminent or catastrophic threats but because the very act of identifying hazard created liability. More recently, a Marin County homeowner fought a lawsuit from her neighbors over dozens of late-stage blue gums on her property—the remnants of a nineteenth-century plantation—that allegedly presented a grave and immediate hazard. On appeal, the case went to the state's second highest court. The appellate panel unanimously affirmed that the litigant's blue gums created nuisance and ruled moreover, without scientific evidence, that "the *species itself* is prone to failure and presents a fire hazard."[23]

The discourse about "killer eucs" with "shallow roots" has a counterdiscourse: old eucalypts as "heritage trees" that enhance "quality of life." In some towns—notably Burlingame, Camarillo, and Ramona—landscape preservationists rallied throughout the twentieth century to protect and prolong the life of the historic rows of gum trees that lined the main thoroughfares. These opposing positions—eucs as hazard and eucs as heritage—have caused friction in Santa Cruz, a city squeezed between the ocean and the coastal mountains. Santa Cruz resembles the Berkeley Hills in sociology (a blend of beach bums, university people, and millionaires), topography, and vegetation. Naturalized groves of blue gum envelop many Santa Cruz neighborhoods. According to the city's expansive Heritage Tree Ordinance, first passed in 1989, any plant is eligible for "heritage" status if a) it has historical significance; b) it has horticultural significance (for being beautiful, for being rare, for providing habitat); or c) it is big. By law, any tree with a diameter over 14 inches qualifies for protection. A blue gum can reach that size in less than two decades.

Thanks to the dendrophilic city government, a property owner in Santa Cruz who wants to fell or prune a large blue gum in his yard must first cut through red tape, starting with the application and processing fee. Then a certified inspector has to verify physically whether the tree meets "heritage" requirements. If the inspector decides to grant an exemption and issue a cutting permit, the property owner must agree to a mitigation plan, which may involve replanting an approved tree (after posting a refundable bond with the city), or planting a replacement at an approved municipal site, or making a sizable cash donation to the city's tree trust fund. If the property owner's proposed action affects more than three heritage trees, he or she must additionally pay for the consulting services of an approved arborist.

Stymied by the Heritage Tree Ordinance, one notable landowner lost his cool. After Santa Cruz repeatedly denied his application to remove blue gums from his property, Robert Sward, a former Guggenheim fellow and retired poetry professor, simply hired a chainsaw operator. Sward became a passionate critic of *E. globulus* after a specimen from his neighbor's yard almost crushed his wife in 1996. He wrote a funny-serious poem subtitled "The Tree That Destroyed California" that depicted blue gum as a toxic, flammable, waste-making plant from hell. He flouted the city ordinance—the "Hazardous Tree Ordinance," he called it—and disputed the resulting penalty. In town, some disapproving people called Sward a "plant Nazi." Turning that symbolism around, sympathizers referred to municipal officials as the "green Gestapo." The poet and the city finally resolved their feud in 2003. Sward's neighbors willingly (and legally) reduced the number of eucalypts on their wooded parcel, but the mitigation process turned out to be slow and expensive when officials determined that the not-so-old "heritage" trees sheltered a wildlife-rich riparian zone. To compound the irony, the life-sustaining streamlet below the nonnative plants derived from municipal runoff.[24]

Santa Cruz appears to be in the rear guard. Since the East Bay fire of 1991, more and more agencies and municipalities have reevaluated eucs in the negative and zoned against them. In Southern California, the 280,000-acre Cedar Fire—the largest fire yet in state history, the destroyer of hundreds of homes and fifteen lives in exurban San Diego County in October 2003—prompted fire departments to repeat a claim first heard in the Berkeley Hills: *Eucalyptus* equals menace. Crews removed three thousand trees from the Whittier Hills, east of Los Angeles, to reduce fuel load. Planning commissioners in Temecula, Riverside County, drafted a historic tree ordinance that categorically excluded eucalyptus. The newspaper in Pasadena, a city famous for its love of flowering plants, editorialized on the "dark side" of gums, trees that acted "like some kind of napalm" and "virtual bombs" in fires. News coverage in 2009 of the terrifying bush fires in Victoria, Australia, reinforced this attitude. One major insurance carrier began canceling the policies of California property owners with large eucs in fire-prone areas.[25]

And so, one by one, the Southland's great old gums succumbed to the deliberations of arborists, actuaries, and elected officials. The violent Santa Ana winds of December 2011, a dry windstorm that reached hurricane speed, uprooted hundreds more in one fell swoop. Los Angeles added a new word to its rich lexicon of urban calamity: *Arborgeddon*. Mike Davis, the Southland's resident scholar of disaster, gave a sound bite to the *Times*, warning of a "eucalyptus catastrophe" if California did not raze aged eucs by the thousands. In the immediate aftermath of the storm, the CEO of the L.A. County Arboretum saw opportunity amid the devastation: the Australian section could be replanted with more ecologically appropriate trees that would be "in harmony with Southern California." In 2012, another county-owned arboretum, Descanso Gardens, announced a "new vision" to grow native oaks on acreage cleared of eucalyptus. "We're interested in reclaiming a more natural feeling," the director of horticulture explained to the *Pasadena Star-News*. The reversal was complete. A century before, a distinguished Pasadena horticulturist had pronounced that eucalypts "harmonize so well with the landscape that it is hard to realize that they are of man's planting, not Nature's."[26]

CALIFORNIA NATIVE PLANTS

Most mainstream environmentalists in California now despise gums as flora non grata. Their preference for autochthonous plants trumps their veneration of trees. Vanguard groups such as the California Native Plant Society (1965) worked to increase appreciation and protection of endemic species; later bioregionalists focused on the eradication of weeds, the nemesis of native plants. The first Exotic Pest Plant Council formed in Florida in 1985, and the California chapter—since renamed the California Invasive Plant Council—followed a few years later. In 1996 the council issued the first edition of its "weed list," an inventory of nonnative plants considered ecological threats. By this point, environmentalists had enlarged their conception of "weed" to include shrubs and trees. Tasmanian blue gum made the grade.

In a major story for the magazine *Audubon* in 2002, the environmental journalist Ted Williams called *E. globulus* "America's largest weed." He described a naturalized blue gum forest as a life-killing, soul-killing place, the antithesis of biodiversity. According to him, only poison oak and English ivy survived beneath the trees' toxic fog drip. The canopy appeared to be a dead zone, too, except for hummingbirds, which favored the flowers at their peril. Unlike Australian nectar-feeders, California hummingbirds have short bills, which means they must move in close to reach the sticky flowers. Some tiny birds have been known to suffocate after getting a mouthful of "eucalyptus glue." The eggs and babies of hummingbirds were allegedly at risk as well, because the limbs of blue gums provided hazardous support for nests. Even worse, the bird-killing trees dewatered creeks, sucking away salmon habitat. Williams delivered this indictment list from Bolinas, a self-consciously artsy, earthy village in coastal Marin County, where a "euc war" pitted residents against municipal officials who planned to remove blue gums from the sewage disposal area to reduce the fire danger. Using an effective rhetorical strategy, Williams paired reasonable words from an ornithologist, an arborist, and an ecologist with nutty comments from selected Marin tree huggers, some of whom had been married or given birth under blue gums. These Marinites decried the plant Nazis for their proposed genocide or ethnic cleansing of their old-growth sacred groves.[27]

Native-plant enthusiasts like Williams tend to downplay the true range of scientific opinion about *E. globulus* in California. In truth, the species is not all bad for wildlife. For avians, at least, blue gums seem to be a net gain, especially in urban and urban-proximate settings. The trees provide some of the best available nesting in oceanside cities such as Santa Cruz and bayside cities such as Palo Alto. Colonial waterbirds such as great blue heron, great egret, and double-crested cormorant build within the complex limb structure of mature blue gums. Similarly, old windrows of eucalyptus provide an important nesting habitat for great horned owl and red-tailed hawk. Not all birds benefit, though. From the point of view of acorn-eating and cavity-dwelling birds, blue gum is a worthless substitute for coast live oak. To the extent that gums have invaded hillside oak woodlands and deciduous riparian zones, they have displaced preexisting bird habitats. More often, however, gums have gone wild where oaks were already felled or where native trees never grew. In various forms—isolated rows, contained groves, low-density forests—blue gums can actually enhance avian life by providing new food sources for nectarivorous birds and, more recently, insectivorous birds. An ecological study conducted near Santa Cruz demonstrated that native warblers and kinglets have learned to feed on lerp psyllids.[28]

From an ecological (and fire safety) standpoint, blue gum is most problematic in California when monocultural plantations have grown into extensive high-density closed-canopy forests. Fortunately, this problem is restricted to relatively few locations in the fog belt. And even here, the eucalyptic thickets are hardly allelopathic wastelands. In the hills above Berkeley, a university ecologist has compared an oak woodland to a blue gum grove in the same locale. To determine species richness (number of species present), the scientist took leaf-litter samples, set rodent traps, and conducted a bird inventory. His results contradicted conventional wisdom. While gums do limit growth of understory plants (particularly annuals), they don't inhibit animal life. The dead-looking leaf litter actually teems with life: the folds and cavities create a mosaic of microhabitats. Roughly speaking, the two woodland types have equivalent species richness, though each has one outlier category: oaks support more rodents, eucs support more subsurface invertebrates. The nonnative blue gum forest is not life-killing; it is simply composed differently from a native woodland. Should it therefore be judged on its own merits? "A community has developed around these naturalized citizens, and they deserve credit, too," offered one scientist, noting that blue gums in California benefit amphibians, the most threatened class of life on earth. "At some point in our history, we all come from another place," he continued.

"These trees have been here long enough to be recognized as citizens of the area."[29]

People who dare to defend California eucalypts with ecological desiderata have one charismatic ally: the monarch butterfly. Seven states have designated this orange-and-black beauty as their state insect or state butterfly; by that measure, only the honeybee is more popular. The delicate-looking monarch is in fact phenomenally tough, the only insect that annually travels vast distances like migratory birds—up to 2,000 miles. There is a crucial difference, however. Unlike an individual Canada goose, which may make the same grand circuit many times in a lifetime, each monarch inevitably dies before the journey is complete. Astoundingly, the North American migration occurs in stages over multiple generations. Through some combination of stimuli from temperature, light, and magnetism, millions of monarch progeny find their way from summer milkweed habitat in northern temperate zones to winter tree habitat in subtropical zones. Once they alight in the late fall, monarchs enter a state of "diapause," a period of suspended sexual development and low activity. The insects require conditions not cold enough to freeze, not warm enough to enervate. Colonies of torpid butterflies hang together on leaves or branches, occasionally venturing out in bursts of color to look for nectar. Come February or March, a new generation of butterflies begins the epic flight back to the milkweed.

While monarchs are not imperiled by extinction (they have been introduced to various parts of the world, including Australia), the genetic pool of long-distance migrators faces an uncertain future owing to habitat loss. For this reason, monarch advocates have proposed a new protective category: "threatened phenomenon." Only two main overwintering areas for the monarchs exist—central Mexico's forested volcanic highlands and coastal California's eucalyptus belt. The montane destination is highly concentrated, whereas the maritime habitat consists of hundreds of scattered roosts, some permanent, others temporary, from Mendocino in the north to Ensenada in the south. The maritime population is smaller and probably less itinerant; many of the butterflies never leave California. The relationship between the two migratory streams remains unclear; the conventional thinking that the Rockies divide the butterflies into separate "western" and "eastern" populations may not be true. It has even been suggested that the annual monarch migration to Mexico is a recent adaptation that accompanied a population explosion that followed the enlargement of open-ground milkweed habitat in eastern North America because of deforestation caused by American settlement.[30]

Historical records about California's monarchs in the period before eucalypts are nonexistent. Presumably the introduction of gums benefited the population by extending its habitat. Of native trees, Monterey pine and Monterey cypress originally provided the best roosts, but those species had an extremely limited natural range. The third main native host, coast redwood, did not occur naturally south of Big Sur and disappeared from many coastal canyons as a result of logging. From the monarchs' point of view, the simultaneous introduction of *Eucalyptus* was a fortunate coincidence. Unlike pines, cypresses, and redwoods, eucalypts sport flowers; better yet, they bloom in winter, when the travel-weary butterflies need nectar. Unlike California sycamore, the only native tree south of Big Sur that might have hosted colonies, gums keep their leaves year-round, providing better sites for attachment and protection.

Over the twentieth century, several California cities established traditions around the annual monarch migration. Pacific Grove, "Butterfly Town, U.S.A.," staged a yearly parade (with children dressed up in wings) and established a tax-supported monarch grove sanctuary. City code authorizes a $1,000 fine for anyone caught in the act of "butterfly molestation." Coastal state parks—notably Pismo State Beach and Natural Bridges State Beach—once boasted eucalyptus groves with even larger monarch populations. But in the opening years of the new millennium, Santa Cruz's yearly Welcome Back Monarchs Day at Natural Bridges attracted fewer and fewer butterflies. A combination of drought, herbicide use, and habitat loss probably accounts for the decline. There seems to be less milkweed growing in coastal

California. To make things worse, many of Natural Bridges' large eucs fell down after the Monterey pines that sheltered them became sick with pitch canker. Prohibited by state policy from planting nonnative species, rangers have added Monterey cypresses as windbreaks for surviving gums.

The greater number of butterfly groves are privately owned. Some have been developed, others spared thanks to easements. Conservation on the coast does not come cheap. It took two cooperating land trusts drawing $20 million from various sources, including individuals, foundations, federal grants, state grants, and a statewide bond initiative that specifically earmarked funds for monarch habitat, to save Ellwood Mesa, a 127-acre relict of Ellwood Cooper's horticultural operation near Santa Barbara. Meanwhile, a large portion of Nipomo Mesa, the old haunt of euc-booster Theodore Lukens, morphed into a "resort-lifestyle community" called the Woodlands. Although the developer destroyed thousands of trees, he advertised the preservation of a 20-acre remnant as a butterfly preserve.

Monarchs get most of the attention, but they are hardly the only lepidopterans affected by California's changing biodiversity. Many butterflies have adapted to anthropogenic influence by switching from native to nonnative host plants. According to an expert at UC Davis, fourteen of thirty-two local species rely entirely on nonnatives. "If we were to remove all alien plants, we would lose 40 percent of the butterfly species in Davis," he says.[31] "Butterfly gardeners" in the Golden State would be wrong to assume that native flowers bring the best results. At the same time, certain introduced plants, including the same flowering gums that help monarchs, do in fact hurt native butterflies. In the Bay Area, three endangered insects fit in this category: callippe silverspot, San Bruno elfin, and mission blue. None are large, spectacular, or well known like the monarch. Each species relies on a unique host plant for laying eggs and raising young. Their habitat—native grassland and coastal scrub—has been severely compromised by development and vegetative invasion.

The future of this lepidopterous trio is tied to San Bruno Mountain, the massif that separates the city of San Francisco from the rest of the peninsula. This isolated uplift, 1,314 feet high, the northernmost extension of the Santa Cruz Mountains, has become even more of an ecological island now that cities completely encircle it. Houses and eucalypts infringe on some of its steep slopes, too. The summit, a 4-mile-long east-west ridge, remains undeveloped except for an antenna complex. It could have turned out differently. In the 1960s conservationists fought off pro-growth forces that wanted to shave off the summit to obtain fill for an expansion of San Francisco International Airport. Then, in the 1970s, much of the privately owned mountain was slated for residential and commercial expansion. After battling the developer, San Mateo County agreed to approve the project in exchange for other land. The deal broke down in 1976 when the U.S. Fish and Wildlife Service listed the mission blue butterfly as endangered. Using the expansive powers of the Endangered Species Act (1973), the federal government could have shut down all development. Instead, the interested parties crafted a compromise— something called a "habitat conservation plan" (HCP). As allowed by Congress in 1982, this exemption to the Endangered Species Act permitted the "incidental taking" of critical habitat even as it set aside the larger portion (81 percent) of the 3,000-acre mountain as a park to be jointly managed by the county and the state. Private landowners on the mountain would be required to pay a small annual mitigation fee toward a species recovery program administered by a third party—in this case, an environmental consulting firm in Palo Alto.

The first permit of its kind, the San Bruno Mountain HCP became the model for endangered species conflict resolution throughout the nation. Like most prototypes, this one had flaws. Some of the best butterfly breeding grounds were sacrificed outright to housing. Moreover, the protected acreage did not automatically provide good habitat for mission blues. By the 1980s, nonnative plant species had largely crowded out the deciduous perennials required by the tiny butterfly. In reality, then, habitat conservation required habitat creation.

One such project began with the removal of 63 acres of Tasmanian

blue gum, a naturalized grove that lined Guadalupe Canyon Parkway, the winding connector between Daly City and Brisbane, along
the northern flank of the mountain. In 1995, with the blessing of local
officials and environmentalists, workers began clear-cutting. "We
don't call it logging," said one overseer. "It's habitat restoration activity." A Sierra timber company did the job for free in exchange for the
logs, which it sold to Japanese pulp mills. Accustomed to regulations
that restricted timbering, a chainsaw operator marveled at the situation: "You can't hardly cut down a tree in the forest anymore without
getting arrested." He spoke too soon. The sight of the slash operation
turned many local supporters into opponents. These eucalypts "are as
native as you and I," said one letter to the editor. The author referenced the Vietnam War trauma of My Lai: *We had to destroy it to save
it.* Others likened the scene to post-eruption Mount St. Helens. After
the city of Brisbane filed for a restraining order, park officials agreed
to set aside 15 acres of blue gum near the entrance for aesthetics.[32]

For restorationists, cutting eucalyptus is the easy part. The next
step, making a coastal prairie, requires a continuing budget line and a
dedicated workforce. Native plants do not perforce spring up to succeed the trees. People must tend the old-new habitat. That's because
nonindigenous vegetation such as gorse, broom, blackberry, and ivy
now dominates lowland temperate California, particularly its relict
grasslands. Once established, these invasive ground-cover plants are
much harder to remove than blue gums. Fire helps. Not only does
wildfire keep down invasive ground cover, it promotes the growth of
the mission blue's host plants. In historic times, when *ranchos* instead
of condos covered the peninsular hills, the butterflies could always
find some ground where recent flames had created prime habitat for
early succession species like lupines. Their natural haunt has now
shrunk to San Bruno Mountain, Twin Peaks, and the Marin Headlands. The presence of new houses on San Bruno makes fire management challenging. In 2003 a controlled burn went out of control and
came within 150 feet of a neighborhood. At the end of the HCP's
initial thirty-year permit, the mission blue population remained

endangered. The underfunded mitigation program accepts weekend volunteer workers who literally garden in the nature preserve: they uproot weeds and plant lupines by hand.[33]

Angel Island has likewise experienced the uncertainty of grassland restoration. The first phase of gum removal occurred in 1990 using helicopter logging, a low-impact but very expensive method. Budgetary constraints delayed the second, larger phase until 1995–1997. This time California State Parks used conventional logging skidders. To stack the mess of slash for burning, rangers borrowed inmates from nearby San Quentin Prison. Predictably, the project's aesthetic effects elicited a new round of complaints about "ethnic cleansing." A letter writer from Berkeley claimed that Angel Island was being "reduced to a semi-arid desert with large swaths abandoned to scrappy 'native vegetation'—environmentalist buzz-words cynically invoked to subdue those plagued with post-colonialist guilt and/or Anglo-Saxon self-loathing." In truth, the native vegetation proved to be insufficiently scrappy. At phase one sites, nonnative herbaceous plants invaded the logged acreage despite the addition of tens of thousands of container-grown native shrubs. Park rangers felt compelled to mow Italian thistle, burn French broom, and apply herbicide to ice plant (a transplant from South Africa). The one native species that performed well, coyote brush, performed *too* well, outcompeting other natives, lowering biodiversity. Early results at phase two sites brought more discouragement. Native grasses colonized first, but over the long, dry summer that followed, noxious nonnatives such as bull thistle expanded and dominated.[34]

The San Francisco metropolitan region ranks among the world's most fertile experiment grounds for ecological restoration. This gateway to the Pacific is important because it is a complicated hybrid landscape—natural and artificial, wild and cultivated, native and nonnative, populous and uncrowded. The Bay Area includes dense cities, sprawling suburbs, and low-density exurban developments alongside deep ocean waters, shallow bays, rivers, deltas, islands, hills, mountains, beaches, tidelands, forests, grasslands, and chaparral. In addition, San Francisco–Oakland–San Jose boasts the most ample greenbelt of any urban complex in the United States. The combination of intractable topography, progressive politics, and incredible wealth presented opportunities in the twentieth century to create a multiagency system of parks, wildlife refuges, and open-space preserves. Now land managers face difficult choices: When and where is it worth the effort to remove nonnative vegetation? After removal, do we want to create something new, or do we want to try to restore the land to a simulacrum of an earlier state? If so, which one? Before the Indians? The Spanish? The Americans? Before Tasmanian blue gum? Management questions become more vexing when the public feels emotional about the outcome. In urban-fringe places such as Don Edwards National Wildlife Refuge and the Peninsula Watershed of the San Francisco Public Utilities Commission, officials have quietly removed many blue gums, but in San Francisco proper, efforts to remove old trees have generated considerable controversy.[35]

One hot spot is the Presidio, a former Spanish, Mexican, and American military base that occupies the northwest corner of the peninsula near the Golden Gate Bridge. At 1,491 acres, the Presidio is slightly larger than Golden Gate Park, which itself is slightly larger than Central Park. Even before the U.S. Army decommissioned the base in 1994, San Franciscans viewed the Presidio as a de facto recreational ground. After coming close to selling it off, Congress transferred the property to the national park system as part of GOGA. However, the Republican majority dictated that the new Presidio must pay for itself and created a public corporation, the Presidio Trust, to oversee the property. Today the Presidio offers a mixture of residential, retail, commercial, and recreational space surrounded by historic sites and wildlife habitat. The trust has authorized the removal of hundreds of eucalypts, pines, and cypresses to open up view corridors and to foster native plant growth. At the same time, the trust is obligated by the Interior Department's "Guidelines for the Treatment of Cultural Landscapes" to sustain 300 acres of "historic forest" that recreate the look of the original windbreak planted by the army in the late nineteenth century. Sustaining means something different from preserving: blue gums are being replaced by visually similar species of *Eucalyptus* that are less messy and less invasive.[36]

Discord erupted in 2002 when a separate government agency got involved in the remaking of the Presidio. The U.S. Fish and Wild-life Service bears the responsibility for creating recovery plans for all federally listed endangered species. One such species is San Francisco lessingia, an unspectacular yellow flowering plant in the aster family that grows only in the sand dunes of San Francisco, a formerly broad habitat that has been almost entirely paved over. In 1996 the Park Service uncovered a 12-acre remnant of the dunes at Lobos Creek in the Presidio. The lessingia immediately made a localized comeback. Hoping to build on that success, the Fish and Wildlife Service proposed to extend the Lobos Creek dunes. The only thing standing in the way was a large group of blue gums that shaded a path frequented by joggers and dog walkers. An influential newspaper columnist immediately lambasted the recovery plan. He told San Franciscans that the government had designs to clear-cut a majestic century-old grove in order to bring back an ugly "weedlike" plant. What sounded better, sandstorms or leafy tranquillity? He characterized the issue as a battle between reasonable tree huggers and zealous "sand-huggers."[37]

In the public's mind, the federal restoration proposal at the dunes blurred with a separate restoration effort administered by the San Francisco Recreation and Parks Department, an agency that manages 3,500 acres in 230 parks and open-space preserves. In the late 1990s the department initiated its Natural Areas Program, which identified about 1,000 acres within thirty-two of its units as "natural." On these lands, the agency planned to remove nonnative trees—notably blue gum—and promote native vegetation. Unfortunately, poor PR and misinformed criticism initially created the impression that the greenery of Golden Gate Park would be clear-cut. In truth, less than 5 percent of the city's crown jewel had been rezoned. Even so, some neighborhood groups opposed any cuts anywhere; they wanted to "integrate" the blue gums instead of "exterminating" them. (And they didn't want to give up any place where they could take their dogs off leash.)

Across the bay, euc lovers accused the University of California of discrimination against immigrant trees. In 2004 UC Berkeley initiated an ambitious ten-year plan to remove some 25,000 eucalypts from its property as a fire prevention measure. Above campus, the flagship school owns 850 acres of slopes and canyons. "The forests and the wildlands around the campus are our equivalent of the New Orleans levees," said the manager of UC's Office of Emergency Preparedness. In Claremont Canyon, the removal of eucs revealed 250 coast redwoods planted by Rotarians in the 1970s. Student and neighborhood volunteers have since added hundreds of seedlings from the fire-resistant native species. The goal is to recreate one of the forested microhabitats that once existed in the shady glens of the East Bay hills. On the sun-exposed slopes, meanwhile, the university wants to take down all trees and bring back native shrubs and grasses. A clear-cutting plan got the green light in 2005 when UC won a grant from the Federal Emergency Management Agency, but it straightaway stalled owing to administrative obstacles: a few gum-dwelling endangered species and one obstreperous neighborhood association that demanded a "species neutral" rather than "eucaphobic" approach to fire control. The group compared gums in the hills to WMDs in Iraq—a minor threat exaggerated into a crisis by scaremongers. A contemporaneous proposal by UC San Francisco to reduce the tree cover on Mount Sutro ran into similar opposition.[38]

To fight the various federal, state, and municipal restoration programs, dendrophilic activists in the Bay Area used new social media; they created websites and blogs with names like Death of a Million Trees and Save Mount Sutro Forest. In 2002, after hearing from angry constituents, San Francisco supervisor Leland Yee introduced a pair of resolutions calling for greater public oversight of the city's official natural areas. The supervisor also wrote an editorial decrying the "xenophobia" of the program: "Plants and trees without the proper pre-*Mayflower* lineage are called 'invasive exotics' and are wrenched from the soil to die . . . How many of us are 'invasive exotics' who have taken root in the San Francisco soil, have thrived and flourished here, and now contribute to the diversity of the wonderful mix that constitutes present-day San Francisco?"[39] These comments had added rhetorical power coming from a Chinese-born politician who had immigrated to San Francisco, become a citizen, and adopted an English forename that recalled the famous California politician Leland Stanford (who, it should be said, pandered to the anti-Chinese sentiment of his period). At the same time, Yee's comments—like all the others about "veggie racism" and "biological nativism"—defied logic. Trees are not the same as people. Nonnative plants are not analogous to immigrants. Our socially and legally constructed differences of race, culture, ethnicity, and nationality have no parallel in other life-forms. Biologically, they are fictions.

INVASION OF THE NONNATIVES

Scientists deserve part of the blame for this rhetorical confusion, this conflation of social and ecological discourses. Academics representing conservation biology and a subdiscipline, invasion biology, have emphasized—and often exaggerated—the negative impacts of nonnative species. It is no coincidence that the negative public reappraisal of California eucalypts since 1991 concurred with a global environmental policy debate on "bioinvasion."

Although *invasion* and *invasiveness* are meant to be technical terms, biologists have struggled to define them with precision. *Invasion* builds on the older concepts "succession" and "colonization." An invader is a colonizing species that moves beyond its former range, spreading in spectacular fashion, resulting in ecological transformation. In other words, invasive species are outstanding in time and space: they alter things quickly and widely. Infamous faunal examples include European rabbit and cane toad in Australia, brown tree snake in Guam, and Nile perch in Lake Victoria. The most damaging invasions may be invisible: fungi can decimate forests and crops (consider the Irish potato famine); microbes such as West Nile virus and avian influenza can produce epidemics. Plants invade, too. Look no further than kudzu in the U.S. South.[40]

Nineteenth-century British biogeographers codified the basic language of biological invasion, and in doing so they borrowed from established legal terms: *native, denizen, colonist,* and *alien*. Although Victorian scientists did not place normative values on these taxonomic categories, the words retained political connotations. In Darwin's imperial-sounding formulation, the "immigration" of fit "colonists" could beat out less fit "aboriginal species." Invasion was intrinsic to natural selection. Darwin's friend and ally Sir Joseph Hooker spoke about the "invaded" regions of the globe where "Old England plants" had "asserted their supremacy over and displaced a certain number of natives of the soil," just like their "fellow-emigrants and fellow-colonists," the Anglo-Saxons.[41]

A century after Darwin, as the empire waned, a British biologist reconceptualized invasion as unnatural and unfair and deliberately repoliticized the language of biogeography. Charles Elton originally wrote *The Ecology of Invasions by Animals and Plants* (1958) as a series of BBC radio lectures. In popular style, Elton called attention to "exotic" species notorious in America, such as gypsy moth and chestnut blight fungus, and others destined for infamy, such as Dutch elm disease (another fungus). Elton's primary mode of speech was martial: the necessity of war against the advance guard of an aggressive enemy horde whose impact could explode like a nuclear bomb. During World War II, Elton had worked with the military to reduce populations of nonnative rodents that damaged Britain's food supply. In peacetime, too, Elton wanted to apply science to policy.

Elton came before and after his time. His practical approach resembled that of Progressive-era conservationists, who focused on the moral hazard of environmental mismanagement. Elton's postwar contemporaries in ecology instead favored theoretical research and neutral language, and they mainly ignored *The Ecology of Invasions*.

His brand of applied science went against the trend of professional-ization. But when the subfield of invasion biology dissociated from the larger field of ecology in the 1980s and 1990s, policy-minded scientists revived Elton's approach, commemorated him as a found-ing founder, canonized his book, and redeployed his militaristic met-aphors. To publicize the impacts of nonnative species and to draw attention to their new discipline, invasion biologists spoke of dan-gerous trespassers that needed to be barred at the gate or defeated in battle. They referred to nonnative species by the etymologically cor-rect but culturally loaded term *aliens*. With scientists from the United States, Britain, South Africa, Australia, and New Zealand pushing the agenda, the invasion of alien species moved to the forefront of global environmental consciousness. The International Council for Science's committee SCOPE (Scientific Committee on Problems of the Environment) created a special advisory group on biological invasions in 1983. Numerous international conferences followed. Two new professional journals appeared in the late 1990s, and the Union of Concerned Scientists added invasive species to its short list of core policy issues. Of ecological issues, only climate change received more scrutiny at the dawn of the new millennium.[42]

In this same period, scientists, conservationists, politicians, and the media embraced the concept of biological diversity (often shortened to *biodiversity*), a reworking of the "web of life" idea. After its pop-ularization in 1980, biodiversity caused a paradigm shift, a new way to measure and also to value life on earth. Conservation biologists took it as their charge to preserve native biodiversity in remaining natural areas, while invasion biologists focused on preventing non-native species from transforming those same areas. These scientists-activists conceptualized biodiversity as an interdependent three-tiered structure—genetic diversity, species diversity, and habitat diversity—and described bioinvasion as a threat to all three levels. They maligned unwanted species as "biological pollution" or "green cancer," part of the "evil quartet" of human impacts that cause extinction (the antithesis of biodiversity), and they likened out-of-place biota to one of the four horsemen of the environmental apocalypse.[43]

Invasion biology quickly made a mark in geopolitics. At the United Nation's Earth Summit in Rio de Janeiro in 1992, scores of nations signed the Convention on Biological Diversity, which included a provision calling on member nations to "prevent the introduction of, control or eradicate those alien species which threaten ecosystems, habitats or species." To provide treaty nations with scientific expertise, the UN established the Global Invasive Species Programme in 1997. Likewise, in 2000, the World Conservation Union, an international body composed of nation-states and NGOs, passed "guidelines for the prevention of biodiversity loss caused by alien invasive species." Although the United States declined to ratify the Earth Summit treaty, President Clinton created the Invasive Species Council in 1999. Earlier in the decade, the Congressional Office of Technology Assessment published *Harmful Non-indigenous Species in the United States*, a hefty report that estimated annual losses to America's commercial farms, forests, rangelands, and fisheries in the billions of dollars. More recently, NASA teamed up with the U.S. Geological Survey to monitor "the single most formidable threat of natural disaster of the 21st century" with the Invasive Species Forecasting System.[44]

Journalists aided the ascension of invasion biology. Long before the mainstream press gave sustained attention to global warming, it publicized invasive species. Unlike climate, an impassive and impersonal force, invasive species can be anthropomorphized. Going well beyond the pseudo-objective language of "invasive exotics," U.S. media outlets published countless sensationalized stories about floral and faunal immigrants, illegal aliens that hide as stowaways on boats, sleepers that lurk in the landscape for years before irrupting in a reproductive frenzy, exotic life-forms that can survive—even thrive—in extreme conditions where other things won't live. The press tended to focus on poster species such as "Japanese" kudzu vines swallowing the South, "Russian" zebra mussels clogging the Great Lakes, "Africanized" killer bees crossing the Mexican border, and "Chinese" snakehead fish threatening Chesapeake Bay. These and other nonnatives have been described as ugly, dirty, messy, unclean, dangerous, unruly, foreign, inassimilable, overreproductive, insatiable, voracious, predatory, swarming. In news reports, people wage battles against bioinvasions that threaten to assault, bombard, or overrun the landscape. Eradication requires battle plans and tactics.[45]

A number of humanistic scholars have spoken out against this language, arguing that when ecologists use racially charged language to describe scientific phenomena, they unwittingly reinforce the rhetorical foundations of social inequality. A few critics have gone one or two steps further, accusing ecologists of complicity in racism and xenophobia. Did you know, they ask, that the Nazis sponsored a native plants program? With a nod to conspiracy theory, naysayers also note that important early research in invasion biology came out of South Africa. (In truth, this had little to do with apartheid and a lot to do with the fact that South Africa, like California, is an isolated Mediterranean ecozone with a large number of endemic species that have been endangered by the ecological consequences of sea-based trade and colonization.) Less rashly, biohumanists have issued reminders that we humans and our domesticated plants and animals are invasive, too. Instead of denying the world we live in, why not, they say, develop a tolerance or appreciation for "mongrel ecology"? Why not instead call it "recombinant" or "cosmopolitan" ecology? Why not try to love our "rambunctious garden"? "Here's to multihorticulturalism," says Michael Pollan.[46]

This earnest debate is more about the present than the past. In U.S. history, at least, native plant advocacy and xenophobia have rarely occurred together. Many leading conservationists in the late nineteenth and early twentieth centuries were in fact racists, xenophobes, and even eugenicists, but these men *supported* plant introductions more often than they opposed them. The mission of state and federal land managers included procuring, propagating, and distributing useful species. Afforestation was synonymous with conservation. Not

until the Progressive era did Congress establish federal bureaucra-
cies to enforce new plant quarantine laws (to combat real commercial
threats to agriculture in the form of insects and insect-borne diseases)
and new immigrant exclusion laws (to fend off perceived societal
threats to the republic). These two state projects had correlations but
no direct links.

In California history, botanical xenophobia rarely appears in the
expected places. For example, Abbot Kinney, one of the great champions of eucalyptus planting, wrote a book about the "religion of reproduction." In it he argued for the spiritual calling and the civic duty
of procreative sex. Educated married couples of "old stock"—white
people he referred to as "native Americans"—needed to reject con-
traception so that the nation would not be overrun with the illiterate
children of hyperreligious immigrants of undesirable races. Yet Kinney did not draw any analogies to the plant kingdom. When Golden
State farmers initially turned against blue gum in the 1880s, they did
not compare unwanted specimens to despised foreigners such as the
Chinese. (Likewise, during the two world wars, jingoistic Americans
did not call for a war on German ivy or for the removal of the Japanese cherry trees from the National Mall.) More recently, during
the Angel Island controversy, the pro-euc lobby passed up the perfect opportunity to invoke the troubled history of American citizenship. From 1910 to 1940 the federal government used the island as an
immigration station—a small West Coast analogue to Ellis Island.
During the exclusion era, the government detained tens of thousands
of Chinese here, often for long periods. Eucalyptophiles easily could
have compared the removal of immigrant trees to the deportation
of unwanted immigrants. Instead, these "antinativists" asked vaguely
racist rhetorical questions like "Should we give back Angel Island to
the Indians while we're at [eucalyptus removal]?"[47]

Hoping to avoid more outcomes like Angel Island—the language
of science boomeranging and working against the goals of scientists—
many ecologists have expressed a desire to invent new terminology
or to return to a more value-neutral language. Various words are

available to describe an ecological newcomer; arranged on a continuum of political correctness, they are *new, novel, introduced, allochthonous, nonnative, nonindigenous, exotic, foreign, immigrant, alien*. The taxonomy of belonging can be extended even further. Recently arrived species can be divided into three subcategories based on the propagule, or initial release: *transplants* (purposefully introduced by humans), *accidentals* (inadvertently introduced by humans), and *colonizers* (arrived without direct human intervention but with human facilitation). Biotic introduction requires a species to overcome a barrier or requires that barrier to fall. *Alien species* by definition make the journey as piggybackers, with humans assisting as their carriers or vectors. This is why invasion biologists draw a distinction between their subdiscipline and classical biology, which concerns "natural" migrations and autocolonization.

It's tempting to think of human-facilitated introductions as automatically worse than "natural" ones. However, from a purely scientific point of view, the nature of the pathway or conduit is beside the point. It only matters what the donor species does to the recipient environment. The majority of introductions fail outright. Other propagules reproduce at first but eventually die out; ecologists call them *casuals* or *adventives*—or, more awkwardly, *transients, escapes*, or *waifs*. Relatively few of these populations manage to survive and establish themselves as *naturalized species*. When ecological communities are less than fully packed—that is, when unutilized resources remain available and when carrying capacity can be increased—niche opportunities exist. Certain naturalized species seize the moment. Having left behind enemies, having shed pathogens and pests, they enjoy high competitive performance. They increase rapidly and widely: they *invade*. In pure ecology, invasiveness is measured in terms of speed and scale. But in applied ecology—policy and law—invasiveness is defined by harm, a concept nearly impossible to quantify except in dollars. Harmfulness or noxiousness can also have aesthetic, psychological, and cultural components, but the economic ones get priority. According to the executive order that created the National Invasive

Species Council, an invasive species is "an alien species whose intro-duction does or is likely to cause economic or environmental harm or harm to human health."[48]

Scientists, despite their aversion to imprecision, mostly accept a division between harmful and benign invasiveness. Benign invad-ers fail to bother people, whereas injurious invaders—so-called weeds, plant pests, problem plants, nuisance species, or biological pollutants—grow to be a bother. They may seem ugly or useless. They may compromise crops or water supply. In rare cases, they may dis-place other species, destabilize the existing ecological community, and promote secondary invasions. These kinds of pests have been called *transformers* or *ecosystem engineers*. Government agencies and environmental groups have created blacklists of the "most unwanted," the "top offenders," the "world's worst," and the "Hall of Shame."

Numerically speaking, the nuisance of transformers could be much worse. There is an order of magnitude difference (often misleadingly called the "tens rule") between the number of plants imported and the number that take root as introductions, another order between intro-duced plants and naturalized plants, and yet another between natu-ralized plants and those populations that become successful enough to be termed invasive. Finally, only a fraction of those invasive popu-lations will produce transformative effects, thus facilitating additional introductions and ultimately the creation of novel ecosystems—a multiplying effect known as *invasional meltdown*. Transformers are the great, noxious exception. Of the conservatively low estimate of five thousand vascular plant species introduced to the lands of the United States, only a few score have caused widespread harm. Most naturalized populations have become integrated into existing ecolog-ical communities; they provide "ecosystem services"; they seem to fit. After some period of time—how long is the contentious question—naturalized populations judged to be nonharmful might also be deemed native. In the very long term, the species might even deserve to be appended to the list of America's estimated 17,000 "original" autochthonous plants. Ultimately that is a value judgment.[49]

Considered among the thousand-plus established alien vascular plants in California—two-thirds of which originated in Eurasia— *Eucalyptus* seems relatively benign. Of the 374 species in the genus that have been introduced since the 1850s, only 18 have naturalized, and only one of those, *E. globulus*, has become a nuisance, and then only at the urban-wildland interface along the fog belt of the central coast and Bay Area, and there only after humans gave it an enormous head start with plantations. Even in these locations, self-sustaining feral forests have not grown dramatically beyond the boundaries of the original plantings. In the Golden State the blue gum has never been especially invasive; rather, it used to be especially *desirable*. Other vegetation imported to California for ornamental purposes has spread far more widely or densely—for example, periwinkle, English ivy, ice plant, pampas grass, and tamarisk. Unlike Scotch and French broom, Tasmanian blue gum is not a true problem plant. It cannot be considered a paradigmatic invader, or even a noteworthy one. A state survey of floricultural experts revealed a wide range of opinion about the severity of the eucalyptus threat to the state's wildlands, in marked contrast to the unanimous negative evaluation of brooms. The authoritative *Encyclopedia of Biological Invasions* makes note of the "enigmatic" low invasiveness of eucalypts worldwide—"orders of magnitude less successful as invaders than pines."[50]

Even problem plants are not innately problematic. A species can be invasive in one habitat, not in another. Almost any life-form, given the right opportunity, would invade. Where a species "originally comes from" is far less salient than how a given population functions here and now. Native plants, too, can become weeds—homegrown invaders. In short, people object to invading populations rather than invasive species. Or, to be most precise, people have problems with individual ecological networks. Invasion is a relationship, not an autonomous external force.[51] The relationship is contingent: it occurs only in the right place at the right time. Local stress—erosion, for example—can increase local invasibility. At the same time, global changes such as rising temperatures and carbon dioxide levels can produce small-scale effects that favor certain species. Such *disturbances* open invasion windows. Thus the rapid influx of a novel species may be less a function of the species itself than of habitat change. A previously noninvasive introduced plant can suddenly become invasive following a long lag time—as long as a century—if and when environmental conditions change. Many invasive species expand widely only after humans give them thousands of second chances, creating artificial *propagule pressure*. A few species, notably Eurasian annual grasses such as common wild oat (introduced to California by the Spanish), may inherently possess high invasion potential, but mostly it's hard to predict which nonnatives will "outperform" natives. It depends on context. Because of myriad contingent factors, ecologists cannot develop a general theory of invasion. They are better at identifying risk; describing the set of environmental conditions—the trigger point—that induces invasion; and forecasting a range of consequences.

In California, wise ecosystem management demands uncommon subtlety and humility. It's politically expedient to say that nonnative species are unnatural and unmistakable: *Once an exotic, always an exotic*. It's harder to explain—harder to accept—the truth that nativeness is a weak, imprecise category, even more so when paired with political geography. For example, Monterey cypress is no more essentially Californian than Tasmanian blue gum is essentially Australian. A term such as *California native plant* is misleading, if not meaningless, given that the somewhat arbitrary political boundaries of the U.S. state (which exclude Baja California) encompass numerous ecological subregions.

People often define *weed* as a "plant out of place" without bothering to define the spatial and temporal boundaries of place. Practically all species left their home range at some point in their past. Species colonization, like extinction, is inherent in evolution: successful species by nature move beyond their place of nativity. Mass redistribution events happened when continents or oceans became connected for the first time; two outstanding examples are the Trans-Beringian Biotic Exchange (across the Bering Strait) and

the Great American Biotic Exchange (across the Panamanian isthmus). Considering this deep history, one might reconceive recent
anthropogenic introductions of fast-spreading species as "shortcuts
in evolutionary time" or "an abnormal acceleration of the Darwin-
ian process."[52]

Ecologists have abandoned their old models of climax, stasis, and
stability in favor of dynamism. They may soon jettison the concept
of nativeness, too. Life on Earth is constantly changing, they say;
nonequilibrium is natural. At the same time, nearly all life scientists
believe there is something disquieting about our contemporary global
experiment—the "great reshuffling." Earth has probably never experienced anything like the frequency, scale, speed, success rate, simul-
taneity, and cumulative impact of recent and current species shifting.
Homo sapiens is less destroying the biosphere than rearranging it. Rare
seeds, exotic pets, cuttings, spores, and germs: they all move around
through trade and war, colonialism and consumerism. In planes and
in cars, in container boxes and in the ballast water of cargo ships,
"portmanteau biota" escape their bounds by the millions—a Noachian
carnival. And because of rampant ongoing habitat change, peregri-
nators have unprecedented opportunities to naturalize in the "global
weed patch." We inhabit an increasingly out-of-place world where
weeds are the norm rather than the exception, a "post-wild" world
that defies the hard-and-fast dichotomy of native and nonnative.[53]

Every definition of nativeness requires a somewhat arbitrary temporal marker, an equivalence to the expulsion from Eden, before
which anthropogenic change is considered natural, or less unnatural,
or at least categorically different. When did *Homo sapiens* become the
original invasive species? Some ecologists push the baseline back to
the beginning of the "Anthropocene"—to the Neolithic Revolution—
when humans started domesticating plants and animals and thereby
began altering the biosphere. Others point to the end of the last gla-
cial epoch as a more appropriate reference. In the United States, land
management agencies such as the Park Service typically use "European contact" or the "dawn of the age of exploration" as the end of

status quo ante. This is questionable, for we can't know exactly what precontact America looked like. The first ecological surveys came long after seaborne globalization. Hundreds or thousands of crypto-genic species (origin unknown) may not be "naturally occurring." This is particularly true of well-traveled ports. Much of the local marine life in San Francisco Bay that Californians consider native is probably "pseudoindigenous" according to invasion biologists.

Like it or not, all our concepts for evaluating ecological change are based on cultural (and therefore changeable) values. The celebrated naturalist Stephen Jay Gould once wrote that the one and only *biological* defense he could concoct for native species was the protection they "afforded against our overweening arrogance." We can know how native flora behaves in its existing habitat, but we can never know the long-term consequences of introductions into new habitats. Only a small percentage of novel species will become nuisances, but we are bad at predicting which ones. Although Gould considered the biological argument to be "no mean thing," he added an *ethical* defense: by privileging natives, we discourage "the botanical equivalent of McDonalds' uniform architecture and cuisine" and promote a "maximal amount of local variety." Most people—at least most contemporary people in liberal democracies—value diversity for its own sake. No one likes the sound of the Homogocene, the neologism for the current era of human-facilitated species shifting. To flatten the world with sameness seems unethical. It goes against the current of evolution.[54]

SENSE OF PLACE, AGAIN

There is one last complication: variety and homogeneity look different at different scales. From the global economic point of the view, California is more homogenous because of its eucalypts. Blue gum and river red gum have been planted in every Mediterranean environment. For seemingly every climate, there is some commercial eucalyptus species. Countries as different as Portugal and Madagascar contain large plantations; Brazil, China, and India have the largest. As of 2010, approximately 20 million hectares of the world (an area larger than Washington State) consist of cultivated *Eucalyptus*. Because eucs can be grown from seed, can be placed in dry and degraded soils, and can be coppiced at short intervals, they have excited the imaginations of entrepreneurs and social engineers. Stalin endorsed the trees for the Soviet Union's Black Sea region. The apartheid government in South Africa created eucalyptus farms on lands forcibly appropriated from blacks. In developing countries, the United Nations promoted various species of gums for fuel and for pulp; the UN's Food and Agriculture Organization sponsored a "world eucalyptus conference" in Rome in 1956 and again in São Paulo in 1961. The FAO also published two massive eucalyptus textbooks. In the mid- to late twentieth century, state foresters in India, Thailand, and various African nations worked with the World Bank to bring plantations to poor rural regions. In the same era, the Brazilian government offered tax incentives to corporations to create monocultural forests on the deforested Atlantic seaboard. São Paulo–based Aracruz Celulose achieved economic success. But in general, eucalypts failed to meet the unrealistically high expectations of state planners in the twentieth century. A Tree of Hope can all too easily become a Tree of Disappointment: the pattern has been repeated the world over. California is merely one chapter in this global history.[55]

Now let's change the point of view from economics to landscape aesthetics. It turns out that the ornamental and symbolic adoption of *Eucalyptus* is as rare as its economic utilization is common. Outside Australia, there are only two places—California and Israel—where the trees evoke feelings of belonging. The Golden State and the Jewish state make an intriguing pair, two Mediterranean ecozones that have beckoned settlers with ideas of promise, fruitfulness, and renewal, two polities where nonnative trees have been naturalized by colonizers on a very large scale. Early Zionists "redeemed" their ancient homeland by draining malarial swamps and replacing them with groves. Trees served symbolic as well as practical purposes. Zionists imagined their prospective nation as a tree and understood tree planting as a metaphor for reestablishing roots. *Eucalyptus* was the early favorite—so much so that local Arabs began calling it "the Jews' tree." Gum seeding continued into the British Mandate period and beyond. In the 1950s the state of Israel used fast-growing eucs as a "security grove" at the checkpoint to Jordan-controlled East Jerusalem. As a whole, though, *Pinus* replaced *Eucalyptus* as the favored genus for afforestation in the national period. Israelis went so far as to set pine forests on top of obliterated Palestinian villages. To some extent, eucalypts still function as Zionist symbols; patriotic Israelis have canonized a 1960s folk song called "The Eucalyptus Grove." By contrast, olive trees have strong competing associations with Arabs. Cultivated olives can, moreover, function as legal markers of Palestinian landownership. For this reason the Israeli government and militant settlers have uprooted thousands of olives over the years. In the 1980s, during the intifada, tree-minded Palestinians countered by burning and otherwise destroying thousands of pines and eucs propagated by the Jewish National Fund.[56]

Finally, let's move to a purely American perspective. The presence of emblematic gums sets California apart from the other forty-nine states. The only other state with conspicuous eucalypts is Hawai'i, and residents of the Aloha State have never employed them as symbols. Only in California can you drive on boulevards and highways ornamented with rows of gums. In this and so many other ways, the Golden State is unique, a de facto country in itself. Newcomers may have no idea that the trees are not native in the first place. Global biodiversity is invisible at a local scale. Most Americans are aware only of variety between regions, since they live nation-bound lives. Citizens of the United States generally avoid cosmopolitanism. In relation to the wealth and power they wield, they may know less about the world than any other people on the planet.

The gum-inspired sense of local belonging felt by older Israelis and Californians has an olfactory as well as a visual component. A 1946 editorial by the *San Francisco Chronicle* called the "strange aroma" of the "shaggy eucalyptus" the "essence of the land, lively and heady and vigorous . . . We would not trade it for all the maples in Central Park." For many West Coast residents and expatriates, the subtle blend of sea salt and tree oil—the "benedictions of fragrance"—is the distinguishing smell of home. The Canadian singer-songwriter Joni Mitchell easily acclimated to Laurel Canyon, a canopied neighborhood in the Hollywood Hills famous for having hosted a who's who of rock-and-roll icons. Looking back, Mitchell said, "The things that were pleasant about the '60s were pleasant in Laurel Canyon. The things that were horrendous about the '60s were horrendous in Laurel Canyon, you know, so it had its ups and its downs, but the smell of the canyon is beautiful. All eucalyptus. And there's a different smell here than in any other neighborhood it seems like to me. I get nostalgic coming back into it." As science and experience tell us, our sense of smell is neurologically linked to memory. A resident of Marin County told a story in the 1980s about a family that had relocated to Buenos Aires. Whenever the children felt a pang of homesickness for Mill Valley, California, they opened a memento bag of eucalyptus "acorns" and breathed in the good air.[57]

An Aussie would not necessarily have the same response. The people of the commonwealth feel ambivalent about their gums. In the eighteenth and nineteenth centuries, settlers generally considered them ugly and useless. The great Australian historian Keith Hancock put it simply: "The invaders hated trees." To create pastoral lands in New South Wales, British colonizers girdled thousands upon thousands and left them standing—a crude killing method called "ring-barking." On city streets, they were more likely to use English shade tree species. Only after Europeans and Americans expressed enthusiasm for the therapeutic and economic values of gums did the majority opinion slowly begin to change. In the early twentieth century, when Australian nationalism emerged, "gumsuckers" tried to turn *Eucalyptus* into a patriotic emblem, but in the end the genus proved to be less lovable than the *Acacia* genus, known there as wattle. The golden wattle is the nation's official "floral emblem"; the tree's blossom even gets its own holiday, National Wattle Day. To the extent that Aussies now rally around a eucalyptus species, they celebrate mountain ash, which rivals California's coast redwood as the world's tallest plant. Mostly leveled by logging in its Victorian and Tasmanian habitats, mountain ash has inspired environmental activism. Blue gum lacks such currency. You do not find it adorning the avenues of Sydney, Melbourne, or Canberra. Instead it is the foremost colonial tree in the world. In places such as India, it stinks of neocolonialism, and rural villagers—ostensible beneficiaries of state-sponsored afforestation— have reacted against it. In Portugal in the 1980s, rural opponents of cellulose plantations referred to blue gum as the "fascist tree." The Golden State may be the only place where the species has engendered affection and love.[58]

That most Californian of modern-day activities, driving alone on a highway, windows down, approaches perfection with the help of a blue gum canopy. The light is breathtaking, the smell invigorating. Who wouldn't wish for a convertible? On the off-coastal portion of the Pacific Coast Highway from Point Reyes Station to Bodega Bay—the dairy country of Marin and Sonoma counties—the driver steers in and out of eucalyptic galleries. In the distance, tall windrows line the golden-brown hillsides under an azure sky. On a late summer day, if traffic cooperates, no ride could be more joyful.

Even among detractors, one usually detects a grudging appreciation for the frowzy magnificence of a giant blue gum. *Eucalyptus* has joined a short list of floral genera that Americans either love or love to hate. Tumbleweeds and dandelions, disparaged non-American plants that have nonetheless been sentimentalized, also fit this category. As symbionts of settler societies, these naturalized nonnatives can function as emblems of the postsettlement landscape. Like most Americans, they belong and don't belong.

In September 2001—a time of sadness, rage, and patriotism following the misdeeds of foreign terrorists, a time when citizens of the United States, a civically defined nation composed of immigrants, began emphasizing the un-American idiom of "homeland"—a Ventura man, a welder, became possessed by an idea: he and his family would paint the Stars and Stripes on a giant plastic tarp and, trespassing under cover of fog, take it to the hill above town where two broad blue gums grew in splendid isolation. Venturans refer to this official county landmark as Two Trees. Not only did the pair symbolize the local sense of homeland, they bore a symbolic resemblance to the lost Twin Towers. The family tied their domestic flag to the tree-masts. From the town below, it looked as though Old Glory was suspended in midair between two resolute guardians that had weathered the storms of life. The sight brought tears to the eyes of Venturans. No one considered it strange to fly the American flag between "Australian" trees after 9/11.[59]

Many of the controversies surrounding California gums stand in for two societal (and often personal) questions that nag at state residents: *How long must we live here before we can consider ourselves Californians? What, if anything, about this place is permanent?* Even in the context of a fast-growing immigrant nation with high rates of transience, the Golden State induces dizziness. Everyone, it seems, grew up somewhere else; everything, it seems, was built last year. Habitually, Californians both celebrate this impermanence (as freedom, innovation, progress) and bemoan it (as alienation, shallowness, rootlessness). As minorities have become the overall state majority, countless multigenerational "native" Californians, including many Chicanos, have become estranged from their hometown or even the whole state. Old-timers feel like outsiders. In the 1980s and 1990s many cars in the state sported bumper stickers that read WELCOME TO CALIFORNIA . . . NOW GO HOME. No one likes the idea of the familiar becoming unfamiliar. In a realm of relentless demographic and geographic change, there is something comforting about massive trees— oaks or eucs or any other kind. That feeling of comfort might even be enhanced by the knowledge that some of these familiar, deep-rooted denizens of the landscape originated elsewhere. As one "old-timer" resident of Bolinas argued, "Anyone who has lived in California over

50 years is a Calif. Native, so, since our eucalyptus trees are over 100 yrs. old, they are a native tree!"[60]

Implicitly gum apologists compare their favorite plant to coast live oak, the quintessential California native. What eucalypts are to the history of settlers and immigrants in California, oaks are to the history of native peoples. As every schoolchild learns, presettlement subsistence economies relied on acorns from oaks. To this day, the sight of a gnarled oak on a brown hillside suggests indigenousness, permanence, and belonging. Coast live oak and Tasmanian blue gum are the yin and yang of California flora, two grand plants that occupy similar ecological and emotional niches and provide contrasting metaphors for belonging to the land.

Californians arguably attach too much significance to *Eucalyptus*. The recent "monstering" of blue gum has been so effective that even garden writers sometimes call the species "plain evil."[61] Why have eucalypts received a disproportionate amount of attention and opprobrium? Why has Tasmanian blue gum become a symbol of bioinvasion in California? Partly it's because the trees tend to be found in highly visible locations near or within cities. As urban or urban-proximate organisms, eucs have long been associated with infrastructural problems such as disrupted sewers, buckled sidewalks, impeded power lines, littered yards, obstructed views, increased insurance rates, and exposed liabilities. The other reason for their fame and infamy is almost too obvious: eucalypts are distinctive-looking trees, and trees can function as symbols in a way that grasses and shrubs cannot. They can be easily individuated and anthropomorphized. They can be imagined as grandfathers, as guardians, as adopted sons, as foreigners, as immigrants, as naturalized citizens, as illegal aliens. Trees supply building material for homes and also for mythologies and metaphors. In California, *Eucalyptus* has proven malleable in its metaphorical applications; it can function as a blank signifier onto which people project their ever-changing ideas and anxieties. Unlike introduced olives, citruses, and palms—Old World plants with deep symbolic roots in Judeo-Christian-Islamic cultures of the West—

antipodean trees meant nothing in California before Californians gave them meaning.

The number of eucalypts in the state will never return to the historic high of the mid-twentieth century.[62] The arboreal veterans from the pioneer generation—those that still remain—approach the end of their life cycle. This twilight moment provides Californians with an opportunity for reflection. Introducing gums was, in retrospect, a beautiful mistake. In nature preserves like Channel Islands National Park and fire-prone neighborhoods like the Berkeley Hills, it makes perfect sense to eradicate them or to thin their numbers. On Southland metropolitan streets, legacy eucs do present a hazard—not because of their inherent nature but because of their advanced age. But in other places—agricultural lands, highways, campuses, large urban parks—gum trees ought to be maintained as vital elements of the biocultural landscape. Here they should be tended and replanted. One does not have to be nostalgic for the period of American conquest to appreciate *Eucalyptus* as part of California's heritage. Gum trees connect us to a lost era when forward-thinking horticulturists and progressive city planners, for all their faults and excesses, thought holistically about people and nature and labored to make the environment healthier and lovelier. The Golden State would be grayer without its blue-green trees.

PART THREE

CITRUSES:
THE INDUSTRY OF
GROWTH

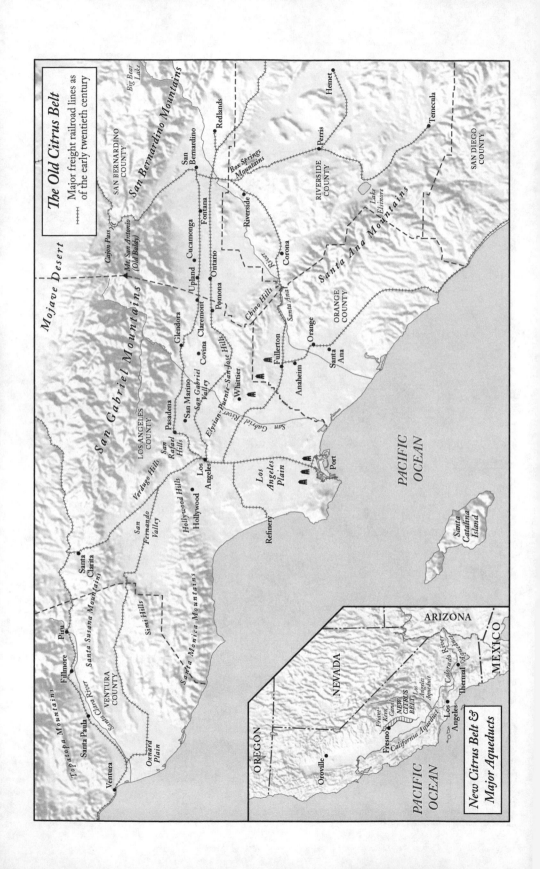

The Old Citrus Belt

Major freight railroad lines as of the early twentieth century

New Citrus Belt & Major Aqueducts

THEODORE ROOSEVELT FANCIED HIMSELF AN HONORARY westerner, but not until May 1903 did he travel to California, America's westernmost state. The president of the United States spent his first night neither in San Francisco, the state's leading city, nor in its upstart southern rival, Los Angeles. Instead, Roosevelt stayed over in Riverside, a small but singularly affluent citrus colony. In fact, according to an 1895 survey by the financial newspaper *Bradstreet's Weekly*, Riverside was America's richest place per capita.

The town donned its party garb for the president. Red, white, and blue lights hung across Main Street. A giant portrait of T.R. had been raised to the roof of one building. Stars and Stripes waved everywhere. From the train depot to downtown, Roosevelt traveled in a carriage decorated, courtesy of a local women's club, in "an exquisite scheme of color," with flowers everywhere, even on the wheels. At the head of palm-lined Victoria Avenue, the head of state got out of the aromatic carriage and dedicated a newly transplanted 45-foot palm in memory of the late queen of England. At the end of a parade route bordered with schoolchildren, Roosevelt gave a short speech, his sixth of the day. He commended Riversiders for creating a "veritable little Paradise." The sight of so many fair-skinned youngsters pleased the blue-blooded president, who never missed an opportunity to talk about the dire fertility contest between Anglo-Saxons and immigrants of "inferior" races. "I like your stock and I am glad it is not dying out," the Rough Rider declared. The crowd burst into applause. "It is a good thing to grow citrus fruit," he continued, "but it is even a better thing to have the right kind of citizenship." Riverside exemplified the "higher life which must be built upon material prosperity."[1]

All that prosperity derived from a single genotype—not human but floral. It came from a tree varietal called Washington navel, which bears sweet and seedless fruit. California's entire winter crop of oranges, the most valuable fruit in America, had been propagated from two cuttings shipped from Washington, D.C., to Riverside around 1873. By 1900 growers had, through grafting, created some 5 million cloned progeny from these two donor specimens. The historical society in Riverside eventually acquired one of the "parent trees" and donated it to the town's leading establishment, the Mission Inn, a complex that evoked California's Spanish past, with Orientalist touches like Japanese lanterns for good measure. (After Teddy Roosevelt slept here in 1903, the hotel continued to have a special place in Republican lore: Richard Nixon, who grew up nearby, married Pat in the Presidential Lounge; and Ronald and Nancy Reagan spent their first honeymoon night here.) The proprietor of the Mission Inn scheduled the ceremonial replanting of the parent tree to coincide with the presidential visit. Early in the morning, before catching the train to Los Angeles, Roosevelt, sporting a three-piece suit and top hat, approached the rather anemic, nondescript plant, which sat next to a pile of dirt in the hotel's inner courtyard. The principal of the historical society (son and namesake of Riverside's founder) told the president that this "little tree" was the progenitor of plenty. "The fruit of this tree is so perfect, its descendants so numerous, its posterity so great, its family so enormous, that we believe it merits your unqualified approval." Taking hold of the shovel, Roosevelt replied, "I am glad to see, Mr. North, that this tree shows no sign of race suicide."[2]

Subsequently the inn's owner mailed an annual box of oranges to T.R., the nation's eugenicist in chief, and displayed for hotel guests a framed letter from the California railroad and real estate baron

Henry E. Huntington: "I agree with you, he [Roosevelt] should always have the first and best of the yield. If there is any tree in the world which should appeal to our President and excite his admiration and esteem, it is this fine old parent of an unexampled progeny which, could it speak to him would proudly say: 'LOOK AT ME! for I am the exemplification of a great principle worthily championed by you. Race suicide has no place in my family. I AM A TRUE AMERICAN.'"[3]

The language of racial and sexual virility belied the truth about this fruiter. Citriculture requires fertility treatment on an industrial scale. Without human intervention, commercial-grade varieties would soon go extinct. The sexual progeny of even the best citrus plants are heterogeneous—and typically unmerchantable. For this reason, growers don't propagate citrus trees straight from seed. They *build* them. Riverside's famous navels were not just clones but organic fusions, one varietal budded onto the rootstock of a different kind. The picturesque scenery around Riverside—even rows of evergreens laden with "golden globes"—could never have grown naturally. Citrus groves are among the world's most intensive crops, requiring huge inputs of capital and labor, not to mention fertilizers and pesticides— and, in California, imported water. The Golden State's orange and lemon growers grafted the industrial onto the horticultural. In pursuit of a fruitful dream, they ultimately created something less than Arcadian: a landscape of social inequality, racial injustice, and environmental pollution. To fight winter freezes, orchardists burned millions of gallons of crude in heaters, fouling the air. The white men and women who owned these "citrus ranches" depended on Chinese, then Japanese, and finally Mexican field hands to do the heavy, dirty work. They also relied on highly educated plant technicians. Southern California—Riverside in particular, with its state-funded experiment station—became the global hub of citrus pomology.

The creation of the "Orange Empire" is a remarkable story of business and biological innovation. Before growers succeeded, they worked through economic false starts, technical challenges, and ecological calamities. Productivity was not inevitable. Nor would it be permanent. Today Los Angeles and Orange counties, including towns named Arcadia, Pomona, Garden Grove, and Orange, lack a single commercial citrus grove. Riverside is now less famous for fruit than for foreclosures and smog. The current center of California orange production, the San Joaquin Valley, faces the impending threat of a devastating insect-borne disease. The problem of perishability affects trees and groves and whole economies, not just fruit.

CHAPTER 5

Orange Revolution

SPECIAL FRUIT

No other fruit tree matches citrus for romance and legend. Storytellers of old spoke of Hercules and his Twelve Labors. For the penultimate exploit, the hero traveled to the western edge of the horizon—the place where Atlas held up the sky—to find the sacred fruit tree tended by nymphs, the Hesperides. The tree, part of Hera's private orchard, bore golden apples that imparted immortality. By tricking Atlas into helping him, Hercules managed to abscond with magical fruits. Whether or not Grecian narrators had sweet oranges in mind, later listeners made the connection. The Roman term for oranges was mythologically literal: *pomum aurantium* (golden apple). Today the scientific name for an orange fruit is hesperidium.

Botanists generally recognize only three parent or true species in the genus *Citrus*: citron, pomelo, and mandarin. The other varieties are hybrids: sweet orange comes from a cross of pomelo and mandarin; grapefruit comes from sweet orange and pomelo; and so on. Hybridization occurs in one of three ways. People can manually cross citrus through assisted sexual reproduction, transferring pollen from one plant to another and seeding from resulting fruit. This kind of trial-and-error, wait-and-see experimentation requires great patience. Alternatively, people can hunt for desirable varieties that appear spontaneously on eccentric tree branches—mutations known as bud sports or chimeras. In the atomic age, plant breeders gained a third technique: bombarding seeds with radiation to induce mutations. (The popular Rio Red grapefruit came into being at Brookhaven National Laboratory on Long Island.) Once a desirable varietal has been created or discovered, it must be asexually copied to be perpetuated. Citrus hybrids are unstable: sweet orange seed may sprout into a sour lemon. Only grafting produces uniform, predictable results.

Humans domesticated the *Citrus* genus at least four thousand years ago in its native tropical habitat in the Malay archipelago and Southeast Asia. The genus traveled westward in stages—first citron, then sour orange, lemon, and finally, much later, sweet orange. Flora followed the paths of traders, conquerors, and refugees. After Alexander the Great vanquished Persia and India in 330 BCE, his Macedonian army brought back citron, the "Persian apple" or "fruit of Media." For centuries this was the only common citrus species in Europe. Its fruit is dry and unpalatable, but its thick rind (usually eaten candied) has many medicinal properties; hence the Latinate name, *Citrus medica*. Groves of the bushy, thorny tree became a familiar sight on the Italian peninsula and Sicily during the reign of Roman emperors. The Jewish diaspora aided the Mediterranean diffusion of citron, for the Torah identified it as one of the four species required for the annual mitzvah at the Feast of Tabernacles (Sukkot). Whereas citron followed the path of Jews, sour orange followed that of Muslims, who introduced it and lemon to Iberia. The Spanish word *naranja* derives from an Arabic word, which came from a Persian word, which itself originated as a Sanskrit word. The renowned mosques in Córdoba and Seville featured courtyards planted with sour orange, also known as Seville orange—the main ingredient in marmalade. From the Arab territories around Jerusalem, crusaders brought back all kinds of plunder, including varieties of oranges, lemons, and limes. But the sweet orange, the familiar fruit that makes orange juice, didn't appear in Europe until roughly 1400 and didn't become common for two hundred years more, centuries after the Chinese mastered its cultivation. Over time, though, the "China orange" was renamed. Medieval growers in Iberia and the Mediterranean supplied northerners with sweet "Portugal oranges" for Christmas celebrations.

In northern climes, citrus cultivation required special-purpose greenhouses called orangeries. Large panes of glass became technologically feasible in the seventeenth century, a huge improvement over the mica and selenite panes used by earlier Roman engineers. Auxiliary heating supplemented solar radiation. Orangeries were architectural and horticultural showcases for aristocrats like the Medicis. The last king of Poland, Stanisław II, oversaw the construction of an orangery at the royal gardens in Warsaw. But no one eclipsed the Sun King, Louis XIV of France, in conspicuous cultivation of citrus. After the monarch imprisoned his superintendent of finances, he seized the marquis's hundreds of oranges and transplanted them to his new palace city, Versailles. Royal arborists scoured the Mediterranean for outstanding specimens to add to Louis's collection. Visitors needed the king's permission to walk among his fruit. Using ingenious wheeled machines, the gardeners of Versailles rotated trees from the orangery to the palace so that blossoms continually perfumed the palatial corridors. In the Hall of Mirrors, the evergreens sat in solid silver tubs.[1]

During the Columbian Exchange, the historical era when plants, animals, pathogens, and persons crisscrossed the Atlantic—the opening stage of what we now call globalization—oranges came on board. Columbus himself brought citrus seeds to Haiti on his second voyage, in 1493. Portuguese colonizers took the sweet orange to Brazil, and Spaniards introduced it to New Spain. As Catholic missionaries radiated outward from Mexico City, they carried seeds and cuttings with them. In the decades and centuries after Spaniards made a beachhead in Florida in 1565, their orchards went wild in the favorable subtropical climate. Americans of the mid-nineteenth century topworked Florida's feral oranges—that is, pruned them down to their rudimentary forms and budded proven varieties onto the trunks and rootstocks—to create near-instant commercial orchards.

Orange trees came to California with Spanish Franciscans, who founded a string of coastal missions starting at San Diego in 1769. Every mission featured a garden, and several included citruses. Only the mission at San Gabriel owned a true orchard—roughly four hundred sweet oranges on 6 acres. Planted around 1804, the orchard fell into disrepair after secularization in 1834 (which followed Mexican independence the decade before). When the Anglo-American grower William Spalding visited San Gabriel in the 1880s, fewer than thirty of the original trees remained, a collection of old, sick, half-dead, stubby plants with their living bark reduced to thin strips.[2]

In the years immediately following the breakup of the mission system, San Gabriel served as a kind of free nursery. In 1834 the French-born Jean-Louis Vignes transplanted (*pilfered* may be a better word) thirty-five sweet oranges from the mission grounds to his vineyard outside the pueblo of Los Angeles. This caught the attention of his neighbor William Wolfskill. An ex-trapper from Kentucky, Wolfskill had fashioned a good life in northern Mexico, first trading on the Santa Fe Trail, later growing fruits and nuts in Los Angeles. Following a familiar pattern for immigrant men, Wolfskill attained social status by converting to Catholicism, marrying the daughter of a prominent Californio family, and earning Mexican citizenship. In 1841, following Vignes's example, Wolfskill appropriated scions from San Gabriel for his own commercial orchard—almost certainly the first for-profit citrus operation in California. Supposedly some of his acquaintances ridiculed the enterprise. The Kentuckian got the last laugh. He expanded his grove to 70 acres, the largest citrus grove in North America at the time. After the Gold Rush, he sold oranges and lemons to San Francisco as well as to the mining camps, where forty-niners worried about scurvy. Wolfskill faced competition from Tahiti and Hawai'i, but his relative business success inspired imitators, who planted orange, lemon, lime, and citron in newly created Los Angeles County. However, no one could match him for quantity and quality. In 1859 Wolfskill won the state fair prize for best oranges. As of 1862 he owned about two-thirds of the 25,000 oranges in California.[3]

By himself Wolfskill did not transform the new "Southern California" (formerly Alta California) into a citrus region. As of the 1860s, the area around the Los Angeles pueblo was famous instead for its vineyards, nourished by ditches (*zanjas*) and harvested by indigenous peons. Wolfskill himself owned an extensive vineyard. Southland vintners like him and especially Vignes (who had the perfect name for the business) shipped their wine—strong, sweet stuff like port and brandy—by boat to San Francisco, where for a time it outcompeted wine from Sonoma and Napa counties. The prospect of throngs of alcohol-deprived miners paying premium price for vino inspired many French entrepreneurs, including friends and relatives of Vignes, to set up shop along the Los Angeles River in the 1850s—so many that the neighborhood became known as French Town. The earliest city seal of Los Angeles featured a bunch of grapes; one of the city's early English-language newspapers was called the *Southern Vineyard*. As late as the 1870 census, Los Angeles County led the nation in wine production, and its forty-three wineries accounted for almost half of the local gross product. In Anaheim, German-run wineries produced a whole line of drinks, from hock to sherry to claret to muscatel. A period guidebook properly referred to Los Angeles and Anaheim as "grapetowns."[4]

Viticulture and citriculture were just two of many agricultural experiments carried out by post–Civil War Anglo-American entrepreneurs in the strange yet promising "semi-tropical" climate of Southern California. These newcomers benefited from the economic effects of the great drought of 1862–1865, which devastated Mexican-American sheep and cattle ranching and the export trade in tallow and hides. In the legal realm, agricultural interests gained the decisive upper hand in 1872 thanks to California's "no-fence law," which permitted agricultural land to go unfenced and shifted the burden to ranchers for livestock damage to crops. White settlers—

many of them Union and Confederate veterans in search of a fresh start—acquired former grazing land (*ranchos*) and tried beekeeping (*bee ranching* in local parlance) or raising cash crops such as opiate poppies, castor-oil plants, ramie, cotton, coffee, and sugarcane. To promote sericulture, the legislature offered a bounty on plantations of mulberry trees until the program threatened to bankrupt the state. The pioneer historian Hubert Howe Bancroft wrote of the silkworm "bubble" and the "fiasco in tobacco" in the 1860s and 1870s. Smitten with "fruit fever," would-be growers tried to establish any number of exotic crops in Los Angeles County, including bananas, plantains, pineapples, coconut, and mango. The climate proved too dry. For about three decades after the Civil War no one knew which economic plants would prevail. Wolfskill shrewdly hedged his bets. He tended tens of thousands of grapevines as well as groves of peaches, quinces, apples, figs, walnuts, almonds, chestnuts—and the oldest eucalypts in Los Angeles.[5]

For ranchers, extensive land conferred power; for intensive growers, power flowed from water. To commercially cultivate Mediterranean or tropical fruit in the semi-arid Southland required irrigation. Since few people possessed the means to develop waterworks on their own, California fruit growers worked cooperatively. The Anaheim Water Company, founded in 1857 by German immigrants, provided one model. The grape-raising, winemaking colonists of Anaheim pooled their money, built check dams and canals, then allocated the water from the Santa Ana River proportionally according to share ownership. This kind of nonprofit enterprise—private governance, really— was called a mutual water company. It minimized conflict between neighbors by forming and enforcing rules about when, where, and for how long irrigators could draw water.[6]

Anaheim may have been the earliest, but Ontario (1881) was the most famous irrigation colony in California. It took its name from the Canadian home of its founders, the brothers George and William Chaffey. A brilliant and innovative engineer, George used a dam, a tunnel, and miles of underground cement-lined pipes, all built by Chinese laborers, to deliver water by gravity and produce hydropower while at it. He captured the subterranean flow of San Antonio Creek where the stream discharged from the mountains. The brothers Chaffey mastered social engineering, too. They wanted only the best people—starting with middle-class white family men—to buy 10-acre blocks and water shares in "the Model Colony." Property deeds forbade the sale of liquor. Ostensibly Ontario was the only California settlement to open a newspaper office before a saloon. It contained a profusion of churches—the Chaffeys gave them free lots—as well as a public library, a hotel, and a college. Four rows of trees, including eucalypts and palms, lined a grand central avenue named after a Greek mathematician. Euclid Boulevard and its streetcar service terminated at the Southern Pacific Railroad station, where a fountain showed off the town's water supply. Ontario boasted telephone service and one of the first electric streetlight systems in the world. Picturesque orchards of peaches, pears, apples, and oranges encircled this urbane village—a "modern Arcadia"—beneath Old Baldy, the highest point in the Sierra Madre (now called Mount San Antonio and the San Gabriel Mountains). No wonder that Ontario won universal accolades. Opportunity lured the Chaffeys to Australia, where they tried and failed to replicate their California success.[7]

The colonizers of the San Gabriel and San Bernardino valleys self-consciously distanced themselves from the older image of Anglo-California settlement: lucre-crazed single men rushing to the Sierra gold fields. Colonies promised family-friendly social order—for a price. To borrow an analogy from the great social critic Carey McWilliams, buying into a fruit colony in the nineteenth century was like purchasing a home in an exclusive subdivision in the twentieth. Founding settlers self-selected. For example, Pasadena, initially called the Indiana Colony, was settled by Hoosiers, Whittier by Quakers. Many colonists shared a common identity as health seekers: they hoped to solve their pulmonary problems in the warm, dry air.

One leading booster spoke of the "fruit belt and sanitarium of South-ern California" and praised orchard work as suitable even for female invalids.[8]

For the history of citrus, the most important settlement was Riv-erside, located about 60 miles east of Los Angeles. In March 1870 John Wesley North of Knoxville, Tennessee, issued a call to create "a Colony for California." He invited "all persons of good charac-ter" to join him. He envisioned a haven for "intelligent, industrious and enterprising people." His planned community would feature schools, churches, reading rooms, a library, and a lyceum—"all the advantages which a first class Town affords." Later that year, North founded the Southern California Colony Association, which chose a location above the Santa Ana River, near the planned route of the southern transcontinental railroad. The colony bought the tract—part of a former Mexican land grant—from the failed California Silk Cul-ture Association. Improvements came slowly at first. "The first time I saw Riverside," recalled one old-timer, "it had a future and a ditch, and the future was in the ditch!" North's subscribers built a canal to siphon upstream water from the river and experimented with many crops, including opium, grapes, peaches, and walnuts. Orange seed-lings came from Los Angeles and, when demand exceeded supply, from Tahiti (via San Francisco). Early colonists were as inexperienced with tropical horticulture as they were unfamiliar with the Mediter-ranean climate. Crops failed. Grasshopper infestations in 1873–1875 decimated young plants, including citrus. The environment seemed to mock the pioneer expression, "When our groves are in full bearing, we shall be as rich as mud." All in all, Riverside might have followed the fate of the prior silk colony were it not for one lucky event: the introduction of the navel orange.[9]

The navel's story functions as the creation myth of Southern Cali-fornia's Orange Empire. It entered local lore as well as history books in no small part because its two main characters, a married couple, were Riverside's original eccentrics. Eliza Tibbets (née Lovell, born 1823), a self-made spiritual omnivore, practiced idiosyncratic forms of

Swedenborgianism, spiritualism, and ultimately Catholicism. Before moving to the West, she worked as a healing medium in Manhattan. At séances, wearing a ceremonial robe, Eliza channeled her guiding spirit, an American Indian maiden named Floating Feather. Eliza's clients included a commodities broker named Luther Tibbets, who wanted to contact his late wife. Eliza helped with that and more. She and Luther had an affair. Eliza left her husband, secured a divorce (her second), and married Luther, who abandoned his second wife, the sister of his dead spouse. Luther's temperament combined rashness, stubbornness, and idealism. The first chronicler of Riverside's history described him as a "good man" who was nonetheless "insane on law matters" with his "mania" to reform the world. For example, following the Civil War, Luther hatched a plan to colonize Virginia with progressive, self-sufficient settlers. He dreamed of creating a model community for the New South, of bringing racial tolerance and Yankee energy to a stagnant region. After multiple run-ins with the law, including an arrest, the "nigger man" received threats from the KKK. He and Eliza and their children (a complicated blended family) decamped for D.C. just one year after arriving.[10]

The Tibbetses occupied the left end of the spectrum of people attracted by John North's call to colonize California. They liked the idea of building a new community in "fresh" land. Eliza, like many arrivals, hoped to cure her asthma in the Far West. Her husband arrived first, in late 1870, even before the completion of the first canal. Technically he was a squatter, not a colonist: he claimed a parcel of the unsurveyed "government tract" just outside the colony—dry land that initially lacked irrigation rights. The rest of the family followed later, probably in 1873, when Eliza was fifty. New acquaintances commented on her resemblance to Queen Victoria. In Riverside, Luther contemplated various business schemes, but in the meantime the Tibbets family needed a garden. They ordered a variety of specimens for transcontinental delivery—tobacco, grapes, plums, and oranges.

The citrus came from Eliza's D.C. friend William Saunders, the USDA's chief botanist and landscape designer. Around 1869, after hearing word of a promising navel varietal in Brazil, Saunders wrote a letter to the U.S. consulate asking for some cuttings. Navels originally came from Goa, on the western coast of India. The Portuguese, who claimed Goa as one of their viceroyalties, introduced this local variety—then called Selecta—to northeast Brazil. Navel oranges seemed like the perfect cash crop: easy to peel, firm yet juicy, sweet and delicious, and distinctive-looking. The name navel references the characteristic bulge at one end of the fruit, which looks something like a distended belly button (actually an embryonic second fruit encased above the main fruit). The fruit's only downside was seediness. Then, sometime in the early to mid-nineteenth century, nature gave business a gift. A Selecta tree in Cidade de São Salvador da Bahia de Todos os Santos (City of the Holy Savior of the Bay of All Saints, or Bahia for short) underwent a spontaneous mutation. One branch on one tree started producing the same fruit with minimal seeds. Brazilian growers grafted pieces of the virgin-birth branch onto other rootstocks, and by this method of mechanical replication they eventually created whole orchards of the "Bahia orange."[11]

The first shipment to Saunders died. On a second try, ten or twelve cuttings survived. The botanist grafted them onto rootstock in a government greenhouse near the Capitol. Once established, these oranges provided budding material for the creation of new trees distributed by the USDA. Two or three of these plants went to California at the request of Eliza. They managed to survive the journey across the Great Plains, Rocky Mountains, Great Basin, and Sierra Nevada, ending up in Gilroy, near San Jose. A stagecoach picked up the package and took it as far as Los Angeles. Eliza and Luther transported the seedlings the final distance, driving a buckboard farm wagon equipped with backless, springless, uncushioned seats.

It's not clear exactly when the fruiters arrived (1873 is the year commemorated), and there's no evidence for or against the most legendary scene in Riverside history: Eliza sustaining them with pail after pail of dishwater. Surely the Tibbetses had no inkling of the future value of their acquisition. The oranges themselves looked stunted, weak—

all-around unimpressive. But a few years later, at bearing age, the fruit looked and tasted fantastic and separated neatly into sections— without seeds! It was the perfect eating or table orange (as opposed to a juice orange). Friends and neighbors immediately asked for cuttings.

When the "Tibbets navel" won first prize at the inaugural Riverside citrus fair, held in a specially constructed public hall in 1879, people of means took note. The next year, E. J. "Lucky" Baldwin, the entrepreneur best known today for founding the Santa Anita Park racetrack, laid out a 75-acre navel grove. About the same time, a British syndicate planted a large spread in the Arlington Heights district of Riverside. In 1885, when both groves came into bearing to great financial reward, everyone in the Southland who grew winter oranges hurried to switch from seeded fruit to seedless, from seedling trees to grafted. As part of this orange rush, growers tore out thousands of walnuts, almonds, and prunes, "the most expensive firewood they have ever used." Orange grove expansion coincided with the great regional real estate boom of 1886–1888. In the words of one Pasadenan, the eastern gentleman smitten with "California fever" imagined he would "lie under an orange-tree in the middle of winter, when you fellows here are freezing! When I get thirsty all I have to do is kick the tree, and down comes a ripe, juicy orange!"[12]

In Riverside, citrus seemed like a particularly good investment in 1886, when work started on a new canal and when the Santa Fe Railway initiated direct service to town. Now fruit could be shipped directly to eastern and midwestern locations, including that year's Chicago Citrus Fair. The navel had the additional advantage of bearing in winter, when consumer demand peaked. As the secretary of the State Board of Horticulture bragged, the California navel was not just the "king among oranges" but the "autocrat of the price list."[13] The varietal attracted wealth from afar: by the early 1890s Arlington Heights was an enclave of wealthy English expatriates. Riverside acquired so much name recognition that orange packers from distant California regions labeled their fruit as coming from there. At the same time, growers from nearby colonies objected when Riversiders

made talk of their "Riverside navel." After some quarreling, California horticulturists renamed the Selecta mutation formerly known as
Bahia orange as Washington navel.

For a few years, Luther Tibbets enjoyed the ultimate seller's market: the only source belonged to him. He cultivated his oranges for
buds, not fruit. He turned down offers of $10,000 for his two prize
plants. In 1882 an assessor valued his property—in effect, the trees—
higher than Riverside's hotel.[14] To protect against the pruning knives
of thieves, Luther installed a padlocked gate to his enclosure and
strung barbed wire around each tree. At peak price, he could sell each
tiny bud for a silver dollar. With this new income source, he and Eliza
bought a fine new buggy with comfortable seats. For sartorial adornment, "Seedless Orange Tibbets" alternated between a top hat and a
derby (with a veil attached to the front rim to protect his chronically
weak eyes from the sun and his irritable nose and throat from dust).
Eliza took to carrying a parasol. In public, she dressed in a way that
played up her resemblance to the queen of England. Like all nouveau
riche Anglo-Californians, the Tibbetses hired a Chinese servant to
cook their meals (and watch their trees when they were away).

Good times never last. By selling genetic material, Luther ensured
the obsolescence of his business. Each bud, once grafted to a rootstock, became a tree with hundreds, then thousands of near-identical
buds. Strangely, Luther did not invest in a grove of his own. Instead
he subdivided and sold off his alfalfa fields during the orange rush.
After a correction in the real estate market, the Tibbetses suddenly
couldn't pay their debts. It didn't help that Luther spent a lot of time
and money in court suing others and being sued, getting arrested on
principle, always acting as his own lawyer. He carried on a protracted
feud with a neighbor over water rights. "Litigation was as the breath
of life to his nostrils," recalled one of his contemporaries.[15] When his
money ran out (again) in 1897, the court seized the homestead and
the navels, which by then were historical curiosities, and put on a
foreclosure sale. Under stress, Eliza's pulmonary condition worsened;

she took refuge among friends at a spiritualist community near Santa Barbara, leaving her irascible husband behind to face eviction charges.

THE CITRUS BELT

The Tibbetses did not really belong in the Riverside they unwittingly helped to create. In 1879 a travel writer composed a biting send-up of the colony's horticultural bourgeoisie:

> Many of the Riverside colonists are "eddicated, intellectooal cusses," as an envious San Bernardino farmer termed them. Many of them are invalids, who have a little property, so that they are not obliged to work with their own hands; most of them are a combination of ill-health, intellectuality, and comfortable circumstances. Orange culture is eminently adapted to their condition and circumstances. They can sit on the verandas of their pretty cottages—the refined essences of abstract existences—inhaling the pure air of the equal climate, reading novels or abstruse works of philosophy, according to their mental activity, from day to day, and waiting from year to year for their oranges to grow. Extremes meet. This is the sort of farming agreeable alike to literati and lazzaroni.[16]

Across the Southland, mutual water companies succeeded in attracting a privileged exurban class, a process opposite to the familiar "brain drain." The stereotypical colony shareholder was a man, a recent arrival of advanced age and considerable means. He came to California to breathe easy and recuperate in the sun, and ended up becoming an avocational horticulturist. Although retired from a professional career in the East or Midwest, he itched for a second-act success. This agrarian entrepreneur grew luxury crops for profit using the latest technologies and scientific methods. He was, in a sense, a back-to-the-lander, but without any Ludditism. He did not like to be called a farmer, unless preceded by adjectives such as *high-class* and *gentleman*. He preferred *grower* or *horticulturist* or, better yet, *rancher*. He tended a *grove*, not a mere orchard. His operation comprised just 10 or 20 acres, and one very nice house. This former doctor, lawyer, judge, politician, financier, or merchant wore a suit, not overalls; a hat of felt, not straw. He felt no kinship for the "dirt farmer" or "man with the hoe" who grew staple crops for subsistence using traditional methods. Politically, he was both an antimonopolist and a pro-business Republican. He frequented fraternal business clubs and championed good roads, progressive education, and public utilities. He professed teetotalism, and every Sunday he sat in the pews in a mainline evangelical church. (Riverside contained so many churches that Chinese gave it the nickname Jesus City.) Although he disdained "Chinamen," he employed them and relied on them for truck produce. The fruit rancher mused about creating a "new race" in the colonies. Anglo-Saxons might reach their full civilizational potential in the civilized countryside—*rus in urbe, urbs in rure*. He believed his grandchildren would remember him with honor for "husbanding the water," for redeeming a sagebrush waste, for making the wilderness blossom as a rose, for having a hand in creation. He was, in the pomologist Thomas Garey's words, a "benefactor to his race."[17]

Citrus held a special attraction for such a transplant. Like viticulture, citriculture promised agriculture with amenities. Orange ranchers didn't work all day in the field; managing a grove required more business acumen than heavy labor. Work and leisure occurred within great beauty. In the words of one visitor, the glossy-leaved trees with golden fruit loaded the air "with the perfume of a thousand weddings." Best of all, growers acquired social capital when they invested in citrus. As one Orange County resident recalled, "Father was a farmer when he started out but when he got an orange grove, well, then he became a rancher." Oranges bore not just fruit but *choice* or *elect* fruit. If, as the Gospels said, one could recognize a tree by its fruit, the orange rancher owned the best in the world. Because of its aristocratic history, citriculture held a certain romance, mystique, glamour—and a hint of the exotic. All in all, a citrus ranch offered a perfect combination of artistry and stern cold calculation, country life and city culture, soul-stirring inspiration and princely profits. To claim such a place, wrote William Spalding in 1885, required a love of the beautiful, an enjoyment of the outdoors, a gross desire for the good things of the world, and, along with intelligence and refinement, a shade of cupidity.[18]

At the onset of the navel era, even as speculative capital flooded the region, Southland citrus growers still professed the moral code of the horticultural movement. In 1888 Riverside cohosted the American Horticultural Society when, for the first time, the group held its annual meeting in the Far West. The local host welcomed conventioneers with a florid address that directly compared the parent navel to the Tree of Life ("blooming ambrosial, vegetable gold") and that praised "men of intelligence, brain and culture" for transforming a "God-forsaken country" into Eden. The president of the society then arose to praise the people of Riverside: "We are pleased to note that you are not only raising fruit but homes; *good intellectual* society with all the rapid growth. We are glad to note that not all is for money, but for comfort and better instincts . . . [Y]ou have not lost sight of the higher motive; not only have you great wealth, but a Christian society." The program went on to feature presentations on a variety of arboreal topics, including "Ornamentation of Our Country Homes," the role of the national government in forest protection, and the importance of afforestation (including eucalyptus) in solving the "desert question" in California. A grower from Riverside lectured on oranges. "Until within a comparatively recent period the Latin and Mongolian races have possessed a monopoly of citrus fruit culture," he said. "But now the Anglo-Saxon has entered the field in both continents, and, with his accustomed system and energy, is infusing new life and new ideas into this calling, and, true to the instincts of the race, makes the pertinent inquiry: 'What permanent profit is there in it?'"[19]

Over time, this balance of horticultural interests—the calling of

husbandry and its moral, ornamental, racial, and financial merits—
tilted in favor of the pecuniary. As the navel business engendered
incredible innovation and prosperity, Riverside's ethos began to
resemble industrial capitalism more than tree culture. In 1900, as
befitting a refuge of rank privilege, Riverside (population 8,163) held
the "first street fair west of the Rockies," complete with an automobile
race, polo and golf competitions, a baby show (with separate prizes
for the prettiest white, black, Indian, and Mexican babies), and cake-
walks to the minstrel accompaniment of the Coontown Ragtime
Opera Company. Booths featured every kind of navel fruit display.
The local water companies pooled their resources to create a block-
long diorama of the colony's irrigation system.[20]

Riverside claimed supremacy in the Orange Empire, but a few
other colonies gave it a run for its money. Pasadena, Pomona, Ontario,
Claremont, Whittier, and Redlands were all of a kind—electrified
villages with resplendent public edifices, opera houses, Arts and
Crafts bungalows, Victorian mansions, and tree-lined boulevards.
Pomona commissioned a marble statue of its namesake Roman goddess for display in its library. Pasadena orchestrated the Rose Parade
(1890), which grew more elaborate and renowned each year. The colonies of the Citrus Belt hosted an enviable collection of educational
institutions, including Whittier College (Quaker), Pomona College
(Congregationalist), the University of Redlands (Baptist), and Throop
Polytechnic (Universalist), the forerunner of Caltech. Riverside's tru-
est rival, Redlands, was a late bloomer, a real estate venture that cat-
apulted to the highest echelon of U.S. society after the arrival of
Albert and Alfred Smiley in 1889. The well-endowed Quaker twins
had earned esteem for their annual conferences on the "Indian Problem" held at their hotel resort at Lake Mohonk in the Catskills. In
California, the Smileys opened the grounds of their retirement place
to the public; the view from Canyon Crest Park (better known as
Smiley Heights) became one of the most reproduced scenes in regional
promotional material. "Smiley Heights would make the hanging gardens of Babylon look like a tenement alley," said one travel guide. The

Smileys hosted sitting presidents such as William Howard Taft and industrialists such as Andrew Carnegie; before long, a parade of bigwig easterners built winter hideaway mansions in Redlands and invested in oranges. Borrowing from Carnegie, the Smileys financed a grand library for their retirement town. As of 1902 Redlands claimed to have surpassed Riverside as the richest place per capita. Visitors admired its Mission-style public architecture, its musical venues, its profusion of palms, and its spectacular mountain vistas.[21]

Sociology mirrored geography. The Citrus Belt—in effect, the wealth belt—of Southern California occupied the broad, inclined alluvial fans (known locally as "benches" or "mesas") beneath the San Gabriel and San Bernardino mountains. This sloped land lay just below the water-catching high country. It occupied the topographic interface where surface and subterranean water from the mountains emptied into well-drained granitic soils at the mouths of steep canyons. Gravity made training this water into irrigation canals, and thence into orchards, relatively easy. Foothill growers augmented the canyon flow with scores of upstream artesian wells and several mountain dams. These waterworks were, for their day, engineering marvels. For 11 miles, boasted the local board of trade, the Gage Canal of Riverside ran "around the edge of a mountain, across high aqueducts, and through sixteen tunnels, one of which is seven hundred feet in length." Redlands' water was regulated by Bear Valley Dam (1884), a 64-foot-high masonry arch dam dubbed the "eighth wonder of the world" by engineers for its daringly slender dimensions. (After the reservoir proved too small to handle successive drought years, the irrigation company erected a larger dam to form Big Bear Lake.)[22]

The aquifer zone also functioned as a thermal zone. The land here, like the foothills of the Sierra Nevada, lies below *and above* the normal frost line, since cold air keeps moving downslope to the valley floor. Navel fruits grown on this threshold undergo favorable aesthetic changes. The combination of low humidity and wide temperature swings induces the skin of oranges to turn a consistent desirable color. By contrast, in tropical climates like those of Brazil and Florida, rinds remain green and acquire more blemishes from storms and pests. California's temperature diurnality also promotes sugar accumulation and acid formation, meaning better-tasting fruit. Compared to Florida, California produces fewer oranges of smaller size but with richer, sweeter flavor. Nonetheless, their paramount value comes from their unpalatable rind. Navels from here command a premium price because of their surface beauty. More than any other orange, they *look* orange on the outside; they manifest the mythological golden apple.

While the Citrus Belt flourished, the pioneer orange groves of San Gabriel and Los Angeles deteriorated. One reason was the frenzied real estate market of the 1870s and 1880s, which followed the arrival of one, then two transcontinental railroads. The citrus industry, like every other speculative land enterprise, went on a bender. Schemers and dreamers planted new orange groves quickly and haphazardly with inferior nursery stock, often in subpar soils lacking sufficient water. Meanwhile, land agents bought up many established groves and tore out the fruiters to lay out subdivisions, or stopped maintaining them, with the goal of simply flipping the land. In 1887 a high-minded realtor in Los Angeles complained about the shortsightedness and "most stupid neglect" of his competitors who had uglified the scene. The "destruction of the beautiful orange groves throughout the city" was, he argued, bad business. Eastern tourists could not be expected to put down good money on "weed-overgrown lots covered with dead trees." When the real estate bubble burst the next year, additional groves fell into disrepair. "No one can help deploring the miserable, ragged appearance of the orchards in the suburbs of Los Angeles and Pasadena," wrote a local newspaper in 1888. Pasadena went on to spruce itself up, but tourism replaced horticulture as its mainstay.[23]

Ecological factors additionally devitalized the citruses of Los Angeles. Around 1868 a population of a tiny insect called cottony-cushion scale arrived at the port of San Francisco, probably hitch-hiking on a shipment of acacias from Australia. The insect, native to New Zealand, gradually moved southward. When the scale arrived in Los Angeles County circa 1880, it found an unprecedented feast in the form of citrus groves. Millions of the insects sucked sap from trees, weakening them, causing fruit- and leaf-fall, opening the way for secondary fungal disease and death. The insect's colloquial name derived from the snow-white waxy egg sacs it extruded onto branches. By the mid-1880s the "cottony plague" threatened to destroy all of Southern California's citrus. A prominent grower later recalled how people desperately "scrubbed their trees with brushes and baptized them with all sorts of noxious decoctions," including kerosene, copperas, coal oil, and whale oil soap. The poison baths provided only temporary relief.[24]

California appealed to Washington for technical assistance. Charles Valentine Riley, the chief entomologist of the USDA, took interest in the case and made plans to import from the antipodes one or more "natural enemies" of the scale. After Congress allocated funds to send U.S. diplomatic representatives to the Melbourne Exposition of 1888, the USDA entomologist Albert Koebele got called to Australia as a titular delegate of the State Department. Going well beyond Melbourne, Koebele collected various scale-eaters, both predators and parasitoids, including a species of ladybird. Then, on his way back home, he stopped in New Zealand and there discovered an invasion of that same Australian ladybird gorging on cottony-cushion scale in its native habitat. Koebele gathered adults, eggs, and larvae of the so-called vedalia beetle and packaged them for steamship delivery. At the end of a long Pacific voyage in the ice-house, the first batch of beetles arrived in San Francisco in November 1888, after which a capable USDA agent distributed specimens to the Wolfskill orchard in Los Angeles and two groves in San Gabriel. The beetles immediately went into a predatory and procreative frenzy. By summer, the orchards in San Gabriel had been "cleansed by this wonderful parasite." An astonished grower reported: "People are coming here daily, and by placing infested branches upon the ground beneath my trees for two hours can secure colonies of thousands of the Vedalia." By the end of 1889 the ladybirds had seemingly consumed the entire regional infestation. Not a scale could be found. A resident of

Pasadena marveled at this "deliverance." The "miracle" of vedalia had instantly cured the trees of their "hideous leprosy."[25]

With the cottony-cushion scale in check, Southern California's citrus ranchers began to taste the success they had been anticipating since the 1870s. However, the region's largest city lost its leadership role in horticulture. In the aftermath of the land boom and the scale, "all that was left to Los Angeles of its living border of green and gold was its blackened stumps of trees and the little white corner stakes of the real estate promoters." Established foothill colonies and upstart Orange County assumed control of the industry. In hindsight, some experts viewed the scale invasion as a blessing in disguise. "The insect has made profitable orange-growing on the Pacific coast more difficult and more of a science," wrote the U.S. commissioner of agriculture, "but, by making it impossible at the same time for the shiftless to succeed in their business, it will come to be looked upon as a not unmixed evil." Welcoming the crowd to the second annual state Citrus Fair in Los Angeles in 1891, keynote speaker William Spalding even looked forward to a "renaissance period." The industry was poised, he declared, on the "threshold of a new period of prosperity." The scale crisis had weeded out the badly located orchards and the lazy and careless growers. In the post-ladybird environment, the industry would capture new markets—not just San Francisco but Salt Lake and Denver, and then major distribution centers such as Kansas City, Chicago, and Cincinnati.[26]

Spalding's optimism was ahead of the curve. It took some fifteen additional years to iron out the system. Building on its biological control program, California passed comprehensive quarantine legislation in 1899—a first for the United States. Because of the state's natural barriers of distance and topography, lawmakers felt confident that they could keep out imported fruit and tree material from nations and U.S. states that harbored injurious insects like citrus whitefly, medfly, and Mexican fruit fly. In its early years, though, the program was badly coordinated. The State Horticultural Commission (1883) could declare quarantines, not enforce them. County commissioners did the actual inspections at ports of entry, but only after receiving authorization from the state. To complement quarantines, the citrus industry adopted chemical technologies for bug control. In the 1880s and 1890s state and local governments created a legal and bureaucratic apparatus to oversee such spraying. The legislature authorized county boards of supervisors to appoint and empower panels of horticultural commissioners to inspect orchards, order disinfection, declare noncompliant orchards a nuisance, and, as a final resort, seize the property. These powers were used sparingly at first, and growers resisted them as invasions of property rights. An important test case occurred in 1891, when the State of California brought suit to condemn 325,000 scale-ridden Tahitian oranges detained at the port of San Pedro. When the state prevailed in superior court the following year, the deputy sheriff of Los Angeles County doused the remaining 60,000 crated trees with kerosene and incinerated them.[27]

The potential impacts of invasive insects increased with economic specialization and accompanying genetic homogenization. Back in the 1860s and 1870s, citriculturalists had experimented with dozens of varietals from various distant sources. Early favorites included Malta Blood, Mediterranean Sweet, and Paper Rind St. Michael. Drawing on the expertise of their Chinese workers, growers also imported tree stock from Southeast Asia. But within a decade or two, the varieties narrowed dramatically. For simplicity's sake, one can imagine the state's citrus industry from the 1880s to World War II as a three-crop, three-genome economy: Washington (Bahia) navel orange, Valencia orange, and Eureka lemon. The Eureka, which went on to become the standard yellow fruit in U.S. supermarkets, originated locally, after some trees grown from Sicilian seeds developed a finer fruit—smooth and thin-skinned. In 1877 Thomas Garey, one of the leading nurserymen in Southern California, obtained buds from these superior lemons and went on to propagate and sell them. Around the same time, the Valencia arrived from the Azores via London.

Orange County and the San Fernando Valley eventually specialized in this varietal. Valencia took well to the coastal plain, with its shale and sandstone soils, its higher humidity and milder temperatures.[28]

Agricultural sorting happened all over the Golden State in the closing years of the nineteenth century. The granary era of "bonanza farms" and "wheat kings"—a form of farming caricatured and criticized by horticultural reformers—came to an end. Intensively grown fruits and nuts replaced extensively farmed cereals and forage crops as California's leading agricultural products. In a globalizing market, wheat and barley farmers could no longer compete with Canada, Argentina, Russia, and Australia. To replace staples, Californians introduced a bewildering array of specialty crops. Only now, in the 1890s, did Southland growers substitute citrus wholesale for wine and raisin grapes and begin to phase out stone-fruit trees, including hundreds of thousands of peaches. The area around Anaheim switched to oranges and walnuts after a fungal blight (Pierce's disease, formerly known as Anaheim's disease) suddenly annihilated its vast and valuable vineyards. In this transition period for Golden State agriculture—the "fruit boom"—many newfangled crops fell by the wayside. But by 1900 the "age of gullible experimentation" ended, and growers settled on the handful of species and varieties that maximized profits in their corner of the state. All told, between 1890 and World War I, the Golden State became one of the world's leading suppliers of Mediterranean fruits and nuts. In the Southland, the leading crops came from trees: oranges, lemons, and walnuts. Even as each individual operation became more homogenous, the overall diversity of California's agricultural output increased dramatically. The fruited Pacific Slope introduced the United States, a nation that had so far subsisted primarily on a few bland crops like corn, wheat, and oats, to a succulent cornucopia. The Sonoma County plant breeder Luther Burbank—the "wizard of horticulture," whose fame once rivaled that of his contemporary Thomas Edison—developed hundreds of fruit varietals, some of which, notably plums, became commercial winners. Before California fruit entered the U.S. market, said one booster, "the

summer was a quick flash of strawberries and the winter a long barrage of dried apple pie."[29]

Nineteenth-century agricultural statisticians often doubled as local
boosters and produced unreliable numbers; California's own horticultural commission called the decentralized system a "huge joke." Be
that as it may, citrus statistics reported by the Los Angeles County
assessor provide an accurate sense of the scale of specialty agriculture and its steep growth curve: a little over 30,000 bearing oranges
in 1870; almost 200,000 in 1880; more than 1 million in 1890. By
1900, when the U.S. Census Bureau started assessing "semi-tropical"
fruit, the Golden State boasted over 5 million bearing oranges, a
twentyfold increase over twenty years before. Against considerable
odds, Southlanders had manufactured a Hesperidian garden on an
industrial scale. Although the triumph of specialty crops was good
for California's economy and good for American cuisine, it came at
a moral cost: the horticultural ideal of diversified planting on family
farms reverted to the California norm of monocultural plantations
harvested by seasonal help. One step at a time, horticulturalism shed
its moral, environmental, and patriotic dimensions. At some point
in the early twentieth century, tree culture stopped being a reform
movement and became pure business: horticapitalism.[30]

PROBLEMS OF PLENTY

Placing desirable varietals in favorable conditions was only the first
stage of building California's citrus economy. A citrus is a fruit as well
as a tree. Fruit takes on a separate life once picked from the branch.
As commodities, California oranges and lemons required attention
in packinghouses, rail yards, advertising agencies, and, surprisingly,
lumber mills. The desire to squeeze golden profit from golden fruit
inspired many innovations in business and technology.

Shipping presented one set of challenges. Even with transcontinental railroads, Southern California remained distant from Amer-

ica's major urban markets. In their first few decades of service, the western lines were slow, inefficient, and prone to weather delays and mechanical breakdowns. At major crossroads, operators typically broke up trains and rearranged cars, causing further delays. Oranges with their protective rinds last longer than most perishable crops, but a two-week trip to Chicago in an unventilated car could turn even the best fruits into moldy mush. Climate control, starting with ventilation, was essential for success. The first "orange train" special left Los Angeles in 1886 and, running on an express schedule, delivered a load intact to St. Louis. A better publicity stunt happened in 1892: winter navels went to New York by train, then to Liverpool in refrigerated cargo holds on White Star steamers. Queen Victoria received samples of the shipment; according to the California State Board of Horticulture, Her Majesty sent her acknowledgments, "stating that she had found it very palatable."[31] Ventilated boxcars eventually gave way to refrigerated boxcars, or reefers. In 1906 Southern Pacific–Union Pacific created a subsidiary, the Pacific Fruit Express Company, and ordered more than six thousand reefers. In no time the company became the nation's largest buyer and maker of ice. Workers iced orange trains at various facilities in Southern California, then reiced them at stops such as Tucson and El Paso.

Air-conditioning by itself didn't seal the deal. To recoup infrastructural costs, the California citrus industry needed to sell product year-round. Its navels were a winter-spring crop. To capture the rest of the calendar, growers in Orange County invested in complementary Valencia trees. Although Valencias flower about the same time (spring) as inland navels, their fruits take longer to mature because they need more heat to ripen. (Unlike some fruit, oranges don't get any riper after picking.) On the mild coastal plain, Valencias aren't ready until the following summer or fall, meaning that one year's fruit overlaps another's bloom. This leads to an alternating heavy-light yield, unlike the more consistent but lighter-bearing navels. Compared to inland navel fruit, coast-grown Valencia oranges are not as pretty on the outside, not as easy to peel (because of a thinner rind), and seedier—but arguably tastier.

Once the industry could export table oranges in winter and summer, it cultivated year-round consumer desire in eastern states. The campaign began with what would now be called a "brand refresh" of the Golden State. Fruit growers worked to update the image of California from a region of rowdy Gold Rush camps to refined irrigation colonies. State, local, and corporate entities coordinated their promotions. For example, Southern Pacific transported locally produced citrus publicity trains to the 1884 world's fair in New Orleans— where Riverside oranges won the gold medal, beating out Florida fruit—then to Louisville, then back to New Orleans for another fair. In 1888–1890 the SP sent a different special train, California on Wheels, on a winter tour of eastern and midwestern states, carrying lecturers from the State Board of Trade, promotional publications, and free orange samples. Over the next decade, similar displays traveled to county fairs, national conventions, and international expositions, including Paris (1900) and Buffalo (1901). With legislative funding from 1890 to 1895, California hosted its own annual citrus fair, where every fruit town in the Southland competed to create the most eye-popping entry—an obelisk or pyramid of oranges, an orange pagoda, an orange equine, a solid-orange miniature high school with electric lights. The Santa Fe Railway shipped the second of these fairs to Chicago's Exposition Building, where it became the Citrus Carnival.[32]

No amount of edutainment or refrigeration could solve the most intractable problem of the citrus industry: long-distance merchandising. Orange ranchers faced a paradox of plenty; as they sold more fruit, they made less money. Their trees grew in place, but the fruit therefrom had to travel to faraway places. Since they could be in only one place at a time, they relied on middlemen. In the 1880s, when demand exceeded supply, growers sold their fruit on the tree outright for cash, meaning that the buying merchants assumed the risks of shipping and selling the crop. The equation changed in the early 1890s—the "red ink years"—as orchards rooted during Southern California's real estate boom matured into bearing and bore heavily in a scale-free environment. In a time of oversupply, middlemen gained the upper hand. Brokers could underbid growers or even compel them to accept a consignment arrangement, thereby avoiding responsibility for shipping. Growers on consignment had no control over their product once they paid for the freight. They recouped nothing if their fruit spoiled en route. If their beautiful, sweet, seedless oranges ended up in a glutted regional market, they got pennies on the dollar. There was no nationwide coordination of supply and demand, no government oversight. Brokers failed to keep account books. Growers alleged that dishonest fruit jobbers made false reports of spoiled shipments, then sold the good fruit under the counter. Other rotten merchants pushed underripe or spoiled fruit onto the market, thinking only of short-term profit, not long-term customer loyalty. Shoppers lacked quality assurance. As a consequence, the reputation of all California citrus suffered. The secretary of the Los Angeles Chamber of Commerce denounced this "evil" merchandising system as a "slough of confusion." To compound the chaos, the national economy slipped into a deep depression following the financial panic of 1893. Fewer people were buying luxury goods like oranges. Southland citrus ranchers postponed their expansion plans, which in turn prompted area nurseries to plow up and burn countless thousands of young navels.[33]

Faced with commercial calamity, more and more growers came to the same conclusion: they should band together as an industry and organize a cooperative marketing association. At annual fruit growers' conventions and in monthly meetings of groups like the Los Angeles Pomological Society, citrus men discussed how they might pool their resources and ship and sell their common product in an orderly, efficient way. They agreed on a number of principles: they should codify standards for washing, grading, labeling, and packaging—the prerequisites for branded fruit; they should share packinghouses; and they should cut out middlemen by hiring their own agents, who would

enforce uniform pricing for uniform quality in eastern markets. Such
a nonprofit collective promised greater individual profits. Although
the first local experiment in this type of venture, the Orange Growers' Protective Union (1885), had failed, the follow-up Southern California Fruit Exchange (1893) grew into the powerful California Fruit
Growers Exchange (1905). The CFGE, officially renamed Sunkist in
1952, at long last brought stability to a volatile market.[34]

Despite the depression of the 1890s, California's citrus ranchers
commenced their organizational revolution at a fortuitous time. A
disastrous freeze blasted Florida in the winter of 1894–95, killing or
damaging millions of trees. It took over a decade for the Sunshine
State, which had previously dominated the East Coast market, to
recover from the collapse of its orange industry. Its lemon industry
never revived. With badly concealed Schadenfreude, the *Los Angeles Times* exulted in 1899 that the Golden State possessed "the only
true citrus belt" in the United States. Notwithstanding the incon-
venient fact that Southern California was in the midst of a terrible
three-year drought that left reservoirs empty and orange trees dry
enough to burn, the region held three permanent advantages over
Florida. First and foremost were the vibrant rinds of tempting color.
Second, Golden State citrus bore fruit in the cruel month of April,
when northerners could no longer obtain southern oranges and when
their local produce consisted of root vegetables. Third, California
fruit grew a thicker albedo—the cushiony "white stuff" around the
fruit—which aided long-distance shipping.[35]

The challenge of packing oranges inspired engineers. In 1897–
98 two Riverside inventors patented a mechanized brusher that
became the industry standard for cleaning picked oranges. Around
the same time, two local maestros of mechanics, Fred Stebler and
George Parker, erected competing manufactories to build devices that
washed, polished, graded, sorted, conveyed, lifted, weighed, labeled,
and boxed citrus fruit. The rivals eventually joined forces, and their
consolidated company became a powerhouse (eventually acquired by
the Food Machinery Corporation). All in all, Riverside earned its

reputation as the fulcrum of innovation for automated citrus packing equipment.[36]

Even well-packed fruit spoiled regularly. In fact, as of 1900, up to one-quarter of the CFGE's marketable fruit decayed before reaching its destination. To address this problem, the co-op hired a consultant, G. Harold Powell, a pomologist with the USDA Bureau of Plant Industry who held an advanced degree from Cornell. Starting in 1904, Powell conducted a series of citrus field investigations. He determined that the culprit, blue mold (a fungus in the *Penicillium* genus), first entered the fruit through fingernail scratches, clipper cuts, stem punctures, and other mechanical injuries caused by field workers. At Powell's recommendation, orchardists instituted a series of procedural changes in picking and packing. The new system worked like magic; the spoilage rate plummeted.

Soon Californians did not need eastern experts, for the citrus industry cultivated its own crop. At monthly meetings of the Riverside Horticultural Club, founded in 1895, technophilic growers discussed experimental techniques of orchard heating, pruning, fumigating, and so on. Then, in 1905, the state legislature authorized the formation of a new Southland branch of the University of California's agricultural experiment station (to supersede an earlier station in Pomona). As built, the branch had two locations, a pathology laboratory in Whittier and the Citrus Experiment Station (CES) in Riverside. Over time, the citrus campus—the institutional parent of UC Riverside—grew from 23 acres on Mount Rubidoux to some 1,500 acres, on which grew the world's most comprehensive collection of *Citrus* varietals. With the help of industry lobbying, the station eventually gained the resources to employ hundreds of research faculty and students, who published a small library of technical reports on every aspect of *Citrus*, from plant breeding to orchard management, culminating with the multivolume bible of citrus pomology. In its heyday in the mid-twentieth century, the Riverside station continuously hosted visiting groups of scientists and growers from far-flung regions and nations.[37]

All this research and ingenuity followed the introduction of the Washington navel. In 1902, anticipating the navel's thirtieth anniversary, the *New York Times* noted the "wide ocean of difference between the little arid, seedy, and tough-skinned orange of a generation ago and the large smooth-skinned, sweet, seedless orange of to-day." Riverside's famous fruit had "revolutionized" the orange markets of the world. Before visiting Riverside's "mammoth orange fair," the *Times* reporter took the time to seek out Luther Tibbets, "a homeless, white-haired, tattered public charge."[38] His last public appearance had been at the 1900 street carnival, where, as the "father of the orange," he presided over his own booth. The honor had been tinged with indignity, for the sign on the booth misspelled his name. Now, looking out the window of the county poorhouse, the octogenarian saw a vast grid, some 20,000 acres, of evergreens, almost all of them the progeny of his and his wife's former property. Proposals to allocate a public pension for Luther had foundered, and his only luxuries came from a small purse raised by Riverside's local newspaper. Just weeks after the reporter's visit, Luther passed away, penniless, in the county hospital.

Tibbets just missed seeing the full flowering of the navel business. The final emphatic stimulus came in the form of a targeted ad campaign devised by Lord & Thomas, the Chicago firm owned by the marketing genius Albert Lasker. With Lasker's hired help, the advertising department of the CFGE embarked on the unorthodox plan of using saturation marketing to sell a perishable product. Lord & Thomas and the CFGE wrote the playbook: they invented many of the gimmicks used universally by food advertisers today. The problem of citrus overproduction was reconceived as the opportunity of underconsumption. The CFGE merely needed to convince Americans to consume oranges in quantity all year—to think of oranges as a regular pleasure, not a special holiday indulgence. Using a matching grant from Southern Pacific, the CFGE initiated a test campaign in the winter of 1907–8 in Iowa. California Fruit Special trains carried pamphlets, lecturers, and, best of all, free samples. Billboards announced the coming train and the sales pitch: ORANGES FOR HEALTH, CALI-

FORNIA FOR WEALTH. Color newspaper ads—a rarity at that time—featured a cartoon by the then-popular Ding Darling. When orange sales in Iowa rose 50 percent the next year, the CFGE and Lord & Thomas extended the campaign to other midwestern states and eventually the nation. Sales doubled in the ten years following the Iowa rollout. The exchange began stamping its crates and instructed consumers to "Ask for California Oranges in this Style Box." The premium fruit, individually wrapped in tissue and sealed with a sticker, bore a new trademark: Sunkist. The admen created something most Americans had never encountered: brand-name fruit.

The advertising went on and on. Hoping to keep the tissues on the oranges—thereby cementing brand recognition and preventing the counterfeiting of nonpremium or, even worse, Florida fruit—the CFGE unveiled the original consumer rewards program. The offer: send in twelve wrappers along with twelve cents and get a piece of California Blossom flatware in return. (The exchange briefly ranked as the world's largest buyer of silverware and redeemed over 2 million utensils to customers.) In subsequent years, as part of the classic "Drink an Orange" campaign, the CFGE offered discounted glass juicers prominently marked with the Sunkist name through fruit retailers. Millions were sold. Drugstores and soda fountains began selling fresh-squeezed OJ alongside Pepsi-Cola, both advertised as digestive aids. Following the publicized discovery of vitamin C around 1930, the exchange promoted the Sunkist orange as a preventive and remedial health agent. It ran campaigns like "Sunkist Baby" and "Get Your Vitamins the Natural Way" and produced a "Citrus Fruits for Health" series for CBS radio. It printed free recipe books, produced radio commercials with movie stars, distributed "educational" films to schools, and purchased millions of ad spaces in women's magazines. It also paid for the construction of hundreds of billboards, a neon display at Coney Island, and an illuminated display in Times Square in 1932–33. With this barrage, the CFGE succeeded in linking the image of the Golden State to the image of the orange. Much as the brand Sterling became the standard for silver,

Sunkist became the standard for table oranges. Thanks to admen, the sweet orange completed its trajectory from fruit of the gods to the aristocracy to the bourgeoisie to the average Joe.[39]

To ship all those delicious, juicy, vitamin-packed fruits to every state in the Union required containers—lots of them. Oranges arrived at groceries in wooden crates made of thinly sawed slats of kiln-dried ponderosa pine or sugar pine known as "box shook." In 1907, in an act of downward vertical integration, the CFGE formed a subsidiary, the Fruit Growers Supply Company, to secure affordable timber. The regional price of wood had doubled in the aftermath of the San Francisco earthquake and fire. With funds from a sales fee on every box of citrus, the supply company broke the monopoly of a rival box company. Over the years, Sunkist bought large parcels of timbered land in Siskiyou, Lassen, and Shasta counties, provided loans to struggling lumber mills, and built its own mill and factory. Roughly speaking, for every orange tree harvested in Southern California, a pine tree in the north fell to the ax. By 1945 the supply company owned over 200,000 acres of conifers. In that peak year, loggers, millers, and construction workers processed some 200 million board feet of wood and fabricated over 40 million crates. Just a decade later, the wooden carriers were obsolete, replaced by "carry-home" cardboard boxes and polyethylene bags. Box-shook crates persisted in American homes as ubiquitous poor man's furniture—waste bins, nightstands, bookshelves. These pieces of native California trees that once carried fruit from introduced California trees manifested the far-reaching ecological and economic networks of the citrus industry.[40]

TREE WORKERS

Unlike eucalypts, citruses in the Golden State decline without the constant attention of people. For these tree workers, the empire of the orange was a conditional blessing, depending on the type of contract. Early growers hired two separate, unequal sets of help. First, for technical tree work, citrus ranchers paid top dollar for licensed arborists who followed the latest advice from CES experts. These were the "great men" invoked in John Steinbeck's *The Grapes of Wrath*—"men of understanding and knowledge and skill," the equivalent of chemists, doctors, surgeons. Meanwhile, for seasonal "ranch labor"— harvesting, spraying, branch clearing, irrigating, ditch cleaning, cover-crop gardening, winter heating—owners employed a larger and cheaper population. Great men didn't work nine-hour days going up and down ladders with heavy loads. Such menial jobs went to itinerant white men or members of "lesser races."[41]

In the formative two decades of the fruit industry, roughly 1875 to 1895, Chinese men, together with remnants of the indigenous population, provided most of the hard labor in the San Gabriel and San Bernardino valleys. Native men and women picked, pitted, and dried stone fruit, mainly peaches. Chinese men tended the citrus. Since California's Chinese came from a subtropical region (Guangdong Province) with a long history of citriculture, they knew more about oranges than most colonists, who started their orchards in ignorance. In addition to grove work, Chinese men built the reservoirs, the water tunnels, the canals, and the railroads that enabled the Citrus Belt to prosper. As of 1880, the state's 75,000 Chinese immigrants (predominantly men) accounted for approximately one-twelfth of the total population and roughly one-quarter of the labor force. No immigrant minority in U.S. history was despised so much yet needed so much—"the indispensable enemy," to borrow one historian's apt phrase. In the Southland, horticulturists relied on Chinese workers for house cleaning, laundry, cooking, and table food. "The Chinese had vegetable and fruit wagons and went to all the [citrus] ranches," remembered a Glendora resident. "Things were very cheap and no rancher bothered with a garden."[42]

The famed Riverside colony could not live with or without its "Celestials." At fruit harvest time, the resident Chinese population in combination with the migrant population (housed in a tent city) outnumbered white residents. The situation induced apprehension and disgust. In 1885 the Riverside publisher and booster Luther M. Holt spearheaded a campaign to "drive the Chinamen out and tear down their filthy quarters." He pressed for "war" against the nuisance of Chinatown, an "abominable" place that was "breeding disease in the very heart of town." When Riverside passed a series of anti-Chinese city ordinances—all done in the name of public health—Chinese leaders accepted a plan to relocate the community (around five hundred people) to an arroyo on the edge of town. Developers later tore down the Chinese quarter and built a stately bank building with a clock tower. Holt proudly contrasted Riverside's legal, non-violent, and ostensibly consensual solution with the brutishness in rival Pasadena, where a mob had given "yellow devils" twenty-four hours to leave town, an eviction order punctuated with an effigy of a "Chinaman" hanged by a noose. To prevent an outbreak of violence, Pasadena business leaders called an emergency meeting in the office of Theodore Lukens (the eucalyptophile introduced in Chapter 3) and hastily drew up a restrictive covenant banning Chinese from the civic center. Luther Holt considered Pasadenans foolish to have antagonized their workers unduly. "The Chinese are bad enough," he explained, "but what would become of the raisin crop and the coming orange crop were it not for the Chinese to save it?"[43]

Extreme bias against Chinese immigrants suffused the Pacific Coast states. The federal government condoned the ethnic prejudice with the Chinese Exclusion Act (1882), the Scott Act (1888), and the Geary Act (1892). Cumulatively, these laws denied Chinese entry and reentry rights, classified resident immigrants from China as permanent aliens, and required them to carry registration papers at all times. In the aftermath, Chinese orchard workers became harder to find—and not just because of curtailed immigration, denied reentries, mass deportations, and outmigration to Mexico. Violence played a part. Scores of towns in Washington, Oregon, and California drove their "Mongols," "Chinks," and "coolies" out of town in locally coordinated purges. Anti-Chinese intimidation and foul play came to a head in 1885–86 and again in 1893, the year Redlands' sheriff earned statewide fame for exploiting the Geary Act to arrest and otherwise legally expel the local Chinese population.[44]

In the Golden State, agricultural reformers routinely praised horticulture for its potential to civilize and whiten California, a state with strong "mongrel" and "foreign" elements because of Spanish colonization and the Gold Rush. Amid flowering trees, supposedly, Anglo-Saxon families would take root and thrive. Orchardists always gave lip service to hiring "good white men" with wives and children, as husbands and fathers were assumed to be more responsible and pliant than single, childless men. In practice, though, seasonal workers of this higher grade could never be found in sufficient quantity. To make things worse, the available labor pool of itinerant white men— "hoboes," "bindlestiffs," "tramps," "white trash"—proved unreliable, despite their increasing numbers after the Panic of 1893.

Faced with a shortage of Chinese, citrus ranchers briefly considered importing black laborers from the South, then turned en masse to Japanese immigrants. From the mid-1890s through the World War I era, a period of industry modernization, men from Japan dominated the orchard labor market. Growers considered them more sober and industrious than bindlestiffs and more skillful and careful with their hands. Unlike California's Chinese, Japanese quite often immigrated as families; many workers had wives who could cook for them on site. As a bonus, explained a government commission, "the majority of the pickers of that race own bicycles, so that they can easily reach work at a distance from their camps and can be transferred from one grove to another at a distance with little loss of time." Because Japanese pickers worked in gangs, they could move in coordinated fashion from grove to grove, week to week, according to the demands of the harvest. Immigrant labor contractors, or "bosses," took a cut of their workers' wages, meaning that they had an incentive to offer growers a discount for hiring in bulk. This, in addition to racial discrimination, encouraged a two-tier wage system; Japanese earned less than whites for the same job. In some cases, owners demanded an extra hour from Japanese workers: their nine-hour day amounted to ten.

Although Japanese bosses profited from the below-market compensation of their own people, they also served as advocates; they could
organize work boycotts if citrus ranchers failed to deliver satisfactory
pay. After underbidding their labor to push competitors out of the
market, Japanese pickers in a work gang could strategically demand
changes to their contract, much like a union could.[45]

Riverside cultivated a reputation for being friendly to "Asiatics,"
notwithstanding the 1885 relocation of Chinatown. The town's growers and their families looked forward to each lunar New Year, when
the Chinese residents of the arroyo opened their homes and shared
the festive ambience of lanterns, candles, and firecrackers. During the
depression year of 1893, the editor of the *Riverside Press* denounced
the nonlocal unemployed white men—"hoodlums" and "anarchis-
tic agitators"—who regularly assaulted hardworking Asian immigrants. After an 1896 riot when a group of malcontents kidnapped
and expelled some Japanese laborers, Riverside owners requested (not
the first time) that local police protect their contractors. The colony
became a safe haven and a dumping ground for Japanese ejected from
neighboring communities. In 1910 Riverside's Japanese population
peaked; the 765 residents recorded by the census swelled to some
3,000 at harvest time, when this one ethnic group performed effectively all the grove work. In contrast, white workers formed a slight
majority in nearby Pomona and Redlands, where anti-Japanese prejudice burned hotter. Why was Riverside different? It had something
to do with the influence of the hotelier Frank Miller, a leading town
figure and noted Japanophile. Miller threw annual Japanese-themed
banquets and even received a medal of appreciation from the emperor
of Japan. Riverside's peculiar political economy helped, too. The town
was so incredibly wealthy that Issei (the first-generation immigrants)
could move into merchant-class positions such as grocer, restaurateur,
and gardener without threatening the ruling establishment. Elitism
opened a narrow pathway for acculturation and assimilation.[46]

Outside the relative safety of Riverside, Japanese workers—and
the ranchers who employed them—became targets for hatemongers.

From 1895 to 1905, anti-Japanese violence rocked the Citrus Belt. White men mainly refused to pick fruit alongside "Orientals," and when owners didn't segregate, trouble ensued. In 1904 Riverside's newspaper received a badly written anonymous threat: "be ware to the heathen Jap lovers," for the "10 night caps" would "tair up trees and burn houses of ever man hires Japs to pick oranges." That same year, a gang of men behind a "good-for-nothing Frenchman" ordered the Japanese out of Glendora on penalty of death, and they pulled down the workers' tent camp by the railroad tracks. In response, the immigrant community fortified and armed itself with shotguns. Rather than engage in battle with the Japanese, the "rioters" cut down a mature Valencia and placed a typewritten message on the stump for the owner: "Notice! Notice! Notice! Notice! My dear Mr. Beckwith— This will be repeated if you do not discharge the Japs in your employ at once, only next time we will get more trees." This was a stupid move. In the Citrus Belt, growers might tolerate intimidation against nonwhite workers off the job, but trespass and destruction of private property were beyond the pale. Using basic forensics—only five typewriters existed in Glendora—local police easily apprehended and prosecuted the vandals. In Covina, fed-up landowners stymied an attempted boycott against Japanese workers spearheaded by a white labor organizer. "I would not have hired Japanese if I could have got white men but I couldn't," said one citrus rancher. "I shall protect not only myself, but should any attempt be made to molest them while they are working on my ranch I shall be there with a gun to take care of them."[47]

In the era of Japanese labor, grove managers devised a new work regime. They took cues from industrialists of the Progressive era who enrolled "scientific managers" like Frederick Winslow Taylor to conduct time-and-motion investigations in their factories. When the CFGE hired the consultancy of G. Harold Powell, it asked for advice on improving efficiency as well as reducing spoilage. At Powell's recommendation, workers had to purchase a new kind of clipper with blunt tips and gloves with a strap to keep the clipper in place.

They had to cut the fruit off, across the stem, near the button—no more pulling. Ideally, workers would also use a tripod ladder and pick sides of rows instead of circling around entire trees. Powell also introduced the "Canterbury sack," a large canvas tote worn across the neck and shoulder. This 50-pound sack could be unhooked at the bottom so that oranges and lemons could roll out gently into specially designed boxes. "Handle the fruit like eggs!" instructed foremen. Each worker put his initials on his boxes—checked for abrasive bits of gravel, leaves, and twigs—so that his overseer could do individual quality monitoring. The Canterbury sack had the added advantage of freeing up both hands, since workers no longer carried buckets. To reduce dehydration, heatstroke, and fatigue, all of which contributed to carelessly picked fruit, water boys made rounds in the groves. To encourage even more efficiency, owners instituted a new pay system, which offered an extremely low base wage (below subsistence level) augmented by "bonuses" for quality and quantity. At a state convention in 1908, one grower from Riverside spoke glowingly of how the "Powell era" had ushered in "new money values."[48]

Japanese workers distinguished themselves after the "Powell revolution." They secured the highest wages of any nonwhite seasonal laborers in California and raised the standard picking rate for oranges from forty to seventy boxes per day. Whereas their predecessors, the Chinese, had been driven out of low-wage jobs, the Japanese lifted themselves out. Despite a series of prejudicial statutes—notably the 1913 California Alien Land Law, which forbade "aliens ineligible for citizenship" from owning farmland or leasing it long-term—many Japanese families in the Southland successfully moved on to truck farming. By the 1920s the Issei had largely transitioned out of the citrus industry, presenting a quandary for growers. The existing labor pool could not be refilled because the 1907 Gentlemen's Agreement cut off new immigration from Japan.[49]

As Japanese pickers left the market, CFGE members turned to cheaper, less organized sources of labor. They tried Koreans, Filipinos, and Punjabi Sikhs—disdainfully called "ragheads" and often mistakenly called "Hindus." (In 1909 the *Los Angeles Times* reported on the "serious Hindu invasion" that competed with the Japanese, or "little brown men.")[50] But in the end citrus ranchers turned overwhelmingly to Mexican immigrants. Labor recruiters benefited from the social and economic disruptions of the Mexican Revolution, which pushed tens of thousands of refugees across the border. A U.S. labor shortage during World War I pulled in more. California's agricultural aristocracy lobbied for, and received, an open-door immigration policy vis-à-vis Mexico, even as Congress directed exclusionary laws at Europe and all of Asia. The Golden State's seasonal farm labor population became predominantly Spanish-speaking before the Great Depression, when, for the first time, the United States restricted immigration from Mexico. During World War II, growers augmented the resident immigrant labor force with guest workers under the bilateral Bracero Program. To this day, Mexican nationals make up nearly 100 percent of the citrus-picking crews in California.

Growers justified their switch to Mexican labor with racial as well as economic calculus. One prominent voice, the manager of the agricultural department of the Los Angeles Chamber of Commerce, expressed a strong preference for "the Mexican," by which he meant not "the cholo"—a disparaging stereotype of a street gang member—but instead "the peon of strictly rural habits and Indian descent." The dark-skinned *campesino* "is ignorant of values; he knows nothing of time; he knows nothing of our laws; he is as primitive as we were 2,500 years ago." In short, "he is the most tractable individual that ever came to serve us." Reputedly he would look up to the grower as a *padron*. Also, unlike "the Filipino," who would create a sexual menace by pursuing white women, "the Mexican is never a biological problem. He rarely marries out of his own people. A Mexican man never marries a white woman."[51]

Citrus ranchers succeeded in making their Mexican workforce permanent. Across the Citrus Belt, barrios grew up on the edges of colonies, often astride or beyond the train tracks or in the stream bottoms. Often called "Mexican camps" or "Jimtowns," these *colo-*

nias were essentially semiautonomous villages with no more comforts than rural communities in Mexico. *Colonias* generally lacked services such as paved roads and indoor plumbing. While white residents lived up the slope, barrio residents lived in the lower elevations.[52]

Yet these "peons" didn't always follow the script written for them. Early on, Mexicans orange pickers (sometimes called *naranjeros*) tried their hand at labor activism. In solidarity with Sikh workers and with help from the Industrial Workers of the World, pickers in the Riverside-Claremont district in 1917 went on strike for better wages—and won. The World War I labor market put workers in a position of strength. A follow-up labor action in the San Gabriel Valley in the postwar year 1919 produced different results: police action and community vigilantism carried the day. Nonlocal IWW activists attempted to co-opt the strike, which, in the midst of the nationwide Red Scare, made it easy for growers to cast local Japanese and Mexican fruit pickers as allies or victims of "Russian agitators" and "Bolshevik conspirators." In one instance, a large group of Anglo nightriders arrested thirty-one "disturbers," loaded them onto a truck, and dumped them in the Boyle Heights neighborhood of Los Angeles, where many actual Russians lived. In the strike's aftermath, the editors of the *California Citrograph* suggested that it might be necessary to string "electrified wire entanglements" around orange groves to prevent foreign syndicalists from spiking trunks with copper nails (poison for plants). Growers believed rumors that agents of anarchy stood ready to pour "destroying fluid" on citrus roots. This fear was exaggerated but not baseless. Wobblies in the San Gabriel Valley had threatened to kill trees—the owners' means of production—with knives. And in 1918, as reported by the *Times*, "some miscreant with pronounced I.W.W. proclivities if not an actual member of that disloyal, pro-German organization" had killed about five hundred fruit trees (mostly Bartlett pears) at Tehachapi.[53]

Despite occasional repression and the daily indignities of racism, working conditions on a citrus ranch were, as one undercover investigator wrote in 1914, "perhaps the best that could exist in any seasonal industry." Worse labor exploitation occurred in California's cotton fields, its table-grape vineyards, and its strawberry farms. Compared to most other crops, the orange-picking season lasted a long time; lemons went year-round. In the Southland, *naranjeros* could find near-continuous work with limited migration, working the inland valleys in the fall and winter, harvesting navels, and rotating to the coastal plain in the spring and summer, harvesting Valencias. Most of these pickers were not migrant laborers in the usual sense, for they had a permanent residence. Because packinghouses hired mainly women, the citrus industry offered couples the possibility of cohabiting and raising children. Young sons worked weekends in the groves, harvesting from lower branches and off the ground; these *ratas* (rats) deposited golden fruits in their fathers' field boxes, adding pennies to the family bank. But even with kinfolk to anchor him, an orange picker's life wasn't easy. "People worked in citrus because they had to, not because they liked it," recalled one Mexican American. "Nobody liked it."[54]

MANAGERIAL CONTROL

The era of the "aesthetic millionaire" who treated an orange grove merely "as a plaything, as a diversion, as a pleasure" passed away in the twentieth century. Overcapitalization forced out all but the most professional growers, those who could turn a profit despite inflated property taxes and high interest rates in a region far removed from America's main financial markets. As in most leveraged enterprises, already wealthy people who could afford to lose a bet now and then came to profit most from citrus. High potential rewards came with high starting costs (land, clearing, seedlings) and high fixed costs (water, fertilizer, oil, equipment, crop insurance, fees to the local exchange). Labor costs added up, too. Before World War I, an active retiree on his small-time citrus ranch might complete the harvest with his family and a modest amount of hired help. In the subsequent era, owners gave up sweat. Consolidation in the industry gave rise to larger orchards with more overseers and more workers per acre. Inexorably, horticapitalism altered the horticultural ideal in California. Degree by degree, the colony model of smallholdings in mutual water companies gave way to agribusiness plantations. As of World War I, 30 acres was still considered a large grove, and the majority of growers owned just 5 to 10 acres—enough trees to make a comfortable living. The median for the period between 1915 and 1945 was 17 acres. But a powerful minority—fewer than two hundred owners—controlled upward of 100 acres. The new big players invested in Valencias and lemons, crops with lower profit margins than select navels. Whereas navel-bearing acreage stayed roughly the same (hovering around 90,000 acres) between World War I and World War II, Valencia-bearing acreage doubled to about 140,000, fueled in part by the popularity of fresh-squeezed OJ. As a result, by 1940, roughly 4 percent of California's orange growers owned 40 percent of the total acreage.[55]

With these economic transitions, the geography of citrus changed. On a map, the groves of Southern California now resembled a ring more than a belt. The lemon and Valencia oligarchy established rural spreads of 1,000 to 4,000 acres in Orange County and the San Fernando Valley. In general, the towns that serviced Valencias occupied a different class stratum from the navel colonies. The Valencia zone contained fewer people and poorer amenities. A town like Placentia felt rustic, even hick, compared to genteel Riverside with its palm-lined boulevards. Most of the megagroves postdated the pioneer era of mutual water companies; the Valley got its water from the Los Angeles Aqueduct (1913). In northern Orange County, Charles Chapman, popularly known as the "father of the Valencia orange," almost singlehandedly turned the Fullerton district into a major player that rivaled Riverside and Redlands in citrus production. Farther south, the Irvine Company, the county's largest landowner, converted hundreds of acres of pasture and cropland to oranges and lemons in the first three decades of the twentieth century.[56]

The biggest player of them all, Limoneira Ranch, was tucked away in the Santa Clara River Valley of Ventura County. The company originated in 1893 with a group of eastern investors who had made fortunes in Pennsylvania oil and Sierra Nevada timber and who had initially been attracted to Ventura by petroleum prospects. Citrus proved more profitable. In the first half of the twentieth century, Limoneira was essentially a self-contained company town (including playgrounds, churches, stores) rather than an outgrowth of adjacent Santa Paula. Charles Collins Teague, a grandnephew of one of the oilmen, presided over the operation as president and manager. He practiced a form of business paternalism over his five hundred or so employees, most of them Mexican, all of whom he knew by name. Teague believed that providing housing for workers increased company profits in the long term, for it encouraged marriage and children and created a stable labor force. He hired the Greene brothers of Pasadena, celebrated for their Arts and Crafts architecture, to design his bunkhouses. In the industry, Limoneira cultivated a reputation as the leader in all things—"a sort of lemon Jerusalem." Even in town, Teague's influence loomed large; he and his partners essentially ran Santa Paula's banks, waterworks, the chamber of commerce, and the city council.[57]

Next to C. C. Teague, the leading citrus figure during the Sunkist era of consolidation was G. Harold Powell. Originally the USDA pomologist had come to the West Coast purely as a consultant. He couldn't contain his enthusiasm to be working with "so many big men" like Teague; straightaway he purchased a new black coat and vest in Los Angeles so he could make a good impression. A self-styled "intellectual aristocrat," Powell imagined for himself a brighter future than working with dirt farmers in his native upstate New York. "There is no class of people in the east who approach the orange growers in intelligence and in large business affairs," he wrote to his wife on stationery from the Mission Inn in Riverside, "the finest hotel I have ever stopped at." (During Powell's stay in 1904, the hotel hosted a masquerade ball with full orchestra.) Lured away from the public sector,

Powell eventually moved his family to Southern California. There he became general manager (essentially the CEO) of the CFGE. Now he paid visits to fruit ranchers in his own vehicle, a maroon Marmon touring car with *GHP* painted on the front doors. During World War I, Powell took a partial leave of absence to serve, at Herbert Hoover's request, as the head of the Perishable Foods Division of the U.S. Food Administration. In 1922 this dynamic leader, barely fifty, dropped dead of a heart attack in the dining room of a Pasadena hotel.[58]

Powell personified the transition from tree culture to horticapitalism. He had started out as a student of the Cornell professor Liberty Hyde Bailey, America's preeminent horticultural scientist and rural reformer, an advocate of the country life movement. Whereas Professor Bailey imagined a second life for the U.S. family farm, the times ahead would belong to corporate entities like the CFGE, a well-oiled machine. Three organizational levels existed above the growers: some two hundred packinghouses, a couple of dozen district exchanges, and one central exchange. The first two levels handled picking and packing, hiring and overseeing. Thus a citrus rancher affiliated with the CFGE could farm out almost all his work. The top-level central exchange, based in downtown Los Angeles, handled the large-scale business issues. It expanded in the interwar years to some twenty departments—legal, claims, advertising, transportation, sales, research, industrial relations, insurance, and so on. A board of directors, with one representative from each district, oversaw the whole operation. The sales team divided the nation into six areas, subdivided into various branches. The CFGE formed its own telegraph department (later teletype) to relay market and sales information every working hour to and from scores of branch offices across the country. Only rival meatpackers Swift and Armour spent more on telecommunications bills.

The CFGE was a strange kind of business. Although it handled millions of dollars in fees and brought in millions more in profit, it didn't technically own any capital or property. As a marketing cooperative, it occupied an ambiguous legal category: a nonprofit that enjoyed the same legal standing as a stock corporation, even though it sold no shares and issued no dividends. All its proceeds went back to members. Seeing the advantage of this system, thousands of citrus ranchers "bought in," and each member proudly displayed a personalized green, white, and orange porcelain sign that proclaimed SUNKIST GROWER. The CFGE emphasized federated individualism, not unionism—or, God forbid, communism. The rhetoric of the small, democratic, mutualistic citrus colony persisted in the face of a complex, integrated, oligarchic agribusiness. Buying in didn't ensure equal representation. Instead of one vote per member, the CFGE granted more votes to large growers. By the late 1920s the mega-cooperative controlled the marketing of roughly 75 percent of California's orange crop and virtually all its lemons. In any other sector, this kind of market share would be called a monopoly. However, the Clayton Act (1914) and the Capper-Volstead Act (1922) specifically exempted agricultural cooperatives from antitrust laws—a gift from Congress. The citrus elite were not above seeking, and accepting, further federal assistance. As the great California historian Robert Glass Cleland wrote in 1947, growers "regard a high protective tariff as the keystone of American prosperity" even as they "regard socialism, communism, and the New Deal as synonymous; and condemn all forms of federal aid to the individual—except when such aid is needed by the citrus industry itself."[59]

To advance its political agenda, the CFGE created a subsidiary, the Citrus Protective League, in 1906. This public relations and lobbying firm focused on matters such as railroad rates, customs, and legislation. Charles Chapman, the Fullerton-based "orange king of California," served as president for many years. Lemon growers benefited most from his work, for their crop faced special challenges. In addition to intractable problems of curing (inducing green rinds to turn a desirable yellow color) and storing (holding on to the winter-spring harvest until the great summer demand for lemonade), they had to contend with deep-pocketed foreign competitors in Sicily. The league and the Lemon Men's Club lobbied hard for a duty on Italian lemons, and secured it as part of the Payne-Aldrich Act (1909). Following this tariff, Sunkist growers "sacrificed" one hundred cars of lemons—that is, sold the fruit at an artificially depressed price to sever the connection between U.S. buyers and Sicilian suppliers. As a result of hardball tactics, California lemons jumped from less than 20 percent of domestic consumption in 1900 to more than 80 percent by 1920.

Regarding labor issues, the managers of the CFGE brought a similar hardheaded mindset, albeit tinged with paternalism. For the technical work of pruning lemons—the most unruly of all citrus types—growers paid premium price for experienced Sicilian workers. Picking fruit from the thorny branches was another story: owners went to the cheapest source. In his breezy autobiography, C. C. Teague expressed his view that Mexicans "are naturally adapted to agricultural work, particularly in the handling of fruit and vegetables." They are "good-natured and happy." According to Teague, Mexicans never became public charges or tramps. They resembled the "loyal and dependable" Chinese. The Japanese were quite different—capable and useful, but "lack[ing] the qualities of loyalty and reliability." Nostalgia for the once despised Chinese worker was characteristic of Teague's generation.[60]

Upon Teague's election to the presidency of the CFGE in 1920, the cooperative created an Industrial Relations Department (IRD) to varnish the public image of citrus work and to encourage internal improvements in worker management. IRD provided architectural and building plans for growers and profiled model communities in *California Citrograph*. Likewise, citrus ranchers discussed labor strategies at conferences and meetings sponsored by industry groups such as the Lemon Men's Club. The CFGE singled out Limoneira and the Chase Plantation, an orange and lemon concern in Corona, for praise. Ethan Allen Chase noted in his diary that he had built adobes "down by the canal, out of the way," for his "Mexican help." Such semifeudal benevolence took a variety of forms in the Citrus Belt: rental barracks, rent-free tract homes, or free land on which workers could build their own *campos* out of whatever lumber they could scavenge or afford (with cash or with credit from the ranch). In the prior era, orchardists might offer nonwhite workers only a shack with no bedding or a drafty barn with hay—if they provided any housing at all. By contrast, during the presidency of Teague (1920–1950), large affiliates such as Foothill Ranch in Riverside County practiced corporate welfare: they opened company stores and medical offices (offering goods and services in exchange for company credit), schools for children, home economics classes for women, baseball leagues for men. Did this look like *The Grapes of Wrath*? asked Teague. He publicly condemned the filming of John Steinbeck's novel as a misrepresentation of California's agricultural workers.[61]

The IRD used its resources to sponsor Americanization programs and English proficiency classes for Spanish-speaking citrus workers. The departmental director recommended a practical approach to ESL: "Instead of giving them such sentences as 'See the red hen crossing the street,' give them something about the business in which they derive their livelihood. Let the instructor draw a picture on the board of an orange tree and a man in front of it. A line such as 'See the Mexican picking oranges,' or 'The man is picking oranges the right way.'" An actual IRD lesson plan in "everyday English" included these lines:

> The men put the great white tents over the orange trees.
> The men fill the tents with hydrocyanic acid gas.
> This hydrocyanic acid gas kills all the insects on the trees.
> Insects spoil the fruit.
> Hydrocyanic acid gas kills insects.[62]

Outreach to Mexican workers also took the form of local charities. In Glendora, for example, women's club members created a "Mexican friendly center," which hosted sewing lessons and an annual Christmas party, and sponsored scholarships for "brighter" Mexican boys to attend private school. In Pasadena, Clara Odell of the Woman's Christian Temperance Union directed sanitation, education, and

Americanization campaigns at the women and children of "Sonora town." Thanks to the efforts of female Protestant reformers, Pasadena gained a day nursery, vocational school, settlement house, laundry, and maternity hospital, all for the exclusive use of Mexicans.[63]

The concomitant of selfless Christian maternalism and self-interested corporate paternalism was racist exclusion. In many citrus towns, including Upland—originally part of the famed Ontario colony—the ruling population enforced a western version of Jim Crow. Through the mid-1940s, Mexicans had to travel in segregated streetcars and avoid stores with signs that announced WHITES ONLY. All over Southern California, not just in the Citrus Belt, municipal pools opened their doors to "coloreds" once a week on International Day or Mexican Day—the swim session right before the scheduled draining and cleaning. In movie theaters, Mexicans (and blacks) had to sit against the walls or go to the balcony. Mexican-American children throughout the Golden State attended segregated schools.[64]

Ethnic intimidation could be framed as good civics. Mexican citrus workers watched with foreboding the appearance of the second Ku Klux Klan, a service and fraternal club somewhat like Kiwanis or Rotary International, albeit with virulent antiunion, anti-immigrant, anti-Catholic politics. The Klan built a substantial following throughout the Southland, especially Orange County, in the 1920s. Anaheim, the future home of Disneyland, was for a short and controversial period the KKK's model city in California. In 1924 Anaheim hosted a regional Klan rally and initiation ceremony in its city park, decorated for the occasion with a 30-foot-high cross with electric lights. Hundreds of civic-minded members of the Orange Empire, men and women, donned white hoods over their suits and dresses and swore allegiance to the Invisible Empire.[65]

In the 1930s Orange County witnessed the harshest instance of strikebreaking in the history of California citrus, an event that mocked the managerial benevolence promoted by the IRD. Indeed, the Great Depression inspired all kinds of labor radicalism and anti-unionism in the Golden State. In 1934 the novelist Upton Sinclair campaigned for governor on a socialist platform (End Poverty in California), a bid stifled by the Democratic and Republican establishments, including some high-level politicking by CFGE president C. C. Teague. Two years later came the great orange strike. In its coverage of the Orange County "citrus war," the right-wing *Los Angeles Times* decried the "Communist disorders"—an organized invasion by a gang of Reds under "Moscow's direct order." (Just as fancifully, the Orange County Protective Association accused the strikers of being revolutionary followers of president Lázaro Cárdenas of Mexico.) The *Times* praised the hired muscle and deputized volunteers who repulsed the insurgency. The left-wing social critic Carey McWilliams reported his astonishment at the same scene: "How quickly social power could crystallize into an expression of arrogant brutality in these lovely, seemingly placid, outwardly Christian communities." When unionized orange pickers went on strike, they were "escorted" by police back to the trees and, as the strike continued, threatened with deportation, evicted from homes on county land, rounded up, arrested on trumped-up charges such as loitering and trespassing, jailed in a stockade, sentenced by a kangaroo court. With tacit approval from law enforcement, thuggish vigilantes bombarded labor organizers with tear gas, beat them with clubs, intimidated them with shotguns. The sheriff of Orange County, who owned his own grove, even issued shoot-to-kill orders after strikers attacked strikebreakers. Law enforcers used portable radio sets to coordinate their clampdown. They openly displayed machine guns in courtrooms. To McWilliams this whole "terroristic campaign" against Mexican workers was nothing less than "Fascism in practice."[66]

In normal times, the hand of management did its best to be invisible. Workers—and worker control—almost never appeared in the visual propaganda issued by the Southern California promotion machine. Instead, over and over, postcards and stereoscopic cards and souvenir books—and literally millions of lithographed orange crate labels—showed orderly rows of fruitful trees surrounding tidy country homes, backed by snowcapped mountains, often with a white woman or white child (or a palm) in the foreground. The standard-issue beautiful girls wore expensive or revealing dresses and struck comely poses, sometimes in heels and fur coats. Even the one stock image of workingmen, the postcard view down an orchard row at picking time, with Japanese or Mexicans on ladders, staring at the camera with inscrutable faces, could be whitewashed. In or around the 1940s, the CFGE produced a series of what might be called citrus soft porn: pinups of smiling young women in bathing suits or shorts, balanced on ladders, picking oranges while bending for the camera.[67]

The image of the citrus idyll—*urbs in horto*—persisted in American culture long after the industry moved away from its ideological roots. In *The Grapes of Wrath*, Ma Joad naively anticipates "how nice it's gonna be, maybe, in California. Never cold. An' fruit ever'place, an' people just bein' in the nicest places, little white houses in among the orange trees." As Steinbeck knew from personal observation, the modern horticultural dream was inaccessible to all but the horticapitalists. Even before the Great Depression, the social structure of the Citrus Belt looked like a pyramid. Industrious Mexican picking crews occupied the wide base; above them, to use Carey McWilliams's biting words, sat the "managerial elite" in the orchard overseer's office or the CFGE building in Los Angeles; and finally, on top, lazed the "do-nothings who own the groves." The placid beauty of towns like Pasadena, with its millionaire row on Orange Grove Boulevard—including a mansion owned by William Wrigley, friend and business associate of adman Albert Lasker—concealed a harsh inequality.[68]

Although the commonwealth of Sunkist excluded many, it lifted the entire regional economy. In the words of two economic historians, "Citrus, no less than real estate subdivision and water development, helped to make Los Angeles the preeminent urban center of the twentieth-century American West." Unlike mines and railroads, which tended to move wealth from the U.S. West to the East, citrus enticed eastern money to California. The same was true of the state's oil sector. Together, citrus and petroleum propelled the Southland to global prominence in the early twentieth century. After the completion of the Panama Canal in 1914, California fruit flooded the European market. As of the 1920s, the Golden State's output in oranges regularly exceeded that of Spain, the next leading producer. In Los Angeles County in the interwar era, citrus generated more wealth than airplane manufacturing and filmmaking combined. Growers of premium navels did go through a rough patch during the Depression, when anemic sales forced them to dump carload after carload of perfectly good fruit. Even so, per capita winter consumption of oranges in the United States doubled from 10 pounds per person in 1919–20 to 20 in 1939–40. Sales rallied during World War II, especially for juice-ready Valencias. On the eve of the war, the Southland led the whole world in citrus production; the industry as a whole employed something like 200,000 people statewide and annually shipped out about 50 million boxes of fruit picked from over 20 million trees. California orange growers at their peak in the mid-1940s supplied roughly 60 percent of the U.S. supply and a quarter of the world's. Their fruit ranked as the number-one plant commodity in the nation's most profitable farm state. In the long run, citrus did in fact create more wealth for the Golden State than gold. Horticapitalists reinvested much of that profit in California, jumpstarting a host of other businesses. As the total value of their commodity increased, property values did, too. Long before postwar population pressures, citrus inflated the price of land and housing in Greater Los Angeles.[69]

There were, it should be said, plenty of business failures in oranges and lemons. As C. C. Teague said with approval, the citrus business promoted "the survival of the fittest": "The poorly located, poorly watered, poorly cared for orchards must inevitably drop out of the running." The managerial elite felt no pity for the suckers who bought frost-susceptible land or no-good trees (a scenario parodied in the W. C. Fields film *It's a Gift*). "It is strange," wrote a Riverside pomologist, "how many unsophisticated persons there are in Northern cities who will trustingly send their money by mail to some agent with the request that he 'Be sure to select a nice orange grove for them.'"[70]

Contrary to promotional images about nature-made bounty in

Southern California, citrus was an unnatural outgrowth of the local environment. Sunkist ranchers knew this full well. They narrated their business history as a series of "problems" intelligently solved: the problem of water, of infestation, of overproduction, of packing, of shipping, of merchandising, of advertising, of labor, and so on. Each of these "problems" had been overcome through some combination of capital, science, politics—and occasional brute force. To accomplish this Herculean task—to turn a mostly treeless, semiarid landscape into a pygmy forest of tropical fruit—required the combination of large-scale low-wage labor, enormous capital investment, and technological innovation. As one agricultural historian said in the 1920s, "California fruit production was really an act in industrial creation." Although Los Angeles County contained the most valuable farm country in America, it didn't look "rural." Instead of cows, chickens, barns, and tarpaper shacks, one saw warehouses, concrete canals, telephone and power lines, and oil tanks—all in the service of trees. In the words of a contemporary journalist, "The orange-grower is not a farmer." Rather, he is "a manufacturer whose raw material, soil, water and sunshine, is transformed into the finished product by living trees instead of machinery." What Detroit meant to cars, Riverside meant to oranges. When social critics of the Depression era—people such as John Steinbeck, Carey McWilliams, and Paul Taylor—inveighed against "factories in the field" and "industrialized agriculture," they used the same metaphors as the owners. The citrus was a growth machine.[71]

CHAPTER 6

Cultural Costs

LABORATORIES IN THE GROVE

Imagine the scene, circa 1920: from the Oxnard Plain to the San Fernando Valley, across the wide San Gabriel and San Bernardino valleys, down the gentle coastal plain of Orange County, trees festoon the landscape. A fructuous grid spreads out as far as the eye can see—even rows of identically pruned evergreens with white blossoms and colorful fruit, orchards with eucalyptic windbreaks, mansions with palm-lined driveways, and, tucked away, beyond the gaze of visitors, Mexican shantytowns. This was the Orange Empire. It would not last. In the opening years of the Cold War, Southern California's citrus economy began to debilitate; by the end of the twentieth century, the iconic groves had all but disappeared, replaced by subdivisions, freeways, shopping malls, and warehouses. The Citrus Belt relocated from the Southland to the Central Valley. Push and pull factors account for this immense transplantation of tree stock and the associated economic consolidation. Citriculture is expensive; orange and lemon trees, like cars, require regular maintenance for optimal performance. They must be irrigated, fertilized, pruned, sprayed, fumigated, and heated during cold winter periods. Growers referred to these expenditures as "cultural costs." As costs rose in the postwar period, as land values and tax rates went higher in the Southland, as disease outbreaks afflicted older orchards, owners did the math: it made financial sense to start over in distant Tulare County. The social ecology of citrus once again altered the physical geography of California.

Commercial citriculture in the Golden State began with innovation, not tradition. The retirees, invalids, snowbirds, dabblers, and entrepreneurs who populated the fruit colonies brought little or no background knowledge in agriculture, much less citriculture. The lessons of subtropical Florida didn't apply here. "Of all the fruits, common in California, probably none are grown under a more unnatural environment than is the case with citrus," wrote one expert. "In the wild state the edible species of citrus are usually found growing in partial shade, in hot, humid climates, on soils rich in organic matter and abundantly supplied with water from the heavy rainfall." In semi-arid Southern California, orchardists proceeded in trial-and-error fashion, sharing their successes and failures in horticultural journals and at fruit growers' conventions. Before extension agents began their service, farmers sought advice in letters to Eugene Hilgard, dean of the University of California's College of Agriculture (1868). Later they flocked to farm demonstration trains co-sponsored by the university and Southern Pacific and attended "farmers' institutes," hugely popular events where scientists presented accessible versions of their research and growers gave lectures based on tinkering and occasional large-scale experiments. Many citrus towns enjoyed their own horticultural clubs and pomological societies, partly for sociability, partly for amateur science.[1]

Citruses were notoriously demanding and finicky—the prima donnas of the horticultural world. Their demands began with fertility. California's most valuable tree type, the Washington navel, produced no pollen, few viable ovules, and scarcely any seeds. The varietal's survival depended entirely on human intervention. To make a grove of navels, you started, strangely enough, with seeds of a different kind of orange. You planted them shallowly in a seedbed under lath shelters that offered protection from sunburn and bird beaks. In the second year, you removed the seedlings from the bed and tossed out the slow growers and those with crooked roots and irregular foliage. Perhaps half the total made the cut. You transplanted the good specimens, 12 to 18 inches high, into the open in widely spaced nursery rows. Next came budding. First you cut a "bud stick" (a bud plus a thin layer of supporting tissue) from a navel donor. Then you used a sharp knife to incise a T through the bark of the young host and gently slipped the scion inside the wound. Then you bandaged the union with wax tape. To force the bud to become the lead stem, you partially cut the existing stem at a point above the bud and bent it so it lay on the ground, where it acted as nurse. Once the scion took hold, you cut off the nurse limb. Now the roots of one varietal fed the fruiting branches of another. A speaker at a farmer's institute in 1897 summed it up: "You have taken a bud from a precocious variety of tree, and by uniting it with a seedling root you have produced the most ravenous feeder of the citrus family, and also the most perfect machine for making superb fruit yet known to the business."[2]

One year after budding, nurserymen clipped, excavated, and "balled" all the "grove-ready" trees for sale.[3] Before a shipment arrived, buyers performed a lot of preparatory work. They cleared away native plants and rocks and leveled the land with California-made machines like the "Fresno scraper." If the hardpan was too hard for plowing, they used dynamite charges to create pockets for trees. Growers hired surveyors to mark the location of each planting precisely, or, more cheaply, unspooled a stiff wire as a guide. Citrus ranchers bedded and staked their trees geometrically according to a few systems, such as the square, the triangular, and the hexagonal. A typical acre contained eighty or ninety citruses spaced 20 to 30 feet apart.

To protect young stock, growers bedded eucalyptus, interspersed with cypress, on the perimeter. The quick-sprouting gums blunted the Santa Ana winds—also called "northers," "Cajon winds," and "electrical winds." (According to one local source, the current name derives from Citrus Belt rivalries: in Pasadena they pilloried the winds as "Riversiders," and in Anaheim as "Santa Anas.") These fierce gales,

The California Citrograph

TEN CENTS A COPY
ONE DOLLAR A YEAR

A Monthly Publication Devoted to the Interests of the Citrus Industry

JANUARY, 1929
VOL. XIV, NO. 3

SURVIVING PARENT WASHINGTON NAVEL ORANGE TREE AT RIVERSIDE
This tree and its companion, now dead, have contributed more to the wealth of California than all the gold that has been produced here. This tree is one of the most unique horticultural possessions of the southwest and has been happily set in this attractive parkway in the midst of thousands of beautiful acres of its progeny—a shrine to the citrus industry.—Photo by Avery Edwin Field, Riverside.

The survivor of the two original Washington navel trees in a pocket park in Riverside, 1929. The historic plaque honors Eliza Tibbets, the "mother" of the money tree. In commemoration of golden wealth, arborists have gone to great lengths to keep this plant alive. (Note the inarched roots, the result of reconstructive surgery.)

President Theodore Roosevelt at the Mission Inn in Riverside, 1903, ceremonially replanting the other of the two parent navels. When this tree died in 1922, superstitious locals claimed that its decline had begun soon after T.R.'s death in 1919.

In 1900 an elderly Luther Tibbets, "father of the orange," was trotted out for the Riverside Street Fair. The honor was tinged with indignity, for the sign misspelled his name. A few years later, he died in a poorhouse.

Terraced hillsides with groves of navel oranges west of Riverside, 1905. Southern California fruit growers felt pride that they had "redeemed" an arid "waste."

Growing tropical trees in this climate required elaborate irrigation infrastructure, including dams, artesian wells, tunnels, flumes, canals, and, as shown here, headgates and ditches.

A classic citrus crate label, ca. 1920, with standard iconographic features: an attractive young woman, a lovely homestead, snowcapped mountains under sunny skies, and individually wrapped branded fruit. Hundreds of millions of such images were printed from the late nineteenth century through the 1950s.

One of many examples of a postcard genre that contrasted winter in the East with "winter's summer garden."

A Sunkist promotional image, ca. 1940s. In the fantasy of California sold to tourists and consumers, citriculture did not require nonwhite workers; picking oranges was fun, even sexy.

A more realistic view of grove work, ca. 1880s, showing Chinese workers. Anti-Asian policies at the state and federal levels—plus many local acts of violence and intimidation—pushed out Chinese and later Japanese labor. By the 1920s, Mexican pickers predominated.

Woodcut illustration to Carey McWilliams's "Gunkist," a report on the violent suppression of the 1936 pickers' strike in Orange County.

904:—Orange Groves and Oil Wells, Calif.

In the early twentieth century, citrus and oil were the two leading industries of Southern California. In certain locales, notably Fullerton (*above*), oil derricks rose directly above orange trees. The proximity of wells and refineries to groves encouraged the widespread use of crude oil for orchard heating during winter freezes (*below*). Smudging, the region's original air pollution problem, generated heated local controversy.

A fumigation crew hoists a heavy canvas tent over a citrus tree in preparation for nighttime application of hydrocyanic acid gas. Even though California growers practiced biological control, their commercial oranges and lemons required large doses of fumigation and spraying.

The fate of millions of trees in Los Angeles and Orange counties in the 1950s: a stump puller makes room for development.

which typically descended from the high desert in late fall, uprooted many oranges in 1887 and again in 1891, when orchards glowed in the dark from static electricity and "balls of fire leaped from tree to tree." The desiccating winds caused windburn and tissue collapse in the leaves. In lieu of windbreaks, growers sometimes built individual shelters—simple structures such as burlap on a stake—to protect young trees. They also wrapped newspaper or cornstalks around trunks to prevent wind, sun, and rodent damage. Then they waited. After planting, it took an additional three to five years for citruses to produce marketable fruit. From seeding to fruiting, the process of building a bearing navel took about eight years. Owners had to "bridge the time" before their investment gave returns.[4]

The waiting game cost a pretty penny, because the shallow-rooted tropical trees required regular watering. In California, a navel needed the equivalent of 25 to 40 inches of rain per year. The average annual rainfall in Riverside is around 10 inches, and the average high temperature in midsummer is 95° F, with low humidity. For industrial-scale citriculture, the simple irrigation system used at the San Gabriel Mission and the Wolfskill orchard—watering each tree individually by filling an embanked basin surrounding it—wouldn't suffice. It was superseded by the more technical and expensive "Riverside method": furrows fed by flumes controlled by dams. Irrigation could be too much of a good thing: salt leached from waterlogged soil, causing rot in the roots and lower trunk; the tree oozed dark gooey sap (a condition called gummosis) in response to the fungal disease. Superior groves in the Citrus Belt possessed well-drained sandy loam in addition to senior water rights.

Even the best soil in Southern California behaved differently from tropical forest soil. It lacked the organic richness—the layers of humus—necessary to support a citrus ranch at the commercial level over the long term. Without nutritional inputs, an intensively planted grove declined in productivity within a few years. To address the "fertilization problem," California growers tried cover crops. They sowed vetch (of the pea family) and other leguminous vegetation to fix nitrogen and to create "green humus" they could plow under in spring. But too much tillage caused "plow-sole," a hard, impervious layer a few inches below the surface that interfered with irrigation drainage. To supplement cover crops, citrus ranchers purchased a variety of additives, including animal byproducts: tankage, whale blood, salmon scrap, bonemeal, manure, and bat guano. They also recycled culled fruits and pruned branches from their own trees.

Of all the "problems" of citriculture, pruning inspired the most disagreement. California horticultural magazines carried endless debates between proponents of light cutting and heavy cutting, "thinning out" (removing the whole branch) and "heading back" (cutting to a stub), "high pruning" and "low pruning." Did branch thinning coax "shy bearers" into better fruiting, or did it lead to sunburn, excess suckering, and general devitalization? The pendulum of opinion swung back and forth over the years. In general, growers of the early 1900s pruned far less than the pioneer generation, but neglecting to prune was unacceptable. Left to go "wild," most citruses assume tall columnar forms. Orchardists prefer them stunted and globular. The rationale is simple economics. Beyond a certain size, the cost of maintaining a tree exceeds the added return from increased fruit production. It doesn't pay to spray, fumigate, and harvest the crop on a giant tree with a wild top. As a rule, a navel (a natural semidwarf) requires light pruning, while a Valencia (a much larger tree) requires moderate pruning and a lemon requires heavy pruning. Lemon trees feature irregular and polymorphic growth. Off-type limbs may produce an entirely different kind of citrus fruit. Unruly branches extend in every direction, including spindly shoots and strong horizontal water sprouts called "riders." To avoid tall limbs that could bend or break under the weight of fruit, pruners give lemons characteristic flat tops.[5]

Before commercial fertilization became the norm in the twentieth century, California growers routinely tore out their citruses after twenty or twenty-five years, believing that peak production had passed. They eventually pushed that rotational schedule to fifty

years, with maximum yield at about thirty-five years. By global standards, one half-century of productivity was still unimpressive. California citrus trees produced great profit, but they depreciated (went
"retrograde") faster than those in tropical regions. Decline affected
whole generations of groves, not just individual trees. Oranges and
lemons tended to underperform and sicken when placed in locations
previously used for citrus. In the early twentieth century, horticultural manuals referred to the "replant problem" of "old citrus soils,"
and growers swapped news about the widespread and mysterious
"mottle-leaf malady." Researchers at Riverside's Citrus Experiment
Station (CES) in the early 1930s determined the cause: zinc deficiency. The problem was solved with sprays containing the metallic
element. Today citriculturists use sophisticated leaf tissue analyses to
develop customized fertilization strategies.[6]

What happened when a sick, old grove reached the end of its
productive life cycle? Rather than uproot the trees and start from
scratch—a slow and expensive process—many growers chose to
"rebuild." They started by "topworking"—deheading the trees and
rebudding onto the established trunks and rootstocks. Likewise,
after a freeze or a desiccating windstorm, owners sometimes took the
opportunity to completely "renovate" their citruses. Old, decadent,
or simply underperforming trees were prime candidates for "rejuve-
nation." "Rebuilding" a drone typically cost less than removing it.
Treatments ranged from mild thinning to moderate "dehorning"
(cutting secondary branches to stubs) to extreme "skeletonization"
(removing everything under an inch in diameter). Arborists whitewashed the skeletonized tree to prevent sunburn, creating a Hallow-
een look. Depending on the market forecast, growers might topwork
their oranges into lemons, or vice versa. When choosing new scion
material, they looked for any number of desirable qualities: thorn-
less branches, sweet fruit, seedless fruit, fast growth, heavy fruiting.
Impulsively, they turned to "precocious" trees for bud material. But
citruses that performed outstandingly well in their early years did not
necessarily provide the best genetic material. They might carry viruses

or produce trees with short life expectancies. Lacking good data, growers perpetuated many hidden and slow-developing undesirable traits along with obvious desirable ones. Through normal practices of budding, grafting, and pruning, arborists unwittingly spread diseases such as blossom blight, citrus blast, stubborn disease, and scaly bark.

Growers likewise diluted genetic stock. Take the example of the famous Tibbets navel. This varietal proved to be highly variable ("promiscuous" or "capricious"): the fruit differed from tree to tree, even branch to branch. New bud sports—mutations—occurred as a matter of course. On the mistaken assumption that a navel was a navel, nurseries and orchardists propagated many "off-type" buds. By the second decade of the twentieth century, the Washington navel had spawned at least a couple dozen recognizable and named strains. (One of these, Thomson Improved, enjoyed minor commercial success.) Most navel ranches consisted of a mixture of superior and inferior bearers, true-type and off-type trees. Younger groves generally bore lighter and poorer fruit than the original groves from the 1870s. Many "grandchildren" of the parent trees produced fruit too small or too large, rinds that were coarse or corrugated or wrinkled or otherwise ugly, and fruit of low-grade taste. Many growers feared that the original Tibbets strain was "running out," and they began the search for a replacement.

Into this situation stepped A. D. Shamel of the CES. From 1911 to 1940, he and various colleagues conducted an exhaustive longitudinal study of bud variations on navels. Shamel estimated that 25 percent of so-called Washington navels were off-type and undesirable. By peering into the branches of tree after tree, by slicing and tasting innumerable fruits, he discovered over a hundred limb variations—both "reverting variations" and new mutations. Through tedious use of scorecards, Shamel isolated the "true" Washington navel and amassed data that enabled the California Fruit Growers Exchange in 1917 to create a Bud Selection Department within its Fruit Growers Supply Company. As a service to members, the department distributed over a million true-type navel buds over the next ten years. Simultaneously, growers deheaded tens of thousands of off-type mature trees and rebudded with certified stock. These measures ensured that all Sunkist-brand navel fruit looked and tasted the same. Building on this private program of genetic stabilization, the California Department of Food and Agriculture later instituted a statewide budwood program that issued true-type and virus-free certifications. Thanks to the legacy of Shamel, citrus ranchers could be confident that when they topworked their groves, they had invested in certified buds from selected strains.[7]

Even a well-watered, well-pruned, "pedigreed" tree could encounter major insect trouble. As a warm-climate evergreen with leafy foliage, citrus provides year-round food for any number of pests: whiteflies, blackflies, aphids, mites, spider insects, scale insects, mealybugs, and more. These offenders mainly suck out the sap or the juices from branches, shoots, leaves, or green fruit. Insect-induced sap drainage causes honeydew, which promotes fungal growth like sooty mold, which disrupts photosynthesis and the setting of fruit. Scale insects are among the worst pests because they arm themselves by building protective shelters (the telltale scales). Their infestations can cause leaf drop, fruit drop, fruit discoloration and deformities, and branch dieback. California initially offered a pest-free environment for citrus, but as cuttings and saplings arrived in the mail from distant tropical places, insects came along for the ride. In the first half century of the industry, growers confronted a succession of scale invasions, which they colloquially identified by color: white, black, red, yellow, purple. Many of these armored insects were "gifts" from Florida. Introduced to monocultural settings in the Citrus Belt, the pests fed with abandon.

To eradicate insects, growers deployed two main chemical strategies, gas fumigating and wet spraying. (A third method, dry dusting, was sometimes done by hand or by blower, but not until airplanes were available did it become widely practiced.) Fumigating a tree for scale resembled tenting a house for termite control. Californians first experimented with tents in the 1880s during the cottony-cushion

scale crisis. Under the canvas, they tried adding heat, steam, gun-
powder, tobacco smoke, sulfur, and many other fumes and gases. By
the 1890s growers settled on a favored technique: nighttime application of hydrocyanic acid gas (HCN) under heavy twill or duck tents.
It had to be dark because sunlight caused a photochemical reaction
that burned the tree. Fitting a tent on a 30-foot plant took mental
as well as physical labor. Inventors in the Citrus Belt devised various
derricklike contraptions attached to wagons. This slow, heavy, and
costly approach was eventually replaced with something simpler and
cheaper: flat sheets lifted up on two poles, then pulled into place with
pulleys. For small trees, a bell tent on a hoop could suffice. Large
or small, the octagonal tents featured outside markings to indicate
volume of air space inside. A fumigation gang included a "taper" or
"scheduler" to take measurements and calculate dosage, a "gunner"
to handle the "commissary cart" of chemicals, and two strongmen to
pull and stake tents. Crews worked from 5 P.M. to 6 A.M. in the fall
(the infant season for scale insects), handling up to seventy-five tents
at a time, but more typically twenty per "throw."[8]

HCN killed scale insects, but it caused its own problems: nasty
bluish or greenish residues on trees and granules of cyanide on the
ground. Apparently rodents knew better than to eat them, but birds
mistook them for gravel and swallowed them as gizzard stones to
aid in mastication. In 1907 one bird lover in Pasadena reported that
"thousands" of quail and mockingbirds were "daily dying" around the
recently fumigated benchland groves. If cyanide could burn through
heavy twill, kill songbirds, and ravage armored insects, one wonders
what it did to the long-term health of orchard workers. The scale
of poison application boggles the mind. For example, in late 1916,
the fumigation company of the Pomona-based San Antonio Fruit
Exchange worked eleven gangs seven days a week for four months
fumigating 383,500 trees on just 4,250 acres. This one job used up
eleven train cars of cyanide.[9]

As early as the 1930s, scale insects in California developed resistance to HCN, which underscored the importance of the other

primary artificial control method, spraying with oils. Whereas fumigation poisoned insects, spraying suffocated them. Growers deployed
whale oil first, then haphazardly moved on to unrefined petroleum
oils, which killed more insects but killed more trees, too. Refined oil
emulsions ("distillates") performed better and became the new norm
around 1900. Sprayers added an emulsifying agent such as condensed
milk to kerosene or lubricating oil, then forced the agitated mixture
through a nozzle. Because the resultant petroleum film acted as a
purely physical inhibitor, insects could not develop resistance to it.
Growers complemented oil with various metallic sprays such as Paris
Green (copper, arsenic, and lead arsenate) and, after World War II,
DDT and other organophosphates. Spraying and fumigating went
largely unregulated until 1923, when the horticultural commissioners of the orange-growing counties of Southern California adopted
a common set of regulations that required permits and reports and
banned the work in wind or rain. Growers in the Citrus Belt grudgingly accepted the rules and thereafter grumbled that homeowners in
Los Angeles failed to spray their backyard citrus trees, thus creating
a reservoir for damaging insects. For their part, homeowners objected
when horticultural commissioners fumigated their trees and left the
bill. On one occasion, residents of Hollywood dug up and burned
citruses to protest the de facto tree tax.[10]

Despite ubiquitous application of poisons and sprays, citrus ranchers actually relied less on chemicals than other American orchardists.
Because of the proud memory of the victory against the cottony-
cushion scale, Californians retained exaggerated faith in biological
control, sometimes called the "California method." Unique among
American states, California funded its own biocontrol program separate from the USDA. After the CES added a Division of Entomology
in 1918, Riverside became, thanks to funding from the citrus industry, the world leader in "natural enemy studies." California exemplified "integrated pest management," the combination of chemical
and biological controls. Although most introductions of parasites and
parasitoids failed to produce the desired effects, now and then scien-

tists scored a victory. Citrophilus mealybug, a species first detected in 1913, threatened the industry in the 1920s. Spraying didn't work. Finally a CES researcher went to Australia in 1927 and gathered various predators for introduction. One of these, a kind of ladybird, naturalized easily in California. Technicians propagated the beetles by the tens of millions on potato sprouts housed in insectaries—some run by the state, others run by grower cooperatives or individual large ranches—and released them widely. By 1930 the beetles had checked the mealybug infestation.[11]

Not all nuisances had six legs. In more humid coastal regions such as Orange County, snails caused damage to leaves, buds, and flowers. Various nematodes (tiny worms) devitalized roots. Rabbits nibbled at trunks; gophers chewed on roots. Every large citrus ranch employed a "trouble man," a jack of all trades who could set traps, shoot guns, and apply poison. To kill rodents, the trouble man laced carrots with strychnine or directed car exhaust by pipe into dens. In summer months, unpaved roads adjacent to groves had to be watered regularly to prevent kicked-up dust from ruining the fruit on outside rows.

Growers faced one last problem: how to determine if all this technical work—intensive and expensive—paid off. How could you know if a high-yield tree resulted primarily from good horticulture, good genes, or simply a "soil pocket"? To distinguish between inherent weaknesses and environmental limitations, the CFGE and the CES in the interwar years promulgated a system of "performance records" for individual trees. Diligent owners gave each a unique identifier, a code composed of three numbers indicating grid location: block, row, tree. They painted the numbers on the trunk or hung a metal tag. Each tree received an annual rating on a scale of 1 to 5. "Know the trees and keep a record of them and soon you will know them by number as well as you know your friends and employees by name," advised a manager at Chapman Acres in Fullerton. "See how many trees you have on the pension list . . . Make each tree pay." Using the language of human resource management, industry experts recommended eliminating the citrus that "rides along on the good talents of others," just as a businessman "weeds out" the employee who "does not earn his way, but spends the money of the firm." They spoke of killing the "weaklings" and "drones" and "runts," discarding the "slackers" and "starboarders," running down the "hobo trees," and throwing out the trees that didn't "pay their keep."[12]

Despite many advancements in citriculture in the early twentieth century, something baffling remained. A citrus, like a baby with colic, defied the best parenting manuals. A La Verne man with fifty work years under his belt conceded in 1936: "I used to think I knew what should be done and when, but with so many different ideas advanced on irrigation, fertilization, pruning and pest control, by so many growers of experience and success in the business, I am convinced that no one knows what is best for a citrus tree." The CES pomologist J. Eliot Coit put the conundrum this way: "Trees are like children, every one different and presenting a set of individual problems." To devastating effect, the social critic Carey McWilliams used a different anthropomorphizing metaphor; he likened the California orange tree to "a rather plump middle-aged dowager bedizened with jewels and gems and a corsage of gardenias." Delicate in health, the lady required constant attention from a "whole retinue of servants"; her watering had to be "examined as carefully as the diet of a diabetic."[13]

The most pampered citrus of all was the second of the two parent navels of Riverside (variously called "mates," "grandma and grandpa," and "sisters"). The first one—the tree replanted by Teddy Roosevelt at the Mission Inn—succumbed in 1922, approximately fifty years after its arrival in California. Riversiders turned its wood into mementos and straightaway planted a "son" (also called "daughter" or "granddaughter") at the hotel. The other, widowed tree had taken its place in a pocket park in the middle of the intersection of two major streets, Magnolia and Arlington. As soon as crews installed the "Daddy of Golden Citrus Wealth" in its new home, souvenir hunters began stripping leaves and twigs, forcing the city to hastily erect a fence. Even with protection, this tree came close to dying, too. By the late teens its foliage appeared thin and discolored. The original cuttings from Washington, D.C., had been budded onto sweet orange root-stock, which proved susceptible to foot rot. The citrus had been set too deep, above the "bud union" where the rootstock and scion met. To top it off, the well-meaning custodians had overwatered, overfertilized, "excessively manured," and generally overloved the plant. After a thorough examination in 1918, a team of university experts from the CES recommended immediate surgery. Arborists proceeded to "inarch" the tree—that is, give it a root transplant. Using tissue from multiple sources—sweet orange, sour orange, rough lemon—the tree surgeons grafted aerial roots from the upper trunk down into the ground. At first these new roots looked like soda straws. Later, as they filled out and fused, they resembled a mangrove.[14]

In its new form—a Bahia navel attached to a variety of *Citrus* rootstock, new and old—the surviving parent earned an honorific as California Historic Landmark #20 in 1932. The following year, the State Department of Natural Resources chose this landmark for the installation of its first historic marker. The plaque went next to an earlier one installed in the 1920s by the Daughters of the American Revolution in memory of Eliza Tibbets, "mother" of the California orange industry. Following the deaths of Luther and Eliza, their genetically unrelated children (of different parentages) squabbled over who deserved credit for the heritage trees. Luther lost the memory war. Riversiders preferred to commemorate the navel as a civilizing female force. This could be seen in 1933, the sixtieth anniversary year, when Riverside pulled out the stops for a navel pageant, including a replica of the Tibbets homestead made of oranges, and a heroic tableau performed by schoolchildren that showed Eliza planting the two progenitors. If, as Riversiders liked to say, the historic tree on Magnolia Avenue was a "shrine," it was a shrine to horticapitalism. The trade magazine *California Citrograph* once published cover art that showed the parent growing above piles of gold coins and greenbacks. The caption read: "This tree and its companion, now dead, have contributed more to the wealth of California than all the gold that has been produced here." Literally it was the money tree. Congressional dignitaries received gifts of its fruit, and White House gardeners tended a "granddaughter." In Riverside in early 1949, during a period of freezing cold, the city's superintendent of parks kept a nighttime vigil, working hundreds of hours of unpaid overtime, firing up oil-burning heaters dozens of times to safeguard the floral replicant. No other plant in California, not even the General Grant or the Lone Cypress, was comparably feted and coddled.[15]

TO SMUDGE OR NOT TO SMUDGE

Frost was the dirty little secret of Southland citriculture. No self-respecting booster of the region would outright admit to freezing weather. Every realtor and orchardist claimed that his property lay within the frost-free zone. Land agents advertised "frostless" slopes in the foothills of the Transverse Ranges where cold air supposedly never settled. Whole citrus districts advertised themselves as frost-proof. An extension agent with the University of California remarked in 1899 that the frost line was "quite provokingly flexible."[16] After freezing spells, boosters minimized local losses while exaggerating losses in rival districts.

Coastal Southern California experiences two kinds of cold spells, advective freezes and radiation frosts. In the first, less common case, a large Arctic air mass sweeps down from Canada, into the Great Basin, and over the rim of the Mojave Desert. Some old-timers referred to this kind of cold front as a "Mormon wind." More commonly, the Southland undergoes atmospheric inversion: a low ceiling of warm air in the atmosphere prevents the heavier, colder air on the surface from rising. During radiation frosts, the sky is clear, the wind calm, the humidity low. By rule of thumb, the critical temperature for "citrus pneumonia" is 26° F, though it varies by varietal. Oranges are hardier than lemons, which are hardier than limes. Two consecutive cold winters in 1878 through 1880 destroyed the state's incipient lime industry. One locale or another—so-called frost pockets—drops below freezing every winter in Southern California. Regionwide freezes are less frequent but hardly rare. It is a calculated gamble to grow citrus under such conditions. "The navel orange reaches its perfection of color and flavor only where the days are bright and hot and the nights are cold," explained a Redlands historian. "Like genius and insanity, the margin between success and disaster is narrow and fraught with mischance. Even while the oranges are reaching their acme of tang and color they are at the same time flirting with disaster."[17]

For fighting Jack Frost, orchardists exercise three basic strategies: retain heat, move the cold air, or replace lost heat. Retention requires some kind of barrier to the frigid air. Early citrus ranchers wrapped cornstalks, palm fronds, tule reeds, newspaper, or tarpaper around the trunks of young trees for insulation. But this did nothing to protect fruit. Hoping to diminish the loss of surface heat, growers experimented with temporary or permanent outdoor roofs—propped-up latticework—made of laths, muslin, or burlap. This technique worked best at nurseries with low-height seedbed stock. Occasionally wealthy orchardists installed laths over their full-height trees. Tall and thick windbreaks—typically Tasmanian blue gums alternated with Monterey cypresses—were common yet controversial. Experts disagreed as to whether shelterbelts blocked cold air or trapped it, preventing proper air drainage.

The second strategy, moving cold air—or, more precisely, circulating the warmer upper layer of an inversion into the colder underlayer—requires elevated outdoor propeller fans. Technologically and financially, this solution remained out of reach until the second half of the twentieth century. From the 1890s through the 1950s, orange and lemon growers in Southern California focused on the third strategy: replacement heat. The impacts of heating—and *not* heating— were most evident in 1898, 1913, 1922, 1937, and 1949, when citrus ranchers mobilized in response to the "great white terror." This uneven meteorological cycle produced two secondary cycles, one technological, the other political. Following each deep freeze, local growers redoubled their efforts to develop more efficient orchard heaters while local activists called for new controls on the pollution caused by outdoor heating.

Before oil-fired burners became the norm around 1910, inventors tested countless heat sources. The simple method used in Florida, lighting bonfires in groves, didn't make sense in Southern California for two reasons: the tight spacing of citruses and the general scarcity of firewood. For a time, some Southland growers tried "wet smudges"— that is, feeding a smoldering fire with damp straw or manure to form a dense steamy smoke. They meant to raise the dew point and create a vapor screen against the frost. Straw was scarce, however, and better used for humus. As an alternative, growers placed water pans over coal-oil fires. California's dry air stymied such efforts. Another possible heating method was, paradoxically, freezing. When water freezes, it releases energy. To exploit this energy transfer, orchardists used sprinklers to create a snowlike mist or even a layer of ice; most simply, they tried flooding the groves with irrigation water. A few rich owners experimented with the "warm water method," sending heated water down the furrows. Problems with soil saturation undermined their plans. Schemers drew up complicated blueprints: steam apparatuses that would force hot air from a central heater, automated systems of water vats heated by flames, fog machines. However, low-tech solutions carried the day. Most early adopters simply poured low-grade crude oil—so-called slop distillate—into paper sacks filled with sawdust, or into lard pails, and set them on fire.[18]

Despite lampblack stains left on fruits and blossoms, many growers believed that smoke protected trees. According to theory, smoke acted like a blanket, holding the heat close to the ground, preventing it from radiating into the atmosphere. Conversely, the carbon cloud shielded the chilled fruit from the sun, preventing overly rapid thawing, which could cause spoliation. Skeptics dismissed the smoke theory, and doctors worried about the effects of the blackened air on the "one-lunged people"—all of those tubercular invalids in area sanatoriums who had done so much to publicize the healthy climate of Southern California.

Prominent growers promoted technological improvements. The center of innovation was Riverside, with Everest Ranch the acknowledged leader. Hiram Bond Everest of Rochester, New York, semi-retired here in 1881, having sold his valuable lubricating oil business to Standard Oil. His son managed the orchard while he continued dabbling in the oil racket. In 1887 a special court in Buffalo convicted Everest of plotting to blow up a competitor's factory, a major scandal at the time, known as the "Standard Oil conspiracy." After losing on appeal, the millionaire received a most generous judicial sentence—a $250 fine. Everest lived out his days in sunny California. He enjoyed the means to test various expensive weather control systems: a large-scale latticework, sprinklers on 50-foot masts, hanging wire baskets filled with coal and kindling, and flaring oil burners fed by underground pipes. Electric gauges throughout his orchard measured the temperature precisely.[19]

To determine which method worked best, the Frost Protection Committee of the Riverside Horticultural Club held investigations during various cold spells in the second half of the 1890s. Appointed committee members, gentlemen of certifiable competence and impartiality, gathered with thermometers and notepads in the middle of the night for a series of tests at various orchards. Their final report on the "frost question" stated with confidence that the air of the Citrus Belt *could* be heated but that dry heat held more promise than wet heat. The committee came down on the side of coal and recommended that growers hang fifty baskets per acre. The Limoneira Company took the lead in adopting this method wholesale. Primed with oil and lit on fire, a basket of soft coal—10 pounds in chunks—gave good heat for five hours. Although it did not burn as hot as oil and could not be turned off at will, coal had the advantage of emitting relatively little staining smoke; the all-important fruit remained unblemished. Coal was the fuel of choice for about a decade after the freeze of 1898–99.[20]

In the meantime, area inventors worked on improving the efficiency of oil heaters, better known as smudge pots. The original "devices," garbage cans or lard pails of 1- or 2-gallon capacity, did not provide draft, leading to incomplete combustion and heavy carbon smoke. The second-generation pots featured covered reservoirs, draft tubes, and exhaust stacks. To streamline production, the CFGE tested various designs and selected the so-called Bolton pot as the industry standard. In 1910 the CFGE's Fruit Growers Supply Company purchased 250,000 heaters for resale to Sunkist members. By 1915 roughly 1 million had been placed in groves. Coal was out. The majority of orchards remained completely unprotected, however, and those who purchased oil heaters did not necessarily possess good thermometers, good fuel, or working knowledge about heating techniques and equipment maintenance. Under the best conditions, Bolton pots were not "smokeless," as advertised; they smoked when filled too full, or filled with cheap fuel, or burned too high, or used without cleaning. Orchard workers, including many local teenagers pressed into nighttime service, coughed up black phlegm. Their faces and collars discolored; their nostrils turned oily. A thick grimy blanket blocked the stars from view.

From roughly 1910 to 1950, the arrival of oil dumpers marked the end of the "smudge season" and the beginning of spring in the Southland. It wasn't enough to drain the unused oil and place the heaters in storage. To prevent the pots from rusting, gumming up, or producing excessive smoke, workers had to clean and repaint them. They scraped out the thick, sticky residue of asphalt, getting stained and smelly in the process—the single worst chore on a citrus ranch. As one grower wrote: "A dirty job and we use Mexicans."[21] Come autumn, the workers repositioned and refilled the pots. The stench of slop distillate mixed with the sweet scent of orange blossoms.

Smudge pots got their first big test in early 1913. In anticipation of severe weather, the Santa Fe Railway authorized two special trains— thirty carloads—to rush-deliver 100,000 pots from a manufacturer in West Virginia. The Citrus Protective League secured emergency freight rate relief. Meanwhile, the Riverside Sheet Metal Works made even more heaters. All in all, Southland growers deployed about 2 million on January 5–7, when the freeze hit. The temperature in Riverside dropped to 18° F. Owners struggled to mobilize enough labor and oil to keep their small-capacity pots full and running; many ran out of fuel entirely. The "great freeze" of 1913, the worst yet, killed for good the hoary idea that heavy smoke by itself offered protection. "It looked like fire had swept through the groves," recalled one Riversider. The leaves on the oranges curled up and eventually dropped. Perhaps half the damage came simply from desiccation, for the cold wind blew dry. Many citruses, especially less cold-resistant lemons, split open at the trunk. Southlanders belatedly came to a sensible consensus: their region did not contain any truly frostless areas. "There is no promised land anywhere," said a U.S. Weather Bureau meteorologist to a Riverside audience. After the freeze, the CFGE lobbied for and won a legislative appropriation to enlarge the CES and expand its research into frost protection.[22]

The wealthiest and best-equipped ranches approached cold weather as an opportunity for profit. The National Orange Company of Riverside, a business owned by Ethan Allen Chase, who had earned his first fortune as a nurseryman in western New York, experimented with electric heaters that hung on trees. At Santa Paula, C. C. Teague's Limoneira Company had fortuitously shifted from coal baskets to oil pots the year before. During the three frosty nights in January, the company marshaled sixty men in multiple squads, each with a foreman. Although the ranch lost a lot of lemons, its remaining stock skyrocketed in value owing to the greater losses of unheated competitors. The success of Teague, the leading figure in the industry, convinced other rich growers of the investment value of large-scale heating. Riverside's Arlington Heights Fruit Company, an orange and lemon operation owned by a British syndicate, armed up after the freeze. By 1916 the 554-acre orchard featured oil faucets fed by pipes from an elevated half-million-gallon steel tank, supplemented by an additional twenty-eight tank wagons. Even with this infrastructure, workers relied on 5-gallon oil cans to refill each of the 44,000 firepots by hand—backbreaking work. The operation required 145 men working the night shift with "military precision." To aid "intelligent control," the company placed telephones among the trees.[23]

In the early days of heating, forecasters resorted to flags and fire whistles to alert growers to predicted freezes. Southern Pacific functioned as the de facto weather service. Then, in the early twentieth century, the U.S. Weather Bureau began relaying its regional forecasts and special frost warnings to well-placed individuals in select localities via long-distance telephone. However, regional forecasts had limited value in the topographically diverse Citrus Belt, where frost conditions varied from locale to locale. To compensate, numerous communities created their own frost leagues. For example, on cold nights, the Pomona Valley Frost Protective Association (1910) dispatched its team of motorcycle patrolmen—"modern Paul Reveres"—to ride on circuits, taking records from 136 government-tested thermometers hanging from trees and poles.[24] After each fifty-minute round, a patrolman turned in his records to district headquarters. In the event of a freeze, four (female) phone operators called five hundred numbers on the protective district's member list. In 1917, at the request of Pomona's growers, the Weather Bureau assumed management of local forecasting. The meteorologist Floyd D. Young initially supervised a telephonic chain-message system. His Fruit-Frost Service called in forecasts to key men, who in turn called several more, and so on. In addition, telephone companies allowed subscribers to obtain Young's forecast for free from the operator.

During the deep freeze of January 1922, the telephonic system crashed when too many growers dialed for information and help. The smudging that month precipitated ugliness of unprecedented scope. A pitch-black cloud settled over the coast, grounding sea traffic at San Pedro Bay. No lighthouse burned bright enough to penetrate the oily fog. The air quality deteriorated so much that even the chamber of commerce in Covina, a citrus town, passed a resolution against the exclusive use of oil heaters for frost prevention. In Ontario, a Congregationalist minister discussed the matter from the pulpit. "There is no such thing as a frostless belt," he sermonized. "That notion has been proven a delusion and a dream." The preacher called for the invention of a smokeless smudge pot to prevent damage to bodies and houses. He encouraged each grower to "have the courage to meet losses with philosophy of life that will enable him to keep his balance." Taking an occasional hit from Mother Nature was part of the game: "A rancher must be a man."[25]

Organized resistance to smudge had been building for about a decade. Pomona, the center of frost protection, also inspired the most agitation. As early as January 1912 the city council protested the nuisance caused by burning slop distillate. Residents woke up with aching ears, sore throats, and stopped-up noses. Property owners reported excessive damage from stains. A city committee in 1913 recommended phasing out the "old-styled" Bolton pots—only a few years old—as well the distressingly common stackless pans. It discovered that 40,000 (27 percent) of the orchard "heaters" in the Pomona district were garbage cans. The committee's report led to the first antismudge ordinance. In 1918 Pomona added teeth to its law by forbidding "the creation of smudge or smoke" from burners. Local growers fought back with lawyers. A judge at the Superior Court of Los Angeles heard testimony from doctors and actuaries that favorably compared Pomona to smoke-filled manufacturing cities throughout the world. The case turned on the distinction between smoke and smudge. The judge ruled that the city could ban only the latter. He defined smudge as smoke "heavier than air." The controversy spilled over to Pomona's mayoral election of 1919. The winning candidate favored a ban on smudging within town limits. Two years later Pomona earned the distinction of being the first government to arrest a citrus rancher for "smoking excessively."[26]

The 1922 freeze led to industrywide improvements. With financial support from the CFGE and the other large cooperative, Mutual Orange Distributors, Floyd Young's Fruit-Frost Service went big-time. From 1924 to 1930, Young called in the nightly forecast to a radio station in Los Angeles, which read the data on air as a public service. Then, starting in 1930, the "frost freeze warning man" transmitted directly from his office in Pomona over the airwaves of KNX Los Angeles every evening at 8:00 from November 15 to February 15. More immediately, the smudge of 1922 altered the political and technological landscape. Jolted by criticisms and municipal actions, citrus and walnut growers held a joint "frostless convention" at the American Legion hall in Covina. The organizers sponsored a showcase for local inventors to display prototype models of "smudgeless devices," including several wind machines, called "blowers" or "windjammers" by detractors. Afterward, a group of Covina citrus men pooled their money to build a full-size version of the best-looking model, a machine that combined an airplane propeller with a heater. Taking a more conservative approach, the Fruit Growers Supply Company formed a committee to develop a new standard oil heater with a conical louvered stack for better burning. To secure a bulk discount, the supply company awarded a manufacturing contract to the American Can Company and purchased an estimated 1.5 million units over the next fifteen years for resale to Sunkist members. The 4-foot-high devices with 10-gallon bowls became known as "Supply Co. heaters." Paradoxically, this innovation increased smudge and its problems, for the numerical increase of heaters more than offset the increased efficiency per unit.[27]

On Christmas Day 1924, a smudge cloud again halted sea traffic at the harbor, and a pall covered Los Angeles, "not unlike the gloom which comes with a solar eclipse." A Pacific Electric trolley derailed in the blackness, killing a passenger. After the holiday, the *Times* began speaking out against "the smudge evil." Clean-air advocates called for a statewide bill in Sacramento. At a "torrid" conference held in Ontario, prominent growers, including C. C. Teague, representing the CFGE, confronted angry shopkeepers and housewives. A resident identified as Mrs. C. Durall spoke for many: "We want the citrus industry, but we also want a clean and healthy community to live in. I am a woman and I know smudge is doomed, for I have talked to those who have suffered serious damage and lost their loved ones because of it. You men on the platform, you represent the brains. It is up to you. What are you going to do about it?"[28]

The antismudge campaign, like its opponent, the frost-protection campaign, was Progressivism distilled—a cooperative enterprise that invoked science, technology, and Christian neighborliness. Women's clubs played a key role. Every citrus town, it seemed, engendered its own orchard heater improvement committee, which held investigations, issued reports, and recommended democratic solutions. The consensus: regulation, not prohibition. The University of California joined the cause in 1925 with a major report, *Orchard Heating in California*. Extension agents offered traveling clinics on frost protection and the proper use of heaters, made appearances at county fairs, and published how-to guides. To measure the carbon output of smudge pots, UC experts developed a truck-mounted apparatus. Studies at the CES showed that a new fuel product, a briquette, offered a less polluting alternative. But growers who had invested heavily in oil heaters felt no incentive to convert. As of 1929, smudge pots accounted for over 90 percent of artificial heat in Southern California's citrus orchards. To refill all these heaters just once took over 20 million gallons—a remarkable figure when one considers that over two thirds of orchards still used no heat at all. As a Covina man noted, "The smudge pot is the big growers' game."[29]

In 1931, following another obnoxious smudge season, the state legislature considered a bill, and San Bernardino passed a county-wide ordinance—a first for Southern California—that limited the output of unconsumed solid carbonaceous material, or sooty smoke, at 20 grams of carbon per pound of fuel. Riverside, Los Angeles, and Orange counties replicated the ordinance. "The smudge pot has become passé," pronounced a Covina editorialist in a moment of wishful thinking. "It belongs with the stage coach and the hoopskirt."[30] In fact, some ranchers still burned used tires in the orchards. The carbon limit on heater emissions was practically unenforceable, and unenforced in practice. After growers groused about the economic hardship of upgrading equipment in the midst of the Depression, and after they threatened to challenge in court, cash-strapped Los Angeles County announced an indefinite enforcement delay.

And so the same thing happened again: during the frosty days of January 1932, when the 3.3 million smudge pots of the Citrus Belt belched into action, ugly automobile accidents occurred. In the aftermath, concerned citizens in the San Gabriel Valley formed an Anti-Smudge League. Activism burned strong in El Monte, a town that derived virtually no income from citrus while lying directly in the path of the "dread menace" of the "black curse." The town newspaper urged readers to sign petitions and write letters to county supervisors asking them to enforce the new pollution law. The editorial board gainsaid growers' claims of economic hardship: "Surely, times are hard. And that is just why the merchant can't afford to have his stock merchandise ruined, the householder cannot afford to have his newly painted house blackened, and the pneumonia patient cannot afford to have the smudge oil roll in during the night and snatch away his chance of recovery."[31]

The grievances got even louder in the aftermath of the "big freeze" of January 1937, two separate episodes of multiple days of unprecedented cold. The official thermometer in Redlands reported 18° F; for the first time in recorded history, snow fell in San Diego. Every smudge that had come before paled in comparison. "Somebody slipped when they sent out those smudge pictures that are going the rounds of the eastern press," wrote a local humor columnist. "To carry out the southern California motif they should have had a beautiful girl in a bathing suit lighting the pots." By the end of the month, orchardists had consumed between 80 and 100 million gallons of crude, comparable to the capacity of a modern supertanker. To replenish the fuel supply, railroads rushed trains out of refineries in El Segundo, pooled them together regardless of owner, and placed them ahead of other freight. Rail companies requisitioned any kind of tank car they could find. As a consequence, orchard heaters burned traces of alcohol, fish oil, coconut oil, and molasses along with crude. Railroads had mon-

etary incentive to aid frost control, since hauling fresh fruit constituted a major part of their business. On highways, cars gave up right
of way to caravans of trucks going full speed. County supervisors
authorized an appeal made over local radio for volunteer truckers to
deliver oil from coastal refineries to inland packinghouses. The highway patrol waved on any kind of truck, even unlicensed vehicles without plates, with loads of crude, kerosene, used tires, or anything else
that might burn. In the groves, some panicked growers impulsively
poured oil into irrigation ditches and lit them on fire. As the chill
persisted, blackness engulfed the San Gabriel Valley and blocked the
view of the mountains. White dogs turned gray; blond hair turned
dirty blond. The smoke eventually moved out to the coast and hung
around; the "sea smudge" irritated tourists at the Santa Monica–
Ocean Park–Venice piers. In the Citrus Belt, schools and businesses
announced closures "for the duration of the African fog." As it happened, the Hollywood producer David O. Selznick test-screened the
big-budget Technicolor film *A Star Is Born* in Pomona during the
freeze. Half the cinema audience left in the middle of the movie to
refuel the orchard heaters. Misinterpreting the egress, the movie men
feared a flop. "My God, I shot it too dark," the director supposedly
exclaimed, and rushed upstairs to the projectionist to tell him to turn
up the light. The man in the booth explained that the problem was
the air; smudge from outside had entered the theater through doors
and ventilation ducts.[32]

Of all the "cultural costs" incurred by citrus ranchers, orchard heating was the furthest removed from traditional tree culture and the
most financially risky. In 1937 Southland growers spent an estimated
$7 million (over $100 million in today's dollars) on heating the outdoors. Did that make economic sense? From the point of view of the
CFGE and the railroads, not to mention the oil refineries, the answer
was unequivocally yes. Overall, the damage to fruit and trees in 1937
totaled significantly less than in 1922, despite the much worse freeze.
And losses clustered in certain areas. Growers who did not heat or
who ran out of fuel lost whole groves; well-supplied owners lost little.

Smudging was a good insurance policy for healthy businesses that could already afford it. The misfortune of the less well equipped benefited the wealthy, who could set a higher fruit price because of the overall reduced supply. The 1937 crop brought in only 8 percent less profit than the year before, despite a 30 percent production loss. In other words, the rich got richer because of the short crop. Big-time growers could argue that they weren't just being selfish. Saving their crop preserved jobs for pickers and sorters, who mostly spent their incomes locally. For these reasons, the CFGE contended that the smudging of 1937 aided the whole region. The only thing worse than smudging was not smudging.[33]

Such reckoning elided two glaring costs. One was health. People with respiratory problems, including patients at Southern California's many sanatoriums, voiced grievances about coughing. Dairy farmers in Chino complained about sickened cows. Workers suffered more, but they couldn't speak out for fear of losing their jobs. No one dreaded cold holiday nights more than Mexican orchard hands. Frances Martínez of Corona remembered when her husband, a laborer at a lemon ranch, went smudging in the night: "They would come and bang and bang like the police from door to door to wake you up . . . You heard about the haciendas in Mexico—well, this is no different." To save time, many orchardists chose to refill their pots while lit—a hazardous strategy because the oil-soaked clothing of workers could catch fire. For example, in the San Fernando Valley, eighteen-year-old Juan Velásquez burned to death after a smudge pot exploded next to him in 1937.[34]

The other major cost displaced that winter, the roughly $7 million in smoke damage, was borne by middle-class homeowners and storekeepers. As truckers rushed to get oil to the groves, housewives hurried to wrap their linen in butcher paper and place it in airtight closets. They covered their upholstered furniture with colored sheets; they tried, and mainly failed, to seal windows and doors with tape. The morning after each smudging, they awoke to find a greasy film on floors, walls, ceilings, and curtains. At schools, all surfaces needed scrubbing before classes could resume. In stores, in-stock merchandise depreciated in value because of the grime. Some local merchants advertised postfreeze sales to lure people to spend their "smudge checks"—the bonuses received for nighttime work in the orchards—but only laundries, dry cleaners, and salons truly profited from the blackness of 1937.

As soon as the ice melted and the pall lifted, a new cycle of community reprisals began. The San Gabriel Valley Anti-Smudge League reorganized and produced calculations to suggest that buying crop insurance would be more cost-effective than maintaining a vast heating infrastructure that sat unused for most of the year. Hadn't growers gotten by—and gotten rich—for decades without heating? The industry responded with a variety of defenses and excuses. "Progressive" smudgers blamed the "smudge evil" on retrograde ranchers who used open pails or who didn't clean their heaters properly. Others blamed inertia. "As in the case of flood-protection in the Ohio and Mississippi basins," acknowledged the *Covina Citizen*, "we have to have a flood before we are stirred into remedial action." The *California Citrograph* conceded that a "Pittsburgh atmosphere" pervaded the Southland during 1937 smudge but disputed the health effects. In a weak conciliatory gesture, growers passed a resolution to "develop the facts." They called for greater cooperation instead of legislation. C. C. Teague offered a $5,000 reward (which went unclaimed) for the invention of a superior protective device, and the CFGE directed $10,000 to the University of California for technological research on "fire pots," the new polite term for smudge pots.[35]

Local governments increasingly sided with the antismudge faction. In 1937 Los Angeles County supervisors enacted a stricter ordinance that covered heaters in unincorporated areas. Henceforth, smudge pots could emit no more than 1 gram of carbon per minute, and by 1940 no more than one-half gram. "The day of tire and oil ditch burning is over!" announced the deputy sheriff in charge of enforcement. He sent his five officers into the orchards with mobile equipment to test the efficiency of combustion. Growers needed to replace an estimated 5 million below-standard pots, or 1 million per officer. Enforcement was a Sisyphean task. The county hoped that orchardists would follow their consciences and upgrade to the Leonard return gas stack heater, a modern device (designed by a UC professor) that forced heavy smoke to return to the firing chamber for second combustion. Although it dramatically reduced exhaust, growers resisted immediate adoption because they had already invested heavily in older technology.

Los Angeles's atmosphere changed decisively during World War II. County supervisors suspended enforcement of the new pollution rule and even gave citrus ranchers permission to smudge during air-raid blackouts. Growers tried to put a patriotic spin on it, saying that rows of firelights on a grid might fool the Japanese; the heated orchards, easily mistaken for factories, could draw away enemy fire. Meanwhile, defense industries in and around the city operated at full bore. Something unfamiliar and disagreeable filled the air— an "atmospheric freak," not smoke, not smudge. In 1944 the *Times* resorted to a new word, placed in quotation marks, to explain the acrid gray mist: "smog." The phenomenon irritated the eyes and lungs and lowered a dingy veil over the city. As we now know, smog results from the photochemical reaction of ozone and ultraviolet radiation. Fine particulates ride along. Smudge, by contrast, consists of heavy carbon. Even without understanding the chemistry, Angelenos during World War II could see and smell—and *feel*—the difference between cough-inducing soot and lachrymose "gas attacks." "Smudge and smog are distinct problems," explained the *Times*. This distinction had legal significance, because California's pioneering Air Pollution Control Act (1947) exempted agriculture, and thus smudging, from regulation. "Quite naturally," said one county supervisor, "many people confuse this decades-old annoyance with the more modern menace of industrial smog."[36]

In truth, smudge was industrial, too. Today slow-growth advocates who bemoan the postwar pollution and sprawl of Greater Los Angeles often lament the ruin of an imagined Arcadian landscape.

The notoriety of smog has obscured the memory of the region's original air contamination, which emanated from the Citrus Belt, an
arbo-industrial landscape in which oil and citrus collaborated. From
roughly 1900 to 1950, these were the two leading economic sectors
in Southern California. In the Fullerton district, a forest of derricks
rose directly above oranges on properties leased to oil companies.
The cost-effectiveness of orchard heating (like that of spraying trees)
depended on the health of California's oil economy. As long as local
oil was cheap, residents of the Citrus Belt faced the prospect of a
black Christmas.

The last major cycle of smudge occurred in the late 1940s, when
three consecutive severe winters culminated in a major freeze in January 1949. Responding to grassroots activism, governor Earl Warren signed a bill that revised the Air Pollution Control Act, placing
orchard heating under its purview and giving more enforcement power
to local counties. Almost immediately Los Angeles County passed an
enhanced ordinance that required the county's five thousand citrus
growers to apply for heating permits. Within one year, one-fifth of all
devices had to conform to stringent standards. The local Air Pollution
Control District banned nine kinds of burners outright.

Smudge now entered its twilight phase. Throughout the Citrus
Belt, voter initiatives in 1949–50 mandated the adoption of improved
technology. Shockingly, in Riverside County fewer than 2 percent
of active pots had return stacks for secondary combustion. "We have
waited too long for procrastinating growers to police themselves,"
said a Pomona homeowner. "The smudge they create trespasses in our
homes and within our very bodies." As owners restocked in the new
political atmosphere, manufacturers struggled to meet the demand
for improved models. The laggard change frustrated tens of thousands of recently arrived residents who worked for defense firms and
lived in ramblers in Long Beach, Lakewood, the San Fernando Valley, the San Gabriel Valley, and Orange County. These people had no
historical connection to citrus. Owners of "GI mansions" didn't buy
the argument that what was good for Sunkist was good for Califor-

nia. Suburban housewives raised a stink. A mother in El Monte woke up one cold morning to find her infant's face "coated with an ugly black." "All of our neighbors are desperate," she wrote in a letter to the editor. "We've bought new homes and we want to live happily in them with our children in good health, but it appears from the record that the orange growers have things pretty much their own way and I'm thoroughly disgusted."[37]

In just half a century, a "war on frost" had turned into a "war on smudge." At some point between the freezes of 1912 and 1949, citrus ranchers forfeited the support of the public, who now valued "freedom of the air" more than "freedom from frost." Seeing the handwriting on the wall, wealthy orchardists pledged their support for a bill in Sacramento to codify the 1-gram-per-minute standard. They could absorb the cost and invest in wind machines. In contrast, small-time growers lacked the means to upgrade their equipment, which not long before had been considered state-of-the-art. Tired of the rising cost of oil and the escalating protests of neighbors, small-timers warmed to the idea of selling out when realtors came knocking at their doors.[38]

SUBDIVIDE AND UPROOT

The sell-off happened quickly. After World War II, California's metropolitan growth, already impressive, achieved stupendous scale and momentum. People moved for the jobs and stayed for the climate. In the Southland, aerospace and other defense-related industries turned Los Angeles County into one of the leading industrial centers of the world. "Even before Pearl Harbor," explained *Life* magazine, "Los Angeles was making more furniture than Grand Rapids, canning more fish than Boston, producing almost as many tires as Akron and assembling more automobiles than any city but Detroit." There was no postwar letdown. In the 1950s the state accepted approximately one new resident with every tick of the minute hand. Early in the next decade, in fulfillment of an old prophecy issued by state boosters, the

Golden State eclipsed the Empire State as the nation's most populous. Governor Pat Brown authorized a celebration on December 31, 1962, Population Day, to mark the symbolic moment.[39]

Migrants to the West Coast needed somewhere to live, and most wanted a certain kind of dwelling: a detached house with driveway and yard. This was the new American Dream subsidized by government tax and lending policies. As developers advanced into the Citrus Belt, the cost of land, already high, rose higher. Inflated valuation translated into increased property taxes for growers. Profits from oranges did not rise in tandem. Just the opposite: the costs of heating oil, oil sprays, and water also went up. Aging orchards had to compete with growing cities for the region's scarce water supply. In addition to obvious financial incentives, citrus ranchers had political and familial incentives to sell out. They grew weary of new neighbors carping about smudging and spraying. They griped that postwar suburbanites, unlike the pioneer suburbanites who had founded the citrus colonies, did not share "country" values. Newcomers didn't want to smell the dairy that produced their milk or the pesticide that protected their fruit. At the same time, the children and grandchildren of established growers generally did not take up horticulture; they wanted to inherit citrus wealth, not the citruses themselves. The heated real estate market provided a chance to turn cultural costs into cash.

Syndicates of land speculators, some of them foreigners, bought up scores of small groves as part of a long-term financial strategy. As new owners, they could take a first-year investment tax credit based on the cost of the bearing trees, even if raising fruit did not enter their calculus. Absentee landlords typically stopped spraying, fertilizing, and pruning their arboreal property. They turned off the water as soon the tax-shelter trees stopped paying for themselves. If and when such a neglected grove became a public nuisance, the owner, at the insistence of the county, might hire a bulldozer. The real goal was to flip the land to developers first, thus unloading the cost of orchard demolition.[40]

In the late 1950s and early 1960s Los Angeles County overflowed with citrus detritus after the county's "smog czar" banned outdoor burning. When the city of San Dimas wanted to create a sport fish habitat at a new municipal reservoir, it dumped uprooted oranges, weighted with concrete blocks, from a barge. The dead flora cost less and lasted longer than the alternative, wrecked cars. Outside L.A. County, the Southland's obsolete orchard trees, numbering in the millions, continued to be incinerated on the site of future tract homes, though some developers left one tree per lot as an enticement to buyers. "The labor of cutting up orange trees for firewood is so great that most tract construction companies won't bother with it," explained a reporter. "They bulldoze the trees into a pile and burn them." In Orange County, developers rushed to combust their accumulated dry citrus wreckage, thus avoiding the expense of hauling, before a countywide ban went into effect on New Year's Day 1968. Fly ash filled the air from all the bonfires.[41]

Farther east, in the San Bernardino Valley, the transition away from citrus began during World War II, when the federal government chose Fontana as the site for a giant new steelworks, built by the Kaiser Corporation. After the war, many other industrial plants opened nearby. Neighboring citrus ranchers complained about the consequent deterioration of air quality and expressed worries about fluorine pollution. In fact, the greater contamination problem for area oranges resulted from cars. Sacramento failed to regulate auto emissions until 1966. The exhaust of millions of V8 engines that plied the new freeways of Los Angeles pushed inland. Photochemically turned into smog by the sun, carried eastward by sea breezes, the modern *mala aria* got trapped by the regular atmospheric inversion and the immovable mountain front. Starting in the 1960s, silver-brown gunk invaded each day as a visible front. For weeks at a time, residents of foothill communities such as Upland could not see the peaks in the noontime sun. They began to call themselves "downwinders." Acid deposition ravaged the region's cut-flower industry and its field crops, starting with fragile-leafed celery, lettuce, spinach, and other greens. By the early 1970s, Riverside had received unflattering national attention as the "smog capital of the world." The mayor went so far as to petition governor Ronald Reagan to declare a state of emergency in the basin. Growers who once resisted smudge control now called for stricter smog control. The CES became a leader in studying the effects of air pollution on agriculture. Field crops fared the worst, but the bad air even yellowed the tough green leaves of citruses and compromised fruit yield. "Up to the days of smog, we raised some of the finest lemons in the world," said a Claremont owner.[42]

Even without the stress of air pollution, navels in the San Bernardino Valley would have yielded less and less fruit in the postwar period. Most of the groves were near the end of their fifty-year production cycle. To make things worse, a baffling ailment called "quick decline" afflicted the region. Diseased trees faded, wilted, dropped their leaves, and died, just like that. Early attempts at quarantine failed. Discovered in California in 1939, the malady remained a mystery until 1946, when UCR researchers determined the viral cause. By then the disease had taken root. The CES had no choice but to bulldoze thousands of research specimens in its world-class collection. The virus, known by the poetic name tristeza, infected nursery stock, too; humans became vectors as they bought and sold buds, branches, and roots. There was also a natural carrier, an aphid. The sickness threatened about 70 percent of California's oranges; in the end, about 50,000 acres of citrus statewide needed replacement. Meyer lemons proved to be the most disease-prone, and the state eventually ordered the removal of all Meyers from commercial districts. The industry finally got a handle on quick decline in the 1960s, when the California Department of Agriculture initiated a register of virus-free trees for grafting and budding and UCR developed new virus-resistant rootstock (the Troyer citrange). The surviving parent navel in Riverside required a second round of major surgery to replace its infected inarches with a new set of root grafts.[43]

In the era of smog and tristeza, more than a few growers welcomed suburbanization as a godsend. Instead of paying for the wholesale replacement of dead, dying, and decadent trees on expensive old land, they could cash out and start over on cheaper fresh land. Until 1969 citrus ranchers could take advantage of an IRS loophole that allowed them to deduct moving and development costs from their taxable income. Some stayed put but switched to row crops such as strawberries. These weren't rural traditionalists who wanted to pass on a patrimony of trees; rather, they were unsentimental capitalists who wanted to maximize returns on their property. One major player, Russell K. Pitzer, shifted entirely to real estate development and then philanthropy; he funded the expansion of the Claremont Colleges (including Pitzer College, which has an orange tree on its seal). "I'm sorry to see the orange groves go but they had to make way for an increasing population," he said. Some real estate speculators cynically assumed the guise of growers; they exploited the Williamson Act, a state law from 1965 meant to preserve farmland. Conventionally, appraisers value real property based on "highest and best use," which in postwar California usually meant housing. To avoid this valuation, landowners could enter into Williamson-approved contracts: when a freeholder promised that his property would stay in agriculture for at least ten years, the county promised to appraise on the basis of the rental value for such use. In northern San Diego County, speculators used the act to create minimally maintained citrus orchards of low quality. They could then market their property after ten years of tax-sheltered appreciation.[44]

Acreage numbers convey postwar development trends. The state's overall area of citrus reached its all-time high at roughly 350,000 acres in 1945. It reached its historic low, 250,000 acres, only eleven years later, a reduction equivalent to three San Franciscos. As acreage went out of production and as replacement orchards took time to mature into production, California lost ground in the national citrus economy. Back in 1920 the Golden State had produced three-quarters of America's total orange crop, Florida the other quarter. By 1950 California's share had dropped below 40 percent, second to that of the Sunshine State.[45]

The collapse of the pioneer citrus landscape occurred first in Los

Angeles County, then in Orange County. The symbolic changing of the guard occurred in 1955 with the opening of Disneyland. Walt Disney created a new kind of managed landscape out of a 1,600-acre orange ranch next to the emergent Santa Ana Freeway corridor in Anaheim. Working at whirlwind speed, Disney contractors bulldozed and uprooted most of the four thousand or so Valencias, though they left a few of the gridded trees in place to be part of the amusement park's original landscaping. After carving out the citrus, landscapers added thousands of new trees—subtropical evergreens in Adventureland and temperate deciduous plants on Main Street, U.S.A.—depleting local nurseries. On all sides of Disneyland, commercial and tract housing developments soon replaced the scented groves. "Pretty soon it will be Orange County no longer," wrote a local newspaper. "It will be 'Tract County.'"[46]

As the industrial greenery fell to the blade, older suburbanites in Southern California grew nostalgic. Instead of smudging and fumigation, they remembered the open space, the screen of foliage, the scent of orange blossoms on the breeze. California nature lovers felt a foreboding that the future promised nothing but concrete, sprawl, and smog. They greeted Pat Brown's Population Day with revulsion. Old-timers grumbled that newcomers had no sense of place, no roots, no honor for the past. Three trade books from the second half of the sixties set the tone: Raymond Dasmann's *The Destruction of California*, Richard Lillard's *Eden in Jeopardy*, and William Bronson's *How to Kill a Golden State*. Dasmann described the common sight of trees on wheels: "As orchards of gnarled old olive trees are displaced by subdivisions, experts machine-excavate and box the roots of large trees and truck them away." Lillard criticized "space eaters" such as freeways, factories, drive-in theaters, and shopping malls. Bronson condemned the "mystique of Growth" and labeled home building the "newest extractive industry." "With the possible exception of smog," he wrote, "California faces no environmental crisis more serious than the uncontrolled, ever-accelerating conversion of prime agricultural land to urban uses." The dirge for lost farmland has been heard more or less constantly from the fifties to the present in coastal counties. Joni Mitchell's immortal lyric about a tree museum in a paved-over paradise seems as relevant today as when she recorded it in 1970.[47]

And yet: California agriculture still thrives. The overall story of agriculture since World War II is expansion, not decline. Between 1950 and 2000, while coastal counties lost most of their prime farmland, the state's farmers doubled the overall amount of land devoted to specialty crops. By inflating land prices around Los Angeles, developers, realtors, and home buyers facilitated a major transfer of agricultural wealth into undercapitalized parts of the state. The Citrus Belt did not perish; it moved.

The orange exodus from Southern California happened in two phases, one small and temporary, the other large and permanent. The former occurred on the Southland's outskirts. Even as the citrus industry decayed in Los Angeles and Orange counties, it enjoyed a brief renaissance in parts of Imperial, San Bernardino, and Riverside counties. In the 1950s and 1960s, before the full elaboration of the regional freeway system, growers seized the opportunity to start new groves in areas temporarily beyond the metropolitan fringe. Using improved disease-resistant rootstock, they planted grapefruits, tangerines, and lemons in the Coachella and Imperial valleys. And along the I-215 corridor from Riverside to Temecula, they added grapefruits and oranges. Many such landowners designed their groves to be a one-generation crop—a real estate investment. Before their fruiters became exhausted, their land would be, they hoped, ready to sell to oncoming developers.

The larger movement led out of the Southland altogether. Citrus ranchers followed the earlier outmigration of walnut growers to the San Joaquin Valley (the southern half of the Central Valley), particularly Tulare County. Even in a state of contrasts, Tulare provokes astonishment, with treeless alpine peaks such as Mount Whitney in the Sierra, sequoia groves in the foothills, and expanses of Mediterranean trees in the lowlands. Before the twentieth century, standing water and marshes covered most of the low-elevation land. Road maps still sometimes show the outline of vanished Tulare Lake. When enlarged by spring runoff, Tulare exceeded Tahoe in surface area. Millions of migratory birds on the Pacific Flyway formerly took refuge here, creating one of the great wildlife spectacles in North America. Not anymore. Pioneer-era Californians drained the lake and then pumped the aquifer dry. Agricultural growth stalled until the mid-twentieth century and the arrival of two vast reclamation projects: the Central Valley Project of the U.S. Bureau of Reclamation, which used dams to train the rivers of the southern Sierra into 500 miles of concrete canals (notably the Friant-Kern Canal), and the California State Water Project, which siphoned water from the north to the south in additional canals (notably the California Aqueduct). Thanks to big government, Tulare farmers gained dependable and affordable irrigation water. All the other conditions for premium navel production were naturally occurring in the county's narrow thermal belt. The sloped land leading to the foothills offered well-drained low-alkali soil, excellent air drainage, hot summers, and cool nights. Harvest season here can extend from November all the way to June. Tulare farmers began cultivating citrus as early as the 1890s and invested heavily in navels in the interwar years, but not until the 1960s could they outcompete Southern California.[48]

Taking advantage of the changed situation, farmers enlarged, modernized, and retrofitted. They upgraded the San Joaquin's low-value fields of barley to high-value citrus orchards and table-grape vineyards. They replaced pruners with giant machines with rotating blades. They invested in propane-powered propellers mounted on rotating platforms, the new standard equipment for winter frost protection. The new orchards in Fresno, Tulare, and Kern counties took up greater size—north of 100 acres—than the old hobby groves owned by semiretired colonists in the Southland. Migration facilitated agribusiness consolidation. The CFGE, under its new corporate name, Sunkist, declined in total membership despite adding hundreds of new members. As of 1965, 60 percent of Sunkist growers had not been in business fifteen years before.

Sunkist confronted a paradox in the postwar period. Americans consumed more oranges than ever before—more oranges than any people in world history—but they didn't primarily eat them. They drank them. Frozen OJ concentrate captured the imagination of ordinary Americans even though they weren't the original intended consumers. USDA research into OJ began during World War II as an effort to provide vitamins to soldiers; it continued after the war as a food aid program for Western Europe. Almost immediately Americans embraced the new liquid ration. No breakfast seemed complete without a glass of pasteurized milk and a glass of reconstituted juice. As early as 1949, some 75 percent of U.S. oranges marketed as "fresh fruit" ended up in cans and bottles. Juicing, no longer a salvage operation for low-grade crops, generated huge profits. Almost all the pulped fruit for OJ concentrate and pasteurized juice came from the Sunshine State. Florida's erstwhile disadvantage to California, the unlovely rinds on its oranges, did not matter for concentrate production. Unlike prewar consumers, who squeezed Sunkist fruits on Sunkist extractors or watched the soda jerker at the drugstore do it for them, postwar drinkers of canned Florida juice never saw or touched any oranges.[49]

To compete, Sunkist embarked on a series of food science enterprises, each of which took the cooperative further away from horticulture. The Exchange By-Products Company, originally founded in 1915, became increasingly important to Sunkist's profit stream in the postwar period. It managed a lemon processing plant in Corona and an orange processing plant in Ontario, both of which resembled oil refineries. Using unattractive and thus unmarketable oranges (the "cull") and off-season lemons, these food laboratories created a host of products, including pectin, citric acid, citrus molasses, and cattle feed additives. In 1962 Sunkist technicians developed a process (Perma-Stabil®) to encapsulate essential oils in solid form—an ingredient that showed up on food labels as "natural orange flavor." The cooperative used its flavor capsules to launch a line of frozen concentrates and frozen fruit bars. In the 1970s it even licensed its valuable brand name to junk food purveyors: Sunkist Orange Soda and Sunkist Fruit Gems. Business dealings and a patent portfolio kept the cooperative afloat during an era when it lost hundreds of members through attrition and through new competition with food corporations and grower syndicates.[50]

The romance is gone from Golden State citriculture. Any talk of "Arcadian gardens" seems archaic. No one could mistake dusty, drab Porterville, the seat of Tulare County, for Riverside or Redlands in their glory years. The groves of the San Joaquin Valley exude none of the glamour of the old citrus ranches of Southern California or the current vineyards of Napa Valley. Today a superwealthy semi-retired businessman who wants to dabble in prestige agriculture goes into *Vitis* rather than *Citrus*. Riches can still be made with trees in the interior, only minus the cultural cachet. The kind of respect and wonderment once bestowed upon Southland citrus kings now goes to Silicon Valley tech moguls. The old north-south split in state culture and politics has largely given way to an east-west split between the coast (mostly metropolitan and "blue") and the interior (mostly agricultural and "red").

In Southern California, wistfulness for the fallen Orange Empire has flowered—and may expire—with baby boomers. Angelenos of a certain age reminisce about the halcyon days, half legendary, when freshly laid freeways lacked traffic jams and fruit stands selling all-you-can-drink fresh-squeezed orange juice lined the secondary roads. In 1988 Lawrence Clark Powell, son of CFGE general manager G. Harold Powell, recalled his boyhood in South Pasadena, a "happy time of innocence and ignorance," a time for playing roughhouse outdoors and chanting rhymes like "Ching Chong, Chinaman." "The very things that made it an idyllic land were what attracted the multitudes who were to make it into a sprawling shrouded metropolis," Powell noted with a sigh. "Groves, bean fields and dairylands were mostly lost to towns and cities . . . Paradise lost can never be regained." Some old-timers even spoke fondly of orchard heating and claimed that no one had minded the smudge. "At no time and in no other sort of farming was there greater evidence of attentive care, even affectionate care," declared a local historian. "If a farmer in Iowa sat up all night caring for a sick calf, his California cousin on a wintry night might well be up during all hours caring for his freezing trees." As a gesture to heritage, regional hobbyists of the late twentieth century began collecting smudge pots. Today these rusty heaters can be seen in yards and on porches in nostalgia-afflicted towns such as Redlands. In the 1950s the high school football teams of Redlands and San Bernardino played for the smudge pot trophy, a chromed short-stack orchard heater. In 1972 the mayors of San Dimas and La Verne initiated their own rivalry with their own decommissioned pot. The annual Smudge Pot Bowl has become one of the most intense sports rivalries in the state.[51]

In Redlands and Riverside, local governments made symbolic efforts to preserve fruit trees within town limits. They did not want to be "Anaheimized." In 1979 Redlands by resolution declared citrus a "historical resource," and in 1987 its voters passed a bond measure to purchase widowed groves. By the time the appropriation ran out in 1999, the city had acquired fifteen parcels, 180 acres total. Unfortunately, the old trees cost more to maintain than they made in profit. The outcome in Riverside was much the same. In 1979 its voters authorized the creation of a greenbelt through agricultural easements. But even with tax deductions, favorable zoning, and relatively low-cost water, the greenbelt could not compete against vast new orchards in lower-cost regions and nations. Some of Riverside's last citrus growers sold their greenbelt land—easements intact—to higher-profit wholesale nurserymen who wanted to escape the costs of Los Angeles and Orange counties. Local preservationists eventually succeeded in obtaining enough state funds to establish the California State Historic Citrus Park at a relict orchard outside town.[52]

In Los Angeles County, nonprofit institutions became final owners by default. By the late 1980s the orchards of the San Fernando Valley could be counted on one hand—five groves, 44 acres total, none of them in commercial production. They included a city park, a Catho-

lic high school, and two college campuses. For liability reasons, Cal
State Northridge closed its derelict orchard to the public; then, to
local controversy, the university converted this accidental open space
to parking.[53] In the San Gabriel Valley, the only remaining orange
grove sits in a back corner of the grounds of the Huntington Botanical
Gardens, next to Henry E. Huntington's eucalyptus-shaded mausoleum. The citruses might as well be museum pieces. Visitors do not
have permission to walk the rows or pick the fruit.

In Orange County, the disintegration of the citrus landscape was
even more complete. An illustrative moment occurred in 1978, when
a defunct county-owned grove in Santa Ana became a source of objections: winos camping out, miscreants throwing oranges at cars, an
epidemic of squirrels. The county uprooted the 1,600 trees and, after
securing an exception from the air pollution control district, burned
them. In the 1990s Anaheim built a picnic and play area called Citrus
Park on the site of a former juice factory and planted trees "reminiscent" of oranges. "It's not a good idea to put fruit trees in parks," said
a city official. "People throw it." Historic preservationists, bitter about
northern Orange County's "bulldozer years," petitioned wealthy
exurbs around Irvine to buy relict orchards for heritage reasons. But
no city in Orange County deemed it sensible to enter the business of
boutique farming when it cost something like $2 million up front for
a 3-acre parcel of moribund fruiters. As of 2000, the whole county
contained only about 200 citrus acres, down from the historic peak of
roughly 65,000 (about 13 percent of the total area). Placentia ("home
of the Valencia") now lacks a single grove. The literal "orange curtain"
that once marked the transition from Los Angeles County to Orange
County no longer exists. Today the leading local landmark is probably
the Orange Crush—the largest and most complicated freeway inter-
change in the world.[54]

In southwestern Riverside County, the first cycle of postwar suburbanization initially favored new groves. But in the 1990s owners
here confronted the familiar troika of population growth, inflated
property valuation, and rising water costs. Irrigation accounted for

some 70 percent of expenditures for local farmers, who didn't have the advantage of pioneer growers in colonies such as Ontario, Riverside, and Redlands, with their municipal canal companies. Instead, exurban growers purchased Colorado River water from the Metropolitan Water District, the same agency that serviced Los Angeles. When the price of imported water reached the tipping point, owners turned off the tap and let their trees die. They did not react with surprise or disappointment. "We figured when we put those [trees] in that it would be about 20 years, and we got 30 out of them," said one.[55] Growers called in the bulldozers and the grinders, hoping to make a small profit on green mulch. They expected to make a lot more when the land changed hands. By the early 2000s, even Corona, erstwhile "lemon capital of the world," welcomed the "condo people" who ventured over the coastal mountains to escape the high cost of living near the beach.

Only a few remnants of the Hesperidian garden remain. One can still see grapefruit groves in Imperial County around Thermal, pockets of navels in Riverside County around Temecula, and the historic corridor of lemons and oranges along Highway 126 in Ventura County (where for years residents of towns such as Santa Paula have been saying, "Let's not become another Orange County"). Certain growers have recently profited from the foodie revival of the Meyer lemon, available since 1975 as a tristeza-resistant variety. But scattered citrus towns do not constitute a Citrus Belt. Oranges no longer claim a privileged place in the region's economy and identity. Riverside's parent navel tree, once the object of parades and pageants, stands nearly forgotten in the middle of a busy intersection next to a 7-Eleven, a nail salon, and a taqueria. At downtown's annual Orange Blossom Festival, one may look in vain for a single fruit or juice vendor, a single orange for sale. A booth called the Orange Place sells chocolate ice cream, not orange sherbet. A shaved ice stand doesn't even carry artificial orange flavoring. Here or there you can purchase vintage collectible citrus crate labels, but the only booth that offers information about citrus is the one staffed by white seniors in front of the history museum. The fairgoers, mostly young Latinos, keep walking.[56]

Demographic changes have accompanied landscape changes. Riverside, once a placid domain of white privilege (with designated enclaves for Asians, Mexicans, and Indians), looks like America's future: a metropolitan suburb where minorities are the majority. As of the 2010 census, Latinos composed 49 percent of Riverside's population, and non-Hispanic whites made up only 34 percent. UC Riverside, formed in 1954 from the nucleus of the CES, attracts the most diverse student body in the University of California system. During the long housing boom of the late twentieth and early twenty-first centuries, aspirational working people were drawn to the Riverside area, one of the few places in Southern California where someone of modest means or bad credit could afford a house. The Riverside–San Bernardino metropolitan statistical area grew into one of the fifteen most populous in the nation. Instead of the Orange Empire, new residents referred to their adopted region as the "Inland Empire," or simply "the IE." Unfortunately, when financial crisis and recession hit, debt and mortgage defaults ravaged the region. In recent years, Riverside–San Bernardino has consistently ranked in the national top ten for home foreclosures. The city of San Bernardino declared bankruptcy in 2012. Related financial troubles in California's higher education system forced a delay in the opening of UCR's medical school, which had expropriated some of CES's last remaining citrus groves.

In economic terms, Orange County, better known today as "the OC," fared better. Cities such as Irvine offer a master-planned, amenity-rich suburban landscape with beautifully landscaped shopping malls and easy beach access. Latino gardeners and arborists keep the landscape well groomed. The OC's largest orchard is ornamental—and for private show. William Lyon, a local developer who made a fortune subdividing former Valencia groves, spent some of his wealth acquiring classic cars (including, for a time, the one and only Bugatti Royale Coupe de Ville) and planting 30 acres of oranges on his estate in the gated country club community Coto de

Caza. By contrast, the county's last producing grove depended on the care of a single elderly Mexican-American man. The acreage, part of a former family ranch, had been acquired in 1990 by the city of San Juan Capistrano with funds from a local bond measure for saving farmland as open space. For almost two decades the city allowed Ignacio Lujano, the caretaker of the dying orchard, to continue residing as a tenant. But in 2008 town hall wanted to build a maintenance yard on the underutilized property. After thirty-eight years of devotion to his beloved trees, Lujano, an octogenarian, was evicted.[57]

BUGS IN THE SYSTEM

The new Citrus Belt, like the old one, must adapt. Whether or not consumer preferences for citrus fruits change, the hybrid ecological system—part natural, part artificial—that supports California's citrus trees surely will. Global warming could, for example, result in diminished snowpack, depleted reservoirs, and curtailed irrigation. On the plus side, climate change might extend the growing season and cut short freezes like the ones that devastated Central Valley crops in 1990 and 2007. Crop insurance can cover damages from fluke weather but not from a graver threat, infestation. The cultural costs of insects and insect-borne diseases may yet cripple the industry. The cottony-cushion scale crisis of the nineteenth century has two modern equivalents, Mediterranean fruit fly and Asian citrus psyllid.

Medfly may be the most despised agricultural pest in the world. Some 250 crops, including citrus, can serve as hosts; female flies deposit their eggs under the skin of fleshy fruits and vegetables. As the larvae nibble and burrow, they deposit a fungus that makes the food mushy and inedible to humans. The California Department of Food and Agriculture (CDFA) considers medfly a category A risk to the state's multibillion-dollar farm sector. While many countries, including Europe's leading citrus supplier, Israel, accept medfly as an established and unavoidable nuisance, the United States pursues

a policy of zero tolerance. At great expense, Florida growers elim-
inated the insect in 1929–30, 1956–57, and 1962–63. Californians
first detected the invasive species in 1975 and fought the first major
battle in 1980–1982.

The 1980 outbreak began in the suburban Bay Area. In a coordinated response, scientists at the University of California, the CDFA,
and the USDA released millions of sterilized male flies among
the ranch homes and high-tech campuses of Silicon Valley. But all
the biolabs in the world couldn't supply enough steriles to control the
population. Lest the medflies spread to commercial farming areas,
the USDA urged immediate and preemptive action: helicopters dropping the pesticide malathion on the initial quarantine zones in Santa
Clara, San Mateo, and Alameda counties. Fearing the political costs
of aerial spraying, governor Jerry Brown came down in favor of continued ground spraying, a less effective control method. Bay Area
environmentalists threatened an impeachment campaign if he authorized the bombardment of populated areas with an organophosphate,
a proposal they likened to Agent Orange. Brown's caution produced
its own political and economic costs: members of his own administration defied him, the USDA promised to place the entire state under
quarantine, and various states and nations threatened separate fruit
embargos. In July 1981, to great controversy, the governor reversed
course and approved the air campaign. On more than one occasion,
agitated residents in the fly zone shot bullets in the direction of helicopters. Interpreting the aerial spraying as an admission of failure to
control the outbreak, Florida, Texas, Mexico, and Japan went ahead
and initiated embargos.[58]

The delayed implementation of spraying allowed medflies to spread
to other suburban areas, including Los Angeles County. This represented a major threat to the citrus export industry, since almost all the
harvested fruit made its way to wholesale distributors in Los Angeles
and thence to container boxes for ocean or land transport. Exporters
and importers feared that fruit would become contaminated in transit. The Los Angeles County agricultural commissioner promised an

"all-out, no-holds-barred eradication reaction." Mayor Tom Bradley offered the use of police helicopters. Exterminators mixed malathion and water with molasses, sugar, and yeast to create granules large enough to deter human inhalation and heavy enough to deter wind dispersal. This sticky poison rain fell on quarantined suburban yards in San Gabriel Valley towns such as El Monte, Baldwin Park, West Covina, and Irwindale. State officials begged valley residents not to pick or transport any citrus fruit from home gardens. Drawing on emergency funds from the USDA and the state, the California Conservation Corps stripped fruits from trees and National Guardsmen buried them at landfills. Reservists also conducted enhanced fruit searches at highway stops. The CDFA claimed victory—full eradication—in fall 1982. The final bill for the first California medfly "war" came to roughly $100 million, a minor sum compared to the state's $14 billion farm economy.[59]

Victory did not endure. Medfly populations reappeared more or less every year after 1980, with occasional irruptions. In 1989–90 the state dropped malathion over Los Angeles, Orange, and San Diego counties. A would-be ecosabotage group called the Breeders sent a letter to Mayor Bradley and the *Los Angeles Times* claiming responsibility—probably but not surely a hoax—for spreading medflies in protest of "carcinogenic" pesticides. More conventionally, community groups formed in opposition. In quarantined Corona, residents complained about respiratory problems and rashes after eight aerial bombardments. The state sprayed over the objections of the city, which lost a case before the supreme court in Sacramento. Bowing to political will, the CDFA eventually phased out aerial spraying in favor of the costlier alternative: mass release of male flies sterilized through irradiation. In 1996 the agency unveiled its tax-funded Preventative Release Program. The CDFA contracted with a rearing facility in Guatemala that could produce 450 million sterile pupae per week. Using specially equipped small-prop planes flying at low altitude, technicians unloaded some 125,000 steriles per square mile per week over targeted areas of Southern California. Over the five-year funded life of the program, roughly 75 billion reproductively challenged flies took flight.[60]

There are two competing arguments about medfly population dynamics in California. The outspoken entomologist James Carey contends that *C. capitata* naturalized in the Southland in the 1980s and that each subsequent irruption has resulted primarily from persistent resident populations. The CDFA rejects this analysis. It interprets each outbreak as a new invasion, the result of people illegally carrying fruit into California from foreign countries and Hawai'i. It does stand to reason that medfly larvae find their way into purses, suitcases, and mailers. This would explain why the Southland and the Bay Area, the two subregions with major international airports, regularly host outbreaks. However, airport blitzes in 1991 at SFO and LAX did not turn up flies. The latest evidence from genetic testing points to multiple introductions but does not rule out the likelihood of locally persistent populations. If and when the CDFA acknowledges the establishment of medfly, the citrus industry will have to make major adjustments. Importers could embargo the state's oranges or demand expensive fly-killing fumigation or cold storage. The response would vary from country to country. Japan is particularly sensitive because thus far it has avoided medflies.[61]

Growers in the Central Valley have managed to keep the flies at arm's length. It will be harder, if not impossible, to repel a newer threat: a citrus-killing bacterial disease called citrus greening, or huanglongbing (Chinese for "yellow shoot disease")—HLB for short. Industry representatives commonly use words like *doomsday* and *catastrophe* when discussing the pathogen. One agricultural commissioner ranked the threat of HLB: "On a scale of 1 to 10—15." Although greening always leads to death, it takes months or years for the worst symptoms to manifest. Leaves turn mottled, fruits grow misshapen, rinds remain green, and fruit flesh becomes disgustingly bitter. By the time an arborist notices one infected tree, the whole grove may be afflicted.[62]

To spread from plant to plant, the HLB bacterium requires one of

two species of psyllid (from the same family of insect that has weakened and killed so many eucalypts in California). In North America, the vector is Asian citrus psyllid. This tiny brownish bug lifts its
posterior to a characteristic 45-degree angle as it feeds on bud shoots
and the undersides of leaves. The insect appeared in Florida in 1998
and initially spread through the sale of nursery stock. The Sunshine
State quickly abandoned hope of exterminating the bug and merely
tried to manage the population. The psyllids are so tiny—the size
of a pinhead—that they needn't expend any energy to travel great
distances; they simply ride the wind. Gulf Coast hurricanes have
aided dispersal. By 2005, when HLB arrived separately in Florida, its
insect vector had already naturalized. Nothing could stop the disease.
Growers uprooted and burned millions of trees at a loss of billions of
dollars and thousands of jobs.

From the opposite coast, Californians followed the grim news of
the advancing Asian citrus psyllid. "This could be the death knell for
our industry," said a Redlands grower. "It's the most serious threat,
next to development, that we've ever faced."[63] In the opening years
of the twenty-first century, the insect pushed northward from Central America into Mexico and finally over the border into San Diego
County in 2008. These pioneer insects tested negative for HLB, but
the CDFA spared no precaution. With financial help from the industry (taken from a per-box assessment on oranges), the agency created
a quarantine zone and sprayed all vegetation and soil in a 400-meter
radius from each infected citrus. Most of the problem plants were in
suburban backyard gardens. Despite the speedy state response, the
psyllid migrated northward to Orange and Los Angeles counties
within a year. The CDFA dispatched spraying crews to Echo Park
(near Dodger Stadium), the neighborhood with the highest density
of the insects.

Every day Californians unwittingly give psyllids a lift. Out of
ignorance or sentiment, ordinary people—not smugglers—routinely
violate the state's strict plant importation laws. In multicultural California, many ethnic traditions incorporate leaves from subtropical

Asia, the evolutionary home of *Citrus*. For example, Mexicans often use cuttings from the ornamental orange Jessamine in flower arrangements for Día de los Muertos. Unfortunately, citrus psyllids feed on jessamines, too. Transborder families who visit the United States in October to construct or visit altars may act as assistants to the vectors. Likewise, Chinese Americans may spread the insect by giving gifts of citrus trees, a traditional good-luck gesture, at the lunar New Year, housewarming parties, and other celebrations. Many Filipinos in California illegally import leaves from the malunggay plant for culinary and medicinal purposes. Inspectors with U.S. Customs and Border Protection intercepted psyllid-infested malunggay at SFO and LAX in 2009. That same year, at a FedEx facility in Fresno, a pest-sniffing Labrador retriever, a canine employee of the county agricultural commission, detected a duffel bag containing leaves from curry tree, a regular component of South Asian recipes, Ayurvedic remedies, and Hindu offerings. The spice package, which originated in India, contained ten psyllids. The bugs tested positive for HLB, the first recorded instance in California.

Even before HLB establishes itself in the Central Valley—as it inescapably will—the Asian citrus psyllid may imperil the niche industry of organic citrus. San Diego County contains the highest concentration of USDA-certified organic farms in the nation, including numerous citrus groves. Located in the pathway of psyllids arriving from Mexico, growers face a tough choice: don't use pesticides and potentially lose their trees, or use pesticides and automatically lose their organic certification. "I'd be lying if I said I wasn't already looking at alternatives to citrus," said one in 2009. "Wine grapes are a possibility out here. And houses. That would be a good crop."[64]

The outlook worsened in the following few years. As of summer 2011, the USDA had placed most of Southern California, including all of Ventura, Los Angeles, Orange, San Diego, and Imperial counties, under citrus quarantine. The ruling banned all transfer of nursery stock and required that all fruit be cleaned of leaves and stems. In 2012 the CDFA stipulated that all citrus nursery stock—"mother trees"—

in licensed commercial nurseries must be enclosed in screenhouses or greenhouses with protections such as outward-blowing automated fans at the doors. None of this prevented the first (detected) psyllid from arriving in Tulare County in winter 2012. Nor did the state's program of spraying tens of thousands of suburban trees in Greater Los Angeles make any noticeable difference. "There were too many trees to treat," said UCR's top entomologist.[65] In March 2012, when the USDA announced the long-expected bad news—HLB detected in California—no one was surprised by the location: the suburban San Gabriel Valley in Los Angeles County. The suspected disease source, a graft of a pomelo variety not legally available in the United States, had been received as a gift within a fellowship of gardeners affiliated with the local United Chinese Christian Church. CDFA teams immediately descended on ground zero, removed the diseased tree, and surveyed the neighborhood for citruses, vacuuming psyllids for lab analysis.

At this juncture, spraying the metropolis no longer makes sense. The next line of defense is early detection of the disease. Through ads, the industry asks for the public's vigilance; the USDA has released a "Save Our Citrus" app for smartphones. No one knows the total number of suburban citrus trees; millions seems likely. If every residential yard in Southern California included just one, the total number would rival the vast groves of Tulare County. One of the enduring features of Southland lifestyle—fresh-squeezed juice from the backyard tree—may wither and die in coming years, but not before the sickened plants act as reservoirs for psyllids that will infect distant rural groves. Outdoor living has its costs: the suburbs threaten to displace the orange industry for a second time.

What next? Florida and California growers continue to pour tens of millions of dollars into HLB research, and scientists may yet develop a cure for greening disease, or determine a weakness in the psyllid through gene sequencing, or breed disease-resistant citrus stock through traditional or transgenic methods. Some place their hopes on a genetically modified citrus varietal with genes implanted from spinach. In the meantime, new genetic and chemical tests enable scientists to determine the presence of HLB in trees long before symptoms become visible. Entomologists at UCR's Center for Invasive Species Research express hope in an older technique: bug-eat-bug control. In late 2011, after gaining state and federal clearance, university scientists released the first batch of a parasitoid wasp that uses psyllid nymphs as its host. Originally collected from the Punjab region of Pakistan, the wasp appropriately made its California debut on the campus of UCR. As coordinated by the CDFA, UCR scientists will raise and release many more batches across the state in coming years. If California bides its time, perhaps a solution will be found and Asian citrus psyllid will go down in history like the cottony-cushion scale of the nineteenth century: a temporary bug in the system. It seems equally plausible that Central Valley farm corporations will someday capitulate to HLB and replace their navel groves with a trendy boutique crop, and hire advertisers to convince consumers that this fresh new wonder fruit will make them healthier and happier.

Capitalist industries and landscapes tend to have short lives by design. The ethos: make money while you can; get out while you're ahead. Specialty agriculture, entrepreneurial and unsentimental by nature, means growing consumer-ready food products, not commodity staples. California agribusinesses experiment with new crops all the time as they try to meet or create demand and compete with foreign suppliers. They plant or uproot trees by the millions in response to consumer desires and ecological dictates. Different citrus varietals rise and fall in popularity. Over the first decade of the millennium, Moro blood oranges and Meyer lemons experienced a modest revival; navels and lemons stood their ground (at around 140,000 and 45,000 bearing acres, respectively), while Valencias and grapefruits lost significantly; and tangerines expanded exponentially. California's two top crops in 2010, almonds and wine grapes, hardly mattered as recently as 1970. The state used to be number one in wheat and cotton; it moved on. California has never been committed to any particular crop in the way that Iowa has wed itself (politically and economically) to corn and corn subsidies. The Golden State is committed to making gold.[66]

The plant-based wealth of California still staggers the imagination. As of the 2007 Agricultural Census, farm acreage took up one-quarter of the state (25 million acres). That year, California produced 80 percent of America's table oranges, almost 90 percent of its lemons, and about 25 percent of its total citrus crop. Foreign buyers imported about one-third of its oranges. The value of the state's total citrus crop exceeded $1 billion, topped only by that of grapes, greenhouse plants, lettuce, almonds, hay, strawberries, and tomatoes. It is true that the sweet orange, once the number-one plant commodity in the state, is in danger of dropping out of the top twenty. But California's over-all farm output tops that of every other state—and many nations—and exceeds the global revenue of the Hollywood film industry. The Golden State retains a virtual monopoly on the domestic supply of almonds, walnuts, pistachios, olives, avocados, pomegranates, apricots, plums, nectarines, dates, figs, lemons, kiwi fruit, processed strawberries, canning tomatoes, broccoli, Brussels sprouts, celery, garlic, leaf lettuce, and artichokes. About one-third of the table food in all fifty states derives from one. The winter cornucopia available at every supermarket in America comes largely from the Salinas Valley, the Central Valley, and the Imperial Valley.[67]

The postwar agricultural history of California reinforces an old adage: money follows the path of least resistance. Sometimes that path leads to row houses, sometimes to crop rows. In Napa Valley, land assessment currently favors vineyards over housing lots. Here suburbanization has stalled. Arguably, the postwar housing industry in Southern California helped more than harmed the citrus industry, because it created capital that could be invested in the Central Valley. From 1950 to 2000, the state's total citrus acreage recovered and its total land in farm production dipped only slightly.[68]

By the logic of capital, the current concentration of citrus in and around Tulare County makes sense. The San Joaquin Valley, unlike the contemporary Southland, encourages large-scale intensive farming. Growers here enjoy more space, fewer land and labor costs, lower taxes, looser regulations, and fewer complaints from neighbors. Small wonder that Greater Los Angeles displaced various other high-impact land uses to the Central Valley. In addition to the metropolitan citrus stock, the rural inland received the metropolitan dairy cows. The milk and cheese for Los Angeles used to come from nearby Artesia, then not-so-distant Chino, but finally the same pressures that expelled most citruses expelled most cows. As dairy farmers in Chino sold out and relocated during the boom years of the Clinton-Bush era, they too consolidated. Concentrated animal feeding operations (CAFOs)—animal slums that emit noxious smells and frightening amounts of waste—became the norm in the San Joaquin. At the same time, the state transplanted a whole class of urban people to rural cages. Until reform measures passed in 2011, coastal California exported its prisoners—its gang members, its mentally ill, its three-strikes-you're-out nonviolent petty drug offenders serving life terms—to correctional facilities located at the edges of depressed farm towns along Highway 99, now a prison-and-fruit alley. The state went for broke in the 1980s and 1990s building new prisons and mandating tough-on-crime law enforcement.[69]

Thus the Central Valley in the late twentieth century became a strange place of concentrated wealth and disempowerment, the home of the state's richest vineyards and orchards, its biggest meth labs and trailer parks. The reclusive grower J. G. Boswell made billions here, and the celebrity businesswoman Lynda Rae Resnick made billions more. Almost singlehandedly, Resnick's company POM Wonderful turned pomegranates from an exotic fruit to a familiar and desirable source of "antioxidant superpower." Today the valley's extensive groves of pomegranates, navels, and tangerines are virtually devoid of people, not counting the migrant workers—predominantly illegal immigrants—who arrive at harvest time. The old paternalistic labor relations between citrus ranchers and their semipermanent year-round help has given way to impersonal relations between absentee owners and seasonal employees, still overwhelmingly Mexican. They live in poor, unincorporated communities and suffer from tapwater contaminated by fertilizers, pesticides, and animal waste. As of 2007, Tulare County, the second most profitable agricultural county in America, second only to neighboring Fresno, contained roughly 11 million oranges, and those trees directly supported the employment of more than 12,000 people. For better or worse, the California citrus industry (like the strawberry industry) relies on old-fashioned sweat power. Unlike oranges in Florida, which can be harvested with canopy shaker machines, since the fruit is destined for pulping, California's navels and lemons must be harvested by hand to maximize aesthetics and longevity.[70]

Whether because of HLB or global capitalism, the second flowering of the California citrus industry will eventually end. As long as horticapitalists in the Central Valley can maximize profits tending *Citrus*, they will. As soon as they can't, they won't. From their perspective, an orange grove is simply a highly capitalized organic factory with a planned obsolescence of fifty years. Decadent citrus orchards surely don't deserve to be "saved" like old-growth redwood stands. The whole purpose of commercial citriculture is optimizing returns, not preserving trees. Economies evolve. Tastes change. It's not as if people need to eat and drink cratefuls of oranges. Citrus is not a dietary staple, like corn, wheat, rice, soy, or even bananas. In an age of artificial sweeteners, vitamin pills, nutrient powders, and free-trade tropical fruit, it's hard to say what pressing advantages California oranges retain for health and happiness. Perhaps someday they will return to being occasional indulgences and holiday gifts. It seems inevitable that the senior holders of water rights in the thermal belt of the Central Valley will someday find a higher economic use for their irrigated land.

The second downfall of citrus will temporarily distress local pickers and packers, but will California's urbanites even notice? Will they care if Safeway starts stocking Chinese or Brazilian oranges? Will they grieve the loss of citruses in the San Joaquin Valley? Maybe not. For urban Californians, the San Joaquin is simply a place for driving through as quickly as possible, not counting a pit stop at In-N-Out Burger. On I-5 and Highway 99, speeding motorists pass by millions of fruit and nut trees without much of a sideways glance. People don't form deep emotional attachments to mechanically pruned row plants *as trees*. Compared to eucalypts, which thrive on their own and grow into idiosyncratic landmarks, oranges are weak and generic landscape features. *Citrus* cannot dominate the California scene except as large-scale, high-maintenance monocultural orchards of monotype organisms. Divorced from the enchanting scenery and reformist ideology of the original Citrus Belt, the groves of Tulare County—*hortus sine urbe*—reveal their true nature as botanical factories. They fail to inspire reverence as sequoia groves do.

However, for an aging generation of Californians, the sweet scent of white blossoms may yet conjure up golden memories of a time when the Southland was more green and less crowded—and, some might add under their breath, less Mexican and Asian. This self-serving sentiment ought to be resisted. Californians should understand that citrus ranches fueled the "growth machine" long before freeways and tract developments. And they should know that horticapitalism begat disposable landscapes that yielded pollution, exploitation, and violence in addition to those luscious fruits with perfectly colored rinds.

PART FOUR

PALMS: THE ECOLOGY OF STYLE

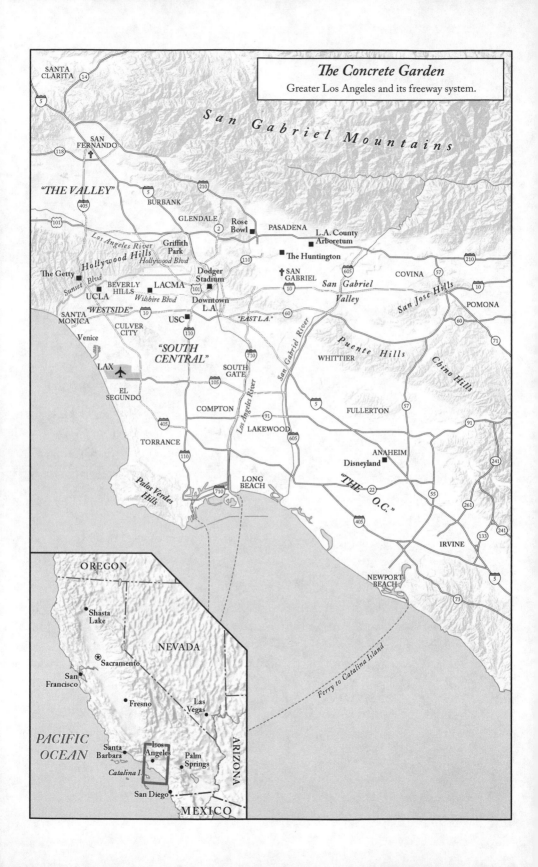

The Concrete Garden
Greater Los Angeles and its freeway system.

SANTA CLARITA

SAN FERNANDO

"THE VALLEY"

BURBANK

GLENDALE

Rose Bowl

PASADENA

L.A. County Arboretum

San Gabriel Mountains

Los Angeles River

Hollywood Hills

Griffith Park

Hollywood Blvd

The Getty

Sunset Blvd

BEVERLY HILLS

LACMA

Dodger Stadium

The Huntington

SAN GABRIEL

COVINA

UCLA

Wilshire Blvd

Downtown L.A.

San Gabriel Valley

San Jose Hills

POMONA

SANTA MONICA

"WESTSIDE"

CULVER CITY

USC

"EAST L.A."

Venice

"SOUTH CENTRAL"

LAX

SOUTH GATE

San Gabriel River

Puente Hills

WHITTIER

Chino Hills

EL SEGUNDO

COMPTON

Los Angeles River

LAKEWOOD

FULLERTON

TORRANCE

ANAHEIM

Disneyland

"THE O.C."

IRVINE

Palos Verdes Hills

LONG BEACH

NEWPORT BEACH

Ferry to Catalina Island

OREGON

Shasta Lake

NEVADA

Sacramento

San Francisco

Fresno

Las Vegas

PACIFIC OCEAN

Santa Barbara

Los Angeles

Palm Springs

ARIZONA

Catalina I.

San Diego

MEXICO

At Chicago's White City, the imperial fantasyland constructed on the quadricentennial of Christopher Columbus, visitors strolled through a series of ostentatious exhibition halls with displays designed to educate, delight, and amaze. The federal government raised a domed building with a neoclassical façade and dignified the rotunda with the severed, eviscerated trunk of a multimillennial giant sequoia. States and territories built exhibits, too, and California did its best to outdo them all. The great Pacific state erected its own domed structure, a mock Spanish mission with Moorish flourishes. Inside the 100,000-square-foot hall furnished with redwood paneling and redwood wainscoting, food and drink—garden produce on redwood counters, wine bottles in redwood display cases—announced the plenitude of California. A banner with gold lettering greeted visitors with a message about the state's admission into the Union in 1850: THEY SOUGHT HER. THEY WOOED HER. THEY WON HER. THEY PLACED HER, THE BRIGHTEST JEWEL THAT NOW GLEAMS IN THE CORONET OF COLUMBIA.

By 1892 sunshine had replaced gold as California's most valuable natural asset. At the fair, the Golden State touted its "semi-tropical" climate with floral displays. Los Angeles donated a young Canary Island date palm—not much visible trunk, but magnificent fronds—and Santa Barbara gave up a pair of mature date palms to accentuate the state building's eastern entrance. California boosters festooned the interior with specimens of azalea, banana, bamboo, and especially palm. Potted trees could be found in every corner, on every parapet and pedestal. Hanging baskets dubbed "air castles" burst with pampas plumes, eucalyptus garlands, and palm fronds. The fair committee intended to "transplant the visitor, mentally, to the semi-tropics."[1] Even the pillars of the dome had been decorated to resemble palms. At the center of this leafy extravaganza, directly beneath the sunlit glass dome, surrounded by fountains, in a triple-terraced ceramic basin, stood the pièce de résistance, a full-sized date palm from San Diego.

The tree came from the grounds of California's first Spanish mission and presidio. According to legend, Junípero Serra, the Franciscan founder of the mission system, planted this palm from seed in 1769. More reliably, it can be said that the display tree rose 40 to 50 feet high and weighed some 45,000 pounds. After lifting the plant out of the ground with a derrick, workers boxed the roots, tied up its fronds, and loaded it onto a train. The living package took up two whole flatcars. Tree tenders dampened the roots several times a day during the weeklong trip to Chicago. Upon arrival, workmen completed the delivery on house rollers pulled by a team of horses. To squeeze the tree into the state pavilion, the men had to remove the extra-large front doors from their hinges. From rail yard to fairground, a crowd followed the exotic specimen. The *Pacific Rural Press* claimed that the arrival of the San Diego palm generated more local excitement than the "monster Krupp gun" from Germany. The tree showed up with a disheveled crown, but recovered enough to impress ticket holders. Every day during the fair, boosters used its trunk as a bulletin board, posting the temperatures at Lake Michigan and Coronado Beach for comparison. "This old tree has come two thousand miles to tell its story of sunshine and soft air," wrote one proud visitor from California.[2]

When Chicago shuttered the White City, the Golden State shipped much of its exhibit, including L.A.'s Canary Island date palm, to San Francisco for another exposition, the Midwinter Fair of

1894. The tree had an agent, Frank Wiggins, the indefatigable secretary of the Los Angeles Chamber of Commerce. William Mulholland, the engineer who brought water to the city, once quipped, "The only way to stop the growth of southern California would be to kill Frank Wiggins." The chamber's hardworking plant, a veteran of two promotional fairs, returned home after its stint in Golden Gate Park. Placed in front of a bungalow at Twelfth and Valenica, the peripatetic palm grew to peak size, towering over the house. "It is the only palm tree in California that has been to Chicago," noted the *Los Angeles Times* in 1936. At this point, the Canary Island date palm retained little value beyond historical curiosity. The newspaper drew attention to the "fading fashion of the palm tree."[3]

In subsequent decades, fashions in trees, like clothes, passed through cycles. Fronded trees came back in style, fell out again, returned once more. Promoters, planners, and developers revert to palms again and again because these plants can signify any number of desirable qualities: health, wealth, warmth, leisure, sophistication, glamour. They enhance California's most valuable, albeit intangible, property—its image. Palms are for the moment the signature trees of Los Angeles, a city built on advertising, a city that promises everyone a makeover. People who deride L.A. scrutinize its extra-tall palms as symbols of glitz, tackiness, and fakery. Throughout California, particularly in Los Angeles, the story of fronds is a field of semiotics—signs and symbols. Palms have been planted here for what they mean, not what they do. Or rather, what they mean *is* what they do.

CHAPTER 7

Cosmopolitan Fronds

DOMESTIC EXOTICA

Palms remain rarities for most Americans. In the late nineteenth century, they seemed positively exotic to migrants to California. In the long run, Californians created homegrown meanings for their palm trees, but initially they turned to familiar, preexisting symbolic categories: the Oriental palm, the tropical palm, and the Mediterranean palm, with their associations with the Near East, the equatorial zone, and the seaside. Worldwide, palms in fact occur in a variety of altitudes and habitats, including temperate mountain regions. They cannot, however, survive in ice-cold or bone-dry conditions. Despite the seemingly favorable climate of coastal Southern California, palms do not occur naturally here. You must go to the state's hottest desert to find its one native palm species and its only example of agricultural palms.

The native tree, California fan palm, occurs in widely spaced stands from Palm Springs in the north to the mountains of Baja California del Norte in the south, with outlier locations in Nevada and Arizona. Most of the stands take root in sheltered canyons with subsurface streams; a few occur in open locations where deep subterranean water makes its way to the surface through cracks in the San Andreas Fault. Over the ages, birds and coyotes spread tree seeds from one isolated oasis to the next. The Colorado Desert—the term for California's portion of the lowland Sonoran Desert west of the Colorado River— contains roughly a hundred fan palm oases. There are single-tree locations such as Una Palma, medium-sized ones such as Oasis of Mara (formerly called Twenty-Nine Palms, a name now associated with the nearby Marine Corps training facility and its liquor-and-tattoo base town), and large ones such as Thousand Palms. Many oases have languished, shrunk, or died in recent decades because of expanding exurbs and falling water tables. The largest stand, and the most visited, is Palm Canyon, which contains more than three thousand trees. The rugged canyon disgorges from San Jacinto Peak, a stunning snow-catcher that rises more than 10,000 feet straight up from the desert floor. From nearby Palm Springs, you cannot see the canyon's mouth; the hidden oasis manages to surprise and delight even repeat visitors. The gorge contains stunning contrasts in colors: ruddy brown-gray rock, bright green fronds, and blackened trunks, the result of past fires.

Palm Canyon belongs to the Agua Caliente Band of Cahuilla Indians, whose mythology prominently includes the trees. In historic times, natives used palms for everything: fronds for thatches, stems for implements, fiber for twine, fruit for food. Cahuillas managed their garden by ritually burning it. They knew how to spread fires without killing the trees. Flames cleared out the mess of dead fronds that made access difficult, and cleaned out insects and rodents that competed for fruit. Fire also stimulated fruit production. It seems probable that Cahuilla caretakers also planted seeds and tended seedlings.[1]

Anglo-Americans exoticized the Cahuilla landscape from practically their first sighting. In 1853 a member of a U.S. railroad survey conveyed surprise at seeing palms in the desert; the scene had "an Oriental aspect; and the similarity was made still more striking by the groups of Arab-like Indians." Around 1900, as Palm Springs became a destination for invalids and health tourists, Americans reverted to tired Old World descriptors: soaking in medicinal water beneath a palm called to mind a Roman or Turkish bath; the colors of Palm Canyon looked like those of Tunisia. The Automobile Club of Southern California encouraged members to drive to Palm Springs for "a taste of Egypt." One enterprising developer instructed his Cahuilla employee to greet tourists at the railroad station in Bedouin garb. In the 1920s the region also attracted full-time residents—fashionable antimodernists seeking a simple life with amenities. Some of them built "gay bungalows" with "oriental color schemes" and villas in the style of Biskra, a resort in interior Algeria. In Hollywood's early years, Palm Springs became the go-to stand-in for every iconic Old World desert—the Sahara, Egypt, Palestine, Arabia, Babylon. In cinematic tales of legionnaires, sheikhs, and belly dancers, California fan palms served as a convenient backdrop.[2]

Meanwhile, in the realm of land management, the palm oases drew comparisons to sequoia groves—unique, isolated, imperiled. Tourists in Palm Springs, like tourists in the Sierra Nevada, disliked the look of blackened tree trunks and worried that traditional Indian-set fires jeopardized the last stands of the native palms. In 1921 a California congressman introduced a bill to reserve Palm Canyon as a national monument. This proposal made it through Congress the next year with the blessing of the National Park Service's director, Steve Mather, who thought the monument would complement Muir Woods. According to the legislation, 1,600 acres of tribal trust land—the oases of Palm, Andreas, and Murray canyons—would become the charge of the secretary of the interior. Even before president Warren Harding signed the authorizing legislation, the *Los Angeles Times* published this headline: "Palm Canyon, Part of Southern California's Little Araby, Becomes a National Park." The boosterish newspaper had already spread misinformation that the canyons composed a small portion of the land of the Cahuillas and "a part which has never been inhabited by them." The *Times* failed to note that the establishment of a monument hinged on the consent of a majority of the Agua

Caliente Band (population: 3,000). When it came time to vote, the Indians refused to relinquish title. Nevertheless, thousands of automobile tourists from Los Angeles came to see "their" new park.[3]

Conditions in the canyon degraded. Campers left behind campfire rings, mounds of tin cans, and soiled tissue paper. Vandals set trees on fire and uprooted barrel cacti to roll down hills. Film crews appropriated fronds to create "Hawaiian" thatched huts; actors washed off greasepaint with oasis water. In response to such abuse, the federal Mission Indian Agency closed the canyon to camping in 1923. This outcome didn't completely agree with the Agua Caliente Band, which relied on film royalties and camping fees for financial stimulus. Midway through 1930, a year when 150,000 people visited Palm Canyon, Cahuillas built a tollgate across the access route. The narrow, pitted road had become a 7-mile traffic jam on fair-weather spring Sundays. The parking lot overflowed. "The place resembles a city dump rather than a famous desert landmark," remarked the county's superintendent of roads.[4]

Palm Springs, having become a fashionable resort for Hollywood stars, wanted to take control of the area's natural attractions. The Chamber of Commerce regularly complained about Cahuilla mismanagement of the hot springs and the canyons, including alleged damage to palms from Indian fires and Indian animals. After World War II, the city began a systematic campaign to beautify its downtown, adding palms and removing Indians—a small-scale municipal case of ethnic cleansing. Using health and building codes, the city "abated" the social threat by evicting Cahuillas from their own land, then burning their condemned homes and razing them to the ground. The band fought off simultaneous federal attempts to coerce them to sell their land and detribalize (a process called "termination"). Despite it all, the natives of Agua Caliente held on to their communal property. In the long run, they benefited financially from the evolution of Palm Springs from an antimodernist retreat to a modernist resort to a snowbird destination to a gay tourist attraction. The Agua Caliente

Band now operates two casinos and manages Indian Canyons as a nature reserve.[5]

Today the entire area looks like an oasis. Plants with fronds adorn every golf course, mansion, spa, boutique, and nightclub in Palm Springs. Over a thousand palms, each with its own illumination, line the main drag, Palm Canyon Drive. During the holiday season, each tree gets festooned with additional fairy lights. The current clientele at Palm Springs is too sophisticated to compare the treescape to the land of the Bedouins. For residual evidence of that kind of thinking, you have to go to the farm-cum-festival town of Indio, located 25 miles southeast on I-10, in the lower Coachella Valley.

Indio contains no palmy oases but many more palms: North America's date industry concentrates here. Date palms count among the oldest cultivated trees in the world; their human-induced sweetness goes back five millennia. Delicious, caloric, and nutritious, dates are essential ingredients in the cuisines of North Africa, the Middle East, and India. Moors brought date palms to Spain, and Spaniards brought them to California—more for Palm Sunday fronds than for fruit. Not until the twentieth century did the local date industry come of age. Indio celebrated its commercial success with a date festival, held first in 1921 and made into an annual event after World War II. The two-week fair became an excuse for all varieties of tacky exoticism. Locals dressed up as Bedouins and rode costumed horses. Teenage beauties competed to become the next Queen Scheherazade. After a matinee at the Ali Baba Theatre, spectators could, down at the fairground, watch camel races and purchase date milkshakes at the Taj Mahal exhibition hall. At night, on the main stage, below mock minarets, community members—and the occasional trained monkey—put on a pageant-play based on the Arabian Nights.[6]

With its fantasy bricolage of India-Persia-Arabia-Sahara, Indio represented a throwback to an Orientalist way of thinking about palms. But the association of palm trees with the Near East (broadly defined) is much older than the colonial gaze. For centuries, palms in the Western imagination primarily suggested three interlocking historical and geographical regions: the Fertile Crescent, Egypt, and the Holy Land. In the shared mythologies of ancient peoples in these regions, the date palm stood in for the Tree of Life. Babylonians cultivated great orchards of dates. Egyptians occasionally built columns in the shape of palms. The Hebrew Bible describes Jericho as the City of Palm Trees and portrays Moses camping at palm oases in the wilderness. On Sukkot, the autumn Feast of Tabernacles, observant Jews make temporary outdoor shelters out of boughs—preferably palm branches—to commemorate the desert sojourn of the Children of Israel. "The righteous shall flourish like the palm tree," says the Book of Psalms. When Christians radically revised the Hebrew Bible, they added a major palm event: Jesus returning to Jerusalem on the back of an ass while excited believers waved fronds and threw down garments and branches to honor the path of the King of Israel. Catholics, Orthodox Christians, and many Protestants ritually reenact this event on Palm Sunday. Where fronds cannot be procured, observant Christians substitute flowers, or branches from other trees, such as olives, willows, and yews.

As European explorer-naturalists pushed into the global south, palm symbolism in the West began to shift away from desert oases, ancient history, and the cradle of civilization. The tropical palm superseded the Oriental palm as an archetype. In the eighteenth century, Linnaeus referred to palms as the "Princes of India" and named the plant order of palms *Principes* (now *Arecales*). As bioprospectors surveyed the flora of the New World, particularly South America, the palm became the key visual shorthand for the tropical unknown. The illustrious Alexander von Humboldt considered palms, banana trees, and tree ferns to be the most characteristic tropical flora; Alfred Russel Wallace referred to palms as "true denizens of the tropics, of which they are the most striking and characteristic feature." Informed by naturalists and explorers, artists sought to create "typical landscapes" of newly discovered tropical regions. The celebrated American landscapist Frederic Church deliberately followed the footsteps of

Humboldt on two art expeditions to equatorial South America and produced several palm-studded canvases. In the painterly hands of Church and other American Romantics, the typical palm could also function as a symbolic tree—the Tree of Life in a New World Eden. At the same time, as a type of the so-called torrid zone, palms suggested an abnormal, potentially dangerous climate, where heat, humidity, and lushness could lead to exhaustion, fever, and disorientation. The slothful, uncivilized world was seemingly replete with palms.[7]

Transplanted to the so-called temperate zone, tropical palms could be domesticated, their negative associations pruned. In royal botanical gardens and private greenhouses, cultivated fronds provided aesthetic escapism. In the 1840s Kew Gardens built the world's largest steel-and-glass greenhouse and amassed an unrivaled palm collection. Many wealthy collectors subsequently built smaller versions of the Palm House at Kew. The financier Jay Gould set the standard in the 1880s when he added a gigantic palm house to his Hudson River estate, with over three hundred varieties inside. Thanks to collectors like Gould, palms began to signify wealth and luxury as well as tropicality. The tourism industry of the Victorian era added more associations—leisure and fun. The designers of the southern resorts of France and England, the inventors of the modern seaside, exploited palmy vegetation. On the Riviera, landscapers favored Canary Island date palm, which became the master floral form for a new archetype, the Mediterranean palm. In the cool British Isles, developers built "winter gardens," enclosed atria decorated with exotic plants. The developers of Torquay, heart of the "English Riviera," mimicked the visual effect of Monaco and Cannes by adding hardy New Zealand cabbage trees to seaside cliffs, passing them off to unsuspecting tourists as subtropical palms.[8]

In the Anglo-American world, the fad for potted fronds—the Mediterranean in miniature—reached its zenith in the Edwardian era. Every luxury hotel worth its name added a "palm court" or a "palm room," an ornate lounge or banquet hall or tearoom with upholstered furniture, a glass ceiling, painted murals in "Pompeiian" style, and tropical-looking plants. To the strains of a "palm-court orchestra"—violin, cello, and piano playing light favorites from Dvořák, Grieg, Herbert, and Lehár, and the ubiquitous "Meditation" from Massenet's *Thaïs*—patrons sat for high tea under the fronds. The trend began in establishments like the Carlton, the Waldorf, and the Cecil in London and the Plaza, the St. Regis, and the Commodore in New York, and spread to the leading hotels of California and many states between. Vacationers could even enjoy palm courts on the water. The "great white fleet" of the United Fruit Company added palm rooms to its Panama liners. The premier cruise ships of the era, the trio of Olympic-class vessels from the White Star Line—RMS *Olympic*, RMS *Britannic*, and RMS *Titanic*—contained lavish, oversized palm courts that combined verdure with opulence. Lesser temples of consumerism, department stores and cinemas, added evergreen rooms of their own. In the United States, upwardly mobile homeowners created miniature tropical zones within their parlors. An editorial from 1907 on the "fad" for palms complained that the "useless" trees were being "nursed, coddled, and reared in the best society" and that "the taste for stunted palms in northern drawing rooms is like the demand for strawberries in January."[9]

STREET TREES AND CITY BOOSTERS

It is one thing to place potted palms in foyers or to set them on seaside promenades. It is quite another to use them, as Los Angeles famously would, as residential street trees. This impulse requires explanation. Trees—much less palms—do not have a long history on the streets of the world's cities. Even Angelenos had to warm up to the idea of palm-lined avenues. When they did, they devised new semiotic categories for plants with fronds: first the semi-tropical palm, later the municipal palm.

In medieval Europe, cities contained no parks within their high walls and no trees on their crooked thoroughfares; instead, wealthy denizens tended fruiters in enclosed gardens. Not until the sixteenth century did Europeans add ornamentals—elms above all—to common spaces. Public verdure appeared first at special-use squares and exterior promenades built on defunct walls or along waterfronts. Newly militarized nation-states ritually paraded their troops down allées, a garden design element adapted for urban use on the edges of cities, beside, beyond, or atop the city walls. People also used allées for lawn games. In commercial areas, meanwhile, the typical road was all roadway, crowded with people, animals, and conveyances, with no designated space for trees. The infrastructure of the modern interior street—crowned pavement, drains, sewers, lamps, and raised sidewalks with trenches cut out for trunks—arrived in the nineteenth century. As European cities modernized their public roads, they greened them up. Beautification signaled the growing power of the state. During the reign of Napolean III, France all but invented the modern tree-lined thoroughfare, the boulevard, when Baron Haussmann redesigned the traffic flow of Paris, forcing wide, straight streets through dense neighborhoods. (Before the "Haussmannization" of urban Europe, *boulevard* had typically referred to a circular road built on the site of deconstructed ramparts.) In the Victorian era, the new Continental street style came full force to England, starting with tree-lined embankments along the Thames.[10]

More often than not, Americans referred to boulevards as *avenues*. Unlike in Europe, the grandest avenues were residential streets— "millionaires' rows" like Commonwealth Avenue in Boston's Back Bay, upper Fifth Avenue in Manhattan, and Euclid Avenue in Cleveland. While the elite enjoyed the best-kempt and most uniform trees, American urbanites of all classes enjoyed greater access to greenery than their counterparts in Europe. The United States boasted more space for planting, more private homeownership, and more volunteerism in the form of civic improvement associations. In the closing decades of the nineteenth century, in the wake of the Arbor Day movement, Americans turned tree planting into a "civic obsession."[11] To the delight and dismay of observers, America's urban canopy resembled its heterogeneous society: a riot of varieties in all states of growth and repair. Homeowners personalized their street front with their favorite plants whether or not the flora matched the look of the neighborhood. Only after municipal street tree divisions and neighborhood covenants became commonplace in the first half of the twentieth century did the urban American treescape lose some of its helter-skelter quality.

The earliest U.S. cities to experiment with palms were located, not surprisingly, in the South. The palmetto or cabbage palm, native to the Southeast and the Caribbean, has been honored as the state tree of South Carolina and Florida. Antebellum visitors to Charleston and New Orleans, the two leading southern ports, admired palmettos on streets and in courtyards. In winter, these fan palms communicated perpetual summer. When the heat and humidity of actual summer arrived, the same trees suggested something ominous: malaria and yellow fever lurked in the "subtropical" Deep South. Racists of the nineteenth century, including many distinguished American thinkers, doubted that the temperate constitutions of white bodies could acclimate to such sultriness. As much as northerners desired tropical flora, they cultivated tropical fear. Northern partisans believed that their region's brisk climate encouraged industry and free labor while the torrid climate of the South sustained the twin evils of laziness and servitude.

Thus the *Southern* in *Southern California* was a vexed descriptor as of 1869, when the United States, newly reunified after the victory of the North, inaugurated the "New West" with the completion of the transcontinental railroad. To introduce Americans to the terra incognita of California, Charles Loring Brace, the social engineer behind the famous "orphan trains," published a travel book. In the preface, he announced that the Golden State possessed a "different climate, a changed flora and fauna, a strange scenery, and new outline of landscape, novel productions, and conditions utterly unknown to our branch of the Anglo-Saxon race." Though Brace pronounced Los Angeles the "most desirable" location for land investment, he added multiple caveats. The climate, "though not oppressive, is ener-vating." The region lacked good water sources and good harbors. Above all, he worried about "the low educational and moral status of the population"—code words for Mexicans and mixed-race families. The counties around Los Angeles "may be considered the 'South' of California," Brace wrote. Southerners made up the majority of white settlers, and they carried the virtues and vices of their home region: "They are warm-hearted, hospitable, slovenly, lazy, and profane." The Californios—another "southern" people—seemed much the same. "Nature has done everything for [the Southland], and man very lit-tle," Brace declared. At the time of his visit in 1867, the regional economy was shifting from ranch animals to specialty fruit. The New Yorker expressed hope for the future: "A combined immigration of Yankees could easily overcome many of the moral disadvantages which result from the 'Southern' and Spanish influences, and . . . make those counties one of the gardens of the world."[12]

The Prussian-born Jewish merchant Harris Newmark, who migrated to El Pueblo de la Reina de los Ángeles in 1853 and lived there until his death in 1916, wrote a classic memoir that described the city's transition from a Mexican pueblo to an Anglo-American com-mercial center. Newmark described muddy, dusty, trash-filled streets devoid of shade. He recalled how vigilantes conducted lynchings on tree branches, but mostly he remembered the "dearth" of arboreal life. A single pepper tree cast the only shade in the plaza, he said. He claimed that Angelenos of the pioneer era had a prejudice against street improvements and that trespassers wantonly killed magnificent hillside oaks for firewood. In the flats below, the Los Angeles Plain, a natural prairie landscape with extensive seasonal wetlands, contained abundant wildlife but little natural verdure. Only by the Los Angeles River and its spillover sloughs did settlers encounter tall leafy plants such as California sycamore, Fremont cottonwood, and a "jungle profuseness" of willows.[13]

Scattered throughout Southern California—a region San Fran-ciscans snidely called the "cow counties"—were ruined Spanish missions, including relict trees. Eighteenth-century Franciscans and their Indian laborers had tended small numbers of date palms (for Palm Sunday fronds) alongside large numbers of olives, citruses, pomegranates, and stone-fruit trees as well as herbs and vines. In 1793 the British captain George Vancouver visited San Buenaventura as part of his Pacific explorations and was impressed by the mission garden, which "far exceeded any thing of that description I had before met with in these regions," with plants from "the temperate as well as torrid zone," all of them flourishing, including date palms he misidentified as "cocoa nut" trees. In pre-railroad Los Angeles, American commentators more than occasionally remarked on the "Oriental air" imparted by these Spanish-era date palms and compared Southern California to the Levant. In 1874 a San Francisco history librarian took a tour of the mission ruins and commented on the "regular" and "inevitable" date palms, always planted in groups of two or three in garden enclosures.[14]

To redefine a region of Mexican ranches and Spanish ruins as the "garden spot of the earth" required a major advertising intervention. The Southern Pacific Railroad, which opened the "valley line" from San Francisco to Los Angeles in 1876, took the lead. The railroad, the state's largest landowner, wanted to sell properties even more than it wanted to sell tickets. To procure real estate publicity, the SP retained the services of eastern authors, photographers, and lecturers. For example, Charles Nordhoff, a reputable journalist, took payments from SP chief Collis P. Huntington to tour the West Coast and write about it approvingly. "The Californians seem to me to enjoy all the advantages of a tropical climate with but a few of its disadvantages," gushed Nordhoff in 1872. "They have about here no malarious fevers, no mosquitoes, no poisonous reptiles; yet their roses bloom all the year round." Nordhoff produced a series of travel pieces for *Harper's*, then compiled them into a book, *California for Health, Pleasure, and Residence*, which became a bestseller. Nordhoff, and the greater SP publicity machine, devised a new regional language for the "South" of California. Unlike "Cuba, Mexico, Brazil, or Central America, and other regions of the South," Nordhoff continued, "California is our own; and it is the first tropical land which our race has thoroughly mastered and made itself at home in. There, and there only, on this planet, the traveller and resident may enjoy the delights of the tropics without their penalties; a mild climate, not enervating, but health-ful and health-restoring; a wonderfully and variously productive soil, without tropical malaria; the grandest scenery, with perfect security and comfort in travelling arrangements; strange customs, but neither lawlessness nor semi-barbarism." In 1873 the founders of the Indiana Colony—today's Pasadena—chose the San Gabriel Valley over Texas, Florida, and Louisiana after reading *California for Health*. Echoing Nordhoff, colonists touted their destination as "the spot unifying the blessings of the tropics without their heat, malaria or enervating influ-ences." Another "journalist" on the payroll of the railroad, Benjamin Truman, the former secretary of president Andrew Johnson, coined a related descriptor to encapsulate the post-frontier charms of the coastal region from Monterey to San Diego: "semi-tropical Califor-nia." This widely repeated phrase suggested balminess, not muggy, sloth-inducing heat; luxuriant flora, not jungle. Like a conservatory with palms, the region offered the exotic domesticated.[15]

Writing in the boom year 1888, the authors of the book *California of the South* claimed to have observed the preliminary racial results—the "fruitage"—of the Southland's horticultural settlements, where migrants had been "culled out from the choicest population of the East." The "law of the improvement of race by selection and elim-ination" was now being intensified by "that other law of the power of climatic surroundings to influence race-development." The state's southern climatic belt seemed destined to produce a civilization on a par with "Græco-Latin civilization."[16]

The reimagined "Southern California"—always written in caps by its promoters—may have been an invention, but physiographically it had some coherence. The region was generally defined as the low-land area between the Transverse Ranges and the Pacific Ocean, from Point Conception on the west, Tehachapi Pass on the north,

San Gorgonino Pass on the east, and San Diego Bay on the south. South of Point Conception, an oceanic and atmospheric divide, the waters are warmer, the fogs rarer, the rains lighter. The formidable Transverse Ranges—the Santa Ynez–Topatopa Mountains, Santa Susana Mountains, San Gabriel Mountains, and San Bernardino Mountains—separate the Southland from the heat and aridity of the San Joaquin Valley and the Mojave Desert.[17]

No matter how one drew the map of Southern California, Los Angeles appeared central, despite its modest attractions. Writing in 1883, a travel writer described the "scarlet berries and fern-like leaves" of the pepper tree as the town's "leading shade and ornament." San Pedro Street featured a "clump of palms," and the courtyard of the principal hotel contained a "single ragged banana." Tourists in search of a good photograph walked to the landmark Twin Palms, two California fan palms joined at the root—a relict of the old pueblo.[18]

The main attraction of Los Angeles was its future. Far ahead of fruit colonies like Riverside, Los Angeles anticipated a post-agricultural economy. In the 1880s this railroad village pioneered a strategy later imitated by Sun Belt boomtowns such as Phoenix, Las Vegas, and Orlando: an economy propelled by regional promotion, real estate speculation, and new home construction. A huge number of home buyers were health refugees and retirees from the Midwest. Their recuperative and restful lifestyle would have been called lazy if carried out by Mexicans. Thanks to in-migration, the population of Los Angeles more or less doubled every decade from the Golden Spike to the Great Depression. Bursts of incredible growth punctuated a half century of remarkable growth. The biggest of the booms began with the completion of Southern Pacific's "southern line" in 1883. Later that year, as if the realtors had planned it, the western sky lit on fire every evening with spectacularly red sunsets (later determined to be an atmospheric result of the Krakatoa eruption). The boom metastasized when the SP's rival, the Santa Fe Railway, arrived in 1886. The two railroads engaged in cannibalizing price warfare: for much of 1887 one could travel from the Lower Mississippi to the Pacific for

twenty-five dollars. Tens of thousands of easterners and midwestern-
ers took excursions to the seat of Southern California to see what the
fuss was about. At the entrance to the SP's new downtown Arcade
Station, a newly transplanted California fan palm greeted the public.
The giant tree came from the historic Wolfskill orchard and vineyard
(see Chapter 5), then being subdivided. The palm announced to arriving passengers that this city would be different by nature.[19]

During the boom years 1886–1888, the atmosphere crackled with
giddiness—the greatest real estate viewing on earth. Promoters recycled an old phrase, *California fever,* to describe the burning desire to
improve one's quality of life. Prospective buyers were greeted, at the
bare minimum, by a brass band. Harris Newmark also saw "fantastic
parades," "elephants and other animals of jungle and forest, as well
as human freaks," and an "endless chain of free lunches." Another
firsthand witness recalled the frenzied mindset of East Coast journalists who ended up being West Coast promoters: "Seeing the land
prosperous, with gold glittering in every palm, and plain mud making
more in five minutes' work than genius could harvest in a month,
it was quite natural for genius to inquire, 'What is there in this for
me?'" Developers took advantage of the existence of Mexican land
grants, or *ranchos,* enormous properties from the pre-American period
that could be bought, sold, and subdivided. They purchased orange
groves in Los Angeles, cut down the trees (sold as cordwood), and
planted realty signs. In a two-year period, developers platted scores
of cities, including one called The Palms. Fortunes were made and
lost. The majority of the paper towns blew away like leaves before the
Santa Ana winds; and still the population of Los Angeles County
tripled, from 33,381 to 101,454, in the decade of the 1880s. One of
the Golden State's great literary voices, Mary Austin, moved from
Illinois to Southern California in 1888. Decades later, in the autobiographical *Earth Horizon*, she remembered being daunted by Los
Angeles and "the wrack of the lately 'busted' boom: the jerry-built
bungalows, the blameless young palms abandoned along with the
avenues they had been planted to adorn. The unwatered palms had a

hurt but courageous look, as of young wives when they first suspect that their marriages may be turning out badly." Austin recoiled from the unimaginative greedy boosterism of Los Angeles, "the miracle-mongering of overgrown vegetation and inflated prices." Nonetheless, she felt "enchanted by the eucalyptus trees. At that time it was plain that the eucalyptus cherished an intention to possess the land."[20]

From the beginning of the great boom, new residents enjoyed the outdoor life by experimenting with flowering evergreens. Southland-ers turned their backs on the familiar broad-leafed deciduous land-scape of Europe and the East—elms, lindens, poplars, chestnuts, maples, and sycamores (plane trees). They did not domesticate the splendid California sycamore. They wanted flora that could adver-tise the "semi-tropical" climate and yet resist the rainless summers and the desiccating autumn winds. Palms were part of the floral mix, but they did not initially dominate the landscape or the imagina-tion. For yard trees, boomers perused seed and nursery catalogs for exotic species that promised flowers and shade. They liked acacias, grevilleas, and, even more, Australian eucalypts, and above all the pepper tree (from the arid zone of South America), with its feath-ery leaves, hanging branches, and bright red berries. The pepper tree served as California's answer to the weeping willow, and the state's pepper-lined streets, with their tunnel-like canopies, offered supe-rior color to equivalent elm-lined streets in the East. More often than gardeners planted palms by themselves, they interspersed them with flowering trees. The boom era's two most celebrated boulevards, Ontario's Euclid Avenue and Riverside's Magnolia Avenue, incorpo-rated palms in combination with eucalypts, pepper trees, grevilleas, and magnolias. Early experiments with California fan palms as uni-form allée trees appeared jarring to many eyes. "Probably most people would prefer a street tree agreeing better with the traditional idea of such an ornament than do the rather more formal outlines of the palm," editorialized the *Pacific Rural Press* in 1893. "Then, too, for shade purposes the palm is about as good as a fish net would be for a bedspread." At that time, one had to visit Santa Barbara (home of the Southern California Acclimatizing Association and the initial center of palm horticulture) or citrus ranches in the San Gabriel and San Bernardino valleys to see conspicuous palm plantings.[21]

At citrus ranches, palms and oranges reinforced each other as symbols of wealth, sunshine, and pleasurable exoticism. The connection was easy to see because the two transcontinentals passed right through the heart of the Citrus Belt, from San Bernardino west into Los Angeles. Tourists recognized that they had entered "semi-tropical" California as soon as they dropped down from Cajon Pass and glimpsed the pointillist grid of dark green citrus foliage, with lines of lighter-colored fronds poking above, marking roads and perimeters. For a closer look, tourists based in Los Angeles could take special guided excursion trains (Santa Fe's Old Kite Route or SP's Inside Track Flyer) on a loop through navel and Valencia towns. Pacific Electric later offered a similar Orange Empire trolley trip through California's "kingdom of the orange." Excursionists saw that growers vaingloriously lined the long driveways at their million-dollar groves with California fan palms. In Riverside, palms likewise paralleled the Gage Canal, the water supply that sustained some of the world's most expensive agricultural real estate. These nonproductive ornamentals drew attention to the elevated status of the citrus rancher.

Orange tours, though important, paled next to the cumulative exposure of citrus crate labels (generally designed in San Francisco). Naturalistic scenes dominated this commercial genre from the 1880s through the 1920s. At groceries across America, millions of consumers passively absorbed the iconography of the "Sunny Scenic Southland" and the semi-tropical palm. One of the master images, which occurred in countless iterations, showed distant snowcapped mountains sheltering a well-tended, fruit-laden citrus orchard, fan palms and flowers in the middle foreground, and often a wholesome child or comely young woman up front. The palms in these five-color lithographs were not resort plants; they didn't signify a seaside vacation.

They contributed one element to a well-rounded whole: sunshine and snow, work and leisure, agriculture and refinement—the suburban horticultural good life.[22]

The same tree type that signaled modernity at citrus ranches signified the quaint past at mission sites. Through commercial photographs, the historic date palms at San Diego and San Fernando became well-known landmarks. San Fernando also boasted the Giant Palms, a trio of California fan palms, the largest cultivated palms in the state, outside the mission walls, where tourists conventionally posed for photographs. In 1888 a visitor purchased a commercial print of a Spanish-era date palm at San Gabriel Mission and wrote upon it, "No single tree ever gave me such a thrill as this solitary palm standing erect & graceful, like a strange being in an atmosphere of its own." When Anglo-Americans began rebuilding this mission in the 1890s, they planted a line of fan palms along the new sidewalk by the old walls. All over the state, architects designed novel buildings in the mix-and-match style of California Mission Revival—adobe, red tile, arcades, towers, parapets, eucalypts, fronds. The Anglo fad for the Spanish fantasy past spread to print and stage; consider San Gabriel's "Mission Play," witnessed by more than 2 million spectators between 1912 and 1929. Or the phenomenal popularity of Helen Hunt Jackson's 1884 romance novel *Ramona*, about a mission-raised mestizo maiden who elopes with an Indian shepherd, which enjoyed a second life as a pageant. In Old Town San Diego, near a building billed as "Ramona's marriage place," Hispanophiles preserved the Serra Tree, ostensibly the "first palm planted in California." Caretakers erected a picket fence around it in 1887 and much later attached guy wires when the tree seemed in danger of falling. In Ventura, the erstwhile "Palm City," members of the Native Daughters of the Golden West spearheaded a successful campaign in the opening years of the twentieth century to preserve a local landmark, a pair of Spanish-era date palms from the former San Buenaventura mission.[23]

Even as newcomers renovated and romanticized the Spanish history of Alta California, they segregated it from the story of the

Golden State. In regional literature, the horticultural colonization of Southern California seemed new, unprecedented—not an extension of the mission gardens but a brand-new start, the "new Eden of the Saxon home-seeker," to use a phrase by Charles Fletcher Lummis, the logorrheic editor of *Land of Sunshine*.[24]

To disseminate this paradisiacal image, professional boosters—a coalition of interests, including railroads, real estate speculators, entrepreneurs, trade associations, civic groups, and honest-to-God true believers in regional destiny—used all media available. In the winters of 1888–89 and 1890–91, Southern Pacific partnered with the California State Board of Trade to send a train car, California on Wheels, to states east of the Rockies. More than a million people visited the decorated train, and left with fruit samples, promotional literature, and memories of gargantuan vegetable specimens. The Los Angeles Chamber of Commerce, founded in 1888, later assumed responsibility for the media train and replaced the SP as Southern California's lead booster. In the visual realm, authors of regional and municipal portfolios always made sure to include photographs of floral novelties such as yard palms and palm-lined allées. Through their selectively chosen "typical views" and "characteristic views," commercial photographers greatly exaggerated the presence of palms in Los Angeles, the "land of promise." Makers of postcards and stereoscopic cards returned again and again to a single vista of a single residential drive near Adams Street, south of downtown—a place variously called Palm Drive, Palm Avenue, and the Avenue of Palms.[25]

To be a booster of Los Angeles required imagination and audacity. In the eyes of conservative investors, the city had "nothing but sunshine." It lacked a port, a navigable river, a ready water supply, timber, coal, or any of the other conventional requirements for a major city with a robust, diversified economy. But the climate! With its perennially perfect weather, how could Los Angeles *not* become the seat of a new empire of wellness? The shock troops for Southern California were the invalids who followed the boosters' call to a fabled land without bronchitis and rheumatism, snow and frost. The center of health tourism, Pasadena, built the region's first two luxury accommodations, the Raymond Hotel (1886) and the Webster Hotel (1890), both landscaped liberally with palms. Because the age of tuberculosis overlapped with the institutionalization of medicine, hundreds of thousands of TB patients from the clammy East followed doctors' orders to recover in California. Until roughly World War II, a medical belt overlapped the Citrus Belt; from Los Angeles to Redlands to Palm Springs, open-air sanatoriums with ornamental palms accepted patients from across the nation. Every ailment, including the disease *du jour*, "nervousness," could be cured in this pacific clime, medical boosters claimed. No miasma, malaria, hay fever, fog, haze, or smoke afflicted the world's unrivaled sanatorium. With characteristic optimism, promoters added floods, earthquakes, and sandstorms to the list of nonexistent phenomena. As one observant tourist noted, the locals "call all Eastern investors 'Tenderfoots,' and when speaking of them use this slang expression: 'We sold them the climate and threw the land in.'"[26]

In the 1890s boosters updated the master climatic descriptor from the clumsy *semi-tropical* to the classy *Mediterranean*, a palmy image with greater connotations of health and civilization. Santa Barbara styled itself as the Pacific Riviera. Regional promoters referred to Southern California as New Greece, America's Menton (after the palm-filled resort town on France's southern coast), and Our Italy. The last phrase came from the distinguished pen of Dudley Warner, the man who with Mark Twain authored the exposé *The Gilded Age*, thereby giving the sordid era its enduring name. A man of his time, Warner exempted himself from scruples; he accepted $10,000 cash from the Santa Fe Railway to write travel essays about the Southland. The railroad lent him a private car to facilitate his winter junket in 1890. Warner's subsequent essays, published in *Harper's*, were profusely illustrated with fronds. "California is the land of the Pine and the Palm," he wrote. This arboreal duo represented the variety and capacity of the state, an American province comparable only to the transition zone from the Alps to the Adriatic. Warner made light of the monotonous weather, scenery, and society in "our Mediterranean region" but urged his readers to reconceptualize monotony as restfulness. Day after day of flawless weather will "take away nervousness and produce a certain placidity, which might be taken for laziness by a Northern observer." For the white race, having industriously reached the "sunset of the continent," Southern California provided a well-deserved "winter of content." Dudley's semi-gilded essays for *Harper's* became the basis of a popular book.[27]

Some people took the Adriatic comparison seriously. In the early years of the twentieth century, J. Waldron Gillespie, a wealthy New York bachelor, built a landmark Italian villa at his vacation estate in Montecito, near Santa Barbara. "Mediterranean eclectic" is perhaps a better descriptor for a country place that included Greek and Spanish details and a bas-relief frieze of King Arthur at the Round Table. Gillespie hybridized the categories of Oriental palm and Mediterranean palm. He gave his retreat a fanciful "Arabic" name, El Fureidis (also the title of an Orientalist novel by a popular American writer of the Civil War era). Instead of grass, the expansive Persian-inspired grounds featured terraces, fountains, pools, and over one hundred palm species. "Can you imagine a picture of Paradise without palms?" Gillespie asked. He remembered falling in love with fronds in Sunday school, looking at pictures of the Garden of Eden. "Many people say that California is unsuited, both climatically and from the point of view of aesthetics, for Palms," he wrote. "Cultivated people" considered the lawny English garden to be the norm, and looked askance at fronds, except in arboretums. Gillespie believed this attitude had to change in Southern California. "Here in the latitude of Morocco, the English garden seems as out of place" as Gothic architecture in India. "We must change our gardening in California in conformity with this climate . . . Plant life that appears harmonious in Sicily should also be appropriate in California. As one hardly imagines a Mediterranean landscape without Palms, so one may feel about California."[28]

Another business transplant from the East, Abbot Kinney, trumpeted the virtues of palms and trees in general. With credentials as

California's first state forester, he promoted widespread cultivation of *Eucalyptus* (see Chapter 3). This idealistic schemer also tried to develop his own private Italy—with palms. Around 1904 Kinney and some partners secured funding for a planned community on the site of Santa Monica Bay's salt marshes. The sea-level city, named Venice of America, featured miles of palm-lined canals plied by real Italian gondolas. Kinney designed his Venice to be a Renaissance city: he built an amphitheater for the performing arts and a lecture hall for the Chautauqua circuit. But not enough buyers wanted to live in this make-believe Mediterranean. It didn't help that poorly circulating canal water created prime mosquito habitat. After a grand opening in 1905, the Italianate development languished. To Kinney's chagrin, his adjacent business venture, the Venice Pier, achieved far more success. The pier (near today's Venice Beach) boasted an aquarium, a natatorium, dance halls, carnival rides, and sideshows. It and several nearby piers became known as the Coney Island of the Pacific. Kinney's boardwalk rather than his canals pointed to the future. By the Depression era, the palms of Southern California would be associated not with refinement but with hedonism.[29]

At the start of the twentieth century, however, the Southland was at the apogee of its midwestern Protestant phase. Hundreds of thousands of amenity migrants from corn states made a deep mark on regional culture—rural piety transplanted to the suburban garden. According to the 1910 census, whites composed 96 percent of the populace of Los Angeles County. According to an old wisecrack, Los Angeles (or Long Beach) was the seaport of Iowa, the westernmost suburb of Des Moines, or Iowa with palm trees. Homeowners projected virtuous affluence and middlebrow refinement with their well-tended bungalow gardens with semi-tropical vegetation. This image appealed to middle-class blacks, too. Thirty-six percent of African Americans in Los Angeles owned homes in 1910, compared to 8 percent in Chicago. After his West Coast tour in July 1913, W. E. B. Du Bois published an essay in *The Crisis* called "Colored California." He began by evoking the mythical image of the Golden State as a "terrestrial paradise" and "the tourist's wonderland, a place of roses and lilies, of palms and giant redwoods." Although he concluded that seg-regated Los Angeles was "not Paradise," Du Bois expressed admira-tion for "the most beautifully housed group of colored people in the United States." For the cover of the California issue, the NAACP magazine showed a smartly dressed black couple (and pet dog) relax-ing under a Canary Island date palm in the well-trimmed front yard of an attractive bungalow.[30]

Angelenos of the early twentieth century expressed their civic pride by using palms—primarily California fan palm and Canary Island date palm—to beautify the grounds of public institutions: schools, libraries, courthouses, hospitals, sanatoriums, asylums, orphanages, post offices. In this way, Southlanders invented a new kind of botan-ical motif, the municipal palm. Los Angeles may have been the first major city to use the palm not just as a symbol of desirable charac-teristics but as a metasymbol for the desirable city itself. Ornamental palms did not bring to mind Hollywood stars or sun-kissed beach girls. Those allurements came later. Before Los Angeles became known as Tinseltown, it earned titles such as Ideal Protestant City and Model Christian Community. (The celebrity evangelist Aimee Semple McPherson bridged the two eras with her radio broadcasts from Angelus Temple, one of America's earliest megachurches.) The city's power structure promoted an antisaloon, pro-business, open-shop, law-and-order morality. In 1913 the chief of police brought in fronds to ameliorate the monotony of the central station's gray corridors. He prettified the entrances, too. Inmates of the jail now pondered their crimes among "palms and hanging baskets of plants, arranged in the most fashionable effects."[31]

For all their enthusiasm for using palms on public and private grounds, Angelenos, and Californians as a whole, were ambiv-alent and inconsistent about using palms as street ornaments. The essayist and noted Italophile Grace Ellery Channing thought that more palms actually threatened the image of Los Angeles as "Our Italy" because new plantings accompanied improved roads for the recently invented automobile—a contradiction to the city's slow-paced "Roman" lifestyle of courtyards, patios, terraces, balconies, and shady rooftop gardens. Channing hated to see street crews tearing out the floral filigree of pepper trees. On new roads, "palms—about as useful as telegraph poles for the purpose—serve as shade trees," she wrote in 1899.[32]

This debate over street aesthetics went on for a couple of decades. The state's preeminent botanist, Professor Willis Jepson of Berkeley, expressed his unalterable opposition to palm-lined roads. The rigidity of street lines demanded the grace of branching trees, he said in 1909. "Palms in our streets are only little more than rigid poles of similar character, and they are extremely obnoxious because of obstructing sidewalks and injuring people's eyes." When preparing the street tree plan for the town of Albany, Jepson banned evergreens and palms; he even raised the specter of sidewalk users getting their eardrums pierced by the sharp ends of fronds. Across the bay, the editorial board of the *San Francisco Call*, a self-declared "advanced missionary for the palm as a street tree," mocked Jepson for his deciduous preferences and questioned his state pride: "If the ideas of our anti-palm professor were applied, the people of our gateway county would strip the orange trees of their yellow fruit and evergreen leaves, so as to make the winter-worn Eastern folk feel at home!" Every city should be a palm city; then California "will get fame not only as the Golden but as the Oriental State." Expressing the opposite viewpoint, the State Board of Forestry distributed an essay by a Bay Area member of the Out Door Art League who condemned the California palm-lined avenue as a "feeble imitation of the tropics" and a "false ideal." In Los Angeles, the park commissioner inspired controversy in 1908 when he grubbed out established deciduous trees at Westlake (now MacArthur) Park and imported subtropical flora as part of a larger makeover program to give each park in the city an individual look. The *Los Angeles Times* protested the "almost shadeless resort—for a palm is not a good tree to walk under, as everybody knows!" The park commissioner acted against the wishes of his colleague, E. J. Harper, the city's first forester. Harper evangelized for more evergreen shade trees—more acacias, laurels, pepper trees, and tulip trees. "I am not a friend of the palm as a street tree," he declared in 1907. "Our California palms, as planted along our sidewalks, are not at all desirable. Their fronds are continually poking you in the face, and are anything but comfortable, then they gather the dust and pour it out upon you, and when they get old, the higher they get the smaller the clump of leaves in proportion to the trunk with its dead leaves hanging alongside, and when you trim them off, you have a pole about as beautiful as a telephone pole."[33]

Although Harper, the mayor's brother and a minister, had weak botanical credentials, his office represented an emerging trend in government nationwide. City foresters advanced the goals of the City Beautiful and Arbor Day movements as well as the social engineering and scientific management impulses of Progressivism. Stated another way, urban forestry was the final outgrowth of the nineteenth-century horticultural movement. As the United States transitioned away from being an agrarian society, city foresters became the caretakers of tree culture, formerly a rural tradition. They were, at least in the ideal, municipal experts like sanitary engineers. The move toward professionalization began in 1893, when New Jersey granted municipalities the authority to create shade tree commissions. Newark and East Orange famously used this new legal power to supervise the addition of thousands of street trees. In 1899 Massachusetts went one step further by requiring all towns to elect tree wardens. Encouraged by the American Civic Association, municipal street tree divisions soon cropped up in urban centers such as Buffalo and Cleveland (two of America's ten largest cities as of 1900). Tree commissions and tree wardens had two main goals, planting and protecting. They called attention to poisonous gas from new underground pipes, electric burns from new overhead electric lines, and above all the "slaughter" and "butchery" and "mutilation" caused by utility companies, which typically cut right through the canopies of established shade trees in order to string their catenary wires. Old trees faced additional urban threats from modern sidewalks, curbs, and streetlights.[34]

In California the governance of street trees first took root in the urbane enclaves of the Citrus Belt. In 1898 the city of Riverside passed an ordinance to protect its mature eucalypts and pepper trees from infrastructural improvements—and from choppers who simply wanted firewood. Over the next ten years, the colony developed a comprehensive planting and management program. After taking a tree census, Riverside officials codified species lists and trimming styles and scheduled regular maintenance by arborists. Riverside's program, the first in the state, and its head, J. H. Reed, attracted positive attention from Progressive planners across the nation. Rival citrus towns, including Redlands, Ontario, Pomona, Corona, and Pasadena, quickly tried to emulate this success. In Hollywood, an orchard town at the time, dendrophiles fought to protect peppers and eucalypts from city engineers who wanted to add parking between the curb and the building line within the business district. In nearby Los Angeles, a leading newspaper made note of Riverside's "shade tree fever." Reform-minded Angelenos hoped for the same. Dana Bartlett, a minister, social worker, and urban theorist, wanted to "ruralize the city." In *The Better City* (1907)—a book with palm fronds on the cover—he dreamed of Los Angeles becoming a "forest city."[35]

Dreaming was the easy part. Tree wardens operated best in small wealthy towns or in large cities with strong central authority, like Sacramento. Neither descriptor applied to Los Angeles. Its original office of city forester performed more advocacy than enforcement. (Harper urged owners to prune trees so that branches "will not mar the plumes on the hats of the ladies.") The city lagged far behind Riverside and Pasadena in planting and maintaining uniform street trees. In the absence of central planning, real estate developers and neighborhood business groups conducted their own tree plantings, and sometimes they chose palms. For example, in 1904 the Highland Park Improvement Association put in some two hundred fan palms and even more live oaks. In the second decade of the century a group of property owners formulated a plan to turn Vermont Avenue, from Griffith Park all the way to San Pedro, into the city's first modern boulevard, with wide lanes and double rows of trees, including palms.[36]

The City Club evaluated the overall progress of the streetscape and issued a mixed report card in 1915. Developers, associations, and to some extent the park department (which had taken over the duties of city forester) had increased the municipal canopy in the decade prior. However, compared to outlying citrus colonies, Los Angeles was still a sun-bleached mess. Trees had been set haphazardly in regard to variety, uniformity, and suitability. Pruning and watering had been neglected. Valiant attempts by owners of subdivisions to plant and maintain uniform street trees came to naught if and when individual lots passed into the hands of owners who didn't care to maintain them. In this era of electrification and telecommunication, the planting of utility poles—processed pine tree trunks—far exceeded the placement of live trees. The former secretary of the Redlands Tree Commission commented on the melancholy spectacle of miles of newly laid-out roads: "If a uniform and heavy planting of [utility] poles is the desired end, the city of Los Angeles has certainly been highly successful, but from any other standpoint, the results leave much to be desired."[37]

Even in the central business district, home of the Southern California semi-tropical promotion machine, palms were surprisingly hard to find. Downtown had inherited some of the oldest, tallest, grandest fan palms in the state, relics of the former Mexican pueblo, but many of these trees fell victim to progress. In the early twentieth century, downtown remade itself into an urban core, the hub of an expanding regional streetcar system. As it added multistory commercial buildings and related infrastructure, the city removed old palms that interfered. Venice of America purchased and transplanted two such specimens. In 1908, with police holding back protestors, the city cut down a historic palm in front of the courthouse to make way for a statue of Stephen M. White, the California senator who helped secure federal funding to build the first port of Los Angeles. In 1914, the landmark Wolfskill fan palm that had been relocated to the Arcade Station was, pending the demolition of the depot, moved again—this time to South Figueroa Street, next to a plaque that proclaimed, IT AND ITS SENTIMENTAL ASSOCIATIONS WILL BE PERMANENTLY PRESERVED. (As of 2012, the all-but-forgotten tree, gaunt and pockmarked, persists at the edge of Exposition Park, in line with the torch of the Coliseum.) Postcard views of downtown Los Angeles from the early automobile era typically show well-trafficked, well-lit streets devoid of greenery. Pershing Square, downtown's only park, did feature some palms in combination with broadleaf trees. But one had to go to Westlake Park, just west of downtown, to see a palm-dominated landscape.[38]

The first attempt to create a modern palm streetscape in the city center failed miserably. In 1915 the Los Angeles County Board of Supervisors authorized the purchase of 1,500 potted palms to line the sidewalks of the shopping district. The board gave the trees to the city, which hired two sprinkling cart attendants to dampen the thirsty roots in the predawn hours. Within months the plants became a source of conflict and embarrassment. The city's park commission wanted to transfer maintenance duties to the county's board of public works. As the agencies feuded, the trees wilted and withered. Vandals smashed the pots and carved their names into the trunks. "Nobody Loves Them," headlined the *Times*. The friendless, neglected palms are "poor civic ornaments," the paper continued; they "line but do not adorn the streets." The county accused the city of passing the buck. "After all we have done to beautify the city," complained the senior supervisor, "the odium of the palms is cast upon us." At a special meeting, a councilman asked, "Who wants the palms?" Nobody answered. As the city continued to evade responsibility, the county announced a tree-lending program for residents. The catch: each borrower would be legally responsible for damage to the tree and its concrete retainer. When no residents came forward, the county simply carted the sorry palms to a vacant lot near Juvenile Hall and sold them off at eight dollars apiece.[39]

Los Angeles paled next to Sacramento—located almost 400 miles north—in shade trees and subtropical vegetation. "The palm in this city is to be seen at its perfection—and it is everywhere, too," bragged the editors of the *Sacramento Bee* back in 1894. Palms of all kinds adorned the Capitol Park, the Plaza, and "hundreds upon hundreds of front yards." Fast-forward to 1922, when the *Times* editorialized on the state of L.A.'s canopy: "Our streets, with the exception of a few palms and various attempts at 'mission style' architecture, might be located in St. Paul or St. Louis. Many blocks are entirely without street trees, or a straggling lot of varied and unsuited specimens are shown. In some sections fine trees set out years ago have been cut down to make way for sidewalks or wires." Improvements to South Figueroa (near today's Staples Center) compelled the city to cut down a landmark California fan palm in 1924. The tree dated to the Spanish period. Nailed to its trunk, high up and out of reach, hung an oversized ceremonial "key to the city." Supposedly a locksmith once lived at the base of the tree and made the key on commission. The city eventually returned the key to its maker, who nailed it to the trunk as a sign. No one could remember the exact details. All in all, the early civic leaders of Los Angeles had been better at advertising palminess than cultivating and tending palms.[40]

FLORA OF THE STARS

In the interwar years, the geography and meaning of the Southland's palm trees changed. Formerly one emblem of many of the Arcadian good life of semi-tropical California, the palm became an essential symbol of metropolitan Los Angeles and a fixture of its expanding network of automobile roads. Palms also became closely identified with motion pictures, movie stars, and the imagined geography known as Hollywood. Thanks to the film industry, palms acquired a novel connotation of glamour. At the same time, because of local changes in the tourism industry, the region's palms acquired a familiar association: seaside recreation.

The urban territory of palms enlarged with economic and demographic growth. The buildup of the Los Angeles Plain reached new crescendos in the first and third decades of the twentieth century. The booms resulted not only from continued advertising and speculation but also from tangible resources, starting with oil. The petroleum fields beneath the basin, first tapped in the 1890s, became integrated into the national market early in the century. Discoveries in the 1920s greatly boosted production. At renowned Signal Hill, near Long Beach, wooden derricks suddenly dwarfed old palms, formerly the tallest things around. To secure the other kind of liquid gold—water—the oligarchy of Los Angeles diverted the entire watershed of the Owens River from the eastern slope of the Sierra to the Pacific coast. The audacious Los Angeles Aqueduct—the "greatest municipal undertaking in the world," according to the chamber of commerce—opened in 1913. It quickened metropolitan growth and nourished new orange groves in the San Fernando Valley. The following year, the Panama Canal instantly made Los Angeles a major sea shipping hub; in advance, the man-made Port of Los Angeles expanded. Oil and citrus went out by barge; redwood lumber for housing came in. The year 1914 also witnessed the release of the first big-budget Hollywood studio film, a western. Thanks to energy, transportation, and entertainment, Los Angeles County blossomed into a diversified economy and attracted light manufacturing.

Lured by the "inexhaustible supply of twenty-two karat climate" and the strong economy, over 1 million migrants came to the county in the twenties, more than doubling the population. Los Angeles eclipsed San Francisco and joined the ranks of the ten most populous cities in the nation. Working-class people with little or no education could secure a pensioned job at a tire plant, obtain a loan for a starter bungalow, and fill the backyard with laying hens and pomegranates. Touting the "industrial metropolis," a real estate developer in East Los Angeles printed a promotion showing brawny workers returning home to beautiful streets lined with palms and parked cars. New migration streams, including Mexicans, Filipinos, and black and white southerners, added diversity to the widely dispersed metropolitan area. Seizing the moment, Los Angeles aggressively enlarged. In the ten years after the completion of its aqueduct, the city annexed some 300 square miles, a fourfold increase, and swallowed up the unincorporated San Fernando Valley ("Los Angeles's Louisiana Purchase," the historian Kevin Starr calls it). Just beyond the city's ungainly boundaries were film towns such as Culver City, manufacturing towns such as South Gate, oil extraction towns such as Fullerton, oil transportation towns such as Whittier, and oil refinement towns such as El Segundo. A privately owned light rail mass transit system tied them all together. Pacific Electric Railroad, founded in 1901, became the world's largest interurban transportation system, with over 1,000 miles of track covering four counties. Trolleys, like oil, created incentives for new and dispersed real estate development. Long before the freeway system, the outlines of sprawl took shape.[41]

Two towering businessmen who profited from the "fragmented metropolis" carried on love affairs with fronds. The owner of Pacific Electric, Henry E. Huntington, collected rare books and exotic plants at his baronial estate in suburban Los Angeles County. He moved there for good after the San Francisco earthquake and firestorm of 1906. As the inheritor of the Collis P. Huntington railroad fortune, Henry sold the ruins of his uncle's Nob Hill property, but not before taking a large pair of fire-singed Canary Island date palms that had managed to survive. The trees became part of the younger Huntington's new manor in San Marino. This transplantation from north to south, from city to suburb, was emblematic. As a trolley car and real estate magnate, Huntington facilitated the low-density growth of

Greater Los Angeles. Taking advantage of the local climate, he and his grounds superintendent amassed a world-class arboretum of palm and cycad specimens.[42]

On at least one occasion, Huntington got in a bidding war with his only local rival, the oil tycoon Edward Doheny (the man fictionalized in the 2007 film *There Will Be Blood*). Doheny lived in a palm-fringed Gothic Tudor–Mission Revival mansion, complete with bowling alley, near the University of Southern California. To beautify his grounds, Doheny bought and transported two historic date palms from downtown that stood in the way of a planned office building. Each 8-ton tree required a team of twelve horses to move. In 1913–14 Doheny tore down his hothouse to build a state-of-the-art aviary and palm room with 50-foot-high glass walls. The indoor tropical habitat contained a "Roman" *tepidarium* equipped with a gondola. Orchids, palms, and cycads surrounded the pool. To complete the project, Doheny's plant broker went to Mexico and Central America and even used dynamite to dislodge one large specimen so it could be placed on a railway car. (The Doheny estate, in its current form as Mount St. Mary's College, retains many legacy palms.)[43]

Beyond the private arboretums of Doheny and Huntington, the palm landscape of Greater Los Angeles did not sport much variety. To this day, only a handful of species compose the majority of plantings. In the Spanish, Mexican, and early U.S. periods, the predominant species were date palm and especially California fan palm. The latter had several advantages: affordability, accessibility (the southern transcontinental pushed right through its habitat zone), and fast growth. Botanists honored this remarkable tree with a genus name, *Washingtonia*, previously reserved for giant sequoia. The species name, *filifera*, means "thread-bearing" and refers to the large quantity of cottony filaments that unravel from the sharp edges of the fronds. The most impressive thing about a mature, wild-growing California fan palm is its mat of used-up fronds, which looks something like a giant shaving brush (or perhaps a wizard's beard). Its leaves prefer dry air. In the relative humidity of Los Angeles, including the elastic shoulder season Angelenos call "May gray" and "June gloom," California fan palms struggle to fend off fungal diseases; many urban specimens develop anemic, yellowish crowns. For ornamentation, the palm's sturdy, upright build—nature-made columns—makes up for its naturally dull grayish trunk.

During the real estate buildup from the 1870s through the 1920s, preference gradually but decisively shifted to Canary Island date palm, in the *Phoenix* genus. (Don't be confused by the name: unlike a true date, the fruit is inedible for humans.) This species may be the most majestic palm in the world. A mature Canary has a globular crown, 25 to 40 feet wide, with one hundred to two hundred glossy green fronds that can reach lengths of 20 feet. It may grow as wide as tall. Unlike most palms, it casts a deep shade. For midwestern transplants to California, Canary Island date palms looked elegant and provided romantic associations with the Riviera, all without costing too much. In the first couple of decades of the century, a new homeowner habitually planted a showy pair on either side of the walkway to the front door. Where city officials failed to create a palmy streetscape, residents rose to the occasion. In 1910 America's great horticultural expert Liberty Hyde Bailey identified Canary Island date palm as the "most popular palm for the masses" and noted that "in Los Angeles and vicinity they may be counted by tens of thousands." A decade and a half later, Charles Saunders, a Pasadena travel and garden writer, remarked that the "passion for planting this tree amounts to almost a state characteristic." "Pro-palmist" residents added the species indiscriminately, haphazardly, as single specimens or in rows or pairs, without much thought to future growth. Incongruously, they placed *Phoenix* next to cypresses, birches, and oddities such as Norfolk Island pine. "Supersensitive souls have told us more than once that they can stand most mixtures in California's landscaping until it comes to Palms; these, they say, with a shudder, these are the unpardonable sin," continued Saunders. "Nevertheless, a campaign in the Golden State to prohibit advertising would have about as much chance of success as one to forbid a Californian's adorning his fifty-foot lawn with a couple of

Canary Island date palms. Lolling in his shirt sleeves beneath those generous fronds, he is dead sure he is in Los Angeles, not Oshkosh, and that is what he wants to be certain of."[44]

Tree wardens objected to heterogeneity on the grid. In cities and towns with street tree commissions, uniform planting became the norm, in contrast to the alternating style of the pioneer period (typically Tasmanian blue gum interspersed with California fan palm). For the ornamentation of avenues, Canary Island date palm grew in favor while an old favorite, the pepper tree, fell into official disrepute because it acted as a reservoir for black scale, an insect that damaged citruses. In Southern California, county horticultural commissioners ordered the spraying and cutting of infected pepper trees. Around 1910 many cities in the Citrus Belt converted pepper drives to palm drives wholesale. When Ontario considered removing all the peppers from famed Euclid Boulevard, the proposal elicited a "storm of protest" from local clubwomen. In Los Angeles, the *Times* editorial board opposed the "total destruction" and "mutilation" of the city's pepper trees, with "the wonderful feathery foliage and the gorgeous scarlet berries"—a "powerful magnet for attracting the wealth and fashion of the East" as well as a beloved marker of home. These "trusty friends" of a quarter century had become an "integral part of life in the sunny Southland." This pioneer-era affection would not last. By 1930 Los Angeles banned street plantings of the species.[45]

In the era of oil and electricity, as the economy and the population diversified, Los Angeles began to shed its Iowa-with-fronds reputation. The city didn't, however, abandon the image of the palm. The chamber of commerce adjusted its boosterism, incorporating the machine into the garden. Manufacturing as well as agriculture thrived in "nature's workshop." Thanks to industry, the "climatic capital of the New World" had become the "southwestern metropolis," the "largest city in the western Americas." City boosterism reached its zenith in the 1920s, when the chamber began assembling a huge stock photograph collection that showed, among other things, business buildings landscaped with palms. On western Wilshire Boulevard, where the city gave way to fields, billboards and palms announced future growth. In *The Boosters*, a 1923 satirical novel by a mass-market writer, one of the main characters, an architect newly relocated from New England, mocks the favorite tree of promoters: "Oh, damn the palms!" In Los Angeles, the "ghastly dusters" looked funereal and depressing, like "great mummies in their shrouds of dead fronds." They exist only "to advertise the climate—to make the tourists feel they're getting their money's worth." By the end of the novel, however, the architect has acclimated to Los Angeles sufficiently that he "now fancied a slender species that suggested a hula-hula dancer."[46]

The film industry augmented the sex appeal of palms. Between 1910 and 1915, for various legal and technical reasons, Southern California supplanted New York and New Jersey as the nation's motion picture capital. By the 1920s, companies such as Warner Brothers, Paramount, Universal, and Metro-Goldwyn-Mayer operated enormous studios that included stockpiles of potted palms for sets. At the studio gates, beneath planted palms, photographers could capture views of silent-era stars such as Rudolph Valentino and the young Joan Crawford. For glamour shots, cameramen went to the world-famous Cocoanut Grove, Los Angeles's premier nightclub, where stars danced the Charleston and held court at reserved tables. A faux Moroccan banquet hall within the Ambassador Hotel, the Cocoanut Grove contained dozens of full-sized synthetic palms populated by stuffed monkeys—leftover props from Valentino's hit *The Sheik*. This showcase room, complete with a waterfall and table lamps shaped like palms, hosted a succession of galas in the 1930s, including the Ball of All Nations during the Tenth Olympiad, and multiple Academy Awards ceremonies. For film openings—a more frequent photo-op ritual—movie stars could pose in the palm-filled courtyard of Grauman's Chinese Theatre. The iconic pagoda-shaped "film temple" opened in 1927 with the debut of Cecil B. DeMille's *The King of Kings*, a New Testament epic filmed on location at the Thousand Palms oasis near Palm Springs.

Stars themselves could be hypnotized by palms. Joan Crawford, arriving fresh from Kansas City, recalled "a limousine waiting, with a chauffeur, and we drove out a long, long way through streets lined with palm trees. An infinity of palms trees. In nothing flat I discovered that the pretty young girls in film business were just as numerous."[47] To escape the hoi polloi, luminaries of the silent screen moved to secluded westside neighborhoods such as Brentwood or the nearby master-planned city Beverly Hills. In advance of residents, developers built the luxury Beverly Hills Hotel, a Mission Revival building surrounded by a pygmy forest of palms. The diligent street tree division of Beverly Hills laid out a succession of monotype plantings: Elm Drive, Maple Drive, Palm Drive, and so on. Although residential lots went up for sale starting in 1914, Beverly Hills didn't become a successful development and a recognizable place-name until the original celebrity power couple, Mary Pickford and Douglas Fairbanks, set up house in the 1920s.

In 1927–28, at the height of her popularity as "America's sweetheart"—a level of worldwide fame on a par with Marilyn Monroe's in the 1950s—Pickford lent her star power to the cause of tree planting in Los Angeles. Writing for the magazine of the chamber of commerce, she called it "criminally inexcusable" that so many of the city's street trees had recently been torn out for road-widening projects in service of the automobile. Pickford recommended slender palms for business streets so that drivers like herself could window-shop from their seats. She seconded the chamber of commerce's proposals for a reconstituted office of city forester and a citywide tree-planting program. The most photographed woman in the world even spoke at city hall in favor of the palmification of one of Hollywood's thoroughfares, Sunset Boulevard. This long east-west artery winds its way from downtown to Beverly Hills to the beach. At the time, the boulevard resembled a scenic byway through half-built suburbs punctuated by commercial districts. Clumps of pepper trees lined the dirt road. As part of a paving project, the city proposed to widen the boulevard and replace the peppers between Normandie and Fairfax with five hundred even-age, evenly spaced palms. As allowed by the California Street Tree Planting Act of 1915 (an update of a law first passed in 1893), city councils could order the addition or removal of trees for the public interest or convenience, paid for by special assessment, provided that a majority of property owners did not formally protest. This was the first time Los Angeles tried to exercise this arboreal authority.[48]

In the real Hollywood (annexed by Los Angeles in 1910), not everyone favored the plan. "The much beloved little actress lives in Beverly Hills and evidently has little knowledge of the future in store for Hollywood if its progress is halted by well meaning lovers of the beautiful," wrote one property owner in protest. "It is for the citizens of Hollywood to decide whether it shall become the center of business life of a great and growing city or whether it shall become a pretty little suburb of beautiful trees." Most striking from today's perspective, the opposition did not equate palms with Hollywood or connect Hollywood to the film industry. "I can see no reason why Sunset Blvd should be the only business street in the city to have trees making it look like a country town," complained one businessman. Another protested "the Babbitizing of our Boulevard."[49]

Perhaps it goes without saying that Pickford's opponents lost the fight. Thanks to the dispersed industry known as "Hollywood," the Los Angeles neighborhood Hollywood went on to become renowned for palms. That association is now a major asset to the city. Millions of tourists come to Hollywood to see what they already imagine it to be. Palmy Sunset Boulevard conjures images of glamour and grit, convertibles and streetwalkers, clubs and boutiques, neon signs and billboards. No one anymore would associate its even rows of palms with conformism or country life.

For better or worse, conventions of urban and architectural design did not hamper Los Angeles in the interwar years, the pivotal period for metropolitan development. The fast-growing city was a paradox: an antiurban metropolis, a planned accident. Angelenos in the twenties embraced cars like no previous people in the world, including Detroiters. In 1920 Los Angeles contained one car for every 3.6 residents (compared to a 1:13 ratio for the nation); a decade later, the ratio was two cars for every three residents. The resulting traffic jams and parking woes on the narrow streets of the central business district exceeded the worst traffic today. The interurban electric train system simultaneously bolstered downtown—because the lines all converged there—and undermined it. The decentralized growth that accompanied the interurban tracks encouraged outlying residents to seek out transportation alternatives. The Pacific Electric trains were notoriously slow and crowded, inadequately scheduled, and ineptly managed. It didn't help that trolleys, lacking dedicated lanes, routinely got stuck in car traffic. Under pressure from real estate speculators and the public, who voted in favor of the Major Traffic Street Plan in 1924, Los Angeles widened and expanded its road network and laid the political foundation for the future freeway system. Various planners drafted models for alternative urban growth—a high-rise core surrounded by ample green space; a collection of decentralized garden cities; a system of parks and parkways. These progressive plans lost out to a radical consensus: an autocentric horizontal metropolis limited only by the mountains and the sea. The grid would be filled in in scattershot fashion according to the free market and permissive zoning. Newly paved car roads, lined with billboards and palms, led to empty intersections with unbounded futures. Prior to houses came the gas pumps—filling stations in the style of Spanish missions, Georgian manors, and fairy-tale cottages.[50]

To eyes habituated to the streets of London and New York, the arbo-architectural landscape of Los Angeles seemed strange and insipid. In 1930 the English travel writers Jan and Cora Gordon described the "crude, eye-aching newness" of roadside scenery: "One could drive for almost sixty miles among raw towns and hot dog stalls," with billboards everywhere and a "petrol-station every five minutes without intermission." They drove "straight road after straight road, bordered everywhere with grass plots, thin palms, aloes, and bungalow courts." Much like outdoor advertisements and drive-in restaurants, the City of Tomorrow's flora signaled a distinctive—and

Palm Canyon near Palm Springs, the most visited native palm
oasis in California. Despite past attempts to federalize the land,
the canyon remains the property of the Agua Caliente Band of
Cahuilla Indians. In this photograph from the 1920s, the rooftops
of touring cars can be seen in the parking area above.

Two of the San Fernando Mission's once renowned California fan palms, arboreal remnants of the Spanish period.

A California fan palm being moved in 1888 from San Pedro Street—the edge of the former Wolfskill citrus orchard (then being subdivided)—to the entrance of the Southern Pacific Railroad depot in Los Angeles. Note the eucalyptus row in back.

Above and bottom left: This residential street—known interchange-
ably as Palm Drive and Avenue of Palms—was for decades the most-
photographed palm row in Los Angeles. The street was falsely advertised
as typical of the city. *Bottom right*: What remains of the same row of Mexican fan palms—the city's oldest, tallest street palms. They are orphaned
within the compound of the Orthopaedic Hospital next to the Harbor
Freeway.

Three views of Canary Island date palms. *Upper left*: The tree that traveled to and from the Chicago World's Fair towers over a bungalow in Los Angeles. *Upper right*: The "Colored California" edition of the NAACP's magazine, showing middle-class African Americans living the L.A. dream. *Below*: City Hall in Compton before the Long Beach earthquake of 1932, when the city was affluent, white, and relatively well shaded. (Now 75 percent nonwhite, Compton is a poor city with few street trees, palms or otherwise.)

Feathery queen palms in the Hollywood Hills overlooking a film premiere—an image widely reproduced on postcards.

The Cocoanut Grove, for many years the leading club in Los Angeles and the venue for multiple Academy Award ceremonies in the 1930s.

Four contemporary views of Southern California palms. *Clockwise from upper left*: Mexican fan palms fastened to a modernist office building (the former headquarters of Getty Oil) on Wilshire Boulevard; the dangerous work of a freelance palmskinner; a graffitied palm trunk at Venice Beach; the remains of a Canary Island date palm after wilt disease.

Two kinds of ready-made palm. *Above*: A palm-shaped cell-phone tower under construction at Preserved Treescapes International, the "world's leading manufacturer of inherently fire-retardant preserved and replica trees." (Note eucalypts in background.) *Below*: Mature Mexican fan palms from a Borrego Springs nursery go out for delivery.

Two kinds of urban palm. *Above*: Canary Island date palms line the Embarcadero, San Francisco. The waterfront was redesigned after the 1989 Loma Prieta earthquake. *Below*: The great Mexican fan palm oasis at the narrows of the Los Angeles River, 2010. The grove has since been chainsawed to stumps.

for some, absurd—experiment in urban form. After an exploratory visit, Edmund Wilson mocked the city's "mixturesque beauty": "A wee wonderful Swiss shilly-shally snuggles up beneath a bountiful bougainvillea which is by no means artificially colored . . . Those fine palms with their stiff tousled wigs are like Topsy, they just growed."[51]

The palminess of Southern California could be both intoxicating and fatiguing to recent migrants. "We used to go down to the Capitol Theater in Sioux City, Iowa, and sit there and watch Bing Crosby movies," recalled one transplant, "and I said, 'Man, is that what it's like out there? I got to get out there!' See how naive we were. Why, hey. They could paint those palm trees in the back of those movie sets as fast as you could leave." In the canonized Los Angeles novel *Ask the Dust* (1939), by John Fante, the narrator, a struggling novelist, describes his first day living at Bunker Hill. He sets his typewriter by the latchless window of his dilapidated flophouse and stares out: "I saw my first palm tree, not six feet away, and sure enough I thought of Palm Sunday and Egypt and Cleopatra, but the palm was blackish at its branches, stained by carbon monoxide coming out of the Third Street Tunnel, its crusted trunk choked with dust and sand that blew in from the Mojave and Santa Ana deserts." For two days he sits at his desk, staring out the window; the only words he can type are "palm tree, palm tree, palm tree." James M. Cain, author of *The Postman Always Rings Twice* and *Double Indemnity*—the bases for two classics of film noir—spent most of the thirties and forties as a Hollywood screenwriter before moving back to his native Maryland. To see the real Southern California, wrote Cain, you must "wash out the palm trees, half visible beyond the tap dancing platform. Palm trees are here, but they are phonies, planted by people bemused with the notion of a sub-tropical climate, and they are so out of harmony with their surroundings that they hardly arrest your notice."[52]

The plebeian aesthetic of Los Angeles, including its auto palms, could be refashioned to meet upper-class tastes. Two landmark buildings on Wilshire Boulevard, a wide thoroughfare from downtown to Santa Monica built expressly for cars, may serve as examples. In

1929 the members of Congregation B'nai B'rith, including the four Polish-born Warner brothers, dedicated a Byzantine-style domed synagogue worthy of the grandest Holy Land epic from a Hollywood studio. Feather palms lined the streets approaching Wilshire Boulevard Temple, and fan palms flanked its entrance. The location, 4 miles west of congested downtown, in sight of agricultural fields, was far from central, and that was the point. Unlike New York and Chicago, Los Angeles welcomed a centerless future. The same year, just down the road, Bullock's luxury department store, an art deco masterpiece with a 241-foot-high tower and accenting palms, opened its doors to the city's most discriminating shoppers. They, like templegoers, expected to drive; the store's main entrance faced the ample free parking lot in the rear.

During the Great Depression and the simultaneous climax of the studio system, palm trees became even greater objects of fantasy. Filmmakers utilized fronds and other packaged symbols of the carefree life to divert the masses. Even before the *South Pacific* era, when film audiences included American GIs returned from Pacific tours of duty, Hollywood studios produced many musicals set in "tropical paradises" such as Hawai'i, Cuba, and Brazil. The great "ethnic" star of the era, Carmen Miranda (a Brazilian of European extraction), sang and danced—with fruit on her head—to a backdrop of palm and banana trees and retired to a Beverly Hills home with a swimming pool fringed with palms. In 1936 a local movie theater impresario opened the Tropics, one of the first fashionable restaurants in Beverly Hills. Filipino bar staff served up stiff cocktails to beautiful people in the palm-and-bamboo outdoor patio. A second Tropics opened near Hollywood and Vine in 1939. In post-Prohibition Los Angeles, movie stars—and the photographers who trailed them—frequented a number of Polynesian-themed clubs, including Ken's Hula Hut, Zamboanga South Sea Club, and the Seven Seas, opposite Grauman's Chinese Theatre. (In the other entertainment capital, New York, the fashionable Copacabana opened in 1940 with pillars remade into make-believe palms with white trunks and velveteen fronds.) The international craze for rumba spawned Cuban bars, too, with the inevitable palm decor. Middlebrow eateries also took the tropical turn. One of the pioneers in the fashion, King's Tropical Inn in Culver City, served up "world-famous" fried chicken and squab among fronds. In 1939 Clifford Clinton, the owner of the landmark chain of Clifton's cafeterias in downtown Los Angeles, remodeled his Olive Street location and renamed it Pacific Seas. The layered façade of the themed cafeteria featured cascading water and live tropical flora. Inside, patrons ate meat and potatoes under synthetic palm trees, neon fronds, grass-thatched huts, and jungle murals. Clinton, a Christian teetotaler, banned alcohol but allowed the needy to dine in paradise for free.[53]

For a real Pacific getaway, Angelenos of the interwar years traveled a mere 25 miles offshore to Santa Catalina Island, one of the eight Channel Islands. The 76-square-mile landmass had once belonged to the heirs of Phineas Banning, one of the great entrepreneurs of boom-era Los Angeles. In 1919 the Banning family sold the isle to the even wealthier William Wrigley of Chicago. The "king of chewing gum" established a spring training facility for the Cubs on his ocean property and transformed the harbor village of Avalon from a local getaway to a nationally known resort. (Wrigley also owned a mansion in Pasadena with palm trees in the yard and a painting of palm trees above the master bedroom mantel.) Wrigley's resort plans garnered the enthusiastic support of the All-Year Club of Southern California, a booster organization founded in 1921 by downtown businessmen, including Harry Chandler of the *Times*. The club worked to attract tourists and conventioneers to Los Angeles in the summer, not just winter. Hollywood did its part, too, by using Catalina as a film set and planting palm trees at the island's isthmus for props. In newsreels and magazines, vacationing movie stars could now be seen waterskiing ("aquaplaning") and playing on the beach. Catalina joined the Cocoanut Grove as a recognized "playground of the stars." Avalon possessed more sophistication than Venice Pier or Coney Island. Wrigley enforced architectural standards, limited the town's size at 1 square mile, and banned cars. To create an ambiance of dignified pleasure, he built a singular circular building—a sound-equipped movie theater on the ground floor, a dance hall above—in Mission-Moorish-Adriatic-Venetian style. He called it the Casino, using the older Italian meaning of the word; the facility offered no gambling. Philip Wrigley, who assumed control of the island in 1932 upon his father's death, added landscaping to the Casino. He autho-rized one hundred full-sized palm trees around the building and the boardwalk leading to it. Barges brought the trees across the channel, and tractors and derricks lifted them into place. The sight of sea-side fronds, an international symbol of leisure, greeted visitors as they embarked from the ferry. The new Avalon referenced the Riviera but welcomed the masses; Wrigley wanted a "resort for Everyman." Vis-itation to Avalon reached approximately 700,000 in 1930, easily sur-passing that of Yosemite, California's most famous national park. A 1937 survey of tourists conducted by the All-Year Club suggested that Santa Catalina Island was the single greatest attraction in the state.[54]

While tourists traveled to seaside Southern California to relax under tall palms, regional exporters sent small palms in pots to desti-nations throughout the country. In the 1930s nurseries based in Los Angeles filled practically the entire national demand. The best variety for low-light indoor conditions was the fashionable kentia palm, a species endemic to Lord Howe Island, a tiny isle between Australia and New Zealand. Thanks to the Port of Los Angeles, Southland nurserymen captured the import market for kentia seed. After ger-minating and tending seedlings for four years, growers distributed palms to cocktail bars, hotel lounges, wedding halls, and floral shops across the United States. In 1935 alone some 300,000 potted kentia palms left Los Angeles in heated railcars.[55]

A federal quarantine dating to 1918 on foreign-grown bamboo and banana trees encouraged Californians to rely even more on nursery-grown palms for outdoor landscaping effects. For explicitly "tropical" and "Oriental" looks, Hollywood turned to queen palm, a native of Brazil—smaller, greener, and softer than the California

fan palm. This was the variety on view in the courtyard of Grauman's Chinese Theatre and on the patios of tiki rooms on the Sunset
Strip. Santa Barbara had practically monopolized the species in the
late nineteenth century, but San Diego eventually adopted it widely,
thanks to the influential gardener Kate Sessions, and Los Angeles
ultimately mimicked the look. A garden writer for the *Los Angeles
Times* stated in 1931 that queen palm was "no doubt the most widely
known and admired of our palms." Urban merchants liked them as
street trees because they didn't grow huge and because their lacy
fronds didn't obstruct views. Today there are probably more queens in
Southern California than *Phoenix* and *Washingtonia* combined. Australia's king palm, genetically distinct but morphologically similar to
queen palm, later joined the list of common street species. Another
distinctive tree type is pindo palm, which has blue-gray fronds that
shoot straight up, then curve down steeply toward the trunk. The
strangest-looking common species is windmill palm, which, in the
words of Charles Saunders, "slipped in from China, in spite of California's anti-Chinese sentiments." Gardeners used to call it "sore-throat
palm" because its trunk resembles a scratchy woolen scarf. Although
relatively unattractive, this hardy dwarf species allows cooler parts of
California to participate in tropical-themed landscaping. Landscapers often use it or Mediterranean fan palm—another small, hardy
plant that grows well in clumps—to ornament traffic medians.[56]

But the iconic palm of Los Angeles—the tree that came to define
the city's postwar treescape—was Mexican fan palm (*Washingtonia
robusta*), a species that never earned special praise for beauty or elegance. A mature specimen looks scoliotic next to its close evolutionary cousin, California fan palm (*W. filifera*). Also known as skyduster
palm, *W. robusta* can reach twice the height of *W. filifera*. Its thin
trunk, mainly grayish brown, sports some chestnut red near the top.
Its disheveled crown contains about thirty bright green fronds, each
composed of roughly fifty segments. Native to Baja and Sonora, *W.
robusta* tolerates cold somewhat less than *W. filifera* but adapts better
to coastal environments. It is exceptionally hardy. As an added advan-

tage, Mexican fan palm seeds have always been cheaply available in California.[57]

For these practical reasons, presumably, Los Angeles chose Mexican fan palm as a featured species for its first comprehensive tree-planting program. In 1931 the recently created Division of Forestry of the Department of Parks announced a ten-year plan to set tens of thousands of trees along hundreds of miles of roads. As part of the program, Los Angeles conducted its first survey of the urban canopy. At the time, over 60 percent of Los Angeles streets lacked trees, unsurprising given that the city added well over 100 miles of paved roads each year. Of the limited street-side greenery on older streets, acacias alone accounted for 20 percent.[58] For new roads, the division chose not to reproduce the familiar street trees from the boom era—acacias, eucalypts, and pepper trees. In the age of streetside parking, sidewalks, sewers, and utility poles, all three of these leafy, rooty growers acquired bad reputations. Palm trees, on the other hand, held out the promise of symbiotic infrastructure: they could provide beautification without dropping fruit, buckling concrete, breaking pipes, or snapping wires.

To save money, the city appealed to the civic pride and pecuniary interest of its citizenry. "The Way to Rising Property Values Is Lined with Trees," trumpeted a city-issued pamphlet for residents and business owners. It urged Angelenos to obtain a permit and plant a tree by the sidewalk in front of their home; the permitting process would ensure uniformity. If a neighborhood group pledged in writing to take care of sidewalk trees (doing the planting and watering), the city arranged to deliver seedlings. The brochure noted that street trees were good for tourism because they added "an air of stability to our city."[59]

City hall also initiated a tree-planting program using unemployment relief bonds; four hundred men stranded by the Depression gained temporary work. In just six months, they spruced up L.A. in time for the Olympic Games of 1932. Priority went to major automobile arteries that would serve as gateways for visitors. The Major

Boulevard Planting Program encompassed twenty-eight designated boulevards and avenues, including place-names now familiar to every local driver: Ventura, Colorado, Wilshire, Beverly, Figueroa, Vermont, Western, Crenshaw. As part of the Master Tree Plan, the urban foresters divided Los Angeles into seven districts and sent out postcards to residents informing them of incoming plants and asking for assistance. The trees would die without regular hose watering.[60]

And so it was that the Great Depression and the Tenth Olympiad propelled L.A.'s second era of palm planting to peak florescence. The first era, coincident with the city's preautomobile real estate booms, left a scattered landscape of palms, dominated first by California fan palm and then by Canary Island date palm, in private yards and driveways and at special civic zones such as avenues, parks, and edifices. Now, by contrast, miles and miles of standardized automobile roads that cut across agricultural, residential, commercial, and industrial tracts featured uniform sidewalk installations of *W. robusta*. Water for these desert oasis plants came from distant desert streams via the Los Angeles Aqueduct and the Colorado River Aqueduct (1939). A new artificial landscape took shape—a fan palm every 40 to 50 feet. The additions were designed to be monocultural, but nurseries and workers couldn't always differentiate between *Washingtonia* seedlings, and a certain percentage of *W. filifera* slipped in. Decades later, the difference would become clear, as the spindly Mexican fan palms grew well past their straighter, shorter, stockier cousins. At first, though, the little plants didn't look like much—spiky tufts on sticks. But with each passing year they grew taller, eventually pushing above the single-story homes and storefronts of the low-profile metropolis, growing taller still, becoming ultra-flora, reaching up toward the endless California sun.

CHAPTER 8

Aesthetic Infrastructure

SUNBELT DESIGN

In the postwar era, sidewalk palms grew into symbols of urban Los Angeles. Tall ranks of Mexican fan palm became familiar fixtures on the horizon, generic landmarks, the original skyscrapers of the horizontal metropolis. The entertainment industry magnified their stature. Advertisements, telecasts, television shows, movies, song recordings, and music videos produced in Southern California made ready use of street palm imagery. A telephoto shot of a row of lanky palms became shorthand for L.A.—America's dream factory, the most filmed locale in the world. Long after the city's street tree division gave preference to other species and genera, private developers, architects, and landscape designers utilized Mexican fan palms for the mass communication of desirability. The "L.A. look" transcended Los Angeles: shopping malls, gated communities, and casinos in places such as Orange County and Las Vegas mimicked and exaggerated the fashion for high-rise fronds. Ultimately, fan palms meant less to Angelenos than to outsiders and their *idea* of L.A. In 2006, when the City of Los Angeles officially discouraged fan palms as street trees, the world reacted in disbelief. People could not imagine "SoCal" without the shabby-chic Mexican fan palm. Even in San

Francisco, a city with a distinctive palm history, the image of L.A. now affects the way that people interpret an urban plant with fronds.

"Fashions in trees change year by year like styles in women's dress," remarked a *Los Angeles Times* writer in 1942. According to him, the rage for palms had subsided. The tropical trees didn't match the architectural styles of the day, English manor houses and Cape Cod cottages. "The present trend is away from the bizarre and exotic." During the serious times of World War II, Angelenos even worried about dangers posed by palms. Very few of the tens of thousands of street palms planted in previous decades had ever been trimmed. The dried-up fronds formed thick mats of flammable material, a stockpile of fuel that conceivably might have been eyed by the Japanese for incendiary attack. In 1942 hundreds of residents petitioned the city council to ameliorate this public safety hazard. Many petitioners felt angry that the board of park commissioners had ordered residential "owners" of municipal street palms to remove dead fronds. This job required special training and equipment; for novices, it would be "fraught with danger and hazard to life and limb." The city attorney later advised the board that it had overreached its authority.[1]

In the immediate postwar era, Southland planners and builders eschewed trees like Canary Island date palms and Mexican fan palms. In a time of mass-produced small lots, these large-form trees didn't seem to fit. "Several decades ago as Los Angeles was developing its suburbs there was a vogue for lining the streets with long rows of evenly spaced palms or dotting front lawns with sentinels," explained a garden writer for the *Times* in 1953. As these palms grew higher and higher, they fell out of favor; "we realized they were grotesque and lonely." She advised home landscapers to use modest-sized varieties such as windmill palm and to set them in groups, thus avoiding the lollipop effect. The developers of Lakewood, an instant suburban city of 70,000 people in ranch houses, the western equivalent to Levittown, Long Island, didn't use any palms. Lakewood's list of approved species instead included throwbacks such as pepper trees and acacias. Prefab communities designed for veterans—and reserved for whites according to racially restrictive covenants—popped up like dandelions in the San Gabriel Valley and Orange County. Walnut and avocado orchards around Whittier fell before the bulldozer. Within the boundaries of the City of Los Angeles, the development frontier shifted to the San Fernando Valley, where developers tore out citrus orchards and their eucalyptic windbreaks. The succeeding residential landscapes of "the Valley" contained many broad-leafed trees and few palms. The trendiest plant of the 1950s and 1960s in Southern California was the "rubber tree" (*Ficus elastica*), with its striking aerial and buttress roots. (Cities would later tear out ficus en masse because of sidewalk buckling.) When Walt Disney opened the gates of Disneyland in 1955, visitors streamed through Main Street, U.S.A., an idealization of a (white) midwestern small town. The deciduous trees on Main Street looked modest and conventional, not Californian. The only section of Disneyland with conspicuous palms was Adventureland, home of the Jungle Cruise.[2]

Even as landscapers downplayed palms on the new suburban streets of Greater Los Angeles, tourism promoters played them up the same old way. The All-Year Club continued its long tradition of wintertime "sunshine ads" in cold states. Predictably, these newspaper spots portrayed Los Angeles as an ideal winter destination, a region of oranges and palms. The advent of color television aided the cause. On 1 January 1954, NBC inaugurated coast-to-coast color broadcasting with coverage of the Tournament of Roses Parade, the floral procession in Pasadena that began on palm-lined Orange Grove Boulevard. The contemporaneous advent of passenger flights also aided the cause. In 1953 the Los Angeles Junior Chamber of Commerce welcomed service to and from Boston with the donation of a potted palm to Logan Airport. Around 1960 United Airlines advertised its service to Los Angeles with eye-grabbing posters showing fan palms backing a blond beauty in a bathing suit with shadows of fronds on her bosom.[3]

Despite the energetic advertising, the image of L.A. as a sunny lotusland dimmed a bit in the mid-twentieth century. The 1965 riots in Watts, widely described as a "ghetto with palms," gave a long-lasting bad name to a swath of the metropolis: South Central. The whole basin's reputation for smog replaced its former reputation for healthy air. The vaunted freeway system, which seemed like Autopia when construction began in the 1940s, was as early as the 1960s derided as the "biggest parking lot in the world" (a quip often attributed to the comedian Bob Hope). Meanwhile, rival destinations beckoned with winter warmth and palms. The same airlines that made winter vacationing in Los Angeles more convenient opened up competition. Chicagoans and New Yorkers could now visit south Florida or the Caribbean with unprecedented ease. The Sunshine State aggressively courted and successfully captured much of the eastern market for winter tourism. Of America's cities, only Miami Beach could match Los Angeles in its symbolic identification with palm trees. "Let me tell you, to me when I came here the first time, I had a feeling that I had come to Paradise," recalled Isaac Bashevis Singer about Miami. "First of all the palm trees."[4] Coconut-rich Honolulu joined the contest for tourists in 1959, when Hawai'i became the fiftieth state and Boeing introduced the 707.

Even hot desert environments competed with Mediterranean L.A. for snowbirds, vacationers, and retirees. Most famously, the Del Webb corporation turned an expanse of saguaro cactus into the first master-planned retirement community, an age-restricted, self-contained complex with golf courses, shopping malls, medical facilities—and absolutely no schools and associated taxes. The original Sun City, located north of Phoenix, Arizona, opened in 1960 and became the template for many other leisure communities, including one in Riverside County. For Del Webb, palms became a trademark landscape element. At Scottsdale, Arizona, Las Vegas, Nevada, and the latest "playground of the stars," Palm Springs, California, leisure developers relied heavily on outdoor palms—and indoor air conditioning—to create an idealized environment. In the restruc-

tured geography of the postwar Sunbelt, the palms of Los Angeles, and especially Catalina Island, seemed less special and alluring
than before.[5]

Greater Los Angeles thrived nonetheless because it attracted so
many workers. In the 1950s the metro area, which now included
scores of municipalities, entered another long boom, more or less
coincident with the Cold War, and transformed its identity yet again.
Now, in addition to entertainment, oil, transport, and light manufacturing, boosters emphasized aerospace. Thanks to defense contracts, the GDP of Los Angeles County eclipsed that of many small
countries. Area labs and factories designed and produced an awesome
arsenal of fighters, bombers, missiles, and rocket boosters. Dozens of
high-tech companies started, expanded, or relocated here, where a
mighty river of defense appropriations disgorged.[6]

The city continued to expand horizontally, engulfing the remaining open spaces, citrus ranches, horse pastures, dairy farms, and low-
density neighborhoods. After Los Angeles lured the Dodgers away
from Brooklyn in 1957, it facilitated the depopulation of Chávez
Ravine, a semirural barrio in the Elysian Hills that had earlier been
slated for a federal housing project. Developers razed the homes and
gardens of evicted Mexican residents, terraformed the ravine into a
platform, and built Dodger Stadium (1962) at the center of an Olym-
pian parking lot. Obligatory groupings of mature fan palms lined
the outfield pavilions. Although the Dodgers' new home overlooked
downtown, there was no easy way to get there. Chávez Ravine had
been chosen for its proximity to several freeways, not its proximity to
the city center. Downtown Los Angeles declined to near irrelevancy
after the electric trolley system, the interurban Red Cars and then the
municipal Yellow Cars, suspended operation in the early 1960s. The
dealings of General Motors contributed to the shutdown—the subject of congressional investigation, conspiracy theories, and the film
Who Killed Roger Rabbit? (1988)—but the consumer choices of city
residents did so even more. As early as 1910 Los Angeles boasted the
highest per capita car ownership in the world. The freeway system

built in the 1940s and 1950s cemented the new order. In a sign of the times, downtown sacrificed the tree cover at Pershing Square to ease the construction of what was, on opening day in 1952, the nation's largest underground parking structure. The relandscaped park consisted of a lawn lined with palms—a "see-through, walk-through park" where the LAPD could easily curtail political rallies, drug deals, and gay encounters. Palms facilitated urban surveillance.[7]

In the early jet age, palm trees often took expressly architectural forms. While residential landscapers turned away from fronds, commercial designers and high-end architects embraced them. Throughout the metropolis, corporate draftsmen used palms as elements in their drawings, models, and finished projects. Aerospace firms such as North American Aviation built clean-lined modernist buildings with palms as accents. It became standard to group the logolike trees in twos or threes, often at angles crossing each other, even bracketed to the sides of buildings. This accessorizing effect could be seen at drive-in theaters and car washes as well as corporate headquarters such as the Capitol Records Tower (1955), high-end accommodations such as the Hotel Statler (1952) and the Beverly Hills Hilton (1955), and government buildings such as the Parker Center (1955), the new home of the LAPD. Architects even designed portico and awning holes to allow sidewalk palms to intersect buildings. In Palm Springs, some of the America's best modernist architects built homes for L.A.'s jet set and incorporated palms and native rocks into their designs. A California fan palm growing out of a trellis that enclosed and sheltered a free-form pool became a familiar design leitmotif at the desert resort.[8]

Plants such as these did not belong to the garden, the seaside, or even the street. They grew out of architecture. The idea was to complement the beauty of concrete and glass, not hide its ugliness. In Los Angeles, building designers placed mature palms close to tall exterior walls so they would cast interesting shadows throughout the day. Select parts of the city—notably Wilshire Boulevard—went vertical in the fifties, adding multistory office towers and apartments (but no more public housing units, a "socialist" proposal defeated by voters). Vertical is relative: from 1905 to 1957, the city enforced a height restriction of thirteen stories or 150 feet. On mid-Wilshire, the oil billionaire J. Paul Getty razed the shade-covered mansion formerly occupied by his ex-wife (the film location for *Sunset Boulevard*) and erected a new corporate headquarters—an exposed block tower—with fan palms all but touching the building, held in place by cable supports.

On the suburban fringe, designers used perpendicular palms to break up the otherwise severe horizontality of large-form asphalt and concrete. Angelenos flocked to freeway-access regional shopping centers with vast parking lots placed in front—no longer in back as at Bullock's on Wilshire. This new, stark landscape, which appeared fresh and modern in the fifties, featured little landscaping except for palm trees, which resembled aestheticized light poles. One early example of this arbo-architectural landscape was Valley Plaza (1951) in the eastern San Fernando Valley. The exemplar was the international airport (1961), the transportation hub of Cold War Los Angeles. In its expanded and redesigned form, LAX featured a futuristic air traffic control tower and the instantly iconic Theme Building, a restaurant-observatory that looked like a Martian flying saucer on a landing pad. From the bar, patrons sipped cocktails while looking out on a sea of blacktop dotted with island groups of palms.[9]

Fronded trees, along with California modernism, fell out of favor with 1960s commercial designers. The dormancy lasted longer than the dry spell after the tropical 1930s. "Palms were very popular in the 1950s," recalled the distinguished landscape architect Emmet Wemple, "and then they became a real *no*." Many suburban Angelenos went to local garden stores for dwarf palms to adorn their new backyard swimming pools—as of the early sixties, Southern California contained roughly one-third of all such pools in the nation—but professional landscapers and arborists temporarily shunned fronds, and cities used them reluctantly. When the diseased queen palms on Wilshire Boulevard in Beverly Hills needed to be replaced in the

1960s, the city stirred up controversy by choosing Mexican fan palms over its initial choice, ficus.[10]

In collective memory, the 1960s Southland means youth culture and the craze for surfing. Hollywood released seven *Beach Party* films from 1963 through 1966, not to mention the *Gidget* franchise. The teenage beach shows did not feature a lot of palm scenery, but cumulatively they probably reinforced the palmy image of Los Angeles in popular consciousness, as did the Beach Boys' hit single "California Girls," with its line about dolls, sand, and fronds.[11]

Away from the beach, thousands of streetside palms looked anything but modern, sleek, and fun. By the 1960s the mass plantings from the twenties and thirties reached heights of 50 feet or more. Thousands had never been trimmed, and their unkempt "beards" reached all the way to the ground. Worked on by gravity, a mat of dead, dingy fronds might collapse partway down the trunk, only to get snagged on the leaf stalks. Los Angeles boulevards with rows of Mexican fan palms in various states of shedding appeared rather disheveled. In the Citrus Belt, the palms were older, taller, and even shaggier. These combustible pillars attracted pyromaniacs and copycat vandals. From the early 1940s through the late 1960s, "gangs of youths" regularly attacked palmy avenues and driveways; they converted bearded palms into "Roman torches of terror," destroying property and disrupting telephone and electric lines. By cover of night, "long-haired" hooligans lobbed bottles of flaming liquid onto palm trees from the windows of moving cars, and plenty of well-adjusted children in broad daylight used clothespin-and-rubber-band guns to launch strike-anywhere matches into desiccated fronds. In rapidly suburbanizing towns such as Pasadena, Covina, and Redlands, firefighters, police, and utility crews rushed from one scene of arbo-vandalism to another.[12]

Despite clear infrastructural advantages—no sidewalks buckled by roots, no storm drains clogged by deciduous leaves—palms create their own maintenance problems, mostly related to fronds. Some species of crownshaft palms, such as king palm and queen palm, are "self-cleaning," meaning that each leaf base has two abscission zones. The used-up fronds drop freely in regular fashion as part of the growth cycle. But fan palms and certain feather palms, like Canary Island date palm, behave differently. Their leaves stay on the trunk until gravity or wind suddenly releases one or a bunch. In autumn, after the Santa Ana winds, the palm-lined streets of Los Angeles become obstacle courses. A downed frond, unlike a dainty maple leaf, looks like a dislodged piece of organic machinery. Weighing several pounds even when dry, palm debris can easily dent a car. To mitigate airborne damage, tall streetside fan palms should be trimmed at least once every five years. Trimmers must beware of wildlife when they approach the crown. In and around Pasadena, noisy flocks of tropical parrots—escaped pets gone feral—have colonized the sheltered, fruit-filled canopies of palms. Rats, too, take refuge in these natural middens. If a tree becomes intolerably infested with rodents, municipal street tree crews may install a belt—a plate of smooth steel or aluminum—around the trunk, thus denying traction to tiny climbing feet. But only wealthy cities such as Pasadena, Beverly Hills, and Santa Monica can afford regular palm trimmings and rat poison applications. Long Beach pioneered this approach in 1948, when its health department placed poison in more than four thousand rat-infested palms. A few years later, its board of supervisors characterized palms as "fire hazards and nesting places for rats."[13]

In Los Angeles, the superintendent of street trees reached his limit with palms in the mid-1970s. Despite constant complaints about rodent eyries, he had to lengthen the interval between maintenance visits to each of the city's approximately 48,000 palms because of budget cuts. Hoping to lessen the labor on future rotations, city contractors known as "palmskinners" removed the bottom layer of green fronds as well as the brown skirt. These "bad haircut" palms looked ridiculous at first, resembling an upright pen with a green nib. (Unintentionally, the "hurricane trim" diminished the crown's cantilevering support and increased the likelihood that healthy fronds would collapse.) As an additional cost-cutting measure, Los Angeles began to give away cut fronds, thus reducing disposal fees. Officials had noticed Jewish residents on the trail of palmskinners, picking up fallen fronds. Observant Jews prefer palm material for sukkahs, the shelters used for outdoor eating during the weeklong Feast of Tabernacles. Los Angeles decided in effect to sponsor the Jewish holiday. On a designated day in the fall, it freely distributed long, feathery leaves from Canary Island date palms—10,000 or more each year—at a city parking lot.[14]

If even low-maintenance street trees such as fan palms require expensive maintenance, why not go the next step? Why not plastic trees? Los Angeles County conducted such an experiment in 1972 on a 1.7-mile stretch of Jefferson Boulevard near Loyola Marymount University. A culvert project beneath the roadway had removed the soil available to trees in the median. To compensate, county crews installed 1-foot-deep concrete planter boxes. To fill them, the county board of supervisors appropriated $35,000 for nine hundred plastic plants, including about one hundred steel-supported palms, as well as fake junipers, Chinese laurels, magnolias, and various flowers such as birds of paradise. The road department set the artificial flora in crushed rock and arranged them in clusters for artistic effect. "Take that, Joyce Kilmer," quipped the *Los Angeles Times*.[15]

The pseudo-trees became an instant scandal. The city and county received hundreds of phone calls and comment letters and formal protests from garden clubs, which quickly came up with long lists of flowers and shrubs that could grow in 1 foot of topsoil. Letters to the editor maligned the inert monstrosities: *What about the maintenance of the human spirit? In the interest of economy, I suggest we have real trees and plastic supervisors. This is just another example of the reason why outsiders refer to our city as "Tinseltown, U.S.A." and why all of L.A. is identified as the "Phony Glamour Capital of the World."* A nighttime prankster attached plastic birds to some of the trees. Less amusingly, vandals destroyed about fifty of the fakes by trampling them, sawing them, and attempting to burn them. Reeling from the controversy, the road department "halted all plastic plantings." However, the median

ornaments would remain "as long as they survive." The veteran columnist Jack Smith reported that the palms looked "clean and shiny"
as well as "stiff and indestructible." Alas, even space-age plastic was
no match for the industrial-strength smog of Los Angeles. County
workers resorted to cleaning the faux palms with spray detergent once
a month. Finally, in 1976, the road department rooted out the entire
beautification because of plastic degradation. "The road grime and
the atmosphere destroyed [the trees]," explained the commissioner.[16]

In the environmentally conscious 1970s, when redwood debates
regularly made the news and housewives defended suburban eucalypts, tree huggers even fought for urban palms. Activists in the Hancock Park neighborhood of Los Angeles in 1972 successfully agitated
to "save our palms" on Highland Avenue from a project to widen the
road and create left-hand turn lanes. "When workmen showed up
to mark a number of the 40-year-old palm trees for the saw," wrote
Jack Smith, "the householders rushed forth from their peep-holes like
tribesmen defending their virgin daughters." Residents erected signs
on their lawns with messages like PALMS UP, HANDS OFF. In response,
the city council canceled the work contract, and the cultural heritage board declared the trees to be a "historic-cultural monument."
Later that year, the city of Camarillo in Ventura County designated
its palms along U.S. 101 a cultural heritage landmark in an attempt
to stymie plans by Caltrans to widen the road. The town had already
tried the same tactic with its gateway eucalypts. This time the strata-
gem failed: the palms were uprooted and relocated.[17]

In Los Angeles, the defining environmental issue of the 1970s
was smog. The dread pollution filled the interior air basins, rose up
into the mountains, and caused acid rain and ozone damage to pines.
This ecothreat inspired local teenager Andy Lipkis, who founded an
ecology club, the California Conservation Project, in 1973. Lipkis's
lifelong activism began in the San Bernardino Mountains, where he
planted trees at summer camps. Banners for his project read, SMOG
KILLS TREES! TREE PEOPLE SAVE TREES. In time, Lipkis moved his
ecological concerns to the city. He wanted Los Angeles to be famous

for its urban forest, not just its palms. The city needed leafy trees for air quality, he said, for energy conservation, and for neighborliness. A dynamic community organizer, Lipkis secured volunteer labor from civic and corporate organizations and free saplings from agencies such as the U.S. Forest Service. His new group, TreePeople, announced an ambitious goal in 1981: 1 million trees in the ground by 1984, the year the Olympics would return to Los Angeles. The project focused on leafy deciduous species, as suggested by its slogans, "Turn Over a New Leaf, Los Angeles" and "Urban Releaf." In a complementary effort, a corporate-sponsored civic group called Los Angeles Beautiful oversaw tree plantings along high-profile streets that would serve as Olympic gateways. The group's chairman knew about the 1931 precedent but didn't want to follow it exactly: "One of the things they planted at that time were palm trees—the same ones that have now turned into 200-foot telephone poles."[18]

To see new systematic palm plantings in 1980s California, one had to go to Orange County, where the Irvine Company put the finishing touches on its edge cities and master-planned amenity enclaves. The owner of roughly 100,000 acres—the last *rancho* in the coastal Southland to be developed—the company became the state's leading planter of palms and the curator of its most uniform palm landscape. Ironically, the company's initial master plan had prohibited fronds, as seen at Newport Center, also known as Fashion Island, a high-end entertainment and shopping complex within a circular parking lot that functioned as an alternative to a downtown. The original Fashion Island (1967) played down the pizzazz. "The concept then was to give the Center an eastern look, with sycamores selected as the principal street trees," explained the company's vice president of urban design in 1985. "It didn't work out well. The climate wasn't right, the trees didn't flourish, and many of them are now dying." The VP spoke at the unveiling of a "Mediterranean" redesign plan for the "renaissance" of the Newport Center. Besides new retail space and an atrium court, the plan called for a triple row of eight hundred mature Mexican fan palms to line the main circle road as well as Canary Island date palms near the shops. The VP lauded palms as being affordable to maintain, distinctive, and dramatic, while in keeping with the "informal ambiance" of nearby Newport Beach. A short time later, the Irvine Company broke ground on a new civic/shopping center, the Irvine Spectrum Center. "By selecting palm trees, we're making a statement," said the director of the project. "We're telling potential tenants and developers that Irvine Spectrum is a professional environment. Palm trees provide an orderly, consistent, high-tech look." Irvine was a real estate brand, and its "consistent landscaping palette" communicated education, wealth, and quality. The company used its signature tree to create a "sense of identity" and a "hierarchy of place."[19]

The palmification of Irvine Ranch during the 1980s signaled a commercial trend. All over Southern California, developers returned to palms. In downtown Los Angeles, fronded plants were meant to communicate a sense of revival, a historic touch of class. In the Reagan years, real estate interests renewed their fitful effort to "clear the slums" and "take back" the city center from the homeless, the dealers, the junkies, and the hardworking immigrants who called it home. From the 1960s to the 1980s, downtown had shifted northwest to Bunker Hill, originally a residential neighborhood. With the old Victorians razed and proposals for public housing defeated, the hill became the bedrock for the city's first skyscrapers. In the name of seismic safety, much of downtown's affordable apartment stock was demolished and replaced with high-end commercial space. Fortress offices in the Wells Fargo Center (1983) looked down onto a dozen Canary Island date palms; luxury rooms in the Sheraton Grande (1983) overlooked one hundred Mexican fan palms. A few blocks to the east, out of sight and out of mind, thousands of unemployed persons, many of them veterans of the Vietnam War, set up semi-permanent residence in single-occupancy hotels, shelters, sidewalk tents, and cardboard boxes. The occasional raggedy palm amid the squalor of skid row mocked the California Dream.

The same real estate forces that built up Bunker Hill pushed low-density palm-lined developments to the city's edge. In the go-go eighties, the exurban frontier reached into Ventura, Riverside, and San Diego counties. One old-timer in Ventura bemoaned the arrival of "trendoid" palms and expressed nostalgia for the former "country" look of eucalyptus. Developers plowed ahead. Shopping centers in Rancho Cucamonga, starter castles in Temecula, gated one-way streets at walled-in country club neighborhoods in Rancho Mirage: they all demanded palms, preferably mature ones that added instant verticality to design schemes. During this rush, the largest palm grower in Southern California sold out his entire mature stock. "It seemed every damn hotel in Los Angeles revamped their grounds and went art nouveau with palm trees," he said at the time. "Architects are like sheep—every architect in Southern California is drawing palm trees now." Queen palms sold best, followed by Mexican fan palms. To meet the demand for full-sized specimens, tree brokers went bioprospecting. They paid cash to owners of small bungalow lots in established neighborhoods who had inherited a hard-to-see 60- or 80- or 100-foot palm tree. In the Southland, it became common to see newly trimmed palms, their fronds tied up like a ponytail and their roots boxed up, piled in stacks on a flatbed. When Steele's Motor Lodge, a venerable palm-shaded motel on Ventura Boulevard, closed its doors, it unloaded its trees to a broker; he in turn marketed them to Fashion Island in Newport Beach, the new Xerox Center in Santa Ana, and a savings and loan in Sherman Oaks. In San Diego, opportunists known as "scouts" or "spotters" or "locators" conducted palm cruises in older, poorer neighborhoods. After buying large specimens for low prices, they flipped them to new homeowners in the Irvine-like neighborhood near La Jolla known as the Golden Triangle. More than once, brokers uprooted rows of palms from municipal streets in San Diego County, disingenuously claiming legal permission.[20]

The trendiness of fronds, and the iconic stature of the L.A. fan palm, could be measured by imitation. In 1987, shortly before the stock market crashed, the World Financial Center, a commercial real estate complex in Lower Manhattan with tenants such as Lehman Brothers, added a final floral touch to its Winter Garden, an extravagant atrium within a luxury mall that boasted views of the Twin Towers on one side and the Hudson on the other. New York's largest "public" indoor space after the main concourse of Grand Central Terminal, the Winter Garden contained a square array of sixteen 45-foot-tall Mexican fan palms. The project architect praised "the subtle interplay between architecture and vegetation." His "living columns" came from Borrego Springs, California.[21]

WILTED CROWNS

The ability of Los Angeles to maintain its allure came into doubt in the 1990s. A full century of promotion and growth had stretched the city to the limit. As of the 1990 census, Greater Los Angeles, a five-county metro complex, burst at the seams with 14.5 million people, roughly half of the state's residents. Los Angeles County alone contained 8.9 million, one-third of them foreign-born. One of the most diverse cities on the planet, the so-called capital of the Third World, Los Angeles was an inspiring social experiment when it worked. When it didn't, the metropolis seemed to portend America's disunited future. The 1992 riots—a week of unrest following the acquittal of white LAPD officers who had been videotaped beating black motorist Rodney King—put a wrench in the L.A. promotion machine. TV cameras broadcast images of young black men attacking symbols of white authority as well as of Latinos, Koreans, and African Americans clashing with each other in shared neighborhoods. Rioters overturned cars, ransacked businesses, and started fires. Just hours after the verdict, the writer Lisa Alvarez saw a teenager pouring gasoline onto the base of a palm near LAPD headquarters. Alvarez remembers speaking out in defense of the plant as the boy reached for his matchbook: "'Listen, lady,' he says, leaning close. 'It's not a real tree. It's a fake one. They're all fake.' He swings his arms toward the city trees that stand at attention in their little plots of dirt. 'They shouldn't be here. I'm taking this one out. Don't worry. It'll be all right.'" This palm, and many others, burned like giant matchsticks that evening. "In a matter of chaotic hours," opined the city's newspaper, "the image of Los Angeles was transformed from palm trees and movie stars to burning buildings and looters." Ad agencies claimed solemnly that the value of the L.A. brand had been seriously compromised.[22]

A run of bad luck followed the Rodney King uprising: 1993 brought winter floods followed by the worst fall fire season on record. To cap it off, the Northridge earthquake of January 1994 caused financial losses in the billions, killed more than sixty, left some 25,000 home-less, and reinjured the city's psyche. (The scandalous O. J. Simpson trial of 1994–95 didn't help.) In the wake of sequential disasters, peo-ple left Los Angeles in unprecedented numbers. They relocated in the face of unemployment, natural disaster, smog, crime, traffic. The good life of the sunny Southland seemed increasingly inaccessible. A national recession lingered in the region because of closures of Cold War military bases and cutbacks in aerospace defense contracts. In this time of stress, California voters passed Proposition 187, an initia-tive designed to deny all social services to illegal immigrants.[23]

To the surprise of many, the Golden State's stock rebounded within a few years. As the millennium approached, the California Dream metastasized with the technology and real estate sectors. Even shop-ping centers in unsexy Fresno decided to splurge on L.A.-style palms. Palm delivery trucks made repeat trips to booming San Jose and the high-tech campuses of Silicon Valley. The landscaped trees denoted irrational exuberance. Realtors and real estate speculators went back to work with advanced financial instruments, such as subprime mortgages. No land was deemed unfit for McMansions with palms. Incredibly, the megalopolis known loosely as L.A. now extended not just to adjacent coastal areas but up and over the Transverse Ranges to Antelope Valley, the rim of the Mojave Desert. More than a few commuters drove luxury Hummers.

In the Coachella Valley, the date palm industry lost and gained ground during the housing bubble of the early 2000s. As sleepy desert towns such as Cathedral City and Palm Desert morphed into country

club communities for snowbirds, growers pulled out of the northern
part of the valley. Some went out of business; others regrouped and
started new orchards in the southern end of the valley, near Mecca
and Thermal, out of the (current) development zone. Major growers
interpreted the move as a win-win: with profit from selling their land
and their older, less productive trees, they could set up larger orchards
with younger, more productive ones. An 80-foot-tall date palm is past
its prime and expensive to harvest. As a landscaping element, however, a palm of such height commands a tall price. With Las Vegas
casinos driving the market, growers determined that any date palm
over 30 feet made more money on a flatbed truck than in the ground.
Many reconceived their business as short-term agricultural production and long-term ornamental production. They harvested fruit and
fashion.

The real estate racket in Vegas brought forth a landscape of gro-
tesqueries. In the blink of an eye, a gambling town became a resort
metropolis. Leveraged by big banks, dozens of themed casinos rose
from the desert floor, each more spectacularly and proudly ersatz than
the last—Thebes, Venice, Paris, New York. Sin City developers used
fan palms for glitzy effect. "It's phenomenal. It's just unbelievable,"
said one landscaper in 1997. "Every project that we're doing requires
palm trees." Vegas seemed intent on outdoing Hollywood and Disneyland as dreamlands and supplanting Los Angeles as the entertainment capital of the world. The city redesigned and beautified Las
Vegas Boulevard, including the Strip, with thousands of fan palms.
Developers added full-height palms to their already extravagant golf
courses, fountain plazas, and lake resorts. To meet the demand, tree
brokers scoured the entire Southwest for exceptional specimens. They
could buy for $1,000 and sell on delivery for ten times more. Casi-
nos, including one called the Palms, outbid other institutional buyers.
"Vegas has priced just about every municipality out of the market,"
said the chief forester of Los Angeles in 2004.[24]

When the global finance system seized up a few years later, thousands of residents of Southern California and Clark County, Nevada,

defaulted on homes with palmy views. Some desperate homeowners, behind on their mortgages, tried to cash in their yard palms. During the Great Recession of 2007–2009, the owner of a palm nursery in San Diego got so many telephone calls from prospective sellers that he composed a special page on his company's website. People "often think they are sitting on a gold mine," he wrote. He dismissed the "urban legend" of the palm tree sold in Las Vegas for a small fortune after being snapped up by a palm broker for a pittance.[25]

Of the common species, the only palm with high resale value was Canary Island date palm. The price, already high because of size and beauty, rose higher owing to disease and mortality. Palms are not especially long-lived; ornamental specimens of most species cannot be expected to last more than a century. In general, palms fall victim to molds and fungi rather than bacteria and viruses. The worst pathogen so far is a variety of fusarium wilt (a fungus) that attacks Canary Island date palm. It arrived in California in the 1970s and became a major problem in the 1990s. The going price for a mature tree ($2,500) doubled, then quadrupled, as the fungal epidemic spread. Garden crews unwittingly spread the wilt with frond cutters and grass trimmers before they made it standard practice to sterilize the tools. The disease took months or years to run its course, but the outcome was always fatal. Older leaves turned yellow, then a desiccated brown, often in irregular patterns, before the whole crown finally wilted or fell off. The decapitating fungus persisted in the soil for several years, negating the possibility of replanting the same species. The worst-hit neighborhoods included some of the wealthiest—Capistrano Beach, Corona del Mar, Beverly Hills. In Los Angeles, the loss of Canary Island date palms in neighborhoods such as Hancock Park affected the popular Sukkot giveaway. The "frond frenzy" had become so successful by 1990 that the city set a hundred-item limit and required people to preorder through a Jewish temple. After years of declining supply, the city ended the tradition in 2007. The sense of uncertainty about the future of Canary Island date palm in Southern California deepened in 2010, when the California Department of Food and

Agriculture announced the discovery of red palm weevil, an invasive species from Southeast Asia—the "world's worst pest of palm trees."[26]

The simultaneous decline of eucalypts and palms gave Southland cities the opportunity to rethink the urban canopy. When selecting species for street planting, arborists make scientific calculations along with fiscal and aesthetic judgments. The ideal tree, in addition to being disease-resistant, drought-tolerant, and low-maintenance, provides "ecosystem services" such as atmospheric filtering, pollution sequestering, noise muffling, rain absorption, and shade. Utility companies like trees for bringing down the temperature of large cities, thereby protecting the power grid. The urban heat island in Los Angeles is the worst in the United States. Vast tracts of exposed pavement absorb heat from the inescapable sun, raising the ambient temperature, motivating people to activate air conditioners, thereby creating more heat and more pollution. For temperature abatement, Mexican fan palms perform poorly, for they cast precious little shade. As of 2006, the canopy coverage for Los Angeles was around 20 percent (compared to a calculated national average of 27 percent for urban areas and 33 percent for metropolitan areas). Merely by excluding a handful of leafy neighborhoods like Brentwood and Sherman Oaks, L.A.'s ranking dropped much lower.[27]

To address the problem, Antonio Villaraigosa, Los Angeles's first Mexican-American mayor since 1868, announced in 2006 an initiative called Million Trees L.A. The mayor dubbed Los Angeles the "dirtiest big city in America." He pledged to add a million new trees to public property with the help of cooperating agencies, businesses, community groups, individual volunteers, and nonprofits such as TreePeople. The mayor portrayed the initiative as a matter of social justice as well as smart growth. The distribution of shade and greenery in metropolitan Los Angeles almost perfectly overlapped the distribution of wealth. Rich cities such as Santa Monica, Beverly Hills, West Hollywood, and Pasadena enjoyed dense urban canopies, as did neighborhoods on the tony west side of Los Angeles. The canopy cover in Bel Air, for example, exceeded 50 percent. In stark contrast, the city's poor areas—South Central, East L.A., and the eastern San Fernando Valley—baked in the sun. Council District 15, a long, thin area from Watts to the harbor, contained less than 10 percent canopy coverage. In conjunction with Million Trees L.A., the representative of District 15, Janice Hahn, proposed that the bureau of street services should review its practice of species selection. Palms are "technically a type of grass and not trees," her motion said. The councilwoman sought to limit the use of tall palms. She singled out Mexican fan palm as "not optimal." Although an "emblematic part of Los Angeles," the species provided few of the benefits required of the modern urban street tree; it should be phased out in favor of more manageable and "more aesthetic" queen palm and king palm.[28]

The city council considered Hahn's motion in late 2006 and passed it two weeks later. The international media hyped and mangled the story. Confusing the wilt-afflicted Canary Island date palm with all species, the Associated Press misreported that "the city's palm trees—as much a symbol of L.A. as the automobile, movie stars, and the beach—are vanishing." The *New York Times* stated dramatically that Los Angeles had "declared them [palms] the enemy of the urban forest and wish that most would disappear." News outlets throughout the world uncritically repeated such claims; in the echo chamber of the Internet it became conventional wisdom overnight that the "symbol of Los Angeles' laid-back lifestyle" was headed for the chopping block for being an "urban menace." Letter writers and bloggers erupted. *Would Nike phase out its trademark Swoosh? Would Paris remove the Eiffel Tower?* Barraged with questions, Los Angeles issued clarifications. "The story wasn't true," said a council member. "We're not getting rid of our palms. We still love our palm trees." Most reporters missed key details: the council had addressed only fan palms (not all palms) and had even issued an exception to its "discouragement" (not ban) on that type of tree. Mexican fan palm was just fine where "it would be consistent with existing plantings in the area or specifically requested by a Council office or community group." In other words, iconic streets such as Sunset Boulevard and Hollywood

Boulevard would not get a makeover. Tourists would continue to see palms where they expected to see palms.[29]

Landscape designers in Southern California also signaled their ongoing commitment to palms as features of gateways and gathering places. The new Grand Park (2012) near Los Angeles City Hall uses fronds liberally. Privatized civic spaces such as Universal City-Walk (1993, expanded in 2000), Downtown Disney (2001), and the Hollywood & Highland Center (2001) likewise show off palms. The complex in Hollywood (including a new home for the Academy Awards, the Dolby—formerly Kodak—Theatre) succeeded in gentrifying a designated tourist zone. The adjacent palm-lined Hollywood Walk of Fame began to attract more trinket dealers than drug peddlers, much as Times Square mutated from a seedy adult district to a corporatized fun zone. Downtown Los Angeles also turned a corner in the opening decade of the new millennium; ahead of Grand Park, the city added loft apartments, a supermarket, the Cathedral of Our Lady of the Angels (2002), Walt Disney Concert Hall (2003), boutique and luxury hotels, and the "entertainment campus" known as L.A. Live (2007–2010). Located next to the Convention Center, L.A. Live accommodates a limited number of palms, strategically located. Whenever TV camera operators broadcast the Grammys or the NBA playoffs from the adjacent Staples Center, they turn to these well-placed trees for framing shots. Similar telegenic palms can be found at the Rose Bowl, the Coliseum, Angel Stadium, and, of course, Dodger Stadium. In the camera's misleading gaze, fan palms seem to be everywhere in the metropolis.

After each victory, the Dodgers and the Lakers blast over the loudspeakers Randy Newman's "I Love L.A.," just as the Yankees play Sinatra's version of "New York, New York." Newman's song begins by mocking New York's weather, then moves on to celebrate L.A.'s automobile landscape. When the narrator, driving a convertible with a redhead by his side, talks about the view of trees, there's no question what kind of trees he means. (The video for the song shows a row of Canary Island date palms.) The song comes from an album called

Trouble in Paradise (1983), and the bouncy tune conceals a hard edge. The lyric ends with a call and response: Newman shouts the name of a street, and the public replies, "We love it!" The streets in question are not sexy like Rodeo Drive. Instead, Newman sings the praises of Sixth Street, which passes through East L.A., and Century Boulevard, which passes through Watts. Such unglamorous neighborhoods sport some of the most impressive trees in the metropolis. Improbably tall Mexican fan palms line the sidewalks of bungalow streets in middle-class and working-class neighborhoods in the vast area of the city (mis)labeled South Central. Although palms are numerically less prevalent here than in Beverly Hills, they have much greater visibility given that no other foliage occupies the upper view frame. Motorists on the 105 and 110 freeways can't miss these skydusters on their way to or from LAX. The bursts of green floating above the concrete sound barriers constitute everything most visitors, and most white residents, will ever see of neighborhoods where millions of Latinos and African Americans live, work, and tend their yards.[30]

Regardless of their actual ubiquity, palms impart a metropolitan sense of place. They have persisted as symbolic landscape features through many transformations of the city since the 1870s, while other symbols have declined or been turned upside-down. A region once promoted for its perfect air, its placid climate, and its cohesive white Protestant populace is now popularly imagined as a smoggy urban wasteland of natural disaster and social disunion. Even if you love L.A., there's no guarantee that your city will look the same ten years from now. In 1975 the *Los Angeles Times* editorialized on the importance of palms in the context of obsolescence: "We have lost Angel's Flight, the Big Red Cars and the Chili Bowls. We have lost most of the grand old Victorian mansions on Bunker Hill and the baroque theaters and office buildings in the downtown district. We have lost the monstrous horse-heads pumping oil all over town. We have lost the mountains to the smog, the citrus groves to the bulldozers." Los Angeles retained precious little, grotesque or uplifting, to give itself a peculiar identity, wrote the editorial board. Only the tall palms remained. They had outlasted and outgrown the arboreal competition, the shade trees from the pioneer period. As late as 1941, the writers of the Work Projects Administration, in their famous guidebook series, described an urban arboreal trio: "Three kinds of trees—palm, eucalyptus, and pepper—against stucco walls and red tiles, are as characteristic of Los Angeles as are the elms and maples above the white frame farmhouse of New England." Today few Angelenos can see, much less identify, a pepper tree. Some of the last great specimens from the nineteenth century succumbed to smog in the 1960s. Relict eucalypts are more noticeable, but the gum scene overall has greatly receded. Innumerable eucs capitulated to postwar developers, and more recently to drought, insects, winds, and city crews under advisement from lawyers.[31]

Mexican fan palms have fared better. Long after Los Angeles stopped adding them systematically, the old municipal plantings grew more and more prominent. The even rows from the early automobile era reached epic height by the Reagan years, becoming iconic skyline features. As the trees hit 80 or 100 feet, becoming some of the tallest palms in the world, the city morphed beneath them. Vacant lots filled in. New freeways gutted old neighborhoods. In southeast Los Angeles, near the intersection of the Harbor and Santa Monica freeways, the city's oldest fan palm allée, the once-famous Avenue of Palms from postcards and promotional views, persisted amid development. A portion of the double row survived because long ago it had been incorporated into the courtyard of the fenced-in Orthopaedic Hospital. Motorists leaving the 110 at Adams Boulevard, a formerly posh, now dilapidated neighborhood, look up at this orphaned floral ornament from the 1870s.

In an ocean of change, old palms act as visual and historical beacons. They connect the Spanish, Mexican, and American periods. They occur along the entire cross-section of the metropolis: in rich and poor neighborhoods, on the seaside, on the flats, in the hills, at the mountain front. They manage to look Californian next to red-tiled civic buildings, redwood bungalows, modernist houses and office

towers, concrete sound barrier walls, and taco trucks. In a city disparaged for its shortage of communal space, a tall *Washingtonia* functions
something like public property, a row of skydusters something like
public art. Festive residents wrap lights on their sidewalk fan palms
at Christmas. Beyond that, it's hard to say what utility a 100-foot-
tall fan palm—a trunk without branches or leaves—provides for any
individual owner. However, by tending the plant, the owner preserves
a visual amenity for countless thousands of fellow Angelenos who see
the crown lit up at sunset. Almost on par with the mountains and
the Pacific, the altitudinous Mexican fan palm unifies this city of
fragments.

Pessimists argue that L.A. long ago jumped the shark, that
the "most advertised city in the world" fell victim to its own self-
promotion. Los Angeles may be a lot nicer than most places, but the
gap between promotional paradise and urban reality—the abiding
subject of L.A. literature—has widened over time. "My colleagues
and I always were looking for the perfect Los Angeles logo, a singular image to evoke the city in all its wonder and misery," wrote a
Times editor in 1992. "We tried out a lot of them, but never did we
do better than a palm tree with bullet holes." The crime fiction writer
Jonathan Kellerman has spoken of "the whole southern California
thing, what I call the malignance behind the palm trees: where you
have the beautiful weather and ambience but there's always a sinister
evil lurking." Fairly or not, Los Angeles has gained infamy for its
failed school system, its skid row, its gridlock and gang violence. The
frontier of boosterism has moved to other regions, where derricks still
suck oil from the earth. To experience newfangled palms, one must
visit Dubai, the Las Vegas of Arabia. In the shallows of the Persian
Gulf, the desert emirate has attempted the kind of preposterously
bold real estate project that L.A. boosters of old would have lauded.
In 2001, at the height of the global real estate mania, Dubai began
construction on the first of three palm-shaped archipelagos. The first
one, Palm Jumeira (finished before the credit crunch forced changes
to the project), accommodates Babylonian mansions on gated, palm-

lined streets. The outline of the megapalm can be seen with Google Earth—or from the observation deck of Burj Khalifa, the tubular skyscraper that claimed the title of world's tallest structure.[32]

If Dubai's Palm Islands represent the future of urban design, Los Angeles should consider itself lucky to be left behind. Perhaps a more livable, more organic city will yet emerge from the horizontal concrete grid. With enough smart infill and enough mass transit, Los Angeles might even become a model urban village center. If a palm tree can symbolize most anything desirable, why not this: a new, better city?

THE PLASTICITY OF TREES

By now it should be clear that a California palm tree is not just a plant. It is a signpost. It conveys at least three layers of meaning: the particular significance of California; the more general category "palm"; and the generic category "tree." People may enhance the signification through architectural placement or cosmetic trimming of the organic form. But the tree-as-signpost doesn't even have to be organic; California palm trees come in a variety of synthetic and artistic forms.

Most dictionaries define *tree* as a large, perennial, single-trunked, woody plant. This is misleading, for a palm tree contains no wood. Botanists themselves do not bother to distinguish trees from non-trees. Instead, they divide plants into more precise categories, such as angiosperms (flowering plants) and gymnosperms (nonflowering). Angiosperms comprise two diagnostic types, monocots and dicots. Monocots, including palms, are less complex than dicots. They develop from a single embryonic leaf, have basic flowers and no secondary growth (wood). The rootstock is adventitious, meaning that the underground shoots develop independently; the tree has no radicle, or primary root. The simplicity of monocots enhances their agricultural tility. As crops, they supply us with essential carbohydrates—think bananas, yuccas, and edible grasses (rice, wheat, maize, cane). From a botanist's point of view, a palm is not so different from a giant stalk of grass.

Cut though a palm and look inside: you see no grain, no growth rings. Instead the cross-section resembles a fiber-optic cable. The trunk consists of hundreds of tubes bundled together in a pattern, packed tightly at the edge and loosely at the center. A peripheral ring of rigid (lignified) tissue in combination with a flexible core creates incredible tensile strength. Like fishing poles, palms can bend over almost to the ground without snapping. This is how they survive hurricanes when woody trees collapse. Unlike, say, an oak, a palm tree doesn't increase in diameter each growing season. The trunk achieves maximum girth in the first few years—the establishment phase. In the words of one horticultural guide, a palm is "overbuilt mechanically and hydraulically when young in anticipation of future support requirements."[33] After completing its outward growth, the tree only increases upward; it doesn't add a single vascular bundle to its girth.

The future of the plant depends on one active lead, the meristem. If the meristem gets damaged, or if the crown falls off, the palm dies. Each new frond—a megaleaf—emerges sequentially from the same place, shooting upward in closed position, then slowly unfurling, like an umbrella. Most fronds on tree-sized palms take one of two general forms. The *palmate* leaves on a fan palm resemble an origami fan; the *pinnate* leaves on a feather palm resemble an oversized ostrich plume, with leaflets attached to a midrib. Whatever the shape, the frond consists of three parts: the blade (containing all the leaflets), the petiole or stem, and the sheath or leaf base. Protected by a thick cuticle, fronds may persist for years; they are the longest-lasting as well as the largest leaves in the plant kingdom. On fan palms, the used-up, dried-out fronds may hang around for many additional years, forming a thick mat that goes by several playful names—skirt, beard, shag. Beneath and below the skirt, the trunk has no bark, simply a tough rind. A palm blackened by fire will stay black. Lacking vascular cambium, it cannot heal from surface damage. Nothing on a palm regenerates.

The base of an old trunk resembles the leg of a circus elephant, with cracked, furrowed skin. In another sign of old age, the adventitious roots may cause basal swelling and burst through the outer rind like a mess of worms.

Never mind Webster's; palms do count as trees. The best definition of *tree* is simply a single-trunk plant filled with human meaning. Trees are floral organisms we honor as individuals, as analogies to humans. A bonsai tree may be tiny, but it has the proportions and character of emblematic megaflora, so we call it a tree. As a symbolic category, treeness varies somewhat from culture to culture. In many indigenous languages of the tropics, palms do not count as trees. In European languages they typically do. When a singular nonwoody plant looms large in the landscape, or in the imagination, the only fitting English word is *tree*. Does it matter that Joshua tree is a yucca? Should it matter that saguaro (a dicot) has no leaves? Tree ferns, dragon trees, bananas, bamboos, pandans, and certain agaves are examples of monocots that have, like palms, earned honorific arbo-reality. Like cetaceans and marsupials in the mammalian kingdom, palms are ambiguous organisms that challenge categorization. Not all palms can be called trees, but many palms appear more treelike than the woody plants called shrubs or bushes.[34]

In the wild, desert fan palms typically cluster in close stands where the frond litter piles up thick—a scene too messy to be called a grove, too compact to be called a forest. In California's cities, ornamental specimens look very different; their arborescence has been enhanced through wide, uniform spacing and heavy grooming. The normative trim depends on the species and the fashion. Today palmskinners usually leave a small beard on a California fan palm but rarely on a Mexican fan palm. In Palm Springs, the city gives palms on Palm Canyon Drive, the main drag, a distinctive look by trimming the ends of the full skirts straight across, like a hemmed garment—what arborists formerly called the "petticoat style." Because of their simple morphology, single-species rows of palms can be turned into uniform aesthetic statements. City street tree divisions even provide diagrams of trees to pruners; these architectural drawings specify angle requirements and crown coverage. The prevailing aesthetic calls for heavy grooming. In 1926 a Southern California gardener criticized the "passion—shall I say a perverted passion—for artificial neatness [that] inspires most people to shave the trunks of the accumulation of dead foliage and leave them naked to the elements." In Riverside, in contrast, it was historic practice to leave the petioles on fan palm trunks, creating a spiky texture and a wicker pattern. But by 2006 the "booted" style seemed shabby and old-fashioned, and the city slicked its palms over the protests of preservationists. Throughout California, it became fashionable in the 1990s to buzz-cut the lower branches of Canary Island date palms to expose the "pineapple"—the bulbous shape formed by the leaf bases on the crown—and to sand the trunk to a finish reminiscent of brushed steel.[35]

The relationship between style and morphology begins when the plant goes in the ground. Landscapers set in palms geometrically, at angles, in pairs or clusters. Dwarf palms arranged like bouquets of flowers can be seen in many medians. In Beverly Hills, Palm Springs, and Las Vegas, one commonly finds fan palms planted together in a *V* shape. As the paired trees grow, they straighten into inverted bowlegs. Palms can also be placed contiguous to buildings at an acute angle—with cable supports, if necessary—to produce dramatic shadows and interesting lines. As a garden critic once complained, a slanted palm looks "more like a tipsy playboy than a prince."[36]

The look of a palm tree requires a lot of invisible human labor. Trimming palms is among the most hazardous jobs in Los Angeles—riskier than patrolling the streets as a police officer or answering emergencies as a firefighter. Imagine being harnessed to a 1-foot-wide trunk 40 feet in the air, using a chainsaw to release heavy fronds armored with sharp edges and barbs. Nesting rats, scorpions, or hawks may attack you from the crown. Most dangerously, the dead fronds may have self-detached. When you tug on one, the whole woven mass—the "frond ring"—may slough off, collaring your body to the trunk, asphyxiating you by pushing your chin into your chest, if not choking you with released dust. Using bucket trucks or mobile cranes is much safer, albeit costlier. Municipal governments enter into contracts with licensed crews for trimming jobs, but private homeowners typically hire the cheapest climber, who may be unskilled, untrained, undocumented, and uninsured. A vocation once performed by middle-class Japanese Americans was turned over to immigrant Mexicans in the last quarter of the twentieth century. In Southern California between 2000 and 2010, over a dozen palm-skinners died on the job, men with surnames such as Guadarrama, Galvez, Valdez, Velázquez, Hernández, and Rodríguez.[37]

Over the twentieth century, palms in California moved from the realms of horticulture and urban forestry to those of architecture and urban design. Planners and builders can treat palm trees like mass-produced construction material because of their simple root system. Unlike a woody plant with a radicle, a mature palm can be popped out of the ground, laid on an eighteen-wheeler, and relocated as the market demands. For this reason, palm nurseries must guard against thieves in the night. A root ball of a 1-foot radius usually suffices to keep a 60-foot-high fan palm alive. Rare, valuable specimens might be bought, sold, and moved multiple times in their lives. Members of the common species are fungible; nurseries raise them in standardized containers. Like orchids, palms can be precisely monetized. When an ornamental palm dies, a replacement of the same height and same look can be delivered in days. These organisms might as well be plastic. They can be planted and transplanted almost at will; they can be ordered in bulk for street delivery; they can be trimmed and groomed to design; they can be harnessed to buildings, lifted onto rooftop patios. Landscaping with palms is the only way to instantly achieve a mature treescape.

In many parts of the world, the utility of palms as a source of food and cooking oil far exceeds their symbolic value. But in North America, almost all the cultivated palms—the exception being date palms in the Colorado/Sonoran Desert—are grown for their ornamental and semiotic appeal. They have monetary value as carriers of human meaning; they add amenity value to real property. Like programmed music in a shopping mall, palms perform commercial work on a subliminal level. Even the most botanically illiterate person registers a palm tree. In silhouette or from a great distance, its shape is immediately recognizable. The palm lends itself to photography and graphic design, and its iconic shape shows up again and again in ad campaigns for hard liquor and beach tourism. Since at least the Victorian era, landscapers and advertisers have used palms to signify a core set of desirables: sunshine, leisure, and affluence.

Palms don't even need to be organic or living to fulfill their symbolic function. Consider the prefabricated embalmed palm, a Golden State innovation. An Orange County company called Nature Preserved began "building" palm trees in 1984. Its patented process is ingenious. The company immerses trimmed fronds in a preservative; with coaxing, the cells in the fronds exchange their natural fluid for the synthetic fluid, which contains green dye and a color fixer. The treatment suspends decay. As the company says, it's the real thing, just no longer alive. The limited-warranty trees can keep their shape and feel for up to a decade. Workers create a simulacrum by installing preserved fronds on top of a vertical support (made of fiberglass, steel, or plastic) covered with pieces of real palm rind—usually Mexican fan palm because it's easy and cheap to obtain from the waste trimmings of local growers. For commercial real estate owners committed to palms, preserved trees may represent a significant long-term cost savings. Modular and lightweight, they can be installed in no time without a crane. They can be customized to fit any space. Undead flora requires no trimming, watering, heating, or lighting and no load-bearing floors with drainage. Occasional dusting suffices. The constructed trunks are seismically fit, and the embalming material contains a fire repellent, meaning the trees meet all building codes. The trunks can even accommodate surveillance cameras, an advantage in Las Vegas. Nature Preserved got its breakthrough job in 1989 contributing some two hundred fan palms to the "tropical rainforest" atrium at the entrance to the Mirage, the first of the Vegas megaresorts. Later clients included the Luxor, Mandalay Bay, and the Las Vegas International Airport. Under its new corporate name, Preserved TreeScapes International, the California tree-building firm has shipped preserved palms to climate-controlled casinos, cruise ships, hotels, airports, and malls all over the world, including a number of projects in the United Arab Emirates. The company, now based in San Diego County, offers both "botanically correct" palms and fantasy palms with curvy trunks and mix-and-match floral parts from different species. To withstand outdoor conditions such as those for rooftop bars, PTI recently introduced a line of purely fabricated replica palms cast in metal from molds of trees.[38]

Another kind of fake palm, the cell-phone tree tower, entered the mass market in the nineties, starting in Southern California. Cell-phone coverage increased exponentially after 1996, when the Telecommunications Reform Act prohibited local governments from using health concerns to block out cell-phone companies. However, cities could still regulate the placement and look of towers. Concealment technology, also called "stealthing," appeared first in wealthy coastal areas where zoning laws or community standards precluded conventional utility poles. Pines and palms are the two most common "genera" for stealth poles. The zoning commissioner of Los Angeles, a veteran of many NIMBY battles, became infatuated with the idea of palm towers while riding the Jungle Cruise at Disneyland. Not surprisingly, some of the companies that went on to produce tree towers also did work for theme parks. Turning a relay tower into a presentable palm can double or triple the cost, and many companies at first cut corners. Early models looked bizarrely stiff, upright, and angular. In isolation, such a 60-foot metal "palm" called more attention to itself than a regular utility pole. A city planner for San Diego, having seen plenty of bad examples, learned to pose demanding questions to commercial applicants, right down to the "species" of tower and type of frond. "We don't want people driving by saying, 'Look at that fake tree,'" she said in 1999. "We want it to blend in so that nobody notices it at all." To meet the demand, suppliers began offering metal and plastic fan palms with skirts of dead fronds or sculpted growth balls that mimicked the pineapple look created by overzealous pruners. Top-end models came with fronds made from molds of real plants. It became good practice to place stealth towers in combination with organic palms. From a distance, they blend in quite well. Despite these improvements, some amenity-rich communities prefer true concealment—placing antennae within steeples and so on. "We don't do fake trees," sniffed a city planner in Santa Barbara.[39]

Palm trees exist in pure artistic form, too. The simple shape of a fan palm can be converted into design, like the logo of California Pizza Kitchen, more easily than that of most trees. Along the 91 freeway, bas-relief palms decorate the concrete noise barriers. Drive to Venice Beach and you will see fan palms on every kind of trinket, T-shirt, and souvenir for sale on the boardwalk. As graphics, their silhouettes appear endlessly on billboards and movie posters. Drawing inspiration from the generic and the commercial, Ed Ruscha reduced L.A. palms to their stylistic essence in his limited-edition art book *A Few Palm Trees* (1971), which consisted of blocked-out photographs—nothing but gray-scale trunks and fronds on plain white paper—above small-print text identifying the street location. Ruscha's photographs look like headshots or mug shots, or both. Another famous Pop artist, David Hockney, first found renown for his acrylic paintings of Los Angeles pool scenes. His most reproduced canvas, *A Bigger Splash* (1967), shows, in addition to the eponymous splash, a pair of stylized fan palms above a modernist house whose glass walls permit views of distant urban palms. Today palmy Pop art can be seen every day on California's freeways. When the state authorized the special California Arts License Plate in 1994—a fund-raiser for arts programs—it commissioned Wayne Thiebaud to create the image. The celebrated painter answered the request with an image of an orange sun setting into the ocean by a beach lined with palms.[40]

Los Angeles's two major art centers exhibit oppositional relationships with popular culture and palm landscaping. The Getty Center (1997), home of the J. Paul Getty Trust, the wealthiest museum in the world, lacks palms altogether. Fronds would seem lowbrow at the Brentwood acropolis, devoted almost exclusively to Continental art. As designed by Richard Meier, the Getty's Italian travertine buildings are airy yet earthy, grounded yet flowing. The garden, designed by Robert Irwin, has perennial flowers and deciduous trees that change with the seasons. Down in the flats, the Los Angeles County Museum of Art brashly celebrates fronds. "The palm tree has become a powerful cultural object, an iconic image that has drawn legions of people to a beguiling version of paradise," gushes LACMA's youthful director. The museum complex takes up a block on Wilshire Boulevard's Miracle Mile, a former department store district once advertised as the "Fifth Avenue of the West," where groupings of fan palms rise out of the median. For the 2008 opening of a new contemporary art pavilion, LACMA commissioned Robert Irwin (the same Irwin who worked for the Getty) to create a courtyard sculpture garden composed of living palms. Irwin went around the country collecting specimens from brokers, collectors, and growers. "You realize you can buy a great tree—I mean a *great* tree—for, like, five thousand dollars," Irwin said. "And to do a sculpture on the scale of that would cost more than five thousand dollars just to put the foundation in." Irwin and his collaborator Paul Comstock spoke of "curating" and "hanging" the potted palms. "We tried to create a museum collection of palm trees much like visiting a Picasso art show," explained Comstock. To enter LACMA visitors pass through a permanent installation of more than two hundred vintage Los Angeles cast-iron light poles ("Urban Light" by Chris Burden) arranged in rows of uniform height, like palms on a street grid. The utility poles date to the 1920s and 1930s, the heyday of the fan palm. At night, the installation illuminates the rows of fan palms that border the buildings at LACMA. Side by side, the palms and the poles announce their shared dual status as aesthetic infrastructure and infrastructural art. No other city would create a public art space like this. No other plant could perform such labor.[41]

BEYOND L.A.

When a California palm tree occurs outside its "natural habitat"—the concrete streets of the southern coast, the canyon oases of the Colorado Desert—people may react with ambivalence or resistance. Many Californians beyond L.A. object to the local presence of fronded trees because they associate this floral type with "Los Angelization."

California's normative palm zone does not perfectly align with the mild weather zone. Fronds look fine in Shasta Lake, the northernmost city in the sun-drenched Sacramento Valley, but at the same latitude, in mild but foggy Humboldt County, palm trees look "wrong" in the midst of redwoods. Most people feel the same cognitive dissonance when they encounter "tropical" palms (actually cold-tolerant varieties) in Washington State and British Columbia. At first glance, it seems bizarre to see "L.A." plants in Seattle and Vancouver. Palms somehow belong in Sacramento, but somehow don't in the foothills of the Sierra Nevada, a short distance to the east. Placerville, located between Sacramento and Lake Tahoe on U.S. 50, lies beyond the psychic palm curtain. The issue came up when California's most beloved fast-food chain, In-N-Out Burger, came to town. Since 1970 this Southland company has for one of its corporate logos used two palms at crossed angles—X marks the spot, in homage to the film *It's a Mad Mad Mad Mad World* (1963). (The company also prints graphical palms on cups and containers.) At almost all its locations, In-N-Out has made the logo real by planting pairs of fan palms, often yoked together for cross-support. Because Placerville's municipal landscaping plan did not allow palms at business addresses, the city denied In-N-Out's tree permit. Some years later, a local manager for the restaurant went ahead and installed the missing botanical logo. Alerted to the infraction, the city council voted in 2006 that the restaurant had to remove the nonnative trees. Community standards trumped brand identity. Palm trees looked too much like L.A. and the OC for this historic Gold Rush town.[42]

Palms grow quite well in the Bay Area, to the surprise of many first-time visitors. It's easy to forget that San Francisco sits at a latitude below the Mason-Dixon Line. It may not be particularly warm in winter, but neither is it cold. In fact, the city may feel warmer in January than July; midsummer, the tourist season, brings fog. "The coldest winter I ever spent was a summer in San Francisco," Mark Twain supposedly said. Another quip, this one attributed to W. C. Fields, contends, "San Francisco is the only place where you can freeze to death while sitting under a palm tree smelling your roses." The hilly city encompasses various microclimates, formerly called "banana belts" and "pneumonia gulches." When Haight-Ashbury bathes in fog all day, the Castro may well soak in the sun.[43]

San Franciscans today have a love-hate relationship with palms. In former times, love prevailed. As the financial and commercial capital of Gilded Age California, the City by the Bay possessed the money and the pretension to carry out showcase plantings of palms before Los Angeles did. In 1894 the city welcomed visitors to the California Midwinter Fair, the brainchild of M. H. de Young, co-owner of the *San Francisco Chronicle*. As we have seen, the exposition transported a large portion of the palmy state exhibit from the previous year's world's fair in Chicago. To supplement the foliage, fair organizers took out ads in local newspapers asking gardeners to donate mature palms for the cause of boosterism. The fairgrounds, built in the eastern part of Golden Gate Park, became known as Palm City. The trees signified warmth and wealth during the winter of America's worst economic depression to date. A contemporaneous gift to the city, the Sutro Baths—the giant pleasure dome built by a millionaire former mayor—featured fronds along its grand staircase. Around the turn of the century, the city set Canary Island date palms along one side of Union Square, the hub of the shopping and theater district. Nearby, the city's most exclusive hotel, the Palace, vaunted its enclosed palm garden. On Nob Hill, the address of business tycoons, the president of the Contra Costa Water Company paid for the transport of a 56-foot-tall palm all the way from Los Angeles in 1903. One of the hill's mansion owners, Leland Stanford, former senator and governor (and president of Southern Pacific), also owned a sprawling ranch on the San Francisco Peninsula. When the Palo Alto Stock Farm became Stanford University in the 1880s and 1890s, Senator Stanford and his landscape architect, Frederick Law Olmsted, laid out a grand entrance, Palm Drive. The avenue led to the Main Quadrangle, which featured palm groupings and the imposing Memorial Church with its mosaic of Jesus sermonizing to the multitudes under palms. All in all, the Bay Area as of 1900 contained more professionally landscaped fronded trees than Los Angeles County.[44]

In the earthquake and firestorm of 1906, San Francisco lost many of its best houses and trees. It never regained its position as California's leading city. But it did rebuild, and did so with a palmy flourish. After the temblor, downtown replanted *Phoenix* palms at the corners of the redesigned Union Square. At the city's northern waterfront, the Panama-Pacific International Exposition of 1915 showed off the phoenix-like rebirth of the city. This wonderland of façades (of which only the Palace of Fine Arts remains) was adorned with countless eucalypts and five hundred mature transplanted palms. After going through the main entrance, visitors—some 19 million total—walked down the Avenue of Palms on their way to the Horticulture Palace. John McLaren, the superintendent of Golden Gate Park, oversaw the landscaping. His agents traveled throughout the Bay Area collecting 20- to 40-foot-high palms donated by private owners. When the fair shut down, the city redistributed the trees to locations such as Dolores Street. San Francisco carried out one last prewar palm-planting project in 1939–40 to mark the completion of the Golden Gate Bridge and the Bay Bridge. The Golden Gate International Exposition, built on the specially constructed Treasure Island, featured an obligatory Palm Avenue.[45]

Treasure Island marked the end of an era. From the 1940s through the 1970s, while the *Washingtonia* of Los Angeles grew taller and the Southland metropolis grew bigger, San Francisco's palm landscape withered. Palms didn't even make the list of approved street trees when the department of public works founded a tree-planting division in 1955 to rectify the dearth of shade in the city. San Francisco's streets were (and still are) remarkably shade-free for a major American city (not counting the major afforestation projects at Golden Gate Park and the Presidio). Guidebooks of the late nineteenth century called it "the treeless city." "The streets here are barren & beeless & ineffably mud[d]y and mean looking," complained John Muir in 1879. "A Eucalyptus bush on every other corner, standing tied to a painted stick . . . may help heavenward a little, but how little amid so muckle downdragging mud!" The paucity of greenery can partly be attributed to the position of the city on a sandy peninsula with limited water and strong wind. Also, since the summers were "unpleasantly cool, the people want all the sunshine obtainable, and dislike trees which obstruct the solar rays," explained one guide. In this context, pioneer-era palms at prominent locations such as Nob Hill appeared even flashier.[46]

A comeback for palms began in the 1980s. First came plantings of Canary Island date palm at institutions such as the San Francisco Zoo, San Francisco State University, and the University of San Francisco. The palmy revival became a resurgence in the 1990s, the onset of the second gilded age, when the coffers of San Francisco grew in tandem with the Internet technology sector. Flush with cash, the city added Canary Island date palms around the intersection of Market and Castro to complement the revival of the historic F streetcar. Most impressively, the city transformed the look of the Embarcadero. The 1989 Loma Prieta earthquake created an opportunity to dismantle the unsightly double-decker elevated freeway at the bay shore. The city now wanted a historic-looking promenade—vintage streetcars and lampposts, views of the bay—without the historic sights and smells of the old working waterfront. The most distinctive element of this New Urbanist redevelopment plan took a page, ironically, from car-crazed Los Angeles: a double row of evenly spaced fan palms lining the median.

The $1 billion beautification project begged for controversy. Francis Violich, an emeritus professor of planning at UC Berkeley, called the proposed palms "incongruous, incompatible and monotonous," a "slenderized, resurrected version" of the freeway columns that would "imprison" waterfront views like "bars of a giant cage." Comment letters flooded the department of public works during the "great palm fracas" of 1992. Tree haters engaged in proxy L.A. bashing. Palms suggested crassness, trashiness, vulgarity, narcissism, shallowness. They would make refined San Francisco look like *Bay Watch, Miami Vice*, or *Hawaii Five-0*. Stop the Los Angelization of the Bay! Concurrent to the Embarcadero controversy, residents of the wealthy Marina District, the former world's fair site, defeated a separate project, already funded, to plant Mexican fan palms. When representatives of the Mission, a poor neighborhood dominated by Latinos, heard about these unwanted palms, they put in a successful request at city hall and happily added the "offensive" trees to their streets.[47]

More often than not, the forces of arboreal gentrification beat out the forces of arboreal snobbery. In 1995 San Francisco added several species of palms to the list of approved street trees and proceeded to set specimens at designated urban gateways. Private enterprise extended the palm revival. In 2000 the San Francisco Giants opened their new red-brick ballpark at the end of the redesigned Embarcadero. Landscapers placed twenty-four mature Canary Island date palms in the stadium's plaza, 24 being the jersey number of Hall of Fame center fielder Willie Mays. The bayside ballpark, like the promenade, was a popular success. The fracas abated. The 2-mile-long Embarcadero with over two hundred tall palms—something like a sanitized version of Ocean Boulevard in Santa Monica—looked charming, at least until fusarium wilt started to disinvigorate the trees.[48]

Ambivalence about palms crops up in Southern California, too. Many towns outside Los Angeles would rather not be associated with L.A. For example, in 1995 the city council of Santa Clarita objected to a developer's plan to landscape a Mission-style shopping center with date palms. City ordinances allowed palm as "accents" but not as "dominant features." "This is a Tree City USA, which means we plant trees here, trees with leaves or needles," said a councilwoman. "Palm trees provide no shade, no air; they do nothing." The city's arborist agreed: "Santa Clarita is more known for canopy-type trees. It's an identity thing." Local controversy accompanied Pasadena's recent removal of its signature rubber trees, relicts of a past fashion trend, from its main commercial street, Colorado Boulevard, in favor of trendy fan palms and ginkgoes. (Before the ficus, the featured tree was queen palm; traditions don't last long, even in Pasadena.) In 2008, when Whittier finalized plans to renovate and beautify its uptown district, it ruled out palms. "We want a Midwest downtown feel," said one planning commissioner. "I think people when they see palm trees interpret it as Hollywood, Sunset Boulevard, west side of Los Angeles or a more hip Beverly Hills type of feel."[49]

Certain Southland towns honor palms as signifiers of local heritage unrelated to Los Angeles. In Orange County, La Palma and Orange have recently planted palms in an attempt to restore the historic look of their commercial districts and revive business. In Redlands, rows of tall fan palms—the boundary lines of former citrus orchards—stand as reminders of past affluence. Of California cities, probably only Beverly Hills boasted more palms per mile of road than Redlands in its glory days. In the post-citrus era, Mexican fan palm assumed the role of emblematic tree. At city hall's insistence, the developers of Citrus Plaza, a shopping center that replaced an orange grove, installed hundreds of palms as landscaping. As the final groves go on the real estate market, Redlands tries its best to relocate historic palms to other locations. But only so much public money can be spent on old trees. Unfortunately, many of Redlands' palms reach such heights—100 feet and up—that they threaten to interfere with high-voltage electric lines. State law requires that trees growing within 18 inches of power lines be trimmed, topped, or removed.[50]

Just a few miles away, in the mountain-front city of San Bernardino, palms have radically different associations. Despite being one of the oldest settlements in California, San Bernardino does not have old money. The city entered a tailspin following the 1994 closure of a nearby air force base. Downtown is a wreck. Only the wealthy hillside neighborhoods look like advertisements of the California Dream. This section of San Bernardino became antipalmist after the Old Fire of October 2003 destroyed hundreds of mountain-front homes. Fan palms turned into flamethrowers as Santa Ana winds lofted burning fronds hundreds of feet into the air. In the aftermath, San Bernardino banned palms for landscaping new homes in the designated hazard zone; it gave away city-owned street palms to any tree brokers who would take them; and it offered incentives to residents to remove palms from their yards. Never mind that the city's own logo featured a palm tree under a blazing sun. "They are just giant matchsticks as far as I am concerned," said the councilman representing the foothills. He dismissed the palmy associations with Hollywood and tropical paradise as passé.[51]

In fact, fronds can reference a wide variety of California motifs—not just Hollywood but the Citrus Belt, the semi-tropics, the Mediterranean, the South Pacific, Mission Revival, modernism, futurism. At well-designed sites such as Fashion Island, palm plantings stay on message; at lesser sites such as the Grove, the trees telegraph identity crisis. Here on Beverly Boulevard in Los Angeles, a perimeter of tall fan and date palms announces a high-class mall, yet the retail space is designed to be a pedestrian-only "main street" (accessed via parking garage), complete with deciduous trees. Compounding the floral confusion, potted palms and cycads adorn store entrances. Developers in Southern California, a region that values self-invention and self-promotion, just can't kick the palm habit. As one horticultural expert has said, "No other plant can produce an automatic response in a person to say: 'I'm somewhere different. I've changed. I'm a new man.'" In 1995 LAX opened a new control tower whose shape was meant to evoke a palm. "The [airport] wanted a real civic monument that symbolizes one's arrival and departure from Los Angeles," said one of the lead architects. Loudly aspirational buildings as different as the Hearst Castle near San Simeon, the Mormon temple in San Diego, the Crystal Cathedral in Orange County, and the Church of

Scientology Celebrity Centre International in Los Angeles have all turned to live palms for landscaping. It does not seem coincidental that both of California's big-time private universities, Stanford and USC—two institutions with highly entrepreneurial cultures—have spent a small fortune on palm landscaping. A palm-lined entrance drive with cycling and jogging lanes would look frivolous at most of the world's top research universities, but it fits at Stanford, a school that has always emphasized the pursuit of bodily perfection through outdoor recreation.[52]

For California "establishing shots," cinematographers reflexively turn to fronded trees. Billions of people who have never visited the Southland have consumed cinematic images—stylized, idealized, sensationalized—that include palms in the frame. "I remember the palm trees in Los Angeles," said a teenaged Michael Jackson. "When we moved there, from Gary [in 1969], my brothers and I had never seen a real palm tree before, only on television."[53] Many scenes meant to telegraph "Hollywood" or "L.A." are actually Beverly Hills streets such as Beverly Drive and Doheny Drive, palm allées that aren't even representative of Beverly Hills. In the 1940s and 1950s, whenever a medium- or low-budget film required a shot of an airport with palms, cameramen went to the Long Beach Municipal Airport. (This stopped in 1957, when the trees were removed as a safety precaution.) On film, the "L.A. palm" may signify any number of desirables. In surfer movies and in *Baywatch*, the world's most popular TV show of all time, the trees suggest sunshine and sex. On Oscar night and in reality shows, palms proclaim glamour. In sit-coms and serials like *Beverly Hillbillies* and *Beverly Hills 90210*, they signify new money. The passive, cumulative effect of thousands of cinematic productions set in L.A. has cemented the correlation between metropolis and palm. This Hollywood impact is both impossible to measure and impossible to overstate.

Out on the streets, the same trees that proclaim "L.A." make it harder for Hollywood to portray other places. Greens crews work to create "ND" (nondescript) vegetation out of the city's floral riot. They strip the fruit from exotic trees; they add fake bark and leaves to the trunks of palms. Cinematographers choose angles that exclude palms, editors crop them out, and if necessary, special-effects engineers digitally remove them. "You can shoot Anywhere, U.S.A., here, as long as you avoid palm trees," said a location manager. "That's our biggest bane, the palm tree, because if you see it, it's either Southern California or Florida." Websites devoted to exposing film goofs list dozens of Hollywood productions ostensibly set in cold temperate cities where palms can be seen fleetingly in the background, revealing the Oz-like artifice. Fillmore, a picturesque town in the lemon-growing Santa Clara River Valley of Ventura County, looks something like an idealized midwestern town, except for the king palms lining Central Avenue. "Fillmore would do the film industry a tremendous favor by letting them buy up those palms and replace them with something less Southern Californian," said one location scout. "Palm trees are our nemesis."[54]

At this point, the *idea* of the L.A. skyduster is more robust than the city's actual plantings, which are old and impermanent. The tall Mexican fan palms literally cannot be replaced with equivalent trees. Over the decades, all the nursery stock of *Washingtonia robusta* has to some extent hybridized with *W. filifera*. (Some nurseries sell a cultivar with the cheeky name *filibusta*.) As a result, none of the young trees available for purchase will reach as high as the original sidewalk rows. To achieve such verticality, one would need to collect seeds from wild trees in the Sonoran Desert of Mexico, grow them, and wait a century. Los Angeles contains scanty midheight fan palms to succeed the old plantings on the skyline. The city's baby boom generation did not create a palm succession system. The essayist Rochelle Gurstein confesses that "for a long time now, whenever I've gone to Los Angeles, I've been alarmed by how impossibly tall the palm trees have grown." The trees dwarf everything, and the sight fills her with gloom. Her "sense of foreboding" comes from the "perfect uniformity of their extreme height," meaning they came into being at the same time and that they will, along with the author's generation, pass away as a group. Already the palms "barely share the world with us," and soon they will be gone.[55]

Almost all of the skydusters lean southward, pulled by the angle of the sun, pushed by the Santa Ana winds. Many of the city's tall Mexican fan palms curve so much that their fronds fly above the median rather than the sidewalk. Suspended above the grid, catching the last rays of the sun, their greenery appears to float on air. People have compared such trees to Q-tips, lollipops, chicken feet, flagpoles, mops on handles, shrubs on trunks, pompoms on telephone poles, Spanish exclamation points, fireworks shooting into the sky, Dr. Seuss drawings, and triffids. In *City of Night*, a formative novel about the gay underground, John Rechy described "long, long rows of phallic palm-trees with sunbleached pubic hair." With their anorexic trunks and plucked crowns, they match the look of so much prospective talent trying to make it in Hollywood. They are both "fabulous and phony-looking," to quote Jack Smith.[56]

By 2050 Southern California's tallest and most impressive palms will be located in Orange County and the Inland Empire. Los Angeles will become even more horizontal as it loses countless palms— perpendicular axes. In vertical cities such as São Paulo and Hong Kong, such street palms never would have become visible in the first place. It's not that Los Angeles ever possessed so many palms; rather, its built environment was ideal for seeing *Washingtonia* palms. Plant surveys in the 1980s estimated that palms accounted for only 2 percent of all floral species in the urbanized Los Angeles Basin and less than 1 percent of the areal vegetative cover. In a more recent study of street trees, Mexican fan palm accounted for just 7 percent of Los Angeles's total, despite being the second most common species. The space that palms take up in the urban imagination is way out of proportion to the space they take up on the urban street. But air space is a different matter. The quantitative measure of tree canopy cover does not take into account visual prominence or vegetative verticality. The palm-studded skyline of Los Angeles is otherwise unoccupied except for the movement of searchlights, police helicopters, and the endless line of jet planes lining up for their descent into LAX. Unlike the palmettos of Charleston, South Carolina, which grow to just the right size for three-story Colonial double houses, airborne Mexican fan palms look fantastically out of place in a low-profile city. Jean Baudrillard, in his oblique travelogue *America*, pronounced that Los Angeles is "in love with its limitless horizontality, as New York may be with its verticality." The gaze of the French theorist fixed on the "long-stemmed palm trees, swaying in front of the electronic billboard, the only vertical signs in this two-dimensional world."[57]

There simply isn't much architectural competition. For a city so large and important, contemporary Los Angeles offers few landmarks instantly recognizable to the masses. Number one is the Hollywood sign, a leftover, truncated advertisement for a real estate development called Hollywoodland. Few buildings make the list. Most of the city's great architectural sites are private homes. Before Walt Disney Concert Hall (designed by Frank Gehry), only a handful of edifices achieved iconic status, including Grauman's Chinese Theatre, City Hall, and Griffith Observatory. The modern skyline of downtown Los Angeles has become somewhat recognizable by virtue of media overexposure, but the skyscrapers on Bunker Hill could not be more unremarkable. Besides downtown and the west-side commercial neighborhood Century City, Los Angeles contains few tall buildings, period. In films and TV shows about Los Angeles, the most distinctive landmarks are actually linear strips: Sunset Boulevard, Mulholland Drive, the beach, and above all the multilane freeway with its multilevel exchanges. Like the L.A. palm row, the L.A. freeway is generic and linear. Both features—the two greatest design elements of the twentieth-century metropolis—lend themselves to cinematic viewing. To convey the essence of Los Angeles, filmmakers turn again and again to tracking shots of these two lines of lines, one horizontal, the other vertical. Another cinematic cliché, something that passengers landing in LAX after sunset can watch live from cabin windows, is the gigantic flat illuminated power grid, the mother of all motherboards. In the priceless words of director Roman Polański,

"There's no more beautiful city in the world . . . provided it's seen by night and from a distance."[58]

Without tall palms swaying in the onshore breeze, the horizontality of the city seems generic, fungible, almost devoid of content to many outsiders and newcomers. In his iconoclastic appreciation of Los Angeles, the architectural critic Reyner Banham divided the city into zones; of these, the central suburbs, "great plains of Id," appeared most daunting because they were "Anywheresville/Nowheresville." If it weren't for the "occasional palm-tree," the townscape would look just like "Kansas City or Denver or Indianapolis," he wrote. This formulaic comparison has now been around for almost a century. The great bandleader Hoagy Carmichael remembered getting this advice upon his arrival in Southern California: "Kid, it's just Newark, New Jersey, with palm trees." Similarly, Bob Hope referred to the San Fernando Valley as "Cleveland with palms." (Hope came of age before the Rust Belt.) After wartime and postwar growth and immigration, and after the riots of 1965 and 1992, the comparison shifted to troubled inner cities: "Detroit with palm trees" or "South Bronx with palm trees." "I hated being in Los Angeles," said the singer of the veteran New York garage rock band the Fleshtones. "It was appalling, an amorphous mess of suburban sprawl, like some endless Long Island with palm trees and taco stands." Easterners miss the point: Los Angeles is supposed to be anything you want to imagine with palm trees. No wonder that Katy Perry, a SoCal pop star who revels in her own self-referential artificiality, wore skin-tight minidresses with sequined palms and printed palms while promoting her single "California Gurls," which went on to reach #1 on the *Billboard* Hot 100 in summer 2010.[59]

Even though Los Angeles will lose its distinguishing skydusters— its best skyscrapers—the city will not lack for fronded trees anytime soon. They are too popular, too pliable. Palms have been able to survive multiple transformations of the metropolis and multiple turns of the fashion cycle because they are horticulturally and symbolically plastic. They can be planted, uprooted, and replaced at will. They accommodate a variety of positive associations. One of the finalists for California's 2005 commemorative U.S. quarter-dollar tried to pack the state's leading emblems into one small circle—the Golden Gate Bridge, the Hollywood sign, redwoods, and palms. Millions of people have seen such an artificial mash-up in real life at Disney California Adventure in Anaheim. As long as the Golden State has enterprises in the business of selling paradise, palms will remain fixtures. It is a matter of image maintenance as much as landscape maintenance. Unlike eucalypts and citruses, formerly integral, now quaint, parts of the Southland landscape that have been systematically displaced, palms manage to feel contemporary; they fit with the urban street and the entertainment and information economies.

If Los Angeles were to experience a cataclysm—and Hollywood has depicted many possibilities, including earthquakes, volcanoes, killer insects, evil aliens, and criminal gangs—at least one palm species would persist. *Washingtonia robusta* has so far proven resistant to fusarium wilt and most other palm diseases. Like the coyote, this trickster tree has naturalized in urban habitat. Its robustness is phenomenal. All over the city, you see fledgling Mexican fan palms growing in the cracks of sidewalks, on the gravelly edges of roads, in the tangle of plastic bags at chain-link fences. They take root in the waste spaces, the no-man's-lands between freeways and behind warehouses. By some miracle, tiny fronds, electric green, push up through caked asphalt in parking lots. As one columnist remarked, only Mexican fan palm has this "junkyard-dog quality." The species shows up on weed lists; conservation biologists consider it moderately invasive.[60]

Until recently, one of the most amazing places in Los Angeles was a grove with no name. It grew at the narrows of the Los Angeles River, where the streamlet moves from the San Fernando Valley to the coastal plain through a gap in the Elysian Hills. On the south side of the narrows, a brownfield—a former railyard—is slowly being remade into Rio de Los Angeles State Park, a much-needed recreational resource for a park-poor neighborhood, the linchpin of an ambitious plan to turn the concrete river corridor into a greenway. Near the tracks, beyond a broken barbed-wire fence, below a levee, roughly eighty Mexican fan palms stood tall and straight. Seeds from street trees in the Valley had floated down municipal drains and taken root at the narrows, one of two stretches where the straitjacketed stream, designed by the U.S. Army Corps of Engineers to flush floodwater out to sea, accumulated enough sediment to support riparian life. The scene was beautifully incongruous. Critics of Los Angeles often use its river as the symbol of nature's death in the city.[61] Hollywood comes to the desolate ditch to capture scenes of murder and mayhem, apocalypse and alienation. But filmmakers never come to the narrows, which shelters egrets and herons—and Mexican men casting lines for fish. Except for the concrete walls, the graffiti, the abandoned shopping carts, and the high-voltage transmission lines, the palm grove here resembled a natural oasis in a desert canyon. Fronds rustled in the breeze; their shadows played on the levee. When I visited in 2010, the scent of smoke coated the air: these towering palms had endured a recent fire, probably arson. They nonetheless looked healthy and strong. When I returned in 2012, all but two of the mature palms had been chainsawed to stumps. Teenagers played paintball among plastic trash and arboreal debris. Despite the clear-cutting, numerous seedlings remained. The "invasive species" persisted. Along with the adaptable immigrants who presently mow the lawns, rake the leaves, clip the shrubs, and trim the trees of metropolitan Los Angeles, the indomitable Mexican fan palm will surely be around for the city's next tomorrow.

Epilogue

IN 1848 TWO EVENTS CHANGED CALIFORNIA FOREVER: THE conquest of Mexico and the discovery of gold. Taking the view from the tree canopy, I have chronicled some of the long-term consequences of this seismic shift. I narrated how migrants to the Golden State marveled at the primeval forest landscapes of the Sierra Nevada and North Coast and devised new ways to exploit and preserve indigenous megaflora. Then I showed how American newcomers, in their attempts to realize the California Dream—and to rectify the profligacy of the Gold Rush era, including wasteful use of sequoias and redwoods—cultivated a profusion of nonnative flora in parts of the state that seemed woodless. Proponents of the horticultural movement believed that by increasing and diversifying the tree cover of the Far West, they were forcing the spring of a new civilization. The great homegrown philosopher and historian Josiah Royce, a product of the Gold Rush era, praised tree planting and climate for encouraging the development of the "somewhat Hellenic type" on the Pacific Coast. In 1900, writing from his post as professor at Harvard, Royce rearticulated the horticultural dream of county life in California: "Very readily, if you have moderate means, you can create your own quiet estate at a convenient distance from the nearest town. You may cover your house with a bower of roses, surround yourself with an orchard, quickly grow eucalyptus as a shade tree, and with nearly equal facility multiply other shade trees. You become, on easy terms, a proprietor, with estate and home of your own."[1]

The florescence of nonnative plants in California correlated with the subjugation of certain native species. People noted this inversion at the time. In 1854, on the first page of the first issue of California's first farm journal, the editor James Warren, a forty-niner from Massachusetts, published a memorial to Congress asking for an agricultural college. The state's pacific environment presented an opportunity, declared Warren, "hitherto unknown, or granted to anyone in the civilized world." He foresaw the fulfillment of manifest destiny in floral terms: barren hillsides soon to be covered by vines and figs, and, in concomitant manner, "many a towering mountain, upon whose lofty summit now stand, in all their pride and glory, those giants of the forests, that like that wonder of the age, 'the Mammoth Tree,' the woodman will no longer spare, these too must give place to that onward march of the Anglo-Saxon race, o'er mountain, hill and valley, and marking its progress onward along the Pacific, by civilization, cultivation and christianization, even till it reaches and penetrates China."[2] Today at the ports of Los Angeles and Oakland one can see a blemished version of this prophecy fulfilled: Chinese supertankers offloading electronics and plastics and taking on scrap metal, used cardboard, and the occasional container box of wine and oranges.

Of the myriad kinds of trees propagated by the millions in nineteenth-century California, eucalypts, citruses, and palms had the most significant, long-lasting effects. Each arboreal type transformed the state in one or more major realms—aesthetics, economics, semiotics. These trees also worked together. Falcate foliage, orange blossoms, and fronds operated for many decades as mutually supportive symbols of the "Sunny Southland"; together this floral triumvirate made an indelible impression on visitors. A typical reaction came from the pen of Charles Augustus Stoddard, a noted Presbyterian minister and the editor of the *New York Observer*, who took a western winter trip in a sleeper train in 1893. Writing with a mixed tone of wonderment and irony, Stoddard recalled waking up to the sound of hard, cold rain:

An Orange Ranch.

We were in California, in the midst of the wonderful orange groves of Riverside, which have no equal in the world. Piles of oranges lay on the ground as far as the eye could see through the vistas of the orchards. The trees were laden with the golden fruit. Huge eucalyptus trees in full and fragrant flower, palms of all sorts, vegetation rank and rich and green, and all the more impressive from the desert dream from which we woke to this wonderful reality, was all about us. This is California, the land of gold, the paradise of climates, the home of health, the retreat for the aged who would live forever, and for the invalid who dreads to die.[3]

Pioneer evergreens manifested fertility and plenitude, but they did not, in the long run, exemplify another environmental quality attributed to California: longevity. The towering rows of aromatic gums have receded from farms and highways; Riverside's solid gold orange groves have tarnished; L.A.'s celebrity sidewalk palms have begun their exit from the stage. Consider, too, the Santa Clara Valley, the erstwhile "garden of the world." Once renowned for apricots, cherries, and an endless supply of prunes, the area around San Jose is now universally known as Silicon Valley, home of Apple. In the biblical sense, *Trees in Paradise* narrates creation *and* expulsion. It lays out multiple long-term failures of the U.S. horticultural movement. Recall how eucalypts went from being symbols of conservation, health, and domesticity to symbols of folly, hazard, and invasion. Or how citrus growers abandoned the ideal of diversified plots in favor of monocultural plantations. Or how palms, despite being championed by middle-class home gardeners and urban foresters, primarily became instruments of property developers and tourism promoters.

A few critics were always cynical about the Golden State's floral exuberance. In 1905 Henry James, an inveterate Atlanticist, made a report to his sister from San Diego. California "has completely bowled me over," he wrote, "such a delicious difference from the rest of the U.S. do I find in it. (I speak of course all of nature and climate, fruits and flowers; for there is absolutely nothing else, and the sense of the shining social and human inane is utter.) . . . I live on oranges and olives, fresh from the tree, and I lie awake nights to listen, on purpose, to the languid list of the Pacific." By the Depression era, the fruitful landscape no longer appeared so placid. In *The Grapes of Wrath,* John Steinbeck described "the little golden oranges on the dark green trees; and guards with shotguns patrolling the lines so a man might not pick an orange for a thin child, oranges to be dumped if the price was low." Over time, more and more people came around to Joan Didion's view, expressed in *Slouching towards Bethlehem* (1968), that citrus foliage is "too lush, unsettlingly glossy, the greenery of nightmare; the fallen eucalyptus bark is too dusty, a place for snakes to breed." Didion wrote as a native daughter, but her pessimism was positively un-Californian. True believers always anticipate that the California Dream will survive, revive, adapt. Who knows, it may even outlast the forest landscapes that inspired it and the horticultural landscapes it inspired. Ideologies adapt to disturbance better than most plants.[4]

Those betting against the Golden State may point to climate models. Even without the wild card of anthropogenic carbon emissions, climate history is not on California's side. Dendrochronologists have compiled a sequoia tree-ring chronology going back nearly four thousand years. According to the growth rings, the period from 1850 to 1950—California's first century as an American state—had the lowest frequency of drought for any hundred-year period in the past two millennia. In other words, American horticulturists got very, very lucky. They arrived just in time for the milk and honey. A similarly prolonged wet period is not likely to recur anytime soon—though if it did, it might begin abruptly, like a step instead of a ramp. Tree-ring scientists have learned from giant sequoias that the "transition from almost drought-free periods to those of very frequent extreme droughts has, on occasion, occurred almost as a step-function"—that is, a revolutionary regime change.[5]

Using advanced techniques, climatologists have recently created a gridded dataset of tree-ring chronologies from various drought-sensitive species all over western North America. These networked data point to past instances of subcontinental "megadrought." Even the worst dry spells in recorded California history pale next to the years 936, 1034, 1150, and 1253 CE, all of them part of an epic period of desiccation lasting from approximately 800 to 1300, a regional effect of the so-called medieval warm period. According to scholarly consensus, this megadrought contributed to the breakdown of ancestral Puebloan societies in the Southwest—the people who abandoned Chaco Canyon and Mesa Verde.[6]

Could California decompose? In the nineteenth century, the remains of the Spanish missions fascinated Americans. "It seemed to be gradually going to ruin and decay," recalled a Yankee sailor of his 1843 visit to the mission outside Monterey, the Mexican capital of Alta California. "The adobe walls, that inclosed [sic] a small garden, which must have been very handsome when the priests were a power in the land, were falling apart, and but few flowers and little fruit could be seen, where once there was an abundance of both."[7] After the U.S.-Mexican War and the Gold Rush, Californians created their own garden on a much larger scale in the lowland enclosure bounded by the mountains and the sea. Here some future people may discover a vast horticultural ruin—the skeletons and stumps of millions of fruiters. If tomorrow the "Big One" were to strike, if torrents or terrorists were to destroy major levees, dams, or aqueducts, lowland California's position as the cornucopia of North America would almost instantly change. Without an elaborate reclamation infrastructure to divert snowmelt from the Sierra and the Rockies to fields, orchards, and cities, large areas of the Golden State would regress to a weedy savannah. Even without a slow or sudden disaster, population and resource pressures may someday force semi-arid cities such as Los Angeles and San Diego to phase out water-thirsty trees and adopt xeriscaping. The biogeographic legacy of the horticultural movement will not last forever.

The creation of the garden of California was a miracle for plants and insects; for animals, it was a holocaust. In order to implant the flowering groves and floral suburbs of the Central Valley, the Santa Clara Valley, the Salinas Valley, and Greater Los Angeles, reclamationists drained millions of square miles of wetlands ("tule lands"), filled in countless vernal pools, and captured entire rivers—dammed them, siphoned them away, lined them in concrete. Critical habitat vanished along with liquid topography: Tulare Lake is gone; Owens Lake has become a dry, dusty salt pan; just over the border, in Mexico, the delta of the Colorado River is a parched ecological disaster. By reallocating mountain streams, Americans destroyed the marsh habitat of fish, amphibians, and water-loving mammals, not to mention millions of migratory wildfowl on the Pacific Flyway. The former treeless landscape of lowland California, like the prairie of the Great Plains, quaked with animals.

Today California is the only U.S. state that flies a flag that calls attention to faunal extinction. The emblem of the short-lived Bear Flag Republic was retained after the Gold Rush and annexation; the "great California bear" or the "biggest bear in America" suggested that everything in the Golden State was outsized. Settlers reflexively associated the California grizzly, an endemic subspecies, with the Big Tree. An exceptionally massive, gnarly specimen in Mariposa Grove—the most photographed sequoia of the nineteenth century, and the one most often called the oldest tree in the world—became known as the Grizzly Giant. The animal metaphor did not inspire mammalian empathy. The first guardian of the grove, Galen Clark, aimed his rifle at any bear that dared to pass his way. In the Sierra Nevada, loggers who cut sequoias sometimes propped ursine carcasses on stumps for posed photographs. Throughout California, Gold Rush settlers caught grizzlies for gladiatorial bear-and-bull fights or for traveling menageries and ruthlessly killed them with traps. The "king of bears" didn't stand a chance. In 1914 the Boone and Crocket Club, whose membership overlapped with those of the American Bison Society, the American Council for the Conservation of Whales, and the Save-the-Redwoods League, called for the preservation of "the Sequoia of the animal kingdom in America." By then the final museum trophy had already been taken. The last reported California grizzly sighting occurred in 1924 in Sequoia National Park. The Grizzly Giant now looms over a depauperate forest.[8]

Extinction lasts forever; nothing else does. The tree rings of sequoias remind us that individuals, nations, even whole civilizations may flower and perish during the life of a single California plant. The longevity of the state's introduced gums, citruses, and palms is more comparable to a human's duration. By considering both time scales, we can better appreciate the landscape Americans cultivated in California—its beauty, its penalty, and its fragility. Growers themselves were astonished by what they had wrought. "We expected to find a tropical country," recalled Charles Collins Teague, long-serving president of the California Fruit Growers Exchange and overseer of the largest citrus ranch in the state. "I am not sure, but I rather think we expected to find monkeys climbing through the trees. At least we expected to find tropical vegetation, and we were not prepared for the brown hills that confronted us, which we have since learned to love, nor for the absence of trees."[9]

Trust the horticulturist: California's genius may be green, but its underlying beauty is brown.

Common and Scientific Names of Species

PLANTS

Acacia	*Acacia* spp.
American chestnut	*Castanea dentata*
Bamboo	*Bambusoideae* subfamily
Banana	*Musa* spp.
Bermuda grass	*Cynodon dactylon*
Bougainvillea	*Bougainvillea* spp.
Bristlecone pine	*Pinus longaeva*
Bull thistle	*Cirsium vulgare*
Bushy yate	*Eucalyptus lehmannii*
California bay	*Umbellularia californica*
California fan palm	*Washingtonia filifera*
California incense-cedar	*Calocedrus decurrens*
California sycamore	*Platanus racemosa*
Canary Island date palm	*Phoenix canariensis*
Cassava	*Manihot esculenta*
Citron	*Citrus medica*
Citrus	*Citrus* spp.
Coast live oak	*Quercus agrifolia*
Coast redwood	*Sequoia sempervirens*
Coastal scrub oak	*Quercus dumosa*

Coconut palm	*Cocos nucifera*
Common wild oat	*Avena fatua*
Coral gum	*Eucalyptus torquata*
Coyote brush	*Baccharis pilularis*
Curry tree	*Murraya koenigii*
Dandelion	*Taraxacum* spp.
Date palm	*Phoenix dactylifera*
Dawn redwood (Chinese redwood)	*Metasequoia glyptostroboides*
Douglas fir	*Pseudotsuga menziesii*
Dwarf blue gum	*Eucalyptus globulus compacta*
Elm	*Ulmus* spp.
English ivy	*Hedera helix*
English (European) yew	*Taxus baccata*
Eucalyptus	*Eucalyptus* spp.
Flooded gum	*Eucalyptus rudis*
Forest red gum	*Eucalyptus tereticornis*
Fremont cottonwood	*Populus fremontii*
French broom	*Genista monspessulana*
Giant sequoia (Big Tree)	*Sequoiadendron giganteum*
Ginkgo	*Ginkgo biloba*
Golden wattle	*Acacia pycnantha*
Grevillea	*Grevillea* spp.
Ice plant	*Carpobrotus edulis*
Interior live oak	*Quercus wislizeni*
Jacaranda	*Jacaranda* spp.
Jarrah	*Eucalyptus marginata*
Joshua tree	*Yucca brevifolia*
Kentia palm	*Howea forsteriana*
King palm	*Archontophoenix alexandrae*
Kudzu	*Pueraria lobata*
Lebanon cedar	*Cedrus libani*
Lemon-scented gum	*Corymbia citriodora* (formerly *E. citriodora*)
Magnolia	*Magnolia* spp.

Malunggay	*Moringa oleifera*
Mandarin	*Citrus reticulata*
Manna gum	*Eucalyptus viminalis*
Marijuana	*Cannabis sativa*
Mediterranean fan palm	*Chamaerops humilis*
Mexican fan palm	*Washingtonia robusta*
Mexican (key) lime	*Citrus aurantifolia*
Monterey cypress	*Cupressus macrocarpa*
Monterey pine	*Pinus radiata*
Montezuma cypress	*Taxodium mucronatum*
Mottlecah	*Eucalyptus macrocarpa*
Mountain ash	*Eucalyptus regnans*
New Zealand cabbage tree	*Cordyline australis*
Norfolk Island pine	*Araucaria heterophylla*
Orange jessamine	*Murraya paniculata*
Osage orange	*Maclura pomifera*
Palmetto (cabbage palm)	*Sabal palmetto*
Palmyra palm	*Borassus* spp.
Pampas grass	*Cortaderia selloana*
Pepper tree	*Schinus molle*
Periwinkle	*Vinca major*
Pindo palm	*Butia capitata*
Pomelo	*Citrus maxima*
Ponderosa pine	*Pinus ponderosa*
Potato	*Solanum tuberosum*
Queen palm	*Syagrus romanzoffiana*
Red-flowering gum	*Eucalyptus ficifolia*
Red ironbark	*Eucalyptus sideroxylon*
River red gum	*Eucalyptus camaldulensis* (formerly *rostrata*)
Rose mallee	*Eucalyptus rhodantha*
Rubber tree	*Ficus elastica*
Sagebrush	*Artemisia tridentata*
Sago palm	*Metroxylon sagu*

Saguaro	*Carnegiea gigantea*
San Francisco lessingia	*Lessingia germanorum*
Scotch broom	*Cytisus scoparius*
Silver dollar gum	*Eucalyptus polyanthemos*
Silverleaf mountain gum	*Eucalyptus pulverulenta*
Sugar gum	*Eucalyptus cladocalyx* (formerly *corynocalyx*)
Sugar pine	*Pinus lambertiana*
Swamp mahogany	*Eucalyptus robusta*
Tamarisk (salt cedar)	*Tamarix ramosissima*
Tanoak	*Notholithocarpus densiflorus*
Tasmanian blue gum	*Eucalyptus globulus*
Tumbleweed (Russian thistle)	*Salsola tragus*
Vetch	*Vicia* spp.
Walnut	*Juglans regia*
Western hemlock	*Tsuga heterophylla*
White fir	*Abies concolor*
White ironbark	*Eucalyptus leucoxylon*
Windmill palm	*Trachycarpus fortunei*
Wine grape	*Vitis vinifera*
Yellow pine	*Pinus* spp.

INVERTEBRATES

Asian citrus psyllid	*Diaphorina citri*
Black scale	*Saissetia oleae*
Callippe silverspot butterfly	*Speyeria callippe callippe*
Citrophilus mealybug	*Pseudococcus calceolariae*
Citrus whitefly	*Dialeurodes citri*
Cottony-cushion scale (white scale)	*Icerya purchasi*
Eucalyptus longhorned borer (ELB)	*Phoracantha semipunctata*
Glassy-winged sharpshooter	*Homalodisca vitripennis*
Gypsy moth	*Lymantria dispar*

Lemon gum psyllid	*Cryptoneossa triangula*
Mediterranean fruit fly (medfly)	*Ceratitis capitata*
Mexican fruit fly	*Anastrepha ludens*
Mission blue butterfly	*Icaricia icarioides missionensis*
Monarch butterfly	*Danaus plexippus*
Red gum lerp psyllid	*Glycaspis brimblecombei*
Red palm weevil	*Rhynchophorus ferrugineus*
San Bruno elfin butterfly	*Callophrys mossii bayensis*
Teredo (shipworm)	*Teredo navalis*
Vedalia beetle (cardinal ladybird)	*Rodolia cardinalis*

VERTEBRATES

Bald eagle	*Haliaeetus leucocephalus*
Bison	*Bison bison*
Brown tree snake	*Boiga irregularis*
California grizzly	*Ursus arctos californicus*
Cane toad	*Bufo marinus*
Coho salmon	*Oncorhynchus kisutch*
Coyote	*Canis latrans*
Double-crested cormorant	*Phalacrocorax auritus*
European rabbit	*Oryctolagus cuniculus*
Great blue heron	*Ardea herodias*
Great egret	*Ardea alba*
Great horned owl	*Bubo virginianus*
Marbled murrelet	*Brachyramphus marmoratus*
Nile perch	*Lates niloticus*
Northern spotted owl	*Strix occidentalis caurina*
Passenger pigeon	*Ectopistes migratorius*
Red-tailed hawk	*Buteo jamaicensis*

PATHOGENS

Blossom blight	*Colletotrichum* spp.
Blue mold	*Penicillium italicum*
Chestnut blight	*Cryphonectria parasitica*
Citrus blast	*Pseudomonas syringae*
Citrus greening (huanglongbing or HLB)	*Candidatus Liberibacter* spp.
Citrus gummosis (foot rot)	*Phytophthora* spp.
Dutch elm disease	*Ophiostoma* spp.
Fusarium wilt	*Fusarium oxysporum* f. sp. *canariensis*
Pierce's disease	*Xylella fastidiosa*
Pine pitch canker	*Fusarium circinatum*
Scaly bark (psorosis)	*Citrus leprosis virus*
Stubborn disease	*Spiroplasma citri*
Sudden oak death	*Phytophthora ramorum*
Tristeza (quick decline)	*Closterovirus*

Further Reading

For natural histories of trees, leaf through Peter Thomas, *Trees: Their Natural History* (2000); Colin Tudge, *The Tree: A Natural History of What Trees Are, How They Live, and Why They Matter* (2006); Nalini M. Nadkarni, *Between Earth and Sky: Our Intimate Connections to Trees* (2008); and the works of Diana Beresford-Kroeger. On the significance of arboreal raw material, consider Joachim Radkau, *Wood: A History* (2012).

For the visually oriented, Thomas Pakenham has produced three beautiful large-format books under the series title *Remarkable Trees*. Seek out Cédric Pollet, *Bark: An Intimate Look at the World's Trees* (2010), for its unusually lovely pictures. James Balog, *Tree: A New Vision of the American Forest* (2004), takes nature photography to new heights and complements Tim Palmer, *Trees and Forests of America* (2008). Fred Hageneder has recently authored several attractive books that blend historical, scientific, spiritual, and artistic approaches; titles include *The Heritage of Trees*, *The Meaning of Trees*, and *The Spirit of Trees*. Two recent compendia, nicely illustrated, are Hugh Johnson, *The World of Trees* (2010); and Allen J. Coombes, *The Book of Leaves: A Leaf-by-Leaf Guide to Six Hundred of the World's Great Trees* (2010). For remarkable close-up botanical views of ten species common in America, see Nancy R. Hugo, *Seeing Trees: Discover the Extraordinary Secrets of Everyday Trees* (2011).

General works on the religious aspects of trees include J. H. Philpot,

The Sacred Tree; or, the Tree in Religion and Myth (1897); Stephanie Kaza, *The Attentive Heart: Conversations with Trees* (1993); and Nathaniel Altman, *Sacred Trees* (1994). On the sociology of trees, begin with Laura Rival, ed., *The Social Life of Trees: Anthropological Perspectives on Tree Symbolism* (1998); and Owain Jones, *Tree Cultures: The Place of Trees and Trees in Their Place* (2002).

On U.S. horticulture, the touchstone work is U. P. Hedrick, *A History of Horticulture in America to 1860* (1950), which has been bountifully updated by Philip J. Pauly, *Fruits and Plains: The Horticultural Transformation of America* (2008). On plant introductions, see Claire Shaver Haughton, *Green Immigrants: The Plants That Transformed America* (1978); Stephen A. Spongberg, *A Reunion of Trees: The Discovery of Exotic Plants and Their Introduction into North American and European Landscapes* (1990); Michael Pollan, *The Botany of Desire: A Plant's-Eye View of the World* (2001); and Londa Schiebinger, *Plants and Empire: Colonial Bioprospecting in the Atlantic World* (2004). On street trees, the authoritative source is Henry W. Lawrence, *City Trees: A Historical Geography from the Renaissance through the Nineteenth Century* (2006). See also Hui-Lin Li, *The Origin and Cultivation of Shade Ornamental Trees* (1963); and Arthur Plotnik, *The Urban Tree Book: An Uncommon Field Guide for City and Town* (2000). For an examination of the arborist profession, read Richard J. Campana, *Arboriculture: History and Development in North America* (1999).

Many authors have recently written about single famous tree types: Michael P. Cohen on bristlecone pines; Thomas Pakenham on baobabs; Peter Crane on ginkgoes; Allen M. Young on cacao trees; Jennifer L. Anderson on mahoganies; Thomas J. Campanella on American elms; Lawrence S. Earley on longleaf pines; Katharine Anderson on live oaks and ceibas in Louisiana and Guatemala; both Esmond Harris and James Jeanette on oaks in Britain; William Bryant Logan on oaks generally; Susan Freinkel on American chestnuts; Richard Mabey on European beeches; and both Robert Bevan-Jones and Fred Hageneder on European yews. John Vaillant, *The Golden Spruce: A True Story of*

Myth, Madness, and Greed (2005), narrates the life and death of a single mutant Sitka spruce.

For ancient history, consult Russell Meiggs, *Trees and Timber in the Ancient Mediterranean World* (1982); and Richard Hayman, *Trees: Woodlands and Western Civilization* (2003). On forests in the Western tradition, see Robert Pogue Harrison, *Forests: The Shadow of Civilization* (1992); and Simon Schama, *Landscape and Memory* (1995). For more on European woodlands (somewhat different from forests), check out Roger Deakin, *Wildwood: A Journey through Trees* (2007); and the books of Oliver Rackham. The best global overview of forest use and forest clearing is Michael Williams, *Deforesting the Earth: From Prehistory to Global Crisis* (2003).

For syntheses of forest use and forestry in the United States, go to Thomas R. Cox, *The Lumberman's Frontier: Three Centuries of Land Use, Society, and Change in America's Forests* (2010); Michael Williams, *Americans and Their Forests: A Historical Geography* (1989); and Thomas R. Cox et al., *This Well-Wooded Land: Americans and Their Forests from Colonial Times to the Present* (1985). On the history of the contemporary eastern forest, see Ellen Stroud, *Nature Next Door: Cities and Trees in the American Northeast* (2012), and Christopher Johnson and David Govatski, *Forests for the People: The Story of America's Eastern National Forests* (2013). For a tree-centered take on U.S. history, read Eric Rutkow, *American Canopy: The Role of Trees in the Shaping of the Nation* (2012), which complements Donald Culross Peattie, *A Natural History of Trees of Eastern and Central North America* (1950). For historical reflections on the nation's vernacular treescape, see Gayle Brandow Samuels, *Enduring Roots: Encounters with Trees, History, and the American Landscape* (1999); and Jeffrey G. Meyer with Sharon Linnea, *America's Famous and Historic Trees: From George Washington's Tulip Poplar to Elvis Presley's Pin Oak* (2001). Barbara Bosworth, *Trees: National Champions* (2005), features pictures of plants that have earned recognition on the National Register of Big Trees.

For an unsurpassed survey of the arboreal life of the U.S. West, written with old-fashioned verve and illustrated with gorgeous block prints, go find Donald Culross Peattie, *A Natural History of Western Trees* (1953). For the Golden State, the classic work is Willis Linn Jepson, *The Silva of California* (1910). For a layperson's botany manual on the state's urban forest, see Matt Ritter, *A Californian's Guide to the Trees among Us* (2011). For more technical information, refer to Charles Hatch, *Trees of the California Landscape: A Photographic Manual of Native and Ornamental Trees* (2007). On the natural history of California, see Elna S. Bakker, *An Island Called California: An Ecological Introduction to Its Natural Communities*, rev. ed. (1984); Philip Fradkin, *The Seven States of California: A Natural and Human History* (1995); and the *California Natural History Guides* from the University of California Press, which includes a volume on trees and shrubs. For an elegiac imagining of California's presettlement environment, lovingly illustrated, take in Laura Cunningham, *A State of Change: Forgotten Landscapes of California* (2010).

For a one-volume historical overview of the Golden State, see Kevin Starr, *California: A History* (2007). For innumerable more details—a de facto encyclopedia of Anglo-American California in narrative form, a florid tour de force—browse through Starr's multivolume series, *Americans and the California Dream*, from Oxford University Press. For stark contrast, read Tomás Almaguer, *Racial Fault Lines: The Historical Origins of White Supremacy in California*, rev. ed. (2008); or pore over Joan Didion's California writings, especially *Where I Was From* (2003). Another good complement is David Wyatt: *The Fall into Eden: Landscape and Imagination in California* (1986) and *Five Fires: Race, Catastrophe, and the Shaping of California* (1997). The idiosyncratic works of Rebecca Solnit—a combination of nature writing, creative nonfiction, history, memoir, cultural criticism, and political activism—are vital for thinking about the California scene. For bibliographic essays on California historiography, consult William Deverell and David Igler, eds., *A Companion to California History* (2008).

On the origins of the myth of California in cartography, fiction, and art, see Dora Beale Polk, *The Island of California: A History of the*

Myth (1991); and Claire Perry, *Pacific Arcadia: Images of California, 1600–1915* (1999). For a readable survey of Alta California, go to Stephen G. Hyslop, *Contest for California: From Spanish Colonization to the American Conquest* (2012). One of the best books (among many) on the California missions is Steven W. Hackel, *Children of Coyote, Missionaries of Saint Francis: Indian-Spanish Relations in Colonial California, 1769–1850* (2005). On indigenous peoples and the California environment, see M. Kat Anderson, *Tending the Wild: Native American Knowledge and the Management of California's Natural Resources* (2005); and Kent G. Lightfoot and Otis Parrish, *California Indians and Their Environment: An Introduction* (2009).

Of the numerous books on the California Gold Rush, good starting points are Malcolm J. Rohrbough, *Days of Gold: The California Gold Rush and the American Nation* (1997); and Susan Lee Johnson, *Roaring Camp: The Social World of the California Gold Rush* (2000). The best illustrated histories are Peter J. Blodgett, *Land of Golden Dreams: California in the Gold Rush* (1999); and J. S. Holliday, *Rush for Riches: Gold Fever and the Making of California* (1999).

On the post–Gold Rush era, classic works include W. W. Robinson, *Land in California: The Story of Mission Lands, Ranchos, Squatters, Mining Claims, Railroad Grants, Land Scrip, Homesteads* (1948); Leonard Pitt, *The Decline of the Californios: A Social History of the Spanish-Speaking Californians, 1846–1890* (1966); and Albert L. Hurtado, *Indian Survival on the California Frontier* (1988). For more recent analyses, I recommend David Igler, *Industrial Cowboys: Miller & Lux and the Transformation of the Far West, 1850–1920* (2001); and Andrew C. Isenberg, *Mining California: An Ecological History* (2005), which includes a section on redwood logging. For a useful sourcebook, see Carolyn Merchant, ed., *Green versus Gold: Sources in California's Environmental History* (1998). For a provocative reinterpretation of Golden State history (including the citrus industry) from a global perspective, see Bruce Cumings, *Dominion from Sea to Sea: Pacific Ascendancy and American Power* (2009).

On giant sequoia, start with Richard J. Hartesveldt et al., *The Giant*

Sequoia of the Sierra Nevada (1975), which, though dated, is better than the revised edition of 2002; and Dwight Willard, *A Guide to the Sequoia Groves of California* (2000). Walter Fry and John R. White, *Big Trees*, rev. ed. (1938); and Norman Taylor, *The Ageless Relicts: The Story of Sequoia* (1962), are still worth tracking down. Hank Johnston, *They Felled the Redwoods: A Saga of Flumes and Rails in the High Sierra* (1966), has incredible photographs of sequoia logging. For cultural history, see Lori Vermaas, *Sequoia: The Heralded Tree in American Art and Culture* (2003). On matters of size, see Robert Van Pelt, *Forest Giants of the Pacific Coast* (2001); and Wendell D. Flint, *To Find the Biggest Tree* (2002).

On coast redwood, start with Michael G. Barbour et al., *Coast Redwood: A Natural and Cultural History* (2001). For more science, see Reed F. Noss, ed., *The Redwood Forest: History, Ecology, and Conservation of the Coast Redwoods* (2000). For a mixture of science journalism and adventure writing, read Richard Preston, *The Wild Trees: A Story of Passion and Daring* (2007). For remarkable descriptions and technical drawings of various tall trees, look up Robert Van Pelt, *Forest Giants of the Pacific Coast* (2001). For a literary anthology, consult Peter Johnstone, *Giants in the Earth: The California Redwoods* (2001), which includes a terrific photographic gallery on logging. Another great visual resource is Lynwood Carranco, *Redwood Lumber Industry* (1982). For attempts to cover giant sequoia and coast redwood in one volume, see James Clifford Shirley, *The Redwoods of Coast and Sierra* (1936); and Jeremy Joan Hewes, *Redwoods: The World's Largest Trees* (1981).

The standard political narrative of the creation and expansion of Redwood National Park is Susan R. Schrepfer, *The Fight to Save the Redwoods: A History of Environmental Reform, 1917–1978* (1983). For a good journalistic overview from the period, look for Kramer Adams, *The Redwoods* (1969). For rousing accounts of the opening stage of the Headwaters battle, see David Harris, *The Last Stand: The War between Wall Street and Main Street over California's Ancient Redwoods* (1995); and Alston Chase, *In a Dark Wood: The Fight over Forests and the Rising Tyranny of Ecology* (1995). Probably the best-selling redwood book of all time is Julia Butterfly Hill, *The Legacy of Luna: The Story of a Tree, a Woman, and the Struggle to Save the Redwoods* (2000).

For more on the Golden State's conservation history, see, among other titles, Joseph H. Engbeck Jr., *State Parks of California, from 1864 to the Present* (1980); Michael P. Cohen, *The History of the Sierra Club, 1892–1970* (1988); Alfred Runte, *Yosemite: The Embattled Wilderness* (1990); Mark David Spence, *Dispossessing the Wilderness: Indian Removal and the National Parks* (1999); David Beesley, *Crow's Range: An Environmental History of the Sierra Nevada* (2004); Richard Walker, *The Country in the City: The Greening of the San Francisco Bay Area* (2007); Donald Worster, *A Passion for Nature: The Life of John Muir* (2008); Philip Garone, *The Fall and Rise of the Wetlands of California's Great Central Valley* (2011); Matthew Morse Booker, *Down by the Bay: San Francisco's History between the Tides* (2013); and Peter S. Alagona, *After the Grizzly: Endangered Species and the Politics of Place in California* (2013).

For information on the Australian botanical authorities who helped to spread the *Eucalyptus* genus, see Ashley Hay, *Gum: The Story of Eucalypts and Their Champions* (2002). On transpacific plant transfers, refer to Ian Tyrrell, *True Gardens of the Gods: California-Australian Environmental Reform, 1860–1930* (1999), which is also very strong on horticultural and conservationist thought in California. For global histories of the genus, see Robin W. Doughty, *The Eucalyptus: A Natural and Commercial History of the Gum Tree* (2000); and Robert Fyfe Zacharin, *Emigrant Eucalypts: Gum Trees as Exotics* (1978). For a succinct history of recent gum tree politics in California in the context of floral and faunal introductions, see Peter Coates, *American Perceptions of Immigrant and Invasive Species: Strangers on the Land* (2007). For an account of environmental activism in Australia on behalf of the world's tallest gum trees, see Tom Griffiths, ed., *Forests of Ash: An Environmental History* (2001). For a comparative analysis of landscape art and aesthetics, including a section on eucalypts, feast your eyes on Erika Esau's *Images of the Pacific Rim: Australia and California, 1850–1935* (2010).

On citrus, begin with Pierre Laszlo, *Citrus: A History* (2007); and John McPhee, *Oranges* (1966). For more details, search out Samuel

Tolkowsky, *Hesperides: A History of the Culture and Use of Citrus Fruits* (1938); and Giovanni Dugo and Angelo Di Giacomo, eds. *Citrus: The Genus* Citrus (2002). On the citrus business in California, see Douglas Cazaux Sackman, *Orange Empire: California and the Fruits of Eden* (2005); and Walter Reuther et al., eds., *The Citrus Industry*, a highly technical multivolume series published by the University of California Division of Agricultural Sciences.

For a heroic chronicle of the men and women who have labored in California's orchards, read Richard Steven Streets, *Beasts of the Field: A Narrative History of California Farmworkers, 1769–1913* (2004). The earlier classic is Carey McWilliams, *Factories in the Field: The Story of Migratory Farm Labor in California* (1939). On Mexican citrus workers specifically, see Gilbert G. González, *Labor and Community: Mexican Citrus Worker Villages in a Southern California County, 1900–1950* (1994); Matt Garcia, *A World of Its Own: Race, Labor, and Citrus in the Making of Greater Los Angeles, 1900–1970* (2001); and José M. Alamillo, *Making Lemonade Out of Lemons: Mexican American Labor and Leisure in a California Town, 1880–1960* (2006).

On California horticulturists, see David Vaught, *Cultivating California: Growers, Specialty Crops, and Labor, 1875–1920* (1999); idem, *After the Gold Rush: Tarnished Dreams in the Sacramento Valley* (2007); Steven Stoll, *The Fruits of Natural Advantage: Making the Industrial Countryside in California* (1998); and Cecilia Tsu, *Garden of the World: Asian Immigrants and the Making of Agriculture in California's Santa Clara Valley* (2013). For critical studies of California agriculture from a variety of perspectives, turn to Paul F. Starrs and Peter Goin, *Field Guide to California Agriculture* (2010); Julie Guthman, *Agrarian Dreams: The Paradox of Organic Farming in California* (2004); Richard A. Walker, *The Conquest of Bread: 150 Years of Agribusiness in California* (2004); and George L. Henderson, *California and the Fictions of Capital* (1999).

For biographical approaches to state agricultural history, see Mark Arax and Rick Wartzman, *The King of California: J. G. Boswell and the Making of a Secret American Empire* (2003); Peter Dreyer, *A Gardener Touched with Genius: The Life of Luther Burbank*, rev. ed. (1985); and

Jane S. Smith, *The Garden of Invention: Luther Burbank and the Business of Breeding Plants* (2009). For national context, read Alan L. Olmstead and Paul W. Rhode, *Creating Abundance: Biological Innovation and American Agricultural Development* (2008).

On the promotion of California's Southland, still nothing beats the witty erudition of Carey McWilliams, *Southern California Country: An Island on the Land* (1946). Newer studies include William Deverell, *Whitewashed Adobe: The Rise of Los Angeles and the Remaking of Its Mexican Past* (2004); Dydia DeLyser, *Ramona Memories: Tourism and the Shaping of Southern California* (2005); Phoebe S. Kropp, *California Vieja: Culture and Memory in a Modern American Place* (2006); and Lawrence Culver, *The Frontier of Leisure: Southern California and the Shaping of Modern America* (2010). For full-color reproductions of promotional material, enjoy Tom Zimmerman, *Paradise Promoted: The Booster Campaign That Created Los Angeles, 1870–1930* (2008); and K. D. Kurutz and Gary F. Kurutz, *California Calls You: The Art of Promoting the Golden State, 1870 to 1940* (2000). To find promoters turned on their heads, read Mike Davis's justly influential *City of Quartz: Excavating the Future in Los Angeles* (1990) and *The Ecology of Fear: Los Angeles and the Imagination of Disaster* (1998). For a corrective, peruse D. J. Waldie's strangely moving *Holy Land: A Suburban Memoir* (1996).

On the built environment of Los Angeles, classic works include Robert M. Fogelson, *The Fragmented Metropolis: Los Angeles, 1850–1930* (1967); Reyner Banham, *Los Angeles: The Architecture of Four Ecologies* (1971); and David Brodsly, *L.A. Freeway: An Appreciative Essay* (1981). On metropolitan planning, see Greg Hise, *Magnetic Los Angeles: Planning the Twentieth-Century Metropolis* (1997); Greg Hise and William Deverell, *Eden by Design: The 1930 Olmsted-Bartholomew Plan for the Los Angeles Region* (2000); Dana Cuff, *The Provisional City: Los Angeles Stories of Architecture and Urbanism* (2000); and Jeremiah B. C. Axelrod, *Inventing Autopia: Dreams and Visions of the Modern Metropolis in Jazz Age Los Angeles* (2009). On postwar suburbanization in comparative perspective, consult Christopher C. Sellers, *Crabgrass Crucible: Suburban Nature and the Rise of Environmentalism in Twentieth-Century*

America (2012). For a medley of approaches, see William Deverell and Greg Hise, eds., *Land of Sunshine: An Environmental History of Metropolitan Los Angeles* (2005); and idem, *A Companion to Los Angeles* (2010). Of the many L.A. picture books, I recommend Marla Hamburg Kennedy, Ben Stiller, and David L. Ulin, *Looking at Los Angeles* (2005); and Jim Heimann et al., *Los Angeles: Portrait of a City* (2009).

On parks and gardens in California, useful titles include Charles Francis Saunders, *Trees and Shrubs of California Gardens* (1926); Victoria Padilla, *Southern California Gardens* (1961); David C. Streatfield, *California Gardens: Creating a New Eden* (1994); Judith M. Taylor and Harry M. Butterfield, *Tangible Memories: Californians and Their Gardens, 1800–1950* (2003); and Terence Young, *Building San Francisco's Parks, 1850–1930* (2004).

For additional studies of specific California tree types, see Bruce M. Pavlik, Pamela Muick, and Sharon Johnson, *Oaks of California* (1993); Ronald M. Lanner, *Conifers of California* (1999); and Judith M. Taylor, *The Olive in California: History of an Immigrant Tree* (2000). For arresting pictures, see George Haas, *Forcing Nature: Trees in Los Angeles* (2006). There is no monograph on California's palm trees. For more on the palm family, refer to Desmond Muirhead, *Palms* (1961); David L. Jones, *Palms throughout the World* (1995); and Robert Lee Riffle, Paul Craft, and Scott Zona, *The Encyclopedia of Cultivated Palms*, 2d. ed. (2012).

Acknowledgments

I CONCEIVED THIS PROJECT while living for six years at Stanford University—a school with an ostentatious Palm Drive, a Citrus Courtyard in the History Corner of the Main Quad, groves of aromatic eucalyptus, and splendid relict oaks, not to mention a redwood on its seal and a dancing tree as its unofficial mascot. This campus landscape schooled me.

All hail to librarians! To the interlibrary loan staff who post off books, to the information technology specialists who create and maintain digital archives, to the countless people who have scanned documents for me personally and for scholars collectively, including those workers whose stray thumbs I sometimes encounter on my computer monitor—*thank you*.

Above all, I must acknowledge the staff at two institutions, the Huntington Library and the National Humanities Center.

At the Huntington, Susi Krasnoo oriented me; Roy Ritchie allowed to me to have a sunlit office on Mahogany Row; the staff of the Reader Services Department, notably Juan Gomez, cared for my archival needs; and Danielle Rudeen gave me permission to browse the stacks of the botanical library. At some point every research day, I took a walk in the Huntington Botanical Gardens—the most pleasant kind of fieldwork. I thank the gardeners who tend that floral sanctuary.

At the National Humanities Center, a glass building enveloped by second-growth loblolly pine, I benefited from the extraordinary interlibrary loan service run by Eliza Robertson, Jean Houston, and Josiah Drewry. Kent Mullikin oversaw the fellowship program with tact and good humor.

This project could not have been completed without considerable institutional assistance: a Mellon Foundation postdoctoral fellowship administered by William Deverell through the Huntington–USC Institute on California and the West; a summer research grant from the Historical Society of Southern California and the Haynes Foundation; an individual development award from United University Professions; a pair of interdisciplinary initiatives individual grants from Stony Brook University; a writing retreat at Grey Towers National Historic Site; a fellowship from the American Council of Learned Societies; and a tenure at the National Humanities Center supported by the Donnelley Family Fellowship (endowed by Strachan Donnelley) and the Fellows' Fellowship (endowed by past fellows of the center).

My postdoctoral years in Los Angeles overlapped with the Huntington Library fellowships of two historian couples who taught me a lot about life inside and outside the walls of academia. My gratitude goes to Michelle Nickerson and Benjamin Johnson, and to Leslie Tuttle and Jonathan Earle.

At Stony Brook University, otherwise known as the State University of New York at Stony Brook, the history department has been nothing but supportive. My colleague Sara Lipton deserves special recognition for her collegiality and neighborliness. Thank you, Sara, for welcoming this westerner to the American Far East and for elucidating the folkways of Long Island.

I have also been the recipient of gracious hospitality from colleagues who have allowed me to housesit or stay over while researching in the Golden State. I offer my sincerest gratitude to Jon Christensen and Kit Miller, Carolyn Lougee Chappell and David Lougee, Zephyr Frank and Tram Frank, Richard White and Beverly Purrington, Deborah Harkness and Karen Halttunen, Terence Young and Kitty Connolly, and Joseph Boone. On multiple occasions, the wonderful Rebecca Lemon saved the day.

At Sequoia–Kings Canyon National Park, archivist Ward Eldredge kindly guided me through the administrative files. In Los Angeles, Tom Zimmerman shared images from his amazing personal collection and offered valuable research tips. Ellis Farms in Borrego Springs and Preserved Treescapes International in Vista granted me tours of their facilities.

A number of scholars provided feedback on sections of the manuscript: Peter Alagona, Jennifer Anderson, Mia Bay, Matthew Booker, Chad Bryant, Matthew Chew, Lawrence Culver, Janet Fireman, Suzanne Guerra, Donald Hodel, David Igler, Andrew Isenberg, Benjamin Johnson, Thomas Lekan, Sungnome Madrone, Margo McBane, Jenny Price, Matt Ritter, Aaron Sachs, Douglas Sackman, Rachel St. John, Christopher Sellers, Jennifer Seltz, Darren Speece, Ellen Stroud, Tamara Venit-Shelton, Louis Warren, and members of the New York Metro Seminar on Environmental History.

David Schoenbrun supplied me with a tranquil writing retreat and superlative chile colorado, among other gifts of friendship.

My editor, Steve Forman, was genial at every stage. He knows what he's doing. Invariably he helped me compose a more readable book. Assistant editor Justin Cahill smoothed out innumerable wrinkles. My trusted copyeditor, Ann Hawthorne, a marvel of perspicacity, passed away unawares before she could complete my manuscript. I honor her legacy.

My pal Cheburashka, who knows a thing or two about oranges, cheered me up whenever work became a drag.

Magdalena Mączyńska makes everything better. She gave my life a makeover. In addition, she critiqued my manuscript in full, thereby tempering my antiquarianism, checking my grandiloquence, pruning my punning, and calling my bullshit. With just the right amount of teasing, she accepted my incorrigible enthusiasm for grainy photographs of guys standing next to trees. She reads me like an open book. I'm a lucky fool to have met her twice.

I dedicate this work to my departed father, James Lee Farmer, a professor of genetics and a student of all knowledge worth knowing. He is my model for intellectual curiosity and moral integrity. I wish I could get his reader's report. My father was a product of postwar Southern California. At Caltech, of all places, he became a lifelong history buff thanks to faculty member Rodman Paul, a leading state historian. Although Dad spent most of his adult life in Provo, Utah, he preserved fond memories of the citrus and pomegranate trees in the backyard of his childhood home in South Gate, a working-class factory town outside Los Angeles. In Utah Valley, he surrounded my childhood home with a grape arbor and dozens of varieties of stone-fruit trees. Unsatisfied, he built a greenhouse so that he could cultivate subtropical fruit. He told me that the Tree of Knowledge must have been a fig. In a moment of nostalgia, he originated a spot-on Utah bumper sticker: SAM BRANNAN WAS RIGHT. After one of the annual meetings of the Pacific Division of the American Association for the Advancement of Science, Dad went to Muir Woods, and returned to the Great Basin with a *Sequoiadendron* seedling from the gift shop. Despite the dry summer heat and the clay-and-cobble soil, his experimental Big Tree had grown taller than the house by the time I drove west to Palo Alto.

Illustration Credits

First Insert

Page 1: Detail from stereoscopic card, "Top of the Mother of the Forest," ca. 1860s. New York Public Library.

Page 1: "The Mother of the Forest," stereoscopic card, 1866. New York Public Library.

Page 2: "The Stump and Trunk of the Mammoth Tree of Calaveras," lithograph, 1862. Courtesy of the Bancroft Library, University of California, Berkeley.

Page 2: C. C. Curtis: Felling the Mark Twain, 1891. Courtesy Sequoia–Kings Canyon National Park.

Page 3: "California: The Home of the Big Tree," *Country Life in America*, Jan. 1904.

Page 4: A. W. Ericson: Oxen team, n.d. Ericson Photograph Collection, Humboldt State University Library.

Page 4: A. W. Ericson: Steam donkey, n.d. Ericson Photograph Collection, Humboldt State University Library.

Page 5: A. W. Ericson: Trains operated by Excelsior Redwood Company, ca. 1890. Ericson Photograph Collection, Humboldt State University Library.

Page 5: A. W. Ericson: Redwood log with undercuts, n.d. Ericson Photograph Collection, Humboldt State University Library.

Page 6: "'#2 Head Rig Mill B.' The Pacific Lumber Co., Scotia, Calif." Postcard from author's collection.

Page 6: "Cut of Redwood, 15x4 Feet, Sent From Vance's Wood, Humboldt County, to London, England," *San Francisco Call*, 15 Jan. 1899.

Page 7: Bohemian Grove, n.d. Courtesy of the Bancroft Library, University of California, Berkeley.

Page 8: Joel Davis: "Redwood Summer," Eureka, 1990. Courtesy of *The Oregonian*.

Page 8: Aaron R. Maret: Tree-sit on Pacific Lumber land, Humboldt County, June 2004.

Second Insert

Page 1: "Will the California Eucalyptus Solve the Timber Problem of the Nation," *San Francisco Call*, 18 Aug. 1907.

Page 1: "The Miracle Tree," advertisement from *Out West*, Dec. 1909.

Page 2: "Edward Weston, Carmel Highlands, California," 1945. Photograph by Ansel Adams. © The Ansel Adams Publishing Rights Trust.

Page 3: Dorothea Lange: "Nipomo, Calif. March 1936. Migrant agricultural worker's family. Seven hungry children and their mother, aged 32. The father is a native Californian." Library of Congress.

Page 3: Rancho Santa Fe, 1930. San Diego History Center.

Page 4: "The Two Extremes: Beauty, Barrenness," illustration used in "Trees or No Trees Again Becomes Fight Issue in Burlingame," *San Francisco Call*, 8 Aug. 1930. San Francisco History Center, San Francisco Public Library.

Page 4: John Edwin Hogg: Highway near El Toro, Orange County, ca. 1930. Reproduced by permission of The Huntington Library, San Marino, California.

Page 5: Franz Geritz: Cover for *Touring Topics*, Jan. 1926. Automobile Club of Southern California Archives.

Page 6: Oakland Hills, 1991. Courtesy California Emergency Management Agency.

Page 6: George Rose: Exploding eucalyptus, Corona, 1980. Getty Images.

Page 6: Mike Lewis: Eucalyptus longhorned borer beetle.

Page 7: Andrew T. Young: Blue gums, Marin Headlands, 2009. Wikimedia Commons.

Page 7: Mike Baird: Monarch butterflies and eucalyptus foliage, Morro Bay, 2008. Wikimedia Commons.

Page 8: Karl Struss, "Storm Clouds, La Mesa, 1921." Tom Zimmerman Collection. Used by permission of the Struss estate.

Third Insert

Page 1: The California Citrograph, Jan. 1929.

Page 2: Theodore Roosevelt and parent navel tree at Mission Inn, Riverside, 1903. Reproduced by permission of The Huntington Library, San Marino, California.

Page 2: "The Hon. Luther C. Tibbits [*sic*], who planted the first navel orange tree," 1900. Used by permission of Special Collections & Archives, University of California, Riverside.

Page 3: W. C. Mendenhall: Orange groves on terraced hillsides, West Riverside, 1905. U.S. Geological Survey.

Page 3: "Irrigating an orange grove, Riverside, California." Stereoscopic card, 1902. New York Public Library.

Page 4: Corona Belle brand citrus crate label, ca. 1920. Used by permission of the Board of Trustees of the Corona Public Library.

Page 4: "I'll eat Oranges for you, While you throw Snow Balls for me." Postcard from author's collection.

Page 5: Sunkist promotional image, ca. 1940s. Tom Zimmerman Collection.

Page 6: "Orange Blossoms and Orange Picking," ca. 1880s. Reproduced by permission of The Huntington Library, San Marino, California.

Page 6: Woodcut illustration to Carey McWilliams's "Gunkist," *Pacific Weekly*, 20 July 1936. Courtesy of the Bancroft Library, University of California, Berkeley.

Page 7: "Orange Groves and Oil Wells, Calif." Postcard view of Fullerton area from author's collection.

Page 7: Clarence Tucker: Smudge pots, Covina, ca. 1937. Courtesy Covina Valley Historical Society

Page 8: Fumigation tent, n.d. Reproduced by permission of The Huntington Library, San Marino, California.

Page 8: Weldon Field: Stump puller, ca. 1950s. Courtesy Orange County Archives.

Fourth Insert

Page 1: Palm Canyon, ca. 1920s. Reproduced by permission of The Huntington Library, San Marino, California.

Page 2: San Fernando Mission, n.d. Courtesy of University of Southern California, on behalf of USC Special Collections.

Page 2: Wolfskill palm being moved from San Pedro Street to Arcade Station, Los Angeles, 1888. Courtesy of University of Southern California, on behalf of USC Special Collections.

Page 3: "Avenue of Palms, Los Angeles." Half of stereoscopic card, 1894. New York Public Library.

Page 3: Jared Farmer: Harbor Freeway off-ramp at West Adams, Los Angeles, 2010.

Page 4: World's Fair palm tree on West Twelfth Street, Los Angeles, 1936. Courtesy of University of Southern California, on behalf of USC Special Collections.

Page 4: The Crisis, Aug. 1913. Courtesy of the Modernist Journals Project, Brown University.

Page 4: Compton city hall, 1926. Courtesy Los Angeles Public Library.

Page 5: View from Hollywood Hills on film premiere night, n.d. Courtesy of University of Southern California, on behalf of USC Special Collections.

Page 5: The Cocoanut Grove, n.d. Courtesy of University of Southern California, on behalf of USC Special Collections.

Page 6: Jared Farmer: Harbor (formerly Getty) Building, Wilshire Boulevard, Los Angeles, 2010.

Page 6: James H. May: Palmskinner, Rancho Mirage, 2008.

Page 6: Jared Farmer: Dead palm, South Pasadena, 2006.

Page 6: Jared Farmer: Graffitied palm, Venice Beach, 2010.

Page 7: Jared Farmer: Preserved Treescapes International, Vista, 2010.

Page 7: Jared Farmer: Delivery truck, Salton City, 2010.

Page 8: Jared Farmer: Embarcadero, San Francisco, 2011.

Page 8: Jared Farmer: Los Angeles River, 2010.

Notes

WITH THE FOLLOWING NOTES, I tried my best to strike a balance between the minimal and the maximal. I began this project with the goal of writing a short book. I failed. At some point I realized I could spend the rest of my life researching California trees without exhausting the material. Given the proliferation of digitized online sources, I was able to study—in addition to my archival work—thousands of books, pamphlets, and articles, only a portion of which I have cited here. Although I endeavored to provide documentation for every statistic and direct quotation, I left numerous minor factual statements unattributed for the sake of space. Generally I omitted author names from short news pieces. I excluded all page numbers from old newspaper articles in part because the digitized versions are often encoded with misleading numbers depending on the inclusion or omission of editions and inserts. I used the following abbreviations:

Bancroft	Bancroft Library, University of California, Berkeley
CC	*California Citrograph*
CH	*California History*
GC	*Gardeners' Chronicle* (London)
GOGA	Golden Gate National Recreation Area Archives and Records Center, Presidio, San Francisco
GPO	Government Printing Office, Washington, D.C.

HEH	Henry E. Huntington Library, San Marino
JFH	*Journal of Forest History*
JSDH	*Journal of San Diego History*
LAH	*Los Angeles Herald*
LAT	*Los Angeles Times*
NG	*National Geographic*
NYT	*New York Times*
OT	*Oakland Tribune*
PHR	*Pacific Historical Review*
PRP	*Pacific Rural Press*
RPE	*Riverside Press-Enterprise*
SCB	*Sierra Club Bulletin*
SCQ	*Southern California Quarterly*
SDUT	*San Diego Union-Tribune*
SEKI	Sequoia–Kings Canyon National Park Archives, Three Rivers
SFC	*San Francisco Call*
SFCh	*San Francisco Chronicle*
SPO	State Printing Office, Sacramento
UC	University of California
USDA	U.S. Department of Agriculture

Introduction

1. Leonore Kothe, "The Monterey Cypress," *Overland Monthly* 66 (Dec. 1915): 469–73.

2. See "Golf Course Tries to Trademark a Tree," *SFC*, 12 July 1990; "Tree Trademark Claim Stirs Fury," *LAT*, 13 July 1990; "Trees and Trademarks," *NYT*, 2 Aug. 1990; and *Pebble Beach Company v. Laub America Corporation*, U.S. District Court for the Northern District of California (1986). "*Trademark of quality*" is from a sign on 17-Mile Drive; "brand identity" quotation is from the company's website, www.pebblebeach.com, 2012.

3. See "The Last Lone Cypress?" *San Jose Mercury News*, 3 Feb. 1994; and "Lone Cypress Poses Proudly for Generations," *LAT*, 16 May 2002.

4. Willis Linn Jepson, *The Silva of California* (Berkeley, 1910), 157.

5. Lecture described in M. D. Brainard, *Monterey Cypress* (n.p., 1919). Biographi-

cal information and "Dharma" quote from "A Buddhist Prelate of California," *Open Court* 26 (Feb. 1912): 65–70.

6. Frank Soulé et al., *The Annals of San Francisco* (New York, 1845), 362.

7. "The Way They Talk in California," *Horticulturalist* 12 (1857): 314–16.

8. Notable contributions to this literature are Ian Tyrrell, *True Gardens of the Gods: California-Australian Environmental Reform, 1860–1930* (Berkeley, 1999); Philip J. Pauly, *Fruits and Plains: The Horticultural Transformation of America* (Cambridge, Mass., 2008); Richard W. Judd, *The Untilled Garden: Natural History and the Spirit of Conservation in America, 1740–1840* (Cambridge, 2009); and David Curtis Hickman, "Landscapes of Green and Gold: The Environmental Vision of the California Horticulturalists, 1849–1900" (Ph.D. diss., UC Davis, 2011). See also Cecilia Tsu, *Garden of the World: Asian Immigrants and the Making of Agriculture in California's Santa Clara Valley* (Oxford, 2013); John F. Freeman, *High Plains Horticulture: A History* (Boulder, 2008); and Shen Hou, *The City Natural:* Garden and Forest *Magazine and the Rise of American Environmentalism* (Pittsburgh: University of Pittsburgh Press, 2013).

9. See Joachim Radkau, *Wood: A History* (Malden, Mass., 2012).

10. Charles Sprague Sargent, "John Muir," *SCB* 10 (Jan. 1916): 37; John Muir, *The Mountains of California* (New York, 1907), 252.

11. John Muir to Jeanne Carr, fall 1870, John Muir Correspondence, Holt-Atherton Special Collections, University of the Pacific.

12. Hubert Howe Bancroft, *Chronicles of the Builders of the Commonwealth: Historical Character Study*, vol. 3 (San Francisco, 1892), 442.

13. Strentzel quoted in J. P. Munro-Fraser, *History of Contra Costa County, California* (San Francisco, 1882), 59; John Strentzel, "Agricultural and Horticultural Development and Resources," from the "Centennial Papers" series of the *Contra Costa Gazette*, 5 Aug., 23 Sept., 7 Oct., and 14 Oct. 1876, reprinted in *Illustrations of Contra Costa County Co., California, with Historical Sketch* (Oakland, 1879), 13.

14. Louisiana Strentzel diary, 20 March 1881, quoted in Hickman, "Landscapes of Green and Gold," 235.

15. Ezra S. Carr, "Address," in *Transactions of the California Agricultural Society during the Years 1870 and 1871* (Sacramento, 1872), 96; John Muir to Jeanne Carr, 9 Apr. 1879, John Muir Correspondence; John Muir, *Steep Trails* (Boston, 1918), 140–41, originally published in *San Francisco Bulletin*, 7 Sept. 1877.

16. Ray Stannard Baker, "John Muir," *Outlook* 74 (6 June 1903): 365–77, quote on 377.

17. Ezra S. Carr, "Our Forests," in *Transactions of the California State Agricultural Society during the Year 1872* (Sacramento, 1873), 545–46. For a correlative exhumation of nineteenth-century U.S. landscape philosophies and practices, see Aaron Sachs, *Arcadian America: The Death and Life of an Environmental Tradition* (New Haven, 2013).

18. "Funeral Sunday of John Muir," *Berkeley Daily Gazette*, 28 Dec. 1914, 8. The best biography is Donald Worster, *A Passion for Nature: The Life of John Muir* (Oxford, 2008). On the grounds at Martinez, see James K. Agee and P. J. Ryan, "Historic Trees

of John Muir National Historic Site," *JFH* 24 (Jan. 1980): 40–46; and Jeffrey Killion, *Cultural Landscape Report for John Muir National Historic Site*, vol. 1 (Boston, 2005).

Part One: Redwoods

1. See "Housing Slump Hits California Timber Industry like a Buzz Saw," *LAT*, 28 Oct. 2009. California Redwood Company is a subsidiary of Green Diamond Resource Company, formerly known as Simpson Timber Company.
2. Logger quotations from "Redwood Peanut Rejected," *Nevada State Journal* (Reno), 25 May 1977; "Park Protest 'Doomed to Fail,'" *Eureka Times-Standard*, 29 May 1977; and "Redwood Peanut Leads Caravan to Washington D.C. and Meets Hard-Shelled Bureaucrats," *Western Conservation Journal* 34 (June–July 1977): 26–31.
3. "Peanut," *Eureka Times-Standard*, 7 Oct. 1977. See also "Peanut: Orick Soon 'Home-Sweet-Home,'" *Eureka Times-Standard*, 16 Sept. 1977.

Chapter 1. Twilight of the Giants

1. The literature on California's two redwood species seemingly goes on forever; no one can claim to have read it all. For finding aids, start with Emanuel Fritz, *California Coast Redwood: An Annotated Bibliography* (San Francisco, 1957); and the unpublished companion, Emanuel Fritz and George W. Smith, "Bibliography on California Big-tree (*Sequoia Gigantea*)" (1937), copy in Bancroft. See also Lloyd W. Currey and Dennis G. Kruska, *Bibliography of Yosemite, the Central and the Southern High Sierra, and the Big Trees, 1839–1900* (Los Angeles, 1992); and Deborah L. Rogers, "An Annotated Bibliography of the Biology of Coast Redwood" (1997), available online at the Save-the-Redwoods League's website, www.savetheredwoods.org.
2. John Davies, ed., *Douglas of the Forests: The North American Journals of David Douglas* (Seattle, 1980), 160. On El Palo Alto, the historic redwood associated with Portolá (and later Stanford University), see Jared Farmer, "On Emblematic Megaflora," *Environmental History* 15 (July 2010): 533–47.
3. Albert Kellogg, *Forest Trees of California* (SPO, 1882), 23.
4. On the canopy ecosystem, see the many scientific articles authored and coauthored by Stephen C. Sillett, California's first endowed professor of redwood ecology, who is also the main subject of Richard Preston, *The Wild Trees: A Story of Passion and Daring* (New York, 2007). On the former tallest tree in the world, see the special edition of *NG* 126 (July 1964).
5. Fitz Hugh Ludlow, "Seven Weeks in the Great Yo-Semite," *Atlantic Monthly* 8 (June 1864): 739–54, quote on 745.
6. On the ecology of fog, see T. E. Dawson, "Fog in the California Redwood Forest: Ecosystem Inputs and Use by Plants," *Oecologia* 117, no. 4 (1998): 476–85;

S. S. O. Burgess and T. E. Dawson, "The Contribution of Fog to the Water Relations of *Sequoia sempervirens* (D. Don): Foliar Uptake and Prevention of Dehydration," *Plant, Cell and Environment* 27, no. 8 (2004): 1023–34, quote on 1023; and Holly A. Ewing et al., "Fog Water and Ecosystem Function: Heterogeneity in a California Redwood Forest," *Ecosystems* 12 (Apr. 2009): 417–33.

7. Bonnie Johanna Gisel, ed., *Kindred & Related Spirits: The Letters of John Muir and Jeanne C. Carr* (Salt Lake City, 2001), 119.

8. J. M. Hutchings, *In the Heart of the Sierras* (Yo Semite Valley, 1886), 215–16. See also Richard J. Hartesveldt, "The 'Discoveries' of the Giant Sequoias," *JFH* 19 (Jan. 1975): 16–21.

9. John Lindley, untitled lead article, *GC* (24 Dec. 1853): 819–20; *California Farmer*, 4 May 1854, quoted in "The Giant Taxodium of California," *Magazine of Horticulture* 20 (1854): 333; "Dr. C. F. Winslow's Letters from the Mountains. The 'Big Tree,'" *California Farmer* 2 (24 Aug. 1854): 58. On taxonomic nomenclature, see William A. Dayton, "The Names of the Giant Sequoia: A Discussion," *Leaflets of Western Botany* 3 (Apr. 1943): 209–19; and Richard J. Hartesveldt et al., *The Giant Sequoia of the Sierra Nevada* (GPO, 1975), 19–25.

10. Bayard Taylor, *At Home and Abroad: A Sketch-book of Life, Scenery, and Men* (New York, 1862), 45; extract of letter published in *GC* (10 June 1854): 373; lecture by J. Bateman reprinted in *GC* (3 Feb. 1855): 69–70. For a cartoon of mammoth vegetables, see "California 'Products,'" *Hutchings' California Magazine* 3 (Oct. 1858): 192.

11. "Dr. C. F. Winslow's Letters."

12. See Isaac H. Bromley, "The Wonders of the West—I: The Big Trees and the Yosemite," *Scribner's Monthly* 3 (Jan. 1872): 261–77.

13. Caroline M. Churchill, *Over the Purple Hills, or Sketches of Travel in California* (Denver, 1881), 200; Elizabeth Cady Stanton, *Eight Years and More* (New York, 1898), 294. On naming history, see Fern Gray, *And the Giants Were Named* (Three Rivers, Calif., 1975).

14. "Nothing lovable": C. F. Gordon Cumming, *Granite Crags* (London, 1884), 76. "Extreme": Charles B. Turrill, *California Notes* (San Francisco, 1876), 95. "Intense": Thomas Starr King, *A Vacation among the Sierras: Yosemite in 1860* (San Francisco, 1962), 35–36 (originally published in *Boston Evening Transcript*, 12 Jan. 1861). "Average (female) mind": Mrs. Frank Leslie, *California: A Pleasure Trip from Gotham to the Golden Gate, April, May, June, 1877* (New York, 1877), 244. "None of us": Bromley, "The Wonders of the West—I," 267.

15. Horace Greeley, *An Overland Journey, from New York to San Francisco in the Summer of 1859* (New York, 1860), 311–12; King, *Vacation among the Sierras*. Italicized quotes from "The Mammoth Trees of California," *Chambers' Journal* 18 (29 Nov. 1862): 346; Alfred Lambourne, *Pine Branches and Sea Weeds* (Chicago, 1889), 36; Thomas S. Chard, *California Sketches* (Chicago, 1888), 21; Charles Dudley Warner, *Our Italy* (New York, 1891), 160; and "Dr. C. F. Winslow's Letters."

16. Direct quotes from Ludlow, "Seven Weeks in the Great Yo-Semite"; Eli Perkins,

"California's Big Trees," *NYT*, 17 June 1877; *Description of the Mammoth Tree from California, Now Erected at the Crystal Palace, Sydenham* (London, 1857), 6, 13; "The Wellingtonia Gigantea," *Times* (London), 18 Feb. 1859.

17. James M. Hutchings, *Scenes of Wonder and Curiosity in California* (London, 1865), 13; Samuel Bowles, *Across the Continent: A Summer's Journey to the Rocky Mountains, the Mormons, and the Pacific States, with Speaker Colfax* (Springfield, Mass., 1865), 237.

18. King, *Vacation among the Sierras;* "Dr. C. F. Winslow's Letters"; verse quoted in Hutchings, *Scenes of Wonder,* 46–47, and many other period books and articles.

19. Rev. John Todd, *The Sunset Land; or The Great Pacific Slope* (Boston, 1870), 87–88. This passage was later plagiarized in George W. Pine, *Two Wonders of the World: Yo-Semite, Mammoth Trees, and Bird's-Eye View of California* (New York, 1873), 45–46.

20. Alexander von Humboldt, *Views of Nature: Or Contemplations on the Sublime Phenomena of Creation*, trans. E. C. Otté and Henry G. Bohn (London, 1850), 220; "An Immense Tree," *Gleason's Pictorial Drawing-Room Companion*, 1 Oct. 1853, 217; Asa Gray, "On the Age of the Large Tree Recently Felled in California," in *Proceedings of the American Academy of Arts and Sciences* 3 (Boston, 1857), 94–96 (from a lecture delivered in February 1854 after Gray inspected a *sempervirens* specimen in Philadelphia falsely advertised as a Big Tree); Torrey quoted in Berthold Seemann, "On the Mammoth-tree of Upper California," *Annals and Magazine of Natural History* 3 (Mar. 1859): 161–75, quote on 170; J. D. Whitney, *The Yosemite Guide-Book* (Cambridge, Mass., 1869), 154; and J. D. Whitney for the Geological Survey of California, *The Yosemite Book* (New York, 1868), 116. For context, see Richard G. Beidleman, *California's Frontier Naturalists* (Berkeley, 2006).

21. C. B. Bradley, "A New Study of Some Problems Relating to the Giant Trees," *Overland Monthly & Out West Magazine* 7 (March 1886): 305–16, passim.

22. "The Big Trees," *Daily Evening Bulletin* (San Francisco), 5 Aug. 1890; "California's Big Trees," *NYT*, 15 Nov. 1891; John Muir, *The Mountains of California* (New York, 1894), 182; David Starr Jordan, *"California and the Californians" and "The Alps of King-Kern Divide"* (San Francisco, 1903), 49 (quote comes from the latter article, which originally appeared in the regional magazine *Land of Sunshine*); "Our Big Trees Saved," *NG* 31 (Jan. 1917): 1–11. *National Geographic* repeated the claim as late as the May 1951 issue ("Saving Earth's Oldest Living Things").

23. Quote from reprinted lecture by J. Bateman, *GC* (3 Feb. 1855): 70.

24. See Dennis G. Kruska, *Sierra Nevada Big Trees: History of the Exhibitions, 1850–1903* (Los Angeles, 1985).

25. For a photograph of the display, see Ian Leith, *Delamotte's Crystal Palace: A Victorian Pleasure Dome Revealed* (Swindon, Wiltshire, 2005), 40.

26. Cumming, *Granite Crags*, 312; Edward Vischer, *Vischer's Views of California: The Mammoth Tree Grove, Calaveras County, California, and Its Avenues* (San Francisco, 1862). In an otherwise celebratory 1870 portfolio about the progress of California, Vischer included a new, austere portrait of the tree "skeleton," which, in his eyes, stood "in silent accusation against the vandalism of its executioners." See *Vischer's Pictorial of California Landscapes, Tree and Forest Scenes* (San Francisco, 1870). For a

fuller discussion of Watkins and Vischer, see Lori Vermaas, *Sequoia: The Heralded Tree in American Art and Culture* (Washington, D.C., 2003), chaps. 2–3. See also Elizabeth Hutchinson, "They Might Be Giants: Carleton Watkins, Galen Clark, and the Big Tree," *October* 109 (Summer 2004): 47–63.

27. Lowell reprinted in *Crayon* 4 (Mar. 1857): 96; "An Immense Tree," *Gleason's Pictorial Drawing-Room Companion*, 1 Oct. 1853, 217; P. Barry, "The Big Tree of California.—Sequoia Gigantea of Torrey (Wellingtonia Gigantea of Lindley.)," *Horticulturalist* 5 (Sept. 1855): 398–401.

28. Andrew Murray, "Notes on Californian Trees, Part II," *Edinburgh New Philosophical Journal* 11 (Jan.–Apr. 1860): 205–22, quote on 218. On sequoias in Rochester, see W. D. Ellwanger, *A Snuff-box Full of Trees & Some Apocryphal Essays* (New York, 1909).

29. *GC* (1856): 502, 518, 534, 567, 580, 631; commissioner quoted in Hartesveldt, *Giant Sequoia of the Sierra Nevada*, 79. Dozens of articles in European botanical magazines summarized in Fritz and Smith, "Bibliography on California Bigtree." See also Hans Huth, "Sequoias in Germany," *JFH* 20 (July 1976): 146–48. On the poet's sequoia, see Hallam Tennyson, *Alfred Lord Tennyson: A Memoir by His Son* (London, 1906), 417–18.

30. *GC* (29 Nov. 1856): 790, reprinted from the 4 March 1854 issue; response in *GC* (6 Dec. 1856): 805.

31. Details from Gary D. Lowe, *The Big Tree Exhibits of 1870–1871 and the Roots of the Giant Sequoia Preservation Movement*, 2d ed. (Livermore, Calif., 2002). See also J. Otis Williams, *Mammoth Trees of California* (Boston, 1871). On Bierstadt, see Vermaas, *Sequoia*, chap. 4.

32. "An Act Authorizing a Grant to the State of California of the 'Yo-Semite Valley' and of the Land Embracing the 'Mariposa Big Tree Grove,'" 30 June 1864 (13 Stat. L. 325).

33. John Muir, "On the Post-Glacial History of Sequoia Gigantea," in *Proceedings of the American Association for the Advancement of Science* (Salem, Mass., 1877), 242–53, quotes on 246. See also Muir, "The New Sequoia Forests of California," *Harper's New Monthly Magazine* 57 (Nov. 1878): 813–27. Muir's science articles have been collected in Robert Engberg, ed., *John Muir Summering in the Sierra* (Madison, 1984), 121–37.

34. "Protection of Big Trees," *Mariposa Gazette*, 20 Mar. 1874, as quoted in Lowe, *Big Tree Exhibits*, 72. Muir quotes from Engberg, *John Muir Summering*, 96; and John Muir, *Our National Parks* (Boston, 1901), 101. Information on Clark from H. Willis Baxley, *What I Saw on the West Coast of South and North America* (New York, 1865), 494. For an account of Sierra logging in the service of mining, see Dan De Quille, *History of the Big Bonanza* (San Francisco, 1877), chap. 33; and for historical analysis, see Robert Neil Chester, "Comstock Creations: An Environmental History of an Industrial Watershed" (Ph.D. diss., UC Davis, 2009), chap. 4.

35. W. A. Sanders, "The High Sierras," correspondence to editor, *PRP* 18 (13 Sept. 1879): 162. Information on Galen Clark from Baxley, *What I Saw*, 494. See also Henry T. Finck, *Pacific Coast Scenic Tour: From Southern California to Alaska* (New

York, 1890), 104. Photographs of the General Grant in Jackie McDougall Weiner, *Timely Exposures: The Life and Images of C. C. Curtis, Pioneer California Photographer* (Sanger, Calif., 2009). Sequoia National Park later offered access to the Auto Log, and private landowners created several "tunnel trees" in redwood country.

36. *Annual Report of the Secretary of the Interior on the Operations of the Department for the Year Ended June 30, 1879* (GPO, 1879), 29–30.

37. Start with W. W. Robinson, *Land in California: The Story of Mission Lands, Ranchos, Squatters, Mining Claims, Railroad Grants, Land Scrip, Homesteads* (Berkeley, 1948); and Paul W. Gates, *Land and Law in California: Essays on Land Policies* (Ames, 1991).

38. *Annual Report of the Commissioner of the General Land Office for the Year 1886* (GPO, 1886), 95. See also S. A. D. Puter, *Looters of the Public Domain* (Portland, Ore., 1908); and Harold Hathaway Dunham, *Government Handout: A Study in the Administration of the Public Lands, 1875–1891* (New York, 1941), 263–68.

39. On logging in the Kings River drainage, see Hank Johnston, *They Felled the Redwoods: A Saga of Flumes and Rails in the High Sierra* (Los Angeles, 1966); in the Kaweah drainage, see Lary M. Dilsaver and William C. Tweed, *Challenge of the Big Trees: A Resource History of Sequoia and Kings Canyon National Parks* (Three Rivers, Calif., 1990); and in the Tule, see Floyd L. Otter, *The Men of Mammoth Forest: A Hundred-Year History of a Sequoia Forest and Its People in Tulare County, California* (Ann Arbor, 1963).

40. *A Pen Picture of the Kaweah Co-Operative Colony Co.* (San Francisco, 1880). See also Elaine Lewinnek, "The Kaweah Co-operative Commonwealth and the Contested Nature of Sequoia National Park," *SCQ* 89, no. 2 (2007): 141–67; Jay O'Connell, *Co-operative Dreams: A History of the Kaweah Colony* (Van Nuys, 1999); and Robert V. Hine, *California's Utopian Colonies*, rev. ed. (New Haven, 1969), chap. 5.

41. Editor quoted in Hine, *California's Utopian Colonies*, 97. For legal details, see Douglas H. Strong, "The Sierra Forest Reserve: The Movement to Preserve the San Joaquin Valley Watershed," *CH* 46 (Mar. 1967): 3–17; and David Beesley, *Crow's Range: An Environmental History of the Sierra Nevada* (Reno, 2004), chap. 3.

42. Hutchings, *Scenes of Wonder*, 143; "Californian Giants," *Living Age* 52 (14 Feb. 1857), reprinted from *Chambers' Journal*; Leslie, *California*, 246; "In the Matter of the Investigation of the Yosemite Valley Commissioners," testimony, Feb. 1889, in *Appendix to the Journals of the Senate and Assembly of the Twenty-eighth Session of the Legislature of the State of California*, vol. 8, pt. 2 (SPO, 1889), 42–43, 73.

43. On fire in Mariposa, see Hal K. Rothman, *Blazing Heritage: A History of Wildland Fire in the National Parks* (New York, 2007), 18–21; and Alfred Runte, *Yosemite: The Embattled Wilderness* (Lincoln, 1990), 58–63.

44. *A Short Account of the Big Trees of California*, USDA Bulletin 28 (GPO, 1900), 7–8; John Muir, "Save the Redwoods," posthumously published in *SCB* 11 (Jan. 1920): 1–4. On Calaveras Big Trees State Park, see Joseph H. Engbeck, *The Enduring Giants*, 3d ed. (Sacramento, 1988). On early buybacks in Sequoia, see Douglas H. Strong, "The History of Sequoia National Park, 1876–1926, Part II: The Problems of the

Early Years," *SCQ* 48 (Sept. 1966): 265–88. Much of the sequoia land in the Tule watershed reverted to federal ownership around the turn of the century, after the "forest lieu clause" of 1897 allowed claimants whose property had been surrounded by forest reserves to trade their title for land scrip.

45. On Southern Pacific, see Oscar Berland, "Giant Forest's Reservation: The Legend and the Mystery," *SCB* 47 (Dec. 1962): 68–82; Douglas H. Strong, "The History of Sequoia National Park, 1876–1926, Part I: The Movement to Establish a Park," *SCQ* 48 (June 1966): 137–67; and Richard J. Orsi, *Sunset Limited: The Southern Pacific Railroad and the Development of the American West, 1850–1930* (Berkeley, 2005), 363–64, 370–71. On the General Noble, see Sara Delavergne Price, "How the Big Tree Was Sent to Chicago," *Frank Leslie's Popular Monthly* 35 (June 1893): 728–34; and Donald J. McGraw, "The Tree That Crossed a Continent," *CH* 61 (Summer 1982): 120–39.

46. See Johnston, *They Felled the Redwoods*; and Robert Zimmerman, "Log Flume," *American Heritage of Invention and Technology* 14 (Fall 1998): 58–63.

47. Walter Fry and John R. White, *Big Trees* (Stanford, 1930), 19–20; George B. Sudworth, *Forest Trees of the Pacific Slope* (GPO, 1908), 141.

48. Henry Seidel Canby, "The Last Stand of the Redwoods," *Harper's Monthly Magazine* 131 (June 1915): 46–58, quote on 58.

49. "Reminiscences of Mendocino," *Hutchings' Illustrated California Magazine* 3 (Oct. 1858): 146–60, 177–81, quote on 154; Kellogg, *Forest Trees of California*, 26; *History of Humboldt County, California, with Illustrations* (San Francisco, 1881), 140; W. G. Bonner, "The Redwoods of California," *Cassier's Magazine* 6 (July 1894): 195–213, quote on 199. Statistic from *First Biennial Report of the California State Board of Forestry* (SPO, 1886), 138.

50. Willis Linn Jensen, *The Trees of California*, 2d ed. (Berkeley, 1923), 16.

51. See Leslie M. Freudenheim, *Building with Nature: Inspiration for the Arts & Crafts Home* (Salt Lake City, 2005). One of the leading architects of the movement was Bernard Maybeck. Later modernist architects such as Harwell Hamilton Harris and Richard Neutra (in southern California) and William Wurster (in the Bay Area) also favored redwood. In fact California modernism has been called the Redwood School of architecture. The neorustic modernist Sea Ranch style of the 1960s also depended heavily on *S. sempervirens*.

52. Quote from a Pacific Lumber promotional postcard (n.d.) in the author's collection. Statistic from "Casket Shells Large Redwood Users," *Timberman* 57 (Nov. 1955): 86–90. See also "Redwood Casket Parts," *Western Wood Worker and Furniture Manufacturer* 3 (July 1929): 19, 22.

53. See R. F. Luxford and L. J. Markwardt, *The Strength and Related Properties of Redwood*, USDA Technical Bulletin 205 (GPO, 1932); W. LeRoy Neubrech, *California Redwood (*Sequoia sempervirens*) and Its Uses*, U.S. Department of Commerce Trade Promotion Series 171 (GPO, 1937); James M. Leaver, *California Redwood: Its Production and Uses* (Chicago, n.d.); and Redwood Manufacturers Company, *A Handbook of Information for Hydraulic Engineers Relating to Remco Redwood Pipe* (San Francisco, 1926).

54. See Stephen Tobriner, *Bracing for Disaster: Earthquake-Resistant Architecture and Engineering in San Francsico, 1838–1933* (Berkeley, 2006), 142–44, 207, 235; Elizabeth Hull, "Redwood in the 1906 San Francisco Earthquake & Fires: A Photo Essay," *Forest History Today* (Spring/Fall 2006): 36–41; and Pacific Lumber Company, *California Redwood* (San Francisco, 1915). *Wall Street Journal* quoted in "Redwood's Claims as a Fire Resistant Substantiated," *American Lumberman*, 26 May 1906: 25. Timber yield data from "Lumber Production, by Species: 1869–1996," in *Historical Statistics of the United States, Earliest Times to the Present: Millennial Edition Online*, ed. Susan B. Carter et al. (New York, 2006), table Db438.

55. See Lynwood Carranco and John T. Labbe, *Logging the Redwoods* (Caldwell, Id., 1975); Lynwood Carranco, *Redwood Lumber Industry* (San Marino, 1982); Alan K. Brown, *Sawpits in the Spanish Redwoods* (San Mateo, 1966); Alice Holmes and Wilbur Lawson, *Mills of Mendocino County: A Record of the Lumber Industry, 1852–1996* (Ukiah, 1996); and Frank H. Baumgardner III, *Yanks in the Redwoods* (New York, 2010), chap. 7.

56. See A. L. Kroeber and E. W. Gifford, *World Renewal: A Cult System of Native Northwest California*, University of California Anthropological Records 13, no. 1 (Berkeley, 1949), 92; Peter Nabokov and Robert Easton, *Native American Architecture* (New York, 1989), 292; and Lynn Huntsinger and Sarah McCaffrey, "A Forest for the Trees: Forest Management and the Yurok Environment, 1859 to 1994," *American Indian Culture and Research Journal* 19, no. 4 (1995): 155–92.

57. Martin F. Schmitt, ed., *General George Crook, His Autobiography* (Norman, 1946), 14–16. For context, see William F. Strobridge, *Regulars in the Redwoods: The U.S. Army in Northern California, 1852–1861* (Spokane, 1994).

58. Bret Harte, "Indiscriminate Massacre of Indians: Women and Children Butchered," *Northern Californian*, 29 Feb. 1860. Quote on local tax from Brendan C. Lindsay, *Murder State: California's Native American Genocide, 1846–1873* (Lincoln, Neb., 2012), 210. On the massacre, see Ray Raphael and Freeman House, *Two People, One Place* (Eureka, 2007), 155–88. On terminology, see Benjamin Madley, "California's Yuki Indians: Defining Genocide in Native American History," *Western Historical Quarterly* 39 (Autumn 2008): 303–32.

59. On violence against California Indians, see, in addition to Lindsay, *Murder State*, books by Frank H. Baumgardner, Lynwood Carranco and Estle Beard, Sherburne F. Cook, Robert F. Heizer, Chad L. Hoopes, Albert L. Hurtado, Jack Norton, George Harwood Phillips, James Rawls, and Clifford E. Trafzer and Joel R. Hyer. On treaties and land rights, see Stuart Banner, *Possessing the Pacific: Land, Settlers, and Indigenous People from Australia to Alaska* (Cambridge, Mass., 2007), chap. 5.

60. Lillie E. Hamm, *History and Business Directory of Humboldt County* (Eureka, 1890). On Humboldt County's Chinese, see Jean Pfaelzer, *Driven Out: The Forgotten War against Chinese Americans* (New York, 2007), chap. 4.

61. See "Millionaire Astor Explains about His Famous Redwood," *SFC*, 15 Jan. 1899; and Martha Beer Roscoe and Lynwood Carranco, "Lord Astor's Round Table," *Humboldt Historian* 56, no. 2 (Spring 2008): 38–39.

62. See Howard Brett Melendy, "One Hundred Years of the Redwood Lumber Industry, 1850–1950" (Ph.D. diss., Stanford University, 1952); James Michael Buckley, "Building the Redwood Region: The Redwood Lumber Industry and the Landscape of Northern California, 1850–1929" (Ph.D. diss., UC Berkeley, 2000); and Andrew C. Isenberg, *Mining California: An Ecological History* (New York, 2005), chap. 3.

63. On the life and language of workers, see Lynwood Carranco, "Logger Language in Redwood Country," *JFH* 18 (July 1974): 52–59; idem, *Redwood Lumber Industry*; Hyman Palais, "Pioneer Redwood Logging in Humboldt County," *JFH* 17 (Jan. 1974): 18–27; and Daniel A. Cornford, *Workers and Dissent in the Redwood Empire* (Philadelphia, 1987).

64. *First Biennial Report of the California State Board of Forestry*, 137–57, quotes on 150, 148. For a sense of the toll on workers, see Andrew Mason Prouty, *More Deadly than War! Pacific Coast Logging, 1827–1981* (New York, 1988).

65. Charles S. Sargent, *Report on the Forests of North America* (GPO, 1884), 580; *History of Humboldt County*, 24, 140.

66. Willis L. Jepson, "Talk on the Redwood," lecture to the Bohemian Club, 10 June 1920, copy in the Willis Linn Jepson Papers, box 13, University and Jepson Herbaria Archive, UC Berkeley.

Chapter 2. The Perpetual Last Stand

1. For timber counts by acreage and by volume, see *Forest Statistics for the Redwood–Douglas Fir Subregion in California*, Forest Survey Release 19 (Berkeley, 1953); Kass Green, *The Old Growth Redwood Resource: An Historical Review of Harvesting and Preservation* (Oakland, 1985); and Lawrence Fox III, *A Classification, Map, and Volume Estimate for the Coast Redwood Forest in California*, rev. ed. (Sacramento, 1989).

2. Bureau of Corporations, Department of Commerce and Labor, *The Lumber Industry, Part II: Concentration of Timber Ownership in Important Selected Regions* (GPO, 1914), 101–14.

3. See Arthur A. Taylor, *California Redwood Park* (Sacramento, 1912); Frank E. Hill and Florence W. Hill, *The Acquisition of California Redwood Park* (San Jose, 1927); Carolyn de Vries, "Andrew P. Hill and the Big Basin, California's First State Park," *San José Studies* 2, no. 3 (1976): 70–92; idem, *Grand and Ancient Forest: The Story of Andrew P. Hill and Big Basin Redwoods State Park* (Fresno, 1978); Michael L. Smith, *Pacific Visions: California Scientists and the Environment, 1850–1915* (New Haven, 1987), 166–71; and William S. Yaryan, "Saving the Redwoods: The Ideology and Political Economy of Nature Preservation" (Ph.D. diss., UC Santa Cruz, 2002). Quote from Willis Fletcher Johnson, ed., *Addresses and Papers of Theodore Roosevelt* (New York, 1909), 129–30.

4. See John Auwaerter and John F. Sears, *Historic Resource Study for Muir Woods National Monument* (Boston, 2006); Anne F. Hyde, "William Kent: The Puzzle of Progressive Conservationists," in *California Progressivism Revisited*, ed. William

Deverell and Tom Sitton (Berkeley, 1994); and Hal Rothman, *Preserving Different Pasts: The American National Monuments* (Urbana, 1989). Congressman Kent went on to oppose Muir over the San Francisco Water Department's damming of Hetch Hetchy Valley in Yosemite National Park.

5. See Porter Garnett, *The Bohemian Jinks: A Treatise* (San Francisco, 1908); John Van der Zee, *The Greatest Men's Party on Earth: Inside the Bohemian Grove* (New York, 1974); and G. William Domhoff, *The Bohemian Grove and Other Retreats* (New York, 1974). Nixon quote from 13 May 1971, as transcribed in "All the Philosopher King's Men," *Harper's* 300 (Feb. 2000): 22–24.

6. See Jonathan Peter Spiro, *Defending the Master Race: Conservation, Eugenics, and the Legacy of Madison Grant* (Burlington, Vt., 2009); Ronald Rainger, *An Agenda for Antiquity: Henry Fairfield Osborn and Vertebrate Paleontology at the American Museum of Natural History, 1890–1935* (Tuscaloosa, 1991); Brian Regal, *Henry Fairfield Osborn: Race and the Search for the Origins of Man* (Burlington, Vt., 2002); and Stephen R. Mark, *Preserving the Living Past: John C. Merriam's Legacy in the State and National Parks* (Berkeley, 2005).

7. J. D. Grant, *Redwoods and Reminiscences: A Chronicle of Traffics and Excursions, or Work and Play, of Ups and Downs, during More than Half a Century Happily Spent in California and Elsewhere* (San Francisco, 1973), 142.

8. On the history of the league, see Susan R. Schrepfer, *The Fight to Save the Redwoods: A History of Environmental Reform, 1917–1978* (Madison, 1983). For gender context, see Cameron Binkley, "'No Better Heritage than Living Trees': Women's Clubs and Early Conservation in Humboldt County," *Western Historical Quarterly* 33 (Summer 2002): 179–203. After 1938 state royalties from oil drilling were funneled directly into the park system, covering the operating expenses of the existing redwood parks and facilitating the system's expansion. Over the next few decades, oil revenue (and a follow-up bond issue) allowed California to amass over thirty park units with redwoods. See Paul Sabin, *Crude Politics: The California Oil Market, 1900–1940* (Berkeley, 2005), chap. 4; and Joseph H. Engbeck Jr., *State Parks of California, from 1864 to the Present* (Portland, Ore., 1980).

9. See, for example, Madison Grant, "Saving the Redwoods," *NG* 37 (June 1920): 518–38; Albert W. Atwood, "Redwood Dividends," *Saturday Evening Post* 197 (25 Apr. 1925): 10–11, 169–70, 173; and idem, "Redwood Investments," *Saturday Evening Post* 197 (23 May 1925): 20, 161–62, 165–66, 171, 173.

10. Henry Fairfield Osborn, "Sequoia—the Auld Lang Syne of Trees," *Natural History* 19 (Dec. 1920): 599–613, quote on 604; Madison Grant, "Saving the Redwoods: An Account of the Movement during 1919 to Preserve the Redwoods of California," *Zoological Society Bulletin* 22 (Sept. 1919): 91–118, quote on 91. Mary Cynthia Dickerson was Osborn's ghostwriter. See also *Saving the Redwoods*, the league's annual report. For context, see Gabrielle Barnett, "Drive-By Viewing: Visual Consciousness and Forest Preservation in the Automobile Age," *Technology and Culture* 45, no. 1 (2004): 30–54; and David Louter, *Windshield Wilderness: Cars, Roads, and Nature in Washington's National Parks* (Seattle, 2006). On the road itself, see John Robinson,

"The Redwood Highway, Part II," *California Highways and Public Works* (July–Aug. 1964): 24–33.

11. Grant, *Redwoods and Reminiscences*, 25, 85, 69, 209. On conservationists and eugenics, see Alexandra Minna Stern, *Eugenic Nation: Faults and Frontiers of Better Breeding in Modern America* (Berkeley, 2005). On Madison Grant in particular, see Spiro, *Defending the Master Race*; and Matthew Pratt Guterl, *The Color of Race in America, 1900–1940* (Cambridge, Mass., 2001), 14–67. Other league members active in the eugenics movement included Henry Fairfield Osborn, Vernon Kellogg, and Charles Goethe.

12. Grant, "Saving the Redwoods: An Account of the Movement," 92, 94; memorial speech quoted in Spiro, *Defending the Master Race*, 292.

13. Madison Grant, *Preserve an America Worth Fighting For* (Berkeley, 1921). On its website, the Save-the-Redwoods League has a list of all the memorial trees and groves.

14. "California's Big Trees," *NYT*, 15 Nov. 1891; Abbot Kinney, "The Forests of California," *Californian* 1 (Feb. 1892): 115–28, quote on 118.

15. See Samuel Trask Dana and Myron Krueger, *California Lands: Ownership, Use, and Management* (Washington, D.C., 1958), 190–92; and *Fourth Biennial Report of the State Forester of the State of California* (SPO, 1912), 72–89.

16. Vance paraphrased in Lillie E. Hamm, *History and Business Directory of Humboldt County* (Eureka, 1890), 201; supervisor quoted in Emanuel Fritz, *The Development of Industrial Forestry in California* (Seattle, 1960), 22. See also Alfred Powers, *Redwood Country: The Lava Region and the Redwoods* (New York, 1949), 111–14.

17. "California's Fight for Redwoods," *SFCh*, 8 Dec. 1924. On cutover lands, see Warren T. Clarke, *Agriculture in Cut-over Redwood Lands*, California Agricultural Experiment Station Bulletin 350 (Berkeley, 1922); and Arnold Newton Weber, "Redwood Cut-over Lands and Their Use" (master's thesis, UC Berkeley, 1926). On early reforestation efforts, see *Ninth Biennial Report of the State Board of Forestry of the State of California* (SPO, 1923), 7–26; W. R. Schofield, "Reforestation in the Humboldt Redwood Belt," *Journal of Forestry* 27 (1 Feb. 1929): 168–75; S. B. Show, *Timber Growing and Logging Practice in the Coast Redwood Region of California*, USDA Technical Bulletin 283 (GPO, 1932); and Hubert L. Person, *Commercial Planting on Redwood Cut-over Lands*, USDA Circular 434 (GPO, 1937).

18. On Fritz, see Elwood R. Maunder and Amelia R. Fry, "Emanuel Fritz: Teacher, Editor, and Forestry Consultant," interview, Santa Cruz, 1972, available at the Internet Archive (www.archive.org); and Alston Chase, *In a Dark Wood: The Fight over Forests and the Rising Tyranny of Ecology* (Boston, 1995), chap. 3. For a succinct expression of Fritz's approach to forestry, see Emanuel Fritz, "Redwood Crop 'Rotations' Mean 20–25-Year Returns," *Ukiah Journal-Press-Dispatch*, 22 Nov. 1950, 7.

19. For the report leading up to the Forest Practice Act, see California Forestry Study Committee, *The Forest Situation in California* (SPO, 1945). On the subsequent regulatory system Fritz helped to create, see T. F. Arvola, *Regulation of Logging in California, 1945–1975* (Sacramento, 1976).

20. For a statistical portrait of the industry in the postwar boom years, see Henry J. Vaux, *Timber in Humboldt County*, California Agricultural Experiment Station Bulletin 748 (Berkeley, 1955). See also Lynwood Carranco, *Redwood Lumber Industry* (San Marino, 1982); and the special issue of *Western Conservation Journal* 14 (May–June 1957). On the tree farm movement, see Eric Rutkow, *American Canopy: Trees, Forests, and the Making of the Nation* (New York, 2012), 285–87; and Emily K. Brock, "Tree Farms on Display," *Oregon Historical Quarterly* 113 (Winter 2012): 526–59.

21. See John Robinson, "The Redwood Highway, Part III," *California Highways and Public Works* (Sept.–Oct. 1964): 14–23; Henry Sadler, "Winter Damage in Redwoods Parks," *SCB* 41 (Oct. 1956): 12–13; Peggy Wayburn, "The Tragedy of Bull Creek," *SCB* 45 (Jan. 1960): 10–11; and Alex Calhoun, "Must Logging Destroy Streams?" *SCB* 47 (Dec. 1962): 60–67.

22. See the two separate reports by Rudolf W. Becking, both titled *The Ecology of the Coastal Redwood Forest and the Impact of the 1964 Floods upon Redwood Vegetation* (Arcata, Calif., 1967 and 1968), copies in Redwood Subject File, Forest History Society Research Center, Durham, N.C.; Edward C. Stone and Richard B. Vasey, "Preservation of Coast Redwood on Alluvial Flats," *Science* 159 (12 Jan. 1968): 157–61; and Jeffrey F. Mount, *California Rivers and Streams: The Conflict between Fluvial Process and Land Use* (Berkeley, 1995), 227–45. For a pictorial account of the 1964 flood, see Stuart Nixon, *Redwood Empire* (New York, 1966), 234–47.

23. See Binkley, "'No Better Heritage than Living Trees'"; Charles Willis Ward, *Humboldt County, California: The Land of Unrivaled Undeveloped Natural Resources on the Westernmost Rim of the American Continent* (Eureka, 1915), 23–25; Samuel T. Dana and Kenneth B. Pomeroy, "Redwoods and Parks," *American Forests* 71 (May 1965): 3–32; Helen Gahagan Douglas, "The Proposed Roosevelt Redwood Forest," *National Parks* 21 (Apr.–June 1947): 16–22; Amelia Fry, "Helen Gahagan Douglas Project, Volume 4: Congresswoman, Actress, and Opera Singer," interview, 1973, 117–20, Bancroft (also available at the Internet Archive); and Powers, *Redwood Country*, 145–49.

24. See National Park Service, *The Redwoods: A National Opportunity for Conservation and Alternatives for Action* (Washington, D.C., 1962); the special edition of *NG* 126 (July 1964); and California State Legislature, *Conflict in the Redwoods* (Sacramento, 1967).

25. "Special Message to the Congress: Protecting Our Natural Heritage," 30 Jan. 1967, *Public Papers of the Presidents of the United States, Lyndon B. Johnson*, vol. 4 (Washington, D.C., 1968), 97; *Wall Street Journal*, 26 Jan. 1968. Reagan, who spoke at a meeting of the Western Wood Products Association in San Francisco on 21 March 1966, has been pervasively misquoted as having said, "If you've seen one redwood, you've seen them all."

26. On the twists and turns of the legislative history, see Schrepfer, *Fight to Save the Redwoods*, supplemented by Michael McCloskey, "The Last Battle of the Redwoods," *American West* 6 (Sept. 1969): 55–64; Edward C. Crafts, "Men and Events behind the Redwood National Park," *American Forests* 77 (May 1971): 20–27; Robin W. Winks,

Laurance S. Rockefeller: Catalyst for Conservation (Washington, D.C., 1997), 85–94; Edgar Wayburn, *Your Land and Mine: Evolution of a Conservationist* (San Francisco, 2004), 131–71; Michael McCloskey, *In the Thick of It: My Life in the Sierra Club* (Washington, D.C., 2005), 65–83; and Thomas G. Smith, *Green Republican: John Saylor and the Preservation of America's Wilderness* (Pittsburgh, 2006), 250–65.

27. Summarized from Arcata Redwood, Louisiana-Pacific Corporation, and Simpson Timber Company, "Protecting Redwood National Park," 13 Sept. 1976, copy in scrapbook 4, item 219, Dewitt Nelson Collection ("The Politics and Propaganda of Expanding the Redwood National Park"), Forest History Society Research Center; and *Proposed Expansion of the Redwood National Park: The Industry's View* (1975), scrapbook 3, item 75, ibid.

28. For contrasting viewpoints on park enlargement, see C. R. Batten, "The Second Battle of the Redwoods," *Reason* 11 (Oct. 1979): 18–23; and Tom Turner, *Wild by Law: The Sierra Club Legal Defense Fund and the Places It Has Saved* (San Francisco, 1990), 65–81; as well as *Forest Management and Redwood National Park* (GPO, 1976). On the legal issues, see Thomas Lundmark, "Regulation of Private Logging in California," *Ecology Law Quarterly* 5, no. 1 (1975): 139–88; Henry J. Vaux, "The Regulation of Private Forest Practices in California: A Case Study in Policy Evolution," *JFH* 30 (July 1986): 128–34; and Stephanie S. Pincetl, "The Peculiar Legacy of Progressivism: Claire Dedrick's Encounter with Forest Practices in California," *Forest and Conservation History* 34 (Jan. 1990): 26–34.

29. "Emanuel Fritz: Some Call Him 'Mr. Redwood,'" *Eureka Times-Standard*, 19 May 1977; "Statement of Emanuel Fritz to House Subcommittee on National Park and Insular Affairs," 15 July 1977, typescript in scrapbook 6, item 359, Dewitt Nelson Collection; Robert A. Jones, "After a Long and Bitter Battle, a Clear Victory for the Redwoods," *Smithsonian* 9 (July 1978): 38–45, quote on 43.

30. See Edward George and Dary Matera, *Taming the Beast: Charles Manson's Life behind Bars* (New York, 1998), 43; and Jess Bravin, *Squeaky: The Life and Times of Lynette Alice Fromme* (New York, 1997), 271.

31. "Harvesters of Redwoods Face Crisis in Way of Life," *Sacramento Bee*, 28 Nov. 1977. In his memoir, Edgar Wayburn portrayed the convoy as a waste of fuel during the energy crisis and a public relations fiasco: "The peanut log became a symbol of the industry's desecration of the nation's most magnificent tree." *Your Land and Mine*, 169.

32. On Arcata, see "Town Divided by a Redwood Curtain," *LAT*, 23 June 1977; and Dan Sealy, Suzanne Guerra, and John Amodio, "Redwood National Park Expansion, Woodstock, Earth Day, and the Kent State Massacre," in *Rethinking Protected Areas in a Changing World: Proceedings of the 2011 George Wright Society Biennial Conference on Parks, Protected Areas, and Cultural Sites*, ed. Samantha Weber (Hancock, Mich., 2012), 290–96.

33. On economic theory, see James K. Agee, "Issues and Impacts of Redwood National Park Expansion," *Environmental Management* 4, no. 5 (1980): 407–23; and Peter Berck and William R. Bentley, "Hotelling's Theory, Enhancement, and the Taking of the Redwood National Park," *American Journal of Agricultural Economics*

79 (May 1997): 287–98. For the industry's point of view, see John L. Walker, "Tall Trees, People, and Politics: The Opportunity Costs of the Redwood National Park," *Contemporary Policy Issues* 2 (Mar. 1984): 22–29.

34. "Eureka a Victim of the Redwood War," *LAT*, 8 Mar. 1978. On the deindustrialization of the North Coast, see Edwin Kiester Jr., "A New Park Saved the Tall Trees, but at a High Cost to the Community," *Smithsonian* 24 (Nov. 1993): 42–55. For a wider overview, see Ray Raphael, *More Tree Talk: The People, Politics, and Economics of Timber* (Washington, D.C., 1994).

35. Emanuel Fritz, "Some Popular Fallacies Concerning California Redwood," *Madroño* 1 (July 1929): 221–24.

36. See Thomas A. Spies and Sally L. Duncan, *Old Growth in a New World: A Pacific Northwest Icon Reexamined* (Washington, D.C., 2009); Chase, *In a Dark Wood*; and Nancy Langston, *Forest Dreams and Forest Nightmares: The Paradox of Old Growth in the Inland West* (Seattle, 1995).

37. On early Earth First!, see Dave Foreman, *Confessions of an Eco-Warrior* (New York, 1991); Christopher Manes, *Green Rage: Radical Environmentalism and the Unmaking of Civilization* (Boston, 1991); Susan Zakin, *Coyotes and Town Dogs: Earth First! and the Environmental Movement* (New York, 1993); and Keith Woodhouse, "A Subversive Nature: Radical Environmentalism in the Late-Twentieth-Century United States" (Ph.D. diss., University of Wisconsin, 2010).

38. See Ray Raphael, *Cash Crop: An American Dream* (Mendocino, 1985); and Beth Robinson Bosk, ed., *The New Settler Interviews*, vol. 1: *Boogie at the Brink* (White River Junction, Vt., 2000).

39. See Jack Held, "Scotia, the Town of Concern," *Pacific Historian* 16 (Summer 1972): 76–92; Hugh Wilkerson and John Van der Zee, *Life in the Peace Zone: An American Company Town* (New York, 1971); and Ray Raphael, *Edges: Backcountry Lives in America Today on the Borderlands between the Old Ways and the New* (New York, 1976), 43–53.

40. Quoted in David Harris, *The Last Stand: The War between Wall Street and Main Street over California's Ancient Redwoods* (New York, 1995), 16.

41. Murphy quoted in *Sustained-Yield Forest Policy, Part I: The Redwoods and the Raiders*, California State Legislature Joint Hearing (Sacramento, 1988), 7. For details of the buyout, see *Corporate Takeovers: Hearings before the Subcommittee on Oversight and Investigations of the Committee on Energy and Commerce, House of Representatives*, 100th Cong., Serial No. 100-116 (GPO, 1988); and Harris, *The Last Stand*.

42. See Harry DeAngelo and Linda DeAngelo, "Ancient Redwoods and the Politics of Finance: The Hostile Takeover of the Pacific Lumber Company," *Journal of Financial Economics* 47 (Jan. 1998): 3–53.

43. See Judi Bari, *Timber Wars* (Monroe, Maine, 1994); Daniel Faber, ed., *The Struggle for Ecological Democracy: Environmental Justice Movements in the United States* (New York, 1998), 248–71; and Kate Coleman, *The Secret Wars of Judi Bari: A Car Bomb, the Fight for the Redwoods, and the End of Earth First!* (San Francisco, 2005).

44. On Redwood Summer, see Chase, *In a Dark Wood*; and Harris, *The Last Stand*.

For context, see Richard White, "Are You an Environmentalist or Do You Work for a Living? Work and Nature," in *Uncommon Ground: Toward Reinventing Nature*, ed. William Cronon (New York, 1995), 171–85.

45. See Darren Speece, "From Corporatism to Citizen Oversight: The Legal Fight over California Redwoods, 1970–1996," *Environmental History* 14 (Oct. 2009): 705–36. On the current regulatory environment, see Sharon E. Duggan and Tara Mueller, *Guide to the California Forest Practice Act and Related Laws: Regulation of Timber Harvesting on Private Lands in California* (Point Arena, Calif., 2005). For historical context, see Stephanie S. Pincetl, *Transforming California: A Political History of Land Use and Development* (Baltimore, 1999); and Dana and Krueger, *California Lands*.

46. See Patrick Beach, *A Good Forest for Dying: The Tragic Death of a Young Man on the Front Lines of the Environmental Wars* (New York, 2003); and Joan Dunning, *From the Redwood Forest: Ancient Trees and the Bottom Line: A Headwaters Journey* (White River Junction, Vt., 1998).

47. See Julia Butterfly Hill, *The Legacy of Luna: The Story of a Tree, a Woman, and the Struggle to Save the Redwoods* (San Francisco, 2000); and *Butterfly* (2000), dir. Doug Wolens.

48. For more complete narratives of the Headwaters campaign, see Darren Speece, "Defending Giants: The Battle over Headwaters Forest and the Transformation of American Environmental Politics, 1850 to 1999" (Ph.D. diss., University of Maryland, 2010); Alessandro Bonanno and Douglas H. Constance, *Stories of Globalization: Transnational Corporations, Resistance, and the State* (University Park, Pa., 2008), 171–89; John Berger, *Forests Forever: Their Ecology, Restoration, and Protection* (Chicago, 2008), 166–87; and Douglas Bevington, *The Rebirth of Environmentalism: Grassroots Activism from the Spotted Owl to the Polar Bear* (Washington, D.C., 2009), 41–109. For a cultural studies perspective, see Richard Widick, *Trouble in the Forest: California's Redwood Timber Wars* (Minneapolis, 2009). EPIC has posted detailed case histories on its website, www.wildcalifornia.org.

49. Quoted in William E. Marks, *The Holy Order of Water: Healing the Earth's Waters and Ourselves* (Great Barrington, Mass., 2001), 149–50.

50. On the post-Hurwitz outlook for logging, see Joel K. Bourne Jr., "Redwoods: The Super Trees," *NG* 216 (Oct. 2009): 28–59. On indoor marijuana, see Mark Arax, *West of the West: Dreamers, Believers, Builders, and Killers in the Golden State* (New York, 2009), 177–214.

51. "The best idea" motto originated in 1983 with Wallace Stegner and has been widely appropriated, notably by Ken Burns.

Part Two: Eucalpyts

1. *LAT*, San Fernando Valley section, 10–11 Apr., 19 Apr., and 21–22 Apr. 1970. For context, see Adam Rome, *The Genius of Earth Day: How a 1970 Teach-In Unexpectedly Made the First Green Generation* (New York, 2013).

2. "The Trees That Captured California," *Sunset* 117 (Aug. 1956): 44–49. Other historians have investigated the regional introduction of eucalypts: Robert LeRoy Santos, "The Eucalyptus of California," *SCQ* 80 (Summer 1998): 105–44; Gayle M. Groenendaal, "California's First Fuel Crisis and Eucalyptus Plantings" (master's thesis, California State University at Northridge, 1985); Kenneth M. Johnson, "Eucalyptus," *Out West* 6 (Oct. 1971): 41–49; Leland G. Stanford, "San Diego's Eucalyptus Bubble," *JSDH* 16 (Fall 1970): 11–19; Viola Lockhart Warren, "The Eucalyptus Crusade," *SCQ* 44 (Mar. 1962): 31–42; Frank William Purdy Jr., "Eucalyptus Cultivation in California, 1853–1900" (master's thesis, Sacramento State College, 1968); and Jacqueline Anna Lanson, "Eucalyptus in California: Its Distribution, History, and Economic Value" (master's thesis, UC Berkeley, 1952). A remnant of Humboldt County's gum row on U.S. 101 is still there, a survivor of freezes in 1932 and 1972, though Caltrans recently cut down several of the historic trees because of aviation safety concerns.

Chapter 3. Immigration and Naturalization

1. "Firewood," *California Culturist* 3 (July 1860): 19–20.
2. See James C. Williams, *Energy and the Making of Modern California* (Akron, 1997), chap. 3.
3. "Sugar Gums Solve Forest Protection as Demonstrated on Whittier Hills," *Covina Argus*, 6 Apr. 1917.
4. On the founder of the *California Farmer*, see Walton E. Bean, "James Warren and the Beginnings of Agricultural Institutions in California," *PHR* 13 (Dec. 1944): 361–75.
5. Ellwood Cooper, *Forest Culture and Eucalyptus Trees* (San Francisco, 1876), 30, 16.
6. E. O. Essig, *A History of Entomology* (New York, 1931), 587.
7. Ezra S. Carr, "Forest-Planting, a Source of Wealth," *California Horticulturist* 3 (Feb. 1873): 50–52.
8. T. B. Merry, "Australasian Arboriculture," in *Transactions of the California State Agricultural Society during the Year 1893* (SPO, 1894), 125–30, quote on 125; N. P. Chapman, "Fruit vs. Wheat," in *Fourth Biennial Report of the State Board of Horticulture* (SPO, 1894), 172; Ezra S. Carr, *The Patrons of Husbandry of the Pacific Coast* (San Francisco, 1875), esp. 46–53. For fuller discussions of the ethos, see Ian Tyrrell, *True Gardens of the Gods: Californian-Australian Environmental Reform, 1860–1930* (Berkeley, 1999), chap. 2; and David Curtis Hickman, "Landscapes of Green and Gold: The Environmental Vision of the California Horticulturalists, 1849–1900" (Ph.D. diss., UC Davis, 2011), chap. 4.
9. R. W. Home et al., *Regardfully Yours: Selected Correspondence of Ferdinand von Mueller*, 3 vols. (Bern, 1998–2006), 2:582.
10. On Mueller and his colleagues in the British Empire, see Margaret Willis, *By Their Fruits: A Life of Ferdinand von Mueller, Botanist and Explorer* (Sydney, 1949); Ashley Hay, *Gum: The Story of Eucalypts and Their Champions* (Potts Point, New South

Wales, 2002); and Home, *Regardfully Yours.* For context, see Michael A. Osborne, "Acclimatizing the World: A History of the Paradigmatic Colonial Science," *Osiris* 15 (2001): 135–51; and Richard Drayton, *Nature's Government: Science, Imperial Britain, and the "Improvement" of the World* (New Haven, 2000).

11. *The Eucalyptus Globulus, from a Botanic, Economic, and Medical Point of View, Embracing Its Introduction, Culture, and Uses—Translated from the French of J.-E. Planchon* (GPO, 1875), 20. On colonial trees, see also R. J. Streets, *Exotic Forest Trees in the British Commonwealth*, rev. ed. (Oxford, 1962). On medical geography in nineteenth-century California, see Linda Nash, *Inescapable Ecologies: A History of Environment, Disease, and Knowledge* (Berkeley, 2006), chaps. 1 and 2.

12. Cooper, *Forest Culture and Eucalyptus Trees*, 43; Robert E. C. Stearns, *On the Economic Value of Certain Australian Forest Trees, and Their Cultivation in California* (San Francisco, 1872); "The Eucalyptus Tree," *NYT*, 3 May 1874.

13. "The Eucalyptus and Its Mission," *PRP*, 10 Oct. 1874, 233. On Delano, see "Sanitary Influences of Trees—No. 2," *PRP*, 5 Apr. 1879, 227. On Sacramento, see E. Gregory McPherson and Nina Luttinger, "From Nature to Nurture: The History of Sacramento's Urban Forest," *Journal of Arboriculture* 24 (Mar. 1998): 72–88.

14. See Kenneth Thompson, "The Australian Fever Tree in California: Eucalypts and Malaria Prophylaxis," *Annals of the Association of American Geographers* 60 (June 1970): 230–44.

15. "Eucalyptus Groves," *California Horticulturist* 4 (Apr. 1874): 114; "Eucalyptus Wood," *PRP*, 3 Nov. 1877, 273.

16. "Important Points on Eucalyptus," *PRP*, 25 Aug. 1877, 122. On gums in the Southland, see Ludwig Louis Salvator, *Los Angeles in the Sunny Seventies: A Flower from the Golden Land*, trans. Marguerite Eyer Wilbur (Los Angeles, 1929), 75–76. See also Walter Lindley and J. P. Widney, *California of the South: Its Physical Geography, Climate, Resources, Routes of Travel, and Health-Resorts* (New York, 1888), 325–26.

17. *The Argonaut* (San Francisco), 22 Apr. 1877.

18. "The Shadow on Blue Gums," *PRP*, 5 Apr. 1879, 232.

19. "Tree Culture Experiments," in *First Biennial Report of the California State Board of Forestry* (SPO, 1886), 227–29.

20. Quotes from *PRP*: 2 Dec. 1882, 429; 29 Sept. 1883, 261; 26 Jan. 1884, 73; 31 Dec. 1887, 527; 9 Dec. 1882, 444; and 4 Feb. 1882, 82.

21. See *Third Biennial Report of the California State Board of Forestry* (SPO, 1890), Part I, 17–50, and Part II, 25–31; and, for context, Gerald D. Nash, "The California State Board of Forestry, 1883–1960," *SCQ* 47 (Sept. 1965): 291–99; and Frederica Bowcutt, "Tanoak Target: The Rise and Fall of Herbicide Use on a Common Native Tree," *Environmental History* 16 (Apr. 2011): 197–225.

22. George McGillivray, "The Economic Value of the Eucalyptus," *Overland Monthly* 12 (Nov. 1888): 449–58, quote on 456. See also "The Eucalyptus in California," *Chemist and Druggist* 40 (30 Jan. 1892): 145.

23. See Terence Young, *Building San Francisco's Parks, 1850–1930* (Baltimore, 2004), 73–74, 84–87, 107–11.

24. William W. Winn, "The Joaquin Miller Foundation," *CH* 32 (Sept. 1953): 231–

41, quote on 234. On the Sutro Forest, see Richard Brandi, "Farms, Fire and Forest: Adolph Sutro and Development 'West of Twin Peaks,'" *Argonaut* 14 (Summer 2003).

25. "Evils of the Eucalyptus," *SFCh*, 19 Mar. 1893; "No Eucalyptus Trees Allowed," *SFCh*, 11 Apr. 1900.

26. Emma H. Adams, *To and Fro in Southern California* (Cincinnati, 1887), 249.

27. Jeanne C. Carr, "Some Experiments in Forestry," *PRP*, 3 July 1880, 3; idem, "Floral Culture," in *Annual Report of the State Board of Horticulture of the State of California* (SPO, 1890), 122–24. See also Charles Francis Saunders, *The Story of Carmelita: Its Associations and Its Trees* (Pasadena, 1928).

28. Abbot Kinney, "Our Forests: Their Destruction and Its Dangers," in *Third Biennial Report of the State Board of Horticulture* (SPO, 1888), 118.

29. Abbot Kinney, *Eucalyptus* (Los Angeles, 1895), 65, 24–25; *Transactions of the American Horticultural Society*, vol. 5 (Indianapolis, 1888), 275.

30. Alfred James McClatchie, *Eucalyptus Cultivated in the United States*, USDA Bureau of Forestry Bulletin 25 (GPO, 1902). As late as 1895, a former riverboat captain recalled that in Sacramento "they used to lay in quinine for family stores . . . just as they would tea, coffee, or sugar, but that period has passed by, never to return; and the blue gum of Tasmania is to be thanked for it." Merry, "Australasian Arboriculture," 126.

31. Whiting quoted in Tyrrell, *True Gardens of the Gods*, 76; Louis Margolin, *Yield from Eucalyptus Plantations in California*, California State Board of Forestry Bulletin 1 (SPO, 1910).

32. Joachim Radkau, *Nature and Power: A Global History of the Environment*, trans. Thomas Dunlap (Cambridge, 2008), 233. On the second Board of Forestry, see Gerald Nash, *State Government and Economic Development: A History of Administrative Policies in California, 1849–1933* (Berkeley, 1964), 308–16.

33. William L. Hall, *The Waning Hardwood Supply and the Appalachian Forests*, USDA Forest Service Circular 116 (GPO, 1907). For context, see David A. Clary, *Timber and the Forest Service* (Lawrence, 1986).

34. Stephen J. Pyne, *Fire in America: A Cultural History of Wildland and Rural Fire* (Princeton, 1982), 188.

35. Sarah Cooper, "Floral Culture," *PRP* 38, 16 Nov. 1889, 457.

36. F. D. Cornell, "As It Was—the Eucalyptus Industry—as It Is," *Grizzly Bear* 4 (Apr. 1909): 10–11; idem, "Hickory's Younger Brother," *Sunset* 22 (Mar. 1909): 274–82, quote on 282. Endorsements in A. R. Heath, *The Eucalyptus Hardwood Trees of California* (Chicago, 1912).

37. Advertisements by eucalyptus companies can be found in the back pages of most state and regional magazines in 1909, as well as in newspapers from San Francisco and Los Angeles. A prime example is the notice by the American Forestation Company of Los Angeles that appeared in *Out West* 31 (Dec. 1909): 1050–53.

38. "The Value of Eucalyptus Trees," *Forestry Society of California Bulletin* 5 (1909); George B. Lull, "The Eucalyptus Situation in California," *Grizzly Bear* 4 (Mar. 1909): 1. Information on investigations from "Eucalyptus Growing," *OT*, 12 Aug. 1909.

39. George W. Peavy, "The Eucalypts in California," *California Weekly*, 30 Apr. 1909, 363–64; 14 May 1909, 395; 28 May 1909, 427–28; and 11 June 1909, 449–50.

40. G. B. Lull, letter, *California Weekly*, 18 June 1909, 479; *A Handbook for Eucalyptus Planters*, State Board of Forestry, Circular 2 (SPO, 1908); Norman D. Ingham, *Eucalyptus in California*, UC Agricultural Experiment Station Bulletin 196 (SPO, 1908); Richard J. Orsi, *Sunset Limited: The Southern Pacific Railroad and the Development of the American West* (Berkeley, 2005), quote on 308; C. H. Sellers, *Eucalyptus: Its History, Growth, and Utilization* (Sacramento, 1910).

41. Earle Labor, Robert C. Leitz III, and I. Milo Shepard, eds., *The Letters of Jack London*, vol. 2 (Stanford, 1988), 919, 952, 978, 1007; *The Hardwood Situation*, broadside, copy in Jack London Papers, box 582, folder 2629, HEH; Jack London, *Burning Daylight* (New York, 1910), 255–56.

42. Railroads throughout the country experimented with tree plantations in this period; see Sherry H. Olson, *The Depletion Myth: A History of Railroad Use of Timber* (Cambridge, Mass., 1971), 80–94.

43. "To Investigate Eucalyptus Tales," *OT*, 10 July 1910; H. S. Betts and C. Stowell Smith, *Utilization of California Eucalypts*, USDA Forest Service Circular 179 (GPO, 1910).

44. The association published a journal, *Water and Forest*, and a booklet, *Should the Forests Be Preserved?* (San Francisco, 1903).

45. Muir's card is reproduced in Erika Esau, *Images of the Pacific Rim: Australia and California, 1850–1935* (Sydney, 2010), 219. Biographical information from Shirley Sargent, *Theodore Parker Lukens, Father of Forestry* (Los Angeles, 1969); Ronald F. Lockmann, "Improving Nature in Southern California: Early Attempts to Ameliorate the Forest Resource in the Transverse Ranges," *SCQ* 58 (Winter 1976): 485–95; idem, "Forests and Watershed in the Environmental Philosophy of Theodore P. Lukens," *JFH* 23 (Apr. 1979): 82–91; Theodore Lukens Papers, esp. box 2, HEH; and Lionel A. Sheldon, "Forestation in Southern California: The Eucalyptus," *Rural Californian* 31 (July 1908): 241. John Muir admired the *Eucalyptus* genus so much that he once traveled Down Under to hunt for tall specimens. See P. J. Ryan, "John Muir and the Tall Trees of Australia," *Pacific Historian* 29, nos. 2–3 (1985): 124–35.

46. Abbott Kinney, "Forest Culture," in *Annual Report of the State Board of Horticulture* (SPO, 1890), 149; Tyrrell, *True Gardens of the Gods*, 13.

47. Edward N. Munns, "Resumé of Eucalyptus Planting on the Angeles National Forest," typescript, 1915, Bancroft.

48. "Sugar Gums Solve Forest Protection."

49. For context, see Peter L. Reich, "Dismantling the Pueblo: Hispanic Municipal Land Rights in California since 1850," *American Journal of Legal History* 45 (Oct. 2001): 353–70.

50. All information and quotations come from clippings in the Max Watson Scrapbook, San Diego History Center. For a contemporary profile, see Walter V. Woehlke, "Out of Humanity's Cesspool," *Technical World Magazine* 18 (Jan. 1913): 500–508.

51. See Mike Davis, Kelly Mayhew, and Jim Miller, *Under the Perfect Sun: The San*

Diego Tourists Never See (New York, 2003), 169–97; Richard Steven Street, *Beasts of the Field: A Narrative of California Farmworkers, 1769–1913* (Stanford, 2004), chap. 24; and Kevin Starr, *Endangered Dreams: The Great Depression in California* (Oxford, 1996), chap. 2.

52. See Albert Wilson, "The Story of Two Careers, One of a Tree, and the Other of a Man," *Journal of the California Horticultural Society* 22 (Oct. 1961): 143–49.

53. H. D. Tiemann, "Eucalyptus Lumber," *Hardwood Record*, 25 Sept. 1913, 20–34; and 10 Oct. 1913, 20–23.

54. Jepson quoted in "Street Trees of California," *PRP*, 2 Sept. 1905, 148–49. Kinney quotations from *Eucalyptus*, 42; and *Third Biennial Report* of the State Board of Forestry, Part II, 27.

55. Charles Francis Saunders, *With the Flowers and Trees in California* (New York, 1914), 38; A. H. Crofut to U.S. Department of Forestry, 6 Jan. 1919, MSS 77/95 c, carton 3, Woodbridge Metcalf Papers, Bancroft.

56. T. P. Lukens, *Eucalyptus Growing in California for Profit*, leaflet, 1914, copy in National Agricultural Library, Washington, D.C.; "T. J. Gillespie and the Eucalyptus Industry," *Overland Monthly* 53 (Apr. 1909): 359–60.

57. See Sherry H. Olson, "Commerce and Conservation: The Railroad Experience," *Forest History* 9 (Jan. 1966): 2–15; and idem, *Depletion Myth*.

58. Woodbridge Metcalf, *Growth of Eucalyptus in California Plantations*, UC Agricultural Experiment Station Bulletin 380 (Berkeley, 1924), 6–7.

59. "Value of Windbreaks Shown on Big Tract," *LAT*, 1 Mar. 1925; "Blue Gum's Elected: It Will Have Life Job at Fontana," *LAT*, 27 Mar. 1932. See also John R. Lundemo, "Value of Effective Windbreak to Citrus Orchard," *CC* 6 (Jan. 1921): 76–77. On firewood, see, for example, "The Eucalyptus Wood-lot Solves Farm Fuel Problem," *LAT*, 29 Jan. 1922.

60. "Blue Gum Trees Held Menace to Water System," *OT*, 21 Aug. 1921; "Trees Inclined to Evil Invite Reformer's Axe," *OT*, 20 Nov. 1921.

61. Direct quote from "The Versatile Eucalyptus, California's Adopted Tree," *LAT*, 5 June 1927. Composite (italicized) quotes from *LAT*, 16 Feb. 1929, 26 July 1931, 2 July 1933, and 24 Oct. 1937. For a more tempered view from the editors, see "The Blue Gum's Place," *LAT*, 11 Apr. 1926.

62. Theodore Payne, "The Eucalyptus in California: The Eucalyptus Centennial 1956," *Golden Gardens* (Jan. 1957): 9–12. See also idem, *Theodore Payne in His Own Words: A Voice for California Native Plants* (Pasadena, 2004).

63. "Shows Beauty of Eucalyptus," *SFC*, 19 Feb. 1907; "Cadenasso, Noted Painter, Is Dead," *OT*, 11 Feb. 1918, 2.

64. "The 'Eucalyptus' School," *LAT*, 16 Sept. 1928; J. Smeaton Chase, *California Coast Trails: A Horseback Ride from Mexico to Oregon* (Boston, 1913), 18. For context, see Kenneth R. Trapp and Leslie Greene Bowman, eds., *The Arts and Crafts Movement in California: Living the Good Life* (New York, 1993); Nancy Dustin Wall Moure, "Impressionism, Post-Impressionism, and the Eucalyptus School in Southern California," in *Plein Air Painters of California: The Southland*, ed. Ruth Lilly Westphal (Irvine, 1982), 4–15; and Esau, *Images of the Pacific Rim*. In 1909, when the bickering

heirs of the Sutro estate in San Francisco discussed selling the timber rights to the Sutro Forest to a logging company, women from the Outdoor Art League, a local conservation group also active in redwood preservation, objected to the proposed sale on aesthetic grounds.

65. See Adam Arenson, "Ansel Adams's *Eucalyptus Tree, Fort Ross*: Nature, Photography, and the Search for California," *CH* 82 (Winter 2005): 10–25, 62–65. On hangman's trees in California, see Jared Farmer, "Witness to a Hanging: California's Haunted Trees," *Boom* 3 (Spring 2013): 70–80.

66. On San Diego, see Nancy Carol Carter, "Trees of Balboa Park," *JSDH* 56 (Summer 2010): 137–53.

67. *Garden and Forest* 3 (12 Mar. 1890): 123; "Should Berkeley's Trees Be Cut?" *SFC*, 25 Feb. 1900; Heather Henter, "Tree Wars: The Secret Life of Eucalyptus," *@UCSD* 2 (Jan. 2005). Currently Santa Cruz Island has the tallest gum tree in California—indeed, the tallest eucalypt outside Australia and the tallest flowering plant in the Americas, at nearly 250 feet.

68. See Donald Price, "The Stanford Arboretum," typescript (2001), Special Collections, Green Library, Stanford University; Julie Cain and Roxanne Nilan, "Every Tree, Shrub, and Vine: Leland Stanford's Arboretum, 1879–1905," *Sandstone and Tile* 27 (Spring/Summer 2003): 15–30; Ronald N. Bracewell, *Trees of Stanford and Environs* (Stanford, 2005); August 1910 letters to and from Timothy Hopkins, in Board of Trustees Supporting Documents, box 5, folder 8, Stanford University Archives.

69. Advertisement reprinted at www.outsidelands.org/forest-hill-broadsheet.php. On Rancho Santa Fe, see Phoebe S. Kropp, *California Vieja: Culture and Memory in a Modern American Place* (Berkeley, 2006), chap. 4.

70. George Taylor, "Art and Architecture at the San Francisco Exposition" and "The City of the Golden Gate," *Building*, 12 Feb. 1915, 110–11. For a thorough discussion of landscape aesthetics, beautifully illustrated, see Esau, *Images of the Pacific Rim*. On architecture, see David Gebhard, "The Spanish Colonial Revival in Southern California (1895–1930)," *Journal of the Society of Architectural Historians* 26 (May 1967): 131–47; Karen J. Weitze, *California's Mission Revival* (Santa Monica, 1984); and Arrol Gellner, *Red Tile Style: America's Spanish Revival Architecture* (New York, 2002).

71. See Richard R. Mathison, *Three Cars in Every Garage: A Motorist's History of the Automobile and the Automobile Club in Southern California* (Garden City, N.Y., 1968).

72. Alice Koons, "Ours by Adoption," *LAT*, 2 July 1922. On the Glendale tree fight, see *LAT*: 28 Feb. 1918, 16 July 1926, 20 July 1926, 13 Aug. 1926, 24 Sept. 1927, 3 May 1930, 23 June 1930, and 9 Sept. 1930. Burlingame's shaded 4-mile stretch of El Camino had been landscaped by John McLaren in 1873 with eucalypts and elms. In the late twentieth century, the elms all died from Dutch elm disease, leaving just the towering roadside gums—now one of the last rows of its kind in the state. In 1975 San Mateo County designated the tree row as a heritage grove, and in 2012 it secured its designation as a national historic site.

73. H. Dana Bowers to Woodbridge Metcalf, 15 May 1961, MSS 73/180 c, carton 18, Woodbridge Metcalf Papers, Bancroft.

74. Richard G. Lillard, *Eden in Jeopardy: Man's Prodigal Meddling with His Environ-*

ment: The Southern California Experience (New York, 1966), 77–78; Harold Gilliam, "This Land," *SFCh*, 18 July 1965. For context, see Christopher C. Sellers, *Crabgrass Crucible: Suburban Nature and the Rise of Environmentalism in Twentieth-Century America* (Chapel Hill, 2012).

75. "Housewives Open Drive to Block Tree Removal," *LAT*, 30 Jan. 1963. Other details from *LAT*, San Fernando Valley section: 2–9 July 1971, 15–16 July 1971, 18 July 1971 (source of engineer's quote), 23–24 July 1971, 22 Oct. 1971, 12 Jan. 1972, 14 Jan. 1972, and 22 May 1973.

Chapter 4. Natives, Aliens, and (Bio)diversity

1. "First Eucalyptus Seeds Brought Here in 1840's," *OT*, 9 May 1952; "Eucalyptus: The Beloved Failure," *LAT*, 13 Oct. 1974. On the Sierra Club tradition, see Jeffrey Killion, *Cultural Landscape Report for John Muir National Historic Site*, vol. 1 (Boston, 2005), 180.

2. Louis Allen, "Peril of the Oakland Hills," *OT Magazine*, 25 June 1922.

3. "2 Million Trees Killed in Freeze Pose Threat," *LAT*, 4 Feb. 1973.

4. "Astounding Cost of the Dead Eucalyptus," *SFCh*, 22 July 1973.

5. "Hill Area Holocaust Is Feared," *OT*, 2 Feb. 1973.

6. "Predisaster Assistance for Eucalyptus Tree Fire Hazard," hearing before the Subcommittee on Forests of the Committee on Agriculture, House of Representatives, 93rd Cong., 1st sess., 29 May 1973, Serial No. 93-P (GPO, 1973), 19; "House Kills Bay Area Tree Removal Bill," *LAT*, 12 Sept. 1973.

7. "Eucalyptus Menace in East Bay Hills," *SFCh*, 19 Apr. 1977. See also "New Eucalyptus Trees Sprouting in the Hills," *OT*, 17 July 1971; J. K. Agee et al., "Eucalyptus Fuel Dynamics, and Fire Hazard in the Oakland Hills," *California Agriculture* 27 (Sept. 1973): 13–15; and *The Vegetative Management Plan for the Eucalyptus Freeze Affected Areas in the Berkeley-Oakland Hills* (Alameda, 1974).

8. Quote from "Energy: Search Branches Out to the Eucalyptus," *LAT*, 24 Nov. 1981. See also Richard B. Pearce, "Eucalypts: Energy Tree of the Future," *American Forests* 89 (Jan. 1983): 30–34, 54; Eliseo O. Mariani et al., *The Eucalyptus Energy Farm* (Washington, D.C., 1978); and *Proceedings of a Workshop on Eucalyptus in California*, USDA Pacific Southwest Forest and Range Experiment Station General Technical Report PSW-69 (Berkeley, 1983). Two corporate landowners, Tejon Ranch in Southern California and Simpson Timber Company in the north, experimented with eucs as energy. Even for these large concerns, the biomass boom busted. Simpson converted its would-be energy farm in the Sacramento Valley into a 10,000-acre pulp operation. At the end of the first eight-year cutting cycle in the mid-1990s, the plantation boasted over 6 million trees, almost exclusively river red gum.

9. Italicized passages excerpted from letters in box 2 of Collection RMPNR-07-01, GOGA.

10. Comment letters reprinted in appendix to Douglas D. Piirto et al., *Strategies for Eucalyptus Management at Montaña de Oro State Park* (San Luis Obispo, 1987).

11. "State Parks Get Back to Nature," *San Jose Mercury News*, 20 Aug. 1987.

12. "Angel Island Eucalyptus Facing Loggers' Ax," *SFCh*, 9 Sept. 1987; "Spare Those Trees," *San Francisco Examiner*, 28 July 1987; "State Hatchet Job: Angel Island's Eucalyptus Trees," *San Francisco Examiner*, 9 Sept. 1988; John G. Trezevant to David K. Boyd, 8 Oct. 1987. Boyd, the senior environmental scientist at the Marin District of the DPR in Petaluma, lent me his files on Angel Island. Many of the public comments were reprinted in Jones & Stokes Associates, Inc., "Restoration of Angel Island Natural Areas Affected by Eucalyptus," Final Environmental Impact Report, State of California Department of Parks and Recreation (July 1989). See also Walter E. Westman, "Park Management of Exotic Plant Species: Problems and Issues," *Conservation Biology* 4 (1990): 251–60; Margaret Azevedo, "Of Eucalyptus and Ecology," *California Waterfront Age* 6 (Winter–Spring 1990): 16–20; and California Department of Parks and Recreation, "Focused Environmental Study: Restoration of Angel Island Natural Areas Affected by Eucalyptus" (July 1988).

13. See J. Gordon Routley, *The East Bay Hills Fire, Oakland-Berkeley, California*, U.S. Fire Administration Technical Report Series, FEMA (Washington, D.C., 1992); Peter Charles Hoffer, *Seven Fires: The Urban Infernos That Reshaped America* (New York, 2006), 258–306; and Margaret Sullivan, *Firestorm! The Story of the 1991 East Bay Fire in Berkeley* (Berkeley, 1993).

14. Edward Tenner, *Why Things Bite Back: Technology and the Revenge of Unintended Consequences* (New York, 1996), 196–205. I consulted *OT*, *SFCh*, and *San Jose Mercury News* for the last week of October 1991. On comparative fuel loads of gums, bays, and oaks, see Golden Gate National Recreation Area and Point Reyes National Seashore, *Eucalyptus: A Transcontinental Legacy* (GPO, 2006).

15. "Beetle Threatens State's Eucalyptus," *SFCh*, 9 June 1986.

16. See T. D. Paine and J. G. Millar, "Insect Pests of Eucalypts in California: Implications of Managing Invasive Species," *Bulletin of Entomological Research* 92 (Apr. 2002): 147–51.

17. "Eucalyptus Trees See Summer of Suffering in Insect Infestation," *SDUT*, 4 Sept. 2000.

18. Quote from "California a Paradise for Pests as Well as People," *LAT*, 9 Apr. 2000. Details from Donald L. Dahlsten et al., "Imported Parasitic Wasp Helps Control Red Gum Lerp Psyllid," *California Agriculture* (Oct.–Dec. 2005): 229–34.

19. Paine quoted in Zoë Corbyn, "California's Bioterror Mystery," *Failure Magazine*, 1 Aug. 2012, www.failuremag.org. See also Timothy D. Paine, Jocelyn G. Millar, and Kent M. Daane, "Accumulation of Pest Insects on Eucalyptus in California: Random Process or Smoking Gun," *Journal of Economic Entomology* 103, no. 6 (2010): 1943–49.

20. Accident reportage from *LAT*, 26 Sept. 1983, 20 Nov. 1990, 25 Apr. 1998, 28 Apr. 1998, and 20 June 2001; *Student Life* (Pomona), 3 Mar. and 21 Apr. 2000; and *LAT*, 16 Sept., 17 Sept., and 22 Sept. 2011.

21. "The Deadly Beauty of San Diego's Eucalyptus Trees," *SDUT*, 9 Jan. 2003; "Shadows Cast over Towering Eucalyptuses," *SDUT*, 8 Jan. 2003; and Ernie Grimm, "Parks Coddle Killer Trees," *SanDiegoReader.com*, 13 Feb. 2003. See also "Eucalyptus Safety in Spotlight after Woman's Death," *Orange County Register*, 24 Sept. 2011.

22. Willis L. Jepson, 15 Sept. 1942, field book 67, pp. 15–18, University and Jepson Herbaria Archives, UC Berkeley; "Tree Statistics," UC Tree Failure Report Program, http://groups.ucanr.org/treefail.

23. *Way v. Wolff*, Case A125581, Court of Appeal of California, First Appellate District, Division Four, 30 Mar. 2010, available through LexisNexis under "2010 Cal. App. Unpub. LEXIS 2333." Italics mine. For other examples of lawsuits involving eucs, see Randall S. Stamen, *California Arboriculture Law* (Riverside, 1997).

24. See "Tempest in the Treetops," *LAT*, 17 Sept. 2002; "Blue Gum Blues No More," *LAT*, 27 Feb. 2003; and "Beware Woodsy Dream House," *SFGate*, 5 Aug. 2003. For context, see Martin Peter Poriss, "Eucalyptus Globulus (Also Known as the 'Tasmanian Blue Gum Eucalyptus') and the Santa Cruz, CA, Heritage Tree Ordinance," 1992, copy in Special Collections, UC Santa Cruz; and Chris J. Magyar, "Eupocalypse Now," *Good Times* (Santa Cruz), 23 July 2008.

25. "Some Gum Trees Have to Go," *Pasadena Star-News*, 29 Jan. 2009; "Officials Confirm Dropped Policies," *Laguna Beach Coastline Pilot*, 2 Sept. 2010.

26. "Lessons of 'Arborgeddon,'" *LAT*, 15 Dec. 2011; "L.A. County Arboretum's Fallen Trees Open a Door to the Future," *LAT*, 6 Dec. 2011; "Descanso Gardens to Plant New Native Woodland," *Pasadena Star-News*, 9 Oct. 2012; Charles Francis Saunders, *With the Flowers and Trees in California* (New York, 1914), 35.

27. Ted Williams, "America's Largest Weed," *Audubon* 104 (Jan.–Feb. 2002): 24–31. See also Rich Stallcup, "Deadly Eucalyptus," *Point Reyes Bird Observer Newsletter* (Fall 1996); and Judith Larner Lowry, *Gardening with a Wild Heart: Restoring California's Native Landscapes at Home* (Berkeley, 1999), 212–16.

28. See Julie L. Lockwood and James J. Gilroy, "The Portability of Foodweb Dynamics: Reassembling an Australian Eucalypt–Psyllid–Bird Association within California," *Global Ecology and Biogeography* 13 (2004): 445–50; and David L. Suddjian, "Birds and Eucalypts on the Central California Coast: A Love-Hate Relationship," paper presented at Ecology and Impacts of Blue Gum Eucalyptus in Coastal California conference, 3 June 2004, accessed through www.elkhornsloughctp.org. Other middle-position commentaries include Achva Benzinberg Stein and Jacqueline Claire Moxley, "In Defense of the Non-native: The Case of the Eucalyptus," *Landscape Journal* 11 (Spring 1992): 35–49; and Bill O'Brien, "Raze Them or Praise Them? Eucalyptus: The Sins of a Few Species Tarnish the Genus," *California Trees* 6 (Winter 1995): 1–4, 12.

29. Dov F. Sax, "Equal Diversity in Disparate Species Assemblages: A Comparison of Native and Exotic Woodlands in California," *Global Ecology & Biogeography* 11 (2002): 49–57; Michael Warren, "Consider California's Eucalypts—Such a Lovely Invader," AP State and Local Wire, 27 Sept. 1999, accessed through LexisNexis.

30. See Robert Michael Pyle, *Chasing Monarchs: Migrating with the Butterflies of Passage* (Boston, 1999); Stephen B. Malcolm and Myron P. Zalucki, eds., *Biology and Conservation of the Monarch Butterfly* (Los Angeles, 1993); and John Lane, "California's Monarch Butterfly Trees," *Pacific Discovery* 38 (Jan.–Mar. 1985): 13–15.

31. Paul D. Thacker, "California Butterflies: At Home with Aliens," *BioScience* 54

(Mar. 2004): 182–87. See also Arthur M. Shapiro, "The Californian Urban Butterfly Fauna Is Dependent on Alien Plants," *Diversity and Distributions* 8 (Jan. 2002): 31–40.

32. "Tree-Cutting Clears Path for Butterflies," *SFCh*, 24 Feb. 1995; "Brisbane Sues over Logging," *SFCh*, 27 Apr. 1995; "Medicine That Kills" (opinion letter), *SFCh*, 9 June 1995.

33. See Ellen McGarrahan, "The Mission Blue Mission," *SF Weekly*, 9 Aug. 1995; Paul McHugh, "San Bruno's Mounting Challenge," *SFCh*, 19 Sept. 2002; and Susan Zakin, "Saving San Bruno Mountain: Butterflies and Bulldozers on an Island of Time," *Bay Nature* (Apr.–June 2002), accessed at www.baynature.org.

34. "Day of the Locust for Trees in the Parks" (opinion letter), *SFCh*, 6 July 1996. See also David Boyd, "Eucalyptus Removal on Angel Island," in *Proceedings, California Exotic Pest Plant Council Symposium* (Sacramento, 1997), 73–75; and Michael Kincaid, "Complications of Exotic Plants in the Natural Vegetative Recovery of *Eucalyptus globulus* Eradication Sites," student paper (1997), Water Resources Center Archives, UC Berkeley. As a fire control measure, the state's eucalyptus removal plan seems to have been vindicated in October 2008, when flames burned 400 of Angel Island's 700 acres yet failed to become an inferno: all the island's historic buildings survived. For context, see Jeffrey D. Corbin, Carla M. D'Antonio, and Susan J. Bainbridge, "Tipping the Balance in Favor of Native Plants: Experimental Approaches to Changing the Exotic: Native Ratio in California Grassland," in *Experimental Approaches to Conservation Biology*, ed. Malcolm S. Gordon and Soraya M. Bartol (Berkeley, 2004), 154–79.

35. For context, see Richard A. Walker, *The Country in the City: The Greening of the San Francisco Bay Area* (Seattle, 2007).

36. Bark from decommissioned Presidio gums has been utilized by the celebrated environmental artist Andy Goldsworthy for an onsite outdoor installation ("Wood Line") commissioned by the trust.

37. Ken Garcia, "Presidio Trees May Be Axed to Save Weed," *SFCh*, 9 Apr. 2002; Ken Garcia, "Sand-huggers Run Amok at Presidio," *SFCh*, 14 May 2002. See also "By the Bay, Old Dunes Vie with Exotic Trees," *NYT*, 9 Mar. 2003; and "In S.F., Tree Huggers vs. Sand Huggers," *LAT*, 29 June 2003.

38. "Thousands of Invasive Trees Cleared in UC Berkeley Fire Project," press release, UC Berkeley, 21 Sept. 2004. See also Michelle Quinn, "Trees, Fires and the East Bay Hills," at www.bayareablogs.nytimes.com, 11 Dec. 2009.

39. "Plan to Save Native Plants Too Toxic for Some," *San Jose Mercury News*, 18 Nov. 2002.

40. For overviews, see Harold A. Mooney et al., eds., *Invasive Alien Species: A New Synthesis*, SCOPE 63 (Washington, D.C., 2005); Alan Burdick, *Out of Eden: An Odyssey of Ecological Invasion* (New York, 2005); Mark A. Davis, *Invasion Biology* (Oxford, 2009); Julie L. Lockwood, Martha F. Hoopes, and Michael P. Marchetti, *Invasion Ecology* (Oxford, 2007); David M. Richardson, ed., *Fifty Years of Invasion Ecology: The Legacy of Charles Elton* (Oxford, 2011); Ian D. Rotherham and Robert A.

Lambert, eds., *Invasive and Introduced Plants and Animals: Human Perceptions, Attitudes and Approaches to Management* (London, 2011); and Daniel Simberloff and Marcel Rejmánek, eds., *Encyclopedia of Biological Invasions* (Berkeley, 2011).

41. Sir Joseph Dalton Hooker, "The Distribution of the North American Flora," *American Naturalist* 13 (Mar. 1879): 155-70, quote on 155. For context, see James Moore, "Revolution of the Space Invaders: Darwin and Wallace on the Geography of Life," in *Geography and Revolution*, ed. David N. Livingstone and Charles W. J. Withers (Chicago, 2005), 106-32; and Matthew K. Chew and Andrew L. Hamilton, "The Rise and Fall of Biotic Nativeness: A Historical Perspective," in Richardson, *Fifty Years of Invasion Ecology*, 35-47.

42. See Mark A. Davis, "Invasion Biology, 1958-2004: The Pursuit of Science and Conservation," in *Conceptual Ecology and Invasion Biology: Reciprocal Approaches to Nature*, ed. Marc W. Cadotte, Sean M. McMahon, and Tadashi Fukami (Dordrecht, 2006), 35-64. For critiques of the field, see Mark A. Davis, Ken Thompson, and J. Philip Grime, "Charles S. Elton and the Dissociation of Invasion Ecology from the Rest of Ecology," *Diversity and Distributions* 7, nos. 1-2 (Jan. 2001): 97-102; David I. Theodoropoulos, *Invasion Biology: Critique of a Pseudoscience* (Blythe, Calif., 2003); Mark Sagoff, "Do Non-native Species Threaten the Natural Environment?" *Journal of Agricultural and Environmental Ethics* 18 (May 2005): 215-36.

43. See Timothy J. Farnham, *Saving Nature's Legacy: Origins of the Idea of Biodiversity* (New Haven, 2007). Jared Diamond coined the term *evil quartet* in 1984.

44. See http://bp.gsfc.nasa.gov/isfs_science.html (accessed May 2009).

45. News stories are too numerous to mention, but here are some of the book titles in this vein: *Alien Invasion: America's Battle with Non-native Animals and Plants* (1998); *Life Out of Bounds: Bioinvasion in a Borderless World* (1998); *Killer Algae* (1999); *Nature Out of Place: Biological Invasions in the Global Age* (2000); *Tinkering with Eden: A Natural History of Exotics in America* (2001); *A Plague of Rats and Rubbervines: The Growing Threat of Species Invasions* (2002); *Feral Future: The Untold Story of Australia's Exotic Invaders* (2002); *Aliens in the Backyard: Plant and Animal Imports into America* (2005); and *Super Species: The Creatures That Will Dominate the Planet* (2010). For context, see Daniel Simberloff, "A Rising Tide of Species and Literature: A Review of Some Recent Books on Biological Invasions," *Bioscience* 54 (1 Mar. 2004): 247-54. For a case study in media sensationalism, see Eric Jay Dolin, *Snakehead: A Fish Out of Water* (Washington, D.C., 2003).

46. For critiques of language, see Banu Subramaniam, "The Aliens Have Landed! Reflections on the Rhetoric of Biological Invasions," *Meridians* 2, no. 1 (2001): 26-40; Brendon M. H. Larson, "The War of the Roses: Demilitarizing Invasion Biology," *Frontiers in Ecology and the Environment* 3 (2005): 495-500; and Charles R. Warren, "Perspectives on the 'Alien' versus 'Native' Species Debate: A Critique of Concepts, Language and Practice," *Progress in Human Geography* 31 (Aug. 2007): 427-46. On the Nazi connection, see especially Gert Groening and Joachim Wolschke-Bulmahn, "Some Notes on the Mania for Native Plants in Germany," *Landscape Journal* 11 (Fall 1992): 116-26; and, for a challenging critique, Frank Uekötter, "Native Plants: A

Nazi Obsession?" *Landscape Research* 32 (June 2007): 379–83. For defenses of non-natives, see Michael Pollan, "Against Nativism," *NYT Magazine*, 15 May 1994; Jonah H. Peretti, "Nativism and Nature: Rethinking Biological Invasion," *Environmental Ethics* 7 (May 1998): 183–92; Mark Sagoff, "What's Wrong with Exotic Species?" *Report from the Institute for Philosophy and Public Policy* 19, no. 4 (1999): 16–23; and Emma Marris, *Rambunctious Garden: Saving Nature in a Post-Wild World* (New York, 2011), chaps. 6–7. For contrary views, see Sarah Johnson, comp., *Bioinvaders: Themes in Environmental History* (Cambridge, 2010); Daniel Simberloff, "Confronting Introduced Species: A Form of Xenophobia?" *Biological Invasions* 5, no. 3 (2003): 179–92; and William O'Brien, "Exotic Invasions, Nativism, and Ecological Restoration: On the Persistence of a Contentious Debate," *Ethics, Place and Environment* 9 (Mar. 2006): 63–77.

47. Abbot Kinney, *The Conquest of Death* (New York, 1893). As the value of California's specialty fruit crops grew, anxiety about the economic impact of plant pests and diseases—not nonnative plants per se—grew as well. This led to the state's first plant quarantine law in 1881. That this law came the year before the Chinese Exclusion Act seems coincidental. On federal plant quarantine laws, see Philip J. Pauly, "The Beauty and Menace of the Japanese Cherry Trees: Conflicting Visions of American Ecological Independence," *Isis* 87 (Mar. 1996): 51–73; and idem, *Fruits and Plains: The Horticultural Transformation of America* (Cambridge, Mass., 2007). On the connections—and increasing lack thereof—between xenophobia and biophilia in the United States, see Peter Coates, *American Perceptions of Immigrant and Invasive Species: Strangers on the Land* (Berkeley, 2007), which includes a section on Golden State eucalypts.

48. The 1999 order greatly expanded on the preexisting legal categories *injurious wildlife* and *noxious weeds* established by Congress in 1900 and 1974, respectively.

49. On terminology, see David M. Richardson et al., "Naturalization and Invasion of Alien Plants: Concepts and Definitions," *Diversity and Distributions* 6 (Mar. 2000): 93–107; Mark A. Davis and Ken Thompson, "Eight Ways to Be a Colonizer; Two Ways to Be an Invader: A Proposed Nomenclature Scheme for Invasion Ecology," *Bulletin of the Ecological Society of America* 81 (July 2000): 226–29; Petr Pyšek et al., "Alien Plants in Checklists and Floras: Towards Better Communication between Taxonomists and Ecologists," *Taxon* 53 (Feb. 2004): 131–43; Robert I. Colautti and Hugh J. MacIsaac, "A Neutral Terminology to Define 'Invasive' Species," *Diversity and Distributions* 10 (Mar. 2004): 135–41; Anna Occhipinti-Ambrogi and Bella S. Galil, "A Uniform Terminology on Bioinvasions: A Chimera or an Operative Tool?" *Marine Pollution Bulletin* 49 (Nov. 2004): 688–94; and Jannike Falk-Peterson et al., "On the Numerous Concepts in Invasion Biology," *Biological Invasions* 8 (Sept. 2006): 1409–24. On the "tens rule," see Mark Williamson, *Biological Invasions* (London, 1996), 31–44. The concept applies less well to animals (especially vertebrate predators) than to plants. In some contexts, the "rule" is simply wrong; see Jonathan M. Jeschke and David L. Strayer, "Invasion Success of Vertebrates in Europe and North America," *Proceedings of the National Academy of Sciences* 102 (May 2005): 7198–7202. Plant species estimates are from Edward T. LaRoe et al., eds., *Our Living Resources: A*

Report to the Nation on the Distribution, Abundance, and Health of U.S. Plants, Animals, and Ecosystems (Washington, D.C., 1995), 200–209.

50. Marcel Rejmánek and David M. Richardson, "Eucalypts," in *Encyclopedia of Biological Invasions*, ed. Daniel Simberloff and Marcel Rejmánek (Berkeley, 2011), 203–9. For the total number of plant introductions, see "Invasive Alien Plants in California: 1993 Summary and Comparison with Other Areas in North America," *Madroño* 41, no. 3 (1994): 161–77. For the tally on eucs, see Matt Ritter and Jenn Yost, "Diversity, Reproduction, and Potential for Invasiveness of Eucalyptus in California," *Madroño* 56, no. 3 (2009): 155–67. On low-level plant recruitment in the Southland, see J. B. Kirkpatrick, "Eucalyptus Invasion in Southern California," *Australian Geographer* 13 (Nov. 1977): 387–93. On attitudes of experts, see Cheryl A. Wilen et al., "Survey of University of California Academics' Attitudes Regarding the Impact of Escaped Horticultural Introductions on Wildlands," *Journal of Extension* 44 (Feb. 2006), accessed at www.joe.org.

51. See Paul Robbins, "Comparing Invasive Networks: Cultural and Political Biographies of Invasive Species," *Geographical Review* 95 (Apr. 2004): 139–56.

52. Quotes from John Rodman, "Restoring Nature: Natives and Exotics," in *In the Nature of Things: Language, Politics, and the Environment*, ed. Jane Bennett and William Chaloupka (Minneapolis, 1993), 147; and E. O. Wilson, *The Future of Life* (New York, 2002), 45. See also Brendon M. H. Larson, "Thirteen Ways of Looking at Invasive Species," in *Invasive Plants: Inventories, Strategies and Action*, ed. David R. Clements and Stephen J. Darbyshire, Topics in Canadian Weed Science 5 (Sainte Anne de Bellevue, Québec, 2007), 131–56. For a smart history of "happenstance plants," see Zachary J. D. Falck, *Weeds: An Environmental History of Metropolitan America* (Pittsburgh, 2010).

53. On species shifting, see Anthony Ricciardi, "Are Modern Biological Invasions an Unprecedented Form of Global Change?" *Conservation Biology* 21 (Apr. 2007): 329–36. For a contrarian voice, see Geerat J. Vermeij, "Invasion as Expectation: A Historical Fact of Life," in *Species Invasions: Insights into Ecology, Evolution, and Biogeography*, ed. Dov F. Sax, John J. Stachowicz, and Steven D. Gaines (Sunderland, Mass., 2005), 315–39. "Portmanteau biota" belongs to Alfred Crosby; "weed patch" comes from Clinton N. Jenkins and Stuart L. Pimm, "How Big Is the Global Weed Patch?" *Annals of the Missouri Botanical Garden* 90 (Spring 2003): 172–78.

54. Stephen Jay Gould, "An Evolutionary Perspective on Strengths, Fallacies, and Confusions in the Concept of Native Plants," in *Nature and Ideology: Natural Garden Design in the Twentieth Century*, ed. Joachim Wolschke-Bulmahn (Washington, D.C., 1997), 11–19. The biologist Gordon Orians coined *Homogocene* in 1994; Charles C. Mann helped popularize it in *1493: Uncovering the New World Columbus Created* (New York, 2011).

55. See Robin Doughty, *The Eucalyptus: A Natural and Commercial History of the Gum Tree* (Baltimore, 2000); Brett M. Bennett, "The El Dorado of Forestry: The Eucalyptus in India, South Africa, and Thailand, 1850–2000," *International Review of*

Social History 55, supp. S18 (2010): 27–50; and idem, "A Global History of Australian Trees," *Journal of the History of Biology* 44, no. 1 (2011): 125–45. Cultivation data from G. Iglesias-Trabado and D. Wilstermann, "*Eucalyptus universalis*: Global Cultivated Eucalypt Forests Map 2008," http://git-forestry.com/download_git_eucalyptus_map .htm. In the U.S. South, major timber companies have recently gained preliminary approval from the USDA for large-scale planting of genetically modified eucalypts. Biotech engineers at ArborGen introduced desirable foreign genes to create the patented Freeze Tolerant Eucalyptus. Opponents of the new "FrankenForests" have pointed to California's experience with *E. globulus*. In response, ArborGen notes that it specifically avoided the species with the bad regional reputation. The company even goes out of its way to defend blue gums. "That they have not taken over the entire landscape of California should be considered as proof that the species is not only manageable, but imminently [*sic*] containable," reads the FAQ section of its website. "All species of plants, given enough time and the right environment[,] can become naturalized, which does not mean it is invasive. The California Eucalyptus scenario is a very good example." See "Eucalyptus Facts," www.eucalyptusfacts.org (accessed Jan. 2013).

56. See Sandra M. Sufian, *Healing the Land and the Nation: Malaria and the Zionist Project in Palestine, 1920–1947* (Chicago, 2007), esp. 40–41; Shaul Ephraim Cohen, *The Politics of Planting: Israeli-Palestinian Competition for Control of Land in the Jerusalem Periphery* (Chicago, 1993); and Irus Braverman, *Planted Flags: Trees, Land, and Law in Israel/Palestine* (Cambridge, 2009).

57. "The Smell of Eucalyptus," *SFCh*, 11 Nov. 1946; Saunders, *With the Flowers and Trees in California*, 40; Joni Mitchell, radio interview by Jim Ladd, 29 Dec. 1980, transcript accessed at www.jonimitchell.com/library; Albert G. Miller to Brian O'Neil, 19 Mar. 1986, box 2, Collection RMPNR-07-01, GOGA.

58. W. K. Hancock, *Australia* (London, 1930), 30. See also Ashley Hay, *Gum: The Story of Eucalypts and Their Champions* (Potts Point, New South Wales, 2002); Robert Fyfe Zacharin, *Emigrant Eucalypts: Gum Trees as Exotics* (Melbourne, 1978); Geoffrey Curgenven Bolton, *Spoils and Spoilers: A History of Australians Shaping Their Environment*, 2d ed. (North Sydney, 1992), chap. 4; Tim Bonyhady, *The Colonial Earth* (Carlton South, Victoria, 2000); Tom Griffiths, *Forests of Ash: An Environmental History* (Cambridge, 2001); and Libby Robin, "Nationalising Nature: Wattle Days in Australia," *Journal of Australian History* 26, no. 73 (2002): 13–26. On South Asia, see N. C. Saxena, *India's Eucalyptus Craze: The God That Failed* (Thousand Oaks, 1994); and Doughty, *The Eucalyptus*, chap. 7. On Portugal, see Lars Kardell, Eliel Steen, and Antonio Fabiao, "Eucalyptus in Portugal: A Threat or a Promise," *Ambio* 15, no. 1 (1986): 6–13.

59. "Going Out on a Limb for Liberty," *Ventura County Star*, 26 Sept. 2001.

60. Mary Water to Brian O'Neil, 9 Nov. 1986, box 2, Collection RMPNR-07-01, GOGA. For a nostalgic assessment of the "vanishing" eucalyptus landscape, see Peter Fish, "The Lost Tree," *Sunset* 219 (July 2007): 40D. For another appreciation, see

"Eucalyptus: Invader Also Holds Bay Area Identity," *SFCh*, 30 Nov. 2011. Sadly, coast live oak faces its own dire ecological threat—an invasive microbe that causes a disease known as sudden oak death.

61. "Evil Plants: A Cautionary Tale about Invasive Species," *Monterey County Herald*, 21 Feb. 2009. For comparison, see Matthew K. Chew, "The Monstering of Tamarisk: How Scientists Made a Plant into a Problem," *Journal of the History of Biology* 42, no. 2 (2009): 231–66.

62. Precise acreage numbers are lacking. As estimated in Teresa L. Bulman, "The Eucalyptus in California," *Fremontia* 16, no. 1 (1988): 9–12, California contained 200,000 acres of eucalyptus plantings in 1978.

Part Three: Citruses

1. *California Addresses by President Roosevelt* (San Francisco, 1903), 17–18.

2. See "President Replants Riverside's Treasured Tree," *LAT*, 9 May 1903; and "The President and Party Arrives" and "Roosevelt Plants Original Navel Orange Tree," *RPE*, 9 May 1903. The Mission Inn was originally called the Glenwood Inn.

3. Letter from Huntington to Frank Miller, 17 Mar. 1905, quoted in Minnie Tibbets Mills, "The Man and the Tree: Epic of the Navel Orange and Luther C. Tibbets," typescript, 1942, pt. II, 2, HEH.

Chapter 5. Orange Revolution

1. See May Woods and Arete Swartz Warren, *Glass Houses: A History of Greenhouses, Orangeries and Conservatories* (New York, 1988); and Sylvia Saudan-Skira and Michel Saudan, *Orangeries: Palaces of Glass—Their History and Development* (Cologne, 1998).

2. William A. Spalding, *The Orange: Its Culture in California* (Riverside, 1885), 6–9.

3. See Iris Higbie Wilson, *William Wolfskill, 1798–1866: Frontier Trapper to California Ranchero* (Glendale, 1965); and Anthony J. Lorenz, "Scurvy in the Gold Rush," *Journal of the History of Medicine and Allied Sciences* 12 (Oct. 1957): 473–510.

4. James S. Hittel, *Resources of California* (San Francisco, 1863), 200. Census data from "The History of the Wine Industry in California," typescript, 96, HEH. On the wine period in Southern California, see Thomas Pinney, *A History of Wine in America: From the Beginnings to Prohibition* (Berkeley, 1989), 243–58, 285–315; Ernest Peninou and Sidney Greenleaf, *A Directory of California Wine Growers and Wine Makers in 1860* (Berkeley, 1967); Cleve E. Kindall, "Southern Vineyards: The Economic Significance of the Wine Industry in the Development of Los Angeles, 1831–1870," *SCQ* 41 (June 1959): 26–37; Vincent P. Carosso, *The California Wine Industry: A Study of the Formative Years* (Berkeley, 1951); Irving McKee, "The Beginnings of California Winegrowing," *SCQ* 29 (Mar. 1947): 59–71; Mrs. A. S. C. Forbes, "Los Angeles When It Was

the 'City of Vines,'" *Annual Publication of the Historical Society of Southern California* 15, pts. 2–3 (1932): 336–46; Frona Eunice Wait, *Wines and Vines of California: A Treatise on the Ethics of Wine-drinking* (San Francisco, 1889); and the annual reports of the Board of State Viticultural Commissioners. On labor in the vineyards, see George Harwood Phillips, *Vineyards & Vaqueros: Indian Labor and the Economic Expansion of Southern California, 1771–1877* (Norman, 2010), esp. chaps. 12–13; and Richard Steven Street, *Beasts of the Field: A Narrative History of California Farmworkers, 1769–1913* (Stanford, 2004), chaps. 5 and 7.

5. *The Works of Hubert Howe Bancroft*, vol. 24: *History of California, 1860–1890* (San Francisco, 1890), 34. On silk bounties, see Gerald Nash, *State Government and Economic Development: A History of Administrative Policies in California, 1849–1933* (Berkeley, 1964), 73–75. On the changing economic scene from a contemporary Anglo perspective, see J. M. Guinn, "From Cattle Range to Orange Grove," *Annual Publication of the Historical Society of Southern California* 8, pt. 3 (1911): 144–57. On fencing, see Hazel Adele Pulling, "California's Fence Laws and the Range-Cattle Industry," *Historian* 8 (Spring 1946): 140–55; and Nash, *State Government and Economic Development*, 71–72. For an overview of the structural changes that permitted the transition from grazing to agriculture, see H. F. Raup, "Transformation of Southern California to a Cultivated Land," *Annals of the Association of American Geographers* 49 (Sept. 1959): 58–78; Paul W. Gates, ed., *California Ranchos and Farms, 1846–1862* (Madison, 1967); and Andrew C. Isenberg, *Mining California: An Ecological History* (New York, 2005), chap. 4.

6. Another, less successful pioneer model, the irrigation district, was a creation of state and local government. See Donald J. Pisani, *From the Family Farm to Agribusiness: The Irrigation Crusade in California and the West, 1850–1931* (Berkeley, 1984), chap. 9; and Norris Hundley Jr., *The Great Thirst: Californians and Water—A History*, rev. ed. (Berkeley, 2001), chap. 3.

7. See J. A. Alexander, *The Life of George Chaffey: A Story of Irrigation Beginnings in California and Australia* (Melbourne, 1928); Ian Tyrrell, *True Gardens of the Gods: Californian-Australian Environmental Reform, 1860–1930* (Berkeley, 1999); Jessica B. Teisch, *Engineering Nature: Water, Development and the Global Spread of American Environmental Expertise* (Chapel Hill, 2011); Bernice Bedford Conley, *Dreamers and Dwellers: Ontario and Neighbors* (Montclair, Calif., 1982); Paul Jason Prescott Sandul, "Harvesting Suburbs: Recalling the Suburban Side of California's Agricultural Colonization" (Ph.D. diss., UC Santa Barbara, 2009); and E. O. Moeller, *The Ontario-Cucamonga-Etiwanda Colonies: The Banner Fruit District of Southern California* (San Francisco, 1902).

8. Carey McWilliams, *Southern California: An Island on the Land* (New York, 1946), 215. On Pasadena, see James H. Madison, "Taking the Country Barefooted: The Indiana Colony in Southern California," *CH* 69 (Fall 1990): 236–49. For a regional overview, see Oscar Osburn Winther, "The Colony System of Southern California," *Agricultural History* 27 (July 1953): 94–103. On the connections between therapeutics

and horticulture, see L. M. Holt, *The Great Interior Fruit Belt and Sanitarium of Southern California* (San Bernardino, 1885); and John E. Baur, "The Health Seekers and Early Southern California Agriculture," *PHR* 20 (Nov. 1951): 347–63.

9. North's broadside reproduced in Tom Patterson, *A Colony for California: Riverside's First Hundred Years* (Riverside, 1971), 19. Other quotes from James H. Roe, "Notes on Early History of Riverside, California" (1900), typescript, 6, 10, HEH.

10. John Brown Jr. and James Boyd, *History of San Bernardino and Riverside Counties*, vol. 1 (Madison, 1922), 430; *Fredericksburg News*, 22 Oct. 1867, quoted in Patricia Ortlieb and Peter Economy, *Creating an Orange Utopia: Eliza Lovell Tibbets and the Birth of California's Citrus Industry* (West Chester, Pa., 2011), 29–30. I gleaned additional biographical details from Mills, "The Man and the Tree"; Minnie Tibbets Mills, "Luther Calvin Tibbets: Founder of the Navel Orange Industry of California," *SCQ* 25 (Dec. 1943): 126–61; Tom Patterson, "Spiritualist Introduced Seances, Navel Orange Farming to Riverside," *RPE*, 14 July 1984; and Patterson, *A Colony for California*, 139–53.

11. See P. H. Dorsett, A. D. Shamel, and Wilson Popenoe, *The Navel Orange of Bahia*, USDA Bulletin 445 (GPO, 1917); and A. D. Shamel and Carl S. Pomeroy, *The Washington Navel Orange*, Riverside Chamber of Commerce Citrus Publication 3 (Riverside, 1933).

12. Roe, "Notes on Early History of Riverside, California," 33; R. W. C. Farnsworth, *A Southern California Paradise* (Pasadena, 1883), 29.

13. B. M. Lelong, *A Treatise on Citrus Culture in California* (SPO, 1888), 8–9.

14. Mills, "The Man and the Tree," 122.

15. Edward North, "Biographical Sketch of Luther C. Tibbets," typescript, HEH.

16. John Codman, *The Round Trip by Way of Panama* (New York, 1879), 56.

17. Thomas A. Garey, *Orange Culture in California* (San Francisco, 1882), 29. My composite sketch belies the significant number of widowed female grove owners. "Jesus City" is from Great Basin Foundation, ed., *Wong Ho Leun: An American Chinatown*, vol. 1 (San Diego, 1987), 21. For a broad analysis of the "Concordian" search for "urban pastoralism," see James E. Vance, "California and the Search for the Ideal," *Annals of the Association of American Geographers* 62 (June 1972): 185–210.

18. Mrs. Frank Leslie, *California: A Pleasure Trip from Gotham to the Golden Gate, April, May, June, 1877* (New York, 1874), 257; Laura Gray Turner, "Citrus Culture: The Mentality of the Orange Rancher in Progressive Era North Orange County" (Ph.D. diss., UC Irvine, 1995), quote on 139–40; Spalding, *The Orange*, 1.

19. *Transactions of the American Horticultural Society for the Year 1888*, vol. 5 (Indianapolis, 1888), passim.

20. Details on the fair from Brown and Boyd, *History of San Bernardino and Riverside Counties*, 533–37; and "Many Novel Features for the Riverside Street Fair," *SFC*, 11 Apr. 1900.

21. Marshall Breeden, *The Romantic Southland of California* (Los Angeles, 1928), 123. On Redlands, see Lawrence Emerson Nelson, *Only One Redlands: Changing Patterns in a Southern California Town* (Redlands, 1963).

22. Edson D. Hale, *The County of San Bernardino, California, and Its Principal City* (San Bernardino, 1888), 52–54. On irrigation, see William Hamilton Hall, *Irrigation in California (Southern): The Field, Water-Supply, and Works, Organization and Operation in San Diego, San Bernardino, and Los Angeles Counties* (SPO, 1880); and Walter C. Mendenhall, *Ground Waters and Irrigation Enterprises in the Foothill Belt, Southern California*, U.S. Geological Survey Water-Supply Paper 219 (GPO, 1908).

23. "Protest against the Destruction of Orange Groves," *LAT*, 16 Sept. 1887; *Glendora Signal*, 24 May 1888, quoted in Donald Pflueger, *Glendora: The Annals of a Southern California Community* (Claremont, 1951), 101.

24. William Spalding quoted in "The Opening Programme," *LAT*, 11 Mar. 1891. On the infestation, see Richard C. Sawyer, *To Make a Spotless Orange: Biological Control in California* (Ames, 1996), chap. 1; *Biennial Report of the State Board of Horticulture* (SPO, 1884), 43–45; Paul Debach and David Rosen, *Biological Control by Natural Enemies*, 2d ed. (Cambridge, 1991), 140–48; and Claude B. Hutchison, ed., *California Agriculture* (Berkeley, 1946), 244–61.

25. Quotes from *Report of the Secretary of Agriculture*, House Ex. Doc. 1, Part 7, 51st Cong., 1st sess. (GPO, 1890), 336; and *Transactions of the California State Agricultural Society* (SPO, 1891), 383. The story of the red beetle versus the white scale remains *the* textbook example of biological control. Koebele attained hero status in California for rescuing the citrus industry and won many honorifics, to the annoyance and envy of scientific colleagues. The vedalia beetle became a beloved symbol, too, even though it didn't, we now know, deserve full credit. Another one of Koebele's catches, a parasitoid fly, worked in tandem with the more beautiful and conspicuous predator beetle.

26. Guinn, "From Cattle Range to Orange Grove," 155; *Report of the Commissioner of Agriculture for the Year 1886* (GPO, 1887), 492; "Opening Programme," *LAT*, 11 Mar. 1891.

27. See "The Courts," *LAT*, 29 Jan. 1892; "Those Tahiti Trees," *LAT*, 2 Mar. 1892; and "A Big Bonfire," *LAT*, 30 Mar. 1892. Riverside growers sometimes complained about the laxness of enforcement by the Los Angeles Horticultural Commission; see "Tree Inspection," *LAT*, 18 June 1899. For fuller discussions, see Howard Seftel, "Government Regulation and the Rise of the California Fruit Industry: The Entrepreneurial Attack on Fruit Pests, 1880–1920," *Business History Review* 59 (Autumn 1985): 369–402; Sawyer, *To Make a Spotless Orange*, chap. 2; Nash, *State Government and Economic Development*, 146–50; Alan L. Olmstead and Paul W. Rhode, *Creating Abundance: Biological Innovation and American Agricultural Development* (Cambridge, 2008), 252–58; and E. O. Essig, *A History of Entomology* (New York, 1931), 502–38. California's initial quarantine law (regulating viticulture) came in 1881, following the French model. The U.S. Congress didn't pass such an act until 1912. State commissioner of horticulture Elwood Cooper issued the first quarantine order related to citrus in 1905; this ban on imported tree stock from Florida was meant to keep out citrus white fly.

28. For a list of more than fifty orange varieties raised by Garey, see his *Orange Culture in California*, 153. For a period discussion of the merits of various citrus varietals

grown in California, see B. M. Lelong, *A Treatise on Citrus Culture in California* (Sacramento, 1888), 13–44, 73–80, 90–91. For more on the introduction of particular citrus varieties, see Harry M. Butterfield, *A History of Subtropical Fruits and Nuts in California* (Berkeley, 1963). For a sense of the overall size of the state nursery business in the nineteenth century, see Thomas A. Brown, *A List of California Nurseries and Their Catalogues, 1850–1900* (Petaluma, 1993).

29. E. J. Wickson, *Rural California* (New York, 1923), 164. "Gullible": John E. Baur, "California Crops That Failed," *CH* 45 (Mar. 1996): 41–68, quote on 61. For context, see Paul W. Rhode, "Learning, Capital Accumulation, and the Transformation of California Agriculture," *Journal of Economic History* 55 (Dec. 1995): 773–800; Olmstead and Rhode, *Creating Abundance*, chap. 8; and D. V. Fisher and W. H. Upshall, eds., *History of Fruit Growing and Handling in the United States of America and Canada, 1860–1972* (University Park, Pa., 1976), esp. 11–30. On the demise of Southern California's vines, see Carosso, *California Wine Industry*, 127–29; Pinney, *History of Wine in America*, 292–94; and Newton B. Pierce, *California Vine Disease: A Preliminary Report of Investigations* (GPO, 1892).

30. *Monthly Bulletin of the California State Commission of Horticulture* 8 (July 1919): 347. Los Angeles County statistics compiled from various sources, including *Transactions of the California State Agricultural Society*. The 5 million figure is from "The Orange Crop of the United States," *Crop Reporter* 5 (Dec. 1903), 64. For a succinct overview of the development of the industry, see Walter Ebeling, *The Fruited Plain: The Story of American Agriculture* (Berkeley, 1979), 352–61; or, for fuller discussions, Douglas Cazaux Sackman, *Orange Empire: California and the Fruits of Eden* (Berkeley, 2005); and Anthea Marie Hartig, "Citrus Growers and the Construction of the Southern California Landscape, 1880–1940" (Ph.D. diss., UC Riverside, 2001).

31. *Annual Report of the State Board of Horticulture of the State of California* (SPO, 1892), 330.

32. For a description of one of the state fairs, see M. C. Fredericks, "The Orange in California," *Californian* 1 (Apr. 1892): 451–67. On the SP's role in shipping and marketing California fruit, see Richard J. Orsi, *Sunset Limited: The Southern Pacific Railroad and the Development of the American West, 1850–1930* (Berkeley, 2005).

33. Charles Dwight Willard, *A History of the Chamber of Commerce of Los Angeles, California* (Los Angeles, 1899), 114–25. "Red ink": Rahno Mabel MacCurdy, *The History of the California Fruit Growers Exchange* (Los Angeles, 1925), 15. On nursery trees, see "Boom in Orange Trees," *LAT*, 12 May 1896. For context, see Steven Stoll, *The Fruits of Natural Advantage: Making the Industrial Countryside in California* (Berkeley, 1998), chap. 3.

34. See MacCurdy, *History of the California Fruit Growers Exchange*; Ira B. Cross, "Co-operation in California," *American Economic Review* 1 (Sept. 1911): 535–44; G. Harold Powell, *Coöperation in Agriculture* (New York, 1913); and John William Lloyd, *Co-operative and Other Organized Methods of Marketing California Horticultural Products* (Urbana, 1919).

35. "The Only True Citrus Belt," *LAT,* 13 Mar. 1899. On the Sunshine State, see Christian Warren, "'Nature's Navels': An Overview of the Many Environmental Histories of Florida Citrus," in *Paradise Lost? The Environmental History of Florida,* ed. Jack E. Davis and Raymond Arsenault (Gainesville, 2005), 177–200.

36. On Stebler and Parker, see Vincent Moses, "Machines in the Garden: A Citrus Monopoly in Riverside, 1900–1936, *CH* 61 (Spring 1982): 26–35.

37. See Esther H. Klotz, Harry W. Lawton, and Joan H. Hall, eds., *A History of Citrus in the Riverside Area* (Riverside, 1969), 30–36; Alfred M. Boyce, "U.C. Riverside: Outstanding Achievements in Agricultural Research," *California Agriculture* 29 (Jan. 1975): 3–8; Walter Reuther et al., *The Citrus Industry,* vol. 4 (Berkeley, 1978), chap. 5; *Citrus Experiment Station, Riverside, 1907–1982* (Riverside, 1982); and Alfred M. Boyce, *Odyssey of an Entomologist: Adventures on the Farm, at Sea, and in the University* (Riverside, 1987), 363–78.

38. "The First Seedless Oranges," *NYT,* 20 Apr. 1902.

39. On the history of CFGE/Sunkist, see MacCurdy, *History of the California Fruit Growers Exchange*; Irwin W. Rust and Kelsey B. Gardner, *Sunkist Growers, Inc.: A California Adventure in Agricultural Cooperation* (USDA, 1960); and Catherine Merlo, *Heritage of Gold: The First 100 Years of Sunkist Growers, 1893–1993* (Los Angeles, 1994). On the ad campaigns, see Jeffrey L. Cruikshank and Arthur W. Schultz, *The Man Who Sold America: The Amazing (But True!) Story of Albert D. Lasker and the Creation of the Advertising Century* (Boston, 2010), 113–22; Sackman, *Orange Empire,* chap. 3; Susanne Freidberg, *Fresh: A Perishable History* (Cambridge, Mass., 2009), 134–47; and Don Francisco, *Cooperative Advertising: A Social Service as Well as a Powerful Sales Force* (Los Angeles, 1920). For its nonpremium fruit, CFGE used the Red Ball trademark.

40. See Ted W. Nelson, "Citrus Fruit and Forests: The Story of California's Fruit Growers Supply Company," *Forest History Today* (Spring–Fall 2006): 24–28; and Tim I. Purdy, *Fruit Growers Supply Company, Hilt-Susanville-Westwood-Burney: A History of the Northern California Operations* (Susanville, 2000).

41. John Steinbeck, *The Grapes of Wrath* (New York, 1939), chap. 25, para. 3. For a concise overview of labor practices, see Margo McBane and Anthea Hartig, "Oranges on the Plains of Id: The Influence of the Citrus Industry on San Gabriel Valley Communities," *California Politics and Policy* (1998): 9–17.

42. Helen Kennard Bettin, comp., *This I Remember: Reminiscences of Old-Timers of Glendora, California* (City of Industry, Calif., 1990), 126. On Chinese labor in the orange groves, see Great Basin Foundation, ed., *Wong Ho Leun: An American Chinatown,* vol. 1 (San Diego, 1987). For context, see Alexander Saxton, *The Indispensible Enemy: Labor and the Anti-Chinese Movement in California* (Berkeley, 1971); and Sucheng Chan, *This Bittersweet Soil: The Chinese in California Agriculture, 1860–1910* (Berkeley, 1986).

43. Holt in the *Riverside Press and Horticulturalist,* quoted in Great Basin Foundation, *Wong Ho Leun,* 40, 44, 46, 49. On Pasadena, see Michael E. James, *The Conspiracy of*

the Good: Civil Rights and the Struggle for Community in Two American Cities, 1875–2000 (New York, 2005), 28–30. "Yellow devils": J. W. Wood, Pasadena, California, Historical and Personal (Pasadena, 1917), 272–73.

44. See Jean Pfaelzer, Driven Out: The Forgotten War against Chinese Americans (New York, 2007); Street, Beasts of the Field, chaps. 13 and 16; and Patterson, A Colony for California, 194–98. However, the best source on the Chinese in Riverside and the Citrus Belt is Great Basin Foundation, Wong Ho Leun, 1–140, 193–203.

45. On the Japanese in the citrus labor market, see Dillingham Commission, Japanese and Other Immigrant Races in the Pacific Coast and Rocky Mountain States, vol. 2 (GPO, 1911), 215–32, quote on 227; and, for context, Street, Beasts of the Field, chap. 20. Street's magisterial work updates Cletus E. Daniel, Bitter Harvest: A History of California Farmworkers, 1870–1941 (Ithaca, 1981).

46. Riverside Press, 1–7 Sept. 1893. On Riverside's Japanese population, see Morrison Gideon Wong, "The Japanese in Riverside, 1890 to 1945: A Special Case in Race Relations" (Ph.D. diss., UC Riverside, 1977); and Mark Howland Rawitsch, No Other Place: Japanese American Pioneers in a Southern California Neighborhood (Riverside, 1983). Frank Miller had a fascination with American Indians, too. Due in large part to his lobbying, the federal government in 1900 authorized a large boarding school in Riverside. The hotelier saw tourist gold in Indians. See Nathan Gonzales, "Riverside, Tourism, and the Indian: Frank A. Miller and the Creation of Sherman Institute," SCQ 84 (Sept. 2002): 193–222; and Clifford E. Trafzer, Matthew Sakiestewa Gilbert, and Lorene Sisquoc, eds., The Indian School on Magnolia Avenue: Voices and Images from Sherman Institute (Corvallis, 2012).

47. "Dire Threat of the Nightcaps," LAT, 27 Nov. 1904; "Glendora Tree Vandals Treed," LAT, 4 Dec. 1904; "Shall Fruit Rot for Help's Lack?" LAT, 4 Apr. 1906. On anti-Japanese violence, see Street, Beasts of the Field, 499–500. See also Donald Pflueger, Glendora: The Annals of a Southern California Community (Claremont, 1951), 122; and Bettin, This I Remember, 160.

48. J. H. Reed, "The Proper Handling of Citrus Fruits," in Official Report of the Thirty-fourth Fruit-Growers' Convention of the State of California (SPO, 1908), 57. For more details, see H. Vincent Moses, "'The Orange-Grower Is Not a Farmer': G. Harold Powell, Riverside Orchardists, and the Coming of Industrial Agriculture, 1893–1930," CH 74 (Spring 1995): 22–37, 131–33; and idem, "G. Harold Powell and the Corporate Consolidation of the Modern Citrus Enterprise, 1904–1922," Business History Review 69 (Summer 1995): 119–55. See also G. Harold Powell, The Decay of Oranges while in Transit from California (GPO, 1908).

49. In the Santa Clara Valley (today's Silicon Valley), many Japanese became stone-fruit orchardists; see Cecilia Tsu, Garden of the World: Asian Immigrants and the Making of Agriculture in California's Santa Clara Valley (Oxford, 2013).

50. "Hindu Invasion Causes Stir," LAT, 1 Feb. 1909.

51. George P. Clements, "Mexican Immigration and Its Bearing on California's Agriculture," CC 15 (Nov. 1929): 3, 28–29, 31; idem, testimony before the House Committee on Immigration and Naturalization, Western Hemisphere Immigration: Hearings

on H.R. 8523, H.R. 8530, and H.R. 8702, 71st Cong., 2nd sess. (GPO, 1930), 437. For context, see Stephanie Lewthwaite, "Race, Paternalism, and 'California Pastoral': Rural Rehabilitation and Mexican Labor in Greater Los Angeles," *Agricultural History* 81 (Winter 2007): 1–35.

52. On housing, see Camille Guerin-Gonzales, *Mexican Workers and American Dreams: Immigration, Repatriation, and California Farm Labor, 1900–1939* (New Brunswick, 1994), 61–64.

53. Details from Nelson Van Valen, "The Bolsheviki and the Orange Growers," *PHR* 22, no. 1 (1953): 39–50; "Agitators Causing Trouble among Orange Pickers in South," *CC* 4 (Mar. 1919): 129; "Wire Entanglements," *CC* 5 (Dec. 1920): 33; "Russian Reds Are 'Deported,'" *LAT,* 6 Feb. 1919; "Tehachepi [*sic*] Fruit Trees Destroyed," *LAT,* 2 May 1918. For context, see John H. M. Laslett, *Sunshine Was Never Enough: Los Angeles Workers, 1880–2010* (Berkeley, 2012), chap. 3.

54. Gregory R. Woirol, ed., *In the Floating Army: F. C. Mills on Itinerant Life in California, 1914* (Urbana, 1992), 39; Modesto López, quoted in Matt Garcia, *A World of Its Own: Race, Labor, and Citrus in the Making of Greater Los Angeles, 1900–1970* (Chapel Hill, 2001), 162. On the history of Mexican labor, see also Gilbert G. González, *Labor and Community: Mexican Citrus Worker Villages in a Southern California County, 1900–1950* (Urbana, 1994); José M. Alamillo, *Making Lemonade Out of Lemons: Mexican American Labor and Leisure in a California Town, 1880–1960* (Urbana, 2006); and Sackman, *Orange Empire,* chap. 5.

55. Guinn, "From Cattle Range to Orange Grove," 157; Ronald Tobey and Charles Wetherell, "The Citrus Industry and the Revolution of Corporate Capitalism in Southern California, 1887–1944," *CH* 74 (Spring 1995): 6–21, 129–31, median statistic on 14; other statistics from Williamson, "Labor in the California Citrus Industry," 14–16.

56. On Chapman, see Merle Crowell, "Wiped Out at Forty," *American Magazine* 91 (Apr. 1921): 14–15, 106, 109–10; and Charles C. Chapman, *The Career of a Creative Californian, 1853–1944* (Los Angeles, 1976). On the valley, see Laura R. Barraclough, *Making the San Fernando Valley: Rural Landscapes, Urban Development, and White Privilege* (Athens, 2011), chap. 1. On the Irvine Company, see Robert Glass Cleland, *The Irvine Ranch,* rev. ed. (San Marino, 1962), 116–20.

57. "Jerusalem" is from one of Teague's private letters, quoted in Richard G. Lillard, "Agricultural Statesman: Charles C. Teague of Santa Paula," *CH* 65 (Mar. 1986): 2–16. See also Michael R. Belknap, "The Era of the Lemon: A History of Santa Paula, California," *CH* 47 (June 1968): 113–40. Teague also presided over the state's walnut and lima bean cooperatives and served as a member of the Federal Farm Board and the University of California Board of Regents.

58. G. Harold Powell, *Letters from the Orange Empire,* ed. Richard G. Lillard (Los Angeles, 1990), 36–44. See also Lester S. Ivins and A. E. Winship, *Fifty Famous Farmers* (New York, 1924), 166–78.

59. Robert Glass Cleland, *California in Our Time* (New York, 1947), 165–66. California's other important citrus cooperative was Mutual Orange Distributors, which introduced its Pure Gold brand in 1910. The MOD, centered in Redlands, was much

smaller, focusing on select navel oranges. It published its own magazine, *Citrus Leaves*. By the 1930s CFGE and MOD together controlled close to 90 percent of California's citrus crop. On MOD, see Rahno Mabel MacCurdy, V. A. Lockabey, and Richard H. Baker, *Citrus Roots . . . Our Legacy: Selling the Gold*, vol. 1 (Upland, 1999). In 1967 the Supreme Court ruled that Sunkist didn't qualify as an agricultural cooperative under the law because it admitted members who were not producers. Sunkist reorganized the next year. In 1977 the FTC filed a complaint against Sunkist for anticompetitive practices, and in 1980 it reached a settlement with the cooperative.

60. Charles Collins Teague, *Fifty Years a Rancher* (Los Angeles, 1944), 142–44. See also Margo McBane, "The Role of Gender in Citrus Employment: A Case Study of Recruitment, Labor, and Housing Patterns at the Limoneira Company, 1893 to 1940," *CH* 74 (Spring 1995): 68–81.

61. Chase quoted in Alamillo, *Making Lemonade Out of Lemons*, 27. On *The Grapes of Wrath*, see Sackman, *Orange Empire*, chap. 8.

62. "Interesting the Mexican," *CC* 5 (Aug. 1920): 1; Industrial Relations Department, California Fruit Growers Exchange, "Easy Lessons in Everyday English for Citrus Fruit Workers," booklet, 1920, copy in HEH.

63. On Glendora, see Bettin, *This I Remember*, 39–41; on Pasadena, see James, *Conspiracy of the Good*, 142–54.

64. The skating rink in Redlands likewise enforced Mexican Day. On segregated pools, see Lawrence Culver, *The Frontier of Leisure: Southern California and the Shaping of Modern America* (Oxford, 2010), 68–74; and, for context, Jeff Wiltse, *Contested Waters: A Social History of Swimming Pools in America* (Chapel Hill, 2007). For additional local details on segregation, see James, *Conspiracy of the Good*, esp. 140–68, 245–54; Rob Leicester Wagner, *Sleeping Giant: An Illustrated History of Southern California's Inland Empire* (Las Vegas, 2004), 58; Philippa Strum, *Mendez v. Westminster: School Desegregation and Mexican-American Rights* (Lawrence, 2010); and Martha Menchaca and Richard R. Valencia, "Anglo-Saxon Ideologies in the 1920s–1930s: Their Impact on the Segregation of Mexican Students in California," *Anthropology & Education Quarterly* 21 (Sept. 1990): 222–49, which focuses on Santa Paula.

65. Christopher N. Cocoltchos, "The Invisible Empire and the Search for the Orderly Community: The Ku Klux Klan in Anaheim, California," in *The Invisible Empire in the West: Toward a New Historical Appraisal of the Ku Klux Klan of the 1920s*, ed. Shawn Lay (Urbana, 1992), 97–120. .

66. "Vigilantes Battle Citrus Strikers in War against Reds," *LAT*, 11 July 1936; "Nature's First Law," *LAT*, 9 July 1936; Carey McWilliams, "Gunkist Oranges," *Pacific Weekly* 5 (20 July 1936): 38–39, which appeared in revised form in *Southern California*, 220–21, where McWilliams updated the analogy to "Nazi concentration camp." See also Paul Garland Williamson, "Labor in the California Citrus Industry" (master's thesis, UC Berkeley, 1947), 118–33; Clara Huber Engle, "The Orange County Citrus Strike, 1936: Historical Analysis and Social Conflict" (master's thesis, California State University, Fullerton, 1975); Louis Reccow, "The Orange County Citrus Strikes of 1935–36: The 'Forgotten People' in Revolt" (Ph.D. diss., University

of Southern California, 1971); and Gilbert G. González, "The Mexican Citrus Picker Union, the Mexican Consulate, and the Orange County Strike of 1936," *Labor History* 35 (Winter 1994): 48–65. On Sinclair, Teague, and EPIC, see Sackman, *Orange Empire*, chap. 6.

67. See Laurie Gordon and John Salkin, "'Eat Me and Grow Young!': Orange Crate Art in the Golden State," *CH* 56 (Spring 1977): 52–71; and Paul F. Starrs, "The Navel of California and Other Oranges: Images of California and the Orange Crate," *California Geographer* 28 (1988): 1–41. For a visual analysis of a series of illustrated essays in the industry magazine *California Citrograph*, see Andrea M. Hartig, "'In a World He Has Created': Class Collectivity and the Growers' Landscape of the Southern California Citrus Industry, 1890–1940," *CH* 74 (Spring 1995): 100–111.

68. Steinbeck, *Grapes of Wrath*, chap. 10; McWilliams, *Southern California Country*, 218.

69. Tobey and Wetherell, "Citrus Industry and the Revolution of Corporate Capitalism," 18–19. For context, see Richard A. Walker, "California's Golden Road to Riches: Natural Resources and Regional Capitalism, 1848–1940," *Annals of the Association of American Geographers* 91 (Mar. 2001): 167–99. Statistics compiled from USDA Bureau of Agricultural Economics, Foreign Agricultural Service, *Statistics Relating to the Citrus Industry* (Washington, 1933, 1934, 1935–36); California Fruit Growers Exchange, Marketing Research Department, *Statistical Information on the Orange Industry* (Los Angeles, 1940–1945); idem, *Statistical Information on the Citrus Fruit Industry: Oranges, Lemons, Grapefruit* (Los Angeles, 1947); and Hutchison, *California Agriculture*, 217–22. For comparisons of Californian and Mediterranean production, see José Morilla Critz, Alan L. Olmstead, and Paul W. Rhode, "'Horn of Plenty': The Globalization of Mediterranean Horticulture and the Economic Development of Southern Europe, 1880–1930," *Journal of Economic History* 59 (June 1999): 316–52; and Samuel Garrido, "Oranges or 'Lemons'? Family Farming and Product Quality in the Spanish Orange Industry," *Agricultural History* 84 (Spring 2010): 224–43.

70. Teague quoted in Stoll, *Fruits of Natural Advantage*, 50; Coit, *Citrus Fruits*, 356.

71. E. J. Wickson, *Rural California* (New York, 1923), 190; Water E. Woehlke, "In the Orange Country," *Sunset* 26 (Mar. 1911): 251–64, quote on 263. Paul S. Taylor's major work, created with his wife, Dorothea Lange, was *An American Exodus: A Record of Human Erosion* (New York, 1939). For context, see Kevin Starr, *Endangered Dreams: The Great Depression in California* (Oxford, 1996).

Chapter 6. Cultural Costs

1. W. M. Mertz, "Windburning of Citrus Trees," *CC* 9 (Jan. 1924): 85. On the SP's role in agricultural education, see Richard J. Orsi, *Sunset Limited: The Southern Pacific Railroad and the Development of the American West, 1850–1930* (Berkeley, 2005), chap. 11.

2. "Orange Trees—Age of Maturity," *LAT*, 3 Oct. 1897. For more on the history

and science of rootstock, see W. P. Bitters, "Citrus Rootstocks: Their Characters and Reactions," unpublished ms., ca. 1986, available at www.citrusvariety.ucr.edu.

3. The Citrus Belt contained some huge nursery operations. San Dimas Nurseries, started around 1900, was one of the largest; the owner, Robert M. Teague, supplied navel tree stock locally and globally, including to Italy, South Africa, Palestine, India, and New Zealand. See Paul Rippens, *San Dimas* (Charleston, S.C., 2008), chap. 3; and Frank Parkhurst Brackett, *History of Pomona Valley, California, with Biographical Sketches* (Los Angeles, 1920), 359–61.

4. Floyd D. Young, "The 1937 Freeze in California," *Monthly Weather Review* 66 (Oct. 1938): 311–24, quote on 312; "Injurious Effects of the Windstorm of Nov. 20, 1919," *CC* 5 (Apr. 1920), 178. On the 1891 windstorm, see Henry Markham Page, *Pasadena: Its Early Years* (Los Angeles, 1964), 156–57.

5. On pruning, see Robert W. Hodgson, *The Pruning of Citrus Trees in California* (Berkeley, 1923); C. D. McCarty, *Pruning Citrus Trees* (Berkeley, 1974); and Walter Reuther et al., *The Citrus Industry*, vol. 3, rev. ed. (Berkeley, 1973), chap. 7.

6. See L. J. Klotz and H. S. Fawcett, *Color Handbook of Citrus Diseases* (Berkeley, 1948); Walter Reuther et al., *The Citrus Industry*, vol. 4 (Berkeley, 1978), chaps. 1–2; and Pinchas Spiegel-Roy and Eliezer E. Goldschmidt, *Biology of Citrus* (Cambridge, 1996), 167–75.

7. See A. D. Shamel et al., *Citrus-Fruit Improvement: A Study of Bud Variation in the Washington Navel Orange* (USDA, 1918); A. D. Shamel, C. S. Pomeroy, and R. E. Caryl, *Bud Selection in the Washington Navel Orange: Progeny Tests of Limb Variations* (USDA, 1929); and Reuther, *Citrus Industry*, vol. 4, chap. 3. Shamel's colleagues in Riverside also investigated the costly annoyance known as "June drop," the excessive dropping of young small green navel fruit in late spring to early summer. A heat wave in June 1917 caused extreme drop losses throughout the Citrus Belt. See J. Eliot Coit and Robert Hodgson, *The June Drop of Washington Navel Oranges* (Berkeley, 1917).

8. For the most detailed account of the various early methods, both biological and chemical, used to combat insect pests in California, consult E. O. Essig, *A History of Entomology* (New York, 1931). For a historical overview of pest control in California specialty agriculture, see Steven Stoll, *The Fruits of Natural Advantage: Making the Industrial Countryside in California* (Berkeley, 1998), chap. 4. On citrus pest control, see Henry J. Quayle, *Insects of Citrus and Other Subtropical Fruits* (Ithaca, 1938), 446–547; and Walter Reuther et al., eds., *The Citrus Industry*, vol. 5 (Oakland, 1989), 89–147. On fumigation specifically, see R. S. Woglum, "Hydrocyanic-Acid Gas Fumigation in California," *USDA Bureau of Entomology Bulletin* 90, pt. 1 (GPO, 1911); C. W. Woodworth, *School of Fumigation* (Los Angeles, 1915); and R. W. Hodgson, "How Fumigation Methods for Fighting Scale Have Changed," *LAT*, 3 Apr. 1921.

9. "Cyanide Grains Kill Songsters," *LAT*, 25 Aug. 1907. Statistics are from "Trees Guarded at Cost of Seventy Thousand," *LAT*, 5 Jan. 1916; and "More Fumigation at Smaller Cost," *LAT*, 22 Feb. 1916. Some growers applied cyanide whether or not their trees had scale, in the belief that the treatment invigorated the tree and produced

heavier and better fruit. As one cyanide supply company said in an advertisement, *"Fumigation* is as essential to the Citrus Industry as *Iron* is to the *Human System."* See *CC* 7 (July 1922), inside front cover.

10. Period details from "Commissioner's Office Issues Spray and Fumigation Rules," *LAT,* 19 Aug. 1923; and "Men Put Torch to Fine Trees," *LAT,* 7 Dec. 1910.

11. On the mealybug, see Debach and Rosen, *Biological Control by Natural Enemies,* 185–88. On twentieth-century biological control in California, see Reuther, *Citrus Industry,* vol. 4, chap. 6; and Richard C. Sawyer, *To Make a Spotless Orange: Biological Control in California* (Ames, 1996), chaps. 4–6. For a case study of grower-led biological control, see Lawrence Graebner, "An Economic History of the Fillmore Citrus Protective District" (Ph.D. diss., UC Riverside, 1983).

12. Chapman manager quoted in William L. McCulloch, "The Tree as the Unit of Culture," *CC* 7 (Apr. 1922): 189, 220. "Weeds out": "Do Your Trees Make Good," *LAT,* 14 Jan. 1917. See also H. J. Damerel, "The Tree, the Unit of the Citrus Industry," *CC* 8 (Aug. 1923): 338, 357–58; Robert W. Hodgson, *Analyzing the Citrus Orchard by Means of Simple Tree Records* (Berkeley, 1923); and A. D. Shamel, *Citrus-Fruit Improvement: How to Secure and Use Tree-Performance Records* (USDA, 1917/1928). A survey in the early 1920s showed that fewer than half of growers kept *any* records except cash expenses and receipts. Roland S. Vaile, *A Survey of Orchard Practices in the Citrus Industry of Southern California* (Berkeley, 1924), 6.

13. "No One Knows What Is Best for a Citrus Tree, Says La Verne Grower," *CC* 21 (June 1936): 279; J. Eliot Coit, *Citrus Fruits* (New York, 1930), 204; Carey McWilliams, *Southern California Country: An Island on the Land* (New York, 1946), 207–8.

14. See "Parent Tree Is in Serious Condition," *RPE,* 17 Feb. 1918; Herbert John Webber, "Saving the Parent Washington Navel Orange Tree," *CC* 29 (June 1944): 213, 235.

15. Program, Riverside Navel Orange Pageant, 5 May 1933, copy in A. D. Shamel Papers, box 1, folder 31, Special Collections, UC Riverside. A similar parade was held the next year: "Thousands Applaud Spectacular Parade at Riverside Navel Orange Pageant," *LAT,* 5 May 1934. Cover image: *CC* 14 (Jan. 1929). On tree care, see "L. C. Vincent, Guardian of Low Park and Parent Navel Orange Tree, Retires," *RPE,* 27 May 1962.

16. "Lessons from the Frosts," *PRP* 57 (13 May 1899): 293.

17. Edith Barrett Parker Hinckley, *On the Banks of the Zanja: The Story of Redlands* (Claremont, 1951), 118.

18. The following summary of orchard heaters builds on Alan M. Paterson, "Oranges, Soot, and Science: The Development of Frost Protection in California," *Technology and Culture* 16 (July 1975): 360–76. See also Alexander McAdie, "Frost Fighting for Fruit," *PRP* 59 (9 June 1900): 356–57. I read every *LAT* article containing any variant of the word *smudge* and perused the digital archive of local newspapers in Redlands, Covina, and Long Beach. More research awaits; smudging (not restricted to citrus growers) is a surprisingly understudied chapter in California history and environmen-

tal history, even though Alfred J. Toynbee in *A Study of History* (1957) identified it as an example of "Western Man's success in modifying the incidence of laws of non-Human Nature on his affairs" (289).

19. On the court case, see "The Everests Convicted," *NYT,* 16 May 1887; and "Why He Was So Lenient," *NYT,* 30 Oct. 1889. On the orchard, see "Frost in the Orange Groves," *Massachusetts Ploughman* 60 (2 Feb. 1901): 1.

20. On the Riverside tests, see W. H. Hammon, *Frost: When to Expect It and How to Lessen the Injury Therefrom* (Washington, 1899), 22–34; and E. B. Garriott, *Notes on Frost,* USDA Farmer's Bulletin 104 (GPO, 1908), 20–22. On Limoneira, see "Frost Prevention by Coal Baskets," *PRP* 61 (16 Mar. 1901): 164.

21. F. A. Little Ranch (Riverside), scrapbook (1913), photograph 119, Lemon Men's Club collection, HEH.

22. Quotes from Esther H. Klotz et al., eds., *A History of Citrus in the Riverside Area* (Riverside, 1969), 42; and Joan H. Hall, *A Citrus Legacy* (Riverside, 1992), 112. On the 1913 freeze, see H. J. Webber et al., *A Study of the Effects of Freezes on Citrus in California,* UC Agricultural Experiment Station Bulletin 304 (Jan. 1919). On frosts and freezes, and for a history of cold weather protection and forecasting, see Reuther, *Citrus Industry,* vol. 3, 339–406.

23. "Military Precision in Frost Fighting," *PRP* 91 (18 Mar. 1916): 345. On Chase, see J. M. Guinn, *Historical and Biographical Record of Southern California* (Chicago, 1902), 917–18; Elmer Wallace Homes, *History of Riverside County, California, with Biographical Sketches* (Los Angeles, 1912), 562–64; and E. P. Clarke, *Celebration in Honor of the Eightieth Birthday of Ethan Allen Chase* (Riverside, 1912).

24. "Modern Paul Reveres in the Night of Need," *LAT,* 6 Feb. 1916.

25. "Smudge Pots Sermon Topic," *LAT,* 7 Feb. 1922. See also Floyd D. Young, "Notes on the 1922 Freeze in Southern California," *Monthly Weather Review* 51 (Nov. 1923): 581–85.

26. See "Pomona Council Must Abate Smudge Nuisance," *LAT,* 21 May 1913; and "Orchard Heaters Emitting Smoke Lighter than Air May Be Used," *CC* 5 (Nov. 1919): 20.

27. On Young, see Paterson, "Oranges, Soot, and Science"; F. D. Young, "How They Formerly Gave Frost Warnings before Advent of Radio," *CC* 23 (Apr. 1938): 270; and Richard H. Barker, *Citrus Roots . . . Our Legacy,* vol. 2, *Citriculture to Citrus Culture* (Upland, 2004), 80. Details on frostless convention are from *Covina Argus* in 1922: Apr. 14, Apr. 28, May 5, May 12, May 19, June 2. The supply company adopted the design of the Scheu smokeless orchard heater, invented by W. C. Scheu of Upland.

28. "Smudge Pot Pall Blocks Shipping in L.A. Harbor," *OT,* 28 Dec. 1924; "Question of Smudge Elimination Argued at Torrid Meeting," *LAT,* 15 Feb. 1925. On the accident, see "Electric Train Is Overturned," *LAT,* 26 Dec. 1924.

29. Floyd D. Young, "Southern California Orchard Heating Statistics," *CC* 14 (Jan. 1929): 88–89; "Smudge Versus Wind—Which Shall It Be," *Covina Argus,* 30 June 1922.

30. G. F. Rinehart, "To Smudge or Not to Smudge," *Covina Citizen,* 15 Jan. 1931.

31. *El Monte Herald* quoted in "Asked to Enforce Smudging Laws," *Covina Citizen*, 22 Sept. 1932. See also *Covina Citizen*, 29 Sept. 1932; 13 Jan. 1933; and 19 Feb. 1937.

32. Bill Warr, "Warrblings," *Covina Argus*, 29 Jan. 1937; Floyd D. Young, "The 1937 Freeze in California," *Monthly Weather Report* 66 (Oct. 1938): 311–24, quotes on 322, 323; Bob Thomas, *Selznick* (Garden City, N.Y., 1970), 114.

33. Details from Young, "The 1937 Freeze in California."

34. Martínez quoted in José M. Alamillo, *Making Lemonade Out of Lemons: Mexican American Labor and Leisure in a California Town, 1880–1960* (Urbana, 2006), 41. Death reported in *Van Nuys News*, 25 Jan. 1937.

35. "El Monte Doesn't Like the Smudge," *Covina Citizen*, 19 Feb. 1937; "Didn't Affect Bird Life," *CC* 22 (Aug. 1937): 441; "Probe on Smudge Nuisance to Be Launched under Chamber Committee," *Covina Citizen*, 12 Feb. 1937.

36. "Smudge Hailed as Raid Screen," *LAT*, 15 Dec. 1941; "Exhaust Fumes Hang over City," *LAT*, 23 July 1943; "Blanket over Downtown Area Lifts," *LAT*, 24 Sept. 1944; "Smudge and Smog Are Distinct Problems," *LAT*, 14 Feb. 1948; "Law to Control Smudge," *Long Beach Press-Telegram*, 30 Mar. 1949. On the origins of air pollution, see Marvin Brienes, "Smog Comes to Los Angeles," *SCQ* 58 (Winter 1976): 515–32. On the consequences, see Christopher C. Sellers, *Crabgrass Crucible: Suburban Nature and the Rise of Environmentalism in Twentieth-Century America* (Chapel Hill, 2012), chap. 7; Sarah S. Elkind, *How Local Politics Shape Federal Policy: Business, Power, and the Environment in Twentieth-Century Los Angeles* (Chapel Hill, 2011), chap. 2; and Chip Jacobs and William J. Kelly, *Smogtown: The Lung-Burning History of Pollution in Los Angeles* (Woodstock, 2008), though the latter two ignore smudge.

37. "Smog Curbs Put on 5000 Orchardists," *LAT*, 10 Nov. 1949; "Victim of Smudge," *LAT*, 16 Jan. 1949. See also "Smudge Laws: Just One More Obstacle," *San Bernardino Sun*, 24 May 1981.

38. For midcentury orchard heating statistics, see R. L. Adams, *Protecting Citrus Groves from Frost: Costs and Benefits to Growers*, California Agricultural Experiment Station Extension Service Bulletin 730 (1953).

39. Roger Butterfield, "Los Angeles," *Life* 15 (22 Nov. 1943): 102–18. For context, see Kevin Starr, *Golden Dreams: California in an Age of Abundance, 1950–1963* (Oxford, 2009), chap. 15.

40. On a later iteration of absentee ownership, see "Who Owns the Groves?" *San Bernardino Sun*, 24 May 1981.

41. "Southland's Famed Orange Trees Find a New Home—Lake Bottom," *LAT*, 9 May 1965; "Cost of Fireplace Wood Increases; Orange, Walnut Supply Nearly Gone," *Long Beach Independent-Press-Telegram*, 17 Oct. 1963. On the bans, see "County Balks at Tree Burning on Tract Sites," *LAT*, 13 Apr. 1956; and "Builders and Developers Race Against Fire Ban," *LAT*, 28 Dec. 1967.

42. "Valley Citrus Industry Braces for Bleak Future," *LAT*, 3 Mar. 1963. On inland smog, see Calvin Trillin, "Receptor," *New Yorker*, 27 Aug. 1979, 76–80. On field crops, start with Jacobs and Kelly, *Smogtown*, 49–51; and on citrus, see David M. Olszyk, *The Growth and Yield Effects of Ambient Air Pollution on Valencia Orange Trees*,

Statewide Air Pollution Research Center, UC (Aug. 1989). Preautomobile industrial air pollution was a problem for many farmers; for a northern California case study, see Khaled J. Bloom, *Murder of a Landscape: The California Farmer-Smelter War, 1897–1916* (Norman, 2010).

43. Reuther, *Citrus Industry*, vol. 4, 187–89.

44. Gloria Ricci Lothrop, *Pomona: A Centennial History* (Northridge, 1988), quote on 67. On trees as tax havens, see Julie Guthman, *Agrarian Dreams: The Paradox of Organic Farming in California* (Berkeley, 2004), 101–2; and Dennis Kelly, "Williamson Act: Boon or Bust?" *San Bernardino Sun*, 24 May 1981.

45. See Paul F. Griffin and Ronald L. Chatham, "Population: A Challenge to California's Changing Citrus Industry," *Economic Geography* 34 (July 1958): 272–76.

46. "Citrus Areas Peeled for Crop of Houses," *Long Beach Independent-Press-Telegram*, 15 Aug. 1954. On Disneyland, start with John M. Findlay, *Magic Lands: Western Cityscapes and American Culture after 1945* (Berkeley, 1992), chap. 2. Cost figure from "Disneyland Shrubs, Trees Cost $400,000," *LAT*, 23 May 1955.

47. Raymond F. Dasmann, *The Destruction of California* (New York, 1965), 8; Richard G. Lillard, *Eden in Jeopardy: Man's Prodigal Meddling with His Environment—The Southern California Experience* (New York, 1966); William Bronson, *How to Kill a Golden State* (Garden City, N.Y., 1968), 146–48. For a summary of large-scale changes in the agricultural landscape and economy, see H. F. Raup, "Transformation of Southern California to a Cultivated Land," *Annals of the Association of American Geographers* 49 (Sept. 1959): 58–78. The song by Joni Mitchell is "Big Yellow Taxi" from *Ladies of the Canyon* (1970).

48. On ecological change in lowland Tulare County, see William L. Preston, *Vanishing Landscapes: Land and Life in the Tulare Lake Basin* (Berkeley, 1981); and Philip Garone, *The Fall and Rise of the Wetlands of California's Great Central Valley* (Berkeley, 2011). The movement of walnuts from Southern California to the Central Valley preceded that of citrus by a couple of decades. Walnut orchards typically occupied level land—the most desirable property for developers—whereas citrus groves more often occupied sloping land. From 1928 to 1958, the Southland's share of the state's total walnut acreage fell from 66 to 15 percent. See Kenneth Thompson, "Location and Relocation of a Tree Crop—English Walnuts in California," *Economic Geography* 37 (Apr. 1961): 133–49.

49. On Florida concentrate, see Alissa Hamilton, *Squeezed: What You Don't Know about Orange Juice* (New Haven, 2009). Whereas Florida OJ generally went to personal consumers, California OJ generally went to industrial and institutional buyers.

50. On Sunkist and its products, see Catherine Merlo, *Heritage of Gold: The First 100 Years of Sunkist Growers, Inc., 1893–1993* (Los Angeles, 1994); R. T. Will, "Some Phases of the Citrus By-Product Industry in California," *Journal of Industrial and Engineering Chemistry* 8 (Jan. 1916): 78–86; and Glenn H. Joseph, "Citrus Products: A Quarter Century of Amazing Progress," *Economic Botany* 1 (Oct.–Dec. 1947): 415–26.

51. Lawrence Clark Powell, *An Orange Grove Boyhood: Growing Up in Southern*

California, 1910–1928 (Santa Barbara, 1988), 25, 79; Donald H. Pflueger, *Covina: Sunflowers, Citrus, Subdivisions* (Covina, 1964), 149. For another voice from that generation, see Lawrence Emerson Nelson, *Only One Redlands: Changing Patterns in a Southern California Town* (Redlands, 1963).

52. "Anaheimized": "Tract Boom Sparked Friends of Redlands," *Redlands Daily Facts*, 22 July 1977. On land and development issues, see "Greenbelt Doesn't Save Oranges," *RPE*, 16 Sept. 2001; "Saving the Citrus," *RPE*, 6 July 2003; "Development Squeezes Citrus Growers Out of Region," *RPE*, 3 Apr. 2006; and "Citrus Preserve," *RPE*, 29 Apr. 2006. In Glendora, the city and the Glendora Preservation Foundation worked to set aside the small Centennial Heritage Park with its orange trees.

53. "Last of the Citrus: Vast Groves Squeezed Down to 5," *LAT*, 24 Nov. 1988; "Asphalt and Oranges Growth," *LAT*, 2 May 1991; "Step Is Taken toward Saving Orange Grove," *LAT*, 26 Dec. 1991.

54. "No 'Roast' Planned for SA Squirrels," *Santa Ana Register*, 14 July 1978; "New Playground to Lend Greenery in Downtown," *Anaheim Bulletin*, 10 Dec. 1992.

55. "Where Have All the Oranges Gone?" *RPE*, 19 Sept. 1999.

56. The author attended the street fair in 2006. On Ventura County, see "Orange Trees Losing Ground," *LAT*, 24 Oct. 1993; "A History Wilts," *LAT*, 9 Oct. 1995; "Not Like Orange County," *LAT*, 30 Oct. 1991.

57. See Gustavo Arellano, "Last One," *OC Weekly*, 22 May 2008; and "Citrus Grower Faces Eviction," *OC Register*, 11 July 2008. For context, see Edward J. Bachus, "Who Took the Oranges Out of Orange County? The Southern California Citrus Industry in Transition," *SCQ* 63 (Summer 1981): 157–73; and Rob Kling, Spencer C. Olin, and Mark Poster, eds., *Postsuburban California: The Transformation of Orange County Since World War II* (Berkeley, 1991).

58. See Eileen Shields, Claudia Wallis, and Dick Thompson, "Trying to Thwart the Fruit Fly," *Time*, 27 July 1981; and "The Politics of Judging a Scientific Debate," *LAT*, 3 Aug. 1981.

59. "Los Angeles Jumps into Action against Medfly," UPI, 27 Aug. 1981. See also "Will Medfly Strike Again?" UPI, 31 Jan. 1982.

60. On the Breeders, see "Mystery Letter Puts Odd Twist on Medfly Crisis," *LAT*, 3 Dec. 1989; and Jeffrey Alan Lockwood, *Six-Legged Soldiers: Using Insects as Weapons of War* (Oxford, 2009), 233–41.

61. On outbreaks in the 1990s, see, for example, "California Loads Sprayers, Fearing Return of the Medfly," *NYT*, 15 Feb. 1994; "Malathion-Related Complaints Linger," *RPE*, 12 Feb. 1995; and Anne Dawson et al., *California Agricultural Trade: Combating the Medfly Menace* (Monterey, 1998). On fly populations, see James R. Carey, "Establishment of the Mediterranean Fruit Fly in California," *Science* 253 (20 Sept. 1991): 1369–73; Tom Abate, "Is the Invading Medfly Eligible for California Residency?" *BioScience* 43 (Jan. 1993): 3–6; and M. D. Meixner et al., "The Mediterranean Fruit Fly in California: Evidence for Multiple Introductions and Persistent Populations Based on Microsatellite and Mitochondrial DNA Variability," *Molecular Ecology* 11 (May 2002): 891–99.

62. "Pest Worries Tulare County Citrus Growers," *Visalia Times-Delta/Tulare Advance-Register*, 28 Feb. 2009. The ongoing HLB story is too new to have an established literature. I relied on news stories aggregated by LexisNexis and Google News and information at the websites of the USDA and the CDFA.

63. "Insect Poses Dire Threat to Citrus," *San Bernardino Sun*, 28 Jan. 2009.

64. Alastair Blaind, "A Green Threat to Our Groves," *San Diego Reader*, 22 Apr. 2009.

65. "Bug Poses 'Devastating Impact' to Citrus Industry," *San Jose Mercury News*, 16 Feb. 2012.

66. On crops, see the annual state report, *California Agricultural Production Statistics*, at www.cdfa.ca.gov/statistics/.

67. Data from USDA Economic Research Service, "Background Information and Statistics: California's Citrus Industry" (2007), and the websites of the USDA National Agricultural Statistics Service and the CDFA.

68. For a trenchant analysis of trends, see John Fraser Hart, "Specialty Cropland in California," *Geographical Review* 93 (Apr. 2003): 153–70. For production statistics from the late twentieth century, see *California and Arizona Oranges: Acreage and Production Trends, Costs, and Returns*, UC Cooperative Extension Leaflet 2355, rev. ed. (1993). In recent decades global free trade has reordered the citrus market. Florida now struggles to compete with Brazil in the global juice market. Limes sold in the United States mostly come from Mexico.

69. On prisons, see Ruth Wilson Gilmore, *Golden Gulag: Prisons, Surplus, Crisis, and Opposition in Globalizing California* (Berkeley, 2007); and Volker Janssen's forthcoming book from Oxford University Press. On changing labor patterns, see Richard Mines and Ricardo Anzaldua, *New Migrants vs. Old Migrants: Alternative Labor Market Structures in the California Citrus Industry* (La Jolla, 1982). On the valley in general, see Stephen Johnson, Gerald Haslam, and Robert Dawson, *The Great Central Valley: California's Heartland* (Berkeley, 1993); and James J. Parsons, "A Geographer Looks at the San Joaquin Valley," *Geographical Review* 76 (Oct. 1986): 371–89.

70. On Boswell, see Mark Arax and Rick Wartzman, *King of California: J. G. Boswell and the Making of a Secret American Empire* (New York, 2003); on Resnick, see Amy Wilentz, *I Feel Earthquakes More Often than They Happen: Coming to California in the Age of Schwarzenegger* (New York, 2006), 151–200. The overwhelming majority of the citrus acreage in the Central Valley is now located in the southern half (San Joaquin Valley), but Butte, Glenn, and Tehama counties in the northern half (Sacramento Valley) have been growing commercial oranges since the nineteenth century. Oroville's Mother Orange Tree is a state historical landmark. Orangevale, near Sacramento, is another former citrus area.

Part Four: Palms

1. *Final Report of the California World's Fair Commission* (SPO, 1894), 68.
2. "Majestic Palms at San Fernando," *PRP*, 12 Aug. 1893, 117; Charles Edwin Markham, "California at the World's Fair," *California Illustrated* 4 (Nov. 1893): 762–71. See also Charles Edwin Markham, "California at the World's Fair," *Californian* 4 (Nov. 1893): 762–71; and "San Diego's Palm," *LAT*, 11 May 1893.
3. "Frank Wiggins," *American Magazine* 71 (Nov. 1910): 34–35; Timothy G. Turner, "Rediscovering Los Angeles," *LAT*, 31 Aug. 1936. Other sayings, unattributed but popular at the time: "God did much for Los Angeles, but Frank Wiggins did the rest"; and "California was destined by God to be the home of untold millions and Frank Wiggins was His instrument."

Chapter 7. Cosmopolitan Fronds

1. Lowell John Bean and Katherine Siva Saubel, *Temalpakh (From the Earth): Cahuilla Indian Knowledge and Usage of Plants* (Banning, Calif., 1972), 145–49.
2. William P. Blake, "Geological Report," in *Reports of Explorations and Surveys, to Ascertain the Most Practicable and Economical Route for a Railroad from the Mississippi River to the Pacific Ocean*, vol. 5, pt. 2 (Washington, 1857), 95. "Gay bungalows": Helen Ring Robinson, "Palm Canyon—Our Newest National Park," *LAT*, 24 Sept. 1922. For an outstanding example of exoticism, see J. Smeaton Chase, *Our Araby: Palm Springs and the Garden of the Sun* (Pasadena, 1920). On regional tourism, see Lawrence Culver, *The Frontier of Leisure: Southern California and the Shaping of Modern America* (Oxford, 2010).
3. *Report of the Director of the National Park Service* (GPO, 1920), 50–52; headline from *LAT*, 6 Aug. 1922; "Palm Canyon Bill Passed," *LAT*, 13 July 1922. For a fuller discussion, see Rachel Dayton Shaw, "Evolving Ecoscape: An Environmental and Cultural History of Palm Springs, California, and the Agua Caliente Indian Reservation, 1877–1939" (Ph.D. diss., UC San Diego, 1999).
4. "Indians Close Palm Canyon," *LAT*, 28 May 1930. See also "Palm Canyon's Closed to All Picnic Parties," *LAT*, 18 Mar. 1923; and "Compromise Offered in Canyon Row," *LAT*, 19 Feb. 1931. For a description of a traffic jam, see "Palm Canyon Enjoyment Marred," *LAT*, 2 Apr. 1933. For a description of earlier resource abuse, see "Palm Tree Defenders in Protest," *LAT*, 18 Dec. 1923.
5. See Shaw, "Evolving Ecoscape"; *Palm Springs Band of Mission Indians: Hearing before the Committee on Indian Affairs, United States Senate, Seventy-fifth Congress, First Session, on S. 1424 . . . and S. 2589* (GPO, 1937); and Ryan M. Kray, "The Path to Paradise: Expropriation, Exodus, and Exclusion in the Making of Palm Springs," *PHR* 73 (Feb. 2004): 85–126.
6. On the date industry, see Donald R. Hodel and Dennis V. Johnson, *Dates: Imported*

and American Varieties of Dates in the United States (Oakland, 2007), 1–12; David R. Lee, "Date Cultivation in the Coachella Valley, California," *Ohio Journal of Science* 63 (Mar. 1963): 82–87; and Charles C. Cooley, "The California Date Growing Industry, 1890–1939," pt. I, *SCQ* 49 (Mar. 1967): 47–63; pt. II, *SCQ* 49 (June 1967): 167–91. For pictures of the Indio fair, see "Life Goes to a Date Festival," *Life*, 15 Mar. 1948, 154–56.

7. Alexander von Humboldt, *Aspects of Nature* (Philadelphia, 1850), 320; Alfred Russel Wallace, *Palm Trees of the Amazon and Their Uses* (London, 1853), iii–iv. See also Nancy Leys Stepan, *Picturing Tropical Nature* (Ithaca, 2001); Felic Driver and Luciana Martinus, eds., *Tropical Visions in an Age of Empire* (Chicago, 2005); and Katherine Manthorne, "The Quest for Tropical Paradise: Palm Trees as Fact and Symbol in Latin American Landscape Imagery, 1850–1875," *Art Journal* 44 (Winter 1984): 374–82. "Typical landscapes" comes from Bernard Smith, *European Vision and the South Pacific* (New Haven, 1985), 4–5.

8. See Fred Gray, *Designing the Seaside: Architecture, Society and Nature* (London, 2006), 106–14.

9. "The Palm Tree Fad," *Medical World* 25 (Sept. 1907): 365.

10. See Henry W. Lawrence, *City Trees: A Historical Geography from the Renaissance through the Nineteenth Century* (Charlottesville, 2006).

11. Ibid., 246.

12. Charles Loring Brace, *The New West; or, California in 1867–1868* (New York, 1869), 277, 354–55.

13. Harris Newmark, *Sixty Years in Southern California, 1853–1913*, 4th ed. (Los Angeles, 1970), 34, 97, 126, 141, 162, 291, 471. See also Paula M. Schiffman, "The Los Angeles Prairie," in *Land of Sunshine: An Environmental History of Metropolitan Los Angeles*, ed. William Deverell and Greg Hise (Pittsburgh, 2005), 38–51.

14. George Vancouver, *A Voyage of Discovery to the North Pacific Ocean and Round the World*, vol. 2 (London, 1798), 494; Ruth Frey Axe et al., eds., *A Visit to the Missions of Southern California in February and March 1874 by Henry L. Oak* (Los Angeles, 1981), 50, 57, 62. For an example of "Oriental" Los Angeles, see John S. Hittell, *The Resources of California*, 6th ed. (San Francisco, 1874), 76–77. On mission gardens, see Victoria Padilla, *Southern California Gardens: An Illustrated History* (Berkeley, 1961).

15. Charles Nordhoff, *California for Health, Pleasure, and Residence* (New York, 1872), 68, 11; James H. Madison, "Taking the Country Barefooted: The Indiana Colony in California," *CH* 69 (Fall 1990): 236–49, quote on 237; Benjamin C. Truman, *Semi-Tropical California* (San Francisco, 1874). The railroad writers weren't the first to use this kind of language; consider this passage from Bayard Taylor, *At Home and Abroad: A Sketch-Book of Life, Scenery and Men*, rev. ed. (New York, 1862), 197: "California presents the anomaly of a semi-tropical climate, with all the inspiring and invigorating qualities of a Northern atmosphere."

16. Walter Lindley and J. P. Widney, *California of the South: Its Physical Geography, Climate, Resources, Routes of Travel, and Health-Resorts* (New York, 1888), 63–64.

17. Palm Springs and Catalina Island became honorary appendages of Southern California in the twentieth century. For academic studies on regional invention, see the

books by Stephen V. Ward, Dona Brown, Katherine G. Morrissey, and David M. Wrobel. The most trenchant book on the invention of Southern California remains Carey McWilliams, *Southern California Country: An Island on the Land* (New York, 1946).

18. William Henry Bishop, *Old Mexico and Her Lost Provinces* (New York, 1883), 426, 433. On the landmark tree, see "The California Fan Palm," *PRP*, 17 Dec. 1887, 479. It was transplanted to Beverly Park in 1906.

19. See "The New S. P. Depot," *LAT*, 27 July 1888; and "Moving Palm Trees," *Daily Alta California*, 30 July 1888. The following narration of L.A. palms owes much to the pioneering scholarship of David Alan Karnes, "Modern Metropolis: Mass Culture and the Transformation of Los Angeles, 1890–1950" (Ph.D. diss., UC Berkeley, 1991), 18–128. See also Charles Henry Rowan, "Ornamental Plants as a Factor in the Cultural Development of Southern California" (master's thesis, UCLA, 1957); and Warren Techentin, "Landscape: Tree Huggers," in *The Infrastructural City: Networked Ecologies in Los Angeles* ed. Kazys Varnelis (Los Angeles, 2008). Many of my observations and conclusions about street trees have come from long walks in Los Angeles, an unheralded form of fieldwork. My research also encompassed thousands of still visual sources—photographs, postcards, etc. I cannot list all these sources, but I will call attention to four repositories: the Huntington Library, the Seaver Center for Western History Research, the University of Southern California, and the Los Angeles Public Library.

20. Newmark, *Sixty Years in Southern California*, 571; T. S. Van Dyke, *Millionaires of a Day: An Inside History of the Great Southern California "Boom"* (New York, 1890), 114–15; Mary Austin, *Earth Horizon* (Boston, 1932), 185–86. See also Glenn S. Dumke, *The Boom of the Eighties in Southern California* (San Marino, 1944); and Oscar Osburn Winther, "The Rise of Metropolitan Los Angeles, 1870–1900," *Huntington Library Quarterly* 10 (Aug. 1947): 391–405.

21. "Fan Palms as Street Trees," *PRP*, 7 Oct. 1893, 245. For a general description, see William S. Lyon, "Exotic Flora of Southern California," *American Florist* 2 (1 Oct. 1886): 61–62. The pepper tree commonly grown in California since Spanish times, *Schinus molle*, is also called Peruvian pepper tree or Chilean pepper tree.

22. Some examples are Date Palm, Highland Grove, Landscape, Old Mission, Palm Tree, San Fernando Rey, Silver Moon, Southern Cross, Tesoro Ranch, and Twilight brands. For pictorial histories, see John Salkin and Laurie Gordon, *Orange Crate Art: The Story of the Labels That Launched a Golden Era* (New York, 1976); and Gordon T. McClelland and Jay T. Last, *California Orange Box Labels: An Illustrated History* (Beverly Hills, 1985).

23. Harriet Tolman, "Views from a Trip to California, ca. 1887–1889," vol. 2, image 3, Bancroft. On the Spanish fantasy past, see William Deverell, *Whitewashed Adobe: The Rise of Los Angeles and the Remaking of Its Mexican Past* (Berkeley, 2004); Dydia DeLyser, *Ramona Memories: Tourism and the Shaping of Southern California* (Minneapolis, 2005); and Phoebe S. Kropp, *California Vieja: Culture and Memory in a Modern American Place* (Berkeley, 2006). There used to be several date palms at the base of

Presidio Hill in San Diego; the tree displayed at the Chicago Word's Fair was one of these "mission palms" or "Old Town palms." The penultimate specimen collapsed in 1915, and the final Serra Palm—a state-registered landmark—survived until 1957. See Heidi Trent and Joey Seymour, "Examining California's First Palm Tree: The Serra Palm," *JSDH* 56 (Summer 2010): 105–20. There was a different Serra Tree (an oak) at Monterey. On Ventura's now-dead twin palms (since superseded in local land-mark status by Two Trees, mentioned in Chapter 4), see Jill Patrice Dolan, "Preserv-ing the Palms: Ventura's First Landmark and the Women Who Saved It," *Ventura County Historical Society Quarterly* 48, nos. 3–4 (2005): 2–66.

24. Charles F. Lummis, "Gardens of Eden While You Wait," *Land of Sunshine* 2 (Mar. 1895): 63.

25. See Jennifer Watts, "Picture Taking in Paradise: Los Angeles and the Creation of Regional Identity, 1880–1920," in *The Nineteenth-Century Visual Culture Reader*, ed. Vanessa R. Schwartz and Jeannene M. Przyblyski (New York, 2004), 218–32.

26. Ratcliffe Hicks, *Southern California, or the Land of . . . the Afternoon* (Springfield, Mass., 1898), 9. For context, see John E. Baur, *The Health Seekers of Southern Califor-nia, 1870–1900* (San Marino, 1959); and Emily K. Abel, *Tuberculosis and the Politics of Exclusion: A History of Public Health and Migration to Los Angeles* (New Brunswick, 2007).

27. Charles Dudley Warner, "Our Italy," *Harper's* 81 (Nov. 1890): 813–29; idem, "The Winter of Our Content," *Harper's* 82 (Dec. 1890): 39–57. On Warner's business deal-ings, see Kenneth R. Andrews, *Nook Farm: Mark Twain's Hartford Circle* (Cambridge, Mass., 1950), 154–55.

28. Ernest Braunton, "Montecito Estate Made a Sanctuary for Palms," *LAT*, 23 Dec. 1934; Waldron Gillespie, "Why Palms Belong in Southern California," *Garden Magazine* 36 (Dec. 1922): 187–90. See also Kate Greenleaf Locke, "The Gardens of Southern California," *Century Magazine* 76 (Sept. 1908): 716–24; and Robin Kar-son, *A Genius for Place: American Landscape of the Country Place Era* (Amherst, 2007), 285–307.

29. See J. M. Guinn, *California and an Extended History of Los Angeles and Environs*, vol. 1 (Los Angeles, 1915), 456–59; Charlton Lawrence Edholm, "The Seaward Sub-urbs of Los Angeles," *Out West* 30 (May 1909): 423–65; and Dale Samuelson, *The American Amusement Park* (St. Paul, 2001), 43–50. Contemporaneous to Venice of America, a different developer built some islands in the artificial bay at the mouth of the San Gabriel River near Long Beach; he called his canal-and-gondola development Naples.

30. *Crisis* 6 (Aug. 1913): 192–95. On blacks in the city, see Douglas Flamming, *Bound for Freedom: Black Los Angeles in Jim Crow America* (Berkeley, 2005); and Josh Sides, *L.A. City Limits: African American Los Angeles from the Great Depression to the Present* (Berkeley, 2003).

31. "Los Angeles Jail to Have Palms and Ferns," *San Jose Evening News*, 4 Nov. 1913. On early evangelical L.A., see Matthew Avery Sutton, *Aimee Semple McPherson and*

the Resurrection of Christian America (Cambridge, Mass., 2007); and Daniel Mark Epstein, *Sister Aimee: The Life of Aimee Semple McPherson* (New York, 1993). On the subsequent (more southernized) era, see Darren Dochuk, *From Bible Belt to Sun Belt: Plain-Folk Religion, Grassroots Politics, and the Rise of Evangelical Conservatism* (New York, 2011).

32. Grace Ellery Channing, "Italy and 'Our Italy,'" *Land of Sunshine* 11 (June 1899): 24–29, quote on 29.

33. "Objects to Trees That Line Streets," *SFC*, 28 Oct. 1909; "Palms in Oakland," *SFC*, 12 Jan. 1904; "San Jose Takes the Palm," *SFC*, 5 Mar. 1904; "Want Boulevard to Tap Highway," *OT*, 28 Dec. 1910; Miss E. Porter, *Native Growth for Planting in California*, California State Board of Forestry Circular 4 (SPO, 1913); "More Shade Trees, Not Fewer," *LAT*, 12 June 1908; "The Planting of Trees and Their Care," *Pacific Municipalities* 17 (Nov. 1907): 102–8, quote on 105–6 (from an address by Harper to the convention of the League of California Municipalities). For more on Westlake Park, see "Spare the Trees," *Municipal Affairs* 3 (July 1908): 6. On Jepson's plan for Albany, see "Albany Plans to Be Village Beautiful," *OT*, 11 Mar. 1911. C. K. McClatchy, the editor of the *Sacramento Bee* from 1883 to 1936, was another noted urban palm tree booster. See E. Gregory McPherson and Nina Luttinger, "From Nature to Nurture: The History of Sacramento's Urban Forest," *Journal of Arboriculture* 24 (Mar. 1998): 72–88.

34. On the national street tree movement, see Albert Davis Taylor, *Street Trees: Their Care and Preservation* (Ithaca, 1908); William Solotaroff, *Shade-Trees in Towns and Cities* (New York, 1911); Carl Bannwart, "The Movement for City Street Trees—A Survey," *Municipal Review* 4 (Apr. 1914): 238–44; Max Page, *The Creative Destruction of Manhattan, 1900–1940* (Chicago, 1999), 192–206; Thomas J. Campanella, *Republic of Shade: New England and the American Elm* (New Haven, 2003), 110–21; and Robert M. Ricard, "Shade Trees and Tree Wardens: Revising the History of Urban Forestry," *Journal of Forestry* 103 (July–Aug. 2005): 230–33.

35. "Town Has Shade Tree Fever," *LAH*, 13 Apr. 1906; Dana W. Bartlett, *The Better City: A Sociological Study of a Modern City* (Los Angeles, 1907): 30. On Riverside, see J. H. Reed, "Riverside and the Story of the Trees," *California Outlook* 16 (10 Jan. 1914): 10–12; idem, "The Parks and Street Trees of Riverside," *Monthly Bulletin of the California State Commission of Horticulture* 4 (Oct. 1915): 453–55; and Lee M. A. Simpson, *Selling the City: Gender, Class, and the California Growth Machine, 1880–1940* (Stanford, 2004), 94–95. On Hollywood, see Francis William Vreeland, "Confessions from a Tree-Saving Campaigner," typescript, n.d., ca. 1900, Los Angeles Public Library. For additional context on the Progressive roots of the Southland's street trees, see Anthony Allyre Bernier, "The Sidewalk Metropolis: Street Furniture and Pedestrian Public Space in Twentieth Century Los Angeles" (Ph.D. diss., UC Irvine, 2002), 58–84.

36. "Trim Your Trees, Forester Urges," *LAH*, 24 Oct. 1907. See also "Highland Park," *LAT*, 30 May 1904; and "Wide Boulevard to Sea," *LAT*, 26 May 1912.

37. "The Care of Trees in Los Angeles," *American City* 13 (Dec. 1915): 508–9; S. R. Hotchkiss, "Municipal Tree Planting at Redlands," *California Outlook* 16 (21 Feb. 1914): 7–9, 18, quote on 7.

38. On the uprooted palms, see "Historical Palms Are to Be Taken to Venice," *LAH*, 21 July 1905; "Protests Fail to Save Courthouse Palm," *SFC*, 27 Aug. 1908. At Sycamore Grove Park, meanwhile, park crews tore out palms against the objections of residents in Highland Park, the first unincorporated district annexed by Los Angeles. See "'Spare the Palms' Cry Highland Park Residents," *LAH*, 15 May 1908.

39. *LAT*: 15–17 June 1915; 5 Nov. 1915; and 11 Jan. 1916.

40. *Sacramento County and Its Resources; Our Capital City, Past and Present: A Souvenir of* The Bee (Sacramento, 1894), 102; "The Beauty That Might Be," *LAT*, 11 Jan. 1922; "Progress Fells Historic Palm," *LAT*, 25 July 1924.

41. Walter Woehlke, "Los Angeles—Homeland," *Sunset* 26 (Jan. 1911): 3; "Where Will the Workers Live?" advertisement for Montebello Park, *LAT*, 24 May 1925; Kevin Starr, *Inventing the Dream: California Through the Progressive Era* (Oxford, 1985), 64. The standard account of metropolitan growth is Robert M. Fogelson, *The Fragmented Metropolis: Los Angeles, 1850–1930* (Berkeley, 1993), originally published in 1967. On the critical decade, see Mark S. Foster, "The Model T, the Hard Sell, and Los Angeles's Urban Growth: The Decentralization of Los Angeles during the 1920s," *PHR* 44 (Nov. 1975): 459–84; Kevin Starr, *Material Dreams: Southern California through the 1920s* (Oxford, 1990); and Tom Sitton and William Deverell, eds., *Metropolis in the Making: Los Angeles in the 1920s* (Berkeley, 2001).

42. See William Hertrich, *Palms and Cycads: Their Culture in Southern California as Observed Chiefly in the Huntington Botanical Gardens* (San Marino, 1951).

43. MaryAnn Bonino, *The Doheny Mansion: A Biography of a Home* (Los Angeles, 2008), 68–73; "Oil King Buys, Moves Pair of Pioneer Palms," *LAT*, 23 May 1913.

44. Liberty Hyde Bailey, *Cyclopedia of American Horticulture*, vol. 3 (New York, 1910), 1194; Charles Francis Saunders, *Trees and Shrubs of California Gardens* (New York, 1926), 39–63, passim. For a critique of the "ridiculous use of trees" in California, see Mark Daniels, "Green Symbols," *Garden* 33 (Aug. 1921): 364–68. Downtown Los Angeles gained many Canary Island date palms simply by absorbing formerly residential neighborhoods, including parts of Bunker Hill. As the commercial core expanded, developers tore down Victorian houses or built around them and their orphaned palms.

45. "Entire Town Is Against Tree Cutting," *LAT*, 18 Jan. 1912; "Spare Us Our Pepper Trees," *LAT*, 6 Mar. 1911; "Ban Is Placed on Pepper Tree," *LAT*, 19 Feb. 1930. See also "Let's Keep the Trees," *LAT*, 3 Feb. 1912.

46. Mark Lee Luther, *The Boosters* (Indianapolis, 1923), 34–35, 123.

47. Joan Crawford, *A Portrait of Joan: The Autobiography of Joan Crawford* (Garden City, N.Y., 1962), 10.

48. "Mary Pickford Says: Tree Planting Pays Big Dividends," *Southern California Business* 6 (Jan. 1928): 14, 42; "Chamber Acts for Trees," *LAT*, 6 Apr. 1927; "O Coun-

cil, Plant Those Trees," *LAT,* 2 Nov. 1927. For the text of the act, see *Sixth Biennial Report of the State Forester of the State of California* (SPO, 1916), 30–35. As a faded star late in life, Pickford, a Canadian, confessed, "I have come since to dislike the palm trees." Robert Windeler, *Sweetheart: The Story of Mary Pickford* (New York, 1974), 58.

49. City Council files 8868–89, Los Angeles City Archives.

50. See Scott L. Bottles, *Los Angeles and the Automobile: The Making of the Modern City* (Berkeley, 1987), car ownership rates on 93; and Ashleigh Brilliant, *The Great Car Craze: How Southern California Collided with the Automobile in the 1920s* (Santa Barbara, 1989).

51. Jan and Cora Gordon, *Star-dust in Hollywood* (London, 1930), 66, 57; Edmund Wilson, "The City of Our Lady the Queen of Angels: I," *New Republic* 69 (2 Dec. 1931): 67–68. Gore Vidal, *Messiah* (New York, 1954), 45, has one of the best contemptuous lines: "Egypt one knows without visiting it, and China the same; but Los Angeles is unique in its bright horror."

52. Denise S. Spooner, "A New Perspective on the Dream: Midwestern Images of Southern California in the Post–World War II Decades," *CH* 76 (Spring 1997): 44–57, quote on 48; James M. Cain, "Paradise" (1933), in *Writing Los Angeles: A Literary Anthology* ed. David L. Ulin (New York, 2002), 108–9.

53. See Jim Heimann, *Out with the Stars: Hollywood Nightlife in the Golden Era* (New York, 1985). The Polynesian-themed restaurant-bar, invented in Los Angeles, became a national fad in the 1950s after millions of young GIs returned from service in the Pacific. A-frame tiki bars adorned with palms, real or fake, popped up in cities such as Boston, Massachusetts, and Lincoln, Nebraska. See Sven A. Kirsten, *The Book of Tiki: The Cult of Polynesian Pop in Fifties America* (Cologne, 2000); and Kevin Starr, *Golden Dreams: California in an Age of Abundance, 1950–1963* (New York, 2009), 49–52.

54. See Culver, *The Frontier of Leisure,* 83–138; and "Catalina's Changes Begun," *LAT,* 18 Mar 1934.

55. "We're Famous Here for Potted Palms!" *LAT,* 12 Jan. 1936.

56. Helen W. King, "Conjuring Trees," *LAT,* 2 Aug. 1931; Charles Francis Saunders, *With the Flowers and Trees in California* (New York, 1914), 28. On the general absence of queen palm and other "tropical" feather palms in nineteenth-century Los Angeles, see J. C. Harvey, "Notes on Palms," *Transactions and Proceedings of the Southern California Horticultural Society for the Year 1892* (Los Angeles, 1892), 150–54. On Santa Barbara, see E. O. Fenzi [Francesco Franceschi], *Santa Barbara Exotic Flora: A Handbook of Plants from Foreign Countries Grown at Santa Barbara* (Santa Barbara, 1895).

57. On early taxonomic history, see S. B. Parish, "A Contribution toward a Knowledge of the Genus Washingtonia," *Botanical Gazette* 44 (Dec. 1907): 445–54. Some botanists classify *robusta* as a subspecies of *filifera.*

58. See Rowan, "Ornamental Plants as a Factor," 163–64.

59. *The Way to Rising Property Values Is Lined with Trees* (Los Angeles, 1931), copy in Los Angeles Public Library.

60. See "Tree-Planting Program Opens," *LAT,* 29 Mar. 1931; "Tree Planting Plan

Approved," *LAT*, 8 Apr. 1931; and "Vast Planting Plan Launched," *LAT*, 3 Aug. 1931. Mexican fan palm was also the tree of choice for the last great rail station built in the city, Union Station (1939).

Chapter 8. Aesthetic Infrastructure

1. Weldon F. Heald, "Fashions in Trees," *LAT*, 14 June 1942; City Council files 11529 and 11664, Los Angeles City Archives.
2. Peggy Sullivan, "Plain Truth about Palms," *LAT*, 3 May 1953. Lakewood information from Charles Henry Rowan, "Ornamental Plants as a Factor in the Cultural Development of Southern California" (master's thesis, UCLA, 1957), 221.
3. "Palm Gift to Boston Marks Airtourist Run," *LAT*, 1 July 1953. United's graphic designer was Stan Galli.
4. Singer quoted in Deborah Dash Moore, *To the Golden Cities: Pursuing the American Jewish Dream in Miami and L.A.* (Cambridge, Mass., 1994), 2.
5. On Del Webb, see "Palm Trees Trademark of Retirement Cities," *LAT*, 13 May 1962; and John Findlay, *Magic Lands: Western Cityscapes and American Culture after 1940* (Berkeley, 1992). For general context, see Clark Davis, "From Oasis to Metropolis: Southern California and the Changing Context of American Leisure," *PHR* 61 (May 1992): 357–86. For an unparalleled visual sense of Watts, including its palm trees, see *Killer of Sheep* (1977), dir. Charles Burnett.
6. See Richard W. Lotchin, *Fortress California, 1910–1961: From Warfare to Welfare* (New York, 1992).
7. Quote from Lawrence Culver, *The Frontier of Leisure: Southern California and the Shaping of Modern America* (Oxford, 2010), 79.
8. See Adèle Cygelman and David Glomb, *Palm Springs Modern: Houses in the California Desert* (New York, 1999).
9. See Richard Longstreth, *City Center to Regional Mall: Architecture, the Automobile, and Retailing in Los Angeles, 1920–1950* (Cambridge, Mass., 1997); and, for context, John A. Jakle and Keith A. Sculle, *Lots of Parking: Land Use in a Car Culture* (Charlottesville, 2004).
10. Wemple quoted in "Urban Designers Turn Over a New Leaf, So Palm Trees Are 'In' Again," *LAT*, 24 Mar. 1985. On the ficus/palm controversy in Beverly Hills, see *LAT*: 9 Jan. 1966, 16 July 1967, 23 July 1967, 24 Aug. 1967, 29 Oct. 1967, 11 Jan. 1968, and 4 Aug. 1968. Statistic on pools from Remi Nadeau, *California: The New Society* (New York, 1963), 61.
11. See Kirse Granat May, *Golden State, Golden Youth: The California Image in Popular Culture, 1955–1966* (Chapel Hill, 2002).
12. On shaggy trees, see, for example, "Palms Given First Haircut in 45 Years," *LAT*, 23 Sept. 1956. On arson, see *LAT*: 21 Nov. 1941; 28 Nov. 1941; 4 Aug. 1948; 14 Feb. 1950, and 4 Nov. 1962. I read dozens more news items about palm fires in the *Covina Argus* (esp. 1946–47) and the *Redlands Daily Facts* (throughout the 1960s). Under-

timmed trees in urban areas also present fire hazards, as Anaheim learned the hard way in 1982. The Orange County city paid out millions to insurance companies, lawyers, and victims after a firestorm started at the contact point between a city-owned light fixture and the fronds on a street palm. See "Anaheim Settles with Victims of 1982 Firestorm," *LAT*, 12 Sept. 1985.

13. On vermin, see, for example, Charles Abrams, "Rats among the Palm Trees," *The Nation* 170 (25 Feb. 1950), 177–78; and "Affluent Areas Have Attractions for Rats," *LAT*, 28 Apr. 1968. On Long Beach specifically, see "Rats of Any Hue Are Still Rats—the Rats," *Long Beach Independent*, 14 Mar. 1948; "Health Officials Gain Upper Hand in Fight on Rats," *Long Beach Press-Telegram*, 20 Nov. 1949; and "Our City Fathers Remain Calm on Alleged Perils of the Palm," *Long Beach Independent-Press-Telegram*, 19 Oct. 1952.

14. "L.A. Palms—a Frond in Need," *LAT*, 13 Feb. 1975; "A Paper Chase for Palm Fronds Holiday Frenzy," *LAT*, 3 Oct. 1990.

15. "Take That, Joyce Kilmer," *LAT*, 8 Feb. 1972.

16. Details and quotations from *LAT* in 1972: 8–9 Feb., 12–13 Feb., 22–23 Feb., 26–27 Feb., 1 Mar., 24–25 Mar., and 10 May. See also *LAT*, 14 Apr. 1975, and *LAT*, 12 Dec. 1977.

17. Jack Smith, "Holding Out for Palmier Days," *LAT*, 23 Jan. 1972. See also *LAT*, 11 Jan. 1972; 18 Jan. 1972; and 27 Jan. 1972. On Camarillo, see *Oxnard Press-Courier*, 27 Apr. 1972; and 20 Oct. 1973.

18. "An Olympic Greening Takes Root across L.A.," *LAT*, 16 Feb. 1983; "Branching Out," *LAT*, 23 July 1984.

19. Quotes about Irvine from "Newport Center Will Soon Take on a Dramatic Mediterranean Look," *LAT*, 27 Jan. 1985; William F. Schulz, "Palm Trees' Rising Popularity," *Palm Journal* (May 1989), 21–23; and "The Architect of Paradise," *LAT*, 1 Oct. 1995. See also *Irvine Ranch: Different by Design: Images, 1960–2000* (Newport Beach, 2001); and Joel Garreau, *Edge City: Life on the New Frontier* (New York, 1991).

20. Quotes from "A Farewell to Fronds," *LAT*, 5 Sept. 1999; and "Back in Vogue: Landscapers Fan Out for Palm Trees," *LAT*, 23 May 1987. See also "Unmaking of an Oasis," *LAT*, 5 May 1988; Neal Matthews, "Move Those Palms," *Palm Journal* (Mar. 1989): 28–29; "Dispute over Trees Leaves Poway Puzzled," *LAT*, 20 Sept. 1983; and "Imperial Beach Palm Caper Leaves City Officials Frowning," *LAT*, 23 Jan. 1987. For context on exurban development, see Edward J. Blakely and Mary Gail Snyder, *Fortress America: Gated Communities in the United States* (Washington, 1999); and William Fulton, *The Reluctant Metropolis: The Politics of Urban Growth in Los Angeles* (Baltimore, 2001).

21. In 1997 the World Financial Center replaced the trees, which were dying because of insufficient light. In 2001, toxic dust from the collapse of the Twin Towers coated the replacement trees, necessitating a third planting. See "From California, an Indoor Palm Grove," *NYT*, 15 Sept. 1987; Frank Bruni, "Manhattan, Where Palms Sway as Brokers Sweat," *NYT*, 10 July 1997; and "Palms Return to an Island (Manhattan)," *NYT*, 13 Aug. 2002.

22. Lisa Alvarez, "The Burning Tree," *LA Weekly*, 2 May 2002; "Two Faces of L.A.— City's Instant Ugliness Threatens TV Ad Image," *LAT*, 6 May 1992.

23. On recent history, see David Rieff, *Los Angeles: Capital of the Third World* (New York, 1991); and Kevin Starr, *Coast of Dreams: California on the Edge, 1990–2003* (New York, 2004).

24. Quotes from "Vegas Landscapers Betting on Palm Trees," *LAT*, 25 May 1997; and "Palm in Twilight," *LAT*, 8 July 2004. See also "Demand for Palms Soars," *LAT*, 14 Aug. 1999; and "Attractive Attractions," *Fresno Bee*, 2 Sept. 2005.

25. "I Want to Sell My Large Palm!" at www.junglemusic.net/palmadvice/palms -selling-your-large-palm.htm.

26. See, for example, "Countywide Fatal Fungus Is Killing Palm Trees," *LAT*, 29 Aug. 1994; "Beverly Hills Bids a Frond Farewell," *LAT*, 18 Jan. 2003; "Sukkot Is Shedding Fronds," *LAT*, 1 Oct. 2007; and D. R. Hodel, *Pest Notes: Palm Diseases in the Landscape* (Davis, 2009). Many California cities, including Sacramento and Beverly Hills, lost beloved rows of street elms to another fungus, Dutch elm disease, in the 1970s and 1980s. The disease, which had already devastated the elms of the East and Midwest, appeared in the Golden State in 1975.

27. On the governance challenges of urban street trees, with examples from Los Angeles, see Anastasia Loukaitou-Sideris and Renia Ehrenfeucht, *Sidewalks: Conflict and Negotiation over Public Space* (Cambridge, Mass., 2009), 189–217.

28. See Los Angeles City Council, "Motion Limiting the Use of Palm Species in Plantings on City Streets and Medians," 21 July 2006; "L.A. to Be Remade in the Shade," *LAT*, 1 Oct. 2006; and "Planting the Future, One Tree at a Time," *LAT*, 23 Nov. 2006. For data on tree canopy cover, see E. Gregory McPherson et al., *Los Angeles 1-Million Tree Canopy Cover Assessment*, USDA General Technical Report PSW-GTR-207 (2008). By crude ethnic/racial grouping, whites are the best-shaded people in the city, followed by Hispanics, and then, far below, Asians and blacks. See Stephanie Pincetl, "Implementing Municipal Tree Planting: Los Angeles Million-Tree Initiative," *Environmental Management* 45, no. 2 (2010): 227–38.

29. "Fungal Disease Killing L.A. Palm Trees," AP, 17 Oct. 2006; "City Says Its Urban Jungle Has Little Room for Palms," *NYT*, 26 Nov. 2006; "Palm Trees in California Infected with Fungus That Can't Be Avoided, Cured or Diagnosed," CBS Morning News, transcript, 17 Nov. 2006; "Los Angeles to Phase Out Its Palm Trees," *Daily Telegraph*, 28 Nov. 2006; "Obituaries for an L.A. Icon Were Premature," *Washington Post*, 5 Dec. 2006. See also "Fan Palms No Longer Hold Sway," *LAT*, 18 Nov. 2006.

30. The incongruity of palms in the "hood" sometimes shows up in rap. In Ice Cube's "How to Survive in South Central" (from the soundtrack to the 1991 film *Boyz n the Hood*), the narrator pauses after his first description of drive-by shootings and racist cops and tells listeners that this is the real L.A., not the palms and blondes as seen on television. Similarly, in a hip-hop song called "Compton, Compton" (2003), The Game ridicules the image of the laid-back California beach life of palm trees and marijuana.

31. "Let's Not Palm Off Our Past," *LAT*, 14 Feb. 1975; *Los Angeles: A Guide to the City and Its Environs* (New York, 1941), 8; "Smog Blamed for Death of Pepper Trees," *LAT*, 13 Jan. 1966.

32. Peter H. King, "Under the Unlovely L.A. Palms," *LAT*, 28 Jan. 1992; Kellerman quoted in Tom Nolan, *Ross Macdonald: A Biography* (New York, 1999), 413.

33. Timothy K. Broschat and Alan W. Meerow, *Ornamental Palm Horticulture* (Gainesville, 2000), 9.

34. See Roy Ellen, "Palms and the Prototypicality of Trees: Some Questions Concerning Assumptions in the Comparative Study of Categories and Labels," in *The Social Life of Trees: Anthropological Perspectives on Tree Symbolism*, ed. Laura Rival (Oxford, 1998), 57–79.

35. "Pruning Targets Palm Trees," *RPE*, 17 Sept. 2006; Charles Francis Saunders, *Trees and Shrubs of California Gardens* (New York, 1926), 41.

36. Victoria Padilla, *Southern California Gardens: An Illustrated History* (Berkeley, 1961), 243.

37. I found obituaries of tree trimmers using electronic databases of newspapers. California's Division of Occupational Safety and Health keeps statistics. See also Sam Quinones, "Perils among the Palms," *LAT*, 26 Oct. 2006; Rich Magargal, "Beware the Hidden Dangers of Palms," *Tree Care Industry Magazine* 18 (Apr. 2007): 40–43; and Larry Collins, "Palm Tree Rescuers: Hazards for Victims and Responders," *Fire Engineering* 163, no. 5 (2010), available at www.fireengineering.com. For a cinematic depiction of a Mexican palmskinner in Los Angeles, see *A Better Life* (2011), dir. Chris Weitz.

38. See Seth Lubove, "The Pickled Palm Man," *Forbes* 158 (12 Aug. 1996): 86–87; Libby Waldrop, "Spreading Its Limbs," *Retail Traffic*, 1 June 1999; "Faux Palms," *SDUT*, 15 May 1996; and Patricia Scullin, "'Building' the Tree You Need," *Interior Landscape* (Winter 1996): 20–23. In the late 1980s, the timber giant Weyerhaeuser briefly offered a competing line of "Interiorized™" palms.

39. Quotes from "Cell Phone Antennae Hide in Plain Sight," *SDUT*, 9 Nov. 1999; and "Ugly Debates over Cellular Antennas," *LAT*, 5 Aug. 2001. See also "High-Wire Act," *LAT*, 12 July 1998.

40. On the art of the urban palm, see *Los Angeles and the Palm Tree: Image of a City* (Los Angeles, 1984).

41. Quotes from Michael Govan, "The History of Art, Through the Lens of Los Angeles," *Huffington Post*, 2 Dec. 2009; Emma Townshend, "A Nice Green Leaf: Why Palms Trees Are Like Cockroaches," *Independent*, blog extra, 13 Feb. 2008; Susan Heeger, "Palm Pilots," *Los Angeles Times Magazine*, 6 Jan. 2008; and "LACMA Palm Garden More than Landscape," *San Fernando Valley Business Journal*, 17 Mar. 2008.

42. "Palm Trees Must Go, Placerville Panel Says," *Sacramento Bee*, 13 Oct. 2006.

43. See Warren J. Dolby, "Palms in the Microclimates of the San Francisco Bay Area," *Principes* 28 (Apr. 1984): 92–98.

44. On the Midwinter Fair, see "More Palm Trees Wanted," *SFCh*, 20 Dec. 1893.

On the palm from Los Angeles, see "Big Palm Goes North," *LAT*, 25 Feb. 1903. On Golden Gate Park in general, see Terence Young, *Building San Francisco's Parks, 1850–1930* (Baltimore, 2004).

45. See Katy Wilcoxen, "Shaping a Landscape Image: Geography of Palm Trees in San Francisco, 1850s to 1997" (master's thesis, San Francisco State University, 1997).

46. John Muir to Strentzel family, 28 Jan. 1879, John Muir Correspondence, Holt-Atherton Special Collections, University of the Pacific; *Hittell's Handbook of Pacific Coast Travel* (San Francisco, 1887), 80.

47. "S.F. Backs Off Planting Palms on Lombard," *SFCh*, 9 May 1992; "Mission Getting 21 Palms Marina Rejected," *SFCh*, 14 Aug. 1992.

48. See "Palms Pop Up All Over S.F.," *SFCh*, 6 May 2006.

49. Quotes from "Palm Tree Dispute Growing," *Los Angeles Daily News*, 14 Feb. 1995; "City Prefers to Pass on the Palms," *LAT*, 20 Feb. 1995; and "Long-term Removal of Ficus Debated," *Whittier Daily News*, 14 Apr. 2008.

50. "Fronds vs. Needles," *LAT*, 21 May 1998; "Remembering Square's Roots," *LAT*, 2 Jan. 1999; "Cultivating an Image by Putting the Palms Back in La Palma," *LAT*, 21 Feb. 1999; "Planners Fear Development Will Endanger Trees," *RPE*, 13 Feb. 2005; "400 Palms to Be Removed from Redlands," *Redlands Daily Facts*, 21 May 2008; "Redlands May Remove Palm Trees to Make Streets Safer," *RPE*, 21 May 2008.

51. Quote from "Safety, Disease Endanger Inland Palm Trees," *RPE*, 2 Feb. 2007. See also "A Farewell to Fronds?" *San Bernardino Sun*, 15 July 2005; and "Untouchable Fire Threat," *RPE*, 6 Dec. 2006.

52. Expert quoted in "Obituaries for an L.A. Icon Were Premature"; architect quoted in "It's All Under Control," *LAT*, 3 July 1994, 3. See also "Giving Los Angeles an Airport Tower to Write Home About," *NYT*, 21 Mar. 1996.

53. "Michael Jackson's Worldwide Scrapbook," *Ebony Jr.* 4 (June–July 1976): 42–45, quote on 42.

54. Quotes from "Location, Location, Location," *Los Angeles Downtown News*, 10 Sept. 2010; and "Palm Trees Make Fillmore Too Californian for Movie Makers," *LAT*, 11 May 1989.

55. Rochelle Gurstein, "On the Lifespan of Trees," *Raritan* 26 (Winter 2007): 66–70, quotes on 66.

56. John Rechy, *City of Night* (New York, 1963), 87; Smith, "Holding Out for Palmier Days."

57. Statistics from Donald R. Hodel, "Palms over L.A.: Conspicuous by Their Nature, Not Their Numbers," *Principes* 40, no. 2 (1996): 103–11; and E. Gregory McPherson et al., "Expanding Street Tree Canopy Cover and Repairing Sidewalks in the City of Los Angeles," *Western Arborist* 29 (Fall 2003): 22–25; Jean Baudrillard, *America*, trans. Chris Turner (London, 1989), 52.

58. Roman Polański, *Roman on Polanski* (London, 1984), 304. On the sign, see Leo Braudy, *The Hollywood Sign: Fantasy and Reality of an American Icon* (New Haven, 2011). For a brief treatment of the semiotics of L.A. palms, see Virginia Postrel, *The*

Substance of Style: How the Rise of Aesthetic Value Is Remaking Commerce, Culture, and Consciousness (New York, 2003), 109–17.

59. Reyner Banham, *Los Angeles: The Architecture of Four Ecologies* (New York, 1971), 172–73; *The Stardust Road & Sometimes I Wonder: The Autobiographies of Hoagy Carmichael* (New York, 1999), 190; Joe Bonomo, *Sweat: The Story of the Fleshtones, America's Garage Band* (New York, 2007), 150.

60. Robert A. Jones, "Palm Has Armageddon Made in Shade," *LAT*, 13 May 1990.

61. Start with Blake Gumprecht, *The Los Angeles River: Its Life, Death, and Possible Rebirth* (Baltimore, 1999).

Epilogue

1. Josiah Royce, "The Pacific Coast: A Psychological Study of Influence," *International Monthly* 2 (1900): 555–83, quote on 573.

2. *California Farmer*, 5 Jan. 1854, reprinted in E. Louise Peffer, "Memorial to Congress on an Agricultural College for California, 1853," *Agricultural History* 40 (Jan. 1966): 53–56, quote on 56.

3. Charles Augustus Stoddard, *Beyond the Rockies: A Spring Journey in California* (New York, 1894), 49.

4. Percy Lubbock, ed., *The Letters of Henry James*, vol. 2 (New York, 1920), 33; John Steinbeck, *The Grapes of Wrath*, chap. 19; Joan Didion, *Slouching towards Bethlehem* (New York, 1968), 5.

5. Malcolm K. Hughes and Peter M. Brown, "Drought Frequency in Central California Since 101 BC Recorded in Giant Sequoia Tree Rings," *Climate Dynamics* 6 (1992): 161–67, quote on 166. See also Peter M. Brown et al., "Giant Sequoia Ring-width Chronologies from the Central Sierra Nevada, California," *Tree-Ring Bulletin* 52 (1992): 1–14; M. K. Hughes, R. Touchan, and P. M. Brown, "A Multimillennial Network of Giant Sequoia Chronologies for Dendroclimatology," *Radiocarbon* (1996): 225–34; and John T. Austin, *Floods and Droughts in the Tulare Lake Basin* (Three Rivers, Calif., 2013).

6. See Celine Herweijer et al., "North American Droughts of the Last Millennium from a Gridded Network of Tree-Ring Data," *Journal of Climate* 20 (1 Apr. 2007): 1353–76; David W. Stahle et al., "Tree-ring Reconstructed Megadroughts over North America Since AD 1300," *Climatic Change* 83, nos. 1–2 (2007): 133–49; and Edward R. Cook et al., "Long-Term Aridity Changes in the Western United States," *Science* 306 (5 Nov. 2004): 1015–18. The theme of megadroughts has been taken up popularly by Jared Diamond, *Collapse: How Societies Choose to Fail or Succeed* (New York, 2004); and, in regional perspective, by James Lawrence Powell, *Dead Pool: Lake Powell, Global Warming, and the Future of Water in the West* (Berkeley, 2008); and William deBuys, *A Great Aridness: Climate Change and the Future of the American Southwest* (Oxford, 2011).

7. William H. Thomes, *On Land and Sea: California in the Years 1843, '44, and '45* (Boston, 1884), 179.

8. George Bird Grinnell, ed., *Big Game in Its Haunts: The Book of the Boone and Crockett Club* (New York, 1914), 412. On the Golden State's emblematic animal, see Tracy I. Storer and Lloyd P. Trevis Jr., *California Grizzly* (Berkeley, 1955); Susan Snyder, *Bear in Mind: The California Grizzly* (Berkeley, 2003); and Peter S. Alagona, *After the Grizzly: Endangered Species and the Politics of Place in California* (Berkeley, 2013), chap. 1.

9. Charles Collins Teague, *Fifty Years a Rancher* (Los Angeles, 1944), 26–27. Teague arrived in 1893.

Index

Page numbers beginning with 465 refer to endnotes.

firewood, 116–17, 127–28, 138, 143, 153,
    156, 180
flooded gum, 157
flowers of, 118, 134, 157, 191, 194, 195
forest red gum, 131
frost intolerance of, 169–71, 176
gums, 118–19
height of, 119, 127–28, 161, 217
insect infestations of, 112, 169, 180–85,
    186
introduction to California of, 115–16,
    119–20, 123–25, 131, 159, 210, 220
ironbarks, 118, 157
jarrah, 151
leaves of, 117–19, 125, 126–27, 130, 131,
    141, 155–56, 157, 158, 164, 165,
    179, 182–83, 193, 194
lemon-scented gum, 165
manna gum, xxxix, 131, 163, 168
medicinal uses of, 125–28, 131, 484
mottlecah, 157
multiple uses of, 115, 126–28, 136, 139,
    165
natural range of, 118, 186
nesting of birds in, 191–92
plantations, 129, 130, 136–37, 142–44,
    147, 151, 153, 155–56, 166, 169, 174,
    180, 187, 192, 210, 214, 217
planting of, 74, 120–21, 126, 128, 138,
    148–51, 175, 179, 184, 187
rapid growth of, 117, 119, 120, 140–42,
    152, 171, 215
red-flowering gum, 134, 157
red gums, 130, 155
red ironbark, 157, 165
reproduction and spread of, xxx, 112, 115,
    117–18, 155–56, 210
river red gum, 131, 156, 160, 164, 169,
    183, 184, 185, 213
roots of, 117, 129, 133, 156, 160, 171, 186,
    188
rose mallee, 157
San Jose gum, 154
seeds and seedpods of, 116, 118, 120, 124,
    126, 127, 130, 135, 150–51, 158,
    214, 336
silver dollar gum, 157
silverleaf mountain gum, 157
structural hazard of, 112, 169, 172, 179,
    185–90, 220
sugar gum, 131, 135, 147–51, 155, 161
swamp mahogany, 157

Tasmanian blue gum, xxix, xxxvi, 119–22,
    124–25, 128, 130, 131, 136–37, 151,
    157, 161, 165–66, 168–79, 191–93,
    196–99, 207, 210–11, 213, 217,
    219–20, 292, 372
white ironbark, 157
wood, 127, 136, 144–45, 152–54
Eucalyptus (Kinney), 135
"Eucalyptus Grove, The," 215
eucalyptus longhorned borer (ELB), 180–83
Eucalyptus School (art), 159
eucalyptus Timber Corporation, 143, 144
eugenics, 68–72, 206, 224–25
Euphrates River, 63
Eureka, Calif., 51–53, 55, 66, 74, 86, 87, 112
    Carson Mansion in, 53
    Chinese in, 52–53
Everest, Hiram Bond, 294
Everest Ranch, 294
evergreens, xxvi, xxvii, xxxvi, 8, 9, 117–18,
    156, 285, 312
Exotic Pest Plant Council, 190

Fairbanks, Douglas, 374
Fante, John, 377
fascism, 217, 274
Federal Bureau of Investigation (FBI), 88, 97
Federal Deposit Insurance Corporation
    (FDIC), 100
Federal Emergency Management Agency
    (FEMA), 201
Feinstein, Dianne, 100
fertilizer, 156, 225, 266, 278, 281–82, 331
ficus, xxvii, xxxvi, 386, 391, 422
Fields, W. C., 276, 418
fig, xxxiv, xxxvi, 232, 329, 432, 458
Filipinos, 263, 264, 326, 369, 378
Fillmore, Calif., 425
fir, Douglas, xxxiii, 61, 154–55
Fire Island National Seashore, 81
fish, "Chinese" snakehead, 206
Fish and Wildlife Service, U.S., 196, 200
Fisher family, 104
Flintham, Stuart, 147
Florida, 190, 229–30, 243–44, 279, 285, 311,
    348, 351, 387, 425
    citriculture in, 229–30, 243–44, 251, 253,
    256, 293, 311, 315, 322, 325, 327,
    331, 499, 512
fog, coastal, 10, 48, 61, 62, 75, 131, 146, 156,
    192, 210
fog machines, 293